Microsoft® Visual C++®.NET

Don Gosselin

Australia • Canada • Mexico • Singapore • Spain • United Kingdom • United States

Microsoft® Visual C++®.NET

by Don Gosselin

Senior Vice President, Publisher:
Kristen Duerr

Managing Editor:
Jennifer Locke

Senior Product Manager:
Margarita Leonard

Development Editor:
Marilyn Freedman

Production Editor:
Melissa Panagos

Marketing Manager:
Angie Laughlin

Associate Product Manager:
Janet Aras

Editorial Assistant:
Christy Urban

Text Designer:
GEX Publishing Services

Cover Designer:
Abby Scholz

Manufacturing Manager:
Denise Sandler

Printed in Canada

1 2 3 4 5 6 7 8 9 WC 06 05 04 03 02

For more information, contact Course Technology, 25 Thomson Place, Boston, Massachusetts, 02210.

r find us on the World Wide Web www.course.com

ISBN 0-619-01657-4

BRIEF

Contents

TABLE OF

Contents

Preface

Microsoft Visual C++ .NET teaches the skills necessary to create applications in the dynamic Visual C++ development environment. The Visual C++ environment takes the C++ language one step beyond being an object-oriented extension of the C language by adding Microsoft Foundation Classes, or MFCs, the building blocks for Windows applications. Microsoft Visual C++ .NET discusses in detail all of these technologies, while also thoroughly exploring the C++ structure and syntax underlying Visual C++.

Microsoft Visual C++ .NET provides coverage of the necessary basics of C++ programming in the first few chapters, provides detailed information on memory management and class concepts in the middle of the book, and then brings the reader confidently into the Visual environment in the last third of the book.

Organization and Coverage

Microsoft Visual C++ .NET contains 13 chapters that present hands-on instruction in the basics of C++ and Windows application programming. In these chapters, readers with no previous programming experience learn how to plan and create well-structured programs. By the end of the book, users will have learned how to work with basic C++ syntax, such as how to write functions using repetition and control programming structures, and how to use both simple and advanced techniques to debug their programs. Readers also learn more advanced topics, such as how to work with memory management and classes, the basics of Windows API programming, and how to work with MFCs. Additionally, users will learn how to create and work with dialog-based and document-based applications, how to create visual interface components, and how to work with databases.

Each chapter includes a concept lesson, which introduces programming concepts that are presented in hands-on, step-by-step exercises. Each step-by-step exercise provides an opportunity for the reader to apply the knowledge learned in the main text. The combination of text explanations with step-by-step exercises that illustrate the concepts reinforces understanding and improves retention of the material presented. It also provides the user with learning opportunities beyond what might be taught in the classroom.

Readers using Microsoft Visual C++ .NET build applications from the bottom up, rather than using pre-written code. This technique facilitates a deeper understanding of the concepts used in programming with Microsoft Visual C++ .NET. When users complete this book, they will know how to create and modify simple console applications, Windows API applications, and MFC applications and will have the tools to create more complex applications. Readers will also have a fundamental knowledge of programming concepts that will be useful whether they continue to learn more about the C++ language or go on to learn other object-oriented languages.

This edition of Microsoft Visual C++ .NET includes a new chapter on comprehensive memory management techniques, along with greatly improved material in the original chapters. Some of the improvements include new visual illustrations of step-by-step exercises along with enhanced end-of-chapters Programming Exercises and Programming Projects. Additionally, the debugging chapter has been moved earlier in the book in order to give users the tools to successfully debug the projects they create in later chapters.

APPROACH

Microsoft Visual C++ .NET distinguishes itself from other books because of its unique approach, which motivates students by demonstrating why they need to learn the concepts and skills. This book teaches programming concepts using a task-driven, rather than a command-driven, approach. By working through the chapters—which are each motivated by a realistic application—students learn how to create the programs that solve problems they are likely to encounter in the workplace. This is much more effective than memorizing a list of commands out of context.

In addition, Microsoft Visual C++ .NET uses the following teaching techniques:

- The code examples are short; one concept is featured in each code example.
- Variables, functions, and other key language elements are covered earlier than in many other texts, giving users a better understanding of the more advanced concepts and techniques that occur later in the text, allowing them to work on significant projects from the start.
- Debugging concepts are introduced early in order to give users the tools to successfully debug the projects they create in later chapters.
- Text explanation is interspersed with step-by-step exercises.
- Syntax is introduced throughout the text, as necessary.
- C++ applications are built from the bottom up; the user gains a clear picture of how complex programs are built.
- Programming techniques are presented in easy-to-understand lessons.

Features

Microsoft Visual C++ .NET is a superior textbook because it also includes the following features:

- **Read This Before You Begin Page** This page is consistent with Course Technology's unequaled commitment to helping instructors introduce technology into the classroom. Technical considerations and assumptions about hardware, software, and default settings are listed in one place to help instructors save time and eliminate unnecessary aggravation.

- **Step-by-Step Methodology** The unique Course Technology methodology keeps users on track. They always write program code within the context of solving the problems posed in the chapter. The text constantly guides users and lets them know where they are in the process of solving the problem. The numerous illustrations guide individuals to create useful, working programs.
- **Tips** These notes provide additional information—for example, an alternate method of performing a procedure, background information on a technique, a commonly-made error to watch out for, debugging techniques, or the name of a Web site the user can visit to gather more information.
- **Caution** This icon highlights critical safety information for your computer. Follow these instructions very carefully.
- **Notes** Chapters contain Notes designed to expand on the section topic, including resource references, additional examples, and ancillary information.
- **Summaries** Following each chapter is a summary that recaps the essential programming concepts covered in each section.
- **Review Questions** Each chapter concludes with meaningful, conceptual review questions that test users' understanding of what they learned in the chapter.
- **Programming Exercises** These exercises provide users with additional practice of the skills and concepts they learned in the lesson.
- **Programming Projects** At the end of each chapter are additional projects that allow users to practice building complete applications from the ground up.

Teaching Tools

The following supplemental materials are available when this book is used in a classroom setting. All of the teaching tools available with this book are provided to the instructor on a single CD.

Electronic Instructor's Manual The Instructor's Manual that accompanies this textbook includes:

- Additional instructional material to assist in class preparation, including suggestions for lecture topics.
- Solutions to all end-of-chapter materials, including Review Questions and Projects.

ExamView This textbook is accompanied by ExamView, a powerful software package that allows instructors to create and administer printed, computer (LAN-based), and Internet exams. ExamView includes hundreds of questions that correspond to the topics covered in this text, enabling students to generate detailed study guides that include page references for further review. The computer-based and Internet testing components allow students to take exams at their computers, and also save the instructor time by grading each exam automatically.

PowerPoint Presentation This book comes with Microsoft PowerPoint slides for each chapter. These are included as a teaching aid for classroom presentation, to make available to students on the network for chapter review, or to be printed for classroom distribution. Instructors can add their own slides for additional topics they introduce to the class.

Data Files Data files, containing all of the code necessary for steps within the chapters and the Projects, are provided through the Course Technology Web site at *www.course.com*, and are also on the Teaching Tools CD-ROM.

Solution Files Solutions to end-of-chapter questions. Hands-on Exercises, and Projects are provided on the Teaching Tools CD-ROM and may also be found on the Course Technology Web Site at *www.course.com*. The solutions are password protected.

ACKNOWLEDGEMENTS

A text such as this represents the hard work of many people, not just the author. I would like to thank all of the people who helped make this book a reality. First and foremost, I would like to thank Marilyn Freedman, Development Editor, for her outstanding work and for making me a better writer. Next, I would like to thank Margarita Leonard, Senior Project Manager, for her patience and professionalism in managing the production of this book. I would also like to thank Kristen Duerr, Publisher and Jennifer Muroff, Senior Editor. Finally, I would like to thank Melissa Panagos, Production Editor, for getting this book out on time under extraordinary circumstances.

Many, many thanks to the reviewers for their invaluable comments and suggestions, including John Gerstenberg, Cuyamaca College; Morris Goodwin, Stetson University; Chris Howard, DeVry Institute; Judy Jernigan, Tyler Junior College; Rich Trudeau, Terryville High School; and Peter Van der Goes, Rose State College. You truly made this a better book.

On the personal side, I would like to thank my family and friends for their understanding when I disappear for days and weeks on end. Thanks especially to my father for always listening when I needed someone to talk to. A very special thanks to Sydne Stempien, Roxana Cisternas, and everyone else at East-West Karate in San Rafael, California; thank you for not only teaching me patience and focus, but for pushing me, with a rousing cheer, back into the fight.

As always, thanks to my friend and colleague, George T. Lynch, for getting me started. Thanks also goes to my cat, Mabeline, for keeping me company while I write, and to my dog, Noah, for never failing to remind me that a world exists outside of my office. Finally, my most important thanks of all goes to my wonderful Kathy for her eternal patience and support, and for always believing in me.

Read This Before You Begin

To the User

Data Disks

To complete the chapters and exercises in this book, you need Data Disks. Your instructor will provide you with Data Disks or ask you to make your own.

If you are asked to make your own Data Disks, you will need four blank, formatted high-density disks. You will need to copy a set of folders from a file server or stand-alone computer onto your disks. Your instructor will tell you which computer, drive letter, and folders contain the files you need. The following table shows you which folders go on each of your disks:

Data Disk	Write this on the disk label	Put these folders on the disk
Data Disk 1	Chapters 2 and 3	Chapter.02
		Chapter.03
Data Disk 2	Chapters 4 and 5	Chapter.04
		Chapter.05
Data Disk 3	Chapters 6 through 10	Chapter.06
		Chapter.07
		Chapter.08
		Chapter.09
		Chapter.10
Data Disk 4	Chapters 11 through 13	Chapter.11
		Chapter.12
		Chapter.13

When you begin each chapter, make sure you are using the correct Data Disk. Ask your instructor or technical support person for assistance.

Self-Study

You can use your own computer to complete the chapters and exercises in this book. To use your own computer, you will need the following:

- **Visual C++ .NET** This book assumes installation of Visual C++ .NET Standard Edition or Academic Edition. You can also use Professional, Enterprise Developer, or Enterprise Architect editions of Visual C++ .NET with this text. However, you should be aware that these versions include additional features that are not documented in this text. Note that system requirements for Visual C++ .NET vary according to hardware configuration and operating system. Be sure your hardware configuration and operating system meet the minimum system requirements before purchasing an edition of Visual C++ .NET. You can find a listing of the system requirements for each edition of Visual Studio .NET by searching for *Visual Studio .NET Hardware Requirements* in the MSDN Library at *msdn.microsoft.com*.
- **Data Files** You will not be able to complete all the chapters and exercises in this book using your own computer until you have the data files. You can download the files from the Course Technology Web site at *www.course.com*.
- Project disk space. You will need approximately 45 MB of disk space to store the projects you create in this text.

Additional materials designed for this book might be available on the Course Technology Web site. Go to *course.com* and search for this book title periodically for more details.

To the Instructor

To complete all the exercises and chapters in this book, your users must use a set of data files. These files are included in the Instructor's Resource Kit. They may also be obtained electronically through the Course Technology Web site at *www.course.com*. Follow the instructions in the Help file to copy the user files to your computer. You can view the Help file using a text editor, such as WordPad or Notepad.

Once the files are copied, you can make Data Disks for your users or instruct them where to find the files so they can make their own Data Disks. Make sure the files are copied correctly onto the Data Disks by following the instructions in the Data Disks heading found earlier in this section.

Course Technology Data Files

You are granted a license to copy the data files to any computer or server used by individuals who have purchased this book.

CHAPTER

1

INTRODUCTION TO PROGRAMMING AND VISUAL C++

In this chapter you will learn about:

- Computer programming and programming languages
- C/C++ programming
- Logic and debugging
- Creating a new project in Visual C++
- The Visual Studio IDE
- Managing the solution
- Visual C++ Help

There is nothing more difficult to take in hand, more perilous to conduct or more uncertain in its success than to take the lead in the introduction of a new order of things.

Niccolo Machiavelli *The Prince* 1532

COMPUTER PROGRAMMING AND PROGRAMMING LANGUAGES

Creating instructions that control the operation of a computer or computer hardware is called **computer programming**. The instructions themselves are called **computer programs**, **applications**, **software**, or simply **programs**. The pieces of information that a program needs are called **data**. Think, for a moment, about an automobile. The automobile is useless without someone to drive it. If you compare an automobile to a computer, you can see that the computer is useless without a program that drives its hardware.

When you start a program and provide it with the data it needs to function, you are **running**, or **executing**, the program. To develop the comparison to an automobile a little further, you can think of the driver as the program that operates the automobile. The gas and oil that the automobile needs to operate are its data. Figure 1-1 illustrates the concept of how hardware, software, and data all work together to execute an automobile program.

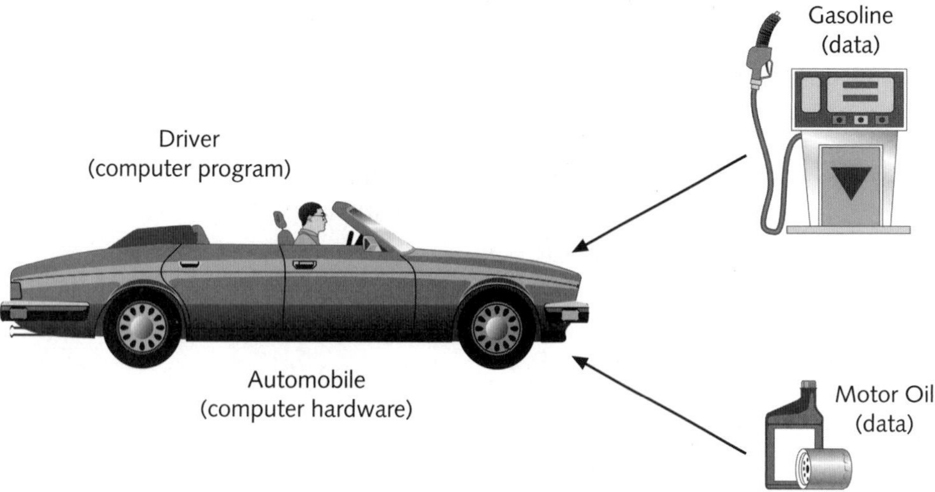

Figure 1-1 Executing an automobile program

The instructions used to create computer programs are called **programming languages**. To understand Visual C++ programming and how it relates to the C/C++ programming languages, it is helpful to know a little background about computer programming and how current programming languages evolved.

Machine and Assembly Languages

The electronic circuitry of a computer is controlled by two simple electronic signals, or switches—an on switch and an off switch. A 1 represents the on switch, and a 0 (zero) represents the off switch. Telling a computer what to do involves writing programs that set these switches to on or off. **Machine language** is the lowest level of computer languages, and programs written in machine language consist entirely of 1s and 0s that control the computer's on and off switches. For example, a program written in machine language may contain lines similar to the following (note that the following code is not an actual program; it just serves to give an idea of how difficult it can be to program with machine language):

```
0 0 1 0 1 0 1 0 1
1 0 0 1 1 0 0 1 1
0 0 1 1 0 0 1 1 0
1 0 0 0 0 1 1 1 1
0 0 1 0 1 1 0 1 0
1 0 0 1 1 1 1 0 0
0 0 1 1 0 1 0 0 1
```

Writing a program in machine language is very difficult because you must understand how the exact placement and combination of 1s and 0s will affect your program. Assembly languages provide an easier (although still challenging) method of controlling a computer's on and off switches. **Assembly languages** perform the same tasks as machine languages, but use simplified names of instructions instead of 1s and 0s. To get an idea of how difficult it can be to program with assembly languages, examine the following assembly code, which only performs some simple numeric calculations.

```
Main proc
   mov ax, dseg
A  integer ?
B  integer ?
C  integer ?
cseg segment para public 'code'
assume cs:cseg, ds:dseg
Main proc
   mov ax, dseg
   mov ds, ax
   mov es, ax
   mov A, 3
   mov B, -2
   mov C, 254
   mov ax, A
   add ax, B
   mov C, ax
```

Machine languages and assembly languages are known as **low-level languages** because they are the programming languages that are closest to a computer's hardware. Each type of **central processing unit (CPU)** contains its own internal machine language and assembly language. To write programs in machine language, a programmer must know the specific machine language and assembly language for the type of CPU on which a program will run. Because each CPU's machine language and assembly language is unique, it is difficult to translate low-level languages from one CPU to another.

High-Level Programming Languages

Because of the difficulty of working with low-level languages, high-level, or symbolic, languages were developed to make it easier to write computer programs. **High-level programming languages** create computer programs using instructions that are much easier to understand than machine or assembly language code because you use words that more clearly describe the task being performed. Examples of high-level languages include C++, BASIC, and COBOL. To understand the difference between low-level languages and high-level languages, consider the following assembly language code that adds two numbers, and then assigns the result to a variable named C:

```
mov A, 3
mov B, 2
add A, B
mov C, A
```

Although easier than machine language, the above assembly language code is still difficult to understand. In comparison, the same task is accomplished in a high-level language using a much simpler statement. For example, the following C++ statement performs the same addition task and assigns the result to a variable named C: `int C = 3 + 2;`. The syntax in C++ is much easier to understand than the syntax in assembly language.

Another advantage to high-level programming languages is that they are not CPU-specific, as are machine and assembly languages. This means that a program you write in a high-level programming language will run on many different types of CPUs, regardless of their machine languages or assembly languages. However, in order to run, programs written in high-level languages must first be translated into a low-level language using a program called a compiler. A **compiler** translates programming code into a low-level format. You need to compile a program only once when you are through writing it or after editing an existing program. When you execute the program, you actually execute the compiled, low-level format of the program. However, each time you make any changes to an existing program, you must recompile it before the new version of the program will execute.

Procedural Programming

One of the most common forms of programming in high-level languages is called procedural programming. In **procedural programming**, computer instructions are often grouped into logical units called **procedures**. In C++ programming, procedures are referred to as **functions**. Each line in a procedural program that performs an individual task is called a **statement**. For example, a checkbook program may contain a series of statements grouped as a function named balanceCheckbook() that balances a checkbook. Another function named sumDeposits() may be used to calculate the total of all deposits made during a single period. A single procedural program may contain hundreds of variables and thousands of statements and functions.

When a procedure or function is referred to in the book, its name is usually followed by two parentheses, as in balanceCheckbook().

Procedures are also called routines or subroutines.

One of the most important aspects of procedural programming is that it allows you to temporarily store pieces of data in computer memory locations called **variables**. The information contained in a specific variable often changes. For example, you may have a program that creates a variable containing the current time. Each time the program runs, the time is different, so the value *varies*. The value of a variable often changes during the course of program execution. For example, a payroll program might assign employee names to a variable named employeeName. The memory location referenced by the variable employeeName might contain different values (a different value for every employee of the company) at different times. Another form of data that you can store in computer memory locations is a constant. A **constant** contains information that does not change during the course of program execution. You can think of a constant as a variable with a *constant* value. A common example of a constant is the value of pi (π), which represents the ratio of the circumference of a circle to its diameter. The value of pi never changes from the constant value of 3.141592.

The statements within a procedural program usually execute in a linear fashion, one right after the other. Figure 1-2 displays a simple procedural program written in BASIC that calculates and prints the average of the numbers 1, 2, and 3. The first two statements in the program create variables named SUM and COUNT. During the course of program execution, the numbers 1, 2, and 3 are added to the SUM variable. The COUNT variable maintains a record of how many numbers are assigned to the SUM variable. Finally, the average is calculated using the statement SUM / COUNT. The last statement, which begins with PRINT, prints the result of the program to the screen.

```
LET SUM = 0
LET COUNT = 0
LET SUM = SUM + 1
LET COUNT = COUNT + 1
LET SUM = SUM + 2
LET COUNT = COUNT + 1
LET SUM = SUM + 3
LET COUNT = COUNT + 1
LET AVERAGE = SUM / COUNT
PRINT "The average is "; AVERAGE
```

Figure 1-2 A procedural program written in BASIC

Object-Oriented Programming

Procedural-based programs are self-contained; most code, such as variables, statements, and functions, exists within the program itself. For example, you may have written a small business program that calculates accounts receivable and accounts payable. To add to the program a new function that calculates the interest on a loan, you must include all the required code within the accounting program, using variables, statements, and functions. If you want to use the interest calculation code in another program, you must copy all of its statements into the new program or recreate it from scratch.

Object-oriented programming takes a different approach. **Object-oriented programming (OOP)** refers to the creation of reusable software objects that can be easily incorporated into another program. Reusable software objects are often referred to as **components**. For example, you could refer to all of the interest calculation code as a single object—which you could then use over and over again just by using the object name. Popular object-oriented programming languages include C++, Java, Visual Basic, and Turbo Pascal. In object-oriented programming, an **object** is programming code and data that can be treated as an individual unit or component. **Data** refers to information contained within variables, constants, or other types of storage structures. The functions associated with an object are referred to as **methods**. Variables that are associated with an object are referred to as **properties** or **attributes**. Objects can range from simple controls such as a button, to entire programs such as a database application. Object-oriented programming allows programmers to use programming objects that they have written themselves or that have been written by others. One of the most powerful features of object-oriented programming is that it allows programmers to use objects in their programs that may have been created in an entirely different programming language.

For example, if you are creating an accounting program in Turbo Pascal, you can use an object named Payroll that was created in C++. The Payroll object may contain one method that calculates the amount of federal and state tax to deduct, another function that calculates the FICA amount to deduct, and so on. Properties of the Payroll object may include an employee's number of tax withholding allowances, federal and state tax percentages, and the cost of insurance premiums. You do not need to know how the Payroll object was created in C++, nor do you need to re-create it in Turbo Pascal. You only need to know how to access the methods and properties of the Payroll object from the Turbo Pascal program. The object-oriented Accounting program is illustrated in Figure 1-3. In the figure, the Accounting program is composed of three separate objects, or components: an Accounts Receivable object, the Payroll object, and an Accounts Payable object. The important thing to understand is that you do not need to rewrite the Payroll, Accounts Payable, and Accounts Receivable objects for the Accounting program; the Accounting program only needs to call their methods and provide the correct data to their properties.

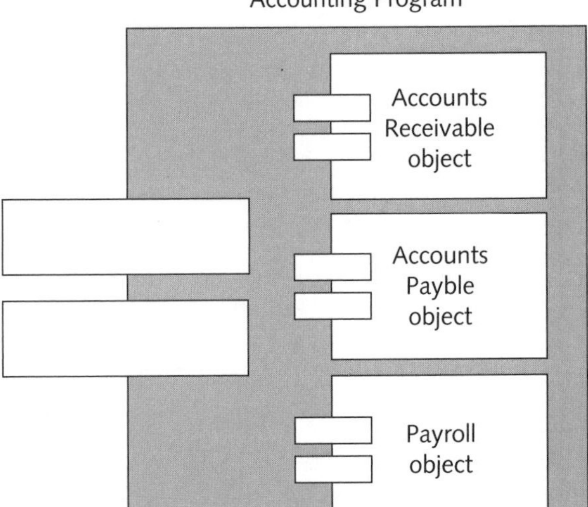

Figure 1-3 Accounting receivable program

The diagram in Figure 1-3, along with other diagrams in this book, is created in Unified Modeling Language, or UML, which is a symbolic language for visually designing and documenting software systems. Each of the symbols in Figure 1-3 is a UML representation of a component.

Objects are **encapsulated**, which means that all code and required data are contained within the object itself. Encapsulation is also referred to as a black box, because of the invisibility of the code inside an encapsulated object. When an object is well written, you cannot see "inside" it—all internal workings are hidden. The code (methods and statements) and data (variables and constants) contained in an encapsulated object are accessed through an interface. An **interface** represents elements required for a source program to communicate with an object. For example, interface elements required to access a Payroll object might be a method named calcNetPay(), which calculates an employee's net pay, and properties containing the employee's name and pay rate.

You can compare a programming object and its interface to a hand-held calculator. The calculator represents an object, and you represent a program that wants to use the object. You establish an interface with the calculator object by entering numbers (the data required by the object) and then pressing calculation keys (which represent the methods of the object.) You do not need to know, nor can you see, the inner workings of the calculator object. As a programmer, you are concerned only with what the methods and properties are and what results to expect the calculator object to return. Figure 1-4 illustrates the idea of the calculator interface.

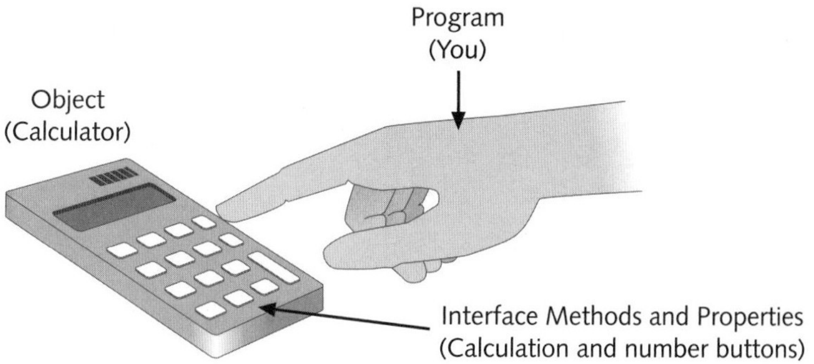

Figure 1-4 Calculator interface

Another example of an object and its interface is a Windows word-processing program. The word-processing program itself is actually a type of object made up of numerous other objects. The program window is called the user interface. The items you see in the word-processing window, such as the menu, toolbars, and other elements, are interface items used for executing methods. For example, an icon that you click to make text bold is an interface element that executes a bold method. The data you provide to the program is the text of your document. You do not need to know how the method works, only what it does. You only need to provide the data (text) and execute the appropriate methods (such as the bold method), when necessary.

In object-oriented programming, the code, methods, attributes, and other information that make up an object are contained in a structure known as a **class**. Programming objects are created from classes. When you use an object in your program, you actually create an instance of the class of the object. An **instance** is an object that has been created from an existing class. In fact, a class is really just a template, or blueprint, from which you create objects. As an example, let's return to the Payroll object mentioned earlier. The Payroll object is created from a Payroll class. To use the Payroll class, you create an instance of the class. Particular instances of objects inherit their characteristics from a class. **Inheritance** refers to the ability of an object to take on the characteristics of the class on which it is based. The Payroll object, for instance, inherits all of the characteristics of the Payroll class. To give another example, when you create a new word-processing document, which is a type of object, it usually inherits the properties of a template on which it is based. The template is a type of class. The document inherits characteristics of the template such as font size, line spacing, and boilerplate text. In the same manner, programs that include instances of objects inherit the object's functionality.

You will learn about object-oriented programming throughout the course of this book.

Consider the class upon which the Payroll object might be based. As mentioned, the Payroll class (upon which the Payroll object is based) may include a method named calcNetPay().The Payroll class may also include a calcFederalTaxes() method, a calcStateTaxes() method, and a deductIRAContribution() method. Some of the properties of the Payroll class may include federalTaxRate, stateTaxRate, insurancePremium, and iraContribution. Each time you create a new instance of the Payroll object, the object inherits its own copies of these methods and objects. For example, a company that generates its payroll once a month would create 12 separate Payroll objects. Figure 1-5 illustrates how the January and February Payroll objects inherit all of the methods and properties of the Payroll class.

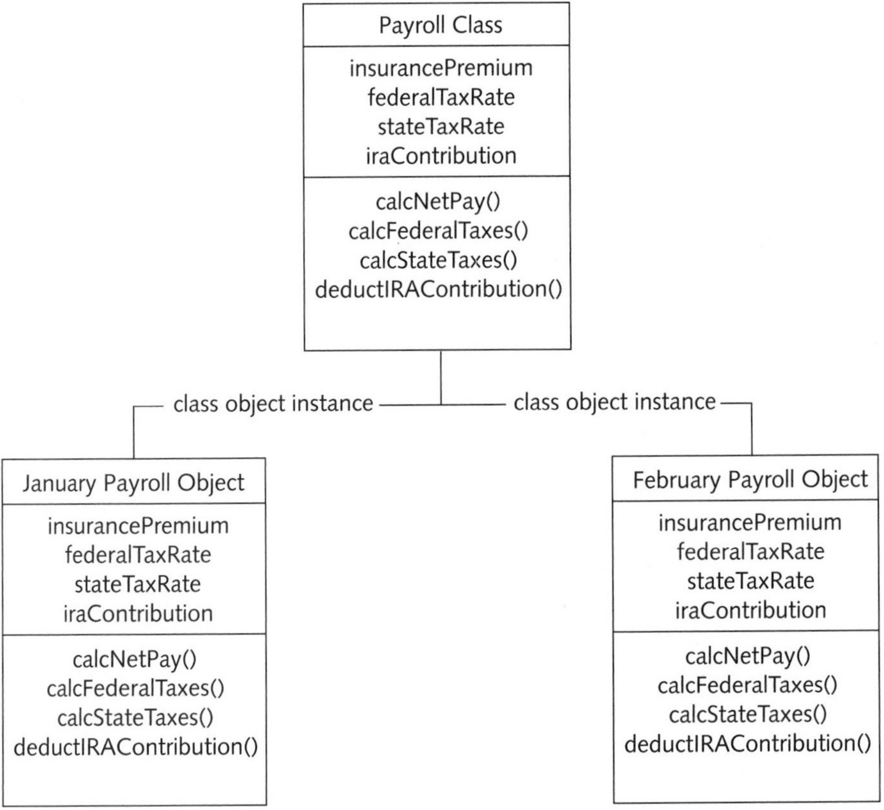

Figure 1-5 Payroll class and objects

Although you will not return to object-oriented programming for several chapters, you need to understand that the classes and objects you can create with C++ are the most important and powerful part of the C++ programming language. In fact, the primary goal of this book is to provide you with a firm foundation in the concepts of classes and object-oriented programming. However, before you can learn about classes and object-oriented programming in detail, you need to understand some of the more basic aspects of C++, such as data types, functions, and decision-making statements. These concepts will be examined in the next few chapters

C/C++ Programming

The term C/C++ refers to two separate, but related, programming languages: C and C++. At Bell Laboratories in the 1970s, Dennis Ritchie and Brian Kernighan designed the procedural C programming language based upon two earlier languages, BCPL and B. In 1985, again at Bell Laboratories, Bjarne Stroustrup created C++ based on the C programming language. C++ is an extension of C that adds object-oriented programming capabilities.

You create C and C++ programs in text files using a text-editing tool such as Notepad. The original program structure you enter into a text file is referred to as **source code**. Once you finish creating your program source code, you use a compiler to translate it into the machine language of the computer on which the program will run. The compiled machine language version of a program is called **object code**. Once you compile a program into object code, some systems require you to use a program called a **linker**, which converts the object code into an executable file, typically with an extension of .exe. Figure 1-6 uses a simple program that prints the text *Hello World* to a console application window to show how source code is transformed into to object code and then into an executable process.

You cannot read object code or the code in an .exe file. The only code format in human-readable form is source code. In Visual C++, you compile and link a program in a single step known as **building**. You will learn how to build a program later in this chapter.

Remember that each computer contains its own internal machine language. The C/C++ compiler you use must be able to translate source code into the machine language of the computer, or platform, on which your program will run. A **platform** is an operating system and its hardware type. For example, Windows operating systems for PCs, Mac OS 10 operating system for Macintosh, and Solaris for SPARC are different platforms. Numerous vendors market C/C++ compilers for various platforms. Some vendors offer complete development environments containing built-in code editors, compilers, and linkers. Microsoft Visual C++ and Borland C++ Builder are examples of C/C++ professional development environments that contain built-in code editors and compilers, as well as many other development tools.

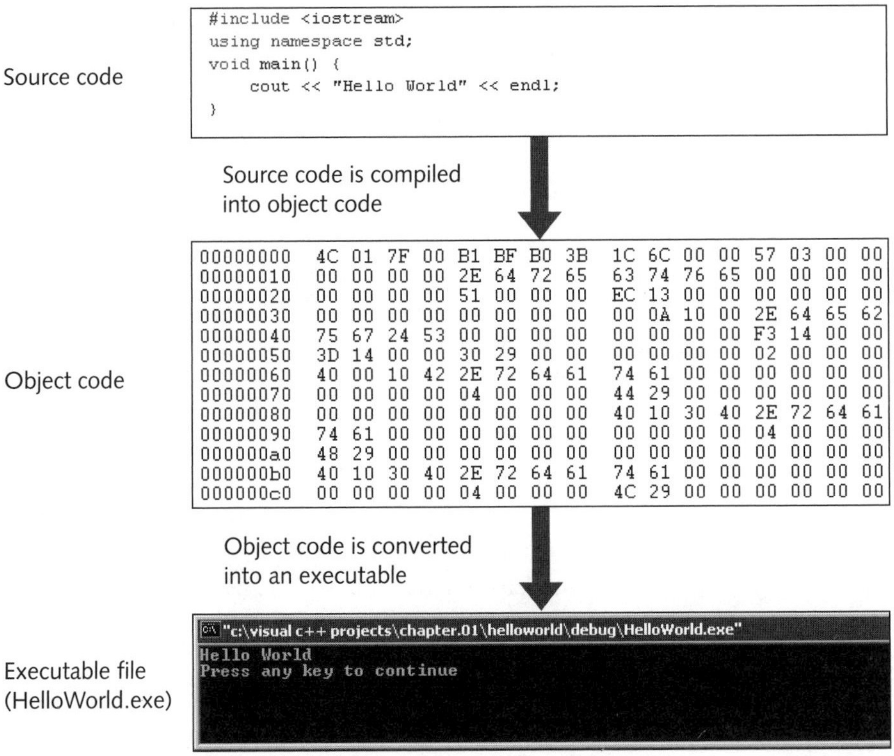

Source code

```
#include <iostream>
using namespace std;
void main() {
    cout << "Hello World" << endl;
}
```

Source code is compiled into object code

Object code

```
00000000  4C 01 7F 00 B1 BF B0 3B  1C 6C 00 00 57 03 00 00
00000010  00 00 00 00 2E 64 72 65  63 74 76 65 00 00 00 00
00000020  00 00 00 00 51 00 00 00  EC 13 00 00 00 00 00 00
00000030  00 00 00 00 00 00 00 00  00 0A 10 00 2E 64 65 62
00000040  75 67 24 53 00 00 00 00  00 00 00 00 F3 14 00 00
00000050  3D 14 00 00 30 29 00 00  00 00 00 00 02 00 00 00
00000060  40 00 10 42 2E 72 64 61  74 61 00 00 00 00 00 00
00000070  00 00 00 00 04 00 00 00  44 29 00 00 00 00 00 00
00000080  00 00 00 00 00 00 00 00  40 10 30 40 2E 72 64 61
00000090  74 61 00 00 00 00 00 00  00 00 00 00 04 00 00 00
000000a0  48 29 00 00 00 00 00 00  00 00 00 00 00 00 00 00
000000b0  40 10 30 40 2E 72 64 61  74 61 00 00 00 00 00 00
000000c0  00 00 00 00 04 00 00 00  4C 29 00 00 00 00 00 00
```

Object code is converted into an executable

Executable file (HelloWorld.exe)

```
"c:\visual c++ projects\chapter.01\helloworld\debug\HelloWorld.exe"
Hello World
Press any key to continue
```

Figure 1-6 Source code to object code to executable process

The C Programming Language

One of the most important programs created with the original C language was the UNIX operating system. Because of its involvement in the creation of UNIX and its subsequent use as the main programming language for the UNIX platform, C was originally used almost exclusively on UNIX platforms. During the 1980s, C compilers were written for other platforms, including personal computers. The first C compilers for other platforms were based on the original version of the language developed by Ritchie and Kernighan. By 1985 numerous C compilers had been created by independent software vendors, many of which did not conform to the original version of the language. To provide a level of standardization for the C language, in 1989 the American National Standards Institute (ANSI) created a standardized version of C that is commonly referred to as **ANSI C**. In 1990, a worldwide standard for the C language named **ANSI/ISO C** was approved by the International Standards Organization (ISO).

One of the great benefits of the C language is that it is much closer to assembly language than other types of high-level programming languages. Being closer to assembly language means that programs written in C often run much faster and more efficiently than programs written in other types of high-level programming languages. Additionally, thanks to the ANSI/ISO standard, the same C program can usually run on many different platforms. However, C's closeness to assembly language can also be a disadvantage. It can make C difficult to use and not ideally suited to certain types of applications, such as graphical applications and object-based programs that you want to use with other programming languages.

The C++ Programming Language

Although C programs are not ideally suited to graphical applications, C++ is a different story. C++ is currently the most popular programming language for developing graphical programs that run on platforms such as Macintosh and Windows. Graphical programs refers to programs with visual components such as dialog boxes, menus, toolbars, and so on. C++ has the ability to create graphical programs because of the object-oriented programming capabilities added by Stroustrup when he first developed the language from its C predecessor. Much of this book explores C++'s object-oriented programming capabilities.

As with the C language, early versions of C++ suffered from a lack of standardization until the worldwide ANSI/ISO C++ standard was approved in 1997. The standardized version of C++ is commonly referred to as **ANSI C++**. The ANSI C++ standard ensures that programs written in C++ are compatible with different compilers and can be run on different platforms.

The ANSI C and ANSI C++ standards define how C/C++ code can be written. The ANSI standards also define **run-time libraries**, which contain useful functions, variables, constants, and other programmatic items that you can add to your programs. The ANSI C++ run-time library is also called the **Standard Template Library** or **Standard C++ Library**. Although the run-time libraries are not actually part of each language's structure, they are required for a compiler to conform to the ANSI C/C++ standards. You can be assured that any of the components of the run-time libraries that you use in your programs will be available to all compilers that support the ANSI C/C++ standard.

Both the C and C++ programming languages are still in use today. In fact, Visual C++ supports both the C and C++ languages. Most of the features of C are also available in C++, which means you can use C++ to write both procedural and object-oriented programs. For this reason, this book focuses primarily on the C++ language.

Visual C++ .NET

Microsoft Visual C++ .NET, or Visual C++ for short, is a Windows-based, visual development environment for creating C and C++ applications. It is part of the Microsoft Visual Studio line of products. Visual C++ contains a built-in code editor, compiler, and other tools for creating programs. You can create both C and C++ applications in Visual C++. The C and C++ language syntax used in Visual C++ conforms to ANSI C/C++ specifications. Actually, Visual C++ itself is *not* a programming language. It is a *development environment* used for creating programs with the C/C++ languages.

Visual C++ supports a number of extensions to the ANSI C/C++ run-time libraries. **Extensions** are new or additional features that have been added to the original run-time libraries.Visual C++ extensions may or may not be supported by other C/C++ compilers, so you cannot be absolutely certain that any programs you write that use the extensions will be able to run on other platforms. For example, Visual C++ extends the C++ language by allowing you to include Microsoft Foundation Classes in your programs. **Microsoft Foundation Classes (MFCs)**, are libraries of classes that can be used as the building blocks for creating Windows applications with Visual C++. It is very important to understand that any Visual C++ programs you create that utilize MFCs will not conform to the ANSI C/C++ standards, and therefore will not be able to run with other vendor's C/C++ compilers. If you need your C/C++ program to be portable to other platforms, you must use only the standard ANSI C/C++ run-time libraries. Nevertheless, MFCs are an extremely powerful feature of Visual C++ because they allow you to create true Windows applications. One of the primary uses of Visual C++ is in the creation of Windows applications, and many of the projects you create in this book will include MFCs and therefore will not conform to ANSI C/C++.

You will learn how to use the various Visual C++ libraries throughout this book.

The visual aspect of Visual C++ is used for designing the user interface of certain types of programs, such as an MFC program. You can also use your mouse to draw some user interface elements of your program, such as the controls in a dialog box, using various Visual C++ tools. Figure 1-7 shows an example of the visual portion of a calculator program that you will work on in later chapters. You will draw the user interface elements shown in the figure using the controls displayed in the Toolbox window.

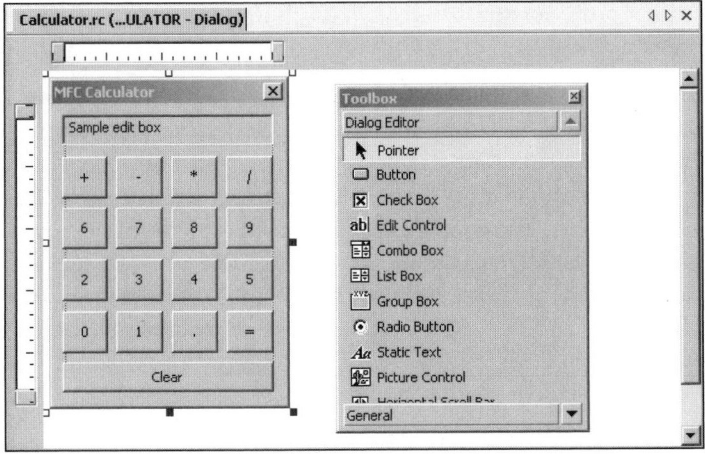

Figure 1-7 Visual portion of a calculator program that you will work on in later chapters

The Microsoft Visual Studio line of development tools includes a platform called the **.NET Framework** that is designed for developing and running Internet applications, primarily Web-based applications and services. As part of the .NET Framework, Microsoft has introduced a new programming language, C# (pronounced C *sharp*). **C#** is an object-oriented programming language based on C/C++ that creates Web-based programs designed to run on the .NET Framework. This text does *not* discuss C#, but focuses on traditional C++ programming. Traditional C++ programs, including Visual C++ programs, are not designed to run on the .NET Framework. Rather, they are designed to run on standard platforms such as Windows and UNIX operating systems. You can find a supplemental chapter online at *www.course.com* that discusses how to use Managed Extensions to write C++ programs that operate on the .NET Framework. **Managed Extensions** are special sets of code that allow traditional C++ programs to function on the .NET Framework.

To locate supplemental chapters and other support material for this book, search on 0-619-01657-4 at *www.course.com*.

If you would like to study the C# language, refer to *Microsoft C#* by Joyce Farrell, published by Course Technology/Thomson Learning.

Logic and Debugging

Each high-level programming language, including Visual C++, has its own **syntax**, or rules of the language. All languages have a specific, limited vocabulary and a specific set of rules for using that vocabulary. For example, you might use the commands *print* or *write* to produce output to the screen. To create a program, you must understand a given programming language's syntax.

To write a program, you must also understand computer-programming logic. The **logic** underlying any program involves executing the various parts of the program in the correct order to produce the desired results. For example, although you know how to drive a car well, you may not reach your destination if you do not follow the correct route. Similarly, you might be able to use a programming language's syntax correctly, but be unable to execute a logically constructed, workable program. Examples of logical errors include multiplying two values when you meant to divide them, or producing output prior to obtaining the appropriate input. The following C++ code contains another example of a logic error:

```
int count = 0;
while (count <= 10) {
   cout << "The number is ";
   cout << count;
}
```

The code in the example uses a `while` statement, which is used to repeat a command or series of commands based on the evaluation of certain criteria. The criterion in the example is the value of a variable named count. The `while` statement is supposed to execute until the count variable is less than or equal to 10. There is no code within the `while` statement body however, that changes the count variable's value. The count variable will continue to have a value of 0 (zero) through each iteration of the loop. In this program, as it is written, a line containing the text string *The number is 0* will print on the screen over and over again.

Do not worry about how the C++ code in the example is constructed. The example is only meant to give you a better understanding of a logical error.

Any error in a program that prevents it from compiling or causes it to function incorrectly, whether due to incorrect syntax or flaws in logic, is called a bug. **Debugging** describes the act of tracing and resolving errors in a program. Legend has it that the term *debugging* was first coined in the 1940s by Grace Murray Hopper, a mathematician who was instrumental in developing the COBOL programming language. As the story goes, a moth short-circuited a primitive computer that Hopper was using. Removing the moth from the computer *debugged* the system and resolved the problem. Today, a bug refers to any sort of problem in the design and operation of a program.

Do not confuse bugs with computer viruses. Bugs are errors within a program that occur because of syntax errors, design flaws, and other types of errors. Viruses are self-contained programs designed to "infect" a computer system and cause mischievous or malicious damage. Actually, virus programs themselves can contain bugs if they contain syntax errors or do not perform (or damage) as their creators envisioned.

Many programming languages and development environments include commands and other features to assist in locating bugs in a program. Visual C++ contains many debugging commands and features, which you will learn about in Chapter 4, "Debugging". To provide you with some debugging skills prior to Chapter 4, debugging suggestions are offered in the Tips feature throughout this book. As you read the debugging tips however, keep in mind that debugging is not an exact science—every program you write is different and requires different methods of debugging. Your own logical and analytical skills are the best debugging resources you have.

CREATING A NEW PROJECT IN VISUAL C++

You will need to store the applications you create in a folder on your hard drive or on a network drive with sufficient disk space. Next, you will create a projects folder named Visual C++ Projects, or some other name that makes sense to you. Regardless of the name you choose in the next exercise for your projects folder, this text refers to it as the *Visual C++ Projects folder* throughout the course of this text.

To create a projects folder for the Visual C++ projects you create in this text:

1. If necessary, start Windows. Open **Windows Explorer** or **My Computer**.
2. Create a folder named **Visual C++ Projects** (or use another name if you like).
3. In your Visual C++ Projects folder, create a folder named **Chapter.01** where you will store the projects you create in this chapter.
4. Close **Windows Explorer** or **My Computer**.

Next, you will start creating a new project that you will use for the rest of this chapter to demonstrate the basic Visual C++ development tools and windows. The project you create in this chapter is for demonstration purposes only.

To create a new Visual C++ project:

1. Click the **Start** button on the taskbar. Point to the **Programs** folder (or the **All Programs** button in Windows XP) on the Start menu. Point to **Microsoft Visual Studio .NET** on the Programs menu, then click **Microsoft Visual Studio .NET**. Figure 1-8 shows how Visual Studio appears when you start it for the first time.

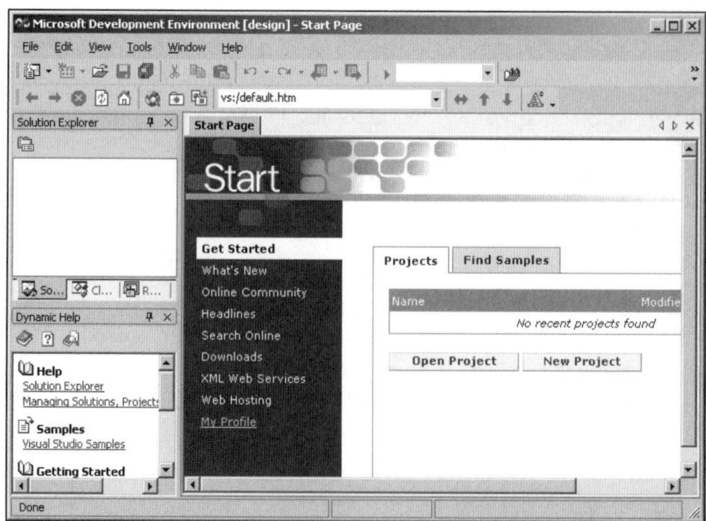

Figure 1-8 The Visual Studio window

2. Click the **New Project** button in the Start Page window or point to **New** on the **File** menu, then select **Project**. If necessary, when the New Project dialog box appears, click the **Visual C++ Projects** folder in the Project Types list. Also if necessary, click the **More** button to display more options in

the New Project dialog box. The caption on the More button changes to Less if all of the options in the dialog box are currently displayed. The Visual C++ Projects folder of the New Project dialog box is shown in Figure 1–9.

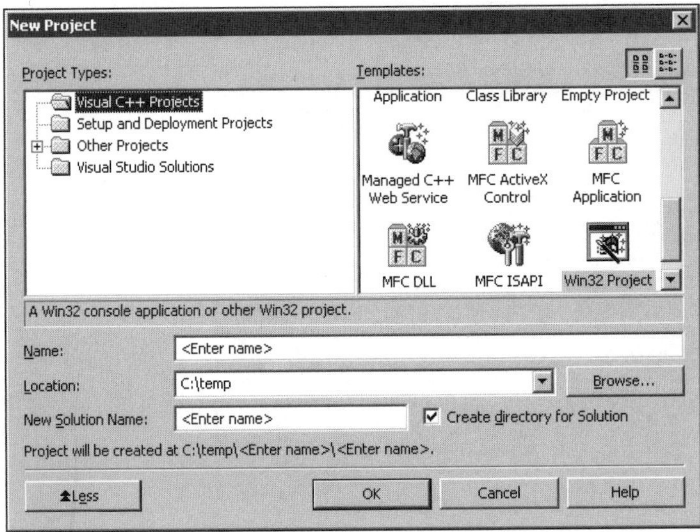

Figure 1-9 The Visual C++ Projects folder of the New Project dialog box

When you first see the New Projects dialog box, you might be intimidated by the many available options. Keep in mind that Visual Studio is a high-level programming environment and that many of the options in the New dialog box are used primarily by professional programmers. By the end of this text, you will understand how to work with many of the Visual C++ options in the New Project dialog box.

3. Scroll through the Templates list and click **Win32 Project**.
4. Next, replace *<Enter name>* in the Name text box with **HelloWorld**. Notice that the name you typed in the Name text box is automatically entered into the New Solution Name text box. What a solution is will be discussed in a moment.
5. Press the **Tab** key to move to the Location text box, type the name of the Visual C++ Projects folder, followed by a backslash and **Chapter.01**, then type another backslash and the text **HelloWorld**. This will create a new folder named HelloWorld in the Chapter.01 folder where the new project will be stored. The Location text box should read `C:\Visual C++ Projects\Chapter.01\HelloWorld`, or something similar if you are using different directory names or drive letters. You can click the button to the right of the Location text box to see the available drives and directories on your computer.
6. If necessary, clear the **Create directory for Solution** check box.

7. Click the **OK** button. The Win32 Application Wizard appears, describing the type of application you are creating. Click the **Application Settings** tab. In this tab, you can select the specific application type and options that you want to create. Figure 1-10 shows the Application Settings tab of the Win32 Application Wizard dialog box.

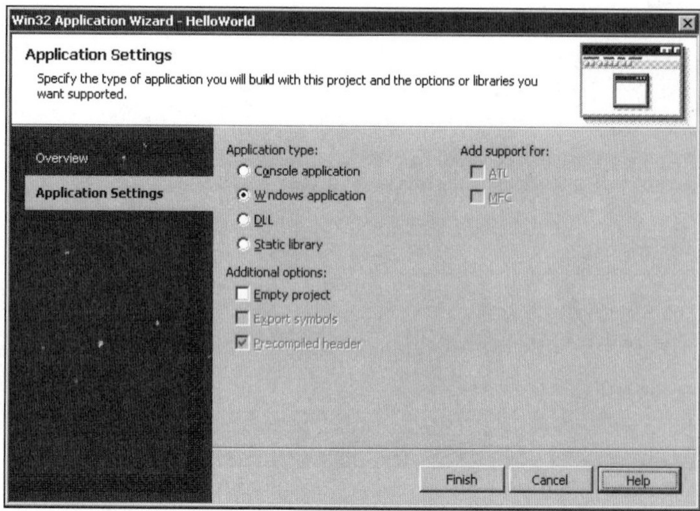

Figure 1-10 Application settings tab of the Win32 Application Wizard dialog box

8. The default Windows application setting type is fine for our purposes, so click the **Finish** button. Visual C++ creates a new project called HelloWorld in the HelloWorld folder in the Chapter.01 folder in your Visual C++ Projects folder. The Integrated Development Environment appears.

The Visual Studio IDE

Visual C++, Visual Basic, Visual C#, and the MSDN Library share a common workspace in Visual Studio called the **Integrated Development Environment (IDE)**. For each instance of the IDE there is a single solution containing one or more projects. A **project** is the application you are creating. A **solution** is also an application, but it is composed of one or more projects. For example, in a large accounting system you may have one project that handles accounts receivables and another project that handles accounts payable. Although both projects can function as independent applications, they are both part of the same accounting solution. Through the IDE you can simultaneously open projects from any combination of Visual Studio development tools. Figure 1–11 shows an example of the HelloWorld project opened in the Visual Studio IDE.

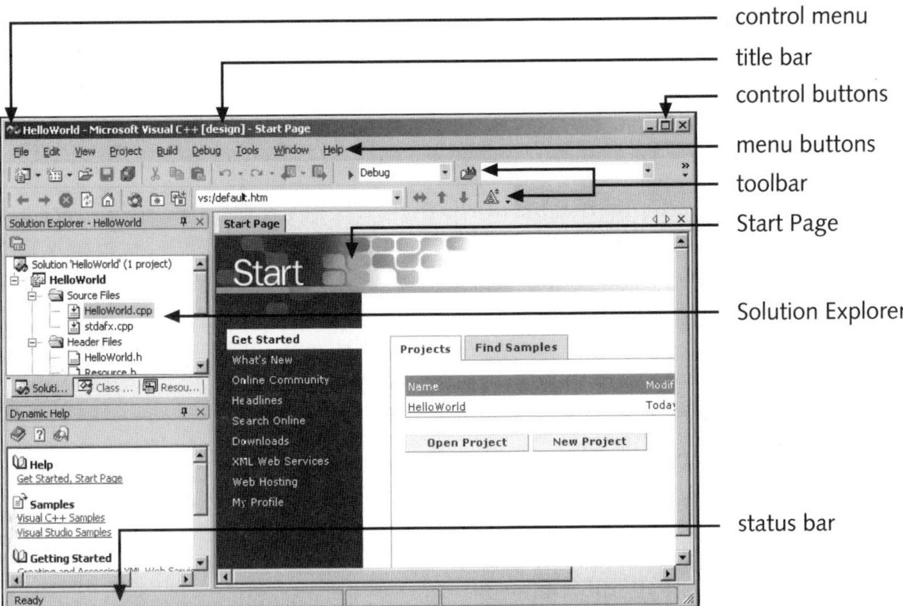

Figure 1-11 HelloWorld project opened in the Visual Studio IDE

Your screen may not look identical to Figure 1–11.

You can customize various aspects of Visual Studio by selecting Options from the Tools menu.

Projects can be part of one solution or part of more than one solution. They can be opened individually within a new solution or as part of an existing solution. Any changes to the project itself are reflected in all solutions in which the project is contained. Note that the solutions you create in this book will all consist of a single project. For this reason, whenever you create a new project, be sure to clear the Create directory for Solution check box.

For the rest of this chapter, you will use the HelloWorld project to learn how to work with several of the basic development tools and windows that are available to a Visual C++ application. You will also learn about the various techniques for managing the files and how to obtain help in Visual Studio .NET. Keep in mind that this chapter introduces only the basic tools and windows that you will need throughout this text. However, Visual C++ includes many other tools and windows than are introduced in this chapter. Some tools and windows are only available to certain types of applications.

Others are somewhat advanced and require a solid understanding of the basics of C++ programming. You will learn about many of the various C++ tools and windows as necessary during the course of your study.

The Start Page

The Start Page appears by default in the IDE whenever you first start Visual Studio. The Start Page allows you to set IDE user preferences and acts as a Web browser window. Links within the Start Page provide quick access to MSDN Online Web pages and newsgroups. MSDN Online is a Web-based version of the MSDN Library. You can also use the Start Page to find or register XML Web services, which allow programs written in different languages and on different platforms to communicate with each other using XML standards. The links within the Start Page window are as follows:

- **Get Started** — Opens existing projects and solutions or creates new ones
- **What's New** — Displays new features in Visual Studio and checks for product updates
- **Online Community** — Provides links to online developer sites and newsgroups
- **Headlines** — Displays links to the latest news in MSDN Online
- **Search Online** — Searches for information in MSDN Online
- **Downloads** — Provides access to MSDN downloads of developer tools, sample code, betas, and product updates
- **XML Web Services** — Accesses a free public registry where you can search for XML Web services to include in your applications
- **Web Hosting** — Offers professional Web hosting services through various Internet service providers (ISPs)
- **My Profile** — Allows you to set your IDE user preferences, including interface and Help options

Several of the Start Page links, including Headlines and Downloads, receive periodic Internet updates. If you are connected to the Internet when you click a link that requires an update, the IDE automatically downloads the necessary information. If you are not connected to the Internet when you click a link that requires an update, the IDE displays the last updated information you received.

You must have a newsgroup reader configured on your system before you can access any newsgroups through the Online Community link.

Next, you will set your IDE user preferences in the My Profile section of the Start Page.

To set your IDE user preferences in the My Profile section of the Start Page:

1. Click the **My Profile** link on the Start Page.
2. If neccesary, select **Visual C++ Developer** in the Profile combo box. Selecting a profile in the Profile combo box automatically sets the options in the Keyboard Scheme, Window Layout, and Help Filter combo boxes. The Keyboard Scheme sets the shortcut keys that you can use within Visual Studio. The Window Layout combo box sets the arrangement of the various windows within Visual Studio. The Help Filter combo box filters the information displayed in the MSDN Library and on the Startup Page. After you select **Visual C++ Developer** in the Profile combo box, the Keyboard Scheme and Window Layout combo boxes should change to *Visual C++ 6*, and the Help Filter combo box should change to *Visual C++*.
3. The Show Help section contains two choices: Internal Help and External Help. The Internal Help choice displays MSDN Library help information within the IDE. External Help displays MSDN Library help in a separate window. Displaying help internally can make the IDE crowded and difficult to work with, so select **External Help** (if necessary). A dialog box appears notifying you that changes will not take effect until Visual Studio is restarted. Click the **OK** button to continue.
4. The last option in the My Profile section is the At Startup combo box, which determines what will appear when you first open Visual Studio. Expand the combo box to see the available options, and if necessary, select **Show Start Page**. Figure 1-12 shows how the My Profile section your IDE should appear.

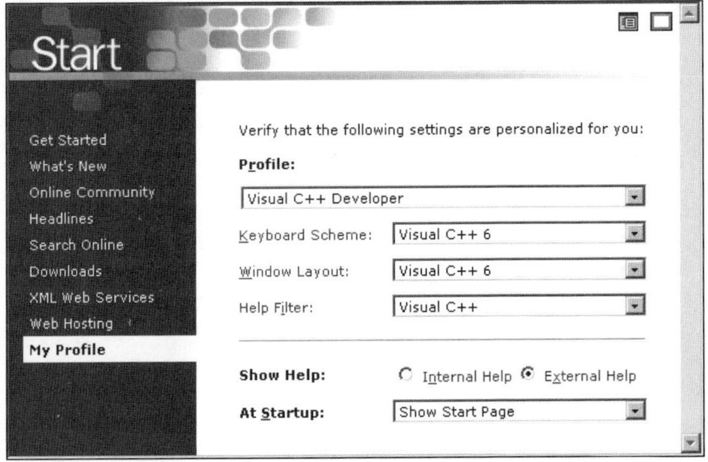

Figure 1-12 Updated My Profile section in Start Page

Changing how Help appears does not take effect until you close and restart Visual Studio. If you needed to change your Show Help option to External Help, be sure to close and then reopen Visual Studio before continuing. Once you reopen Visual Studio, open the HelloWorld project by clicking its name on the Get Started screen on the Start Page.

The Solution Explorer Window

Visual C++ projects are normally composed of multiple files representing a specific type of resource or object. Two of the most common types of files you will use in Visual C++ are C++ source files, with an extension of `.cpp`, and C++ header files, with an extension of `.h`. Other types of files used in a Visual C++ project include resource files, with an extension of `.rc`, which are used for managing visual aspects of a program, such as dialog boxes and toolbars. You use the **Solution Explorer window** in the IDE to manage the various projects and associated files contained in a solution. Projects, folders, and files in the Solution Explorer window appear in a hierarchical list that may remind you of Windows Explorer, or some other type of graphical file management system.

To use the Solution Explorer window to display the contents of the HelloWorld solution:

1. The Solution Explorer window should have appeared automatically when you first created the HelloWorld project. If it did not, select **Solution Explorer** from the View menu. An example of the Solution Explorer window is shown in Figure 1-13.

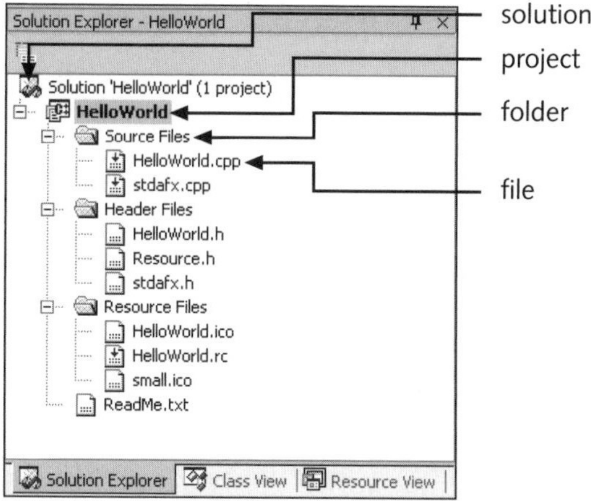

Figure 1-13 Solution Explorer window

2. The first item in the Solution Explorer window is the Solution icon. Beneath the Solution icon is a Project icon for the HelloWorld project. The HelloWorld project contains several folders containing the various files that make up the project. The Plus box and Minus box located to the left of each

folder icon are used for expanding and collapsing folders. The Plus box indicates that an item contains other items that are not currently visible. The Minus box indicates that all items beneath the associated item are currently visible. By default, all of a project's folders are expanded, so you will not see any Plus icons. Try clicking the Minus box next to the Source Files folder. All the files in the Source Files folder are hidden, and the Minus box changes to a Plus box.

The Plus box and Minus box are also used in Windows Explorer for expanding and collapsing drives and folders.

3. Click the Plus box again to redisplay all the files within the Source Files folder. For now, do not worry about what these files are used for; you will learn about the various files types used in Visual C++ throughout the course of this text.

This solution contains only one project, named HelloWorld. If it contained additional projects, they would be located in an alphabetical list beneath the Solution icon.

You can also display the Solution Explorer window by clicking the Solution Explorer button on the Standard toolbar or by pressing Ctrl+Alt+L.

Notice the three tabs that are visible at the bottom of the Solution Explorer window: Solution Explorer, Class View, and Resource View. **Class View** displays project files according to their classes, which are arranged as folders in the project directory. **Resource View** displays the files that are used specifically for building a Windows application. You will work mostly with Solution Explorer for the next few chapters.

The Code and Text Editor Window

Visual C++ has its own built-in editor called the **Code and Text Editor** window. Before diving too deeply into this section, you need to understand that some of the features you will use in the Code and Text Editor window require a knowledge of more advanced programming techniques. For example, some of the features of the Code and Text Editor window apply only to objects that are part of your C++ code. Although the advanced features of the Code and Text Editor window could have been introduced as you progress through the book, it is less confusing to introduce the Visual C++ interface features in one place. For this reason, you will be examining parts of a Windows-based calculator program that you will work on in later chapters. Do not try to understand the advanced code that you will see in this section. Instead, simply try to focus on the features of the Code and Text Editor window that are introduced.

The Code and Text Editor window is called the Code Editor when it displays programming code, and it is called the Text Editor when it displays text that is not associated with any particular programming language. Because you will be using the Code and Text Editor window almost exclusively with C++ code, it will be referred to as the Code Editor from this point forward. The Code Editor window has the same text editing capabilities as other Windows text editors: you can cut and paste, drag and drop, and search for specific text strings. These and other text editing options are available on the Edit menu and the toolbar.

The various types of code elements in the Code Editor window are distinguished by syntax coloring. This color coding makes it easier to understand the structure and code in a C++ program. For example, the default syntax coloring for keywords such as `public` is blue. (You will learn about keywords in the next chapter. For now, you should understand that keywords represent some of the most basic parts of a C++ program.) If you need to locate a statement containing the keyword `public`, you can start by looking at just the blue text. Of course, if you know the specific text contained in the statement, it can be much easier to use the Find and Replace commands on the Edit menu. If you do not know the specific text, syntax coloring can help you greatly limit the lines that you need to examine. Consider a large word-processing document in which you need to locate a piece of text. If you cannot remember the exact text string for which to search, then the Find and Replace command is useless; you would need to examine each line of text in the document manually. Manually searching for text is simpler however, if the specific type of text is indicated by color.

You can change Code and Text Editor options, including syntax color choices, by selecting Options from the Tools menu. The Text Editor folder in the Options dialog box contains options for the Code and Text Editor window. You can select syntax coloring choices in the Fonts and Colors section of the Environment folder.

The Code Editor window uses a feature called **statement completion** to aid in the creation of C++ code. As you are writing code, member lists and parameter information are displayed automatically according to the current object. Members refer to functions and properties that are associated with a particular class. For example, later in this text you will create a class named CCalculator that you will use to create a Windows-based calculator. You will create an object of the class named calc, which you can then use to access CCalculator class members. In order to access class members, you append a period to an object of the class. Once you append a period to an object of the class, statement completion displays a list of the class members, as shown in Figure 1-14. You can then let Visual C++ fill in the rest of a member name for you by double-clicking a name in the list, or by highlighting the name and pressing Enter.

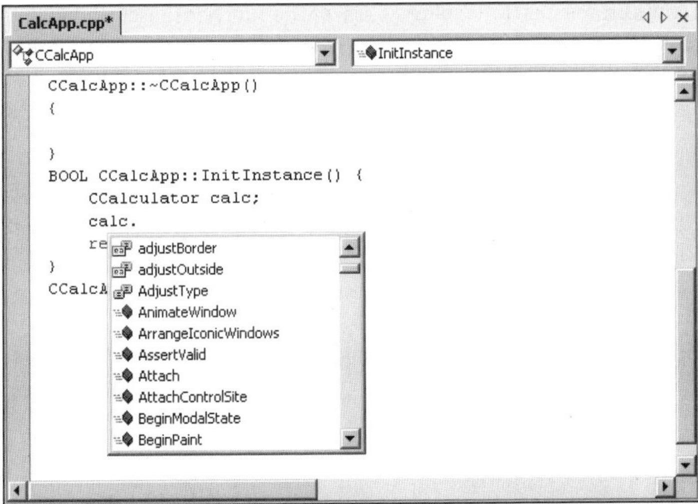

Figure 1-14 Statement completion for a class object

A parameter is a piece of information that is required by a particular function. You enter parameter information into a set of parentheses that follows a function name. Statement completion can help you fill in parameter information. For example, if you type `CreateWindow` and then type the opening parenthesis (, a list of ten parameters accepted by the CreateWindow() function appears. An example of statement completion for the CreateWindow() function parameters is shown in Figure 1–15.

Start Page **HelloWorld.cpp***

(Globals) InitInstance

```
BOOL InitInstance(HINSTANCE hInstance, int nCmdShow)
{
   HWND hWnd;

   hInst = hInstance; // Store instance handle in our global variable

   hWnd = CreateWindow(

   if (!
   {
      return FALSE;
   }

   ShowWindow(hWnd, nCmdShow);
```

HWND CreateWindow (**LPCTSTR lpClassName**, LPCTSTR lpWindowName, DWORD dwStyle, int x, int y, int nWidth, int nHeight, HWND hWndParent, HMENU hMenu, HANDLE hInstance, LPVOID lpParam)

Figure 1-15 Statement completion for the CreateWindow() function's parameters

Don't worry about the exact meaning of any of the functions discussed in this chapter, or exactly how to use class members or function parameters. Simply understand that the Code Editor will assist you in creating statements.

To manually display list members for a class or object, place your cursor anywhere in the class or object name, then select List Members from the IntelliSense submenu on the Edit menu, or press Ctrl+J. To manually display parameter information, place your cursor anywhere in a statement, then select Parameter Info from the IntelliSense submenu on the Edit menu or press Ctrl+Shift+Space.

IntelliSense is a Microsoft technology that automates routine and complex tasks.

A command that is similar to the Parameter Info command is the Quick Info command, which displays syntax information for various types of programming elements, including variables, functions, and objects. To execute the Quick Info command, place your cursor anywhere in the name of a C++ programming element, such as a variable or function name, and then select Quick Info from the IntelliSense submenu on the Edit menu or press Ctrl+K, Ctrl+I.

Shortcut keys that consist of multiple sets of keystrokes, such as the Ctrl+K, Ctrl+I keystrokes that execute the Quick Info command, are called chords. To execute a chord, press the first keystroke combination in the chord, release the keys, then press the second keystroke combination and release the keys again. For example, to execute the chord for the Quick Info command press Ctrl+K, release the keys, then press Ctrl+I and release the keys again.

Figure 1-16 shows an example of the syntax that appears when you execute the Quick Info command while your cursor is within the name of the InitInstance() function.

```
CalcApp.cpp*
CCalcApp                                    InitInstance
#include "calcapp.h"
#include "Calculator.h"
CCalcApp::CCalcApp(void)
{
}

CCalcApp::~CCalcApp(void)
{
}
BOOL CCalcApp::InitInstance() {
     CCalculator c BOOL CCalcApp::InitInstance(void)
     calc.DoModal();
     return FALSE;
}
CCalcApp theApplication;
```

Figure 1-16 Quick Info with the InitInstance() function

You cannot execute the Quick Info command on keywords, which appear in blue in the Code Editor window.

Another tool for writing C++ code is **Word Completion**, which is used to automatically complete class names and other elements according to the first few characters you type. For example, if you type the word `Create`, then press Alt+Right Arrow, a list containing all elements beginning with the word *Create* appears. If the letter or letters you type are unique to a specific element, Visual C++ automatically inserts that element name into your code. For example, if you type `CreateAcc`, then press Alt+Right Arrow, the function name `CreateAcceleratorTable` is inserted into your code because this is the only element that begins with the letters *CreateAc*. You can also use Word Completion by selecting Complete Word from the IntelliSense submenu on the Edit menu.

You can also select the four IntelliSense commands, List Members, Parameter Info, Quick Info, and Complete Word, from a shortcut menu by right-clicking a programming element in the Code Editor window.

Next, you will open a source file in the Code Editor window and examine its contents.

To open a source file in the Code Editor window and examine its contents:

1. Return to the Solution Explorer window in Visual C++ and double-click the filename **HelloWorld.cpp** that should be visible beneath the Source Files folder located directly beneath the Hello World project icon. The HelloWorld.cpp source file should open in the Code Editor window, as shown in Figure 1-17.

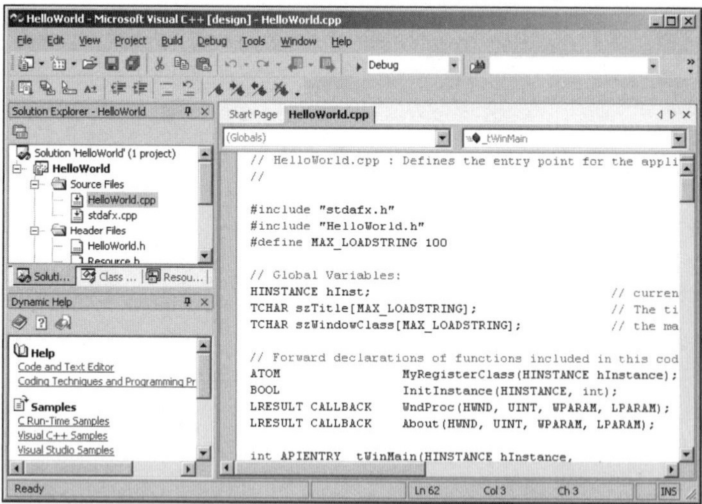

Figure 1-17 HelloWorld.cpp in the Code Editor window

2. Scroll through the document and observe the different color coding that is applied to the various statements in the program. By default, keywords are marked in blue, comments (which are explanatory notes that you place in code) are marked in dark green, and standard statements are marked in black.

The default color choices on your computer may differ from those mentioned in this text.

3. About twenty lines from the top of the file is a statement that includes a function named `_tWinMain()`. Place your cursor anywhere within the function name (_tWinMain) and press **Ctrl+Shift+Space,** or select **Parameter Info** from the IntelliSense submenu on the Edit menu. A list of parameters for the _tWinMain() function appears. This exercise serves only to demonstrate how you can display the parameter list after you have finished typing a statement.
4. Press **Escape** to close the Parameter Info list.
5. In about the middle of the file, you will see several statements that begin with `wcex`. This object is based on the WNDCLASSEX class. Again, don't worry about how to use the WNDCLASSEX class at this point. Our purpose in this section is only to demonstrate the use of the Code Editor window. Place your cursor within any of the wcex object names in any of the statements, and then press **Ctrl+J** or select **List Members** from the IntelliSense submenu on the Edit menu. A list of WNDCLASSEX class members should appear. As with the Parameter Info command, this step only serves to demonstrate how to display class members after you have finished typing the statement.

6. Press **Escape** to close the member list.
7. Scroll a little farther down in the file and place your cursor in the function name ShowWindow within the statement that reads `ShowWindow(hWnd, nCmdShow);`. Display the function syntax information by pressing **Ctrl+K, Ctrl+I**, or by selecting Quick Info from the IntelliSense submenu on the Edit menu. The syntax for the ShowWindow() function should appear. Although the information that appears may not make much sense to you now, as you progress in your C++ studies, you will realize how valuable it is to be able to quickly view the required syntax for a specific type of programming element.
8. Press **Escape** to close the Quick Info list.

Project Properties

A Visual C++ project contains various settings, or properties, that determine how the project appears and behaves. You use the Property Pages dialog box to change the properties of a project. Although many project properties are too advanced for our studies, you will need to change several properties during the course of this book. In order to access the Property Pages dialog box for a particular project, you must have the project selected in the Solution Explorer window. To display the Property Pages dialog box, select the Properties command on the Project menu. Figure 1-18 displays an example of the Property Pages dialog box. Notice in Figure 1-18 the various folders on the left of the dialog box that display the major types of properties. Within each folder are various property categories. Once you select a property category within a folder, the various properties that are available in that category appear on the right side of the dialog box.

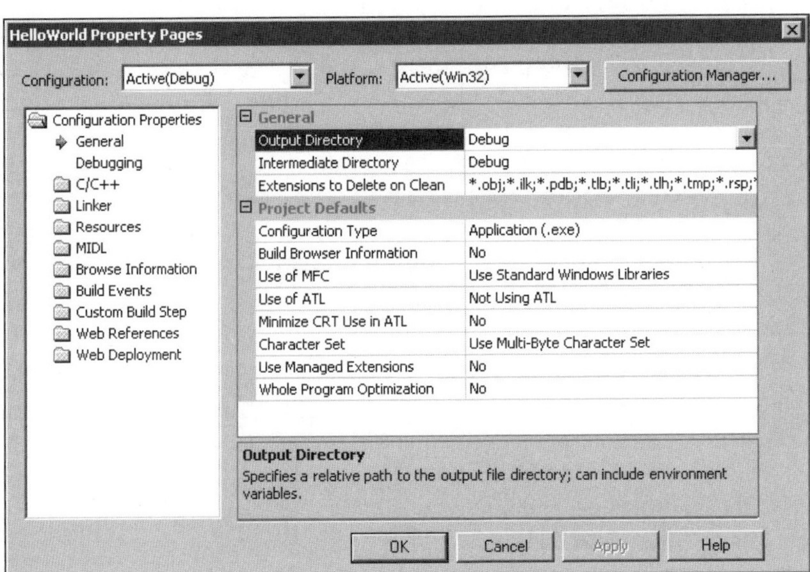

Figure 1-18 The Property Pages dialog box

A project's properties are saved in a file with an extension of .vbproj.

Building and Executing an Application

The tools for compiling a C++ program are located on the Build menu. You have three options for compiling an application: compile C++ source files individually using the Compile command; compile individual projects using the Build <project name> command; or compile all the source files and projects in a solution using the Build Solution command. You use the Compile command when you want to check your syntax while you are writing code. However, you must execute the Build <project name> or Build Solution command at least once in order to create an executable file. For small programs, it is usually easier to select one of the Build commands so that the program is compiled and built in a single step. However, the Compile command is useful if you have a large program with many C++ source files as it allows you to compile only those files that you have modified. Note that even if your file compiles successfully with the Compile command, you must still run one of the Build commands to build the executable file. Because the programs you create in this text will consist of single projects, you can select either the Build <project name> or Build Solution command. This text primarily uses the Build Solution command.

You can execute the Build Solution command by pressing the F7 key and the Compile command by pressing Ctrl+F7.

When you select one of the Build commands, Visual C++ compiles only the files in any of your projects that have changed. However, there may be instances when you must recompile your program, even if you have made no changes to the code. For example, you would need to recompile your entire program if your compiled files became corrupt or if you wanted to perform some final testing before releasing a finished version of your program. You can force Visual C++ to recompile all files in your program, even if they have not been modified, by selecting the Rebuild <project name> or Rebuild Solution command from the Build menu. After running the Build command, you execute a program by selecting the Start Without Debugging command on the Debug menu, or by pressing Ctrl+F5.

When learning a new programming language, an old tradition among programmers is to create a first program that prints or displays the text *Hello World!* To carry on the tradition, you will modify the HelloWorld project so that it displays the text *Hello World!* After adding the appropriate code, you will build and execute the application. As you add the necessary code to the HelloWorld project, remember that the purpose of this

1

chapter is to introduce you to the basics of the Visual C++ IDE. Therefore, do not worry about trying to understand the code you write in this chapter. Instead, simply try to get comfortable with working in the Code Editor window and with building and executing programs.

To modify the HelloWorld project so that it displays the text *Hello World!*:

1. Return to the **HelloWorld.cpp** file in the Code Editor window.
2. Locate the statement in the file that reads `HWND hWnd;`. Place your cursor after the semicolon, press **Enter**, and then type **`HWND hHello;`**. Be sure to type the case of the letters exactly as shown.
3. Four lines down is a statement that begins `hWnd = CreateWindow` and that wraps to a second line. Place your cursor after the semicolon on the second line of the statement, press **Enter**, and then type the following code. Again, be sure to type the case of the letters exactly as shown.

```
hHello = CreateWindow("EDIT", "Hello World!",
  WS_VISIBLE | WS_CHILD, 10, 10, 100, 20,
  hWnd, NULL, hInstance, NULL);
```

The following code shows how the new statements should appear in the file. The new statements you are adding appear in boldface.

```
HWND hWnd;
HWND hHello;
hInst = hInstance; // Store instance handle in our global
   variable
hWnd = CreateWindow(szWindowClass, szTitle, WS_OVER
   LAPPEDWINDOW, CW_USEDEFAULT, 0, CW_USEDEFAULT, 0,
   NULL, NULL,       hInstance, NULL);
hHello = CreateWindow("EDIT", "Hello World!",
       WS_VISIBLE | WS_CHILD, 10, 10, 100, 20,
       hWnd, NULL, hInstance, NULL);
```

4. Next, build the program by pressing **F7** or by selecting **Build Solution** from the Build menu. If your program builds successfully, you should see *Build succeeded* in the status bar. If your program did not build successfully, you will see one or more error messages in the Task List at the bottom of the IDE. (Error messages and the Task List will be discussed shortly.) If you see error messages in the Task List, make sure you entered the case of the letters exactly as shown, and then rebuild the application.
5. After successfully building the project, press **Ctrl+F5** or select **Start Without Debugging** from the Debug menu to execute the program. A simple Windows application executes and displays the single line *Hello World!* in the application window, as shown in Figure 1-19.

Figure 1-19 Hello World application window

6. Select **Exit** from the **File** menu, or click the **Close** button to close the Hello World application.

Next, you need to introduce some errors into the HelloWorld project in order to learn how to work with build messages in the next section.

To introduce some errors into the HelloWorld project in order to learn how to work with build messages in the next section:

1. Delete the semicolon at the end of the `HWND hHello;` statement you added in Step 2. The new statement should now read `HWND hHello`.
2. In the second statement you added, which begins with `hHello = CreateWindow(`, delete the closing parenthesis just before the semicolon at the end of the statement. The new statement should read as follows:

```
hHello = CreateWindow("EDIT", "Hello World!",
  WS_VISIBLE | WS_CHILD, 10, 10, 100, 20,
  hWnd, NULL, hInstance, NULL;
```

Before you build the project, you need to learn how to work with the Output Window and the Task List.

The Output Window

At the bottom of the IDE is the Output window. Visual C++ uses the **Output window** to display its progress when you build a program. The Output window also displays build messages for any types of errors that Visual C++ finds during the build process. You open the Output window by pressing Ctrl+Alt+O, by clicking the Output tab with your mouse, or by selecting Output from the Other Windows submenu on the View menu. Figure 1-20 shows the Output window after successfully building the HelloWorld project.

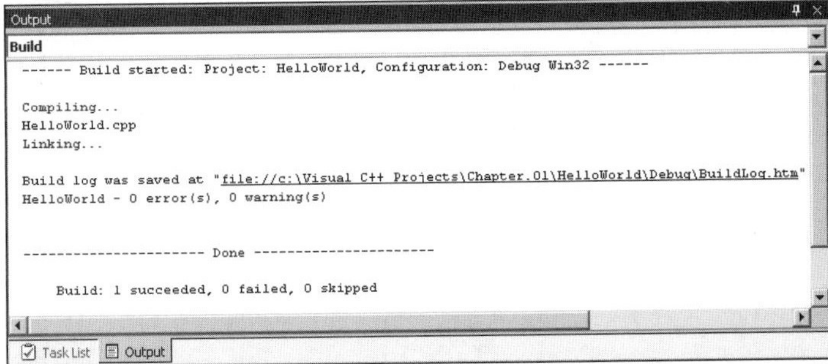

Figure 1-20 Output window after building the HelloWorld project

The Task List

Located next to the Output window in the IDE is the **Task List**, which maintains a list of tasks that need to be completed for a project. The Task List also shows build messages for errors that Visual C++ finds during the build process. Unlike the Output window, which shows build messages as static text, the Task List shows build messages as tasks that need to be completed. Although most of the tasks are automatically generated by Visual C++ (such as build tasks), you can add your own tasks containing notes, items to be completed, and so on. You display the Task List by pressing Ctrl+Alt+K, by clicking the Task List tab with your mouse, or by selecting Task List from the Other Windows submenu on the View menu. Figure 1-21 shows an example of the Task List.

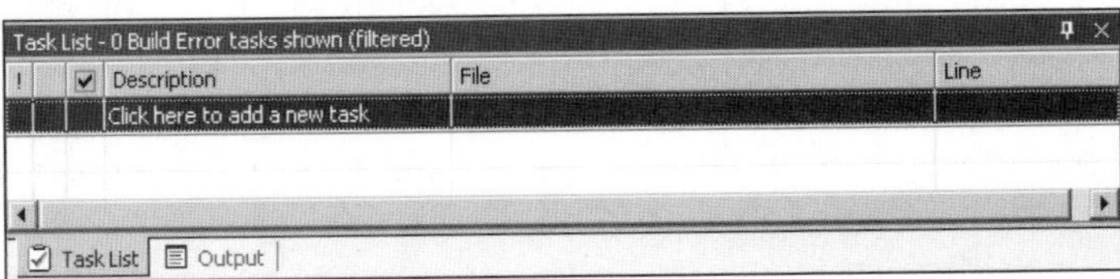

Figure 1-21 Task List

You can filter the tasks appearing in the Task List using one of the predefined views that are available on the Show Tasks submenu on the View menu.

As you can see in Figure 1-21, the Task List contains six columns. The first column indicates the priority level of the task. Clicking the first column displays a combo box with the three priority levels you can choose: Low, Normal, or High. The second column displays an automatically generated icon indicating the task category. (See the topic Task List Views in the MSDN Library for a list of the task category icons that can appear in Task List.) The third column contains a check box used for indicating when a task is complete. The fourth column contains a description of the task. If the task is a build error task, the fifth column shows the name of the file containing the error, and the sixth column shows the location of the error in the file.

You cannot mark certain tasks, such as build errors, as complete by using the Task List check box column. In the case of a build error, you must first correct the code causing the error. Most compiler errors are automatically removed from the Task List once the code is corrected.

Next, you will add a new task to the Task List.

To add a new task to the Task List:

1. Display the Task List by pressing **Ctrl+Alt+K**, by clicking the **Task List** tab with your mouse, or by selecting **Task List** from the **Other Windows** submenu on the **View** menu.
2. Select **All** from the **Show Tasks** submenu on the **View** menu.

The tasks you see that begin with TODO: are automatically generated by Visual C++ for any statements in your code that begin with // TODO:. Statements beginning with //TODO: are automatically generated for certain project types to indicate where you should add your own code to customize a Visual C++ application.

3. Place the insertion point in the Description column where it reads *Click here to add a new task*, and then type **Fix intentionally introduced errors in code**.
4. Click the first column and select a priority level of **High**.

Although an entire chapter is devoted to debugging later in this text, you should know up front that the build messages appearing in the Output window and Task List are your first opportunity to locate bugs in your programs. There are two main types of build messages: compiler error messages and warning messages. **Compiler error messages** occur for any syntax errors in a program. Compiler error messages contain the name of the document in which the error occurred, the line number in the document, and a description of the error. You will learn in the next chapter that functions require opening and closing braces ({}). As an example of a compiler error message, consider the following function that causes a syntax error because it is missing the closing brace (}).

```
void CErrorsApp::incompleteFunction()
{
   CString szMessage = "Missing closing brace";
   AfxMessageBox(szMessage);
```

The syntax error in the preceding code generates the following description:

fatal error C1075: end of file found before the left brace '{' at 'c:\Visual C++ Projects\Chapter.01\Errors\Errors.cpp(111)' was matched

You should use compiler error messages only to find the general location of an error in a program and not as the exact indicator of an error. You cannot always assume that the line specified by an error message contains the actual problem in your program. The challenge with the description for the preceding error message is that it does not exactly say *the function named incompleteFunction() is missing a closing brace*. Instead, the message more vaguely states that the end of the file was found before a matching left brace was found. You need to be able to interpret the meaning of each message depending on the given circumstance. In the case of the missing closing brace, the compiler searched through the entire source file to locate a matching closing brace for the function. The error message appeared because the end of the file was reached before the compiler found the closing brace.

You can quickly jump to the line that raised a build error by double-clicking the build error task in Task List. After double-clicking a build error task, your cursor will be placed in the line that raised the error, and a blue arrow will also point to the line. For example, Figure 1-22 shows the compiler error message that is generated by the missing closing brace, along with the Code Editor window containing the source code file. After double-clicking the build error task in the Task List, the line in the source file that raised the error is identified—in this case the end of the file.

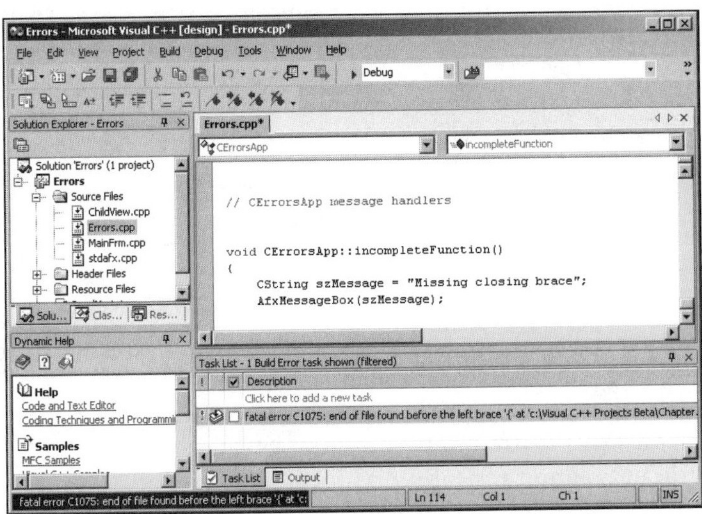

Figure 1-22 Jumping to a statement that raised a compiler error message

Warning messages occur for any potential problems that may exist in your code, but that are not serious enough to cause a compiler error message. One of the more common warning messages you may see occurs when you declare a variable, but do not use it in your program. For example, consider the following code:

```
void calculateProfits() {
   int iPayRate = 15;
   int iNumHours = 40;
   double dGrossPay;
   double dNetPay = (iPayRate * iNumHours) / .20;
}
```

Because the dGrossPay variable is never used, the following warning message appears in the Output window:

warning C4101: 'dGrossPay' : unreferenced local variable

An unused variable is not really a problem in a C++ program. The compiler issues a warning however, about any unused variables and other unused programming elements in order to help you write cleaner and more efficient code.

You will study functions and variables in the next chapter.

The number and severity of warning messages is determined by the Warning Level setting in the C++ folder of the Project Properties dialog box. Figure 1-23 lists the warning levels and their descriptions.

Warning Level	Description
Off	All warning messages are turned off
Level 1	Displays very severe warning messages
Level 2	Displays less severe warning messages
Level 3	Displays moderately severe warning messages
Level 4	Displays all Level 3 warnings along with information warnings

Figure 1-23 Warning levels

Until you are a more experienced programmer, you should leave your warning level set to the default setting of Level 3. You may even want to consider setting your warning level to treat all warnings as errors, which will help you write better code by forcing you to fix all code that raises warnings. If you want to adjust your warning level, first click the Project icon in Solution Explorer, and then select Properties from the Project menu. Click the C/C++ folder in the Project Property Pages dialog box, and then select the General property page. Warning levels are set with the Warning Level combo box. To treat all warning levels as errors, select Yes in the Treat Warnings as Errors combo box. Figure 1-24 shows an example of the General property page of the C/C++ folder in the Project Property Pages dialog box.

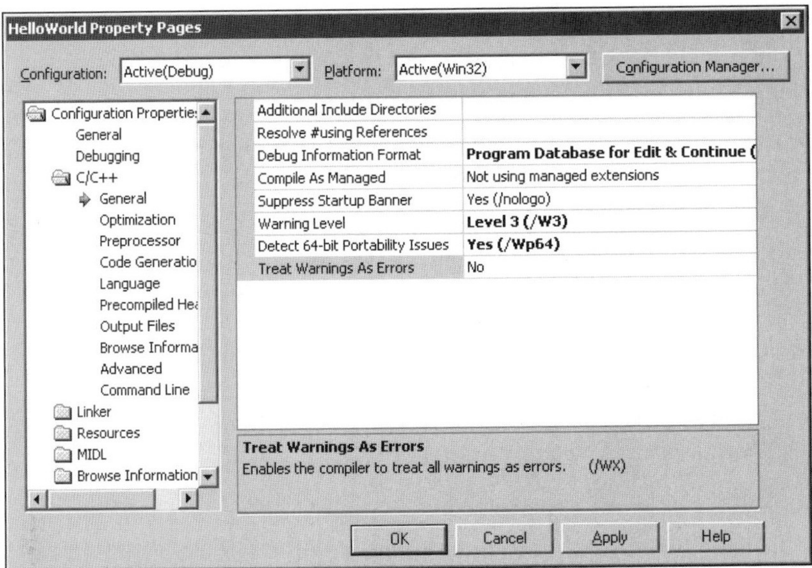

Figure 1-24 The General property page of the C/C++ folder in the Project Property Pages dialog box

Next, you will build the Hello project and observe the build messages in the Task List.

To build the HelloWorld project and observe the build error tasks in the Task List:

1. Return to the HelloWorld project in Visual C++.
2. Select **Build** from the Build menu to rebuild the HelloWorld project.
3. Once your project finishes building, a filter is automatically applied to the Task List so that it shows only build error tasks, as shown in Figure 1-25.

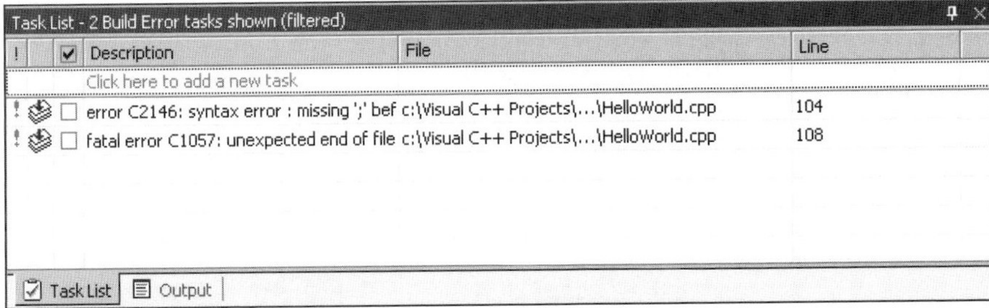

Figure 1-25 Build error tasks in the Task List

4. Double-click the first build error task. Your cursor will be placed in the statement following the `HWND hHello` statement from which you deleted the ending semicolon. Your cursor is placed in the line following the statement with the error because that is where the compiler starts searching for the ending semicolon. Move your cursor to the previous statement and add the semicolon to the end of the line so that it reads `HWND hHello;`.

5. Rebuild the project. You should now receive a single build error task in the Task List for the statement from which you deleted the closing parenthesis. Double-click the build error task, and your cursor will be placed in the statement that is missing the closing parenthesis. Add the closing parenthesis before the semicolon so that the statement reads as follows:

```
hHello = CreateWindow("EDIT", "Hello World!",
  WS_VISIBLE | WS_CHILD, 10, 10, 100, 20,
  hWnd, NULL, hInstance, NULL);
```

6. Rebuild the project again. The project should build successfully.

7. Select **All** from the Show Tasks submenu on the View menu. Click the check box in the *Fix intentionally introduced errors in code* task. The check box should change to the checked state and the task description should be crossed out as follows: ~~Fix intentionally introduced errors in code~~.

Managing Windows

With so many windows available in the IDE, it is easy for one window to hide another. As you work through this book, you will probably find it necessary to move and resize the windows on your screen. Certain types of tool windows in the IDE, such as the Solution Explorer and Output window, can be floating or dockable. A window with its dockable property turned on "snaps" to a default position on the screen. A tool window with its dockable property turned off snaps to the main application window as a tab. By default, the dockable property of a tool window is turned on, and the floating property is turned off. Figure 1-26 shows an example of the Task List window with its dockable property turned off. Notice that it is snapped to the main application window as a tab.

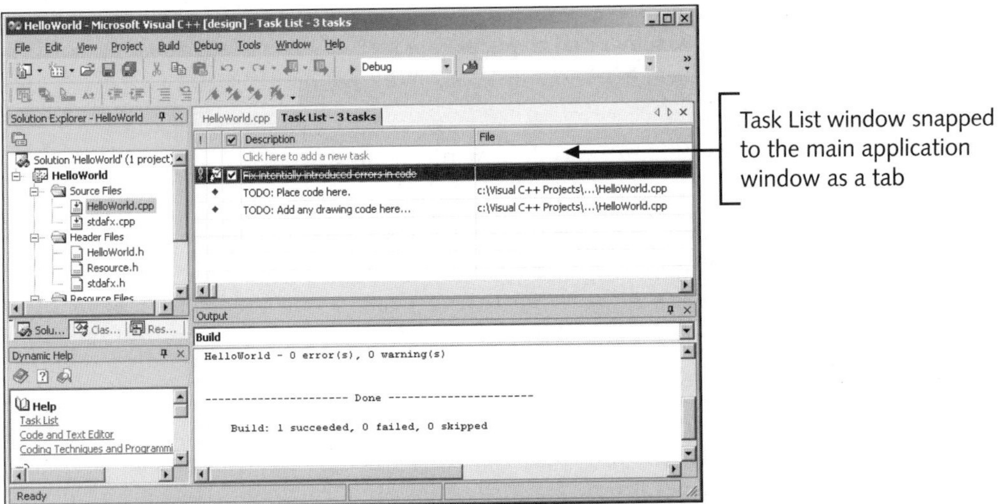

Figure 1-26 Task List window with its dockable property turned off

With its floating property turned on, a window can be dragged as a floating window to any part of the screen. It is usually easier to move a window with the docking property turned off. Figure 1-27 shows an example of the Task List window with its floating property turned on.

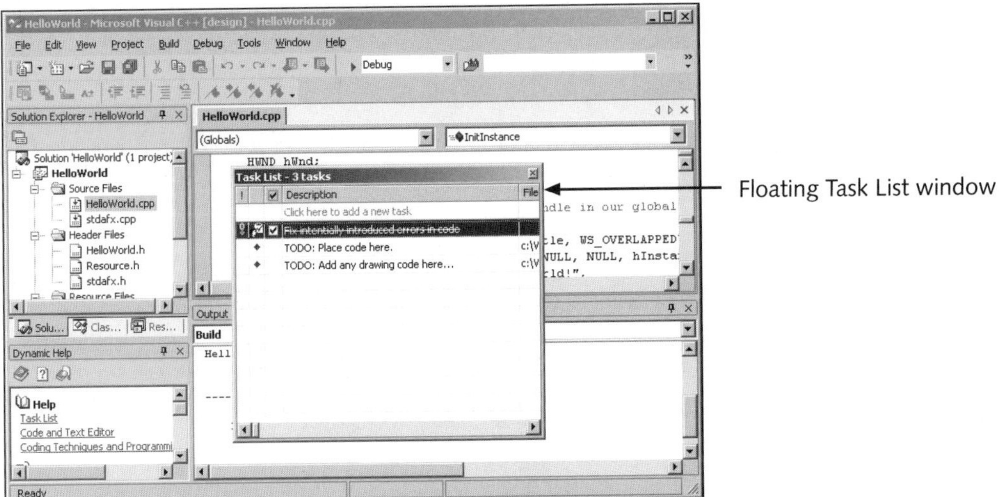

Figure 1-27 Task List window with its floating property turned on

The dockable property is not available for main windows such as the Code Editor or Start Page windows.

If at any point you become completely lost among the various floating and dockable windows that can appear in the IDE, you can start over by resetting your profile in the My Profile link on the Start Page.

To turn the dockable property of a window on or off:

- Activate a window whose docking property you want to change by clicking the window or selecting it from the Window menu, and then select **Dockable** from the **Window** menu. A check mark (√) next to the Dockable menu item indicates that the property is selected. If there is no check mark next to the Dockable property, then the window is not dockable.

To turn the floating property of a window on or off:

- Activate a window whose dockable property you want to change, and then select **floating** from the **Window** menu. A check mark (√) next to the Floating menu item indicates that the property is selected. If there is no check mark next to the Floating menu item, then the window is not floating.

Like windows, toolbars can be floating or docked. To dock a floating toolbar, double-click the toolbar title bar using the left mouse button. To move a floating toolbar, position the mouse cursor over the toolbar title bar, then hold down the left mouse button and drag the toolbar to the desired position. To move a docked toolbar, position the mouse cursor over the move handle that appears on the left side of the toolbar, then hold down the left mouse button and drag the toolbar to the desired position.

To move a floating window:

- Point to the **title bar** of a floating window, click and hold down the left mouse button, then **drag** the window to the desired position.

To resize a floating window:

- Point to the side, corner, top, or bottom of a window, make sure you get a double-arrow pointer, click and hold down the left mouse button, and drag the window until it is the desired size. Dragging the top or bottom of a window resizes it vertically, dragging the left or right side resizes the window horizontally, and dragging a corner resizes the horizontal and vertical dimensions simultaneously.

You can hide a window by selecting the Hide command from the Window menu. For windows in the default docking position, you can select the Auto Hide command from the Window menu. Windows that are auto hidden are visible as a tab at the edge of the IDE. Moving your mouse over an auto-hidden window redisplays the window, and moving your mouse off an auto-hidden window hides it again.

MANAGING THE SOLUTION

In this section, you will learn some basic techniques for working with the Visual C++ solution. You will use these techniques throughout the text, so be sure that you understand them.

Adding Resources to a Project

The various resources that make up projects and solutions are contained in disk files. These include source files and the other types of files that Visual C++ uses in its projects. The files that make up your projects are stored in folders, just like any other files.

It is important that you realize that although a file may be stored in the same folder where other files in a project are stored, the file will not actually be a part of the project until you physically add it to the project within the Visual C++ IDE. For example, consider the Solution Explorer window in Figure 1-28. The Source Files folder contains several files that are stored in a folder named Greeting. Each of the files in the Source Files folder has already been added to the project. The Greeting folder, however, may also contain a file named HelloMoon.cpp that you moved into the folder using Windows Explorer. The Greeting folder would then contain the files listed in Figure 1-29. Adding the HelloMoon.cpp file to the folder using Windows Explorer does not automatically add the file to the project—you must perform that task manually within Visual C++.

Figure 1-28 Solution Explorer window showing the Source Files folder

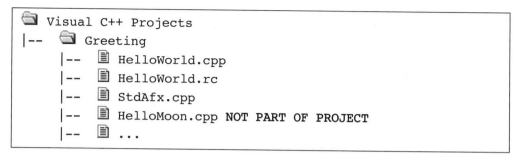

```
Visual C++ Projects
|--  Greeting
     |--  HelloWorld.cpp
     |--  HelloWorld.rc
     |--  StdAfx.cpp
     |--  HelloMoon.cpp NOT PART OF PROJECT
     |--  ...
```

Figure 1-29 Greeting Files folder

Next, you will practice adding a new source file to the HelloWorld project.

To practice adding a new source file to the HelloWorld project:

1. Return to the **HelloWorld** project in Visual C++.
2. Select **Add New Item** from the **Project** menu. The Add New Item dialog box appears, opened to the C++ category, as shown in Figure 1-30.

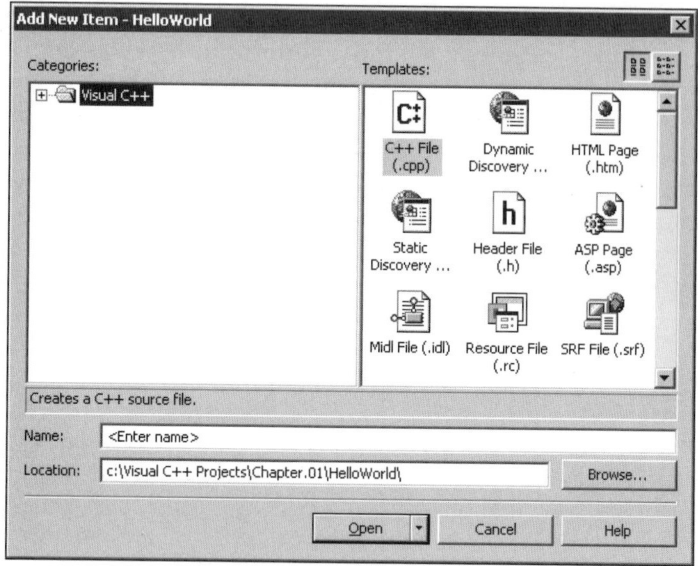

Figure 1-30 Add New Item dialog box

3. Click **C++ File** in the Templates list, and then highlight *<Enter name>* in the Name box. Type **Source2** as the filename, and then click the **Open** button. A new blank file named Source2.cpp opens in the IDE.

To add an existing file to a project, select Add Existing Item from the Project menu.

Adding Projects to a Solution

Solutions are composed of one or more projects. You can add new or existing projects to a solution. For example, you may have created a project that organizes your album collection. Now you are creating a more general music collection solution that organizes all your albums, CDs, and cassettes. Because the album project already exists, you can add it to the music collection solution, along with the CD and cassette projects you will create. You then combine all three projects to create a single music collection solution. This solution is a good example of an object-oriented program. Each project is an object, and you are combining them to create a larger object—the solution.

Next, you will add a new project to the current solution:

To add a new project to the current solution:

1. Select **New Project** from the Add Project submenu on the File menu.
2. In the Add New Project dialog box, select **Win32 Project**. Assign the project a name of **Project2**, and then save it in the Chapter.01 folder in your Visual C++ Projects folder. Click the **OK** button.
3. In the Win32 Application Wizard dialog box, click the **Finish** button. The new project opens in the IDE.

You can also add an existing project by pointing to Add Project on the File menu and then selecting the Existing Project command.

Saving Solutions, Projects, and Files

As you are developing a project and solution, you need to compile and execute your programs to make sure they perform as you would like. Unfortunately, even the most well-thought-out code can cause your computer to freeze or even crash. If your computer crashes—and it probably will—you will lose any unsaved changes to your solution. Therefore, it is good practice to save your solution at regular intervals and especially before compiling and executing a program.

By default, Visual C++ saves changes to all open documents during the build process. However, you must save manually if you make changes to a file contained in a project and then close the file or project without building. Properties and other settings for projects are also contained in physical files on your computer. Solution files have an extension of .sln, and project files have an extension of .vcproj. You must also save projects and solutions if you have made any changes to their properties and settings. Note that saving a project also saves all of the files within that project. Saving a solution saves all of the files within all of the projects it contains.

You can change how Visual C++ saves files during the build process by using the Projects and Solutions category in the General folder of the Options dialog box.

To save the HelloWorld solution:

1. Click the **Solution** icon in Solution Explorer.
2. Select **Save HelloWorld.sln** from the **File** menu.

To save the HelloWorld project:

1. Click the **HelloWorld** Project icon in Solution Explorer.
2. Select **Save HelloWorld.cpp** from the **File** menu.

To save individual files:

1. Activate the window containing the file you want to save or highlight the file name in the Solution Explorer window.
2. Select **Save** ***<file name>***from the **File** menu.

You can also save solutions, projects, and individual files by clicking the Save icon on the Standard toolbar or by pressing Ctrl+S.

Closing Solutions, Projects, and Files

If you have multiple projects and files open, the Visual C++ IDE can become difficult to work with because the screen may become crowded. Therefore, you may find it necessary to close individual projects and files when you are through working with them.

Next, you will close the Source2.cpp file you just added to the project.

To close the Source2.cpp file:

1. Make sure that Source2.cpp is the active window.
2. Select **Close** on the **File** menu.
3. If you make any changes to a file, Microsoft Visual Studio displays a dialog box prompting you to save your changes. You will not see this dialog box if you have not made any changes.

As you work with solutions and projects, you might want to close the current solution or project before opening new ones. For practice, you will now close the HelloWorld solution.

To close the HelloWorld solution:

1. Select **Close Solution** from the File menu.
2. Before closing the solution, Microsoft Visual Studio displays a dialog box prompting you to save any unsaved files. You will not see this dialog box if all of your files have been saved.

You can also close just a project by highlighting the Project icon in the Solution Explorer window and selecting Close on the File menu.

Opening Existing Solutions and Projects

Opening a saved solution opens all of the projects it contains. You can also open a project independently of any solution in which it is contained. Recall that solution files have an extension of .sln, and project files have an extension of .vcproj.

To open the HelloWorld solution:

1. Select **Open Solution** from the File menu. The Open Solution dialog box appears, as shown in Figure 1-31.

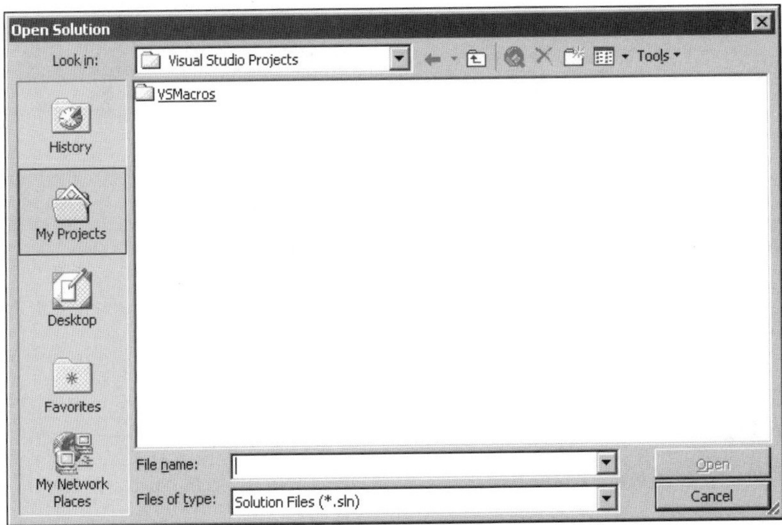

Figure 1-31 Open Solution dialog box

2. Navigate to the Chapter.01 folder in your Visual C++ Projects folder.

3. Click the **HelloWorld.sln** file in the HelloWorld folder, and then click the **Open** button.
4. Now close the solution by selecting **Close Solution** from the File menu.

You can change the default location of your Visual Studio projects by using the Projects and Solutions category under the Environment tab in the Options dialog box.

To open the HelloWorld project:

1. Select **Project** on the Open submenu on the File menu, or press **Ctrl+Shift+O**. The Open Project dialog box appears, as shown in Figure 1-32. For the exercises you perform in this book, be sure to select the Close Solution radio button. You select the Add to Solution radio button only if you want to add a project to the currently open solution.

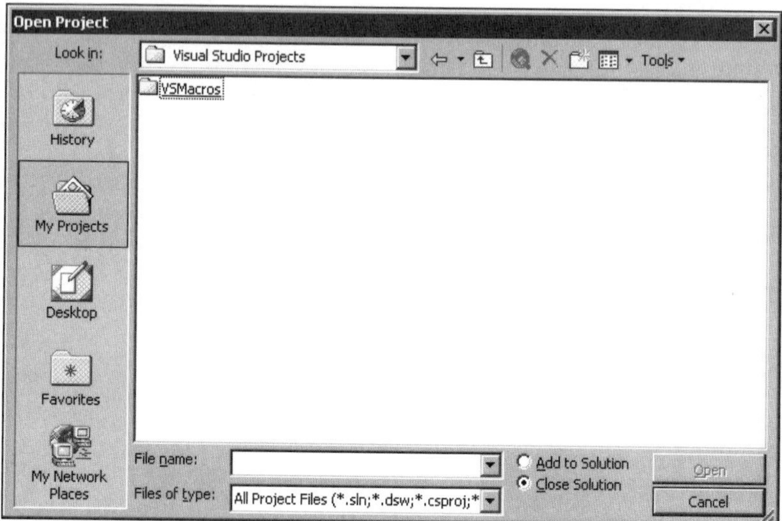

Figure 1-32 Open Project dialog box

2. Navigate to the Chapter.01 folder in your Visual C++ Projects folder.
3. Click the **HelloWorld.vcproj file** in the HelloWorld folder, and then click the **Open** button.
4. Now close the solution by selecting **Close Solution** on the File menu.

You can select recently opened projects and files from the Recent Projects submenu and the Recent Files submenu on the File menu. You can also open a recently opened project by clicking the project name in the Get Started Link on the Start Page window.

In this book, you will be working only with solutions that contain single projects. For this reason, the exercises throughout this book will instruct you to open the individual projects instead of the solutions that contain them. If a solution file exists in the same folder as a project file you open, and if the solution file has the same name as the project file, then Visual C++ opens the solution file as well. This means that if your solutions consist of single projects, opening either the solution file or the project file will perform the same task. If no solution file with the same name as the project exists within the same folder as the project file, then Visual C++ automatically creates a solution file for you, using the name of the opened project.

Exiting Visual C++

You exit the Visual C++ IDE the same way that you exit most other Windows applications.

To exit Visual C++:

1. Select **Exit** from the **File** menu.
2. Before exiting the IDE, Microsoft Visual Studio displays a dialog box prompting you to save any unsaved files in your project. You will not see this dialog box if all of your files have been saved.

You can also exit the Visual C++ IDE by clicking the Close button on the title bar or by pressing Alt+F4.

Visual C++ Help

As you work in Visual C++, there will be many times when you will need to quickly access Help on a particular subject. For example, you may not fully understand what a menu command does, may need help with the syntax of a code function, or would simply like to see an overview of a particular subject. At these times, it can be unproductive (and somewhat frustrating) to thumb through a book or reference guide in order to find the information that will help you. Luckily, Visual C++ (and most good Windows applications) provides several types of help resources. The primary help resources available in Visual C++ are ToolTips, the MSDN Library, context-sensitive help, and dynamic help.

When you are working with toolbar buttons, it is easy to forget what command a particular button represents. **ToolTips** describe the functions buttons perform and can be momentarily displayed next to your mouse pointer for individual buttons. To display a ToolTip for a particular button, hold your mouse pointer over a button for a moment. The ToolTip pops up below and just to the right of your mouse pointer and stays visible until you move your mouse pointer off the button. Figure 1-33 displays an example of the ToolTip for the New Project button on the Standard toolbar.

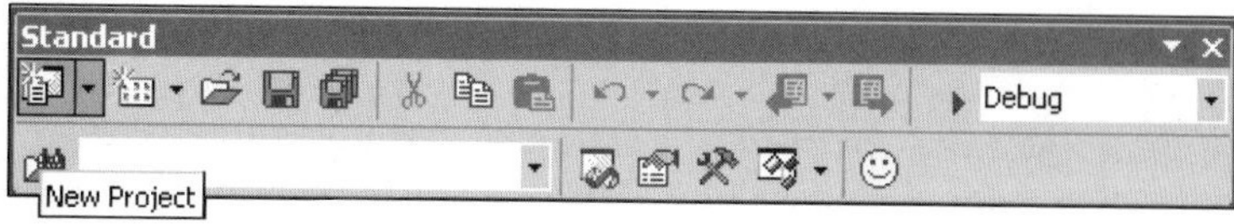

Figure 1-33 ToolTips

For advanced help and reference information, Visual C++ has an online help system, called the **MSDN Library**. All the development tools in Visual Studio share the MSDN Library. As you recall, Visual Studio includes Visual C++, Visual Basic, and Visual C#. The Visual Studio shared online help system can be quite useful if you work with several of these development tools simultaneously or if you are using combinations of the tools to create a single application. For example, you may be developing a C++ application in Visual C++ that includes a project created in Visual Basic. If you need help with both of these tools while creating your applications, it is much more convenient to use a consolidated help system.

You can find an online version of the MSDN Library at *msdn.microsoft.com*

You display the MSDN Library from the IDE by selecting one of the following commands on the Help menu: Contents, Index, Search, Favorites, Index results, or Search results. You can also display the MSDN Library by selecting the Microsoft Visual Studio .NET Documentation command in the Visual Studio .NET folder in the Programs folder in your Start menu. The MSDN Library window contains two panes: the table of contents window and the topic window. The **Table of Contents** window contains four tabs: Contents, Index, Search, and Favorites. The **Contents** tab contains help topics in a table of contents format that is very similar to folders in Windows Explorer or the Solution Explorer window. The **Index** tab is used for browsing a list of key words and topics. The **Search** tab allows you to search for a particular word or phrase. The **Favorites** tab contains your bookmarks for topics of particular interest to you. Help topics selected in any of the Table of Contents window tabs are displayed in the **Topic window**, which is the pane to the right of the Table of Contents window. Also available in the MSDN Library window are a menu bar and toolbar containing various navigation and topic manipulation commands and buttons. Figure 1-34 shows the MSDN Library window opened to the Contents tab and a topic entitled "What's New in Visual Studio .NET."

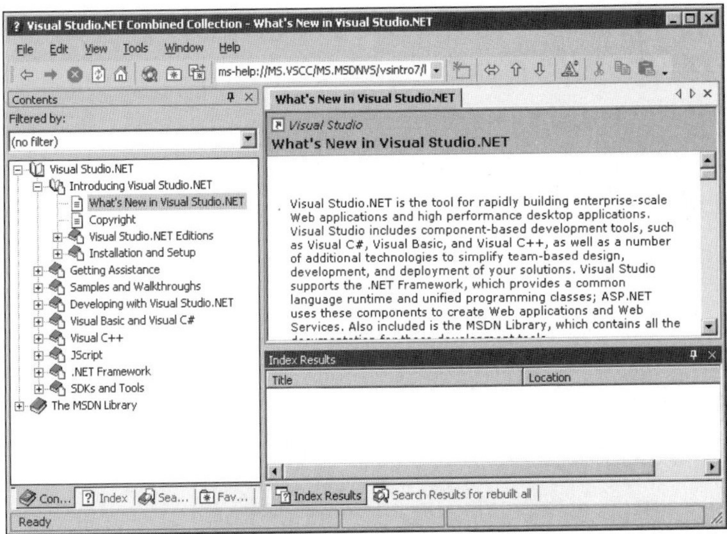

Figure 1-34 MSDN Library

If they are not visible, you can display the tabs in the Table of Contents window by pointing to the Navigation submenu on the View menu and clicking the window you want to work with.

MSDN Library also displays **context-sensitive** help for dialog boxes and programming terms. Rather than searching for a help topic yourself, MSDN Library can automatically display the help topic associated with a selected item. You display context-sensitive help by selecting a control in a dialog box, highlighting a property in the Properties window, or placing your cursor in a keyword or function in the Code Editor window and pressing the F1 key. Various windows such as the Solution Explorer window also display context-sensitive help when you press the F1 key, and many dialog boxes contain a context-sensitive Help button. For example, if you press the F1 key or the Help button when the New Project dialog box is open, Visual C++ displays context-sensitive help.

Dynamic help displays a list of help topics that are relevant to the current window or task. You can display the Dynamic Help window in the IDE by pressing Ctrl+F1 or by selecting Dynamic Help from the Help menu. The topics displayed in the Dynamic Help window change as you navigate through the IDE. For example, if the Code Editor window is active, the Dynamic Help window displays topics that are relevant to working with the Code Editor window. Similarly, if the Task List window is active, the Dynamic Help window displays topics that are relevant to working with the Task List window. Clicking an item in the Dynamic Help window opens the associated topic in the MSDN Library. Although dynamic help is useful when you are first learning about a particular topic, you may find that it takes up too much room in your IDE. For this reason, it is often easier to look up a particular topic yourself in the MSDN Library. Figure 1-35 shows an example of the Dynamic Help window and the topics it contains when the Code Editor window is active.

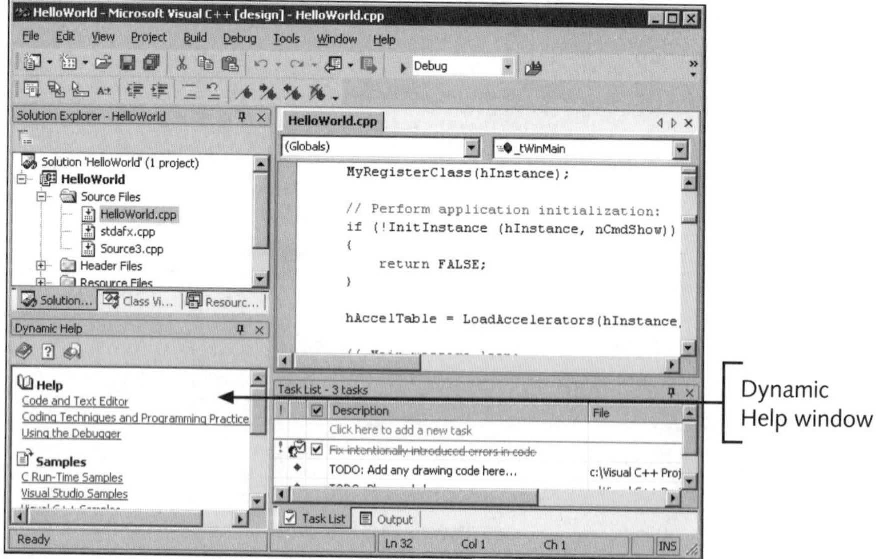

Figure 1-35 Dynamic Help window

CHAPTER SUMMARY

- Creating programs, or the instructions, that control the operation of a computer or hardware is called computer programming.
- The pieces of information that a program needs are called data.
- The instructions used to create computer programs are called programming languages.
- Machine language is the lowest level of computer languages, and programs written in machine language consist entirely of 1s and 0s that control the computer's on and off switches.
- Assembly languages perform the same tasks as machine languages, but use simplified names of instructions instead of 1s and 0s.
- A compiler translates programming code into a low-level format.
- In procedural programming, the computer instructions used in a high-level computer programming language are grouped into logical units called procedures or functions.

- Each line in a procedural program that performs an individual task is called a statement.
- One of the most important aspects of procedural programming is that it allows you to temporarily store pieces of information, called variables, in computer memory locations called variables.
- A constant contains information that does not change during the course of program execution.
- Object-oriented programming (OOP) refers to the creation of reusable software objects that can be easily incorporated into other programs.
- Objects are encapsulated, which means that all code and required data are contained within the object itself. Encapsulation is also referred to as a black box, because of the invisibility of the code inside an encapsulated object.
- In object-oriented programming, the code, functions, attributes, and other information that make up an object are contained in a structure known as a class.
- An instance is a programming object that has been created from an existing class.
- Inheritance refers to the ability of an object to take on the characteristics of the class on which it is based.
- The original program structure you enter into a text file is called source code.
- The compiled machine language version of a program is called object code.
- The standardized version of C++ is called ANSI C++.
- The ANSI C++ run-time library is also called the Standard Template Library or Standard C++ Library.
- Microsoft Visual C++ .NET, or Visual C++ for short, is a Windows-based, visual development environment for creating C and C++ applications.
- Each high-level programming language, including Visual C++, has its own syntax, or rules of the language.
- The logic underlying any program involves executing the various parts of the program in the correct order to produce the desired results.
- Debugging describes the act of tracing and resolving errors in a program.
- The development products in Visual Studio share a common workspace in Visual Studio, called the Integrated Development Environment (IDE).
- For each instance of the IDE there is a single solution containing one or more projects.
- The Start Page allows you to set IDE user preferences and acts as a Web browser window.

- You use the Solution Explorer window in the IDE to manage the various projects and associated files contained in a solution.
- Visual C++ has its own built-in text editor called the Code and Text Editor window.
- The tools for compiling a C++ program are located on the Build menu.
- Visual C++ uses the Output window to display its progress when you build a program.
- The Task List maintains a list of tasks that need to be completed for a project.
- Compiler error messages occur for any syntax errors in a program.
- Warning messages occur for any potential problems that may exist in your code, but that are not serious enough to cause a compiler error message.
- After running the Build command, you execute a program by selecting the Start Without Debugging command on the Debug menu, or by pressing Ctrl+F5.
- Although a file may be stored in the same folder where other files in a project are stored, the file will not actually be a part of the project until you physically add it to the project within Visual C++.
- It is good practice to save your solution at regular intervals and especially before compiling and executing a program.
- Opening a saved solution opens all of the projects it contains. You can also open a project independently of any solution in which it is contained.
- Visual C++ has an online help system called MSDN Library, which all the development tools in Visual Studio share.
- ToolTips describe the function a button performs and can be momentarily displayed next to your mouse pointer for individual buttons.
- MSDN Library also displays context-sensitive help for dialog boxes and programming terms.
- Dynamic help displays a list of help topics that are relevant to the current window or task.

REVIEW QUESTIONS

1. Machine languages write programs consisting entirely of ______________.
    a. bytes
    b. 1s and 0s
    c. As and Bs
    d. magnetic pulses

2. ______________ perform the same tasks as machine languages, but use simplified names of instructions instead of 1s and 0s.
   a. High-level programming languages
   b. 4GL programming languages
   c. Object-oriented machine languages
   d. Assembly languages
3. Programming languages that are closest to a computer's hardware are known as ______________ languages.
   a. low-level
   b. entry-level
   c. rudimentary
   d. primitive
4. Low-level languages are ______________.
   a. programming languages developed by Microsoft
   b. shared only by Windows operating systems
   c. shared by all operating systems
   d. unique to each type of CPU
5. Programming code is converted into a low-level format using a ______________.
   a. modifier
   b. compiler
   c. word processor
   d. systems engineer
6. A(n) ______________ translates programming code into object code.
   a. interpreter
   b. filter
   c. compiler
   d. CPU
7. The rules of a programming language are known as its ______________.
   a. procedures
   b. assembly
   c. syntax
   d. logic

8. Executing the various statements and procedures of a program in the correct order to produce the desired results is called ______________.
   a. reasoning
   b. directional assembly
   c. syntax
   d. logic
9. A(n) ______________ refers to programming code and data that can be treated as an individual unit or component.
   a. icon
   b. procedure
   c. concealed unit
   d. object
10. In object-oriented programming, data and procedures are contained in a structure known as a ______________.
    a. category
    b. container
    c. class
    d. bucket
11. The Visual C++ user interface shared with all members of Visual Studio is called ______________.
    a. Project Explorer
    b. Application Programming Interface (API)
    c. Solution Developer Kit
    d. Integrated Development Environment (IDE)
12. Visual C++ projects are contained within a single ______________.
    a. solution
    b. window
    c. Visual C++ session
    d. project folder
13. ______________ is used for managing the various projects and associated files in a solution.
    a. The Properties Window
    b. Windows Explorer
    c. The Toolbox
    d. The Solution Explorer window

14. Visual C++ uses _______________ to display member lists and parameter information.
    a. build statements
    b. statement completion
    c. online help
    d. spell checking
15. Visual C++ displays build error tasks in the _______________ window.
    a. Task List
    b. Output
    c. Solution Explorer
    d. Compile
16. _______________ errors occur when you enter code that the compiler does not recognize.
    a. Application
    b. Login
    c. Run-time
    d. Syntax
17. When should you save your files?
    a. only when you are finished
    b. after your computer crashes
    c. at regular intervals
    d. it is unnecessary to save your files.
18. If you make changes to files and exit without saving them, Visual C++ _______________.
    a. saves them for you
    b. prompts you to save your work
    c. discards your changes
    d. creates new copies of the files that include the changes
    d. all applications in Windows NT
19. MSDN Library displays context-sensitive help for dialog boxes and _______________.
    a. menu commands
    b. toolbar buttons
    c. programming terms
    d. windows in the IDE

20. Dynamic help ______________.
    a. provides context-sensitive help for dialog boxes
    b. provides context-sensitive help for menu command and toolbar buttons
    c. opens a specific help topic in the MSDN Library, depending on the task you are performing
    d. displays a list of help topics that are relevant to the current window or task

PROGRAMMING EXERCISES

1. What types of information can you think of that could be a constant or a variable? Examples of constants include your name, place of birth, and address, that is, unless you move frequently. List constant values that occur in everyday life.
2. Think of a set of common, related tasks that you can create as either a procedural program or an object-oriented program. One example is cleaning your house. First, list the steps in the proper order required to run the program as a procedural program. Next, break the steps into objects that do not have to be performed in sequential order. What are the attributes and functions of these objects? Can the program be simplified by creating an instance of an existing class? What parts of the program must be run in a procedural fashion?
3. Search the Internet and make a list of vendors that market C++ compilers. What features are available with different vendor's compilers? Are any free compilers available? Also search online editorials and reviews and make a list of C++ development environments such as Visual C++. What are the advantages and disadvantages of the different development environments? Which compilers would you like to use if you were not working with Visual C++, and why?
4. Explain the difference between solutions and projects.
5. Identify the parts of the Visual C++ IDE that are covered in this chapter. Explain what each element is used for and how it is displayed. Also identify the elements that can be customized.
6. Explain what will happen when you select the following types of menu commands:
    a. A menu command followed by an ellipsis (...)
    b. Menu commands followed by an arrow
    c. Menu commands not followed by an ellipsis (...) or arrow
    d. Grayed-out menu commands
7. Identify the different types of Visual C++ help resources and how they are accessed. Describe situations in which each type of help is most appropriate.

CHAPTER

2

C++ PROGRAMMING BASICS

In this chapter you will learn:

- About console applications
- About preprocessor directives
- About the standard output stream
- How to use namespaces
- How to declare variables and constants
- How to add comments to a program
- About functions and scope
- How to work with arrays

Let us watch well our beginnings, and results will manage themselves.

Alexander Clark

PREVIEW: THE HELLO WORLD PROGRAM

As mentioned in Chapter 1, "Introduction to Programming and Visual C++", an old tradition among programmers is that when you learn a new programming language, you create a first program that prints or displays the text *Hello World!*. The tradition of creating a Hello World program is surprisingly addictive. If you are an experienced programmer, then you have undoubtedly created Hello World programs in the past. If you are new to programming, then you will probably find yourself creating Hello World programs when you learn new programming languages in the future. The Hello World program you create in this chapter builds on the original Hello World program by also saying hello to the sun and the moon, as well as printing a line of scientific information about each celestial body.

To preview the Hello World program:

1. Create a **Chapter.02** folder in your Visual C++ Projects folder. (You should have created a Visual C++ Projects folder in Chapter 1.)
2. Copy the **Chapter2_HelloWorld** folder from the Chapter.02 folder on your Data Disk to the Chapter.02 folder in your Visual C++ Projects folder, and then start Visual C++. Point to **Open** on the File menu, and then select the **Project** command. Open the **HelloWorld** project from the Chapter2_HelloWorld folder in the Chapter.02 folder in your Visual C++ Projects folder.
3. Open Solution Explorer window and expand the Source Files folder. Open the **HelloWorld.cpp** file in the Code Editor window, if it is not already open. The HelloWorld.cpp file contains the C++ code that executes the Hello World program. Figure 2-1 shows the HelloWorld.cpp file. The first lines you see, set off with the symbols /* and */, are called comment lines and are used for adding notes to your program. Words marked in blue in the Code Editor window are called keywords and are part of the C++ programming language. Following the comments are #include and using statements that give your program access to some important run-time libraries that enable programs to display information on the screen. The statement after the using statement declares a constant. The next three statements are called function prototypes. The statement that begins with `void main()` is a function that is required by every C++ program. You can think of it as the program starting point. The statements that make up a function are enclosed within curly braces. The main() function statements declare and initialize variables, call custom functions, and print information to the screen. The last three functions in the file are custom functions that are called by the main() function.
4. Build the Hello World program by selecting **Build Solution** from the Build menu or by pressing **F7**. When the project finishes building, execute the program by selecting **Start Without Debugging** from the Debug menu. Figure 2-2 shows how the program appears.
5. Press any key to close the Hello World program window.
6. Select **Close Solution** from the File menu.

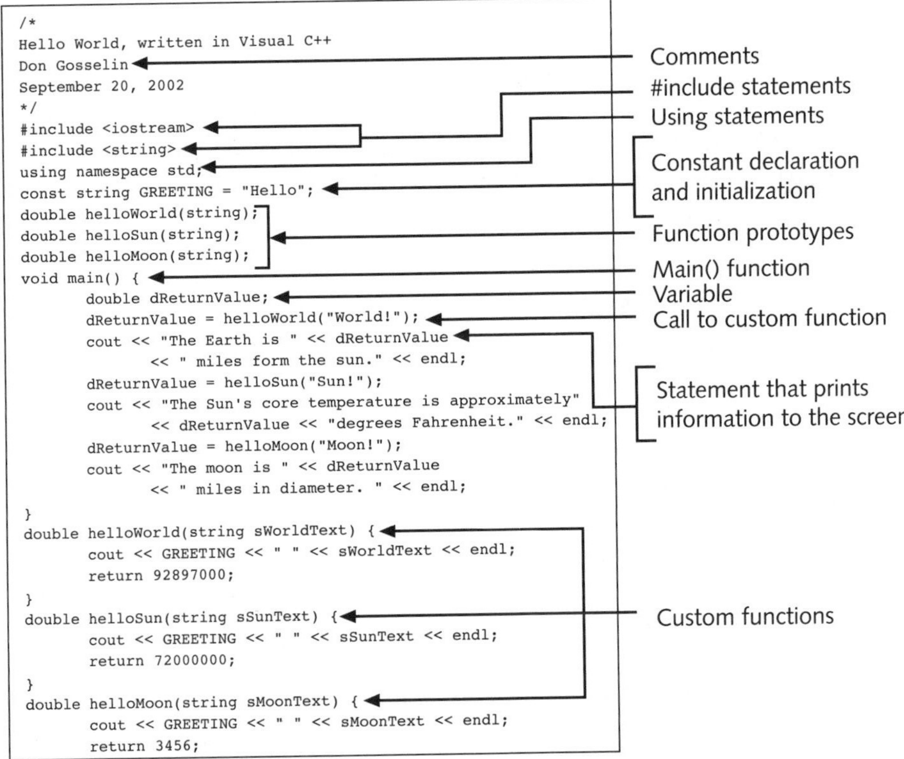
```
/*
Hello World, written in Visual C++
Don Gosselin
September 20, 2002
*/
#include <iostream>
#include <string>
using namespace std;
const string GREETING = "Hello";
double helloWorld(string);
double helloSun(string);
double helloMoon(string);
void main() {
	double dReturnValue;
	dReturnValue = helloWorld("World!");
	cout << "The Earth is " << dReturnValue
		<< " miles form the sun." << endl;
	dReturnValue = helloSun("Sun!");
	cout << "The Sun's core temperature is approximately"
		<< dReturnValue << "degrees Fahrenheit." << endl;
	dReturnValue = helloMoon("Moon!");
	cout << "The moon is " << dReturnValue
		<< " miles in diameter. " << endl;
}
double helloWorld(string sWorldText) {
	cout << GREETING << " " << sWorldText << endl;
	return 92897000;
}
double helloSun(string sSunText) {
	cout << GREETING << " " << sSunText << endl;
	return 72000000;
}
double helloMoon(string sMoonText) {
	cout << GREETING << " " << sMoonText << endl;
	return 3456;
```


Figure 2-1 HelloWorld.cpp

"c:\visual c++ projects\chapter.02\helloworld\debug\HelloWorld.exe"

```
Hello World!
The Earth is 9.2897e+007 miles from the Sun.
Hello Sun!
The Sun's core temperature is approximately 7.2e+007 degrees Fahrenheit.
Hello Moon!
The Moon is 3456 miles in diameter.
Press any key to continue
```

Figure 2-2 Output of Hello World program

INTRODUCTION

The primary goal of this text is to help you learn how to use Visual C++ to create Windows programs—specifically, MFC programs—which requires a thorough knowledge of classes and object-oriented programming. To accomplish this goal, the majority of the chapters in this text are devoted to class and MFC concepts. This book spends relatively little time discussing the basics of the C++ language. However, in this chapter and Chapter 3, "Operators and Control Structures", you will find a fast-paced review of basic C++ programming techniques that you will use throughout the book. In order for you to be successful in this book, you should already be familiar with many of the C++ concepts discussed in the next couple of chapters. If you are not familiar with C or C++ programming, then you should at least have experience with another object-oriented programming language such as Java or Visual Basic.

CONSOLE APPLICATIONS

You already know that C++ programs are constructed within text files. Now you can start examining how the actual nuts and bolts of a program are put together. In this chapter you will create C++ console applications in order to learn the basics of C++ programming. A **console application** is a program that runs within an output window, similar to an MS-DOS command prompt window. Console applications do not use any sort of graphical user interface as Windows applications do. Instead, console applications primarily output text to the screen or receive character input from the user's keyboard.

As a beginner, it is easy to become confused by the large amounts of code that are required for creating Windows applications. For this reason, you will start with console applications because they are the easiest way to demonstrate simple concepts without the distraction of complex Windows code. Although the goal in this text is the creation of Windows programs, you should understand that there are many uses for console applications, particularly in utility programs that do not need extra layers of Windows code and graphical user interface elements in order to function. Even within a Windows environment, you have probably seen several examples of console-style applications, such as installation programs and other applications that do not need a Windows interface.

Next, you will create the Hello World console application project.

To create the Hello World console application project:

1. Return to Visual C++.
2. Point to **New** on the File menu, and then select **Project** or press **Ctrl+Shift+N** to open the New Project dialog box.
3. In the Templates list, click **Win32 Project**.

4. Replace *<Enter name>* in the Name text box with **HelloWorld**. In the Location box, type **c:\Visual C++ Projects\Chapter.02**, replacing c: with the name of the drive where your Visual C++ Projects folder is stored. Be sure to clear the **Create directory for Solution** check box.
5. Click the **OK** button to open the Win32 Application Wizard. In the Win32 Application Wizard, click the **Application Settings** tab.
6. In the Application Settings tab, shown in Figure 2-3, select **Console application** as the application type, click the **Empty project** check box, and then click the **Finish** button. Visual C++ creates a new project called HelloWorld in the HelloWorld folder in the Chapter.02 folder of your Visual C++ Projects folder.

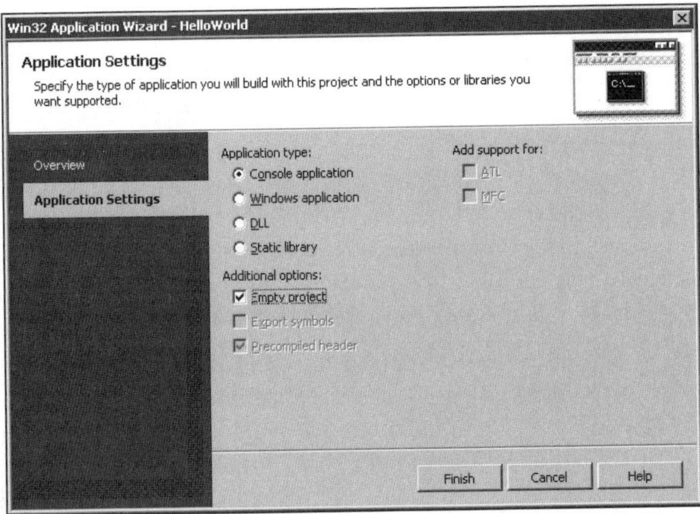

Figure 2-3 Application Settings tab of the Win32 Application Wizard dialog box

The project you just created contains no source files; only the project itself has been created. Before you can start writing code in the Code Editor window, you need to add a source file to the project. Next, you will add a new source file to the Hello World program.

To add a new source file to the Hello World program:

1. Select **Add New Item** from the **Project** menu. The Add New Item dialog box opens.
2. In the Add New Item dialog box, click **C++ File(.cpp)** from the Templates list, replace *<Enter name>* in the Name box with **HelloWorld** as the filename, and then click the **Open** button. The new file opens in the Code Editor window.

PREPROCESSOR DIRECTIVES

Recall from Chapter 1 that the ANSI standards define the Standard C++ Library, which contain useful classes, functions, variables, constants, and other programmatic items that you can add to your programs. Before you can use any of the classes, functions, and other programmatic items in the Standard C++ Library, you must first notify the compiler that you want to use them by adding something called a header file to your program. A **header file**, or **include file**, is a file that is included as part of a program and alerts the compiler that a program uses run-time libraries. One set of classes you will use extensively in the next few chapters are the iostream classes. The **iostream classes** are used for giving C++ programs capabilities to input to and output capabilities from the computer screen and disk files, as well as giving the programs access to printing functions. The header file for the iostream classes is `iostream`. C++ header files contain information and code that allow you to access the objects, functions, code, and data in run-time library classes. Header files get their name because they are usually placed at the "head" (beginning) of a C++ file.

You add a header file to your program by using the #include statement. The **#include statement** is one of several preprocessor directives that are used with C++. The **preprocessor** is a program that runs before the compiler. When it encounters an #include statement, the preprocessor places the entire contents of the designated file into the current file. Preprocessor directives and include statements allow the current file to use any of the classes, functions, variables, and other code contained within the included file.

The syntax for adding a header file is `#include <filename>`. You place each preprocessor directive on its own line. You replace the filename portion of the syntax with the name of the file you want to include. The angle brackets (<>) indicate that the file is one of the C++ run-time libraries or an MFC library file. For example, to include the iostream file, you use the following statement:

```
#include <iostream>
```

Older versions of the Standard C++ Library required you to use an .h extension with header files. The most recent version of the Standard C++ Library eliminates the use of the .h extension. You should be aware that Visual C++ still supports the older version of the Standard C++ Library. In fact, you will probably see older C++ programs that use the .h extensions in their header file declarations. For any programs you create with this book, however, you will use the newer version of the Standard C++ Library that does not require .h extensions in the header file declarations.

Next, you will create the basic structure of the Hello World program by adding the iostream header file to the HelloWorld.cpp source file. You will also add a main() function to the source file. Do not worry about understanding how the main() function works. For now, you should understand that the main() function is the starting point for every C++ program. Functions are discussed extensively later in this chapter.

To add the iostream header file and a main() function to the HelloWorld.cpp source file:

1. Return to the HelloWorld.cpp source file in the Code Editor window in the Hello World program.
2. On the first line of the file, type `#include <iostream>` and then press **Enter**.
3. Type the following code for the main() function:

```
void main() {
  // add code here
}
```

The // add code here statement in the preceding step is called a comment. You will learn about comments later in this chapter.

STANDARD OUTPUT STREAM

Now that you have created the shell of the Hello World program, you will start adding code to make the program work. One of the first coding skills you need to learn when studying a programming language is how to output text to the computer screen. Figure 2-4 shows an example of the output from a simple console application.

```
"c:\visual c++ projects\chapter.02\simple\debug\Simple.exe"
Program type: console application
Created with: Visual C++
Programmer: Don Gosselin
Press any key to continue_
```

Figure 2-4 Output from a simple console application

You create the text you see in Figure 2-4 by sending data to the standard output stream. The **standard output stream** is the destination—usually a screen, file, or printer—for text output. The standard output stream is part of the iostream classes of the Standard C++ Library. For your purposes here, the standard output stream is the console application window.

To send text to the standard output stream, you use the cout (for console output) object. The **cout** object is used for outputting text to the console application window. You must add the iostream header file to your program in order to use the C++ standard output stream cout object. To send data to the standard output stream in C++, you use a statement similar to `cout << "text";`. The insertion operator, <<, is used for sending text to an output device, such as a computer screen, file, or printer. It tells the compiler to send the text on the right side of the statement to the standard output stream (represented by cout) on the left side of the statement.

The text portion of the statement is called a text string. A **text string**, or **literal string**, is text that is contained within double quotation marks. The text string that is sent to the cout object is the text that is printed to the standard output stream. When you want to include a quoted string within a literal string, you surround the quoted text with single quotation marks. For example, `cout << "this is a 'text' string";` writes the text *this is a 'text' string* to the standard output stream. You can send multiple text strings to the standard output stream, provided they are separated by << operators. The statement `cout << "My " << "name " << "is " << "Don Gosselin";` writes the text *My name is Don Gosselin* to the screen.

If you want to add line breaks between strings that are output to the screen, you use the endl i/o manipulator. The **endl i/o manipulator** is part of the iostream classes and represents a new line character. An **i/o manipulator** is a special function that can be used with an i/o statement.

The abbreviation i/o stands for input/output.

The following code shows how to print multiple statements to the standard output stream, separated by line breaks using the endl i/o manipulator:

```
cout << "Program type: console application" << endl;
cout << "Created with: Visual C++" << endl;
cout << "Programmer: Don Gosselin" << endl;
```

Notice that each statement in the preceding example ends with a semicolon. All statements in C++ must end with a semicolon. A statement is not necessarily a single line of code; large statements can span multiple lines. For example, the following statement spans multiple lines of code, yet includes only a single semicolon at the end of the last line:

```
cout << "We, the people of the United States, " << endl
  << "in order to form a more perfect Union, " << endl
  << "establish justice, insure domestic tranquility,
       " << endl
  << "provide for the common defense, " << endl
  << "promote the general welfare, " << endl
  << "and secure the blessings of liberty " << endl
  << "to ourselves and our posterity, " << endl
  << "do ordain and establish this Constitution " << endl
  << "for the United States of America." << endl;
```

You cannot break text strings; all text strings must exist on the same line and include opening and closing quotation marks. If you insert a break in a text string, you will receive a compiler error.

A preprocessor directive is not technically a C++ statement. Rather, it is an instruction to the preprocessor that executes before the program compiles. Because they are not C++ statements, preprocessor directives do not end in semicolons.

You can also place multiple statements on the same line, provided they are separated by semicolons, as in the following example:

```
cout << "Boston is "; cout << "in Massachusetts.";
```

In general, you should place each statement on its own line, unless the statement is too long for the line or placing the statement on multiple lines makes the statement easier to read.

Next, you will add to the Hello World program several cout statements that print text to the screen. Before you do, it is important to keep in mind that the C++ programming language is case sensitive. For example, the statement `Cout<< "My name is Don Gosselin";` will cause an error when you build the project because the compiler does not recognize an object named Cout with an uppercase C; you must enter cout in all lowercase letters. Similarly, the following misspelled statements will cause an error:

```
COUT << "My name is Don Gosselin";
CoUt << "My name is Don Gosselin";
CouT << "My name is Don Gosselin";
```

To add cout statements to the Hello World program:

1. Return to the HelloWorld.cpp source file in the Code Editor window in the Hello World program.
2. Replace the `// add code here` statement in the main() function with the cout statements shown in Figure 2-5.

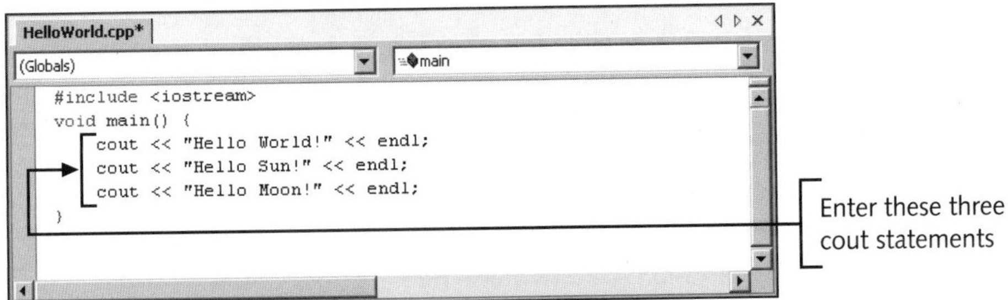

Figure 2-5 Adding cout statements to the main() function

The Hello World program is now essentially complete. Before executing the program, however, you must declare the std namespace, and then compile and build the HelloWorld.exe file.

NAMESPACES

The Standard C++ Library includes many names for the various classes, functions, variables and other code it contains. In addition, you can define your own custom names for the programmatic elements in your applications. Recall from Chapter 1 that code reuse is one of the most important aspects of object-oriented programming. To make code reuse possible, you can include header files in your C++ programs from other programmer's classes or from libraries other than the Standard C++ Library. If you are creating an application that includes headers from the Standard C++ Library and from other code libraries, then it is only a matter of time before your program encounters two elements with identical names. For example, if you accidentally use the name cout for one of the elements in your program, such as a variable or function, the C++ compiler will not know which version of cout to use: the one defined in your code or the one defined in the Standard C++ Library. C++ uses **namespaces** to manage the various names that a program encounters. When you include a Standard C++ Library class, you are also required to declare the std namespace in your program. The **std** namespace contains all of the names that are defined in the Standard C++ Library.

The **using directive** informs your program that you intend to use a namespace. The syntax for the using directive is `using namespace` *`name;`*. For example, to inform your program that you intend to use the std namespace, place the statement `using namespace std;` in your program. The using directive statement needs to be placed before any statement that uses a name defined in that particular namespace. Most programmers place the `using namespace std;` statement immediately after any statements that include classes from the Standard C++ Library, as in the following example:

```
#include <iostream>
using namespace std;
void main() {
        cout << "Hello World!" << endl;
}
```

You were not required to declare the std namespace with older versions of the Standard C++ Library.

Instead of declaring a namespace with the using directive, you can precede a call to a name in the Standard C++ Library with std and the scope resolution operator. The **scope resolution operator** consists of two colons (::) and identifies to which programmatic element another programmatic element belongs. In the case of a name space, the scope resolution operator identifies to which namespace a particular name belongs. Using the scope resolution operator, you can write the preceding example as follows. Notice that both cout and endl are preceded by the std namespace and scope resolution operator.

```
#include <iostream>
void main() {
        std::cout << "Hello World!" << std::endl;
}
```

Later in this book, you will use the scope resolution operator to identify the class to which a particular function belongs.

Although using the namespace and scope resolution operator directly in your statements is useful in small programs, it can become cumbersome in larger programs. It is usually easier to declare the std namespace with the using directive. Therefore, most of the programs you write in this book will declare the std namespace with the using directive.

Next, you will declare the std namespace, and then build and execute the Hello World program.

To declare the std namespace and build and execute the Hello World program:

1. Return to the Hello World program.
2. Declare the std namespace as shown in Figure 2-6.

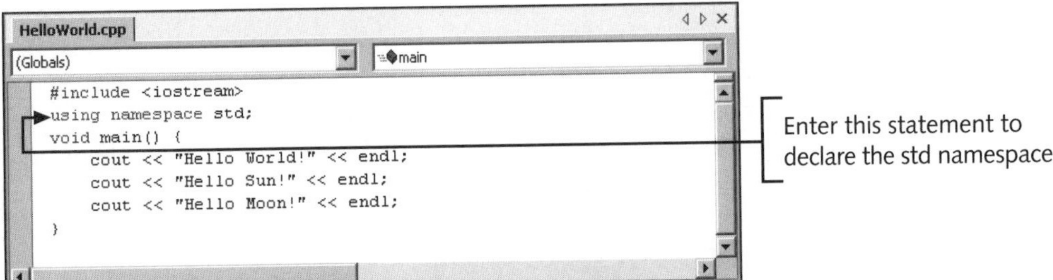

Figure 2-6 Declaring the std namespace in the Hello World program

3. Select **Build Solution** from the **Build** menu. You can view the progress of the compilation and build procedures in the Output window at the bottom of the screen. If your program compiles and builds successfully, the message *Build succeeded* appears in the status bar.

If you receive compilation errors, examine the messages in the Output window. Common errors include using the wrong case and forgetting to end each statement with a semicolon.

4. After your project compiles successfully, run the program by selecting **Start Without Debugging** from the Debug menu. A command window opens and displays the three text strings, as shown in Figure 2-7.

```
"c:\visual c++ projects\chapter.02\helloworld\debug\HelloWorld.exe"
Hello World!
Hello Sun!
Hello Moon!
Press any key to continue
```

Figure 2-7 Output of Hello World Program

5. Press any key to close the command window.

Using cout is the C++ way of writing to the standard output stream, and that is the output method you will use throughout this book. In contrast, in the C language, you write to the standard output stream with the printf() function of the standard input/out (stdio) class. To use the printf() function, you must add the stdio header file to your program. Although you will not use the printf() function in this book, it is important that you understand it because many programmers prefer this method over using the C++ iostream classes. Throughout your career as a C++ programmer, you will certainly see printf() used. If you would like more information on how to use the printf() function, search for the *printf* function topic in the MSDN Library.

VARIABLES

One of the most important aspects of programming is the ability to store and manipulate the values in variables. In C++, you create variables using the syntax `type name;`. The *type* portion of the syntax refers to the data type of the variable. The data type used to create a variable determines the type of information that can be stored in the variable. You will learn about data types shortly. For now, you will learn about a single data type, the integer data type, in order to understand and work with variables. The **integer data type** stores positive or negative numbers with no decimal places or the value 0 (zero). You declare an integer data type using the `int` keyword.

Using a statement similar to `int myVariable;` to create a variable is called **declaring** the variable. You can assign a value to, or **initialize**, a variable at declaration using the syntax `int myVariable = value;`. The equal sign in a variable declaration assigns a value to the variable and is called the assignment operator. This usage is different from the standard usage of the equal sign in an algebraic formula. The value you assign to a declared variable must be appropriate for its data type or you will receive an error message when you compile the project. For example, you must assign to an integer variable a positive with no decimal places, a negative number with no decimal places, or zero using a statement similar to `int myVariable = 100;`. The values you assign to integer data types and other numeric data types are called **literal values**, or **literals**. When assigning literal values to a numeric data type, you do *not* surround the value with quotation marks.

The name you assign to a variable is called an **identifier**, or **variable name**. When naming a variable, you must follow these rules:

1. Reserved words cannot be used for variable names
2. Spaces cannot be used within a variable name.
3. Identifiers must begin with an uppercase or lowercase ASCII letter or an underscore (_)
4. Numbers can be used in an identifier, but not as the first character
5. Special characters, such as $, &, *, or %, cannot be used in variable names.

C++ does not allow you to use a number as the first character in an identifier in order to easily distinguish between an identifier and a literal value.

Reserved words or **keywords** are part of the C++ language syntax. Figure 2-8 lists the C++ reserved words. Reserved words with leading underscores are Microsoft extensions.

__abstract	__alignof	__asm	__assume
__based	__box	__cdecl	__declspec
__delegate	__event	__except	__fastcall
__finally	__forceinline	__gc	__hook
__identifier	__if_exists	__if_not_exists	__inline
__int8	__int6	__int	__int64
__interface	__leave	__m64	__m/28
__m8d	__m/28i	__multiple_inheritance	__nogc
__noop	__pin	__property	__raise
__sealed	__single_inheritance	__stdcall	__super
__try_cast	__try/__except, __try/__finally	__unhook	__uuidof
__value	__virtual_inheritance	__w64	bool
break	case	catch	char
class	const	const_cast	continue
default	delete	deprecated	dllexport
dllimport	do	double	dynamic_cast
else	enum	explicit	extern
false	float	for	friend
goto	if	inline	int
long	mutable	naked	namespace

Figure 2-8 C++ reserved words

new	noinline	noreturn	nothrow
novtable	operator	private	property
protected	public	register	reinterpret_cast
return	selectany	short	signed
sizeof	static	static_cast	struct
switch	template	this	thread
throw	true	try	typedef
typeid	typename	union	unsigned
using declaration, using directive	uuid	virtual	void
volatile	__wchar_t, wchar_t	while	

Figure 2-8 C++ reserved words (continued)

A common practice is to use an underscore (_) character to separate individual words within a variable name, as in `my_variable_name`. Another common practice is to use a lowercase letter for the first letter of the first word in a variable name, with subsequent words starting with an initial cap, as in `myVariableName`. Figure 2-9 lists examples of some legal and illegal variable names.

Legal Variable Names	Illegal Variable Names
my_variable	%my_variable
myVariable	1my_variable
MyVariable	#my_variable
_my_variable	@my_variable
my_variable_example	~my_variable
MyVariableExample	+my_variable

Figure 2-9 Examples of legal and illegal variable names

Variable names, like other C++ code, are case sensitive. Therefore, the variable name myVariable contains different values than variables named myvariable, MyVariable, or MYVARIABLE. If you receive an error when compiling a C++ program, be sure that you are using the correct case when referring to any variables you have declared.

Although you can assign a value when a variable is declared, you are not required to do so. Your program may assign the value later, or you may use a variable to store user input. If you do not initialize your variables, however, they will contain meaningless data, known as garbage. Your program will not run correctly if it attempts to use the garbage data that is stored in a variable that has not been initialized. Therefore, it is good practice to always initialize your variables when you declare them. This can be as simple as assigning a value of 0 (zero) to a numeric variable at declaration time. Regardless of whether you assign a value to a variable when it is declared, you can change the value of a variable at any point in a program by using a statement that includes the variable name, followed by an assignment operator (=), followed by the value you want to assign to the variable. The following code declares an int variable named salary, assigns to it an initial value of 25,000, and prints it using the cout object. The third statement changes the value of the salary variable to 30,000, and the fourth statement prints the new value. The salary variable is declared only once in the first statement.

```
int salary = 25000;
cout << salary << endl;
salary = 30000;
cout << salary << endl;
```

Data Types

In addition to integers, variables can contain many different kinds of values such as the time, a dollar amount, or a person's name. The values, or data, contained in C++ variables are classified into categories known as data types. A **data type** is the specific category of information that a variable contains. The concept of data types is often difficult for beginning programmers to grasp because in real life you don't often distinguish among different types of information. If someone asks you for your name, how old you are, or what the current time is, it makes no difference to you that your name is a text string and that your age and the current time are types of numbers. However, the specific data type of a variable is very important to a programming language because it helps determine how much memory to allocate for the data, as well as the types of operations that can be performed on a variable. Additionally, data types force you to assign the appropriate value to a variable to help prevent programming errors. For instance, consider a variable named weeklySalary that you use to calculate net pay. If a programming language allowed you to assign an inappropriate value, say the employee's name, to the weeklySalary variable, if you later attempted to use the variable in a calculation you would receive an error message or incorrect result, because text cannot be used in numeric calculations. Data types help prevent these kinds of errors from occurring.

Data types that can be assigned only a single value are called **fundamental types** or **primitive types**. The fundamental types supported in C++ are described in Figure 2-10.

Data Type	Description	Example
bool	An integer type that stores a logical value of true or false	true or false
char	Any single character contained within single quotation marks or a numeric ASCII character. Char variables occupy one byte.	'A', 'B', 'C', and so on. The letters *A*, *B*, and *C* are represented in ASCII as 65, 66, and 67, respectively.
int, long int	A four-byte whole number	A value between –2,147,483,648 and 2,147,483,647
short	A two-byte whole number	A value between –32,768 and 32,767
float	A four-byte floating point number	A value between –3.4E+38 and 3.4E+38
double, long double	An eight-byte floating point number	A value between –1.7E+308 and 1.7E308

Figure 2-10 Fundamental C++ data types and their data ranges on 32-bit Windows operating systems

The values that can be assigned to fundamental types vary according to platform. The values shown in Figure 2-10 are for 32-bit Windows operating systems.

For numeric data types, you can easily assign the value of one variable to another variable using the assignment operator-provided that the two variables are of the same data type. The following code declares two variables: januarySalary and februarySalary. A value of 2500 is assigned to the januarySalary variable. Then, the value of januarySalary variable is assigned to the februarySalary variable using the assignment operator.

```
int januarySalary;
int februarySalary;
januarySalary = 2500;
februarySalary = januarySalary;
cout << "Your January salary is $" << januarySalary << endl;
cout << "Your February salary is $" << februarySalary << endl;
```

If you attempt to assign the value of one variable to another variable of a different data type, then you need to be aware of type casting issues. Type casting will be discussed shortly.

If you printed the preceding code, you would see the following two lines printed to the console window:

```
Your January salary is $2500
Your February salary is $2500
```

C++ includes various advanced data types including arrays, pointers, references, and structures. Advanced data types can contain multiple values or complex types of information, as opposed to the single values contained in fundamental data types. You will learn about several advanced data types in the course of this book.

You may occasionally see data type sizes described using bits instead of bytes. Because eight bits is the equivalent of one byte, a 32-bit int data type is the same as a four-byte int data type.

Many programming languages require that you declare the type of data that a variable contains. Programming languages that require you to declare the data types of variables are called **strongly-typed programming languages**. Strong typing is also known as **static typing**, because data types cannot change after they have been declared. Programming languages that do not require you to declare the data types of variables are called **loosely-typed programming languages**. Loose typing is also known as **dynamic typing**, because data types can change after they have been declared. C++ is a strongly-typed programming language. When you declare a variable in C++, you *must* designate a data type. The value contained in a variable can be assigned at declaration or later in the code. You designate a data type by placing the data type name in front of the variable name. The following code illustrates how to declare several different types of variables:

```
int integerVariable = 1157683648;
bool trueOrFalse = true;
char charVariable = 'A';
short shortVariable = 100;
float floatVariable = 2.4e5;
double doubleVariable = 7.2e24;
```

Hungarian Notation

As you learned earlier, you can use any name you like for a variable, provided it doesn't include spaces or special characters, is not a keyword, and starts with a letter or an underscore (_). Variable names, however, do not automatically tell you the data type of a variable—and knowing the data type of a variable is extremely important when it comes to arithmetic calculations or any type of operation for which you need to assign a new value to a variable. For example, if you attempt to use a char variable in an arithmetic calculation, you will receive a compile error because you cannot perform calculations with text. If you have a very long program, you may find it difficult to remember the data type of a variable, or even locate the variable declaration in order to determine the data type. Determining the data type of a variable is even more difficult when you are working with a program written by another programmer.

Many C++ programmers use Hungarian notation to easily identify the data type of a variable. Dr. Charles Simonyi of Microsoft invented **Hungarian notation** as a variable-naming convention for identifying the data types of variables. (Hungarian notation gets its name because Simonyi is Hungarian.) With Hungarian notation, you begin each variable name with a prefix that identifies the data type. For example, the prefix for the integer data type is *i*. If the variable names in a program conform to Hungarian notation then any programmer can clearly identify a variable named, for example, iNetPay as having an integer data type. Figure 2-11 lists the common prefixes of Hungarian notation.

Prefix	Data Type
c	char
i	integer
si	short integer
li	long integer
f	float
d	double
s	string of characters, *not* terminated by a null character
sz	string of characters, terminated by a null character
b	bool
by	single byte
ct	an integer being used as a counter
p	pointer
ar	array
fn	function

Figure 2-11 Common Hungarian notation prefixes

From this point forward, this book uses Hungarian notation when creating variable names. Remember that Hungarian notation is just a convention; you are not required to use it. You can use any naming convention you like, provided you do not violate any of the rules for identifiers. Hungarian notation, however, is an accepted standard. Using it ensures that other programmers will be able to more easily understand and interpret your code—provided they know the Hungarian notation themselves. Similarly, you will be able to more easily work with other programmer's code if you know the Hungarian notation standard.

Integers

Numeric data types are an important part of any programming language, and are particularly useful when doing arithmetic calculations. C++ supports two numeric data types: integers and floating-point numbers. An **integer** is a positive or negative number with no decimal places. The numbers –250, –13, 0, 2, 6, 10, 100, and 10000 are examples of integers. The data types `bool`, `char`, `int`, `long int`, and `short` are all integer data types because they accept only whole numbers with no decimal places. In deciding which integer data type to use, you should always select the smallest type possible in order to conserve memory resources. For example, the `short` data type takes up only two bytes, whereas the `int` data type takes up four bytes. If your variable needs to store only numbers between –32,768 and 32,767, then you should use the `short` data type instead of the unnecessarily larger int data type.

2

Although `bool` and `char` are considered to be integer data types, the values you can assign to them do not necessarily have to be whole numbers. For example, you can assign a value of *true* to a `bool` variable. The values assigned to the `bool` and `char` data types, however, are converted to whole numbers, or integers, before they are stored.

You will learn more about the `bool` and `char` data types later in this section.

By default, integer variables are created with the **signed type modifier**, which allows integers to store both positive and negative numbers. You can specifically designate that an integer is signed using a statement similar to `signed int iVariable;`. However, because integers are signed by default, the statement `int iVariable;` (without the signed type modifier) is equivalent to `signed int iVariable;`.

If you are sure that your integer variable does not need to hold negative numbers, you can use the unsigned type modifier. The **unsigned type modifier** restricts the values assigned to integer variables to positive numbers. To restrict an integer variable to positive numbers, use a statement similar to `unsigned int iVariable;`. Note that when you use the unsigned type modifier, you actually change the range of numbers that can be assigned to the variable. For example, the default range for signed `short` data types is –32,768 to 32,767. This range means that a `short` variable can be assigned any of 65,535 numbers—the amount of numbers in the range. However, if you use the unsigned type modifier, which restricts the variable values to positive numbers, with a `short` variable using a statement similar to unsigned `short iVariable;`, then the range of numbers that can be accepted by the `short` variable becomes 0 to 32,767.

Integers can be written as decimal numbers, octal numbers, and hexadecimal numbers. **Decimal numbers** are the standard numbers used in everyday life that are based on a value of 10 and do not include a leading 0 (zero). Numbers written as decimal integers include 1, 5, 7, 22, and 100. An **octal number** is based on a value of eight and always begins with a 0 (zero) to inform Visual C++ that it is an octal number. Only the numerals 0 through 7 are used with octal numbers. **Hexadecimal numbers** are based on a value of 16 and always begin with the characters 0x or 0X, followed by hexadecimal digits. The numbers 0 through 9, are represented by the numerals 0 through 9 and the numbers 10 through 15 are represented by the letters *A* through *F*. In this book, you will write your integers as decimal numbers.

Floating-Point Numbers

A **floating-point number** contains decimal places or is written using exponential notation. The numbers –6.16, –4.4, 3.17, .52, 10.5, and 2.7541 are all examples of simple floating-point numbers because they contain decimal places. The data types `float`, `double`, and `long double` all contain floating-point numbers. As with the different integer data types, you should use the smallest floating-point type possible in order to conserve memory resources.

Exponential notation, or **scientific notation**, is a way of writing very large numbers or numbers with many decimal places using a shortened format. Numbers written in exponential notation are represented by a value between 1 and 10, multiplied by 10, and raised to some power. The value of 10 is written with an uppercase or lowercase *E*. For example, the number 200,000,000,000 can be written in exponential notation as 2.0e11, which means "2 times 10 to the eleventh power."

The signed and unsigned type modifiers are not used with floating-point variables.

The Character Data Type and Strings

Up to this point, the data types you have seen store only numbers. To store text, you use the **character data type**. You declare a character data type using the reserved word `char`. In contrast to numeric data types, the value you assign to a character data type must be enclosed within quotation marks. To store one character in a variable, you use the `char` keyword and place the character in single quotation marks. For example, you can assign the letter *A* to a `char` variable named cLetter using the statement `char cLetter = 'A';`. Although you use the `char` data type to store characters, it is actually an integer data type. Values assigned to a `char` variable are stored as **American Standard Code for Information Interchange**, or **ASCII**, **characters**, which are numeric representations of English characters. You can assign an ASCII character directly to a `char` variable instead of assigning characters contained in single quotation marks. For example, the statement `char cLetter = 65;` assigns the letter *A* to the cLetter variable because the Unicode character for the letter *A* is 65. Note that when you use an ASCII character, you do not place the value within single quotation marks. Regardless of whether you assign a character in single quotation marks or an ASCII character to a `char` variable, when you retrieve the value of a `char` variable using a statement such as `cout << cLetter << endl;`, the letter value *A* is returned (assuming *A* was assigned to the cLetter variable).

In most circumstances, it is usually easier to assign a letter in single quotation marks to a `char` variable than to look up the appropriate Unicode character.

A `char` variable stores only a single character. If you attempt to store multiple characters in a `char` variable, using a statement similar to `char cCompany = "Microsoft";`, you will receive an error message. However, you will commonly need to use text string variables in your programs to store data such as names, addresses, company names, and so on. There are three methods in Visual C-style of storing text string variables: C-style text strings, the C++ string class, and the MFC CString class. The C-style method of storing text string variables is the oldest method of storing text string variables and is the most widely used. C-style text string variables are also faster than the other two types of string variables, although you will not notice a difference with the simple programs you create in this book. The tradeoff is that C-style string variables are more difficult to use than the other two methods of storing text string variables. Although they are more difficult to use, you should be sure to use C-style text string variables in your programs that require intensive processing of string variables.

The C++ string class method of storing text string variables is a recent addition to the ANSI C++ standard. It is much easier to use than the C-style class method and in the future will almost certainly become the most popular method of storing text string variables in standard C++ programs.

The MFC CString class is used for storing and manipulating text strings in MFC programs. The C-style and C++ String class methods of storing text string variables will be discussed in this chapter. The MFC CString class will be discussed when you start creating MFC programs.

C-Style Strings

To store text string variables using the C-style method, you use the `char` data type. However, you must specify the number of characters that the variable will store by appending a set of brackets and an integer to the end of the variable name using the syntax `char` ***`variable`***`[`***`number`***`] = "`***`string value`***`";`, replacing *number* with the maximum number of characters that will be assigned to the variable. For example, the statement `char szCompany[50] = "Microsoft";` declares and initializes a `char` variable named szCompany that can contain up to 50 characters and assigns to it the text string *Microsoft*.

The szString variable is actually an advanced data type called an array. Because the szString array variable contains a text string, it is referred to as a character array. Arrays will be examined at the end of this chapter. For now, you should understand that an array is an advanced data type that contains a set of data represented by a single variable name. The szCompany variable, for instance, is an array that stores 50 characters represented by a single variable name (szCompany).

When you assign a text string to a character array, C++ automatically adds to the end of the string an extra character called a **null character**, which is represented by \0. The null character marks the end of the text string. You need to be aware of the null character because it uses the last character space in the number of characters you designate for your character arrays. For example, the following code declares a character array named szProgramming that can accept up to 10 characters. The szProgramming variable is then assigned a value of *Visual C++*, which consists of 10 characters.

```
char szProgramming[10] = "Visual C++";
```

If you attempt to compile the preceding code, you will receive an error because there are not enough elements in the character array to store the 10 characters of the Visual C++ string, plus the null character. To make the code work, you need to change the szProgramming variable declaration so that it can contain 11 characters instead of 10, as follows.

```
char szProgramming[11] = "Visual C++";
```

Another reason to be aware of the null character is because it determines the type of prefix you use with the Hungarian notation naming standard. For single char variables, you add a prefix of *c* to the variable name. For character arrays that are terminated by a null character, you add a prefix of *sz* to the variable name. The following code contains declarations for both a single `char` variable and a string `char` variable:

```
char cLetter = 'J';
char szString[25] = "This is a text string.";
```

In Hungarian notation, array names should begin with *ar*. However, because character arrays are also strings of characters, terminated by a null character, you use the Hungarian notation prefix of *sz*.

With C-style text strings, you can initialize the value stored in a character array when you first declare it. However, you *cannot* change the value of a character array at any point in a program using a statement that includes the variable name, followed by an assignment operator, followed by the value you want to assign to the variable. Nor can you use the assignment operator to assign the value of one character array to another character array. For example, in the following code, the szProgramming variable (which is a character array) is declared in one statement, but assigned a value in another statement. The statement that attempts to assign a value to the szProgramming variable using an assignment operator causes an error. The third statement declares another character array variable named szLanguage and assigns to it the value Java. The last statement then attempts to assign the value of the szLanguage variable to the szProgramming variable, which also causes an error.

```
char szProgramming[10];
szProgramming = "Visual C++"; // ILLEGAL
char szLanguage[10] = "Java";
szProgramming = szLanguage; // ILLEGAL
```

Instead to change the value of a character array after it has been declared and initialized, you must use a string function to manipulate the values stored in a character array. String functions will be discussed in Chapter 3, "Operators and Control Structures." For now, only assign values to a character array when you first declare the variable.

Next, you will modify the Hello World program so that the text strings are stored in char variables.

To modify the Hello World program so that the text strings are stored in char variables:

1. Return to the **HelloWorld.cpp** source file in the Code Editor window in the Hello World program.
2. As shown in Figure 2-12, add the statements that declare C-style string variables for each of the text strings. Also, replace the text strings in each of the three cout statements with the name of the appropriate variable.

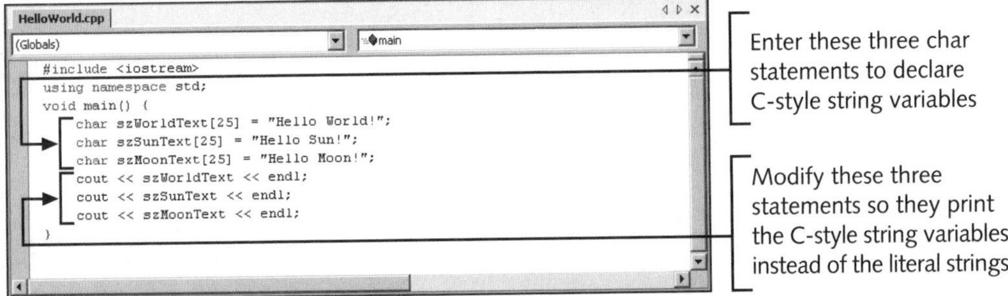

Figure 2-12 C-style string variables added to the main() function

3. Rebuild and execute the program. The console window should appear the same as in Figure 2-7.
4. Press any key to close the console window.

The string Class

The **string class** stores and manipulates text strings in C++. Recall from Chapter 1 that objects are based on classes. This means that you can declare in your code a string *object* from the string *class*. The syntax for declaring a string object is as follows: string sName = "string value";. Notice that the Hungarian notation prefix is *s* and not *sz*. Unlike C-style string variables, C++ does not automatically assign a null character to the end of the text string that you assign to a string class object. Therefore, you use the *s* prefix and not the *sz* prefix with string objects. Before you can declare string class variables, you must first include in your program the string header file using the statement #include <string>.

After you declare a string object, you can work with it the same way you work with a variable. As you will learn later, C++ programmers use the terms *variable* and *object* interchangeably. For now, understand that when a string variable that is declared from the string class is being referred to, the string object is really being referred to.

When you declare a string class variable without initializing it, it is assigned an empty string as its initial value, not the garbage value that is contained in numeric data types that have not been initialized.

With the exception of the brackets and number of characters to store, the syntax for declaring an object from the string class is not all that different from declaring a C-style string variable using the `char` data type. The real difference between the two types of text string variables is in the way you assign values to each variable. You can initialize string class variables at declaration, the same way that you initialize C-style string variables. For example, the following statement declares a string class variable named sProgramming and assigns to it the value *Visual C++* when the variable is first declared:

```
string sProgramming = "Visual C++";
```

Remember that with string class variables, you do not need to declare the number of characters that the variable will contain.

Unlike C-style string variables, you can easily assign a value to a string class variable after declaration using an assignment operator. The following code declares the sProgramming variable in one statement and then uses another statement to assign a value to it:

```
string sProgramming;
sProgramming = "Visual C++";
```

You can also assign the value of one string class variable to another string class variable. The following code declares two string class variables: sProgramming and sLanguage. A value of *Java* is assigned to the sLanguage variable and then the value of the sLanguage variable (*Java*) is assigned to the sProgramming variable using the statement `sProgramming = sLanguage;`.

```
string sProgramming;
string sLanguage = "Java";
sProgramming = sLanguage;
```

If you were to print the sProgramming and sLanguage variables in the preceding code, you would see that they both contain the value *Java*.

Next, you will modify the Hello World program so that the text strings are stored in string class variables.

To modify the Hello World program so that the text strings are stored in string class variables:

1. Return to the **HelloWorld.cpp** source file in the Code Editor window in the Hello World program.
2. As shown in Figure 2-13, include the string header file. Modify the statements that declare the C-style string variables so the variables are declared as string class variables. Be sure to remove the *z* from each of the string variable names so they conform to Hungarian notation. Also, modify the C-style string variables in each of the three cout statements so they reference the string class variables instead of the C-style string variables—you only need to remove the *z* in each of the variable names.

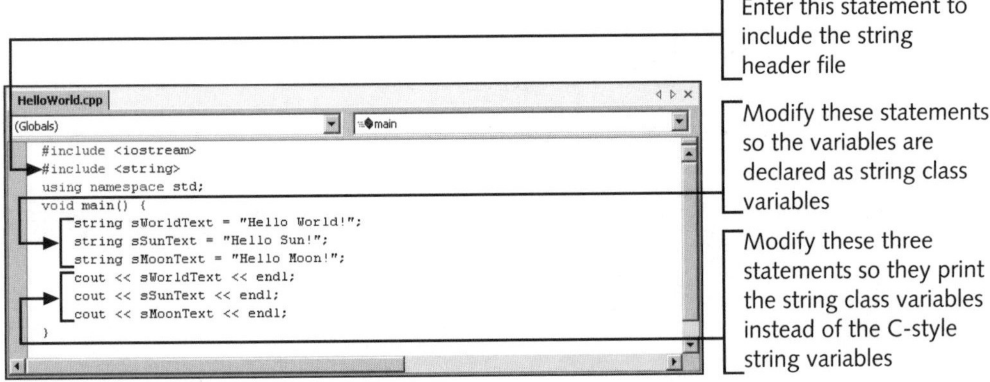
HelloWorld.cpp
(Globals)
main
#include <iostream>
#include <string>
using namespace std;
void main() {
string sWorldText = "Hello World!";
string sSunText = "Hello Sun!";
string sMoonText = "Hello Moon!";
cout << sWorldText << endl;
cout << sSunText << endl;
cout << sMoonText << endl;
}
Enter this statement to include the string header file
Modify these statements so the variables are declared as string class variables
Modify these three statements so they print the string class variables instead of the C-style string variables

Figure 2-13 String class variables added to the main() function

3. Rebuild and execute the program. The console window should appear the same as in Figure 2-7.
4. Press any key to close the console window.

The Escape Character and Escape Sequences

Because you will be using text strings often in your programs, you need to understand a little more of how strings work in C++. As you know, a text string, or literal string, is text that is contained within double quotation marks. Examples of strings you may use in a program are company names, user names, and other types of text. You can use text strings as literal values or assign them to a variable.

If you want to include special characters inside a text string, you need to do so with extra care. Consider the following statement:

```
string sString = "California: the "Golden State"";
```

This statement causes several errors because the Visual C++ compiler assumes that the literal string ends with the double quotation mark before *Golden*. To get around this problem, you include an escape character before the double quotation marks. An **escape character** tells the compiler or interpreter that the character that follows it has a special purpose. In C++ the escape character is the backslash (\). Placing a backslash in front of the special character tells the C++ compiler that the double quotation mark is to be treated as a regular keyboard character, such as a, b, 1, or 2. The backslashes in the following statement tell the Visual C++ compiler to treat the double quotation marks surrounding *Golden State* as regular keyboard characters.

```
string sString = "California: the \"Golden State\"";
```

You can also use the escape character in combination with other characters to insert a special character into a string. When you combine the escape character with other characters the combination is called an **escape sequence**. The backslash followed by a double quotation mark (\") is an example of an escape sequence. Most escape sequences carry out special functions. For example, the escape sequence \t inserts a tab into a string. The null character (\0) you saw earlier is also an example of an escape sequence. Figure 2-14 describes some of the escape sequences that can be added to a string in C++.

Escape Sequence	Character
\b	Backspace
\n	New line
\r	Carriage return
\t	Horizontal tab
\'	Single quotation mark
\"	Double quotation mark
\\	Backslash

Figure 2-14 Escape sequences

Notice that one of the characters generated by an escape sequence is the backslash. Because the escape character itself is a backslash, to include a backslash as a character in a string you must use the escape sequence "\\". For example, to include the path "C:\Personal\" in a string, you must include two backslashes for every single backslash you want to appear in the string, as in the following statement:

```
string sString = "My personal files are in C:\\Personal\\.";
```

Figure 2-15 shows an example of a program containing strings with several escape sequences. Figure 2-16 shows the output.

```
#include <iostream>
using namespace std;
void main() {
   cout << "This line is printed \non two lines." << endl;
   cout << "\tThis line includes a horizontal tab." << endl;
   cout << "My personal files are in c:\\personal." << endl;
   cout << "My dog's name is \"Noah.\"" << endl;
}
```


Figure 2-15 Program containing strings with several escape sequences

```
"c:\Visual C++ Projects\Chapter.02\EscapeSequences\Debug\EscapeSequences.exe"
This line is printed
on two lines.
        This line includes a horizontal tab.
My personal files are in c:\personal.
My dog's name is "Noah."
Press any key to continue
```

Figure 2-16 Output of program containing strings with escape sequences

Boolean Values

A **Boolean value** is a logical value of true or false. You can also think of a Boolean value as being *yes* or *no*, or *on* or *off*. In C++, you use the `bool` data type to contain Boolean values. You can use the words *true* and *false* to indicate Boolean values. You can also use 1 to indicate true or 0 to indicate false. Actually, any integer value other than 0 evaluates to true. However, most programmers use the value 1 or -1 to indicate a value of true. Note that if you use the words *true* or *false*, they are converted to the values 1 or 0 before they are stored in the variable. The following code creates a `bool` variable and assigns several values to it:

```
bool bVariable;
bVariable = true;   // assigns a value of true
bVariable = false;  // assigns a value of false
bVariable = 1;      // also assigns a value of true
bVariable = 0;      // also assigns a value of false
bVariable = -1;     // also assigns a value of true
```

Boolean values get their name from the nineteenth-century mathematician George Boole, who developed the theories of mathematical logic.

Type Casting

The data type of a variable cannot change during the course of program execution. If you attempt to assign a different data type to a variable, you generate a compiler error or warning. If you need to use the contents of a variable as a different data type, you must cast the variable to a new data type. **Casting**, or **type casting**, copies the value contained in a variable of one data type into a variable of another data type. The C++ syntax for casting variables is ***`variable = new_type (old_variable);`***. The *new_type* portion of the syntax is the keyword representing the type to which you want to cast the variable. Note that casting does not change the data type of the original variable. Rather, casting copies the data from the old variable, converts it to the data type of the target variable, and then assigns the value to the new variable. The following code casts an integer variable named *Number* to a float variable named *Number*:

```
int iNumber = 100;
float fNumber;
fNumber = float (iNumber);
```

You can also use the older C syntax for casting variables, *`variable = (new_type) old_variable;`*. This book, however, uses the C++ version.

If you do not explicitly cast a variable of one data type to another data type, then Visual C++ will attempt to automatically perform the cast for you. For example, the following code is identical to the preceding example, except that the intNumber variable is not cast to the float data type before its value is assigned to fNumber. Although you will receive a warning when you compile the program, the value of iNumber will be automatically cast to the float type and assigned to the fNumber variable.

```
int iNumber = 100;
float fNumber;
fNumber = iNumber;
```

How the Visual C++ compiler automatically converts data types is a fairly complex process. If you anticipate that your program will perform operations using multiple data types, you should always manually cast the data type of a variable before assigning its value to a variable of another data type.

Regardless of whether your program uses explicit type casting or automatic type casting, you need to be careful when assigning larger data types to smaller ones. For example, the `short` data type holds values up to 32,768, whereas the `int` data type holds values up to 2,147,483,648. If you attempt to assign the contents of an `int` variable to a short variable, and the value of the `int` variable is less than or equal to 32,767, then the assignment will be successful. If you attempt to assign to a `short` variable a value larger than 32,767, however, the value assigned to the `short` variable will be truncated. Similarly, if you attempt to assign the value of a `float` variable to an `int` variable, the fractional portion of the float variable value will be lost because the `int` data type stores only whole numbers.

In addition to the type casting techniques presented in this section, C++ includes various data conversion functions that you can use to explicitly convert a variable to a different data type. The data conversion functions are found in the stdio.h header. See the Data Conversion Routines topic in the MSDN Library for more information.

Constants

As you learned in Chapter 1, a constant contains information that does not change during the course of program execution. There are two methods of creating constants in C++: the #define statement or the `const` keyword.

The **#define statement** is a preprocessor directive that defines a constant. You place a #define statement at the beginning of a file, just as you do with the #include statement. The syntax for using the #define statement is **`#define`** ***`NAME value`***. For example, to create a constant named COMPANY_NAME that contains the constant value *My Company Name*, you use the statement **`#define COMPANY_NAME "My Company Name"`**. You do not use an equal sign (=) to assign the value to the constant name. Also, as with other preprocessor directives, you do not include a semicolon at the end of the statement. It is common practice to use all uppercase letters for constant names. The following code contains a simple program that defines the COMPANY_NAME constant and outputs the results using cout:

```
#include <iostream>
using namespace std;
#define COMPANY_NAME "My Company Name"
void main() {
   cout << COMPANY_NAME << endl;
}
```

Next, you will use the #define statement to create a constant containing the text *Hello*. You will then combine the constant with text strings that are output to the console window.

To use the #define statement to create a constant containing the text Hello:

1. Return to the **HelloWorld.cpp** source file in the Code Editor window in the Hello World program.
2. As shown in Figure 2-17, add a #define statement to declare a constant named GREETING.
3. In the variable declaration statements, remove the word *Hello* and the space in the literal strings that are assigned to each of the three variables.
4. Finally, modify the output statements so that they output the GREETING constant, a text string consisting of a single space, and the variable.

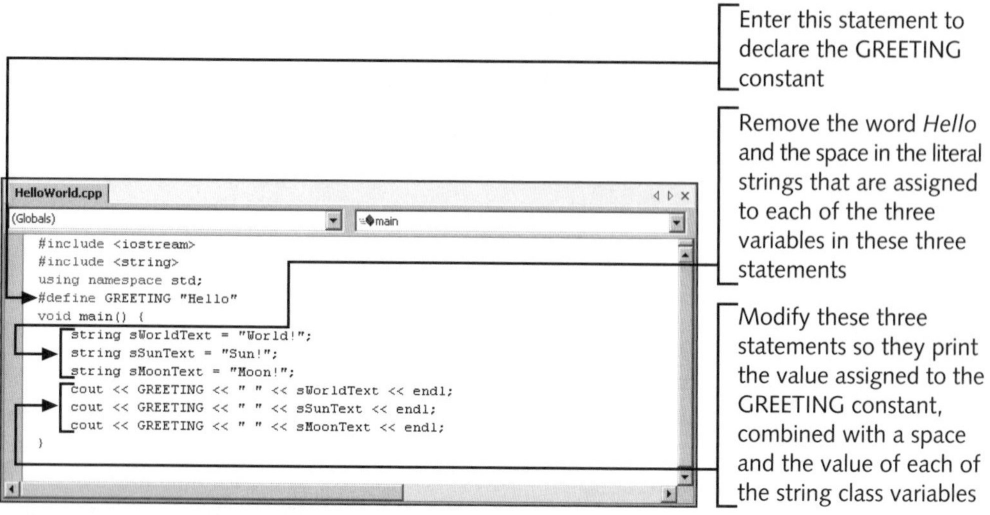
HelloWorld.cpp
(Globals)
main
#include <iostream>
#include <string>
using namespace std;
#define GREETING "Hello"
void main() {
string sWorldText = "World!";
string sSunText = "Sun!";
string sMoonText = "Moon!";
cout << GREETING << " " << sWorldText << endl;
cout << GREETING << " " << sSunText << endl;
cout << GREETING << " " << sMoonText << endl;
}
Enter this statement to declare the GREETING constant
Remove the word Hello and the space in the literal strings that are assigned to each of the three variables in these three statements
Modify these three statements so they print the value assigned to the GREETING constant, combined with a space and the value of each of the string class variables

Figure 2-17 Hello World program modified to use a constant containing the text Hello

5. Rebuild and execute the program. The console window should appear the same as it did before you added the constant.
6. Press any key to close the console window.

You can also create a constant by placing the **const keyword** before the data type in a variable declaration. For example, the statement `const string COMPANY_NAME = "My Company";` also creates the COMPANY_NAME constant. The following code contains the same simple program that declares and outputs the COMPANY_NAME constant, but this time using the const keyword:

```
#include <iostream>
#include <string>
using namespace std;
const string COMPANY_NAME = "My Company";
void main() {
   cout << COMPANY_NAME << endl;
}
```

Note

Unlike constants that are declared with the #define directive, statements that define constants with the `const` keyword must end in a semicolon.

Next, you will use the `const` keyword instead of the #define statement to create a constant containing the text *Hello*. You will then combine the constant with text strings that are output to the console window.

To modify the Hello World program so that it creates a constant with the **const** keyword instead of with the #define statement:

1. Return to the **HelloWorld.cpp** source file in the Code Editor window.
2. As shown in Figure 2-18, modify the `#define GREETING "Hello"` statement so the constant is created with the `const` keyword instead of with the #define statement, so that it reads **`const string GREETING = "Hello";`**.

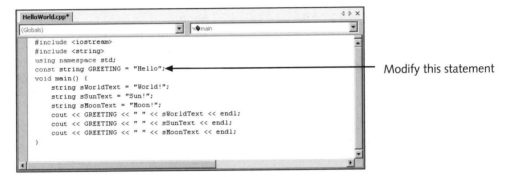

```
HelloWorld.cpp*
(Globals)                         main
#include <iostream>
#include <string>
using namespace std;
const string GREETING = "Hello";   <---- Modify this statement
void main() {
    string sWorldText = "World!";
    string sSunText = "Sun!";
    string sMoonText = "Moon!";
    cout << GREETING << " " << sWorldText << endl;
    cout << GREETING << " " << sSunText << endl;
    cout << GREETING << " " << sMoonText << endl;
}
```

Figure 2-18 The Hello World program after creating a constant with the `const` keyword instead of with the #define statement

Placing a variable or constant declaration outside of a function gives it global scope. You will study scope at the end of this chapter.

3. Rebuild and test the program. The program should function the same as it did with the #define statement constant.
4. Press any key to close the console window.

The #define statement is the oldest method of creating constants in C++. Nevertheless, the `const` method is the preferred method of creating constants for two reasons. First, the #define method does not allow you to declare the data type of the constant. Second, the #define method can be confusing because it does not use standard C++ statement syntax, such as an equal sign, to assign the value to the constant name, or a semicolon to end the statement.

The #define statement is discussed here because some programmers still use it to create constants, and you need to be able to recognize it in a program if you ever come across it.

ADDING COMMENTS TO A PROGRAM

When you create a program, whether it is with C++ or any other programming language, it is considered good programming practice to add comments to your code. **Comments** are nonexecuting lines that you place in your code that contain various types of remarks, including the name of the program, your name, and the date you created the program; notes to yourself; or instructions to future programmers who may need to modify your work. When you are working with long programs, comments make it easier to decipher the structure of the program.

Visual C++ supports two types of comments: line comments and block comments. C++ **line comments** are created by adding two slashes // before the text you want to use as a comment. The // characters instruct the compiler to ignore all text to the end of the line. Line comments can appear at the end of a line of code, or they can exist on an entire line by themselves. C-style **block comments** span multiple lines and are created by adding /* to the first line that is to be included in the block. You close a block comment by typing */ after the last text to be included in the block. The compiler ignores any text or lines between the opening /* characters and the closing */ characters. Figure 2-19 displays a function containing line and block comments.

```
void main() {
     /*
     This line is part of the block comment.
     This line is also part of the block comment.
     */
     cout << "Line comment 1";      // Line comments can
     cout << "Line comment 2";      // follow code statements
     // This line comment takes up an entire line.
}
```


Figure 2-19 Function with line and block comments

Next, you will add comments to the Hello World program.

1. Return to the **HelloWorld.cpp** source file in the Code Editor window.
2. Add the block and line comments shown in Figure 2-20. Be sure to replace *Don Gosselin* and *September 20, 2002* with your own name and the date on which you create the program.

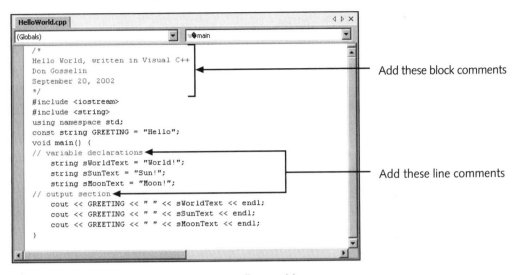

```
HelloWorld.cpp
(Globals)                    main
/*
Hello World, written in Visual C++
Don Gosselin
September 20, 2002
*/
#include <iostream>
#include <string>
using namespace std;
const string GREETING = "Hello";
void main() {
// variable declarations
    string sWorldText = "World!";
    string sSunText = "Sun!";
    string sMoonText = "Moon!";
// output section
    cout << GREETING << " " << sWorldText << endl;
    cout << GREETING << " " << sSunText << endl;
    cout << GREETING << " " << sMoonText << endl;
}
```

Add these block comments

Add these line comments

Figure 2-20 Comments added to the Hello World program

When you create comments in your C++ programs, be sure to use a forward slash (/) and not a backward slash (\). People often confuse these two characters.

3. Rebuild the project, and then execute the program to confirm that the comments do not appear.
4. Press any key to close the console window.

FUNCTIONS

Recall from Chapter 1 that a function allows you to treat a logically related group of C++ statements as a single unit. An example of a function is a series of statements in an accounting program that calculates an employee's net pay. You could execute each statement that calculates net pay one statement at a time. However, it is much easier to execute all of the statements at the same time by executing a function that contains them.

Before you can use a function in a C++ program, you must first create, or define, it. The lines that compose a function within a C++ program are called the **function definition**. The syntax for defining a function is:

```
return_data_type name_of_function(parameters) {
   statements;
}
```

Note that a function definition consists of four parts:

- A reserved word indicating the return data type of the function's return value
- The function name
- Any parameters required by the function, contained within parentheses following the function name.
- The function statements enclosed in curly braces { }

You designate a data type for a function because it is common to return a value from a function after it executes. If you do not need to return a value from a function, then you use a data type of `void`.

Following the `return` data type is the function name. Like variables, the name you assign to a function is called an identifier. The same rules and conventions that apply to variable names apply to function names.

Following the function name are parentheses. Parameters are placed within these parentheses. A **parameter**, or **formal parameter**, is a variable that stores a value that is passed to a function. You can use any data type or class, including the string class, when you define a parameter. Return types and how parameters get their values will be discussed later in this section. For now, the focus will remain on how functions are structured.

For an example of how to use a parameter, consider a function named calculate_square_root() that calculates the square root of an integer variable named iNumber. The function name would be written as `int calculate_square_root(int iNumber)`.

Functions can contain multiple parameters separated by commas. To add three separate number parameters to a function named averageResult() that calculates the average of the numbers, you write the function name as `int averageResult(int iNumber1, int iNumber2, int iNumber3)`.

Functions are not required to contain parameters. Many functions only perform a task and do not require external data.

Following the parentheses containing the function parameters are a set of curly braces containing the function statements. Function statements must be contained within the function braces. The following code is an example of a function that prints the names of multiple companies.

```
void print_names(string sCoName1, string sCoName2,
        string sCoName3) {
        cout << sCoName1 << endl;
        cout << sCoName2 << endl;
        cout << sCoName3 << endl;
}
```

Notice the structure of the function in the preceding example. The opening curly brace is on the same line as the function name and the closing curly brace is on its own line following the function statements. Each statement between the curly braces is indented using a one-half inch tab. This structure is the preferred format among many programmers. However, some programmers prefer placing the opening curly brace on the line following the function name or using spaces instead of tabs for the indentation of statements. Both formats work exactly the same way. Feel free to use whatever function formatting you prefer. You will see both formats used in this book.

You can set the default formatting for your installation of Visual C++ using the Tabs category in the All Languages folder in the Text Editor folder in the Options dialog box.

The main() Function

The starting point for traditional C++ programs is the main() function. The **main() function** is a special function that runs automatically when a program first executes. All C++ programs must include a main() function. All other functions in a C++ program are executed from the main() function. A main() function is created with the exact same structure as other functions, with the exception that it must be named *main*. The compiler knows that the main() function is the first function to execute when your program first loads. If your program does not include a main() function, then it will not execute.

Defining and Calling Custom Functions

You create your own custom function definitions the same way you create main() functions, except that you must use a name other than *main* for the function name. Unlike the main() function, a custom function definition does not execute automatically. Creating a custom function definition only names the function, specifies its parameters, and organizes the statements it will execute. To execute a function, you must invoke, or **call,** it from the main() function or from another custom function.

To call a function, you create a statement that includes the function name followed by parentheses containing any variables or values to be assigned to the function parameters. The variables or values that you place in the parentheses of the function call statement are called **arguments** or **actual parameters**. Sending arguments to the called function parameters is called **passing arguments**. The parameters in the called function definition then take on the value of the arguments that are passed from the calling statement.

The same type casting rules that apply to variables also apply to arguments and parameters that are used within a function. If you pass an argument to a parameter, and the argument and parameter are of different data types, then C++ will attempt to type cast the values for you (if you do not cast them yourself.)

Passing variables or literal values to a function is called passing-by-value. You will learn more about passing-by-value when we start discussing class concepts later in this book.

Figure 2-21 shows a C++ program that prints the name of a company. Figure 2-22 shows the output. Notice that the custom print_company_name() function is called from within the main() function. Also notice that the *My Company* text string is passed from the main() function to the sCompanyName string class parameter.

```
#include <iostream>

#include <string>

using namespace std;

void print_company_name(string sCompanyname) {

     cout << sCompanyName  << endl;

}

void main() {

     print_company_name("My Company");

}
```

Parameter

Argument is passed to the sCompanyName parameter

Argument

Figure 2-21 Custom function definition being called from the main() function

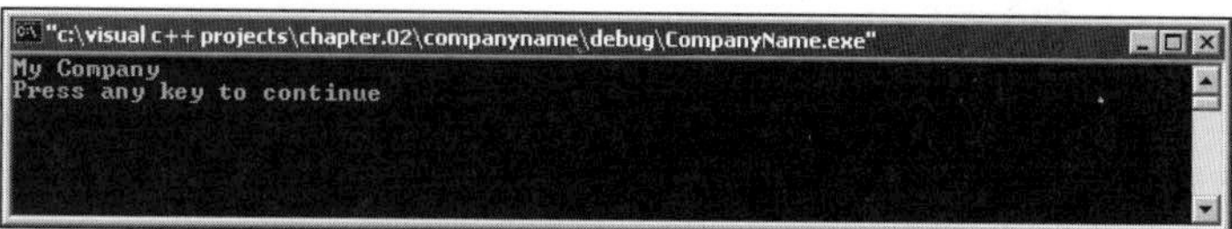

Figure 2-22 Output of the custom function definition being called from the main() function

Next, you will modify the Hello World program so that the text strings, *Hello World!*, *Hello Sun!*, and *Hello Moon!* are printed from separate functions. You will also add to the main() function call statements that execute each function. Each new function will contain a string parameter. As you call each function, you will pass to the string parameter the appropriate text to combine with the GREETING constant: *World!*, *Sun!*, or *Moon!* The program will create the same output that it did before you added the new functions.

To add custom functions to the Hello World program:

1. Return to the **HelloWorld.cpp** source file in the Code Editor window.
2. Delete the statements shown in Figure 2-23 from the main() function.

```
HelloWorld.cpp
(Globals)                                   main
September 20, 2002
*/
#include <iostream>
#include <string>
using namespace std;
const string GREETING = "Hello";
void main() {
// variable declarations
    string sWorldText = "World!";
    string sSunText = "Sun!";
    string sMoonText = "Moon!";
// output section
    cout << GREETING << " " << sWorldText << endl;
    cout << GREETING << " " << sSunText << endl;
    cout << GREETING << " " << sMoonText << endl;
}
```

Delete these statements

Figure 2-23 Statements deleted from the main() function

3. After the main() function, add the three function definitions shown in Figure 2-24.

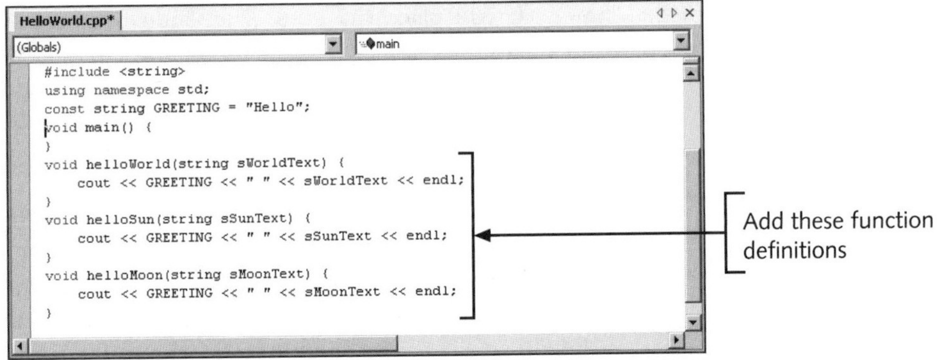
HelloWorld.cpp*
(Globals)
main
#include <string>
using namespace std;
const string GREETING = "Hello";
void main() {
}
void helloWorld(string sWorldText) {
cout << GREETING << " " << sWorldText << endl;
}
void helloSun(string sSunText) {
cout << GREETING << " " << sSunText << endl;
}
void helloMoon(string sMoonText) {
cout << GREETING << " " << sMoonText << endl;
}
Add these function definitions

Figure 2-24 Function definitions added to the Hello World project

4. Finally, add to the main() function the three statements shown in Figure 2-25, which call the three new functions and pass literal strings to them:

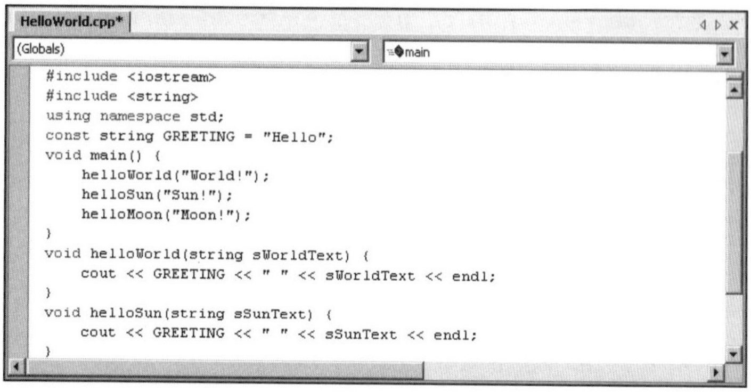

```
HelloWorld.cpp*
(Globals)                                   main
#include <iostream>
#include <string>
using namespace std;
const string GREETING = "Hello";
void main() {
    helloWorld("World!");
    helloSun("Sun!");
    helloMoon("Moon!");
}
void helloWorld(string sWorldText) {
    cout << GREETING << " " << sWorldText << endl;
}
void helloSun(string sSunText) {
    cout << GREETING << " " << sSunText << endl;
}
```

Figure 2-25 Calling custom functions from the main() function

Before you can successfully compile and execute the modified Hello World program, you need to learn about and add function prototypes.

Function Prototypes

Where you place a custom function definition in your source file is critical, and you must always be aware of the choices. If you place any custom function definitions above the main() function (as shown in Figure 2-21), then your program will compile without the problems that can be caused by placement of custom functions. Many programmers prefer to place the main() function at the beginning of the source file, however, because it is the starting point for all other functions within the file. If you place the main() function above any custom functions in your source file, then you must create a function prototype for each function below the main() function. A **function prototype** declares to the compiler that you intend to use a custom function later in the program. If you attempt to call a custom function at any point in a source file *prior* to where its function prototype or function definition appears, then you will receive an error when you compile the project. Figure 2-26 contains a modified version of the program from Figure 2-21. This time the main() function is placed above the print_company_name() function. If you attempted to compile this program, you would receive an error message since the main() function attempts to call the function prior to its function prototype or function definition.

```
#include <iostream>
#include <string>
using namespace std;
void main() {
   print_company_name("My Company");
}
void print_company_name(string sCompanyName) {
   cout << sCompanyName << endl;
}
```

Figure 2-26 Company name before adding a function prototype

In order for the program in Figure 2-26 to work, you must add a function prototype above the main() function. The syntax for a function prototype is ***`return_data_type name_of_function(parameters);`***. A function prototype is essentially the first line of a function declaration without the opening curly brace. Figure 2-27 shows a correct version of the company name program with a function prototype for the print_company_name() function.

```
#include <iostream>
#include <string>
using namespace std;
void print_company_name(string sCompanyName);
void main() {
   print_company_name("My Company");
}
void print_company_name(string sCompanyName) {
   cout << sCompanyName << endl;
}
```

Function prototype

Figure 2-27 Company name after adding a function prototype

You have the option to exclude a parameter name when you declare a function prototype, although you are required to include the parameter data type. For example, in Figure 2-27, you can use either `print_company_name(stringsCompanyName);` or `print_company_name(string);` as the prototype for the print_company_name() function. Although you can exclude a parameter name from function prototype, you must include a name for the parameter in the function definition in order to be able to use it within the body of the function.

Next, you will add function prototypes to the Hello World program for the helloWorld(), helloSun(), and helloMoon() functions.

To add function prototypes to the Hello World program for the helloWorld(), helloSun(), and helloMoon() functions:

1. Return to the **HelloWorld.cpp** source file in the Code Editor window.

2. Add the function prototypes shown in Figure 2-28.

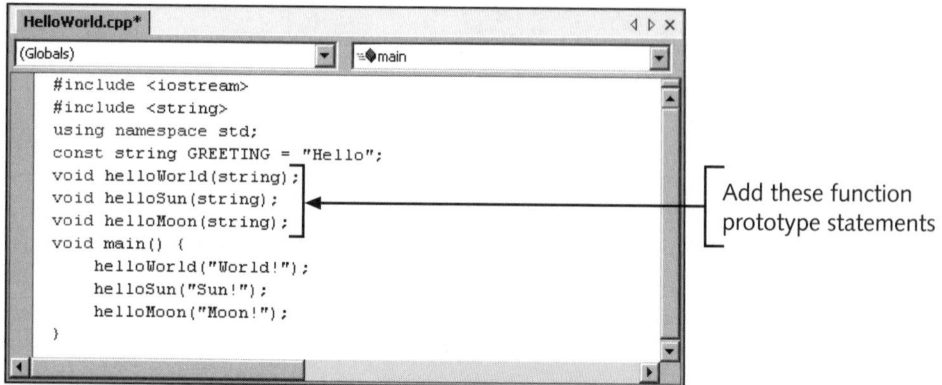
HelloWorld.cpp*
(Globals)
main
#include <iostream>
#include <string>
using namespace std;
const string GREETING = "Hello";
void helloWorld(string);
void helloSun(string);
void helloMoon(string);
void main() {
helloWorld("World!");
helloSun("Sun!");
helloMoon("Moon!");
}
Add these function prototype statements

Figure 2-28 Adding function prototypes to the Hello World project

3. Rebuild and execute the Hello World project. The program should function normally.
4. Press any key to close the console window.

Return Values

In many instances, you may want one function to receive a value from another function that you can then use in other code. For instance, if you have a function that performs a calculation on a number that is passed to it, you would want to receive the result of the calculation. Consider a function that calculates the average of a series of numbers that you pass to it—the function would be useless if you never saw the result. To return a value to a calling statement, you assign the calling statement to a variable. You can use any data type or class, including the string class, as the return type for a function.

Tip

The C++ type casting rules also apply when you assign to a variable the value returned from a function call. If the returned value and the variable are of different data types, then C++ will attempt to type cast the values for you, if you have not already cast them yourself.

The following statement calls a function named average_numbers() and assigns the return value to an integer variable named iReturnValue. The statement also passes three literal values to the function.

```
int iReturnValue = average_numbers(1, 2, 3);
```

To return a value to a variable, you must include the return statement within the called function. The syntax for the return statement is either `return value;` or `return(value);`. This book primarily uses the first syntax example. The program in Figure 2-29 contains the average_numbers() function, which calculates the average of three numbers and stores that value in a variable named iResult. The function then uses the return statement to return the value contained in the iResult variable to the calling statement in the main() function.

2

```
#include <iostream>
using namespace std;
int average_numbers(int, int, int);
void main() {
    int iReturnValue = average_numbers(1, 2, 3);
     cout << iReturnValue << endl;
}
int average_numbers(int iFirstNum, int iSecondNum,
     int iThirdNum) {
     int sum_of_numbers = iFirstNum + iSecondNum
          + iThirdNum;
     int iResult = sum_of_numbers / 3;
     return iResult;
}
```

Return value assigned to the iReturnValue variable

Return statement

Figure 2-29 Average number program

Remember that values passed back and forth between functions must be of the same data type, or C++ will attempt to type cast them for you. Notice that at each stage in the preceding code, the values passed back and forth are of the integer data type.

The variable name that is returned from a function and the variable name that receives the returned value can be the same. For instance, in the preceding examples, the variable name in the return statement in the average_numbers() function and the variable name in the calling statement in the main() function could both be iReturnValue. In addition, when you pass variables as arguments to a function, the passed variables and the parameter names within the function itself can also be the same. If you pass variables to the average_numbers() function instead of the literal values used in the main() function, you can use the statement `average_numbers(iFirstNum, iSecondNum, iThirdNum);`, even though the parameter names within the function itself are *a*, *b*, and *c*. However, most programmers usually use unique names to identify specific variables in their code.

Using unique names to identify specific variables makes it easier to understand a program's logic and assists in the debugging process.

You do not need to receive return values from all functions. For example, you would not need to receive a return value from a function that prints an employee's personal information to the screen or performs some other task that does not create or return a useful value. If you do not need to receive a return value from a function, then you are not required to assign the calling statement to a variable. For instance, if you want to call the average_numbers() function from the main() function to calculate the average of the three literal values, *2*, *3*, and *4*, but do not require a return value, you write `average_numbers(2, 3, 4);` without assigning the statement to the iReturnValue variable.

If you do not want to return a value from a function, then you must use the `void` keyword as the data type in the function definition. If you use any data type other than `void` in a function definition, then you must return a value from the function.

When a function performs a calculation such as an average, you normally want to receive a return value.

Next, you will modify the Hello World program so that the helloWorld(), helloSun(), and helloMoon() functions return values. The helloWorld() function will return the distance of the Earth to the Sun (92,897,000 miles), the helloSun() function will return the Sun's core temperature (72,000,000 degrees Fahrenheit), and the helloMoon() function will return the Moon's diameter (3456 miles). The returned values will be doubles, so you must modify the data type of each function definition, as well as the data type for each function prototype. Each function will continue to print the individual text strings Hello World!, Hello Sun!, and Hello Moon! However, the main() function will print the return value from each function. You will use a `double` variable named dReturnType in order to store the value returned from each function. Note that the values returned from a function are often the result of some sort of calculation or expression evaluation. In this exercise, you will not perform any sort of calculation or expression evaluation because your only purpose is to see how values are returned from calling functions.

To add return values to the Hello World program:

1. Return to the **HelloWorld.cpp** source file in the Code Editor window.
2. Change the data type for the three function prototypes to `double` as shown in Figure 2-30.

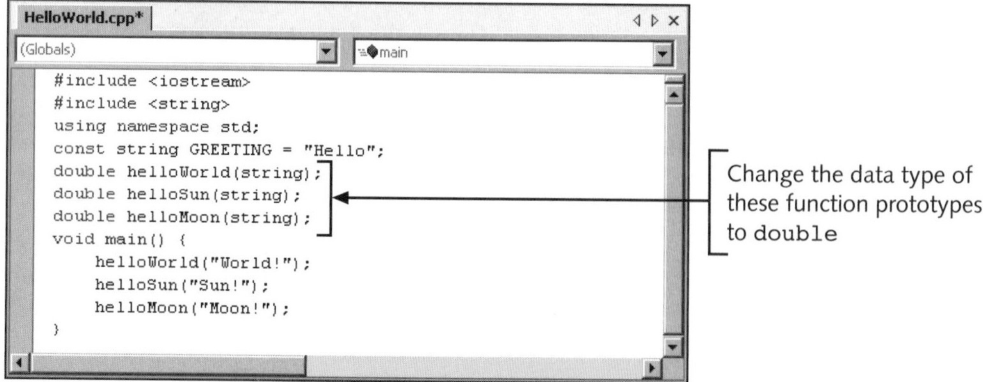

Figure 2-30 The data type for the three function prototypes changed to `double`

3. Declare in the main() function a **`double`** variable named dReturnValue, as shown in Figure 2-31. Also, modify the calls to the custom functions so the return values are assigned to the dReturnValue variable.

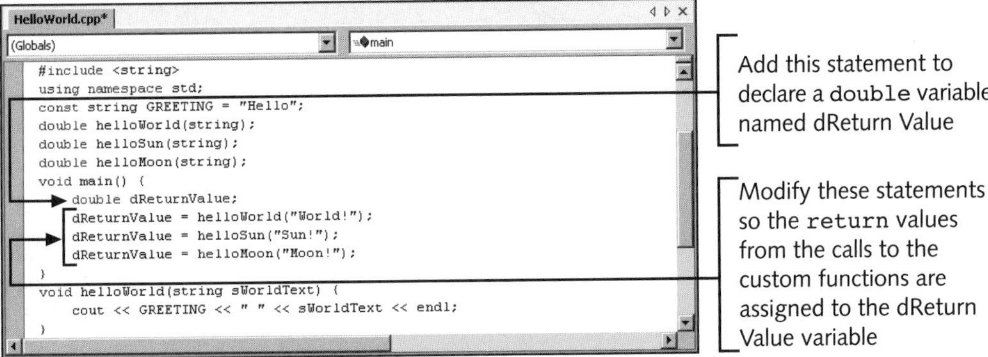

Figure 2-31 `Return` values from the calls to the custom functions in the main() function assigned to the dReturnValue variable

4. Add the statements shown in Figure 2-32 that print the values returned from the custom functions to the screen, along with some descriptive text strings.

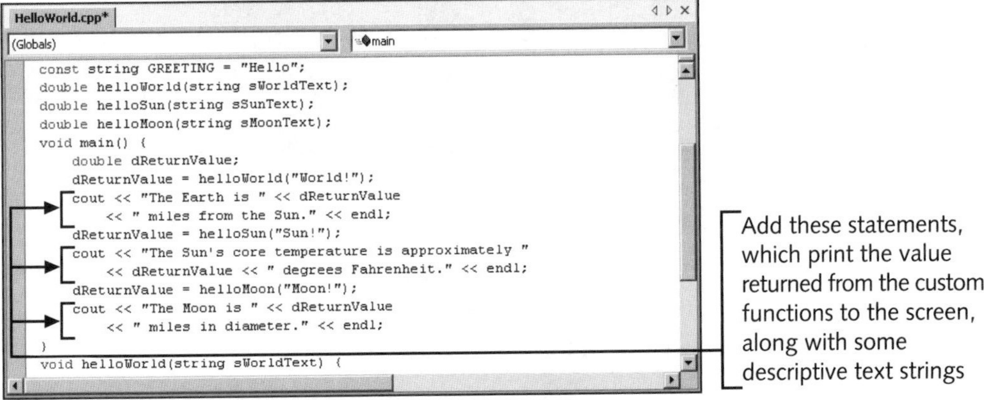

Figure 2-32 Statements that print the value returned from the custom functions to the screen, along with some descriptive test strings

5. Next, change the data types for the helloWorld(), helloSun(), and helloMoon() functions from **`void`** to **`double`**. Also add a **`return`** value of **92897000** to the helloWorld() function, a return value of **72000000** to the helloSun() function, and a **`return`** value of **3456** to the helloMoon() function. Each **`return`** value should appear as the last statement in each function.

The completed helloWorld(), helloSun(), and helloMoon() functions should appear as shown in Figure 2-33.

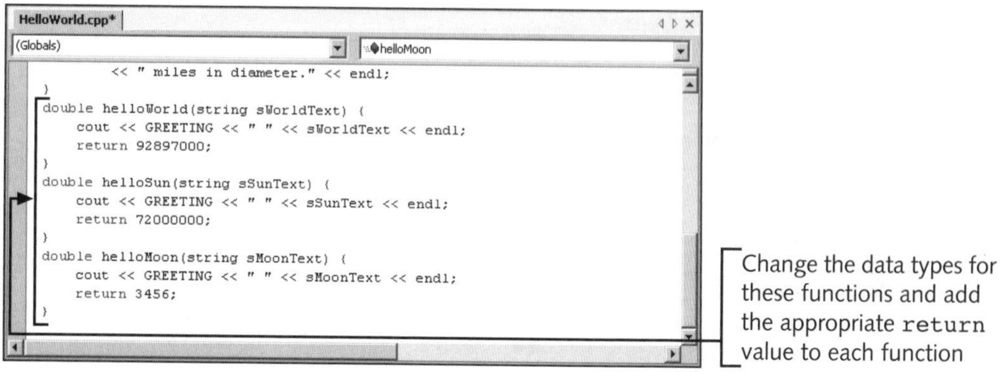
HelloWorld.cpp*
(Globals)
helloMoon
<< " miles in diameter." << endl;
}
double helloWorld(string sWorldText) {
cout << GREETING << " " << sWorldText << endl;
return 92897000;
}
double helloSun(string sSunText) {
cout << GREETING << " " << sSunText << endl;
return 72000000;
}
double helloMoon(string sMoonText) {
cout << GREETING << " " << sMoonText << endl;
return 3456;
}
Change the data types for these functions and add the appropriate return value to each function

Figure 2-33 helloWorld(), helloSun(), and helloMoon() functions modified to include `return` values

6. Rebuild and execute the program. Your command window should appear similar to Figure 2-34.

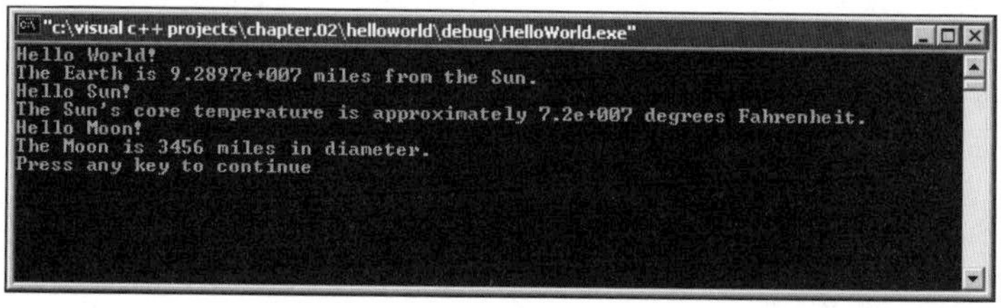
"c:\visual c++ projects\chapter.02\helloworld\debug\HelloWorld.exe"
Hello World!
The Earth is 9.2897e+007 miles from the Sun.
Hello Sun!
The Sun's core temperature is approximately 7.2e+007 degrees Fahrenheit.
Hello Moon!
The Moon is 3456 miles in diameter.
Press any key to continue

Figure 2-34 Output of Hello World after adding `return` values

7. Press any key to close the console window.

Default Parameter Values

When you declare a standard function, you can initialize the function's parameters in its prototype. This allows you to provide default values to the function parameters in the event that users fail to provide arguments when they call the function. The syntax for providing default values to parameters in a function prototype is ***`type functionName(type parameterName = value, ...);`***. Note that you must provide a parameter's name in the function prototype in order to assign default values. For example, the following prototype for a function named downPayment(), which calculates the down payment required for purchasing a home, assigns a default value of 100000 to the dPrice parameter and a default value of .1 to the dPercent parameter:

```
double downPayment(double dPrice = 100000, double dPercent = .1);
```


You do not repeat the initialization statements in the function definition. The definition for the downPayment() function, for instance, would still be written as follows:

```
double downPayment(double dPrice, double dPercent) {
        double dPercentDown = dPercent;
        return dPrice * dPercentDown;

}
```

If the user does not provide any values to a function that defines default parameter values, then the default values will be used in the function. This means that the statement `downPayment();` returns a value of *10000* because the function will use the default parameter values. However, if the user provides arguments when calling the function, the values passed will replace the default values in the function prototype. Therefore, the statement `downPayment(150000, .05);` returns a value of 7500 because the arguments in the function call replace the default parameter values.

The user can exclude individual arguments in order to use the default values assigned to the parameters. However, if you exclude an argument in a call to a function with default parameter values, then you must also exclude all arguments to the *right* of the excluded argument. For instance, you can use the statement `downPayment(200000);` to pass to the dPrice parameter in the downPayment() function a value of *200000*, but use the default value of .1 that is assigned to the dPercent parameter. However, you cannot exclude the first argument and pass only the second argument. For instance, the statement `downPayment(, .08);`, which excludes the first argument, is illegal.

SCOPE

When you use variables and constants in a C++ program, you need to be aware of their scope. **Scope** refers to where in your program a declared variable or constant can be used. Scope is determined by whether a variable or constant is declared within a function or within a command block. First, you will learn about command blocks.

Command Blocks

The functions you have worked with so far have all consisted of statements contained within a set of braces. Commands contained within a set of braces are known as a command block or a statement block. **Command blocks** group statements into a single unit using a set of braces. For example, the following code contains a function whose statements are contained within a command block:

```
void sampleFunction() {
   string sMessage = "Part of a command block.";
   cout << sMessage << endl;
}
```

In the preceding example, the command block contains all of the function statements; the statements then execute as a single unit when the function is called. You can think of a command block as a type of container that holds a series of statements. In the case of a function, you do not need to execute each statement individually. Rather, you call the command block as a unit using its function name.

Multiple statements enclosed in a command block are referred to as a compound statement.

Command blocks are not restricted to use with functions. You can use commands blocks at any point in C++ when you want to group statements together into a single unit. For example, the code in Figure 2-35 contains several command blocks that organize sections of C++ code into units:

```
void commandBlocks() {
   {
      string sFirstMessage = "first command block";
      cout << sFirstMessage << endl;
   }
   {
      string sSecondMessage = "second command block";
      cout << sSecondMessage << endl;
   }
   {
      string sThirdMessage = "third command block";
      cout << sThirdMessage << endl;
   }
}
```

Command block

Figure 2-35 Command blocks

Each command block must have an opening brace ({) and a closing brace (}). If a command block is missing either the opening or closing brace, an error will occur.

The command block examples in Figure 2-35 serve no purpose other than to demonstrate the use of command blocks. Note that it is considered poor programming style to include command blocks in your code that serve no purpose. You should use command blocks in your code only for legitimate reasons, such as when you are using control structures and repetition statements. You will study these topics in the next chapter.

Command blocks have a great deal of influence on the scope of functions and variables. Therefore, you need to use command blocks with care and with a good understanding of the logical flow of your program. You will learn about variable scope next.

Variable Scope

A variable can have either global scope or local scope. Variables that have **global scope** are declared outside of any functions or classes and are available to all parts of your program. Variables that have **local scope** are declared inside a function and are available only within the function in which they are declared. Local variables cease to exist when the function within which they are declared ends. If you attempt to use a local variable outside of the function in which it is declared, you will receive an error message when you attempt to compile the program.

Global scope is also referred to as namespace scope or file scope.

The parameters within the parentheses of a function declaration are considered to be local variables.

Global variables are considered a poor programming technique, especially in large programs, because it can be difficult to understand which functions have modified, or will modify, the value of a global variable. Although there are legitimate reasons for using global variables (which you will learn as you progress through this book), you should instead always use arguments and return values to share data among the functions in your programs.

The code in Figure 2-36 includes a global variable, called sGlobalVariable, and a function named scopeExample() that contains a local variable called sLocalVariable. When the scopeExample() function is called from the main() function, the global variable and the local variable print successfully from within the scopeExample() function. After the call to the function, the global variable again prints successfully from the main() function. However, if you tried to compile the program, you would receive an error message. The main() function is trying to access a variable, sLocalVariable, that is outside of its scope because sLocalVariable is local to the scopeExample() function.

The main() function also contains a command block that declares a variable named sBlockVariable. The sBlockVariable is available only to the command block and not to the main() function. You can think of sBlockVariable as having *very* local scope. You can print sBlockVariable from inside its command block. However, if you attempt to print it from the main() function, which is outside of the command block, you will receive an error.

```
#include <string>
using namespace std;
void scopeExample();
string sGlobalVariable = "First global variable";
void main() {
        scopeExample();
        cout << sGlobalVariable << endl; // prints successfully
   cout << sLocalVariable << endl;       // error message
   {
      string sBlockVariable = "Command block variable."
      cout << sBlockVariable << endl;    // prints successfully
   }
   cout << sBlockVariable << endl;       // error message
}
void scopeExample() {
   string sLocalVariable = "Local variable";
   cout << sLocalVariable << endl;       // prints successfully
   cout << sGlobalVariable << endl;      // prints successfully
}
```

Global variable declaration

Local command block variable declaration

Local function variable declaration

Figure 2-36 Variable scope program

When a program contains a global variable and a local variable with the same name, the local variable takes precedence when its function is called. In the program in Figure 2-37, the global variable sShowDog is assigned a value of *Golden Retriever* before the function that contains a local variable of the same name is called. Once the function is called, the local sShowDog variable is assigned a value of *Irish Setter*. After the function ends, the local sShowDog variable ceases to exist, and *Golden Retriever* is still the value of the global sShowDog variable.

```
#include <iostream>
#include <string>
using namespace std;
void duplicateVariableNames();
string sShowDog = "Golden Retriever";
void main() {
   cout << sShowDog << endl; // prints 'Golden Retriever'
   duplicateVariableNames();
   cout << sShowDog << endl; // prints 'Golden Retriever'
}
void duplicateVariableNames() {
   string sShowDog = "Irish Setter";
   cout << sShowDog << endl; // prints 'Irish Setter'
}
```

Global sShowDog variable declaration

Local sShowDog variable declaration

Figure 2-37 Precedence of variables program

The lifetime of a variable is referred to as the **storage duration**, or **storage class**. There are two types of storage duration: permanent and temporary. **Permanent**, or **static**, storage duration refers to variables that are available for the lifetime of a program. **Temporary**, or **automatic**, storage duration refers to variables that exist only during the lifetime of the command block (such as a function) that contains them. Global variables are always permanent. Local variables are usually temporary.

Although local variables are temporary, they can be made permanent by using the static keyword. When used with a local variable declaration, the **static** keyword changes the variable storage duration to permanent. A local variable declared with the static keyword is not destroyed after its function or command block finishes executing. To create a static local variable, you use a statement similar to `static int variable;`. When working with small programs that are not class-based, it is usually easier to use global variables than static ones. You will see some examples of using static variables when class object manipulation techniques are discussed in Chapter 7, "Object Manipulation".

You can specifically declare variables as temporary with the **auto** keyword, using a statement similar to `auto int variable;`. Because all local variables are temporary by default, however, the auto keyword is unnecessary and rarely used.

INTRODUCTION TO ARRAYS

An **array** is an advanced data type that contains a set of data represented by a single variable name. You use arrays to store collections of related data. When you declare an array, you designate the **dimension**, or number of elements, that you want to store in the array. An **element** is an individual piece of data contained in an array. The syntax for declaring an array is `type name[elements];`. Notice that when declaring an array, you must declare its data type, just as you would with regular variables. Array names follow the same naming conventions as variable names and other identifiers. Because you are using Hungarian notation, array names will have the *ar* prefix. The following statement declares an array named arInterestRates of the `double` data type and designates that it contains five elements:

```
double arInterestRates [5];
```

The numbering of elements within an array starts with an index number of 0. (This numbering scheme can be very confusing for beginners.) An **index number** is an element's numeric position within the array. You refer to a specific element by enclosing its index number in brackets at the end of the array name. For example, the first element in the arInterestRates array is arInterestRates[0], the second element is arInterestRates[1], the third element is arInterestRates[2], and so on. You assign values to individual array elements in the same fashion that you assign values to a standard variable, except that you include the index number for an individual element of the array. The following code assigns values to the five elements within the arInterestRates array:

```
arInterestRates[0] = .065; // first element
arInterestRates[1] = .0675;// second element
arInterestRates[2] = .07;  // third element
arInterestRates[3] = .0725;// fourth element
arInterestRates[4] = .075; // fifth element
```

You use an element in an array in the same manner you use other types of variables. For example, the following code prints the values contained in the five elements of the arInterestRates array:

```
cout << arInterestRates[0] << endl; // prints .065
cout << arInterestRates[1] << endl; // prints .0675
cout << arInterestRates[2] << endl; // prints .07
cout << arInterestRates[3] << endl; // prints .0725
cout << arInterestRates[4] << endl; // prints .075
```

Once you have assigned a value to an array element, you can change it later just as you can change other variables in a program, although you must be sure to include its element number. To change the last element in the arInterestRates[] array from *.075* to *.08*, you include the statement `arInterestRates[4] = .08;` in your code.

You can assign values to array elements when you first create the array using the syntax `type name[elements] = {value1, value2, ...};`. Be sure to place each value you want assigned to the array inside the curly braces { }, separated by commas, and in the order in which you want them assigned to the array elements. For example, the following code assigns values to the arInterestRates[] array when it is created, then prints each of the values using the array element numbers:

```
double arStudentGrades[5] = {.065, .0675, .07,
.0725, .075};
cout << arInterestRates[0] << endl; // prints .065
cout << arInterestRates[1] << endl; // prints .0675
cout << arInterestRates[2] << endl; // prints .07
cout << arInterestRates[3] << endl; // prints .0725
cout << arInterestRates[4] << endl; // prints .075
```

You can use any of the primitive data types as an array data type. As we saw earlier, you can use the char data type to create a character array. The following code, for example, declares a character array with five elements, and then individually assigns a value to each element.

```
char arStudentGrades[5];
arStudentGrades[0] = 'A';
arStudentGrades[1] = 'B';
arStudentGrades[2] = 'C';
arStudentGrades[3] = 'D';
arStudentGrades[4] = 'F';
```

You can access the values stored in a character array by referencing its element number. The following statements for instance, print each of the letter grades stored in the arStudentGrades[] array:

```
cout << arStudentGrades[0] << endl; // prints A
cout << arStudentGrades[1] << endl; // prints B
cout << arStudentGrades[2] << endl; // prints C
cout << arStudentGrades[3] << endl; // prints D
cout << arStudentGrades[4] << endl; // prints F
```

Recall from earlier in this chapter that when working with C-style strings, you are actually creating a character array. For instance, the statement `char szProgramming[11] = "Visual C++";` creates a character array named szProgramming[], consisting of 11 elements. However, in addition to the 10 characters in Visual C++, the last element in the szProgramming[] array is also assigned the null character to indicate that the array contains a text string, not just a collection of individual characters as are stored in the arStudentGrades[] array. Even though the szProgramming[] array was assigned a string (and the null character) instead of individual characters, it is still an array. This means that you can access each individual character stored in the array (the characters in the Visual C++ string, plus the null character) by referencing its element number. For example, the following code prints each of the elements of the szProgramming[] array. Figure 2-38 shows the output.

```
char szProgramming[11] = "Visual C++";
cout << szProgramming[0] << endl;
cout << szProgramming[1] << endl;
cout << szProgramming[2] << endl;
cout << szProgramming[3] << endl;
cout << szProgramming[4] << endl;
cout << szProgramming[5] << endl;
cout << szProgramming[6] << endl;
cout << szProgramming[7] << endl;
cout << szProgramming[8] << endl;
cout << szProgramming[9] << endl;
cout << szProgramming[10] << endl;
```

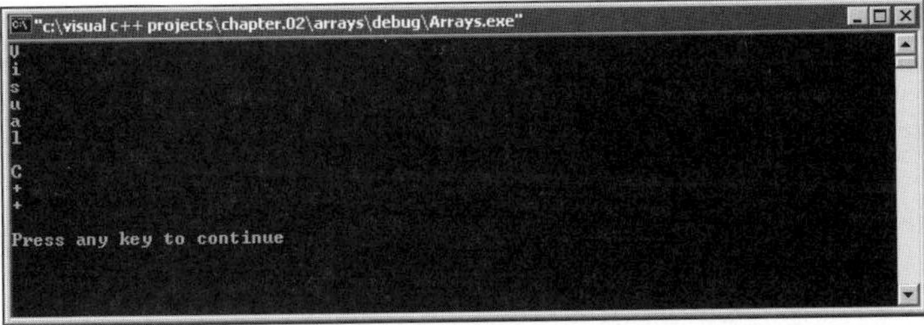

Figure 2-38 Output of the individual elements in the szProgramming [] array

Notice in Figure 2-38 that the null character (in szProgramming[11]) does not actually print. The null character is not really a value that can be displayed, such as *A*, *B*, *C*, or *1*, *2*, *3*. Rather, the null character is a marker that notifies C++ that the end of the text string has been reached.

You will learn about advanced array techniques in Chapter 5, "Introduction to Classes".

CHAPTER SUMMARY

- A console application is a program that runs within an output window, similar to an MS-DOS command prompt window.
- A header file, or include file, is a file that is included as part of a program and alerts the compiler that a program uses run-time classes.
- The iostream classes are used for giving C++ programs input capabilities to and output capabilities from the computer screen and disk files, as well as for printing functions.
- A preprocessor is a program that runs before the compiler and places the entire contents of a designated file into the current file.
- The standard output stream is the destination, usually a screen or file, for text output.
- The cout object is used for outputting text to the console application window.
- A text string, or literal string, is text that is contained within double quotation marks.
- All statements in C++ must end with a semicolon.
- A statement is not necessarily a single line of code; large statements can span multiple lines of code.
- The C++ programming language is case sensitive.
- C++ uses namespaces to manage the various names that a program encounters.
- The std namespace contains all of the names that are defined in the Standard C++ Library.
- The data type used to create a variable determines the type of information that can be stored in the variable.
- The integer data type stores positive or negative numbers with no decimal places.
- The values you assign to integer data types and other numeric data types are called literal values, or literals.

- The name you assign to a variable is called an identifier, or variable name. Identifiers must begin with an uppercase or lowercase ASCII letter or underscore (_). You can use numbers in an identifier, but not as the first character. You are not allowed to use special characters such as $, &, *, or %. Reserved words cannot be used for variable names, and you cannot use spaces within a variable name.
- Reserved words or keywords are part of the C++ language syntax.
- Data types that can be assigned only a single value are called fundamental types or primitive types.
- Programming languages that require you to declare the data types of variables are called strongly-typed programming languages.
- Programming languages that do not require you to declare the data types of variables are called loosely-typed programming languages.
- When you declare a variable in C++, you must designate a data type.
- Hungarian notation is a convention for naming variables so that it is easy to identify their data types.
- An integer is a positive or negative number with no decimal places.
- A floating-point number contains decimal places or is written using exponential notation.
- To store one character in a variable, you use the `char` data type and place the character in single quotation marks.
- You use the `char` data type to store text strings using the C-style method.
- The string class stores and manipulates text strings in C++.
- An escape character tells the compiler that the character that follows it has a special purpose.
- A Boolean value is a logical value of true or false.
- Casting, or type casting, copies the value contained in a variable of one data type into a variable of another data type.
- There are two methods of creating constants in C++: the #define statement or using the const keyword.
- Comments are nonprinting lines that you place in your code to contain various types of remarks.
- The lines that compose a function within a C++ program are called the function definition.
- A parameter, or formal parameter, is a variable, text string, or literal value that will be used within a function.

- The main() function is a special function that runs automatically when a program first executes.
- The variables or values that you place within the parentheses of a function call statement are called arguments or actual parameters.
- Sending arguments to a called function's parameters is called passing arguments.
- A function prototype declares to the compiler that you intend to use a custom function later in the program.
- To return a value to a calling statement, you assign the calling statement to a variable.
- To return a value to a variable, you must include the return statement within the called function.
- Scope refers to where in your program a declared variable or constant can be used.
- Command blocks are used for grouping statements into a single unit.
- Permanent, or static, storage duration refers to variables that are available for the lifetime of a program.
- Temporary, or automatic, storage duration refers to variables that exist only during the lifetime of the command block (such as a function) that contains them.
- An array is an advanced data type that contains a set of data represented by a single variable name.
- When you declare an array, you designate the dimension, or number of elements, that you want to store in the array.

REVIEW QUESTIONS

1. A console application ________________.
   a. contains a graphical user interface like Windows applications
   b. is essentially the same as a Web browser
   c. is a development environment used for creating C++ programs
   d. is a program that runs within an output window, similar to an MS-DOS command prompt window

2. When does the preprocessor run?
   a. before a program executes
   b. after a program executes
   c. before the compiler
   d. after the compiler
3. To include a custom header file within your program, you surround the header file name with ________________.
   a. single quotation marks
   b. double quotation marks
   c. angle brackets
   d. parentheses
4. What is the correct syntax for sending quoted text within a literal string to the C++ standard output stream?
   a. `cout << "The cashier said "May I help you?"";`
   b. `cout << 'The cashier said 'May I help you?'';`
   c. `cout << "The cashier said 'May I help you?'";`
   d. `cout << The cashier said "May I help you?";`
5. What is the correct syntax for printing the statements *Birds Fly*, *Horses Run*, and *Fish Swim* on three separate lines?
   a. `cout << "Birds Fly" << "Horses Run" << "Fish Swim";`
   b. `cout << "Birds Fly" << endl << "Horses Run" << endl << "Fish Swim";`
   c.
   ```
   cout << "Birds Fly";
   cout << "Horses Run";
   cout << "Fish Swim";
   ```
   d.
   ```
   cout << "Birds Fly";
   << "Horses Run";
   << "Fish Swim";
   ```
6. Which namespace manages the names in the Standard C++ Library?
   a. std
   b. stdin
   c. standard
   d. stdname

7. What is the correct syntax for declaring a variable named numberVar, with an integer data type, and assigning to it a value of 100?
   a. `integer numberVar = 100;`
   b. `int* numberVar = 100;`
   c. `int numberVar = 100;`
   d. `integer numberVar = "100";`
8. What is the correct syntax for declaring a variable named textVar, with a character data type, and assigning to it a value of *I like programming*?
   a. `character textVar = "I like programming";`
   b. `char textVar[20] = "I like programming";`
   c. `char textVar = "I like programming";`
   d. `character textVar = "I like programming";`
9. What is the correct syntax for declaring a string class variable named stringVar, with a character data type, and assigning to it a value of *I love New York*?
   a. `string stringVar[25] = "I love New York";`
   b. `string[25] stringVar = "I love New York";`
   c. `string stringVar = "I love New York";`
   d. `stringVar (string) = "I love New York";`
10. Identifiers in C++ can begin with an uppercase or lowercase ASCII letter or ________________.
    a. the dollar sign ($)
    b. an underscore character (_)
    c. a number
    d. the number sign (#)
11. Which is the correct syntax for creating a constant named LAST_NAME, with a value of *Morinaga*, using the #define preprocessor directive?
    a. `#define LAST_NAME = "Morinaga"`
    b. `#define LAST_NAME "Morinaga"`
    c. `#define LAST_NAME "Morinaga";`
    d. `#define(LAST_NAME) = "Morinaga";`
12. Which is the correct syntax for creating a constant named LAST_NAME, with a value of *Morinaga*, using the const keyword?
    a. `#const LAST_NAME = "Morinaga"`
    b. `const LAST_NAME "Morinaga"`
    c. `const char LAST_NAME[25] = "Morinaga";`
    d. `const(LAST_NAME) = "Morinaga";`

13. Which of the following is not an integer?
    a. 7.6
    b. 12
    c. 0
    d. 1
14. Which of the following is not a floating-point number?
    a. -439.35
    b. 3.17
    c. 10
    d. 1.0
15. Boolean values are stored as the values ________.
    a. minimum and maximum
    b. positive and negative
    c. 0 and 1
    d. true and false
16. Which of the following is the correct syntax for including double quotation marks within a string that is already surrounded by double quotation marks?
    a. `"Some computers have \"artificial\" intelligence."`
    b. `"Some computers have "artificial" intelligence."`
    c. `"Some computers have /"artificial/" intelligence."`
    d. `"Some computers have ""artificial"" intelligence."`
17. You create line comments by adding ________ to a line you want to use as a comment.
    a. ||
    b. **
    c. //
    d. \\
18. Block comments begin with /* and end with ________.
    a. */
    b. /*
    c. //
    d. **

19. If you do not need to return a value from a function, then you use a data type of __________.
    a. empty
    b. void
    c. null
    d. You do not specify a data type.
20. When does the main() function execute?
    a. when the program first executes
    b. during the compilation process
    c. only when it is called from another function
    d. the main() function never executes; its only purpose is for declaring variables and function prototypes
21. Where must a function prototype be declared?
    a. inside a function
    b. before the function is called
    c. after the function is called
    d. inside the main() function
22. The syntax for using the return statement is `return` *`value`*`;` or __________.
    a. `return(`*`value`*`);`
    b. `return` *`value`*`();`
    c. *`value`* `return;`
    d. *`value`* `return();`
23. A variable that is declared outside a function is called a __________ variable.
    a. local
    b. class
    c. program
    d. global
24. The lifetime of a variable is referred to as its storage duration or __________.
    a. persistence
    b. storage continuance
    c. storage class
    d. global visibility

25. What must be added to the following code in order for it to compile properly?

```
#include <iostream>
using namespace std;
void main() {
   print_company_name("My Company");
}
void print_company_name(char company_name[50]) {
   cout << company_name << endl;
}
```

   a. A #define processing directive
   b. A global declaration of the company_name variable
   c. A function prototype
   d. An #include directive for the stdio header file

26. The numbering of elements within an array starts with an index number of ________________.
   a. -1
   b. 0
   c. 1
   d. 2

27. What is the correct syntax for creating an integer array with 10 elements?
   a. `int arVariable[10];`
   b. `int arVariable = Array(10);`
   c. `arVariable[] = new Array(10);`
   d. `Array[10] arVariable;`

28. Which of the following refers to the first element in an array named iEmployees[]?
   a. iEmployees[0]
   b. iEmployees[1]
   c. iEmployees[first]
   d. iEmployees[a]

PROGRAMMING EXERCISES

1. Rewrite the following code so that the lines printed from the multiple cout statements print from a single statement:

```
#include <iostream>
using namespace std;
void main() {
cout << "Mark Twain said ";
cout << "'Everybody talks about the weather, ";
cout << " but nobody does anything about it.'" << endl;
}
```

2. Modify the cout statements in the following code so they correctly reference the standard namespace, but do not include a using namespace std; statement:

```
#include <iostream>
void main() {
cout << "New York City";
cout << "is the greatest city";
cout << " in the world!" << endl;
}
```

3. Modify the following statements so the iNumEmployees variable is initialized on the line that declares it:

```
int iNumEmployees;
iNumEmployees = 500;
```

4. Use Hungarian notation to identify the data types of each variable:
   - cData
   - iPeriod
   - siMonths
   - liProjectedFigures
   - fWeeklySalary
   - dGrossRevenue
   - sCompany
   - szStreetAddress
   - bHealthBenefits
   - ctLoop

5. Assign to C-style string variables the literal strings for each of the states that are printed in the main() function in the following code (you do not need to create a variable for the first cout statement). Also, modify the cout statements so they print the variables instead of the literal strings.

```
#include <iostream>
using namespace std;
void main() {
        cout << "The six New England states are: " << endl;
        cout << "Connecticut" << endl;
        cout << "Maine" << endl;
        cout << "Massachusetts" << endl;
        cout << "New Hampshire" << endl;
        cout << "Rhode Island" << endl;
        cout << "Vermont" << endl;
}
```

6. Convert the C-Style string variables that you created in Exercise 5 to string class variables.
7. Discuss the types of information you think should be used as constants. Explain why you think these types of information should be constants and not variables.
8. Rewrite the following code so that it functions correctly when called from the main() function, but *do not use a function prototype.*

```
#include <iostream>
using namespace std;
void main() {
   functionA();
}
void functionA() {
   cout << "printed from functionA()" << endl;
}
```

9. Explain the difference between #define preprocessor directive constants and constants created with the const keyword.
10. Modify the constant in the following code so that it is declared with the **const** keyword instead of using a #define statement. Also, declare the constant as a C-style string variable instead of as a string class variable.

```
#include <iostream>
using namespace std;
#define US_CAPITAL "Washington, D.C."
void main() {
     cout << "The capital of the United States is "
          << US_CAPITAL << endl;
}
```

11. Modify the following code so that the line comments are contained in a single block comment:

```
#include <iostream>
using namespace std;
//        This program was written by
//        Don Gosselin
//        on September 20, 2002
//        in Napa, California
void main() {
        cout << "Output from a C++ program" << endl;
}
```

12. Modify the following code so that the five variables are stored in an integer array. Be sure to use the correct Hungarian notation. After storing the values in the array, write the correct code to print the value stored in each array element.

```
int salary1= 20000;
int salary2= 25000;
int salary3= 30000;
int salary4= 35000;
int salary5= 40000;
```

PROGRAMMING PROJECTS

Save your solutions to the following projects in the Chapter.02 folder in your Visual C++ Projects folder.

1. Create a console application project named PersonalInfo. Within the main()function, use cout statements to print your name, address, date of birth, and Social Security number to the screen.
2. Create a console application project named Continents. Within the main()function, use cout statements to print the names of the continents: Africa, Antarctica, Asia, Australia, Europe, North America, and South America.
3. Create a console application project named Initials that uses cout statements to print your initials in large block letters. Build each block letter out of the same initial letter. Figure 2-39 shows an example of how the program output may appear using the initials *DG*.

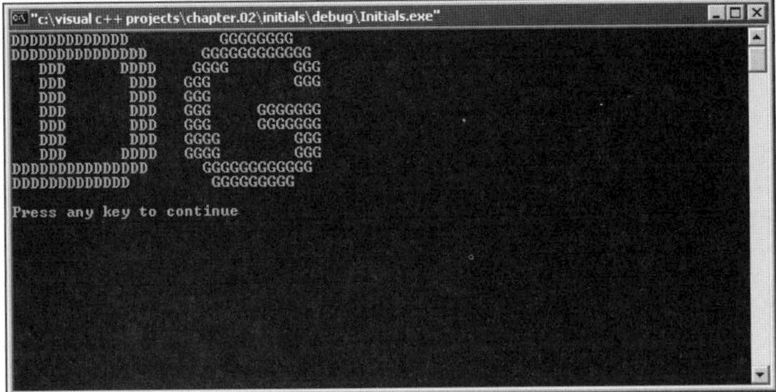

Figure 2-39 Output of the Initials program

4. Create a console application project named Star that uses cout statements to print a large star to the console window using asterisks. Figure 2-40 shows an example of how the program output may appear.

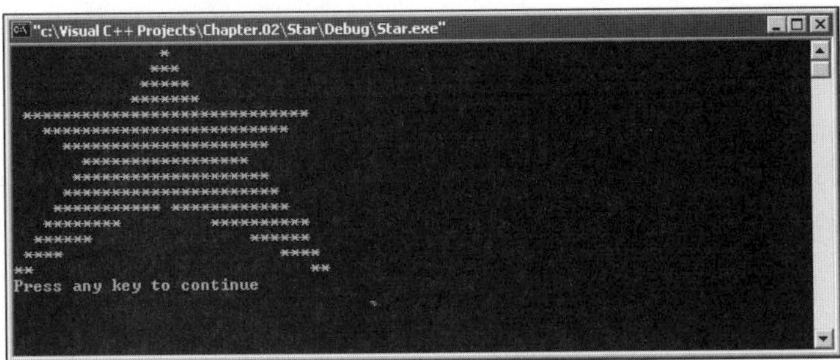

Figure 2-40 Output of the Star program

5. Create a console application project named ExecutiveSalaries. Think of some fictitious names for the top five executive positions at a corporation: chairman, chief executive officer, chief operating officer, chief information officer, and chief financial officer. Within the main() function, declare three variables for each of the executives; one variable should contain the executive's name, another variable should contain the executive's title, and the last variable should contain the executive's salary. Assign each executive's name, title, and salary to his or her respective variables, and then print all of the variables. Each individual executive's name, title, and salary should be printed on its own line.
6. Create a console application project that displays a simplified version of your work history including the names of your former employers, positions within the companies, and dates of employment. Create the employers, positions, and dates of employment in columns. To create line breaks, use an escape character within the string variables. Save the project as WorkHistory.

7. Create a console application project containing personal information including your name, age, the type of car you have, the mortgage interest on your house or loan interest on your car, and whether you have a dog. Use different data types for each variable. Print each piece of information to the screen. Be sure to create items for the `char`, `int`, and floating-point data types. For example, your name will be the char data type, your age will be the `int` data type, and the mortgage interest on your house will be a floating-point data type. Save the project as PersonalInfo2.
8. Create a console application project named CompanyInfo that includes a function named company(). Include three parameters in the company () function: name, products, and motto. Also create a function named employees() that prints the number of employees. Assign the number of employees to a variable within the employees() function. Call the company() function from the main() function and pass values to the name, products, and motto parameters. Print each of the parameters to the screen. Then call the employees() function from inside the company() function and print the number of employees. Combine each printed variable with a descriptive string. For example, when you print the company name, it should read something like *The company name is MyCompany*.

CHAPTER

3

OPERATORS AND CONTROL STRUCTURES

In this chapter you will learn:

- About expressions
- How to use arithmetic, assignment, comparison, and logical operators
- How to work with string functions
- About operator precedence
- How to work with decision-making statements
- How to work with the standard input stream
- How to work with repetition statements

Any intelligent fool can make things bigger, more complex, and more violent. It takes a touch of genius—and a lot of courage—to move in the opposite direction.

E. F. Schumacher

PREVIEW: THE CHEMISTRY QUIZ PROGRAM

In this chapter you will learn about, among other topics, expressions and operators, decision-making statements, and flow-control statements. So far, the code you have written has been linear in nature. In other words, your programs start at the beginning and end when the last statement in the program executes. Decision-making and flow-control statements allow you to determine the order in which statements execute in a program. The special types of C++ statements used for making decisions are called **decision-making structures**. The abilities to control the flow of code and to make decisions during program execution are two of the most fundamental skills required in programming. To learn these concepts, you will create a chemistry quiz, using the different decision-making structures and statements available in C++. Keep in mind that a thorough understanding of all of the topics you study in this chapter will be required in order to complete the remainder of the chapters in this book.

To preview the Chemistry Quiz program:

1. Create a **Chapter.03** folder in your Visual C++ Projects folder.
2. Copy the **Chapter3_ChemistryQuizFinal** folder from the Chapter.03 folder on your Data Disk to the Chapter.03 folder in your Visual C++ Projects folder. Then open the **ChemistryQuizFinal** project in Visual C++.
3. Open the **ChemistryQuizFinal.cpp** file in the Code Editor window, if it is not already open. The file includes the iostream header file in order to provide access to the input and output streams. In the last chapter, you worked only with the output stream and cout statements to write information to the screen. In this chapter you will also receive information from the input stream, using cin statements. Figure 3-1 shows a partial listing of the file. You should recognize many of the statements in Figure 3-1, except for the `for` and `if` statements, which are used for managing the execution of statements in a C++ program.

```
...
          // Question 5
          cout << "5. Select the structure possessed by helium , at room"
               << endl
          << "  temperature and atmospheric pressure;" << endl
          << "\ta. Giant structure of ions" << endl
          << "\tb. Widely spaced atoms" << endl
          << "\tc. Widely spaced molecules" << endl
          << "\td. Giant structure of atoms" << endl;
          cout << "Your answer> ";
          cin >> cInput;                                          <- Cin statement
          recordAnwser (5, cInput);
          cout << endl;
          scoreQuiz();
}
void recordAnwser (int iQuestion, char cAnswer) {                 <- For statement
          arUserAnswers[iQuestion-1] = cAnswer;
}
void scoreQuiz() {
          int iTotalCorrect = 0;
          for (int ctCount = 0; ctCount , 5; ++ctCount) {
                 if (arUserAnswers[ctCount] == arCorrectAnswers[ctCount])  <- If statement
                 ++iTotalCorrect;
          }
          cout << "You scored " << iTotalCorrect
               << " out of 5 answers correctly!" << endl;
}
```

Figure 3-1 ChemistryQuizFinal.cpp

4. Build and execute the Chemistry Quiz program, and then try answering the questions. When you finish answering all of the questions, the scoreQuiz() function executes and uses the `for` statement to score the quiz. Figure 3-2 shows how the program appears in the console window.
5. Press any key to close the Chemistry Quiz program window.

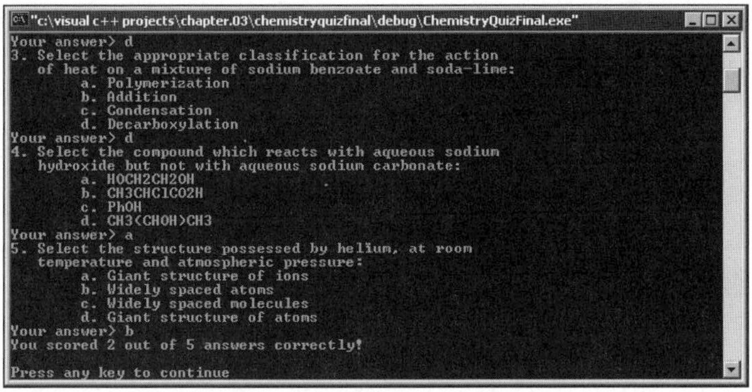

```
"c:\visual c++ projects\chapter.03\chemistryquizfinal\debug\ChemistryQuizFinal.exe"
Your answer> d
3. Select the appropriate classification for the action
   of heat on a mixture of sodium benzoate and soda-lime:
        a. Polymerization
        b. Addition
        c. Condensation
        d. Decarboxylation
Your answer> d
4. Select the compound which reacts with aqueous sodium
   hydroxide but not with aqueous sodium carbonate:
        a. HOCH2CH2OH
        b. CH3CHClCO2H
        c. PhOH
        d. CH3(CHOH)CH3
Your answer> a
5. Select the structure possessed by helium, at room
   temperature and atmospheric pressure:
        a. Giant structure of ions
        b. Widely spaced atoms
        c. Widely spaced molecules
        d. Giant structure of atoms
Your answer> b
You scored 2 out of 5 answers correctly!
Press any key to continue
```

Figure 3-2 Output of the Chemistry Quiz program

EXPRESSIONS AND OPERATORS

Variables and data become most useful when you use them in an expression. An **expression** is a combination of literal values, variables, operators, and other programming elements that can be evaluated by the Visual C++ compiler to produce a result. For example, the Visual C++ compiler recognizes the literal values and variables in Figure 3-3 as expressions.

`"this is a string variable"`	`// string literal expression`
`10`	`// integer literal expression`
`3.156`	`// floating-point literal expression`
`true`	`// Boolean literal expression`
`NULL`	`// null literal expression`
`iEmployeeNumber`	`// variable expression`

Figure 3-3 Literal and variable expressions

You can use operands and operators to create more complex expressions. **Operands** are variables and literals contained in an expression. **Operators** are symbols used in expressions to manipulate operands. You have worked with several simple expressions so far that combine operators and operands. Consider the following statement:

```
iMyNumber = 100;
```

This statement is an expression that results in the literal value 100 being assigned to the variable iMyNumber. The operands in the expression are the *iMyNumber* variable name and the integer value 100. The operator is the equal sign (=) assignment operator. The equal sign operator is an assignment operator because it *assigns* the value (100) on the right side of the expression to the variable (iMyNumber) on the left side of the expression. Figure 3-4 lists the main types of C++ operators.

Operator Type	Description
Arithmetic (+, –, *, /, %, ++,—)	Used for performing mathematical calculations
Assignment (=, +=, –=, *=, /=, %=)	Assigns values to variables
Comparison (==, !=, >, <, >=, <=)	Compares operands and returns a Boolean value
Logical (&&, ll, !)	Used for performing Boolean operations on Boolean operands

Figure 3-4 C++ operator types

Among other types of C++ operators are bitwise operators, which operate on integer values. Bitwise operators treat integers as binary numbers and are a complex topic.

C++ operators are unary, binary, or ternary. A **unary operator** requires a single operand either before or after the operator. For example, the increment operator (++), an arithmetic operator, is used for increasing an operand by a value of one. The statement `iMyNumber++;` changes the value of the imyNumber variable to 101. A **binary operator** requires an operand before the operator and an operand after the operator. The equal sign in the statement `iMyNumber = 100;` is an example of a binary operator. A **ternary operator** requires three operands. C++ includes a single ternary operator, the conditional operator (?:), which will be discussed shortly.

The operand to the left of an operator is known as the left operand and the operand, to the right of an operator is known as the right operand.

Next, you will learn about the different types of C++ operators.

Arithmetic Operators

Arithmetic operators are used to perform mathematical calculations, such as addition, subtraction, multiplication, and division. You can also return the modulus of a calculation, which is the remainder left when you divide one integer by another integer. The C++ binary arithmetic operators and their descriptions are listed in Figure 3-5.

Operator	Description
+ (addition)	Adds two operands
– (subtraction)	Subtracts one operand from another operand
* (multiplication)	Multiplies one operand by another operand
/ (division)	Divides one operand by another operand
% (modulus)	Divides one integer operand by another integer operand and returns the remainder as a whole number

Figure 3-5 Arithmetic binary operators

3

You may be confused by the difference between the division (/) operator and the modulus (%) operator. The division operator performs a standard mathematical division operation on any numeric data type. However, for integer data types, the division operator returns only the number of times that one value can be divided by another value—it does not return the remainder. To return the remainder that results from the division of two integers, you must use the modulus operator. The following code, for instance, uses the division and modulus operators to return the result of dividing 15 divided by 6. The division of 15 by 6 results in a value of 2, because that is the number of times that 6 goes into 14. The modulus of 15 by 6 is 3, because that is the remainder left over following the division. The following code illustrates the difference between the division and modulus operators.

```
int dDivisionResult = 15 / 6;
int dModulusResult = 15 % 6;
cout << "15 divided by 6 is "
  << dDivisionResult << endl;    // prints '2'
cout << "with a remainder of "
  << dModulusResult << endl;     // prints '3'
```

When you divide two floating-point numbers using the division operator, the operation returns the entire result, including the remainder. For instance, the following code returns a floating-point value of 2.5 when a `double` variable containing the value 15 is divided by another `double` variable containing the value 6.

```
double dFirstNum = 15;
double dSecondNum = 6;
double dDivisionResult = dFirstNum / dSecondNum;
cout << "15 divided by 6 is "
  << dDivisionResult << endl;    // prints '2.5'
```

You need to be careful when assigning the results of an integer division to a `double` variable. For example, in the following code, the literal values of 15 and 6 are of the integer data type because they do not include decimals. This means that a standard integer division operation will be performed, which assigns only a value of 2 to the dDivisionResult variable, but not the remainder that is returned in the division operation.

```
double dDivisionResult = 15 / 6;
```

To fix the preceding statement, make each literal value a `double` by simply adding a decimal place of zero to each literal value, as follows:

```
double dDivisionResult = 15.0 / 6.0;
```

Arithmetic operations can also be performed on a single variable using unary operators. Figure 3-6 lists and describes the unary arithmetic operators available in C++.

Operator	Description
++ (increment)	Increases an operand by a value of one
-- (decrement)	Decreases an operand by a value of one
– (negation)	Returns the opposite value (negative or positive) of an operand

Figure 3-6 Arithmetic unary operators

The increment (++) and decrement (--) unary operators can be used as prefix or postfix operators to increase or decrease values. A **prefix operator** is placed before a variable. A **postfix operator** is placed after a variable. The statements ++iMyVariable; and iMyVariable++; both increase iMyVariable by one. The two statements, however, return different values. When you use the increment operator as a prefix operator, the value of the operand is returned *after* it is increased by a value of 1. When you use the increment operator as a postfix operator, the value of the operand is returned *before* it is increased by a value of 1. Similarly, when you use the decrement operator as a prefix operator, the value of the operand is returned *after* it is decreased by a value of 1. When you use the decrement operator as a postfix operator, the value of the operand is returned *before* it is decreased by a value of 1. If you intend to assign the incremented or decremented value to another variable, then whether you use the prefix or postfix operator makes a difference.

You use arithmetic unary operators in any situation in which you want to use a more simplified expression for increasing or decreasing a value by 1. For example, the statement `iNumber = iNumber + 1;` is identical to the statement `++iNumber;`. As you can see, if your goal is only to increase a variable by 1, then it is easier to use the unary increment operator. But remember that with the prefix operator the value of the operand is returned *after* it is increased or decreased by a value of 1, whereas with the postfix operator, the value of the operand is returned *before* it is increased or decreased by a value of 1.

For an example of when you would use the prefix operator or the postfix operator, consider an integer variable named iStudentID that you would use for assigning student IDs in a class registration program. One way of creating a new student ID number is to store the last assigned student ID in the iStudentID variable. When you need to assign a new student ID, you could retrieve the last value stored in the iStudentID variable and then increase its value by 1. In other words, the last value stored in the iStudentID variable will be the next number that you will use for a student ID number. In this case, you would use the postfix operator to return the value of the expression *before* it is incremented, by using a statement similar to `iCurrentID = iStudentID++;`. If you are storing the last assigned student ID in the iStudentID variable, you would want to increment the value by 1 and use the result as the next student ID. With this scenario, you would use the prefix operator, which returns the value of the expression after it is incremented, using a statement similar to `iCurrentID = ++iStudentID;`.

Figure 3-7 shows an example of a simple program that uses the prefix increment operator to assign three student IDs to a variable named iCurStudentID. The initial student ID is stored in the iStudentID global variable and initialized to a starting value of 100. Figure 3-8 shows the output. Figure 3-9 shows the code for the same program, but using a postfix increment operator. Notice that the output in Figure 3-10 differs from the output in Figure 3-8. Because the first example of the program uses the prefix increment operator, which increments the iStudentID variable *before* it is assigned to iCurStudentID, the program does not use the starting value of 100. Rather, it first increments the iStudentID variable and uses 101 as the first student ID. In comparison, the second example of the program does use the initial value of 100 because the postfix increment operator does not increment the iStudentID variable until *after* it is assigned to the iCurStudentID.

```
#include <iostream>
using namespace std;
int iStudentID = 100;
void main() {
     int iCurStudentID;
     iCurStudentID = ++iStudentID; // assigns '101'
     cout << "The first student ID is "
          << iCurStudentID << endl;
     iCurStudentID = ++iStudentID; // assigns '102'
     cout << "The second student ID is "
          << iCurStudentID << endl;
     iCurStudentID = ++iStudentID; // assigns '103'
     cout << "The third student ID is "
          << iCurStudentID << endl;
}
```

Prefix increment operator

Figure 3-7 Prefix version of the student ID program

```
"c:\visual c++ projects\chapter.03\studentids\debug\StudentIDs.exe"
The first student ID is 101
The second student ID is 102
The third student ID is 103
Press any key to continue
```

Figure 3-8 Output of the prefix version of the student ID program

```
#include <iostream>
using namespace std;
int iStudentID = 100;
void main() {
 int iCurStudentID;
 iCurStudentID = iStudentID++; // assigns '100'
 cout << "The first student ID is "
          << iCurStudentID << endl;
 iCurStudentID = iStudentID++; // assigns '101'
 cout << "The second student ID is "
          << iCurStudentID << endl;
 iCurStudentID = iStudentID++; // assigns '102'
 cout << "The third student ID is "
          << iCurStudentID << endl;
}
```

Postfix increment operator

Figure 3-9 Postfix version of the student ID program

```
"c:\visual c++ projects\chapter.03\studentids\debug\StudentIDs.exe"
The first student ID is 100
The second student ID is 101
The third student ID is 102
Press any key to continue
```

Figure 3-10 Output of the postfix version of the student ID program

Assignment Operators

Assignment operators are used for assigning a value to a variable. You have already used the most common assignment operator, the equal sign (=), to assign values to variables. The equal sign assigns an initial value to a new variable or assigns a new value to an existing variable. For example, the following code creates a variable named cMyCar, uses the equal sign to assign it an initial value, and then uses the equal sign again to assign it another new value.

```
string sMyCar = "Ford";
sMyCar = "Corvette";
```

C++ includes other assignment operators in addition to the equal sign. These additional assignment operators perform mathematical calculations on variables and literal values in an expression, and then assign a new value to the left operand. Figure 3-11 displays a list of the common C++ assignment operators, along with an example of each operator and an example of the fully expressed arithmetic operator.

Comparison Operators

Comparison operators are used to compare two operands for equality and to determine if one numeric value is greater than another. A Boolean value of true (1) or false (0) is returned after two operands are compared. Figure 3-12 lists the C++ comparison operators.

Operator	Description	Assignment Operators	Arithmetic Operators
=	Assigns the value of the right operand to the left operand	iNum1 = iNum2;	(not applicable)
+=	Combines the value of the right operand with the value of the left operand or adds the value of the right operand to the value of the left operand and assigns the new value to the left operand	iNum1 += iNum2;	iNum1 = iNum1 + iNum2;
–=	Subtracts the value of the right operand from the value of the left operand and assigns the new value to the left operand	iNum1 –= iNum2;	iNum1 = iNum1 – iNum2;
*=	Multiplies the value of the right operand by the value of the left operand and assigns the new value to the left operand	iNum1 *= iNum2;	iNum1 = iNum1 * iNum2;
/=	Divides the value of the left operand by the value of the right operand and assigns the new value to the left operand	iNum1 /= iNum2;	iNum1 = iNum1 / iNum2;
%=	Modulus—divides the value of the left operand by the value of the right operand and assigns the remainder to the left operand.	iNum1 %= iNum2;	iNum1 = iNum1 % iNum2;

Figure 3-11 Assignment operators

Operator	Description
== (equal)	Returns true if the operands are equal
!= (not equal)	Returns true if the operands are not equal
> (greater than)	Returns true if the left operand is greater than the right operand
< (less than)	Returns true if the left operand is less than the right operand
>= (greater than or equal)	Returns true if the left operand is greater than or equal to the right operand
<= (less than or equal)	Returns true if the left operand is less than or equal to the right operand

Figure 3-12 Comparison operators

The comparison operator (==) consists of two equal signs and performs a function different from the assignment operator, which consists of a single equal sign (=). The comparison operator (==) *compares* values, whereas the assignment operator (=) *assigns* values.

Comparison operators are often used within conditional and looping statements such as the `if else`, `for`, and `while` statements. Although you will not learn about conditional and looping statements until later in this chapter, learning about the conditional operator now will help you better understand how to work with comparison operators. The **conditional operator** (?:) is a ternary operator that executes one of two expressions, based on the results of a conditional expression. A **conditional expression** returns a Boolean value and determines whether to execute a conditional or looping statement. The syntax for the conditional operator is `(`*`conditional expression`*`) ? `*`expression1`*`: `*`expression2`*`;`. If the conditional expression evaluates to true, then *expression1* executes. If the conditional expression evaluates to false, however, then *expression2* executes. The following code shows an example of the conditional operator. In the example, the conditional expression checks if the iValue variable is greater than 100. If the value is greater than 100, then the text *iValue is greater than 100* is assigned to the sResult variable. If the value is not greater than 100, then the text *iValue is less than or equal to 100* is assigned to the sResult variable. Because iValue is equal to 150, the conditional statement returns a value of true and *expression1* executes. This results in *iValue is greater than 100* being printed to the screen.

```
int iValue = 150;
string sResult;
(iValue > 100) ? sResult = "iValue is greater than 100"
   : sResult = "iValue is less than or equal to 100";
cout << sResult << endl;
```

Logical Operators

Logical operators are used for comparing two Boolean operands for equality. Like comparison operators, a Boolean value of true (1) or false (0) is returned after two operands are compared. Figure 3-13 lists the C++ logical operators.

Operator	Description
&& (AND)	Returns true if both the left operand and right operand return a value of true, otherwise it returns a value of false
|| (OR)	Returns true if either the left operand or right operand returns a value of true; if neither operand returns a value of true, then the expression containing the || (OR) operator returns a value of false
! (NOT)	Returns true if an expression is false and returns false if an expression is true

Figure 3-13 Logical operators

The && (and) and || (or) operators are binary operators (requiring two operands), and the ! (not) operator is a unary operator (requiring a single operand). Logical operators are often used with comparison operators to evaluate expressions, allowing you to combine the results of several expressions into a single statement. For example, the && (and) operator is used for determining whether two operands return an equivalent value. The operands themselves are often expressions. The following code uses the && operator to compare two separate expressions:

```
int iFirstNum = 2; int iSecondNum = 3;
bool bReturnValue = iFirstNum==2
&& iSecondNum==3;   // returns true
```

In the above example, the left operand evaluates to true because iFirstNum is equal to 2, and the right operand also evaluates to true because iSecondNum is equal to 3. Because both expressions are true, bReturnValue is assigned a value of true. The statement containing the && operator essentially says "if variable a is equal to 2 AND variable b is equal to 3, then assign a value of true to bReturnValue. Otherwise, assign a value of false to bReturnValue." In the following code, however, bReturnValue is assigned a value of false, because the right operand does *not* evaluate to true:

```
int iFirstNum = 2; int iSecondNum = 3;
bool bReturnValue = iFirstNum==2
&& iSecondNum==4;   // returns false
```

The logical || (or) operator checks if either expression evaluates to true. For example, the statement in the following code says "if a is equal to 2 OR b is equal to 3, assign a value of true to bReturnValue. Otherwise, assign a value of false."

```
int iFirstNum = 2; int iSecondNum = 3;
bool bReturnValue = iFirstNum==2
|| iSecondNum==4;   // returns true
```

The bReturnValue variable in the preceding code is assigned a value of true, because the left operand evaluates to true, even though the right operand evaluates to false. This result occurs because the || (or) statement returns true if *either* the left *or* right operand evaluates to true.

The following code is an example of the ! (not) operator, which returns true if an operand evaluates to false and returns false if an operand evaluates to true. Notice that because the ! (not) operator is unary, it requires only a single operand.

```
bool bValue = true;
bool bReturnValue = !bValue;     // returns false
```

Logical operators are often used to create a **compound conditional expression** that executes a conditional or looping statement based on multiple criteria. As an example of how to create a compound conditional expression, consider the following code, which uses the conditional operator to test whether the value assigned to the iIncome variable falls within the 27% tax bracket. A single tax payer is within the 27% tax bracket if his or her income is between $26,250 and $63,550. The conditional expression in the following code uses the logical OR operator to test the value assigned to iIncome. If the value assigned to iIncome is between $26,250 and $63,550, then the text *You are in the 27% tax bracket* is assigned to the sResult variable. If the value assigned to iIncome is not between $26,250 and $63,550, then the text *You are not in the 27% tax bracket* is assigned to the sResult variable.

```
int iIncome = 35000;
string sResult;
(iIncome > 26250 && iIncome < 63550) ? sResult = "You are
in the 27% tax bracket"
   : sResult = "You are not in the 27% tax bracket";
cout << sResult << endl;
```

String Functions

As you work in C++, you will often find it necessary to manipulate the text strings stored in C-style string variables (character arrays). For example, you may find it necessary to combine the values in a C-style string variable named szFirstName and the values in another C-style string variable named szLastName into a single variable named szName. Or, you may want to assign a new value to a `char` variable after its initial declaration. One of the drawbacks to using a C-style string variable is that you cannot use the assignment operator to assign a new value to a character array after its declaration. Instead, you must use a **string function** to manipulate the character arrays. Although string functions are not precisely "operators," you need to understand them because they are vital to working with strings in your programs. Figure 3-14 lists common string functions.

Function	Description
strcat()	Appends one string to another
strchr()	Finds the first occurrence of a specified character in a string
strcmp()	Compares two strings
strcpy()	Replaces the contents of one string with the contents of another
strcspn()	Finds the first occurrence in a string of a specified character within a specified character set
strlen()	Returns the length of a string
strncat()	Appends characters to a string
strncmp()	Compares characters within two strings
strncpy()	Copies characters from one string into another
strpbrk()	Finds the first occurrence in a string of a specified character in another string
strrchr()	Finds the last occurrence in a string of a specified character
strspn()	Finds the first occurrence in a string of a specified substring
strstr()	Finds the first occurrence in a string of another specified string

Figure 3-14 Common string functions

The functions listed in Figure 3-14 are contained in the cstring header file. (The "c" in cstring indicates that the header file contains functions for working with C-style string variables.) To use the functions, you must add the statement `#include <cstring>` to your program. Two string functions that you will see used in this book are the strcpy() and strcat() functions.

The **strcpy() function** copies a literal string or the contents of a character array into another character array using the syntax `strcpy(`*`destination, source`*`);`. The *destination* argument represents the `char` variable to which you want to assign a new value. The *source* variable represents the literal string or `char` variable containing the string you want to assign to the destination variable.

The **strcat() function** combines, or *concatenates,* two strings using the syntax `strcat(destination, source);`. The *destination* argument represents the character array whose string you want to combine with another string. The *source* argument can be either a character array or a literal string. When you execute strcat(), the string represented by the *source* argument is appended to the string contained in the destination variable.

To successfully assign one string to another using strcpy(), or to concatenate two strings using strcat(), you must make the destination `char` variable large enough. If you do not make the destination `char` variable large enough, then you will either lose data when you call the strcpy() or strcat() functions, or you will receive an error when you attempt to run the program.

The following code shows how to use both the strcpy() and strcat() functions with `char` variables containing a person's name. The first three statements simply declare three `char` variables: szFirstName, szLastName, and szFullName. Next, the strcpy() function assigns values to both the szFirstName and szLastName variables. The value of the szFirstName variable is then assigned to the szFullName variable using the strcpy() function. Finally, strcat() statements assign a space to the szFullName variable to separate the first and the last names, along with the szLastName variable.

```
char szFirstName[25];
char szLastName[25];
char szFullName[50];
strcpy(szFirstName, "Mike");
strcpy(szLastName, "Okayabashi");
strcpy(szFullName, szFirstName);
strcat(szFullName, " ");
strcat(szFullName, szLastName);
```

See the MSDN Library for the complete syntax of other string functions.

String Class Operators

Fortunately, it is much easier to manipulate string class variables. As you know, you can use the assignment operator to easily assign a string directly to a string class variable name by using a statement such as `string sMyString = "This is a text string.";`. Once you have instantiated two string variables, you can assign the contents of one variable to the other by using the assignment operator, in the same way that the assignment operator is used with numeric data types.

Remember that string class variables require that you include the string header file in your program using the statement `#include <string>`— not the cstring header file that is required for C-style string variables to access string functions.

You can also use several operators with string variables, including the + operator and the == and != comparison operators. When used with strings, the plus sign is known as the concatenation operator. The **concatenation operator** (+) is used to combine two strings of the string class. The following code combines a string variable and a literal string and assigns the new value to another variable:

```
string sFirstString = "San Francisco ";
string sNewString;
sNewString = sFirstString + "is in California";
```

The combined value of the sFirstString variable and the string literal that is assigned to the sNewString variable is *San Francisco is in California.*

The comparison operators are useful for determining if string variables contain the same text. For example, the following code contains a conditional operator that compares the values of two string variables. Because the variables do not contain the same string values, the false portion of the conditional operator prints *different cities.*

```
string sFirstCity = "San Francisco";
string sSecondCity = "Los Angeles";
(sFirstCity == sSecondCity) ? cout << "same cities" << endl
     : cout << "different cities" << endl;
```

The following code shows a similar example, but using the != comparison operator. Because the variables do not contain the same string values and the `if` statement uses the != operator, the cout statement *does* execute.

```
string sFirstCity = "San Francisco";
string sSecondCity = "Los Angeles";
if (sFirstCity != sSecondCity)
  cout << "Different cities" << endl;
```

The string header file contains the same string functions that are available in the cstring header file, plus many more. This means that you can use the same functions to manipulate string class variables that you use to manipulate C-style strings. Although this book does not go into detail on the use of string manipulation functions, you will find them invaluable when you need to work with numerous or large text strings in your programs. See the MSDN Library for more information.

Operator Precedence

When creating expressions in C++, you need to be aware of the precedence of an operator. **Operator precedence** is the order of priority in which operations in an expression are evaluated. Figure 3-15 shows the order of precedence for the operators used in C++.

Operator	Order of Precedence	Associativity
::	Scope resolution--highest precedence	None
.	Structure or union member selection	Left to right
->	Pointer to structure member	Left to right
[ ]	Array element	Left to right
( )	Function call	Left to right
++	Postfix increment	Left to right
--	Postfix decrement	Left to right
typeid( )	Type name	Left to right
const_cast	Type cast (conversion)	Left to right
dynamic_cast	Type cast (conversion)	Left to right
reinterpret_cast	Type cast (conversion)	Left to right
static_cast	Type cast (conversion)	Left to right
sizeof	Type cast (conversion)	Right to left
++	Prefix increment	Right to left
– –	Prefix decrement	Right to left
~	One's complement	Right to left
!	Logical NOT	Right to left
–	Unary minus	Right to left
+	Unary plus	Right to left
&	Address	Right to left
*	Indirection	Right to left
new	Allocate program memory	Right to left
delete	Deallocate program memory	Right to left
(type)	Type cast [for example, (float) i]	Right to left

Figure 3-15 Order of precedence for C++ operators

<table>
<tr><th>Operator</th><th>Order of Precedence</th><th>Associativity</th></tr>
<tr><td>*
->*</td><td>Pointer to member (objects)
Pointer to member (pointers)</td><td>Left to right
Left to right</td></tr>
<tr><td>*
/
%</td><td>Multiply
Divide
Remainder</td><td>Left to right
Left to right
Left to right</td></tr>
<tr><td>+
–</td><td>Add
Subtract</td><td>Left to right
Left to right</td></tr>
<tr><td><<
>></td><td>Left shift
Right shift</td><td>Left to right
Left to right</td></tr>
<tr><td><
<=
></td><td>Less than
Less than or equal to
Greater than</td><td>Left to right
Left to right
Left to right</td></tr>
<tr><td>==
!=</td><td>Equal
Not equal</td><td>Left to right
Left to right</td></tr>
<tr><td>&&</td><td>Logical AND</td><td>Left to right</td></tr>
<tr><td>||</td><td>Logical OR</td><td>Left to right</td></tr>
<tr><td>? :</td><td>Conditional</td><td>Left to right</td></tr>
<tr><td>=
*=, /=, %=, +=, -=,
<<=, >>=, &=, ^=, |=</td><td>Assignment
Compound assignment</td><td>Right to left
Right to left</td></tr>
<tr><td>,</td><td>Comma--lowest precedence</td><td>Left to right</td></tr>
</table>

Figure 3-15 Order of precedence for C++ operators (continued)

Operators in the same grouping in Figure 3-15 have the same order of precedence. For operators in different precedence groups, expressions are evaluated on a left-to-right basis with the highest-priority precedence evaluated first. Operators in a higher grouping have precedence over operators in a lower grouping. For example, the multiplication operator (*) has a higher precedence than the addition operator (+). Therefore, the statement `5 + 2 * 8` evaluates to 21. The numbers 2 and 8 are multiplied first for a total of 16, then the number 5 is added. If the addition operator had a higher precedence than the multiplication operator, then the statement would evaluate to 56, because 5 would be added to 2 for a total of 7, which would then be multiplied by 8.

When you perform operations with operators in the same precedence group, the order of precedence is determined by the operator's **associativity**, which refers to the order in which operators of equal precedence execute. For example, the multiplication and division operators have an associativity of left-to-right. This means that the statement 30 / 5 * 2 results in a value of 12 because although the multiplication and division operators have equal precedence, the division operation executes first due to the left to right associativity of both operators. If the multiplication operator had a higher precedence than the division operator, then the statement 30 / 5 * 2 would result in a value of 3 because the multiplication operation (5 * 2) would execute first. In comparison, the assignment operator and compound assignment operators such as *= have an associativity of right to left. Therefore, in the following code, the assignment operations take place from right to left. The variable x is incremented by one *before* it is assigned to the y variable using the *= operator. Then, the value of variable y is assigned to variable x. The result assigned to both the x and y variables is 8.

```
int x = 3;
int y = 2;
x = y *= ++x;
```

Parentheses are used with expressions to change the associativity through which individual operations in an expression are evaluated. For example, the statement `5 + 2 * 8`, which evaluates to 21, can be rewritten as `(5 + 2) * 8`, which evaluates to 56. The parentheses tell C++ to add the numbers 5 and 2 before multiplying by the number 8. (Recall that multiplication and division operations have higher precedence than addition and subtraction operations.) Using parentheses forces the statement to evaluate to 56 instead of 21.

DECISION-MAKING STATEMENTS

When you write a computer program, regardless of the programming language, you often need to execute different sets of statements, depending on some predetermined criteria. You may need to execute different sets of code depending on the time of day, information gathered from a user, the evaluation of a conditional expression, and so on. For example, a doctor's office may use a program that sends out different healthcare reminder notices to people depending on their age. For people under the age of 12, a set of code generates a notice reminding them to get their measles vaccination. For people over 65, another set of code generates a notice reminding them to get their flu shots. The process of determining which statements or in what order statements in a program execute is called **decision making** or **flow control**. The special types of C++ statements used for making decisions are called decision-making structures. The most common decision-making structures include `if`, `if...else`, and `switch` statements.

`if` Statements

One of the more common ways to control program flow is a technique that uses the `if` statement. The **`if` statement** is used to execute specific programming code if the evaluation of a conditional expression returns a value of true. The syntax for the `if` statement is as follows:

```
if (conditional expression) {
    statement(s);
}
```

The `if` statement contains three parts: the key word `if`, a conditional expression enclosed within parentheses, and executable statements. Note that you must enclose the conditional expression within parentheses.

If the condition being evaluated in an `if` statement returns a value of true, then the statement (or statements) immediately following the `if` keyword and its condition executes. After the `if` statement executes, any subsequent code executes normally. Consider the following example. The `if` statement uses the equal (==) comparison operator to determine whether iNum is equal to 5. Because the condition returns a value of true, two lines print. The first line is generated by the `if` statement when the condition returns a value of true, and the second line executes after the `if` statement is complete.

```
int iNum = 5;
if (iNum == 5) // CONDITION EVALUATES TO 'TRUE'
    cout << "The variable is equal to '5'." << endl;
cout << "This text is printed after the if statement.";
```

One method many programmers use in a conditional statement to make it easier to distinguish between the assignment operator (=) and the comparison operator (==) is to reverse the order of the comparison. Instead of writing `iNum == 5` you would write `5 == iNum`. The second example performs the same comparison as the first, but it prevents you from accidentally assigning a value to a variable when you meant to compare the value to the variable. If you assign a value to a variable in an `if` statement, as in `5 = iNum`, a compile error message will be generated.

You can use a command block to construct a decision-making structure that executes multiple statements. The following code shows a program that runs a command block if the conditional expression within the `if` statement evaluates to true.

```
int iNum = 5;
if (iNum == 5) {     // CONDITION EVALUATES TO 'TRUE'
    cout << "The condition evaluates to true." << endl;
    cout << "iNum is equal to 5." << endl;
    cout << "Each of these lines will be printed."
        << endl;
}
```

When an `if` statement contains a command block, the statements in the command block execute when the `if` statement condition evaluates to true. After the command block executes, the code that follows executes normally. When an `if` statement condition evaluates to false, the command block is skipped and the statements that follow execute.

When you build an `if` statement, remember that after the `if` statement condition evaluates, either the first statement following the condition executes, or the command block following the condition executes. Any statements following the `if` statement command or command block execute regardless of whether the `if` statement condition evaluates to true or false.

It is easy to forget to include all of the statements inside a command block that are to execute when an `if` statement evaluates to true. For example, consider the following code.

```
int iIncome = 70000;
string sResult;
if (iIncome > 26250 && iIncome < 63550)
   cout << "Your base tax is $3,637.50" << endl;
   cout << "You are in the 27% tax bracket" << endl;
```


At first glance, the code looks correct. In fact, when the condition evaluates to true, the code seems to run correctly. When the condition evaluates to false, however, the last cout statement runs anyway, printing *You are in the 27% tax bracket.* To fix this problem, enclose the two statements following the `if` statement within a command block as follows:

```
int iIncome = 70000;
string sResult;
if (iIncome > 26250 && iIncome < 63550)  {
   cout << "Your base tax is $3,637.50" << endl;
   cout << "You are in the 27% tax bracket" << endl;
}
```

Now if the condition evaluates to false, both statements will be bypassed because they are contained within a command block.

Next, you will start creating the Chemistry Quiz program you saw at the beginning of this chapter. In this version of the program, each question in the Chemistry Quiz will be scored using a unique function. `If` statements within each question's function evaluate the user's answer and print a response of *Correct Answer* or *Incorrect Answer.*

To start creating the Chemistry Quiz program as a console application:

1. Create a new Win32 Project named **ChemistryQuiz1** in the Chapter.03 folder in your Visual C++ Projects folder. Be sure to clear the **Create directory for Solution** check box in the New Project dialog box. In the Application Settings tab of the Win32 Application Wizard dialog box, select **Console application** as the application type, click the **Empty project** check box, and then click the **Finish** button. Once the project is created, add a C++ source file named **ChemistryQuiz1.cpp**.
2. As shown in Figure 3-16, type the preprocessor directive that gives the program access to the iostream library along with the using directive that designates the std namespace. Also type the function prototypes for each question's scoring function. Each function receives a single argument containing the response gathered from the user. You will learn how to gather input from the user after this exercise.

```
#include <iostream>
using namespace std;
void scoreQuestion1(char);
void scoreQuestion2(char);
void scoreQuestion3(char);
void scoreQuestion4(char);
void scoreQuestion5(char);
```

ChemistryQuiz1.cpp*

Preprocessor directive

Using directive

Function prototypes

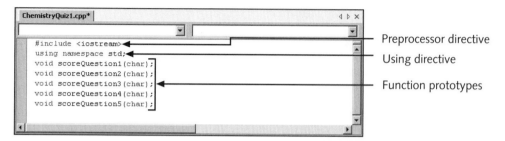

Figure 3-16 Opening statements added to the ChemistryQuiz1.cpp file

3. Add the empty main() function shown in Figure 3-17. You will return to the main() function after learning how to gather input from the user.

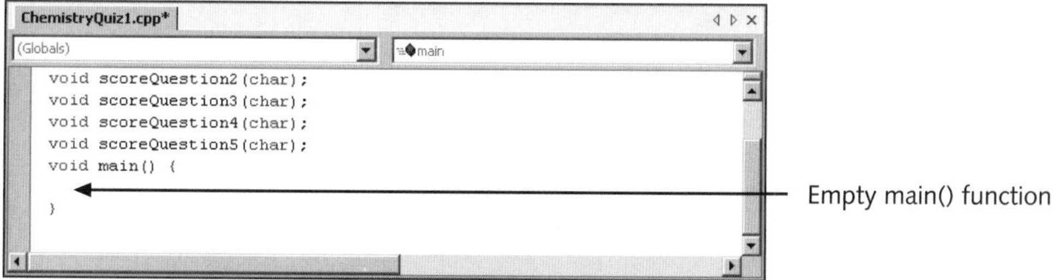

Figure 3-17 Empty main() function

4. After the main() function closing brace, add the following five functions, which score each question. Each function receives a cAnswer variable containing the user's response, which is then evaluated by `if` statements.

```
void scoreQuestion1(char cAnswer) {
     if (cAnswer == 'a')
          cout << "Incorrect Answer" << endl;
     if (cAnswer == 'b')
          cout << "Incorrect Answer" << endl;
     if (cAnswer == 'c')
          cout << "Incorrect Answer" << endl;
     if (cAnswer == 'd')
          cout << "Correct Answer" << endl;
}
void scoreQuestion2(char cAnswer) {
     if (cAnswer == 'a')
          cout << "Correct Answer" << endl;
     if (cAnswer == 'b')
          cout << "Incorrect Answer" << endl;
     if (cAnswer == 'c')
          cout << "Incorrect Answer" << endl;
```

```
        if (cAnswer == 'd')
            cout << "Incorrect Answer" << endl;
}
void scoreQuestion3(char cAnswer) {
        if (cAnswer == 'a')
            cout << "Incorrect Answer" << endl;
        if (cAnswer == 'b')
            cout << "Incorrect Answer" << endl;
        if (cAnswer == 'c')
            cout << "Incorrect Answer" << endl;
        if (cAnswer == 'd')
            cout << "Correct Answer" << endl;
}
void scoreQuestion4(char cAnswer) {
        if (cAnswer == 'a')
            cout << "Incorrect Answer" << endl;
        if (cAnswer == 'b')
            cout << "Incorrect Answer" << endl;
        if (cAnswer == 'c')
            cout << "Correct Answer" << endl;
        if (cAnswer == 'd')
            cout << "Incorrect Answer" << endl;
}
void scoreQuestion5(char cAnswer) {
        if (cAnswer == 'a')
            cout << "Incorrect Answer" << endl;
        if (cAnswer == 'b')
            cout << "Correct Answer" << endl;
        if (cAnswer == 'c')
            cout << "Incorrect Answer" << endl;
        if (cAnswer == 'd')
            cout << "Incorrect Answer" << endl;
}
```

5. Build the project. If you receive any compilation errors, fix them, and then recompile the program. Before you can run the Chemistry Quiz program, you will need to add code that receives input from users.

Standard Input Stream

So far, you have only output information to the console window using the cout object of the standard output stream. There are many situations, however, in which you need to receive information from a user. The **cin** object receives information from the user through the standard input stream. Whereas the standard output stream prints text to the screen or to a file, the **standard input stream** reads information from the keyboard. In other words, the cin object receives keyboard input from the user and returns it to a C++ program. The syntax for using the cin object is `cin >> variable;`. Notice the extraction operator (>>), which points towards the variable. In contrast, consider the syntax for the cout object, `cout << "text";`, in which the insertion operator (<<) points towards the cout object. The **extraction operator** (>>) retrieves information from the input stream. Take a moment to compare the extraction operator (>>) to the insertion operator (<<), which inserts information into the output stream. Essentially, the cout operator sends information towards the cout object (insertion), and the cin object sends information towards a variable (extraction).

A cin statement causes a C++ console application program to pause execution and wait for input from the user. The program starts again once the user presses Enter. Any characters the user entered before pressing Enter are assigned to the designated variable. The keyboard input that can be assigned to a variable using the cin object depends on the data type of the variable. For example, the following code declares an int variable named iNumber, and then uses a cin statement to assign a value to the variable:

```
int iNumber;
cin >> iNumber;
```

The user can enter any number between -2,147,483,648 and 2,147,483,647, because that is the valid range for the `int` data type. If the user enters a floating-point number such as 56.74, however, the number will be truncated to 56 before it is assigned to the iNumber variable because `int` data types cannot store decimal values. A value of 0 (zero) will be assigned if you attempt to assign characters to the iNumber variable. As another example of data types and cin statements, consider the following code:

```
char cLetter;
cin >> cLetter;
```

Because the char data type stores only single characters, if a user types multiple letters, only the first letter typed will be assigned to the cLetter variable in the preceding code. For example, if the user types *Hello* before pressing Enter, then only the letter *H* is assigned to the cLetter variable. If you want to use a cin statement to assign a string to a C-style string variable, then you must first declare the number of characters that will be assigned to the variable. For example, the following code declares two `char` variables, szFirstName and szLastName, to collect a user's name. The variable declaration statements specify 25 as the maximum number of characters to assign to each variable, which should be sufficient to hold the first and last names of most people.

```
char szFirstName[25];
char szLastName[25];
cout << "Enter your first name: ";
cin >> szFirstName;
cout << "Enter your last name: ";
cin >> szLastName;
cout << "Your name is " << szFirstName << " " <<
szLastName << endl;
```

An easier method than using C-style string variables is to use string class variables, which do not require you to declare the number of characters that the variable will hold, as in the following example:

```
string sFirstName;
string sLastName;
cout << "Enter your first name: ";
cin >> sFirstName;
cout << "Enter your last name: ";
cin >> sLastName;
cout << "Your name is " << sFirstName << " " << sLastName
<< endl;
```

Next, you will add to the ChemistryQuiz1 project cout statements that print questions to the screen and cin statements to receive each response and assign it to a string class variable.

To add to the ChemistryQuiz1 project cout statements that print questions to the screen and cin statements to receive each response:

1. Return to the **ChemistryQuiz1.cpp** source file in the Code Editor window in the **ChemistryQuiz1** project.
2. As shown in Figure 3-18, declare a `char` variable in the main() function to hold the response received from cin statements (which you will create next) and a title for the quiz:

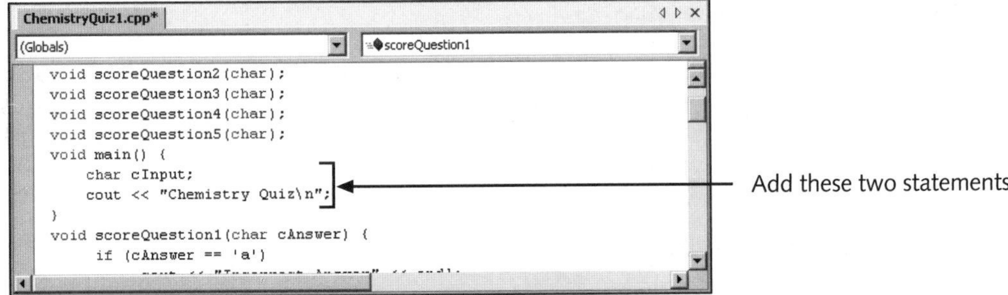

Figure 3-18 Statements added to the main() function

3. Add to the main() function the code for the first question, as shown in Figure 3-19. The code displays the question using cout statements and receives an answer using a cin statement. After the user answers the question, the scoreQuestion1() function executes to score the response. Notice that each answer includes a tab escape character, \t, so that it is indented beneath the question.

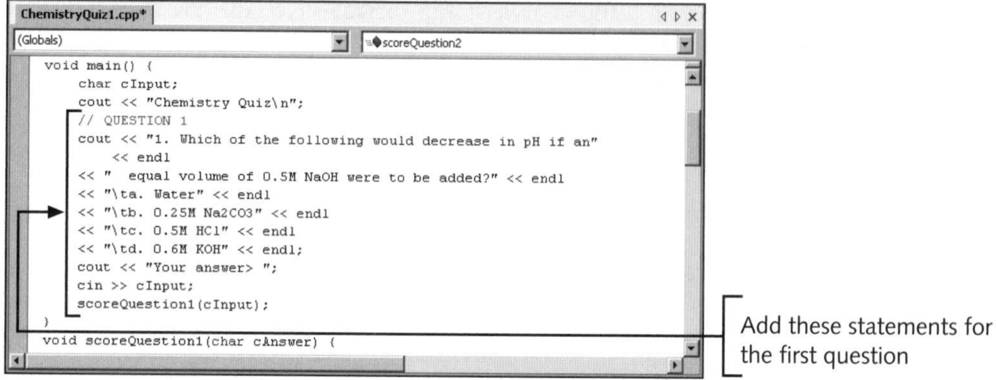

Figure 3-19 Code for the first question added to the main() function

4. Now add the remainder of the questions to the main() function after the code for the first question:

```
// QUESTION 2
cout << "2. Which of the following compounds contain Manganese "
  << endl
<< "  in its highest oxidation state?" << endl
<< "\ta. Mn2O7" << endl
<< "\tb. MnC2O4" << endl
<< "\tc. KMnO5" << endl
<< "\td. K2MnO4" << endl;
cout << "Your answer> ";
cin >> cInput;
scoreQuestion2(cInput);
// QUESTION 3
cout << "3. Select the appropriate classification for the action "
  << endl
<< "  of heat on a mixture of sodium benzoate and soda-lime:"
  << endl
<< "\ta. Polymerization" << endl
<< "\tb. Addition" << endl
<< "\tc. Condensation" << endl
<< "\td. Decarboxylation" << endl;
cout << "Your answer> ";
cin >> cInput;
scoreQuestion3(cInput);
// QUESTION 4
cout << "4. Select the compound which reacts with aqueous sodium "
  << endl
<< "  hydroxide but not with aqueous sodium carbonate:" << endl
<< "\ta. HOCH2CH2OH" << endl
<< "\tb. CH3CHClCO2H" << endl
<< "\tc. PhOH" << endl
<< "\td. CH3(CHOH)CH3" << endl;
```

```
cout << "Your answer> ";
cin >> cInput;
scoreQuestion4(cInput);
// QUESTION 5
cout << "5. Select the structure possessed by helium, at room "
  << endl
<< "  temperature and atmospheric pressure:" << endl
<< "\ta. Giant structure of ions" << endl
<< "\tb. Widely spaced atoms" << endl
<< "\tc. Widely spaced molecules" << endl
<< "\td. Giant structure of atoms" << endl;
cout << "Your answer> ";
cin >> cInput;
scoreQuestion5(cInput);
cout << endl;
```

5. Build and execute the project, then answer the questions. As you select a response for each question, you will immediately learn whether the answer is correct. Figure 3-20 shows the output after answering several questions.

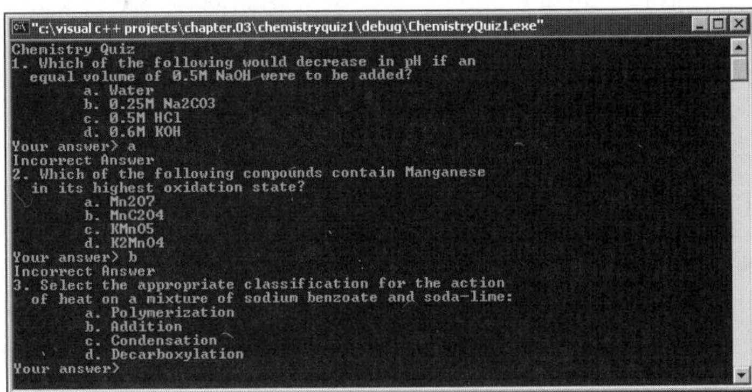

Figure 3-20 Output of ChemistryQuiz1

6. Press any key to close the command window.

`if...else` Statements

When using an `if` statement, you can include an **`else`** clause to run an alternate set of code if the conditional expression evaluated by the `if` statement returns a value of false. For instance, you may have an investment program that uses an `if` statement to evaluate a Boolean variable named bStockMarket. The conditional expression in the `if` statement uses the bStockMarket variable to determine if the user of the program invests in the stock market. If the condition evaluates to true, then the `if` statement prints a list of recommended stocks. If the condition evaluates to false, then the statements in an `else` clause display other types of investment opportunities. An `if` statement that includes an `else` clause is called an `if...else` statement. You can think of an `else` clause as being a backup plan for when the condition of the `if` statement returns a value of false. The syntax for an `if...else` statement is as follows:

```
if (conditional expression) {
    statement;
}
else {
    statement(s);
```

The `else` clause can only be used with an `if` statement. Unlike the `if` statement, the `else` clause cannot be used alone.

A common technique is to combine an `else` structure with another `if` statement. The following code shows an example of a program that gathers a number from a user, assigns it to a variable named iNumber, and then uses an `if...else` structure to determine the size of the number. The opening `if` statement first checks if the iNumber variable is less than or equal to 100. If it is, then the statement following the `if` statement executes. If the conditional expression of the `if` statement evaluates to false, then an `else` structure combined with an `if` statement determines if the iNumber variable is between 100 and 1000. The final `else` structure executes if the number the user enters does not meet the conditional statements in the `if` and `else...if` structures.

```
int iNumber;
cout << "Please enter a positive number." << endl;
cin >> iNumber;
if (iNumber <= 100) {
     cout << "The number you entered is " << iNumber << endl;
     cout << iNumber << " is between 0 and 100" << endl;
}
else if (iNumber > 100 && iNumber <= 1000)  {
     cout << "The number you entered is " << iNumber << endl;
     cout << iNumber << " is between 101 and 1000" << endl;
}
else  {
     cout << "The number you entered is " << iNumber << endl;
     cout << iNumber << " is greater than 1000" << endl;
}
```

The C++ code for the ChemistryQuiz1 project you created earlier uses multiple `if` statements to evaluate the results of the quiz. Although the multiple `if` statements function properly, you can simplify them by using `if...else` statements. Next, you will create a new version of the Chemistry Quiz program that contains `if...else` statements instead of multiple `if` statements.

To create a new version of the Chemistry Quiz program that contains `if...else` statements instead of multiple `if` statements:

1. Return to the ChemistryQuiz1.cpp source file in the Code Editor window and choose **Select All** from the Edit menu. Once the code is highlighted, select **Copy** from the Edit menu. You will copy the highlighted code into a new project, rather than retyping it.
2. Select **Close Solution** from the File menu to close the ChemistryQuiz1 project.
3. Create a new Win32 Project named **ChemistryQuiz2** in the Chapter.03 folder in your Visual C++ Projects folder. Be sure to clear the **Create directory for Solution** check box in the New Project dialog box. In the Application Settings tab of the Win32 Application Wizard dialog box, select **Console application** as the application type, click the **Empty project** check box, and then click the **Finish** button. Once the project is created, add a C++ source file named **ChemistryQuiz2.cpp**.
4. After the ChemistryQuiz2.cpp file opens in the Code Editor window, select **Paste** from the Edit menu to paste the code you copied from the ChemistryQuiz1.cpp file.
5. Because you only need the `if` statement to test for the correct answer, you can group all the incorrect answers in an `else` clause. Modify each of the functions that scores a question so that the multiple `if` statements are replaced with an `if...else` statement. Figure 3-21 shows how the statements for the scoreQuestion1() function should appear. Modify each score Question()function in a similar fashion.

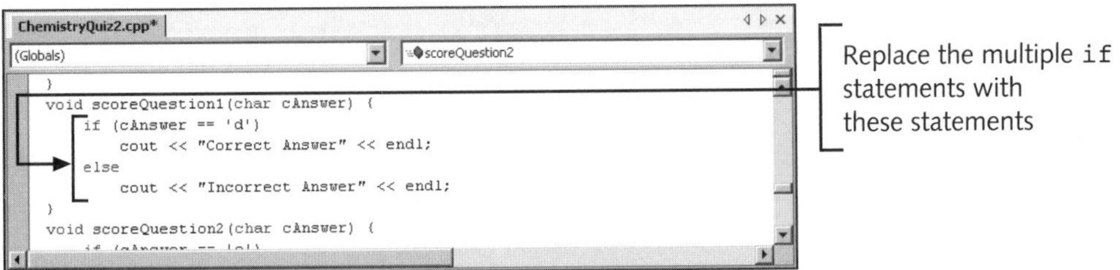

Figure 3-21 ScoreQuestion1() function statements replaced with an `if...else` statement

6. Build and execute the **ChemistryQuiz2** project. The program should function the same as when it contained only `if` statements.
7. Press any key to close the command window.

Nested `if` Statements

When you make a decision with a control structure such as an **`if`** or **`if...else`** statement, you may want the statements executed by the control structure to make other decisions. For instance, you may have a program that uses an `if` statement to ask users if they like sports. If users answer yes, you may want to run another `if` statement that asks users whether they like team sports or individual sports. Because you can include any code you like within the `if` statement or the `else` clause, you can include other `if` or `if...else` statements. An `if` statement contained within another `if` or `if...else` statement is called a **nested `if`** statement. Similarly, an `if...else` statement contained within another `if` or `if...else` statement is called a **nested `if...else`** statement. You use nested `if` and `if...else` statements to perform conditional evaluations in addition to an original conditional evaluation. For example, the following code performs two conditional evaluations before the cout statement executes:

```
int iNumber = 7;
if (iNumber > 5)
    if (iNumber < 10)
        cout << "The number is between 5 and 10." << endl;
```

If either of the conditions in this example evaluates to false, then the program skips the remainder of the `if` statement.

The C++ code in the ChemistryQuiz2.cpp file is somewhat inefficient because it contains multiple functions that perform the same task of scoring the quiz. A more efficient method of scoring the quiz is to use a single function that contains nested decision-making structures. Next, you will create a new version of the Chemistry Quiz program that contains a single function that checks the correct answer for all the questions using nested `if...else` statements.

To create a new version of the Chemistry Quiz program that contains a single function that checks the correct answer for all the questions using nested `if...else` statements:

1. Return to the **ChemistryQuiz2.cpp** source file in the Code Editor window and choose **Select All** from the Edit menu. Once the code is highlighted, select **Copy** from the Edit menu. You will copy the highlighted code into a new project rather than retyping it.

2. Select **Close Solution** from the File menu to close the ChemistryQuiz2 project.

3. Create a new Win32 Project named **ChemistryQuiz3** in the Chapter.03 folder in your Visual C++ Projects folder. Be sure to clear the **Create directory for Solution** check box in the New Project dialog box. In the Application Settings tab of the Win32 Application Wizard dialog box, select **Console application** as the application type, click the **Empty project** check box, and then click the **Finish** button. Once the project is created, add a C++ source file named **ChemistryQuiz3.cpp**.

4. After the ChemistryQuiz3.cpp file opens in the Code Editor window, select **Paste** from the Edit menu to paste the code you copied from the ChemistryQuiz2.cpp file.
5. Replace the five function prototypes with a single function prototype: **`void scoreQuestions(int iNumber, char cAnswer);`**, as shown in Figure 3-22. The scoreQuestions() function will check all of the answers. You will send an answer argument to the scoreQuestions() function, just as you did with the functions that scored each individual question. You will also send a new argument, *iNumber*, which represents the question number, to the scoreQuestions() function.

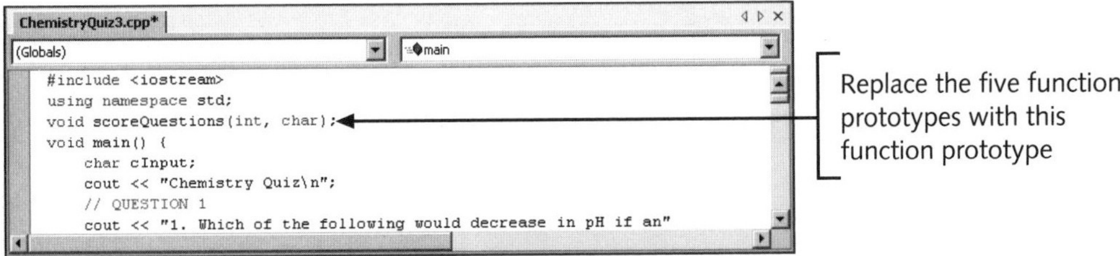

Figure 3-22 Five function prototypes replaced with a single function prototype

6. Delete the five functions that follow the main() function.
7. After deleting the five functions, add the scoreQuestions() function constructor after the closing brace of the main() function: **`void scoreQuestions(int iNumber, char cAnswer) {`**.
8. **Press** Enter and then add the opening `if` statement that checks if the question number is equal to 1. If it is, a nested `if...else` statement evaluates the response.

```
if (iNumber == 1) {
    if (cAnswer == 'd')
        cout << "Correct Answer" << endl;
    else
        cout << "Incorrect Answer" << endl;
}
```

9. Add an `else` clause for question number 2:

```
else if (iNumber == 2) {
    if (cAnswer == 'a')
        cout << "Correct Answer" << endl;
    else
        cout << "Incorrect Answer" << endl;
}
```

10. Add an `else` clause for question number 3:

```
else if (iNumber == 3) {
     if (cAnswer == 'd')
          cout << "Correct Answer" << endl;
     else
          cout << "Incorrect Answer" << endl;
}
```

11. Add an `else` clause for question number 4:

```
else if (iNumber == 4) {
   if (cAnswer == 'c')
        cout << "Correct Answer" << endl;
   else
        cout << "Incorrect Answer" << endl;
}
```

12. Add an `else` clause for question number 5:

```
else if (iNumber == 5) {
   if (cAnswer == 'b')
        cout << "Correct Answer" << endl;
   else
        cout << "Incorrect Answer" << endl;
}
```

13. Add a closing brace (`}`) for the scoreQuestions() function.

14. In the main() function, change the function call for each question to **`scoreQuestions(`*`number`*`, cInput);`, changing the *number*** argument to the appropriate question number. For example, the function call for question 1 should read: `scoreQuestions(1, cInput);`, as shown in Figure 3-23.

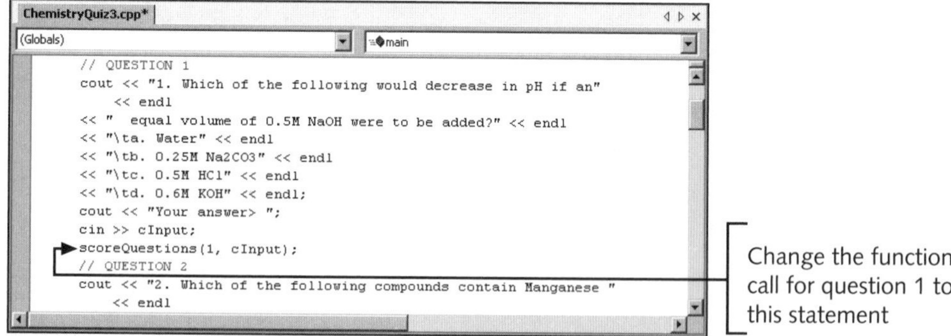

Figure 3-23 Modified function call for question 1

15. Build and execute the ChemistryQuiz3 project. The program should function the same way it did with the multiple `if` statements and the multiple functions.

16. Press any key to close the command window.

An alternative to using nested `if` statements is to use compound conditional expressions.

`switch` Statements

Another C++ statement that is used for controlling program flow is the `switch` statement. The **`switch` statement** controls program flow by executing a specific set of statements, depending on the value returned from an expression. The result returned from the expression must be an integer data type, which includes the `bool`, `char`, `int`, `long int`, and `short` data types. The `switch` statement compares the result returned from the expression to a label contained within the `switch` statement command block. If the value matches a particular label, then statements associated with that label execute. Essentially, a `switch` statement executes a particular block of statements according to the value returned from an expression.

For example, suppose you have a program that determines which sales representative should handle a new customer, based on the customer's ZIP code. The program may contain an integer variable named iZipCode. A `switch` statement can evaluate the iZipCode variable (which is an expression) and compare it to a label within the `switch` statement. The `switch` statement may contain a label for each ZIP code that you need to evaluate. Statements within each label could then assign the correct sales representative name to a string class variable named sSalesRep, along with any other functionality that may be required to set up a new customer account. For instance, if the iZipVariable variable is equal to 94939, then the statements that are part of the 94939 label execute. Although you could accomplish the same functionality using `if` or `if...else` statements, a `switch` statement makes it easier to organize different branches of code that can be executed.

You will receive a compiler error if the expression you evaluate in a `switch` statement is any data type other than `bool`, `char`, `int`, `long int`, or `short`.

A `switch` construct consists of the following components: the keyword `switch`, an expression, an opening brace, a `case` label, the keyword `break`, a `default` label, executable statements, and a closing brace. The syntax for the `switch` statement is as follows:

```
switch (expression) {
     case label :
          statement(s);
          break;
     case label :
          statement(s);
          break;
     ...
     default :
          statement(s);
}
```

The labels within a `switch` statement are called **`case` labels**, and they identify specific code segments. A `case` label consists of the keyword `case`, followed by a constant value, followed by a colon. For `char` labels, enclose each character within single quotation marks, as if you were assigning a new `char` value to a variable. C++ compares the value returned from the `switch` statement expression to the literal value or variable name following the `case` keyword. If the comparison yields a match, the `case` label statements execute. For example, you may have a `case` label similar to `case 3:`. If the value of a `switch` statement expression equals 3, then the `case 3:` label statements execute. Similarly, if you use a `char` variable in the `switch` statement expression, then you would use a label similar to `case 'A':` for each of the characters you want to evaluate.

A `case` label can be followed by a single statement or multiple statements. Unlike `if` statements, however, multiple statements for a `case` label do not need to be enclosed within a command block.

The case labels in a switch statement can contain nested `switch` statements or any other type of decision-making or flow-control statement. In Chapter 9, you will see an example of nested `switch` statements.

Another decision-making structure that works with labels is the `goto` statement. When C++ encounters a `goto` statement, program execution is immediately and unconditionally transferred to a specified label. Although supported in C++, it is considered poor programming technique to use the `goto` statement because it makes program flow extremely difficult to follow. For this reason the `goto` statement is not discussed in this book, and you are encouraged to avoid using it in your programs.

Another type of label used within `switch` constructs is the `default` label. The **`default` label** contains statements that execute when the value returned by the `switch` statement conditional expression does not match a `case` label. A `default` label consists of the keyword `default` followed by a colon.

When a `switch` construct executes, the value returned by the expression is compared to each `case` label in the order in which it is encountered. Once a matching label is found, its statements execute. You can place any statements you like after a `case` label, and you do not need to use command blocks to surround multiple statements that are placed after a `case` label. Instead, C++ knows to execute any statements within a given `case` label until either a break statement is encountered or the `switch` statement closing brace is encountered.

Unlike the `if...else` statement, program execution does not automatically exit the `switch` construct after a particular `case` label's statements execute. Instead, the `switch` statement continues evaluating the rest of the `case` labels in the list. Once a matching `case` label is found, however, evaluation of additional `case` labels is unnecessary. If you are working with a large `switch` construct with many `case` labels, evaluation of additional `case` labels can potentially slow down your program.

It is good programming design to end a **switch** construct once it performs its required task. A **switch** construct ends automatically after C++ encounters its closing brace (}) or when a **break** statement is found. A **break** statement is used to exit **switch** constructs and other program control statements such as **while**, **do...while**, and **for** repetition statements. To end a **switch** construct once it performs its required task, you should include a **break** statement within each **case** label section.

You will learn more about repetition statements later in this chapter.

Figure 3-24 displays an example of a program that uses a **switch** construct. The main() function displays a menu of American cities from which users can choose. The number of the selected city is passed to the cAmericanCity variable in the cityLocation() function and evaluated in a **switch** statement. The **switch** statement compares the contents of the cAmericanCity argument to the **case** labels. If a match is found, a string listing the city's state is returned and a **break** statement ends the **switch** construct. If a match is not found, the value *You did not select one of the five cities!* is returned from the **default** label. Figure 3-25 shows the output.

Next, you will create a new version of the Chemistry Quiz program in which the scoreQuestions() function contains a **switch** statement instead of nested **if...else** statements. Each **case** statement in the modified program checks for the question number from the function number argument. The **switch** statement makes better programming sense because it eliminates the need to check the question number multiple times, as is necessary with an **if...else** structure.

To create a new version of the Chemistry Quiz program in which the scoreQuestions() function contains a **switch** statement instead of nested **if...else** statements:

1. Return to the **ChemistryQuiz3.cpp** source file in the Code Editor window and choose **Select All** from the Edit menu. Once the code is highlighted, select **Copy** from the Edit menu. You will copy the highlighted code into a new project, rather than retyping it.
2. Close the ChemistryQuiz3 project by selecting **Close Solution** from the File menu.
3. Create a new Win32 Project named **ChemistryQuiz4** in the Chapter.03 folder in your Visual C++ Projects folder. Be sure to clear the **Create directory for Solution** check box in the New Project dialog box. In the Application Settings tab of the Win32 Application Wizard dialog box, select **Console application** as the application type, click the **Empty project** check box, and then click the **Finish** button. Once the project is created, add a C++ source file named **ChemistryQuiz4.cpp**.

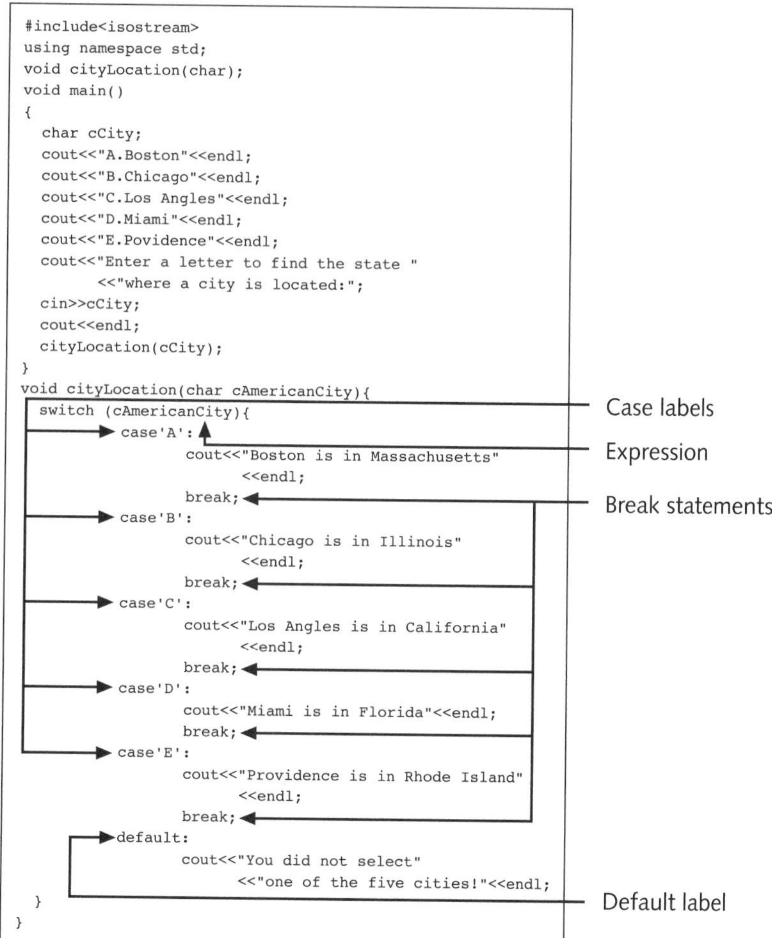

```
#include<isostream>
using namespace std;
void cityLocation(char);
void main()
{
  char cCity;
  cout<<"A.Boston"<<endl;
  cout<<"B.Chicago"<<endl;
  cout<<"C.Los Angles"<<endl;
  cout<<"D.Miami"<<endl;
  cout<<"E.Povidence"<<endl;
  cout<<"Enter a letter to find the state "
        <<"where a city is located:";
  cin>>cCity;
  cout<<endl;
  cityLocation(cCity);
}
void cityLocation(char cAmericanCity){
  switch (cAmericanCity){
         case'A':
                cout<<"Boston is in Massachusetts"
                      <<endl;
                break;
         case'B':
                cout<<"Chicago is in Illinois"
                      <<endl;
                break;
         case'C':
                cout<<"Los Angles is in California"
                      <<endl;
                break;
         case'D':
                cout<<"Miami is in Florida"<<endl;
                break;
         case'E':
                cout<<"Providence is in Rhode Island"
                      <<endl;
                break;
         default:
                cout<<"You did not select"
                      <<"one of the five cities!"<<endl;
  }
}
```


Figure 3-24 Program containing a `switch` statement

```
"c:\visual c++ projects\chapter.03\americancities\debug\AmericanCities.exe"
Enter a number to find the state where a city is located.
1. Boston
2. Chicago
3. Los Angeles
4. Miami
5. Providence

5

Providence is in Rhode Island
Press any key to continue
```

Figure 3-25 Output of program containing a `switch` satement

4. After the ChemistryQuiz4.cpp file opens in the Code Editor window, select **Paste** from the Edit menu to paste the code you copied from the ChemistryQuiz3.cpp file.

5. Change the `if...else` statements within the scoreQuestions() function to the following `switch` statement.


```
switch (iNumber) {
   case 1:
      if (cAnswer == 'd')
          cout << "Correct Answer" << endl;
      else
          cout << "Incorrect Answer" << endl;
       break;
   case 2:
      if (cAnswer == 'a')
          cout << "Correct Answer" << endl;
      else
          cout << "Incorrect Answer" << endl;
       break;
   case 3:
      if (cAnswer == 'd')
          cout << "Correct Answer" << endl;
      else
          cout << "Incorrect Answer" << endl;
       break;
   case 4:
      if (cAnswer == 'c')
          cout << "Correct Answer" << endl;
      else
          cout << "Incorrect Answer" << endl;
       break;
   case 5:
      if (cAnswer == 'b')
          cout << "Correct Answer" << endl;
      else
          cout << "Incorrect Answer" << endl;
       break;
}
```

6. Build and execute the ChemistryQuiz4 project. The program should still function the same as it did with the nested `if...else` statements.

7. Press any key to close the command window.

Repetition Statements

The statements you have worked with so far execute one after the other in a linear fashion. If, if...else, and switch statements select only a single branch of code to execute, then program execution continues on to the statement that follows. But what if you want to repeat the same statement, function, or code section five times, ten times, or one hundred times? For example, suppose you have a program that prompts users for information such as their name or telephone number. If a user does not enter the correct information, then you may want to keep repeating the prompt statements until the user enters the correct information. A **looping statement** repeatedly executes a statement or a series of statements while a specific condition is true. Looping techniques include while, do...while, for, and continue statements.

while Statements

One of the simplest types of looping statements is the while statement. The **while statement** is used for repeating a statement or series of statements as long as a given conditional expression evaluates to true. The syntax for the while statement is as follows:

```
while (conditional expression) {
  statement(s);
}
```

Like the if...else and switch statements, the conditional expression that the while statement tests for is enclosed within parentheses following the keyword while. As long as the conditional expression evaluates to true, the statement or command block that follows will execute repeatedly. Each repetition of a looping statement is called an **iteration**. Once the conditional expression evaluates to false, the loop ends and the next statement following the while statement executes.

A while statement will keep repeating until its conditional expression evaluates to false. To end the while statement once the desired tasks have been performed, you must include code that tracks the progress of the loop and changes the value produced by the conditional expression. You track the progress of a while statement, or any other loop, with a counter. A **counter** is a variable that increments or decrements with each iteration of a loop statement.

Many programmers name counter variables *count*, *counter*, or something similar. The letters *i*, *j*, *k*, and *l* are also commonly used as counter names. Using a name such as *count*, the letter *i* (for *increment*), or a higher letter helps you remember (and lets other programmers know) that the variable is being used as a counter. This book will use the Hungarian notation prefix *ct* with a variable name.

The following code shows an example of a simple program that uses a `while` statement. The program declares a variable named ctCount and assigns to it an initial value of 1. The ctCount variable is then used in the `while` statement conditional expression `(ctCount <= 5)`. As long as the ctCount variable is less than or equal to five, the `while` statement will loop. Within the body of the `while` statement, the cout statement prints the value of the ctCount variable, then the ctCount variable is incremented by a value of 1. The `while` statement loops until the ctCount variable reaches to a value of 6.


```
int ctCount = 1;
while (ctCount <= 5) {
  cout << ctCount << endl;
  ++ctCount;
}
cout << "You have printed 5 numbers." << endl << endl;
```

The preceding code prints the numbers 1 to 5, which represent each iteration of the loop. Once ctCount reaches 6, the message *You have printed 5 numbers.* is printed to demonstrate when the loop ends. Figure 3-26 shows the output.

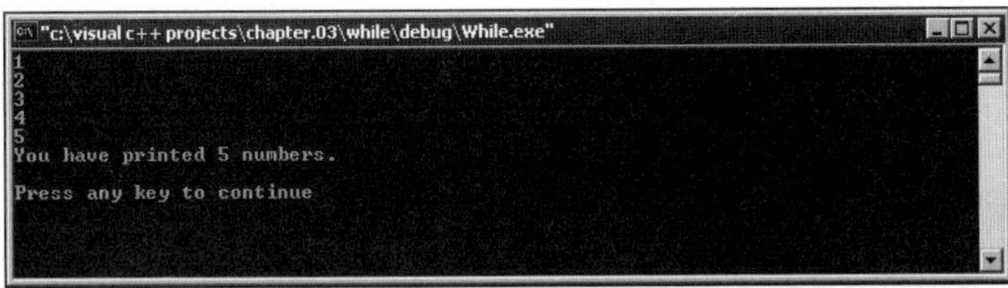

Figure 3-26 Output of a simple `while` statement

The preceding example controls the repetitions in the `while` loop by incrementing a counter variable. However, you can also control the repetitions in a `while` loop by decrementing counter variables. Consider the following program code:

```
int ctCount = 10;
while (ctCount > 0) {
  cout << ctCount << endl;
  --ctCount;
}
cout << "We have liftoff." << endl << endl;
```

In this example the initial value of the ctCount variable is 10, and it is decreased by 1 using the decrement operator (--). While the ctCount variable is greater than 0, the statement within the `while` loop prints the value of the ctCount variable. When the value of ctCount is equal to 0, the `while` loop ends and the statement immediately following it prints. Figure 3-27 shows the program output.

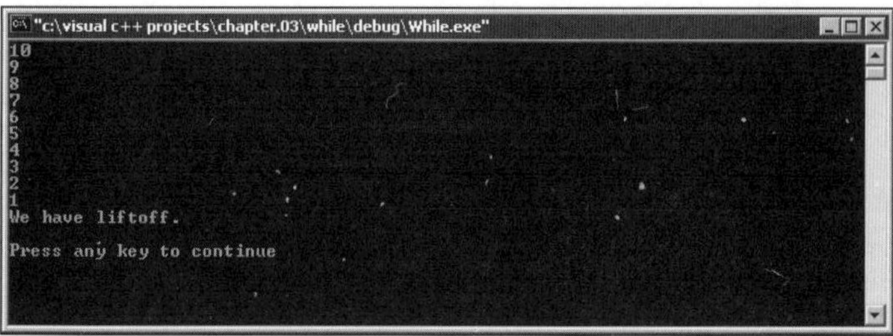

Figure 3-27 Output of a `while` statement using a decrement operator

There are many ways to change the value of a count variable to control the repetitions of a `while` loop. The following example uses the *= assignment operator to multiply the value of the ctCount variable by 2. Once the ctCount variable reaches a value of 100, the `while` statement ends. Figure 3-28 shows the program output.

```
int ctCount = 1;
while (ctCount <= 100) {
  cout << ctCount << endl;
  ctCount *= 2;
}
cout << endl;
```

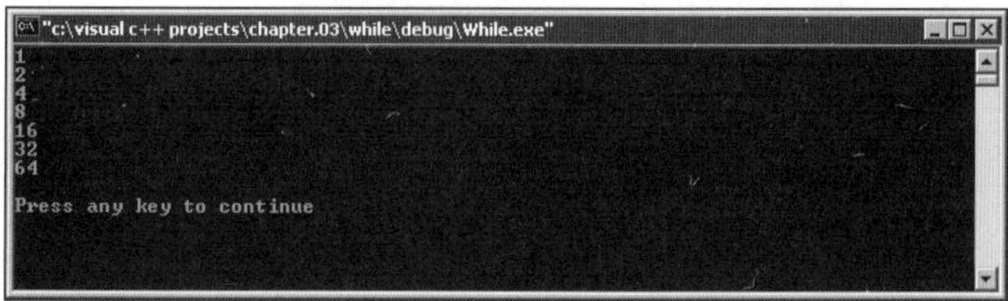

Figure 3-28 Output of a `while` statement using the *=assignment operator

It is important to include code that monitors the conditional expression of a `while` statement. You also need to include code within the body of the `while` statement that changes the value of the conditional expression. If you do not include code that changes the value used by the conditional expression, your program will be caught in an infinite loop. An **infinite loop** is a situation in which a looping statement never ends because its conditional expression is never updated or is never false. Consider the following `while` statement:

```
int ctCount = 1;
while (ctCount <= 10) {
  cout << "The number is " << ctCount << endl;
}
```

Although the `while` statement in the preceding code includes a conditional expression that checks the value of a count variable, there is no code within the body of the `while` statement that changes the value of the count variable. The count variable will continue to have a value of 1 through each iteration of the loop. In this case, the text *The number is 1* prints over and over again, until you close the console application window.

You can end an infinite loop in a console application by pressing Ctrl+Break.

`do...while` Statements

Another C++ looping statement that is similar to the `while` statement is the `do...while` statement. The **`do...while` statement** executes a statement or statements once, then repeats the execution as long as a given conditional expression evaluates to true. The syntax for the `do...while` statement is as follows:

```
do {
   statement(s);
} while (conditional expression);
```

As you can see in the syntax description, the statements execute *before* a conditional expression is evaluated. Unlike the simpler `while` statement, the statements in a `do...while` statement always execute once, before the conditional expression is evaluated.

The following `do...while` statement executes once before the conditional expression evaluates the ctCount variable. Therefore, a single line that reads *The count is equal to 2* prints. Once the conditional expression (ctCount < 2) executes, the `do...while` statement ends because the ctCount variable is equal to 3, which causes the conditional expression to return a value of false.

```
int ctCount = 2;
do {
   cout << "The count is equal to " << ctCount << endl;
   ++ctCount;
} while (ctCount < 2); // CONDITIONAL EXPRESSION
```

Note that this `do...while` example includes a counter within the body of the `do...while` statement. As with the `while` statement, you need to include code that changes some part of the conditional expression in order to prevent an infinite loop from occurring.

`for` Statements

You can also use the `for` statement to loop through code. The **`for` statement** is used for repeating a statement or series of statements as long as a given conditional expression evaluates to true. The `for` statement performs essentially the same function as the `while` statement: if a conditional expression within the `for` statement evaluates to true, then the `for` statement executes and will continue to execute repeatedly until the conditional expression evaluates to false. One of the primary differences between the `while` statement and the `for` statement is that in addition to a conditional expression, you can also include code in the `for` statement constructor to initialize a counter and change its value with each iteration. The syntax of the `for` statement is as follows:

```
for (initialization expression; conditional expression;
update statement) {
   statement(s);
}
```

When C++ encounters a `for` loop, the following steps occur:

1. The initialization expression is started. For example, if the initialization expression in a `for` loop is `int ctCount = 1;`, then a variable named ctCount is declared and an initial value of 1 is assigned to it. The initialization expression is only started once when the `for` loop is first encountered.
2. The condition of the `for` loop is evaluated.
3. If the conditional expression in Step 2 returns a value of true, the `for` loop statements execute, Step 4 occurs, and then the process starts over again with Step 2. If the condition evaluation in Step 2 returns a value of false, then the `for` statement ends and the next statement following the `for` statement executes.
4. The update statement in the constructor of the `for` statement is executed. For example, the count variable may increment by 1.

You can omit any of the three parts of the `for` statement constructor, but you must include the semicolons that separate each section. If you omit a section of the constructor, be sure you include code within the body that will end the `for` statement or your program may get caught in an infinite loop.

The following code displays an example of a `for` statement that prints the contents of an array.

```
#include <iostream>
using namespace std;
void main() {
   char arStudentGrades[5];
   arStudentGrades[0] = 'A';     // first element
   arStudentGrades[1] = 'B';     // second element
   arStudentGrades[2] = 'C';     // third element
   arStudentGrades[3] = 'D';     // fourth element
   arStudentGrades[4] = 'F';     // fifth element
   for (int ctCount = 0; ctCount < 5; ++ctCount) {
     cout << arStudentGrades[ctCount] << endl;
  }
  cout << endl;
}
```

As you can see in the example, the counter is initialized, evaluated, and incremented within the constructor. You do not need to include a declaration for the ctCount variable before the `for` statement, nor do you need to increment the count variable within the body of the `for` statement. Figure 3-29 shows the output of the program.

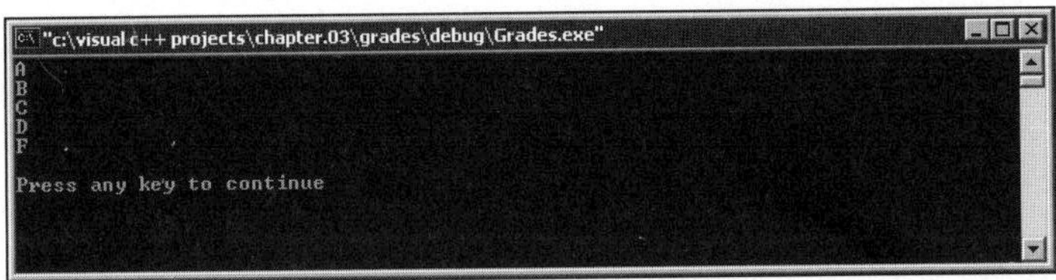

Figure 3-29 Output of a program with a `for` statement that displays the contents of an array

You can create looping statements that are controlled by counters more efficiently using `for` statements than using `while` statements. Using a `for` statement is more efficient because you do not need as many lines of code. Consider the following `while` statement:

```
int ctCount = 1;
while (ctCount <= 5) {
  cout << ctCount << endl;
  ++ctCount;
}
```

You can create the preceding `while` statement more efficiently using a `for` statement as follows:

```
for (int ctCount = 1; ctCount <= 5; ++ctCount) {
    cout << ctCount << endl;
}
```

There are times, however, when using a `while` statement is preferable to using a `for` statement. If you do not use a counter to update the conditional expression or if the counter must be updated from the body of the looping statement, a `while` construction works better than a `for` construction. The following code relies on a value returned from a cin statement, rather than a counter, for program control.

```
char cKey = 'Y';
while (cKey == 'Y') {
  cout << "Press an uppercase Y to redisplay this text. ";
  cin >> cKey;
}
```

You could accomplish the same task using a `for` statement, but in this case the third part of the `for` statement constructor that updates the counter is unnecessary. Therefore, this code is better written using a `while` statement. If you use a `for` statement instead of a **while** statement in the preceding example, you must leave out the update section from the **for** statement constructor. You must also remember to leave in the semicolon that separates the conditional section from the update section. If you leave the update section in the constructor, you could create an infinite loop. The following code performs essentially the same task as the preceding **while** example, but causes an infinite loop because the constructor always changes the cKey variable to *Y* with each iteration. No matter how many times you press any key other than *Y*, the **for** constructor reassigns *Y* to the variable to each time the code repeats, causing an infinite loop.

```
for (char cKey = 'Y'; cKey == 'Y'; cKey = 'Y') {
     cout << "Press an uppercase Y to redisplay this text: ";
     cin >> cKey;
}
```

To make the above **for** loop function correctly without causing an infinite loop, you must remove the update section from the constructor, as follows:

```
for (char cKey = 'Y'; cKey == 'Y';) {
     cout << "Press an uppercase Y to redisplay this text: ";
     cin >> cKey;
}
```

Nested Loops

Just as you can nest **if** and **if...else** statements, you can also nest looping statements. A looping statement contained within another looping statement is called a **nested loop**. You typically nest looping statements when you want to repeatedly execute a statement or a series of statements in addition to an original set of looping statements. One common nested looping example is the output of a right triangle to the console window using a series of asterisks, as shown in Figure 3-30.

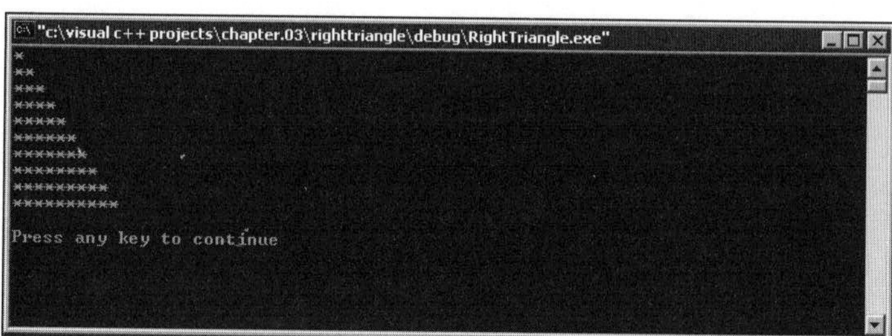

Figure 3-30 Output of right triangle program

You could create the triangle the hard way by using a series of cout statements, as follows:

```
cout << "*" << endl;
cout << "**" << endl;
cout << "***" << endl;
cout << "****" << endl;
cout << "*****" << endl;
cout << "******" << endl;
cout << "*******" << endl;
cout << "********" << endl;
cout << "*********" << endl;
cout << "**********" << endl << endl;
```


An easier method of creating the right triangle is to use one looping statement nested inside of another looping statement. The outer loop iterates 10 times, once for each of the rows in the triangle. Each iteration of the outer loop executes the nested (or "inner") loop. The inner loop executes however many times it is necessary to print the correct number of asterisks for each row, based on a counter variable. For example, for the first row, the inner loop executes once to print a single asterisk to the screen, for the second row, the inner loop executes twice to print two asterisks to the screen, and so on. Figure 3-31 shows an example of the program. Notice that the conditional expression for the inner loop evaluates the inner loop's counter variable (j) against the outer loop's counter variable (i) to determine how many asterisks to print for each row.

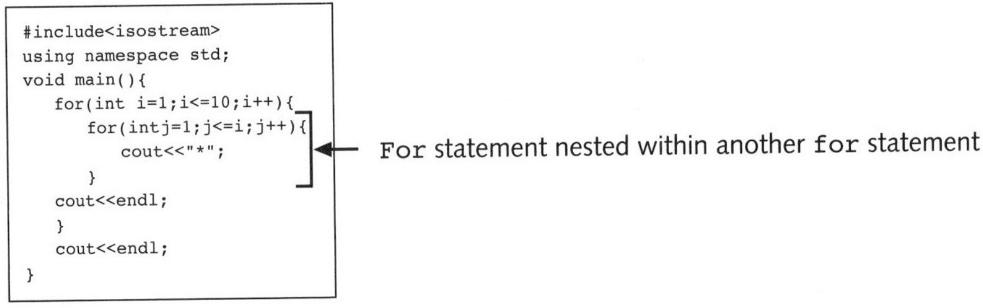

```
#include<isostream>
using namespace std;
void main(){
   for(int i=1;i<=10;i++){
      for(intj=1;j<=i;j++){
         cout<<"*";
      }
   cout<<endl;
   }
   cout<<endl;
}
```


Figure 3-31 Nested loop version of the right triangle program

Figure 3-32 shows a modified version of the right triangle program, but this time the outer loop is a `do...while` loop instead of a `for` loop.

```
#include<isostream>
using namespace std;
void main(){
   int i=1;
   do{
      for(intj=1;j<=i;j++){
         cout<<"*";
      }
   cout<<endl;
   i++;
   }while(i<=10);
   cout<<endl;
}
```

For statement nested within a `do...while` statement

Figure 3-32 Right triangle program with a `do...while` outer loop

Next, you will create a final version of the Chemistry Quiz program that uses a single `for` statement containing a nested `if` statement to score the quiz. Although the `for` statement you create is somewhat more complicated than using the `if`, `if...else`, and `switch` statements, it takes up considerably fewer lines of code. You will also include code that scores the entire quiz after a user is finished, instead of grading the quiz answer by answer.

To create the final version of the Chemistry Quiz program:

1. Return to the **ChemistryQuiz4.cpp** source file in the Code Editor window and choose **Select All** from the Edit menu. Once the code is highlighted, select **Copy** from the Edit menu. You will copy the highlighted code into a new project, rather than retyping it.
2. Close the ChemistryQuiz4 project by selecting **Close Solution** from the File menu.
3. Create a new Win32 Project named **ChemistryQuizFinal** in the **Chapter.03** folder in your Visual C++ Projects folder. Be sure to clear the **Create directory for Solution** check box in the New Project dialog box. In the Application Settings tab of the Win32 Application Wizard dialog box, select **Console application** as the application type, click the **Empty project** checkbox, and then click the **Finish** button. Once the project is created, add a C++ source file named **ChemistryQuizFinal.cpp**.
4. After the ChemistryQuizFinal.cpp file opens in the Code Editor window, select **Paste** from the Edit menu to paste the code you copied from the ChemistryQuiz4.cpp file.
5. Delete the entire scoreQuestions() function, and replace the scoreQuestions() function prototype with the two function prototypes shown in Figure 3-33.
6. Also as shown in Figure 3-33, create two global char arrays: arUserAnswers[] and arCorrectAnswers[]. The arUserAnswers[] array holds the answers selected each time the quiz runs, and the arCorrectAnswers[] array holds the correct response for each of the questions.

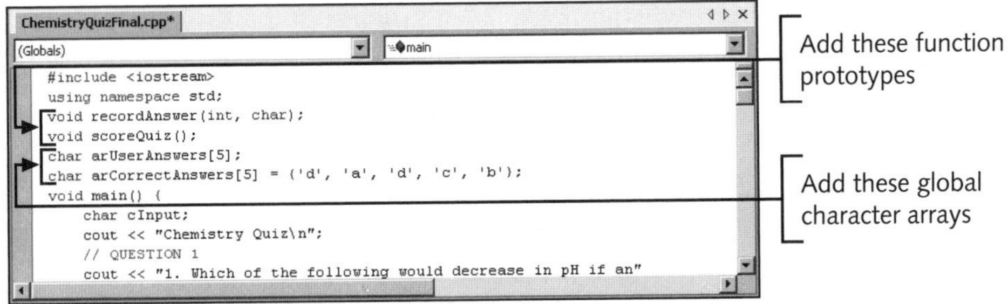

Figure 3-33 The scoreQuestions() function prototype replaced with new code

7. After the main() function, type the recordAnswer() function shown in Figure 3-34, which assigns the response from each question to the appropriate element in the arUserAnswers[] array. The program sends the actual question number (1–5) and answer (a–d) to the function from the main() function. To assign question responses to the correct element, 1 must be subtracted from the question variable because the elements in an array start with 0.

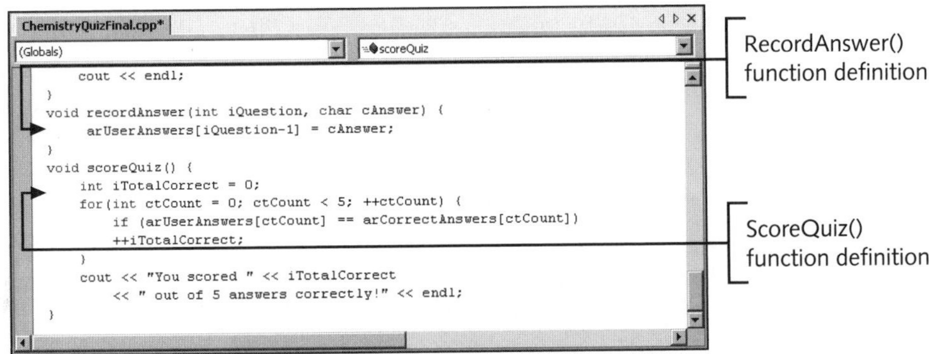

Figure 3-34 New function definitions added to ChemistrtyQuizFinal

8. Type the scoreQuiz() function definition, as show in Figure 3-34. You will call this function at the end of the main() function. Within the scoreQuiz() function, the iTotalCorrect variable will hold the number of correct answers, while the `for` loop scores the quiz. A counter named ctCount is initialized to a value of 0 because 0 is the starting index of an array. The conditional expression checks if ctCount is less than or equal to the number of elements in the arUserAnswers[] array. The ctCount variable is incremented by 1 with each iteration of the loop. The nested `if` statement in the `for` loop compares each element within the arUserAnswers[] array to each corresponding element within the arCorrectAnswers[] array. If the elements match, the iTotalCorrect variable is incremented by 1. The cout statement shows how many questions were answered correctly.

9. In the main() function, change the name of the function called after each question from scoreQuestions() to **recordAnswer()**. Be sure to include the question number and cInput arguments. For example, the statement for question 1 should read `recordAnswer(1, cInput);`.

10. Finally, as shown in Figure 3-35, add the statement **scoreQuiz();** that calls the scoreQuiz() function immediately after the last recordAnswer() function call in the main() function.

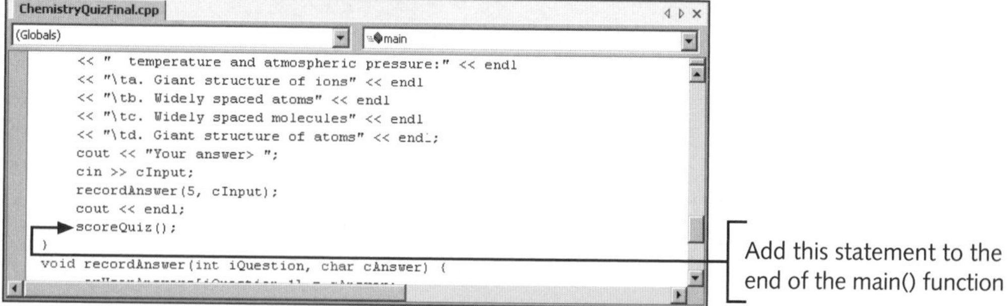

Figure 3-35 The scoreQuiz() function call statement added to the main() function

11. Build and execute the ChemistryQuizFinal project. Test the program by answering all five questions. Your output should appear similar to Figure 3-36, depending on how many questions you answered correctly.

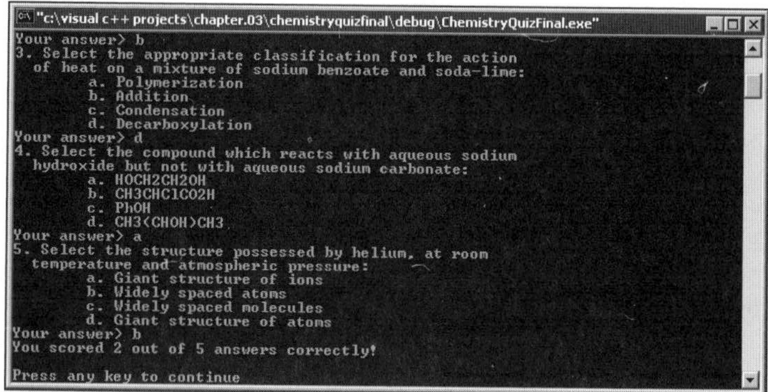

Figure 3-36 Output of ChemistryQuizFinal

12. Press any key to close the command window.

`continue` Statements

Suppose you want a program to loop through the elements of an array containing a list of stocks. For stocks worth more than $10, you want the program to print information to the screen, such as purchase price, number of shares, and so on. You want the program to skip stocks worth less than $10 and move on to a new stock. Earlier you learned that you could use a **break** statement to halt execution of a looping statement. But with a **break** statement, execution leaves the loop altogether and the next statement following the loop executes. Is there a method for stopping and restarting a loop? For instance, in the stocks program, for stocks worth less than $10, you want program execution to stop and restart at the beginning of the loop for the next stock. The **continue** statement halts a looping statement and restarts the loop with a new iteration. You use the `continue` statement when you want to stop the loop for the current iteration, but want the loop to continue with a new iteration. For example, the stocks program may use a `for` statement to loop through the elements of an array containing a list of stocks. For stocks worth more than $10, you print information to the screen, such as purchase price, number of shares, and so on. However, you use the `continue` statement to skip stocks worth less than $10 and move on to a new iteration. The following code contains a `for` loop containing a `break` statement.

```
for(int ctCount = 1; ctCount <=5; ++ctCount) {
   if(ctCount == 3)
       break;
   cout << ctCount << endl;
}
```

The `for` loop in the preceding example contains an `if` statement that checks if the current value of ctCount equals 3. When ctCount equals 3, the `break` statement immediately ends the `for` loop. The output for the preceding `for` loop is as follows:

```
1
2
```

The following code displays the same `for` loop from the previous example, but with a `continue` statement.

```
for(int ctCount = 1; ctCount <=5; ++ctCount) {
   if(ctCount == 3)
       continue;
   cout << ctCount << endl;
}
```

In the preceding example, when ctCount equals 3, the `continue` statement stops the current iteration of the `for` loop, and the program skips printing the number 3. However, the loop continues to iterate until the conditional expression `ctCount <= 5` is false. The output is:

```
1
2
4
5
```

3

CHAPTER SUMMARY

- An expression is a combination of literal values, variables, operators, and other expressions that can be evaluated by the Visual C++ compiler to produce a result.
- Operands are variables and literals contained in an expression.
- Operators are unary, binary, or ternary symbols used in expressions to manipulate operands.
- Arithmetic operators are used to perform mathematical calculations, such as addition, subtraction, multiplication, and division in C++.
- Assignment operators are used for assigning a value to a variable.
- Comparison operators are used to compare two operands for equality and to determine if one numeric value is greater than another.
- The conditional operator (?:) is a ternary operator that executes one of two expressions, based on the results of a conditional expression.
- A conditional expression returns a Boolean value and determines whether to execute a conditional or looping statement.
- Logical operators are used for comparing two Boolean operands for equality.
- You must use a string function found in the cstring header file to manipulate character arrays.
- The concatenation operator (+) is used to combine two strings of the string class.
- Operator precedence is the order of priority in which operations in an expression are evaluated.
- Flow control is the process of determining the order in which statements are executed in a program.
- The `if` statement is used to execute specific programming code if the evaluation of a conditional expression returns true.
- The cin object reads information from the keyboard through the standard input stream.
- The `else` clause runs an alternate set of code if the conditional expression evaluated by an `if` statement returns a value of false.
- An `if` statement contained within another `if` statement is called a nested `if` statement. Similarly, an `if...else` statement contained within an `if` or `if...else` statement is called a nested `if...else` statement.
- The `switch` statement controls program flow by executing a specific set of statements depending on the value returned by an expression.

- A looping statement repeatedly executes a statement or a series of statements while a specific condition is true.
- The `while` statement is used for repeating a statement or series of statements as long as a given conditional expression evaluates to true.
- Each repetition of a looping statement is called an iteration.
- A counter is a variable that increments or decrements with each iteration of a looping statement.
- In an infinite loop, a looping statement never ends because its conditional expression is never updated.
- The `do...while` statement executes a statement or statements once, then repeats the execution as long as a given conditional expression evaluates to true.
- The `for` statement is used for repeating a statement or series of statements as long as a given conditional expression evaluates to true.
- A looping statement contained within another looping statement is called a nested loop.

Review Questions

1. Operators that require an operand before the operator and an operand after the operator are called ____________ operators.
   a. unary
   b. binary
   c. double
   d. multiplicity
2. The modulus operator (%) ____________.
   a. coverts an operand to base 16 (hexadecimal) format
   b. returns the absolute value of an operand
   c. calculates the percentage of one operand compared to another
   d. divides two operands and returns the remainder
3. What value is assigned to the dQuarters variable in the statement `double dQuarters = 10 / 4;`?
   a. 2
   b. 2.0
   c. 2.2
   d. 22

4. What value is assigned to the iReturnValue variable in the statement `iReturnValue = count++;`, assuming that the count variable contains the value 10?
   a. 10
   b. 11
   c. 12
   d. 20
5. What value is assigned to the bReturnValue variable in the statement `bReturnValue = 100 != 200;`?
   a. 100
   b. 200
   c. true
   d. false
6. The operator that returns true if either its left or right operand returns a value of true is the ______________ operand.
   a. ||
   b. ==
   c. %%
   d. &&
7. The ______________ operator is a ternary operator that executes one of two expressions, based on the results of a conditional expression.
   a. assignment (=)
   b. conditional (?:)
   c. equal (==)
   d. greater than (>=)
8. What is the correct syntax for a compound conditional expression that returns true if a variable named iCost is equal to 100 *or* if a variable named iValue is equal to 150?
   a. `(iCost == 100 && iValue == 150)`
   b. `(iCost == 100 || iValue == 150)`
   c. `(iCost == 100 == iValue == 150)`
   d. `(iCost == 100 != iValue == 150)`
9. The ______________ operator is used to combine two strings of the string class.
   a. logical and (&&)
   b. modulus (%)
   c. assignment (=)
   d. concatenation (+)

10. The operator with the highest order of precedence in C++ is the ________________.
    a. assignment operator
    b. addition/subtraction operator
    c. scope resolution operator
    d. parentheses ()

11. What is the value of the expression `4 * (2 + 3)`?
    a. 11
    b. –11
    c. 20
    d. 14
12. Which of the following is the correct syntax for an `if` statement?
    a.
    ```
    if (myVariable == 10);
    cout << "Your variable is equal to 10." << endl;
    ```
    b.
    ```
    if myVariable == 10
    cout << "Your variable is equal to 10." << endl;
    ```
    c.
    ```
    if (myVariable == 10)
    cout << "Your variable is equal to 10." << endl;
    ```
    d.
    ```
    if (myVariable == 10),
    cout << "Your variable is equal to 10." << endl;
    ```
13. An `if` statement can include multiple statements provided they ________________.
    a. execute after the closing semicolon of the `if` statement
    b. are not contained within a command block
    c. do not include other `if` statements
    d. are contained within a command block
14. Which is the correct syntax for receiving user input?
    a. `cin << variable;`
    b. `cin >> variable;`
    c. `stdin << variable;`
    d. `stdin >> variable;`
15. Which of the following statements is true?
    a. An `if` statement must be constructed with an `else` clause.
    b. An `else` clause can be constructed without an `if` statement.
    c. An `if` statement can be constructed without an `else` clause.
    d. An `else` clause cannot be constructed with an `if` statement.

16. The `switch` statement controls program flow by executing a specific set of statements depending on ________________.
    a. the result of an `if...else` statement
    b. the flow control header file that is included in the program
    c. whether an `if` statement executes from within a function
    d. the value returned by a conditional expression
17. When the value returned by a `switch` statement conditional expression does not match a `case` label, then the statements within the ________________ label execute.
    a. `exception`
    b. `else`
    c. `error`
    d. `default`
18. You can exit a `switch` statement by using a(n) ________________ statement.
    a. `break`
    b. `end`
    c. `quit`
    d. `complete`
19. Counter variables ________________.
    a. are used to count the number of times a looping statement has repeated
    b. count the number of times a function starts and stops
    c. are used to count how many times a C++ program has been executed
    d. are used only within `if` or `if...else` statements
20. Which of the following is the correct syntax for a `while` statement?

a.
```
while (ctCount <= 5, ++ ctCount) {
        cout << ctCount << endl;
}
```
b.
```
while (ctCount <= 5) {
        cout << ctCount << endl;
        ++ctCount;
}
```
c.
```
while (ctCount <= 5);

        cout << ctCount << endl;
        ++ctCount;
```
d.
```
while (ctCount <= 5; cout << ctCount << endl) {
        ++ ctCount;
}
```

21. An infinite loop is caused ________________.
    a. when you omit the closing brace for a decision making structure
    b. when a conditional expression never evaluates to false
    c. when a conditional expression never evaluates to true
    d. whenever you execute a `while` statement
22. If a `do...while` statement conditional expression evaluates to false, how many times will the `do...while` statement execute?
    a. never
    b. once
    c. twice
    d. repeatedly—this conditional expression causes an infinite loop.
23. Which of the following is the correct syntax for a `do...while` statement?
    a.
    ```
    do while (ctCount < 10) {
         cout << "Printed from a do...while loop." << endl;
    }
    ```
    b.
    ```
    do { while (ctCount < 10)
           cout << "Printed from a do...while loop." << endl;
    }
    ```
    c.
    ```
    do {
           cout << "Printed from a do...while loop." << endl;
           while (ctCount < 10)
    }
    ```
    d.
    ```
    do {
           cout << "Printed from a do...while loop." << endl;
    } while (ctCount < 10);
    ```
24. Which of the following is the correct syntax for a `for` statement?
    a.
    ```
    for (int ctCount = 0; ctCount < 10; ++ ctCount)
         cout << "Printed from a for statement." << endl;
    ```
    b.
    ```
    for (int ctCount = 0, ctCount < 10, ++ ctCount)
         cout << "Printed from a for statement." << endl;
    ```
    c.
    ```
    for {
         cout << "Printed from a for statement." << endl;
    } while (int ctCount = 0; ctCount < 10; ++ ctCount)
    ```
    d.
    ```
    for (int ctCount = 0; ctCount < 10);
         cout << "Printed from a for statement." << endl;
         ++ ctCount;
    ```

25. When does a `for` statement initialization expression execute?
    a. when the `for` statement begins executing
    b. with each repetition of the `for` statement
    c. when the counter variable is incremented
    d. when the `for` statement ends
26. The ______________ statement halts a looping statement, but instead of exiting the loop construct entirely, it restarts the loop with a new iteration.
    a. `proceed`
    b. `reiterate`
    c. `restart`
    d. `continue`

PROGRAMMING EXERCISES

1. What value is assigned to the iMathResult variable in each the following expressions?
   - `iMathResult = 14 + 2;`
   - `iMathResult = 7 - 14;`
   - `iMathResult = 18 * 4 / 13;`
   - `iMathResult = 37 % 6;`
2. What value is assigned to the bComparison variable in each the following expressions?
   - `bool bComparison = 2 == 3;`
   - `bool bComparison = 2 >= 3;`
   - `bool bComparison = 2 <= 3;`
   - `bool bComparison = (3 > 2) && (2 > 3) ;`
   - `bool bComparison = (2 > 3) || (3 > 2) ;`
3. Rewrite the following code using integer variables and add a modulus statement to return the decimal portion of the division:

```
double dDollars = 100;
double dFrancs = 7;
double dExchange = dDollars / dFrancs;
cout << "There are " << dExchange
  << " French Francs in $100" << endl;
```

4. Rewrite the following statement so the iCurCustomer variable is assigned the contents of iNextCustomer *before* its value is incremented by one:

```
iCurCustomer = iNextCustomer = iNextCustomer + 1;
```

5. Rewrite the following statements using assignment operators:

   - `dValue = dValue + 5;`
   - `dValue = dValue * 14;`
   - `dValue = dValue - 18;`
   - `dValue = dValue / 6;`
   - `iValue = iValue % 5;`

6. Use parentheses to modify the order of precedence of the following code so the final result of idNumber is 581.25. (The result of iNumber using the current syntax is 637.5.)

```
double dNumber = 75;
dNumber = dNumber + 30 * dNumber / 4;
```

7. Rewrite the following **if** statement using the conditional operator:

```
double dInterestRate = 7.5;
if (dInterestRate > 6.67)
   cout << "Your interest rate is higher than the prime
interest rate as of August 2001.";
else
   cout << "Your interest rate is lower than the prime
interest rate as of August 2001.";
```

8. Modify the following code so it uses a compound conditional expression instead of a nested **if** statement:

```
double dGas = 1.57;

if (dGas > 1) {

   if (dGas < 2)

    cout << "Gas prices are between $1.00 and $2.00"
<< endl;

}
```

9. Add code to the following **switch** statement so that after the statements in a **case** label execute, the **switch** statement ends.

```
switch (iAreaCode) {
   case 617:
      cout << "Boston's area code is "
        << iAreaCode << endl;
   case 212:
      cout << "Manhattan's area code is "
        << iAreaCode << endl;
   case 415:
```

3

```
          cout << "San Francisco's area code is "
            << iAreaCode << endl;
         case 813:
          cout << "St. Petersburg's area code is "
            << iAreaCode << endl;
       case 508:
          cout << "Worcester's area code is "
            << iAreaCode << endl;
}
```

10. Rewrite the **switch** statement in the preceding exercise using an **if...else** statement.

11. Modify the **switch** statement from Exercise 6 so that a default value of *You did not enter a valid area code* prints to the screen if none of the **case** labels matches the iAreaCode variable.
}

12. The following code should print the numbers 1 through 100 to the screen. The code contains several logic flaws, however, that prevent it from running correctly. Identify and fix the logic flaws.

```
int ctCount = 0;
int arNumbers[100];
while (ctCount >= 100) {
   arNumbers[ctCount] = ctCount;
   ++ctCount;
}
while (ctCount >= 100) {
   cout << arNumbers[ctCount] << endl;
}
```

13. Use nested loops to print the following pattern to the screen:

```
*******************
*******************
*********
*********
*******************
*******************
*********
*********
*******************
*******************
*********
*********
*******************
*******************
*********
*********
*******************
*******************
```

PROGRAMMING PROJECTS

Save your solutions to the following projects in the Chapter.03 folder in your Visual C++ Projects folder.

1. Write a program that allows a user to enter the length, width, and depth of their swimming pool (for simplicity's sake, assume that the pool does not have a shallow end or a deep end). Calculate the volume of the pool and display a message to the user with the result. Save the project as SwimmingPool.
2. Write a program that allows a user to enter a number of cents. Determine how many dollars the cents make up and print the number of dollars and remaining cents to the screen. Save the project as CentsToDollars.
3. Write a program that allows a user to enter the number of inches it rained during each month of the year. Assign each value to the corresponding element in a 12-element array. Calculate the average yearly rainfall using the array elements, and then print out the rainfall for each individual month, followed by the total yearly rainfall and then the average monthly rainfall. Save the project as Rainfall.
4. Create a program that calculates an employee's weekly gross salary, based on the number of hours worked and hourly wage entered by the user. Compute any hours over 40 as time-and-a-half. Print your results to the screen. Save the project as Wages.
5. You can determine whether a year is a leap year by testing if it is divisible by 4. However, years that are also divisible by 100 are not leap years, unless they are also divisible by 400, in which case they are leap years. Write a program that allows a user to enter a year and then determines whether the year entered is a leap year. Print a message to the user stating whether the year they entered is a standard year or a leap year. Save the project as LeapYear.
6. Any two sides of a triangle must be greater than the length of the third side in order for the segments to form a triangle. For example, 8, 6, and 12 can form a triangle because the sum of any two of the three segments is greater than the third segment. However, 25, 5, and 15 cannot form a triangle because the sum of segments 5 and 15 are not greater than the length of segment 25. Using this logic, write a program that allows a user to enter three integers, one for each side of a triangle. Test whether the three sides can form a triangle. Display a message to the user that states whether their segments can form a triangle. Save the project as Triangle.
7. Create a program that determines sales territories by state. Create a decision-making structure that evaluates a state selected by the user and prints the name of the region where the state is located: North, South, East, West, Midwest, Southwest, and so on. Store the state entered by the user in a string class variable. Print an output statement to the screen that states the sales territory where the state is located. For example, if a user selects California, then print "The state you entered is in the Western sales region" to the screen. What is the best decision structure to use for this type of a program? Save the project as SalesRegions.

8. Write a program that allows a user to enter a number between one and ten. If the number is less than one or greater than ten, prompt the user to reenter a correct number. Once the user enters a number between one and ten, display the number and end the program. Save the project as CheckNumber.
9. When you create a `char` variable and assign to it a letter, you can increase or decrease the letter assigned to the `char` variable by adding or subtracting an integer to or from the variable. For example, if you have a `char` variable named cLetter and you assign to it the letter A, you can change the value of the cLetter variable to B by using a statement similar to `++cLetter;`. With this technique in mind, write a program that uses a looping statement to print out the uppercase letters of the alphabet. You will need to test whether your counter has reached 26—the number of letters in the alphabet. Save the project as Alphabet.
10. Write a program that allows a user to enter a number between 1 and 999. Determine whether the number is a prime number and print your results to the screen. A prime number is a number that can only be divided by itself or by one. Examples of prime numbers include 1, 3, 5, 13, and 17. You will need to use a looping statement to test all division possibilities. Save the project as PrimeNumber.

CHAPTER

4

DEBUGGING

In this chapter you will learn:

- About debugging concepts
- How to use basic debugging techniques
- About the Visual C++ debugger
- How to trace program execution with step commands
- How to trace variables and expressions with debug windows
- How to use the Call Stack window
- About Visual C++ language bugs and debugging resources

If debugging is the art of removing bugs, then programming must be the art of inserting them.

Attributed to Edsger W. Dijkstra

PREVIEW: VISUAL C++ DEBUGGING TOOLS

In this chapter, you will not create any new programs. Instead, you will learn how to use the Visual C++ debugging tools to locate errors in an existing program named Moving Estimator. The Moving Estimator program could be used by a shipping company to calculate the costs of moving a household from one location to another, based on distance, weight, and several other factors. The program is fairly simple and uses various functions to calculate the various types of moving costs, along with a function named calcTotalEstimate() that totals the estimate. You can examine a completed version of the program in the MovingEstimatorNoBugs folder on your Data Disk. You should be able to figure out on your own how the program operates. Figure 4-1 shows an example of the Moving Estimator program running in a console window after some moving costs have been entered.

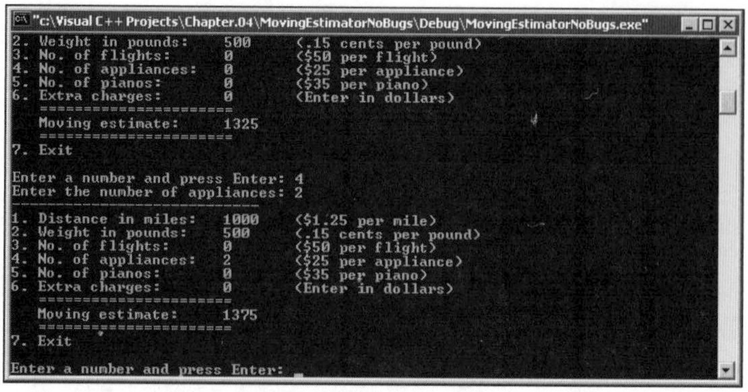

Figure 4-1 Moving Estimator program running in a console window

You will not be working with the version of the program contained in the MovingEstimatorNoBugs folder. Rather, you will work with a version of the program, located in the MovingEstimatorWithBugs folder that contains bugs. You need to use the "buggy" version in order to learn this chapter's debugging techniques. If you get stuck, however, you can use the no-bugs version as a reference.

Some of the most important debugging tools are the "step" tools that help you trace the flow of execution in your program as it executes. Figure 4-2 shows the Moving Estimator program in the IDE as it is paused in break mode. Break mode refers to a temporary pause in program execution. Your program enters break mode once Visual C++ encounters a break point that you set on a statement. Once in break mode, you use the step commands to walk through your program and monitor the results of each statement as it executes. Notice that the Moving Estimator program is still running in the background while you monitor the effects of each statement in break mode. Visual C++ also includes a Debug window, a Debug toolbar, and several debugger windows that assist you in monitoring the values of specific variables in your programs in order to assess their behavior during program execution.

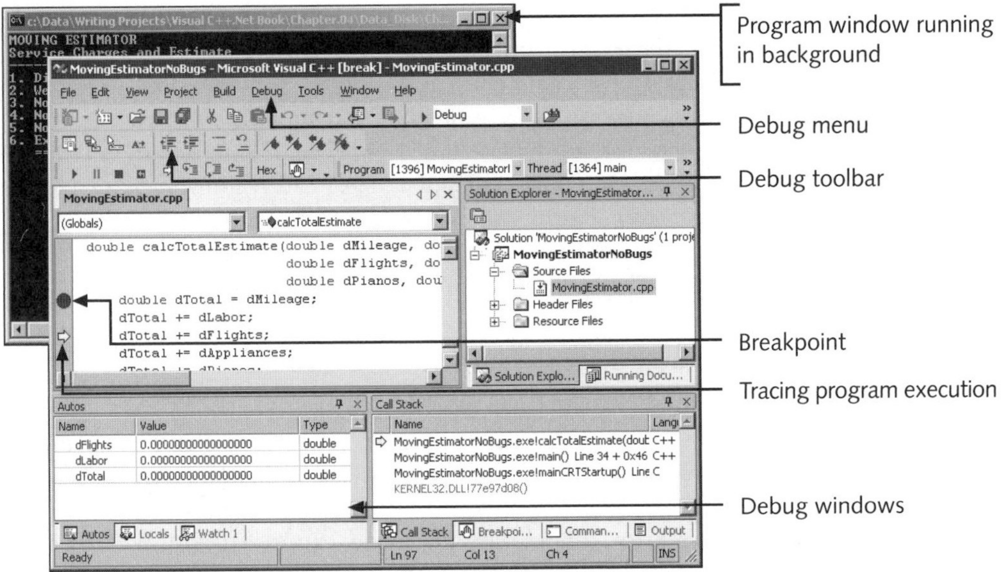

Figure 4-2 Moving Estimator program in break mode

UNDERSTANDING DEBUGGING

Regardless of experience, knowledge, and ability, all programmers create errors in their programs at one time or another. As you learned at the start of this textbook, debugging describes the act of tracing and resolving errors in a program. Debugging is an essential skill for any programmer, regardless of the programming language and the programmer's level of experience. In this chapter, you will learn techniques and tools to help you trace and resolve errors in your Visual C++ programs.

Error Types

Three main types of errors can occur in a Visual C++ program: syntax errors, run-time errors, and logic errors. **Syntax errors** occur when you enter code that the compiler does not recognize. Syntax errors in C++ include invalid statements or statements that are entered incorrectly, such as when a closing parenthesis for a function is missing. Other types of syntax errors include incorrectly spelled or mistyped words. For example, if you were to enter the statement `coute << "Hello World" << endl;`, you would receive a syntax error when you built the program because the cout statement is misspelled as *coute*. Similarly, the statement `Cout << "Hello World" << endl;` also causes a syntax error because the cout object is incorrectly entered with an uppercase *C*. (Remember, C++ is case sensitive.) As you are aware, when you build a project you will receive a build message if your program includes a syntax error. You have probably seen more than your fair share of compiler error build messages in the programs you have been creating. You will examine how to interpret build messages shortly.

If your Visual C++ program encounters a problem while it is executing, the problem is called a **run-time error**. Run-time errors differ from syntax errors in that they do not necessarily represent C++ language errors. Instead, run-time errors occur when your program encounters code that it cannot handle. Some of the most common types of run-time errors occur for numeric calculations. For example, run-time errors occur if you attempt to divide by 0. You will not receive a warning or error message, but the result of the division calculation will be incorrect or erratic. For example, the following code causes a run-time error because the iNumberOfHours variable is set to 0. The dGrossHourlyPay variable is assigned an unusable value of *1.#INF*.

```
double dGrossPay = 1000;
int iNumberOfHours = 0;
double dGrossHourlyPay = dGrossPay / iNumberOfHours;
```

The Visual C++ compiler will warn you of other types of potential run-time errors. For example, another typical run-time error occurs if you attempt to divide by a variable that has not been initialized. You can still execute the program, but you run the risk of raising a run-time error. The following code causes a run-time error because the iNumberOfHours variable is not initialized:

```
double dGrossPay = 1000;
int iNumberOfHours;
double dGrossHourlyPay = dGrossPay / iNumberOfHours;
```

The compiler warns you of the run-time error in the preceding code by raising the following warning message when you build the program:

```
Run-Time Check Failure #3 - The variable 'iNumberOfHours'
is being used without being defined
```

Later in this section you will examine compiler errors and messages at length.

Logic errors are problems in the design of a program that prevent it from running as you anticipate it will run. The logic behind any program involves executing the various statements and procedures in the correct order to produce the desired results. For example, when you do the laundry, you normally wash, dry, iron, and then fold. If a laundry program irons, folds, dries, then washes, you have a logic error and the program executes incorrectly. One example of a logic error in a computer program includes multiplying two values when you mean to divide them, as in the following code:

```
int iDivisionResult = 10 * 2;
cout << "Ten divided by two is equal to "
     << iDivisionResult << endl;
```

Another example of a logic error is the creation of an infinite loop, in which a looping statement never ends because its conditional expression is never updated or is never false. The following code creates a **for** statement that results in the logic error of an infinite loop because the third argument in the **for** statement's constructor never changes the value of the ctCount variable.

```
for(int ctCount = 10; ctCount >= 0; ctCount) {
     cout << "We have liftoff in " + ctCount);
}
```

4

Because the ctCount variable is never updated in the preceding example, it will continue to have a value of 10 through each iteration of the loop, resulting in repeated output of the text *We have liftoff in 10.* To correct this logic error, you need to add a decrement operator to the third argument in the **for** statement's constructor, as follows:

```
for(int ctCount = 10; ctCount >= 0; --ctCount) {
     cout << "We have liftoff in " + ctCount);
}
```

Interpreting Build Messages

As was mentioned at the start of this textbook, the first line of defense against bugs in C++ programs are the build messages that appear in the Task List when the Visual C++ compiler encounters an error during the build process. Build messages are vital to the debugging process. There are two main types of build messages: compiler error messages and warning messages. Compiler error messages occur for any syntax errors in a program. Compiler error messages contain the name of the file in which the error occurred, the line number in the file, and a description of the error. You will find compiler errors most useful when you have a syntax error in a line of code. For instance, consider the following code:

```
void calcMileageCost() {
        int iMiles = 0; double dMileageCost = 0;
        cout << "Enter the mileage: ";
        cin >> iMiles;
        dMileageCost = iMiles * 1.25
}
```

The statement **dMileageCost = iMiles * 1.25** raises the following compiler error message because it does not include an ending semicolon:

```
error C2143: syntax error : missing ';' before '}'
```

Note that you do not receive compiler error messages for logic errors because computers are not smart enough (yet) to identify a flaw in your logic. For example, if you create an infinite loop with a **for** statement, the interpreter has no way of telling whether you really wanted to continually execute the **for** statement's code. Later in this chapter, you will learn how to trace the flow of your program's execution in order to locate logic errors.

Let us consider another example of error messages that do not exactly identify the cause of an error. The `cout << dResult << endl;` statement in the following code causes an error because C++ cannot locate the dResult variable within the scope of the function. The dResult variable is not in scope because it is declared inside the `if` statement. Therefore, it is not visible to the rest of the calculatePercentage() function, which causes the error. Although the `cout << dResult << endl;` statement generates the error because it attempts to access a variable that is not in scope, the real bug in the code is that the dResult variable must be declared outside of the `if` statement.

```
void calculatePercentage() {
     double dAmount = 500;
   double dPercentage = .05;
   if (dAmount < 100) {
         double dResult;
         dResult = dAmount * dPercentage;
   }
     cout << dResult << endl;
}
```

Warning messages occur for any potential problems that might exist in your code, but that are not serious enough to cause a compiler error message. One of the more common warning messages you might see occurs when you declare a variable, but do not use it in your program. For example, consider again the following function, which you first saw in Chapter 1:

```
void calculateProfits() {
     int iPayRate = 15;
     int iNumHours = 40;
     double dGrossPay;
     double dNetPay = (iPayRate * iNumHours) / .20;
}
```

Because the dGrossPay variable is never used, the following warning message appears in the Task List:

```
warning C4101: 'dGrossPay' : unreferenced local variable
```

An unused variable is not really a problem in a C++ program. However, the compiler issues a warning about any unused variables and other unused programming elements in order to help you write cleaner and more efficient code. Although an unused variable will not cause problems, other types of issues that generate warning messages could cause problems. For example, consider the following modified version of the calculateProfits() function:

```
void calculateProfits() {
     int iPayRate = 15;
     int iNumHours = 40.5;
     double dNetPay = (iPayRate * iNumHours) / .20;
}
```

The statement `int iNumHours = 40.5;` causes a more serious warning message because it attempts to assign a floating-point value to an integer variable. This statement will not prevent the program from compiling, but it will result in the loss of data. For this reason, Visual C++ raises the following warning message:

```
warning C4244: 'initializing' : conversion from
'double' to 'int', possible loss of data
```

Next, you will use build messages to help locate bugs in the Moving Estimator program.

To use build messages to help locate bugs in the Moving Estimator program:

1. Create a Chapter.04 folder in your Visual C++ Projects Folder.
2. Copy the **MovingEstimatorWithBugs** folder from the Chapter.04 folder on your Data Disk to the Chapter.04 folder in your Visual C++ Projects folder.
3. Open the **MovingEstimatorWithBugs** project from the MovingEstimatorWithBugs folder in your Visual C++ Projects folder.
4. Highlight the **MovingEstimatorWithBugs** project icon in Solution Explorer and select **Properties** from the Project menu. Click the C/C++ folder in the Property Pages dialog box and make sure that the warning level is set to Level 3. Click **OK** to close the dialog box.
5. Build the project. You should receive 10 build messages.
6. Start with the first message in the Task List, which reads as follows:

   ```
   warning C4518: 'int ' : storage-class or type
   specifier(s) unexpected here; ignored
   ```

7. Double-click the error message, and the MovingEstimator.cpp file opens to the first statement in the main() function. It is not readily obvious from the preceding build message, but the compiler does not recognize the statement because the main() function is missing its opening brace. Fix the problem by adding the missing opening brace to the main() function, as shown in Figure 4-3.

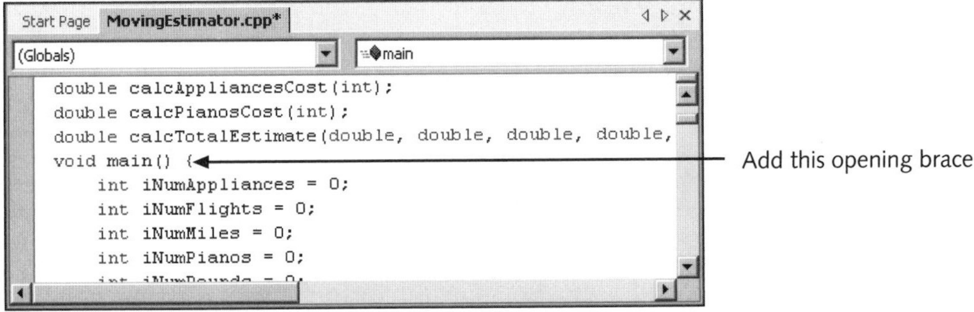

Figure 4-3 Missing opening brace added to the main() function

8. Rebuild the project. This time you should receive 11 compiler error messages and a warning error message. The first compiler error message reads as follows:

   `error C2062: type 'double' unexpected`

9. Double-click the error message, and the header definition for the calcMileageCost() function is highlighted. Again, although not readily obvious, the problem is that the `else` clause in the preceding `while` statement is missing a closing brace. Fix the problem by adding the closing brace, as shown in Figure 4-4.

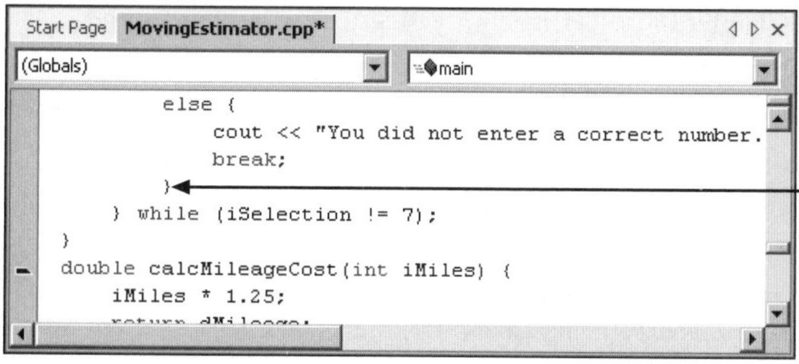

```
        else {
            cout << "You did not enter a correct number.
            break;
        }
    } while (iSelection != 7);
}
double calcMileageCost(int iMiles) {
    iMiles * 1.25;
```

Add this closing brace

Figure 4-4 Missing closing brace added to `else` clause

10. Rebuild the project again. This time you should receive two build errors. The first build message reads as follows:

    `warning C4552: '*' : operator has no effect; expected operator with side-effect`

11. Double-click the warning, which highlights the `iMiles * 1.25;` statement in the calcMileageCost() function. This statement is incomplete and should assign the result of the multiplication operation to the dMileage variable. Modify the statement so that it reads **`double dMileage = iMiles * 1.25;`**.

12. Rebuild the project one more time. You should receive the following build error:

    `error C4716: 'calcTotalEstimate' : must return a value`

13. The preceding error message occurs because the calcTotalEstimate() function does not include a `return` statement. Double-click the preceding error message and the calcTotalEstimate() function's closing brace is highlighted. Fix the problem by adding the statement **`return dTotal;`** before the calcTotalEstimate() function's closing brace.

14. Rebuild the project a final time, and you should receive no more build messages. However, do not try to use the program yet because it still contains plenty of bugs.

BASIC DEBUGGING TECHNIQUES

Although Visual C++ contains a variety of advanced debugging tools, which you will learn about later in this chapter, using advanced debugging tools for simple types of bugs can be overkill. If you know that a bug in your program is being caused by a complicated program design that includes classes and other advanced techniques, then you should use Visual C++'s advanced debugging tools. If you are fairly certain, however, that the bug in your program is being caused by something simple, such as a variable being assigned the wrong value at some point, then you can use some basic debugging tools with which you are already familiar to help you find the error. These basic debugging tools include tracing console application errors with output statements, using comments, and analyzing your logic.

Tracing Console Application Errors with Output Statements

If you are unable to locate a bug in your program using error messages, or if the bug is a logic error that does not generate error messages, then you must trace your code. **Tracing** is the examination of individual statements in an executing program. Although you will use Visual C++'s built-in tracing tools later, one of the simplest tracing tools you can use is an output statement (cout) in a console application. You use output statements placed at different points in your program to print the contents of a variable, an array, or the value returned from a function. Using this technique, you can monitor values as they change during program execution. Output statements are especially useful when you want to trace a bug in your program by analyzing a list of values.

Later in this book, you will create MFC programs that do not use console application windows for their program output. Once you start creating MFC programs, be aware that you can still use console applications to trace code from the programs. Although you cannot actually use MFC classes in a console application, you can use console applications to test the code contained in an MFC program. For example, you may have a function in an MFC program that you want to test separately from the MFC program itself in order to be sure that it is operating correctly. Quickly viewing a list of variable values in a console application window is a simple, yet effective, technique for testing many types of code. Once you are sure the code is operating correctly, you can then plug it back into your MFC program. Simplified, temporary programs that are used for testing functions and other code are called **driver programs**. Driver programs do not have to be elaborate; they can be as simple as a main() function and the function you are testing. They allow you to isolate and test an individual function without having to worry about user interface elements, derived-MFC classes, and other programming constructs that form your application's functionality as a whole.

A testing technique that is essentially the opposite of driver programs is the use of stub functions. **Stub functions** are empty functions that serve as placeholders (or "stubs") for a program's actual functions. Typically, a stub function returns a hard-coded value that represents the result of the actual function. Using stub functions allows you to check for errors in your program from the ground up. You start by swapping stub functions for the actual function definition. Each time you add the actual function definition, you rebuild and test the program. You repeat the process for each function in your program. This technique allows you to isolate and correct bugs within functions, or to correct bugs that occur as a result of how an individual function operates within your program as a whole.

For an example of how to trace a bug using output statements, examine the function in Figure 4-5, which calculates weekly net pay, rounded to the nearest integer. The function is syntactically correct and does not generate an error message. However, it is not returning the correct result, which should be 554.8. Instead, the function is returning a value of 2.50397e+007.

```
double calculatePay() {
     double dPayRate = 20;
     double dNumHours = 40;
     double dGrossPay = dPayRate * dNumHours;
     double dFederalTaxes = dGrossPay * .15;
     double dStateTaxes = dGrossPay * .08;
     double dSocialSecurity = dGrossPay * .062;
     double dMedicare = dGrossPay * .0145;
     double dNetPay = dGrossPay - dFederalTaxes;
     dNetPay *= dStateTaxes;
     dNetPay *= dSocialSecurity;
     dNetPay *= dMedicare;
     return dNetPay;
}
```

Figure 4-5 calculatePay() function with a logic error

To trace the problem, you place the function in a driver program and add an output statement at the point in the program where you think the error may be located. For example, the first thing you might want to check in the calculatePay() function is whether the dGrossPay variable is calculating correctly. To check whether the program calculates dGrossPay correctly, place an output statement in the function following the calculation of the dGrossPay variable, as shown in the driver program in Figure 4-6.

It is helpful to place output statements that are used to trace program execution at a different level of indentation in order to clearly mark them as not being part of the actual function.

Because the dGrossPay variable is calculated correctly as 800, start checking the dNetPay variable by moving the output statement down a few lines. You continue with this technique until you discover the error. The calculatePay() function does not perform properly because the lines that add the dStateTaxes, dSocialSecurity, and dMedicare variables to the dNetPay variable are incorrect. They use the multiplication assignment operator (*=) instead of the subtraction assignment operator (-=). A correct version of the function is shown in Figure 4-7.

```
#include <iostream>
using namespace std;
double calculatePay();
void main() {
     double dReturnValue = calculatePay();
cout << "value returned from calculatePay(): "
     << dReturnValue << endl;
}
double calculatePay() {
     double dPayRate = 20;
     double dNumHours = 40;
     double dGrossPay = dPayRate * dNumHours;
cout << "dGrossPay is " << dGrossPay << endl;
     double dFederalTaxes = dGrossPay * .15;
     double dStateTaxes = dGrossPay * .08;
     double dSocialSecurity = dGrossPay * .062;
     double dMedicare = dGrossPay * .0145;
     double dNetPay = dGrossPay - dFederalTaxes;
     dNetPay *= dStateTaxes;
     dNetPay *= dSocialSecurity;
     dNetPay *= dMedicare;
     return dNetPay;
}
```

Figure 4-6 Output statements in a driver program

```
double calculatePay () {
     double dPayRate = 20;
     double dNumHours = 40;
     double dGrossPay = dPayRate * dNumHours;
     double dFederalTaxes = dGrossPay * .15;
     double dStateTaxes = dGrossPay * .08;
     double dSocialSecurity = dGrossPay * .062;
     double dMedicare = dGrossPay * .0145;
     double dNetPay = dGrossPay - dFederalTaxes;
     dNetPay -= dStateTaxes;
     dNetPay -= dSocialSecurity;
     dNetPay -= dMedicare;
     return dNetPay;
}
```

Figure 4-7 Corrected version of the calculatePay() function

An alternative to using a single output statement is to place multiple output statements throughout your code to check values as the code executes. For example, you could trace the calculatePay() function using multiple output statements, as shown in Figure 4-8. Output statements are placed throughout the function to track the values assigned to the dGrossPay and dNetPay variables. Using the output shown in Figure 4-9, you can then evaluate each variable in the calculatePay() function as the values change throughout the function's execution.

Later in this chapter, you will use more sophisticated tools for tracing the values of variables as they change throughout a program's execution. However, the important thing you should learn from the output statement technique is that tracing gives you an opportunity to evaluate variables at different points in your program in order to locate the cause of an error.

```
#include <iostream>
using namespace std;
double calculatePay();
void main() {
     double dReturnValue = calculatePay();
cout << "value returned from calculatePay(): "
     << dReturnValue << endl;
}
double calculatePay() {
     double dPayRate = 20;
     double dNumHours = 40;
     double dGrossPay = dPayRate * dNumHours;
cout << "dGrossPay is " << dGrossPay << endl;
     double dFederalTaxes = dGrossPay * .15;
     double dStateTaxes = dGrossPay * .08;
     double dSocialSecurity = dGrossPay * .062;
     double dMedicare = dGrossPay * .0145;
     double dNetPay = dGrossPay - dFederalTaxes;
cout << "dNetPay minus federal taxes is "
     << dNetPay << endl;;
     dNetPay *= dStateTaxes;
cout << "dNetPay minus state taxes is "
     << dNetPay << endl;
     dNetPay *= dSocialSecurity;
cout << "dNetPay minus social security is "
     << dNetPay << endl;
     dNetPay *= dMedicare;
cout << "dNetPay minus Medicare is "
     << dNetPay << endl;
     return dNetPay;
}
```

Figure 4-8 calculatePay() function with multiple output statements

```
"c:\visual c++ projects\chapter.04\payroll\debug\Payroll.exe"
dGrossPay is 800
dNetPay minus federal taxes is 680
dNetPay minus state taxes is 43520
dNetPay minus social security is 2.15859e+006
dNetPay minus Medicare is 2.50397e+007
value returned from calculatePay(): 2.50397e+007
Press any key to continue
```

Figure 4-9 Output of calculatePay() function with multiple output statements

Next, you will use output statements to help locate bugs in the Moving Estimator program's calcTotalEstimate() function. The calcTotalEstimate() function should return a total of the dMileage, dLabor, dFlights, dAppliances, dPianos, and dExtras variables. However, you need to be sure that the calculations are being performed properly before you can confidently include the function in the Moving Estimator program. The calcTotalEstimate() function is a very simple function, but, it serves the purpose of demonstrating how to use a driver program to debug a function.

To use output statements to help locate bugs in the Moving Estimator program's calcTotalEstimate() function:

1. Return to the Moving Estimator project in Visual C++, highlight the calcTotalEstimate() function, and then copy it to the Clipboard by selecting **Copy** from the **Edit** menu or by pressing **Ctrl+C**.

2. Select **Close Solution** from the File menu to close the MovingEstimatorWithBugs project.
3. Create a new empty Win32 console application project named **FunctionCheck**. Save the project in the **Chapter.04** folder in your Visual C++ Projects folders. Once the project is created, add a C++ source file named **FunctionCheck**.
4. As shown in Figure 4-10, type the preprocessor directive that gives the program access to the iostream library along with a statement telling it to use the std namespace. Also, add the function prototype for the calcTotalEstimate() function. In this version, the function returns a `double` value for testing purposes instead of being declared with a `void` data type.

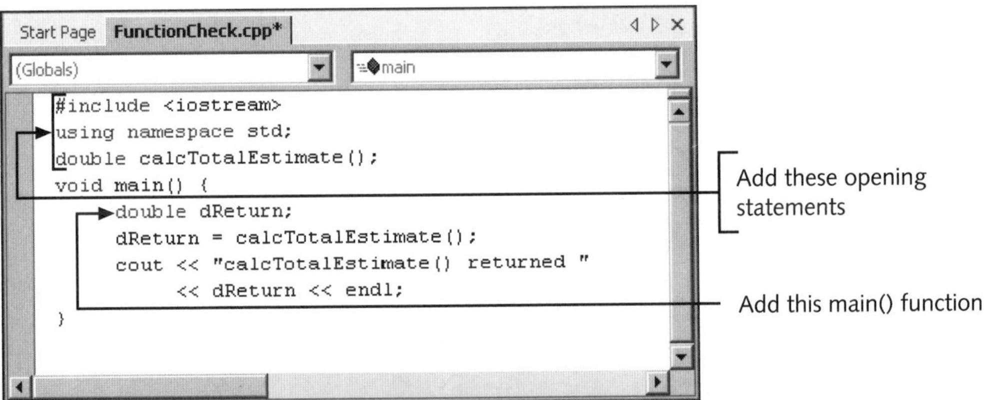

Figure 4-10 Opening statements and main() function added to the FunctionCheck program

5. Also as shown in Figure 4-10, add a main() function, which calls the calcTotalEstimate() function and prints its `return` value.
6. Following the main() function, paste the **calcTotalEstimate()** function, which you copied from the Moving Estimator program, from the Clipboard. Modify its header declaration as shown in Figure 4-11 so that it does not include any parameters.
7. The dTotal variable should be assigned the combined values of the six other variables. Therefore, if each of the other variables contains a value of 100, the dTotal variable should be assigned a total value of 600. To test how the calculations perform under these conditions, add the declarations and assignments for each variable shown in Figure 4-11. In the actual version of the program, the variables receive their values through user input using cin statements in the main() function and are then passed as parameters to the calcTotalValue() function.

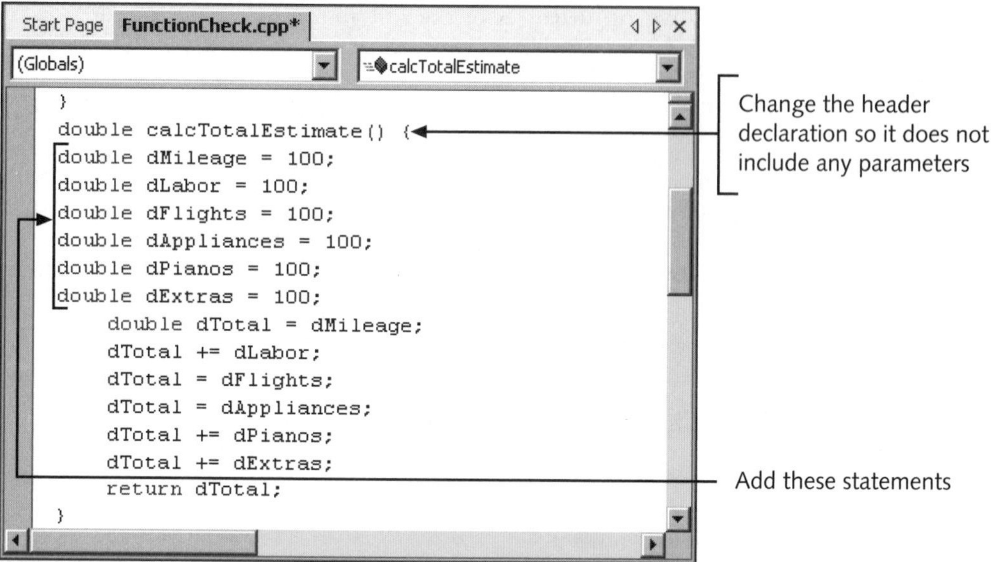

Figure 4-11 calcTotalEstimate() added to FunctionCheck program

8. Next, add to the calcTotalEstimate() function output statements that print the value of the dTotal variable each time it is assigned a new value, along with a statement that returns the dTotal variable:

```
double calcTotalEstimate() {
...
     double dTotal = dMileage;
cout << "dTotal after adding dMileage "
     << dTotal << endl;
     dTotal += dLabor;
cout << "dTotal after adding dLabor "
     << dTotal << endl;
     dTotal = dFlights;
cout << "dTotal after adding dFlights "
     << dTotal << endl;
     dTotal = dAppliances;
cout << "dTotal after adding dAppliances "
     << dTotal << endl;
     dTotal += dPianos;
cout << "dTotal after adding dPianos "
     << dTotal << endl;
     dTotal += dExtras;
cout << "dTotal after adding dExtras "
     << dTotal << endl;
     return dTotal;
}
```

9. Build and execute the program. Your output should resemble Figure 4-12. You can see from the output statement in the main() function that the calcTotalEstimate() function did not return a value of 600. Instead, it returned a value of 300. Looking back over the individual output statements that printed the value of dTotal each time it was assigned a new value, you can see that the dFlightsCost and dAppliancesCost values were not added to the dTotal value, but instead replaced it. As you probably already noticed, the two statements that assign these values to the dTotal value used the assignment operator instead of the += operator. Although this is a very simple example, it does demonstrate how output statements can help you analyze a variable's changing values.

```
"c:\Visual C++ Projects\Chapter.04\FunctionCheck\Debug\FunctionCheck.exe"
dTotal after adding dMileage 100
dTotal after adding dLabor 200
dTotal after adding dFlights 100
dTotal after adding dAppliances 100
dTotal after adding dPianos 200
dTotal after adding dExtras 300
calcTotalEstimate() returned 300
Press any key to continue
```

Figure 4-12 Output of the FunctionCheck program

10. Press any key to close the console window.

11. Select **Close Solution** from the File menu to close the FunctionCheck project.

12. Reopen the **MovingEstimatorWithBugs** project and, if necessary, open the **MovingEstimatorWithBugs.cpp** file in the Code Editor window.

13. Modify the **calcTotalEstimate()** function so that the statements that assign the dFlightsCost and dApplicancesCost values to the dTotal value use += operators instead of the assignment operator, as shown in Figure 4-13, and then rebuild the program.

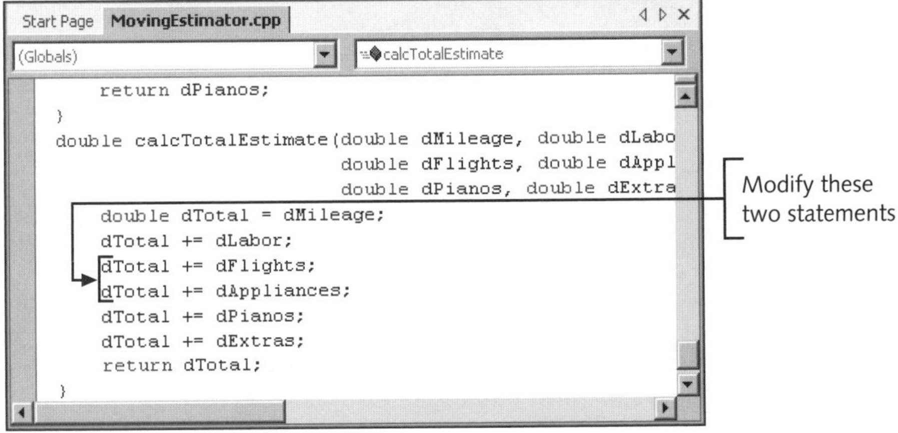

Figure 4-13 Modified assignment statements in calcTotalEstimate()

Using Comments to Locate Bugs

Another method of locating bugs in a C++ program is to comment out lines that you think might be causing the problem. You can comment out individual lines that might be causing the error, or comment out all lines except the lines that you know work. When you receive an error message, start by commenting out only the statement specified by the error message's line number. Rebuild and execute the program, and see if you receive another error. If you receive additional error messages, then comment out those statements as well. Once you eliminate the error messages, examine the commented out statements for the cause of the bug.

The cause of an error in a particular statement is often the result of an error in a preceding line of code.

The last five statements in Figure 4-14 are commented out because they generate compiler error messages stating that dYearlyIntrest is not defined. The problem with the code is that the dYearlyInterest variable is incorrectly spelled as dYearlyIntrest, lacking an *e*, in several of the statements. Commenting out the lines isolates the problem statements.

Although the error in Figure 4-14 might seem somewhat simple, it is typical of the types of errors you will encounter. Often you will see the error right away and not need to comment out code or use any other tracing technique. However, when you have been staring at the same code for long periods of time, simple spelling errors, like yearlyIntrest, are not always easy to spot. Commenting out the lines you know are giving you trouble is a good technique for helping you isolate and correct even the simplest types of bugs.

```
        double dAmount = 100000;
        double dPercentage = .08;
        cout << "The interest rate for a loan "
             << " in the amount of " << dAmount
             << " is " << dPercentage << endl;
        double dYearlyInterest = dAmount * dPercentage;
//      cout << "The amount of interest for one year is "
//      << dYearlyIntrest << endl;
//      double dMonthlyInterest = dYearlyIntrest / 12;
//      cout << "The amount of interest for one month is "
//           << dMonthlyInterest << endl;
//      double dDailyInterest = dYearlyInterest / 365;
//      cout << "The amount of interest for one day is "
//           << dDailyInterest << endl;
```

Figure 4-14 Code using comments to trace errors

Provided that you are working with console applications, you can combine the output statement and comment debugging techniques to aid in your search for errors. Figure 4-15 uses the calculatePay() function as an example of how to use comments combined with an output statement to trace errors. You know that the `var grossPay = payRate * numHours;` statement is the last statement in the function that operates correctly. Therefore, all of the lines following that statement are commented out. You then use an output statement to check the value of each statement, removing comments from each statement in sequential order, and checking and correcting syntax as you go.


```
double calculatePay() {
     double dPayRate = 20;
     double dNumHours = 40;
     double dGrossPay = dPayRate * dNumHours;
cout << "dGrossPay is " << dGrossPay << endl;
//   double dFederalTaxes = dGrossPay * .06794;
//   double dStateTaxes = dGrossPay * .0476;
//   double dSocialSecurity = dGrossPay * .062;
//   double dMedicare = dGrossPay * .0145;
//   double dNetPay = dGrossPay - dFederalTaxes;
//   dNetPay *= dStateTaxes;
//   dNetPay *= dSocialSecurity;
//   dNetPay *= dMedicare;
//   return dNetPay;
}
```

Figure 4-15 calculatePay() function with comments and an output statement used to trace program execution

Next, you will use comments to help locate bugs in the Moving Estimator program.

To use comments to help locate bugs in the Moving Estimator program:

1. First, run the Moving Estimator program and enter the following data:

   ```
   Distance in miles: 400
   Weight in pounds: 900
   No. of flights of stairs: 2
   ```

   After entering the data, a total value of 735 should appear for the moving estimate. Instead, an incorrect value of 3135 appears. In order to locate the code that is causing this problem, you will add comments to the calcTotalEstimate() function.

2. Type **7** and press **Enter** to exit the Moving Estimator program, and then press any key to close the console window.

3. In the calcTotalEstimate() function, add comment lines as follows to all of the statements except the first statement, which assigns the dMileageCost variable to the dTotal variable. When you are finished, rebuild and execute the program.

   ```
   double calcTotalEstimate(double dMileage, double dLabor,
                      double dFlights, double dAppliances,
                      double dPianos, double dExtras) {
        double dTotal = dMileage;
   //   dTotal += dLabor;
   //   dTotal += dFlights;
   //   dTotal += dAppliances;
   //   dTotal += dPianos;
   ```

```
//      dTotal += dExtras;
         return dTotal;
}
```

4. Enter **400** as the Distance in miles value. The correct value of 500 is assigned to the Moving estimate box. Therefore, the problem is not with the dMileage variable. Close the Moving Estimator program.

5. Remove the comment line from the `dTotal += dLabor;` statement, and then rebuild and execute the program.

6. Enter **400** as the Distance in miles value and **900** as the Weight in pounds value. At 15 cents a pound, the total cost of 900 pounds is $135. Adding 135 to the Distance in miles amount of 500 results in 635. Therefore, the program is functioning correctly so far. Close the Moving Estimator program.

7. Remove the comment line from the `dTotal += dFlights;` statement, and then rebuild and execute the program. Enter **400** as the Distance in miles value, **900** as the Weight in pounds value, and **2** as the No. of flights value. At $50 per flight, a value of 2 should only increase the moving estimate by 100, for a total of 735. However, the Moving estimate incorrectly appears as 3135. The program functioned correctly until you tried to call the calcFlightsCost() function. Close the Moving Estimator program.

8. If you scroll to the calcFlightsCost() function, you will see that the function includes an unnecessary statement, `iFlights = 50;`, which causes the calculation error. Do not think this is a trivial example. As you develop your own applications, you will often find yourself adding and deleting statements that can introduce simple, hard-to-detect, bugs in your programs. Delete the `iFlights = 50;` statement from the calcFlightsCost() function, as shown in Figure 4-16.

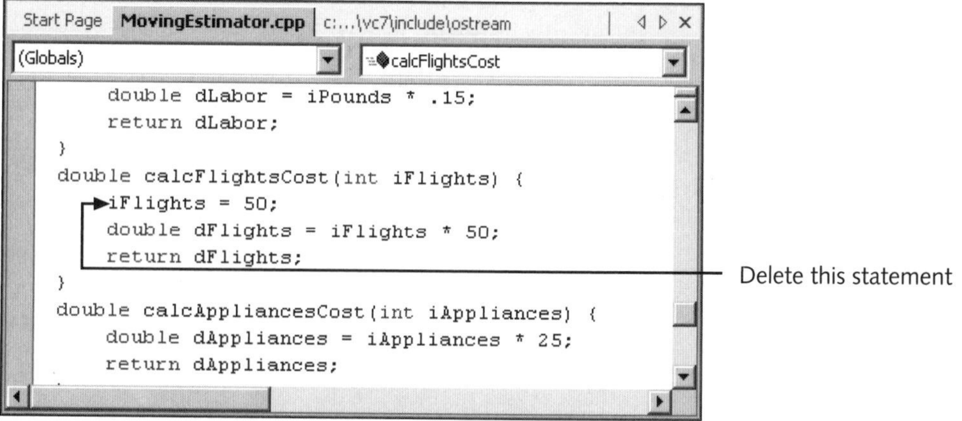

Figure 4-16 Unnecessary statement deleted from calcFlightsCost()

9. Remove the remainder of the comments from the statements in the calcTotalEstimate() function, and then rebuild and execute the program. Enter the data listed in Step 1. The correct value of 735 should appear for the moving estimate value. Do not enter any numbers for the other calculations because the program still contains some errors.


```
"c:\Visual C++ Projects\Chapter.04\MovingEstimatorNoBugs\Debug\MovingEstimatorNoBugs.exe"
2. Weight in pounds:      900      (.15 cents per pound)
3. No. of flights:        0        ($50 per flight)
4. No. of appliances:     0        ($25 per appliance)
5. No. of pianos:         0        ($35 per piano)
6. Extra charges:         0        (Enter in dollars)
   =====================
   Moving estimate:       635
   =====================
7. Exit

Enter a number and press Enter: 3
Enter the number of flights: 2

1. Distance in miles:     400      ($1.25 per mile)
2. Weight in pounds:      900      (.15 cents per pound)
3. No. of flights:        2        ($50 per flight)
4. No. of appliances:     0        ($25 per appliance)
5. No. of pianos:         0        ($35 per piano)
6. Extra charges:         0        (Enter in dollars)
   =====================
   Moving estimate:       735
   =====================
7. Exit

Enter a number and press Enter:
```

Figure 4-17 Moving Estimator program after correcting the calcFlightsCost() function

10. Click the **Close** button to close the Moving Estimator program window.

You might be wondering how to decide where to begin looking for a bug. How do you know to place comments in the calcTotalEstimate() function, or use output statements in a driver program, or use any of the other tools you will examine in this chapter? The answer is that it depends on the program. Every program you write, or rewrite, will be different. You need to determine the most logical place to start debugging based on the design of your program. With the Moving Estimator program, you could have started looking in any of the functions. However, because the program should result in the calculation of a single number, you started at the top by first analyzing the number assigned to the dTotal variable in the calcTotalEstimate() function. If the error you were receiving could not be located in the calcTotalEstimate() function, you could have directed your efforts to the functions that assign values to the variables used by the calcTotalEstimate() function. And if that had not worked, you would have begun examining the main() function and variable declaration statements.

Analyzing Your Logic

At times, errors in your code will be logic problems that are difficult to spot using tracing techniques. When you suspect that your code contains logic errors, you must analyze each statement on a case-by-case basis. For example, the following code contains a logic flaw that prevents it from functioning correctly.

```
bool bCondition = false;
if (bCondition = true)
     cout << "The condition is true" << endl;
else
     cout << "The condition is false" << endl;
```

If you were to execute the preceding code, you would always see the screen output *The condition is true*, although it should print *The condition is false* because the bCondition variable is set to false. If you examine the `if` statement more closely, you will see that instead of using the comparison operator (==) to test the value of the bCondition variable, the conditional expression uses the assignment operator (=). Using the assignment operator in the conditional expression not only assigns a value of true to the bCondition variable, but also returns a value true, causing the body of the `if` statement to execute. For the code to execute properly, the conditional expression must use the comparison operator as follows:

```
bool bCondition = false;
if (bCondition == true)
     cout << "The condition is true." << endl;
else
     cout << "The condition is false" << endl;
```

The following code shows another example of an easily overlooked logic error using a `for` statement:

```
int ctCount = 0;
for (ctCount = 1; ctCount < 6; ++ctCount);
     cout << ctCount << endl;
```

The code should print the numbers 1 through 5 to the screen. However, the line for `(ctCount = 1; ctCount < 6; ++ ctCount);` contains an ending semicolon, which marks the end of the `for` loop. The loop executes five times and changes the value of count to 6, but does nothing else because there are no statements before its ending semicolon. The line `cout << ctCount << endl;` is a separate statement that executes only once, printing the number 6 to the screen. The code is syntactically correct, but does not function as you anticipated. As you can see from these examples, it is easy to overlook very minor logic errors in your code.

THE VISUAL C++ DEBUGGER

Many high-level programming languages have debugging capabilities built directly into their development environments. These built-in debugging capabilities provide sophisticated commands for tracking errors. Up to this point, you have learned how to interpret error messages and correct the statements that cause the errors. As helpful as they are, error messages are useful only in resolving syntax and run-time errors. You have also learned some techniques that assist in locating logic errors. Examining your code manually is usually the first step to take when you have a logic error, or you may use a driver program to track values assigned to a function's variables. These techniques work fine with smaller programs. However, when you are creating a large program, logic errors can be very difficult to spot. For instance, you might have a function that contains multiple calls to other functions, which themselves may call other functions. Attempting to trace the logic and flow of such a program using simple tools such as output statements can be difficult. Visual C++ provides a program called the **debugger** that contains several tools that can help you trace each line of code, creating a much more efficient method of finding and resolving logic errors.

Any messages that are generated while you are debugging an application are printed to the Debug pane of the Output window. You display the Debug pane by selecting Debug from the combo box at the top of the Output window.

You start the debugger by selecting the Start, Step Into, or Step Over commands on the Debug menu or the Run to Cursor command on the Shortcut menu. Any of these commands allows you to enter and work in break mode. **Break mode** temporarily suspends, or pauses, program execution so that you can monitor values and trace program execution. Once the debugger is started, the Modules window appears, new commands become available on the Debug menu, and several debugging windows appear at the bottom of the IDE window. Once the debugger starts, new commands become available on the Debug menu and several debugging windows appear at the bottom of the IDE.

This text instructs you to use the Debug menu to execute commands. However, many of the commands are also available as icons on the Debug toolbar.

Build Configurations

To use the Visual C++ debugger, you need to build a Debug version of your program. A **Debug build** contains additional information that is required by the debugger tools. You can also create a Win32 Release build. A **Release build** does not contain any debugging information. By default when you first create a project, it is set to compile as a Debug build. Debug build is the default setting so that you have debugging information available to you while you are developing your application. Visual C++ places a debug build of your program, along with a .pdb file that contains the debugging information, in a folder named Debug in your project's main folder. In spite of its helpfulness during development, the extra debugging information found in a Debug build slows down your program and makes it unnecessarily large. Once you have completed writing and debugging your application, you create a Release build, which contains only the files necessary for your program to run and doesn't contain the extra debugging information. Visual C++ places a release build of your program in a folder named Release in your project's main folder, along with various settings and information files that are required by the release build. You distribute the files in the Release folder to your clients.

Although you need to build a Debug release of your program to use the Visual C++ debugger, some bugs do not surface until you build and run a release version of your program. Therefore, you should periodically build and test your code using a Release build in order to identify any bugs that do not appear in Debug builds. To change the build setting for your project, select the Configuration Manager command from the Build menu to display the Configuration Manager dialog box, shown in Figure 4-18.

Next, you will make sure your project is set to build a Debug version.

To make sure your project is set to build a Debug version:

1. Select **Configuration Manager** from the **Build** menu. The Configuration Manager dialog box appears.
2. In the Configuration Manager dialog box, be sure that Debug is selected in the Active Solution Configuration combo box, and then click the **Close** button.

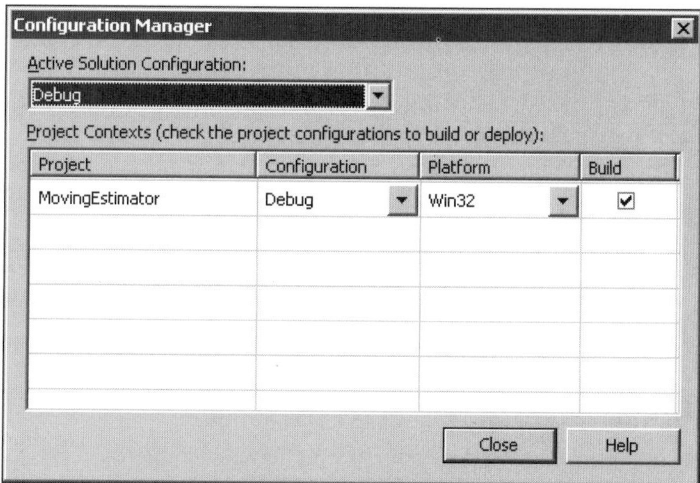

Figure 4-18 Configuration Manager dialog box

Tracing Program Execution with Step Commands

The Step Into, Step Over, and Step Out commands on the Debug menu are used for tracing program execution once you enter break mode. The **Step Into** command executes an individual line of code and then pauses until you instruct the debugger to continue. This feature gives you an opportunity to evaluate a program's flow and structure as it is being executed.

As you use the Step Into command to move through code, the debugger stops at each line within every function. When stepping through a program to trace a logical error, it is convenient to be able to skip functions that you know are working correctly. The **Step Over** command allows you to skip function calls. The program still executes the function that you step over, but it appears in the debugger as if a single statement executes.

The **Step Out** command executes all remaining code in the current function. If the current function is called from another function, all remaining code in the current function executes and the debugger stops at the next statement in the calling function.

You can also trace program execution with the Run to Cursor command on the Shortcut menu, which appears when you right-click a statement. When you select the **Run To Cursor command**, the program runs normally until it reaches the statement where your cursor is located, at which point the program enters break mode. You can then use the Step Into, Step Over, and Step Out commands to continue tracing program execution. The Run To Cursor command is useful if you are sure that your program is functioning correctly up to a certain point in the code.

When a program enters break mode, program execution is not stopped—it is only suspended. To resume program execution after entering break mode, select Continue from the Debug menu. The **Continue command** resumes program execution, which continues until it encounters the next breakpoint. (You will learn about breakpoints shortly.) You can also end a debugging session and halt program execution by selecting the Stop Debugging command from the Debug menu.

Be sure that your C++ files are saved before starting the debugger because certain types of errors that the debugger may encounter, such as memory errors, can cause Visual C++ to crash.

Although you can make changes to code in break mode, they will not take effect while the program is executing. You must end program execution (using the Stop Debugging command), rebuild the project, and then start the program again. You can also select the Restart command from the Debug menu, which stops, rebuilds, and then reexecutes the program in the debugger.

Next, you will practice tracing program execution using the step commands.

To practice tracing program execution:

1. Return to the **MovingEstimator.cpp** file in the Code Editor window.
2. Locate the first `if` statement in the `do...while` loop, right-click with your mouse on the statement that reads `dMileageCost = calcMileageCost(iNumMiles);`, and select the **Run to Cursor** command from the shortcut menu.
3. Execute the program and enter a value for the Distance in miles calculation. As soon as you press Enter after typing the value, program execution enters break mode and a yellow arrow in the margin of the Code Editor window points to the next statement to be processed, as shown in Figure 4-19.

Start Page | MovingEstimator.cpp | c:...\vc7\include\ostream | Disassembly

(Globals) | main

```
        << "7. Exit" << endl << endl;
    cout << "Enter a number and press Enter: ";
    cin >> iSelection;
    if (iSelection == 1) {
        cout << "Enter the mileage: ";
        cin >> iNumMiles;
        dMileageCost = calcMileageCost(iNumMiles);
    }
    else if (iSelection == 2) {
        cout << "Enter the pounds: ";
        cin >> iNumPounds;
```

Figure 4-19 Moving Estimator program in break mode

When you select the Run To Cursor command, the debugger executes all statements before the line that your cursor is in. The statement in the line containing your cursor is the next statement to be processed.

4. Select **Step Into** from the Debug menu. The debugger processes the current statement and transfers control to the calcMileageCost() function.

Most of the commands on the Debug menu can also be executed using keyboard shortcuts or buttons on the Debug toolbar. Each command's keyboard shortcut is listed to the right of the command on the Debug menu. To display a ToolTip for a specific Debug toolbar button, hold your pointer over the desired button.

5. Select **Step Into** from the Debug menu again. The yellow arrow moves to the first statement in the function, `double dMileage = iMiles * 1.25;`. Select the **Step Into** command to execute the first statement. Select the **Step Into** command again to execute the return statement, and then select the **Step Into** command a final time to end the function. Control is transferred back to the `if` statement that called the function.
6. Once control returns to the `if` statement that called the function, execute the **Step Over** command four times, until you reach the cout statement that calls the calcTotalEstimate() function. Click the Step Into command to start the calcTotalEstimate() function.
7. Because you already know that the calcTotalEstimate() function works correctly, select the **Step Out** command from the Debug menu. The rest of the statements in the calcTotalEstimate() function execute normally, and control is transferred back to the `cout` statement that called the function.
8. Finally, select **Stop Debugging** from the Debug menu to halt debugging and program execution.

Another method of tracing program execution in the Visual C++ debugger involves inserting breakpoints into code. A **breakpoint** is a position in the code at which program execution enters break mode. You add a breakpoint to your code by clicking the left margin next to a statement or by right-clicking a statement and selecting Insert Breakpoint from the Shortcut menu. Once a program is paused at a breakpoint, you can use the Step Into, Step Over, Step Out, and Run To Cursor commands to trace program execution. You can also use the Continue command to complete program execution and run to the next breakpoint, or the Stop Debugging command to exit the debugger. Multiple breakpoints provide a convenient way to pause program execution at key positions in your code where you think there could be a bug.

Next, you will practice using breakpoints.

To practice using breakpoints:

1. Return to the **MovingEstimator.cpp** file in the Code Editor window.
2. In the calcTotalEstimate() function, click the margin to the left of the first statement, which reads `double dTotal = dMileage;`. A red circle appears in the left margin of the Code Editor window next to the line containing the breakpoint.
3. Add another breakpoint to the last statement in the function, which reads `return dTotal;`. Figure 4-20 shows how the Code Editor window appears with the two breakpoints.

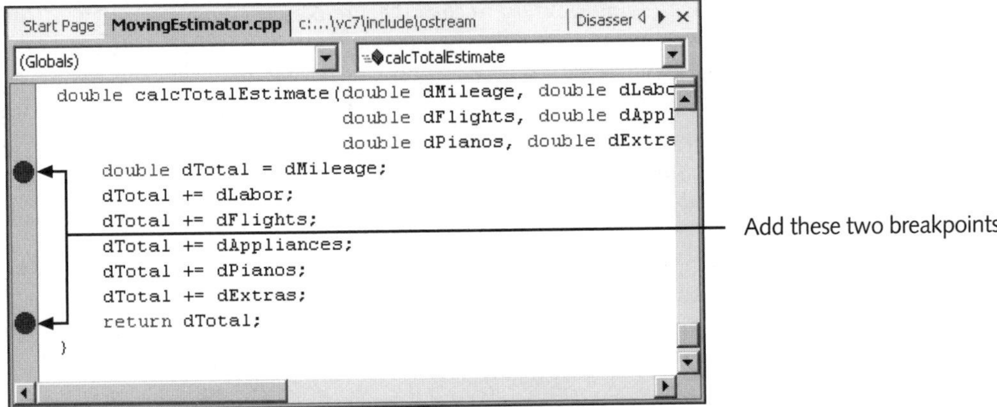

Figure 4-20 Breakpoints in the Code Editor window

You can also add a breakpoint by right clicking a statement and selecting Insert Breakpoint from the Shortcut menu.

4. Select **Start** from the Debug menu. The program starts running, briefly displays the Moving Estimator console window, and then immediately enters break mode and pauses at the first breakpoint. A yellow arrow appears in the margin of the Code Editor window on top of the red circle that marks the breakpoint.
5. Select **Continue** from the Debug menu. The statements between the two breakpoints execute, and then program execution pauses at the second breakpoint.
6. Select **Stop Debugging** from the Debug menu to halt debugging and program execution.

To remove breakpoints from a file:

1. Click the red circle that represents the first breakpoint or right-click the `double dTotal = dMileage;` statement and select **Remove Breakpoint** from the shortcut menu.

Instead of removing a breakpoint, you can enable and disable it by right-clicking the statement containing the breakpoint and selecting Disable Breakpoint from the shortcut menu. A disabled breakpoint appears as a hollow circle in the left margin of the Code Editor window.

2. Repeat Step 1 to remove the second breakpoint in the file.

You can add and remove breakpoints using the Breakpoints window or the New Breakpoint dialog box. To access the Breakpoints window, point to the Windows submenu on the Debug menu and select Breakpoints. To access the New Breakpoint dialog box, select New from the Breakpoints window. You can also use the Breakpoints window and the New Breakpoints dialog box to set the conditions under which a program should pause at a breakpoint. For example, you can set a breakpoint to occur only when the contents of a variable match a specific value.

You can clear or disable all breakpoints by using the Clear All Breakpoints and Disable All Breakpoints commands on the Debug menu.

TRACING VARIABLES AND EXPRESSIONS WITH DEBUG WINDOWS

As you trace program execution using step commands and breakpoints, you might also need to trace how variables and expressions change during the course of program execution. For example, you might have a statement that reads `resultNum = firstNum / secondNum;`. You know this line is causing a divide-by-zero error, but you do not know exactly when secondNum is being changed to a 0 value. The ability to trace program execution and learn the exact location at which secondNum is being changed to a 0 (zero) value allows you to pinpoint the cause of the logic problem. The debugger contains several tools that you can use during break mode to help you trace and analyze variables and expressions. These tools include debugging windows that help you analyze the value of variables during program execution, and the Call Stack window, which helps you trace the calls to your program's functions.

In addition to using the debug windows to learn the value of a variable during program execution, in break mode you can learn the value of a variable by holding your mouse over the variable. An information bubble, similar to a ToolTip, will display the variable's current value. You can also learn the result of an expression by highlighting the expression and holding your mouse over it.

This section discusses only the most common debugging windows that are available in the debugger. However, the debugger also includes numerous additional windows and tools that you can use in your debugging efforts. Feel free to explore the additional debugging capabilities on your own. As you advance in your C++ programming skills, you will find some of the additional debugging windows and tools to be particularly useful.

Monitoring Variables

The debugger contains three windows—Autos, Locals, and Watch—that monitor variables as you step through a program in break mode. In any of these windows, the most recently modified variable is highlighted in red. The Autos, Locals, and Watch 1 windows should appear automatically when you start the debugger. However, you can also display each of the windows manually by pointing to the Windows submenu on the Debug menu and selecting the window you want to work with. In this section, the Autos and Locals windows will be discussed.

Using the Autos Window

If you are stepping through a program and execute a statement that declares `int iSampleVariable =1;`, iSampleVariable comes into scope. When you reach the end of a block in which a variable is declared, the variable goes out of scope. The **Autos window** displays variables within the current statement and the previous statement. You use the Autos window to monitor variables within a specific statement. For example, consider the following version of the calculatePayFunction(). If you are stepping through the function and stop on the statement that appears in boldface, the Autos window will appear similar to the example shown in Figure 4-21. Notice that only the dNumHours and dPayRate variables have been initialized. The large exponential number that you see assigned to the dGrossPay variable has no meaning except to inform you that the dGrossPay variable has not been initialized.

```
double calcHourlyPay() {
     double dPayRate = 20;
     double dNumHours = 40;
```

```
        double dGrossPay = dPayRate * dNumHours;
        double dFederalTaxes = dGrossPay * .06794;
        double dStateTaxes = dGrossPay * .0476;
        double dSocialSecurity = dGrossPay * .062;
        double dMedicare = dGrossPay * .0145;
        double dNetPay = dGrossPay - dFederalTaxes;
        dNetPay *= dStateTaxes;
        dNetPay *= dSocialSecurity;
        dNetPay *= dMedicare;
        return dNetPay;
}
```

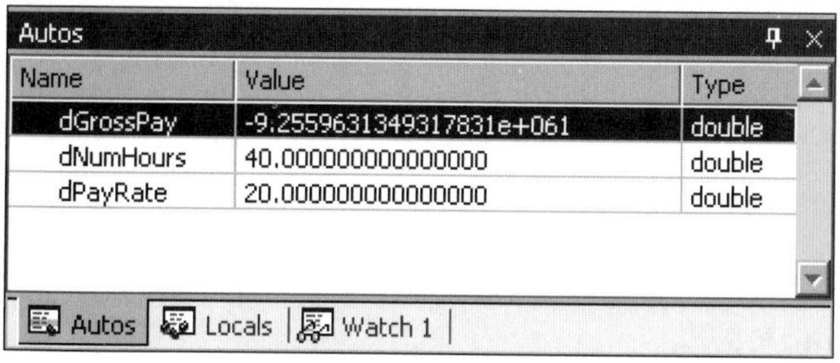

Autos

Name	Value	Type
dGrossPay	-9.2559631349317831e+061	double
dNumHours	40.000000000000000	double
dPayRate	20.000000000000000	double

Autos | Locals | Watch 1

Figure 4-21 Autos window

The Autos window helps you see how different values affect program execution. As you step through code in break mode, you can change the value of a variable in the Auto window by clicking the value in the Value column once, entering a new value, and then pressing Enter. Changing a value in break mode changes the value only for the current instance of program execution.

Using the Locals Window

The **Locals window** displays all local variables within the currently executing function, regardless of whether they have been initialized. The Locals window helps you see how different values in the currently executing function affect program execution. You use the Locals window when you need to be able to see all of a function's variables, regardless of whether they have been assigned a value. You can change the value of a variable in the Locals window by clicking the value in the Value column once, entering a new value, and pressing Enter. Figure 4-22 shows how the Locals window appears when you step through the calculatePay() function and pause at the line that appears in boldface. Even though only the dNumHours and dPayRate variables have been initialized, all of the function's variables are listed in the Locals window.

Next, you will practice tracing variables with the Autos and Locals windows.

To practice tracing variables with the Autos and Locals windows:

1. Open the **MovingEstimator.cpp** file in the Code Editor window.

2. In the main() function, add a breakpoint to the statement that reads `double dMileageCost = 0;`.

3. Execute the program by selecting the **Start** command from the Debug menu. The program starts running and pauses at the `double dMileageCost = 0;` statement in the main() function.

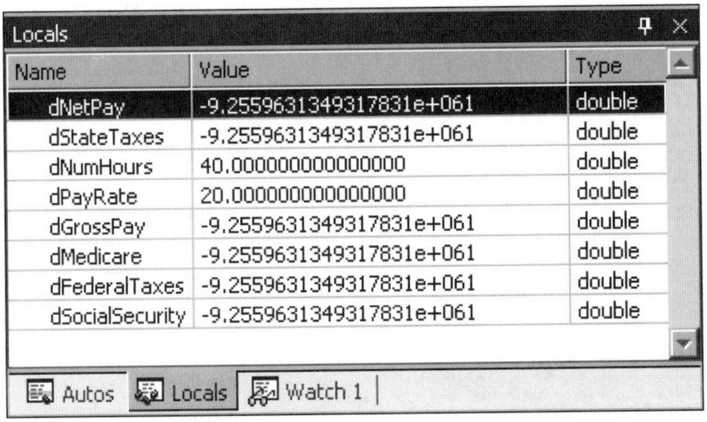

Locals

Name	Value	Type
dNetPay	-9.2559631349317831e+061	double
dStateTaxes	-9.2559631349317831e+061	double
dNumHours	40.000000000000000	double
dPayRate	20.000000000000000	double
dGrossPay	-9.2559631349317831e+061	double
dMedicare	-9.2559631349317831e+061	double
dFederalTaxes	-9.2559631349317831e+061	double
dSocialSecurity	-9.2559631349317831e+061	double

Autos | Locals | Watch 1

Figure 4-22 Locals window

4. If necessary, display the **Autos window** by selecting **Autos** from the Windows submenu on the Debug menu. You should see the dMileageCost and the iNumPounds variable names listed in the Name column. The Value column displays the stored value for initialized values or a garbage number for variables that have not been initialized. For instance, because the iNumPounds variable was initialized to 0 in the previous statement, its value in the Value column appears as 0. However, the Value for the dMileageCost variable contains a garbage number because the current statement has not yet executed.

5. Select the **Step Into** command. The dMileageCost variable is assigned a value of 0. The iNumPounds variable is no longer visible, because it is not within the current statement or the previous statement, and is replaced with the dLaborCost variable, which is part of the current statement.

6. Display the **Locals window** by selecting **Locals** from the Windows submenu on the Debug menu. Notice that all of the variables within the main() function are listed, regardless of whether they have been initialized. Select the **Step Into** command a few more times to observe the values that appear in each variable's Value column as the variable is initialized.

7. Select **Stop Debugging** from the Debug menu to halt program execution.

The Watch Window

The **Watch window** is used for monitoring and changing specific variables that you enter. Unlike the Autos and Locals windows, which automatically show the values of variables according to the current scope, you must manually enter into the Watch window the variables that you want to monitor. You can enter the name of a variable into the Watch window and monitor how the variable changes during the course of program execution. You use the Watch window when you are interested in monitoring only specific variables. You can also enter expressions in the Watch window and observe how their values change as the program executes. For example, if you place the expression `dPayRate * 1.5;` in the Watch window, its value changes as the dPayRate variable changes.

There are four separate Watch windows: Watch 1, Watch 2, Watch 3, and Watch 4. By default, the Watch 1 window automatically appears when you first start the debugger. You display a Watch window by pointing to the Windows submenu on the Debug menu and then pointing to the Watch submenu. In the Watch submenu, click the Watch window you want to work with. Figure 4-23 shows an example of the Watch 1 window.

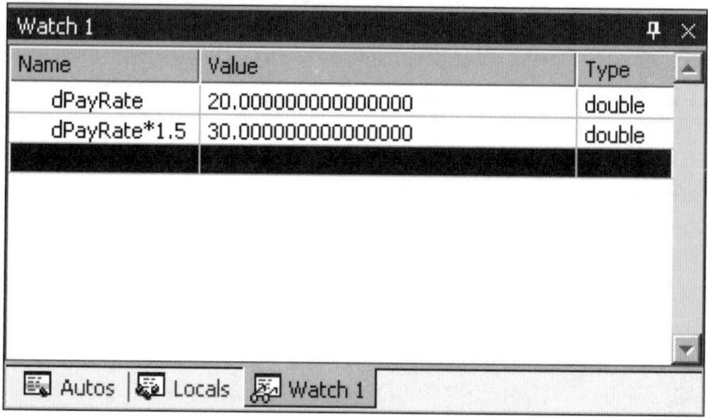

Figure 4-23 The Watch 1 window

You enter variable names and expressions directly into a row in the Watch window, or you can use your mouse to drag a variable or expression onto the Watch window from the Code Editor window or from the Autos, Locals, or This window.

QuickWatch

Another way of watching variables is by using QuickWatch. **QuickWatch** is a dialog box that you can use to quickly examine the value of a single variable or expression. Once you are in break mode, you can display QuickWatch by selecting QuickWatch from the Debug menu. You can then enter a variable name or expression in the Expression edit box and click the Recalculate button to view its value. Alternately, after entering a variable name or expression in the QuickWatch Expression edit box, you can add it to the Watch window by clicking the Add Watch button. QuickWatch is of somewhat limited value because it is a modal dialog box. You must close it in order to continue debugging your application. However, you may find it useful for quickly retrieving a value or calculating an expression. Figure 4-24 shows an example of the QuickWatch window.

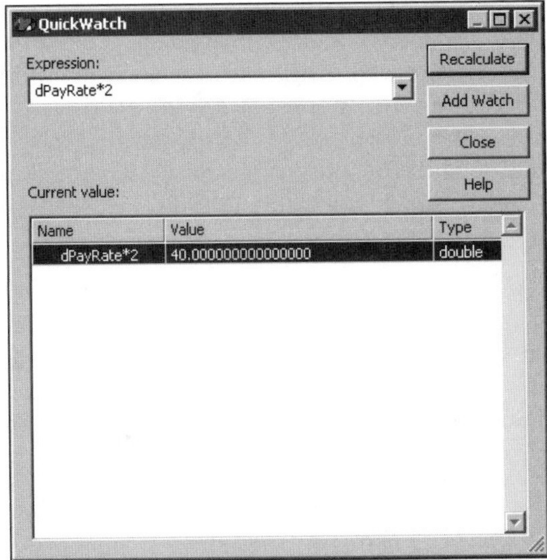

Figure 4-24 QuickWatch window

You can also view the values of variables or expressions by highlighting them in the Code Editor window and then selecting QuickWatch from the Debug menu. The highlighted variable or expression will be added to the QuickWatch window for you.

Next, you will use the Watch window and the QuickWatch dialog box to find a bug in the Moving Estimator program.

To use the Watch window and the QuickWatch dialog box to find a bug in the Moving Estimator program:

1. First, remove all of the breakpoints from the Moving Estimator program by selecting **Clear All Breakpoints** from the Debug menu.
2. Next, rebuild and run the Moving Estimator program, and enter the following data for each of the moving cost calculations.

```
Distance in miles: 1000
Weight in pounds: 500
No. of flights of stairs: 2
No. of appliances: 3
No. of pianos: 2
Extra charges: 100
```

3. After you enter the preceding numbers, the Moving estimate edit box displays a value of 1602. However, you can tell by doing the math manually that the value should be 1670. Because you have already corrected the Distance in miles, Weight in pounds, and No. of flights of stairs calculations, you will start by examining the No. of appliances calculation. You will examine the two values required by the appliances calculation: the iAppliances variable, which receives its value from the dialog box via the UpdateData() function, and the dAppliancesCost variable, which receives the result of the calculation. First, close the Moving Estimator program, enter a breakpoint on the **`double dAppliances = iAppliances * 25;`** statement in the calcAppliancesCost() function, and then select the **Start** command from the Debug menu. The program starts to execute and displays the Moving Estimator console window.
4. Enter the values from Step 2 for the Distance in miles edit box, Weight in pounds, and No. of flights of stairs calculations. Type **4** and then press **Enter** to start the No. of appliances calculation. Enter **3** for the number of appliances and then press **Enter**. After you press Enter, the program enters break mode and pauses on the `double dAppliances = iAppliances * 25;` statement.
5. Before stepping through the function, use the QuickWatch dialog box to examine the values contained in the iAppliances variable by selecting **QuickWatch** from the Debug menu. When the QuickWatch dialog box appears, enter **iAppliances** in the Expression box and then click the **Recalculate** button. The Current value list should display the correct value of *3* for the iAppliances variable. Now, check the result that should be returned by the function by typing **iAppliances * 25** in the Expression box and then clicking the **Recalculate** button. The correct value of *75* should appear in the Current value list. This is the value that should be assigned to the dAppliances variable when the calculation finishes. Click the **Close** button to close the QuickWatch dialog box.
6. Select the **Step Into** command to execute the function's calculation statement.
7. Place the insertion point anywhere within the dAppliances variable and open the QuickWatch dialog box. The dAppliances variable should be automatically entered into the QuickWatch dialog box and the correct value of *75* should appear in the Current value list. Therefore, the problem does not appear to be with the appliances cost calculation. Click the **Close** button to close the QuickWatch dialog box.
8. Select **Stop Debugging** from the Debug menu.
9. Remove the breakpoint from the **`double dAppliances = iAppliances * 25;`** statement in the calcAppliancesCost() function.

10. Next, you will examine the two values required by the piano calculation: the iPianos variable and the dPianos variable, which receives the result of the calculation. Enter a breakpoint on the **`double dPianos = iPianos * 35;`** statement in the calcPianosCost() function, and then select the **Start** command from the Debug menu. The program starts to execute and displays the Moving Estimator window.

11. Enter the values from Step 2 for the Distance in miles edit box, Weight in pounds, No. of flights of stairs, and No. of appliances calculations. Type **5** and then press **Enter** to start the No. of pianos calculation. Type **2** for the number of pianos and then press **Enter**. After you press Enter, the program enters break mode and pauses on the **`double dPianos = iPianos * 35;`** statement.

12 Display the Watch 1 window by pointing to the **Windows** submenu on the **Debug** menu. On the **Windows** submenu, point to the **Watch** submenu and select **Watch 1**.

13. Now, place the insertion point in the Name column of the Watch window and type **iPianos**. Press the **Enter** key, then type **dPianos** in the second row of the Watch window, and press enter again. The iPianos variable should have a value of *2,* and the dPianos variable should a garbage value because it has not yet been initialized. Because the cost to move a single piano is $35, the dPianos variable should be updated to *70* after you execute the **`double dPianos = iPianos * 35;`** statement in the calcPianosCost() function. Figure 4-25 shows the Watch window after entering the two variables.

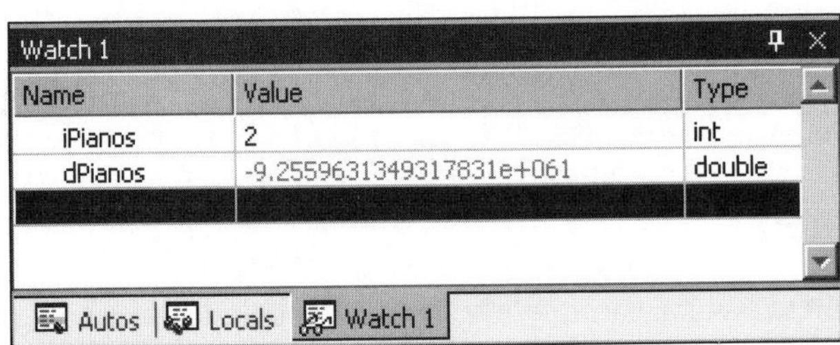

Figure 4-25 Watch window with the iPianos and dPianos data members

14. Select the **Step Into** command to execute the `double dPianos = iPianos * 35;` statement. Notice that the dPianos variable is updated to *70* after you execute the statement. Therefore, the problem is not with the calculation itself. Because the only statement left in the function is the `return` statement, you can conclude that it is the source of the bug. If you are observant, you have probably already noticed that the calcPianosCost() function's `return` statement is incorrectly returning the iPianos variable (which contains the number of pianos to move) instead of the dPianos variable (which contains the result of the calculation).

15. Select **Stop Debugging** from the Debug menu and remove the breakpoint from the `double dPianos = iPianos * 35;` statement.
16. Modify the incorrect return statement in the calcPianosCost() function as follows so that it returns the dPianos variable:

    ```
    return dPianos;
    ```

17. Rebuild and execute the program, and then enter the values from Step 2. The program should now function correctly, calculating a Moving estimate of 1670.
18. Close the Moving Estimator console window.

THE CALL STACK WINDOW

When you are working with a C++ program that contains multiple functions, the computer must remember the order in which functions are executed. For example, if you have a main() function that calls an accountsPayable() function that calls an accountsReceivable() function, the computer must remember to return to the accountsPayable() function once the accountsReceivable() function finishes executing, and then return to the main() function once the accountsPayable() function finishes executing. Similarly, if the accountsReceivable() function calls a depositFunds() function after it has been called by the accountsPayable() function, then the computer must remember to return to the accountsReceivable() function when the depositFunds() function finishes executing, then return to the accountsPayable() function once the accountsReceivable() function finishes executing, and finally return to the main() function after the accountsPayable() function finishes executing. The **call stack** refers to the order in which functions execute in a program. Each time a program calls a function, the function is added to the top of the call stack, then removed once it finishes executing.

The ability to view the contents of a call stack is very useful when you are tracing logic errors in large programs with multiple functions. For example, you might have a variable that is passed as an argument among several functions. At some point, the variable is being assigned the wrong value. Viewing the call stack, along with using tracing and other debug windows, makes it easier to locate the specific function causing the problem. When you enter break mode to debug a program, functions are automatically added to and removed from the Call Stack window as you step through your program. You display the call stack when you are in break mode by selecting Call Stack from the Windows submenu on the Debug menu.

Next, you will step through some of the functions in the Moving Estimator program to observe the contents of the Call Stack window.

To step through some of the functions in the Moving Estimator program to observe the contents of the Call Stack window:

1. Return to the **MovingEstimator.cpp** file in the Code Editor window.
2. Right-click in the cout statement in the main() function that calls the calcTotalEstimate() function, and select the **Run To Cursor** command from

the shortcut menu. The program starts executing and then enters break mode when it encounters the statement that calls the calcTotalEstimate() function.

3. Display the Call Stack window by selecting **Call Stack** from the Windows submenu on the Debug menu. The Call Stack window includes several function calls required by the system, including the call to the mainCRTStartup(). At the top of the call stack is the last function call to the main() function.

4. Select the **Step Into** command to execute the calcTotalEstimate() function. The calcTotalEstimate() function call is added to the Call Stack. Your Call Stack window should resemble Figure 4-26, although there may be some additional items on the Call Stack, depending on your system.

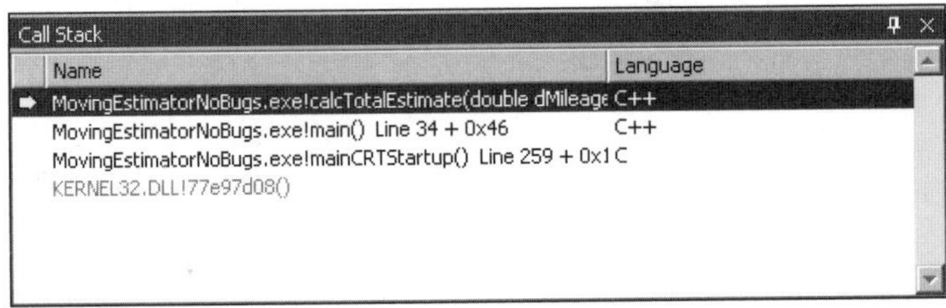

Figure 4-26 Call Stack window in the Moving Estimator program

5. Select the **Step Out** command, the calcTotalEstimate() function finishes executing. Control is transferred back to the main() function, and the calcTotalEstimate() function call is removed from the Call Stack window. Functions will continue to be added and removed from the Call Stack window in this manner for the duration of the program.

6. Select **Stop Debugging** from the Debug menu to end debugging mode.

C++ Language Bugs and Debugging Resources

If you have tried everything you can think of to fix a bug in your program, consider the possibility that you might be encountering one of the known bugs in Visual C++. Bugs can occur with Visual C++'s implementation of the C++ language or with the Visual C++ application itself. To see a list of known bugs in Visual C++ (as well as in other Microsoft development tools), visit the MSDN Bug Center at *http://msdn.microsoft.com/bugs/*. You can view lists of known bugs and suggested workarounds. You can also view a list of perceived bugs, which appear to be bugs to some users, but are really part of Visual C++'s design. If you find what appears to be an undocumented bug in Visual C++, you can submit a bug report at *http://support.microsoft.com/support/visualc/report/default.asp*. But before you submit a bug report, be sure that the problem does not already exist in the bug list and be sure that you can reproduce the bug. Sometimes a problem may occur because your computer is out of memory or you are experiencing other system problems. Microsoft would certainly have its hands full if it received a bug report every time a programmer received an error in his or her application that was caused by a faulty computer or system problem.

Note that the manufacturer of a software program is not always the first to know about a bug in its product. Innovative users often discover bugs first and then report them to a program's creator. These users also usually love to share their bug discoveries with other users. Take advantage of the many Visual C++ programmers who are often more than happy to help you solve a problem or track down a bug. You can find help on many different Web sites, in newsgroups, and in the special forums of Internet service providers such as CompuServe, Prodigy, and America Online.

Chapter Summary

- Syntax errors occur when you enter code that the compiler does not recognize.
- If your Visual C++ program encounters a problem while it is executing, the problem is called a run-time error.
- Logic errors are problems in the design of a program that prevent it from running as you anticipate it will run.
- Tracing is the examination of individual statements in an executing program.
- One of the simplest tracing tools you can use is an output statement (cout) in a console application.
- You can use comments in your code to help locate bugs.
- Visual C++ provides a program called the debugger that contains several tools that can help you trace each line of code, creating a much more efficient method of finding and resolving logic errors.
- Break mode temporarily suspends, or pauses, program execution so that you can monitor values and trace program execution.
- A Debug build contains additional information that is required by the debugger tools.
- A Release build does not contain any debugging information.
- The Step Into, Step Over, and Step Out commands on the Debug menu are used for tracing program execution once you enter break mode.
- When you select the Run to Cursor command, the program runs normally until it reaches the statement where your cursor is located, at which point the program enters break mode.
- The Autos window displays variables that have been initialized within the current scope.

- The Locals window displays all local variables within the currently executing function, regardless of whether or not they have been initialized.
- The Watch window is used for monitoring and changing specific variables that you enter.
- QuickWatch is a dialog box that you can use to quickly examine the value of a single variable or expression.
- The call stack refers to the order in which functions execute in a program.
- If you have tried everything you can think of to fix a bug in your program, consider the possibility that you may be encountering one of the known bugs in Visual C++.

Review Questions

1. ______________ errors occur when you enter code that the compiler does not recognize.
   a. Application
   b. Logic
   c. Run-time
   d. Syntax
2. If a program encounters a problem while a program is executing, that problem is called a(n) ______________ error.
   a. application
   b. logic
   c. run-time
   d. syntax
3. ______________ errors are problems in the design of a program that prevent it from running as you anticipate.
   a. Application
   b. Logic
   c. Run-time
   d. Syntax
4. Which of the following statements would cause a syntax error?
   a. `cout << "" <<;`
   b. `AfxMessageBox("Hello World")`
   c. `return TRUE;`
   d. `CMainWindow curWin;`

5. Which of the following functions would cause a run-time error?

   a.
   ```
   double calcMarginPercent() {
          double dGrossProfit = 100;
          double dNetProfit = 100;
          double dMargin = dGrossProfit - dNetProfit;
          double dMarginPercent = dMargin / dGrossProfit;
          }
   ```
   b.
   ```
   double calcMarginPercent() {
          double dGrossProfit = 200;
          double dNetProfit = 100;
          double dMargin = dGrossProfit - dNetProfit;
          double dMarginPercent = dMargin / dGrossProfit;
          }
   ```
   c.
   ```
   double calcMarginPercent() {
          double dGrossProfit = 200;
          double dNetProfit = 100;
          double dMargin = dGrossProfit - dNetProfit;
          double dMarginPercent = dMargin / dGrossProfit;
          }
   ```
   d.
   ```
   double calcMarginPercent() {
          double dGrossProfit = 0;
          double dNetProfit = 100;
          double dMargin = dGrossProfit - dNetProfit;
          double dMarginPercent = dMargin / dGrossProfit;
          }
   ```

6. Which of the following `if` statements is logically incorrect?

   a.
   ```
   if (count < 5)
          cout << count << endl;
   ```
   b.
   ```
   if (count =< 5)
          cout << count << endl;
   ```
   c.
   ```
   if (count == 5);
          cout << count << endl;
   ```
   d.
   ```
   if (count == 5) {
          cout << count << endl;
   }
   ```

7. Which of the following statements would cause a compiler error message?

   a. `int iNumber = 3.12;`

   b. `double dNumber = 3.12;`

   c. `float fNumber = 3.12;`

   d. `bool bNumber = 3.12`

8. Which of the following statements would cause a compiler warning message?
   a. `int iNumber = 3.12;`
   b. `double dNumber = 3.12;`
   c. `float fNumber = 3.12;`
   d. `bool bNumber = 3;`

9. ________________ refers to the examination of individual statements in an executing program.
   a. Trailing
   b. Tracing
   c. Tracking
   d. Commenting
10. Simplified, temporary programs that are used for testing functions and other code are called ________________.
    a. test kits
    b. stub functions
    c. driver programs
    d. dynamic link libraries
11. ________________ mode temporarily suspends, or pauses, program execution so that you can monitor values and trace program execution.
    a. Break
    b. Stop
    c. Suspend
    d. Wait
12. Which build version do you use when debugging a program?
    a. Win32 Debug
    b. Win32 Check
    c. Debug
    d. Release
13. Which build version do you use when distributing a program?
    a. Win32 Complete
    b. Win32 Release
    c. Debug
    d. Release

14. Which command executes an individual line of code and then pauses until you instruct the debugger to continue?
    a. Step Into
    b. Step Out
    c. Step Over
    d. Continue
15. Which debugger command executes all the statements in the next function?
    a. Step Into
    b. Step Out
    c. Step Over
    d. Continue
16. Which debugger command executes the rest of the commands in a function and moves to the next statement following the statement that called the current function?
    a. Step Into
    b. Step Out
    c. Step Over
    d. Continue
17. Which debugger command resumes program execution until it encounters the next breakpoint?
    a. Continue
    b. Proceed
    c. Exit Debug
    d. Go
18. A(n) ________________ is a statement in the code at which program execution enters break mode.
    a. stop marker
    b. breakpoint
    c. pause position
    d. interrupt
19. The ________________ window displays all local variables within the currently executing function, regardless of whether they have been initialized.
    a. Auto
    b. Locals
    c. This
    d. Scope

20. The ______________ window is used for monitoring and changing specific variables that you enter.
    a. Trace
    b. Immediate
    c. Variables
    d. Watch
21. The order in which functions execute in a program is the ______________.
    a. execution chain
    b. procedure heap
    c. call stack
    d. method batch

PROGRAMMING EXERCISES

1. Manually locate and correct the syntax errors in the following code:

```
#include <iostream>;
#include <string>
using namespace std;
string cityLocation(int iAmericanCity);
main()
{
     int iCity = 0;
     string sState;
     cout << "Enter a number to find the state
          where a city is located. << endl;
     cout << "1. Boston" <<;
     cout << "2. Chicago" << endl;
     cout << "3. Los Angeles" << endl;
     cout << "4. Miami" << endl;
     cout << "5. Providence" << endl << endl;
     cin >> iCity;
     cout << endl;
     sState = cityLocation(iCity);
     cout << sState << endl << endl;
}
string cityLocation(int iAmericanCity) {
     switch (iAmericanCity)
          case 1:
               return "Boston is in Massachusetts";
               break;
          case 2:
               return "Chicago is in Illinois";
               break;
```

```
            case 3:
                 return "Los Angeles is in California";
                 break;
            case 4
                 return "Miami is in Florida";
                 break;
            case 5:
                 return "Providence is in Rhode Island";
                 break;
       default:
                 return "You did not select one of the five
cities!";
}
```

2. The following code should print the values *1*, *2*, *4*, and *5* to the screen. Instead, the code prints only *1* and *2* to the screen. Find the error in the code.

```
for(int ctCount = 1; ctCount <=5; ++ctCount) {
     if(ctCount == 3)
          break;
     cout << ctCount << endl;
}
```

3. The following code should output the two statements within the `if` statement. Instead, it only prints the single statement contained in the `else` clause. Identify the error and rewrite the code:

```
int iNum = 5;
if (iNum = 5) {       // CONDITION EVALUATES TO 'TRUE'
     cout << "The condition evaluates to true." << endl;
     cout << "iNum is equal to 5." << endl;
}
else
     cout << "The condition is false." << endl;
}
```

4. Use build errors to identify the bugs in the following code:

```
#include <iostream>
using namespace std;
void main() {
  cout << "Mark Twain said" endl;
  cout << "Everybody talks about the weather," << endl;
  cout << "but nobody does anything about it." << endl
}
```

5. Use build errors to identify the bugs in the following code. Be sure to test all of the code branches in the getLetterGrad() function to ensure that the program contains no bugs.

```
#include <iostream>
#include <string>
using namespace std;
void main() {
    int iGrade;
  cout << "Please enter a numeric grade: " ;
    cin >> iGrade;
  string sEarnedGrade = getLetterGrade(iGrade);
  cout << "The equivalent letter grade is "
        << iGrade << endl;
}
string getLetterGrade(int iGrade) {
  if (iGrade < 45);
        sGrade = "F";
  else if (iGrade < 50);
        sGrade = "D";
  else if (iGrade < 55);
        sGrade = "D+";
  else if (iGrade < 60);
        sGrade = "C-";
  else if (iGrade < 65);
        sGrade = "C";
  else if (iGrade < 70);
        sGrade = "C+";
  else if (iGrade < 75);
        sGrade = "B-";
  else if (iGrade < 80);
        sGrade = "B";
  else if (iGrade < 85);
        sGrade = "B+";
  else if (iGrade < 90);
        sGrade = "A-";
  else;
        sGrade = "A";
}
```

6. The following program should calculate the mileage charges for a car rental company. The company charges 30 cents per mile for all miles up to 100, and then 20 cents per mile for any additional miles. Use output statements to find the bugs in the program.

```
#include <iostream>
using namespace std;
void main() {
    int iMiles = 0;
  double dMileageCharge = 0;
  const double dStandardMiles = 0.30;
    const double dExtraMiles = 0.20;
    cout << "Enter the number of miles you have driven: ";
    cin >> iMiles;
    if iMiles <= 100;
        dMileageCharge = iMiles * dStandardMiles;
    else
       dMileageCharge = dStandardMiles * 100;
       dMileageCharge = (iMiles - 100) * dExtraMiles;
    cout << "Your total mileage charge is $"
       << dMileageCharge << endl;
}
```

7. The following code should print the days of the week. Instead, it prints only Tuesday through Sunday, and an indecipherable value is printed after *Sunday*. Use comments to locate the bugs and make the appropriate changes.

```
#include <iostream>
#include <string>
using namespace std;
void main() {
     string sDaysOfWeek[7];
     sDaysOfWeek[0] = "Monday";
     sDaysOfWeek[1] = "Tuesday";
     sDaysOfWeek[2] = "Wednesday";
     sDaysOfWeek[3] = "Thursday";
     sDaysOfWeek[4] = "Friday";
     sDaysOfWeek[5] = "Saturday";
     sDaysOfWeek[6] = "Sunday";
     int ctCount = 1;
     do {
          cout << sDaysOfWeek[ctCount] << endl;
          ++ctCount;
     } while (ctCount <= 7);
     cout << endl;
}
```

8. The following program should print a rectangle composed of asterisks, based on the height and width entered by the user. However, when you execute the program, only the first row of asterisks prints. The correct number of lines for the height of the rectangle print to the screen, but they are empty. Use one of the Debugger's Step commands and one of the variable monitoring windows, such as the Autos window, to trace the variables in the program in order to identify the problem.


```
#include <iostream>
using namespace std;
void main() {
    int iHeight = 0;
  int iWidth = 0;
  int iHeightCount = 1;
  int iWidthCount = 1;
  cout << "Enter the height of the rectangle: ";
  cin >> iHeight;
  cout << "Enter the width of the rectangle: ";
  cin >> iWidth;
    cout << endl;
    while (iHeightCount <= iHeight)
    {
        while (iWidthCount <= iWidth)
        {
            cout << "*";
            ++iWidthCount;
        }
        cout << endl;
        ++iHeightCount;
    }
    cout << endl;
}
```

9. The following program should keep a running sum of the integers entered by the user. Instead, the program keeps printing only the last number entered. Use the Watch window to monitor the value of the iSum variable in order to identify the problem.

```
#include <iostream>
using namespace std;
void main() {
  int iNumberEntered = 0;
  int iSum = 0;
  char cSelection;
  do {
       cout << "Enter a number: ";
       cin >> iNumberEntered;
       int iSum = iNumberEntered;
       cout << "The sum of the numbers you entered is: "
             << iSum << endl;
```

```
            cout << "Press 'y' to enter another number "
                  << "or any other key to exit: ";
            cin >> cSelection;
    } while (cSelection == 'y');
}
```

Programming Projects

1. The Chapter.04 folder on your Data Disk contains copies of some of the projects and end of chapter exercises you created earlier in this text. However, all of the programs contain errors. Use any of the debugging skills you have learned in this chapter to correct the errors. You may review earlier chapters to see how each program should function—but *do not* do so to copy or review the correct syntax. Use these exercises as an opportunity to test and improve your debugging skills. The projects for you to correct are as follows:
   - Chapter2_HelloWorld
   - Chapter3_ChemistryQuizFinal
2. Many advanced programming languages, including C++, include a feature known as exception handling, which allows programs to handle errors as they occur in the execution of a program. Search the MSDN Library for exception-handling topics and explain how you would use exception handling in your projects.
3. Visual C++ gives you the option of compiling and linking your project from the command line. How do you go about building a project from the command line? What additional debugging features, if any, exist for command-line compilation? Refer to the Compiling and Linking topic in MSDN Library for your answer.
4. One of the most important aspects of creating a good program is the design and analysis phase of the project. Conducting a good design and analysis phase is critical to minimizing bugs in your program. Search the Internet or your local library for information on this topic. Then explain how you should handle the design and analysis phase of a software project.
5. Equally important to minimizing bugs during software development is the testing phase. Search the Internet or your local library for information on software testing. Then design a plan for thoroughly testing your Visual C++ programs. How would you use driver programs and stub functions in your testing plan?
6. Visit Microsoft's Bug Center at http://msdn.microsoft.com/bugs/ and study the different types of bugs and errors in Visual C++ that are currently known. Write an analysis of the different categories of bugs and include information such as the category of error and what sort of fix, if any, exists for each bug.

CHAPTER

5

INTRODUCTION TO CLASSES

In this chapter you will learn:

- About object-oriented programming and classes
- About information hiding
- How to use access specifiers
- About interface and implementation files
- How to use Visual C++ class tools
- How to prevent multiple inclusion
- How to work with member functions

Out of chaos comes order.

Friedrich Nietzsche (1844–1900)

PREVIEW: THE RETIREMENT PLANNER PROGRAM

In this chapter and the next few chapters, you will study classes, which is perhaps the most important topic in C++ programming. Recall from Chapter 1, that classes are structures that contain code, methods, attributes, and other information. In this chapter you will create a Retirement Planner program to learn how to work with basic class techniques.

To preview the Retirement Planner program:

1. Create a **Chapter.05** folder in your Visual C++ Projects folder.
2. Copy the **Chapter5_RetirementPlanner** folder from the Chapter.05 folder on your Data Disk to the Chapter.05 folder in your Visual C++ Projects folder. Then open the **RetirementPlanner** project in Visual C++.
3. The Chapter5_RetirementPlanner folder in the Chapter.05 folder in your Visual C++ Projects folder contains two C++ source files and a C++ header file. First, open the **CalcSavings.cpp** file in the Code Editor window. This file is a Win32 console application with a main() function that displays and gathers information. You should be able to recognize most of the code. The CalcSavings.cpp file will be used for demonstrating how to work with the class that will provide the Retirement Planner program's functionality. Close the **CalcSavings.cpp** source file.
4. Open the **RetirementPlanner.h** header file. This file contains variable declarations and function prototypes, as illustrated in Figure 5-1. The file also contains some new preprocessor directives, along with two labels—public and private—that determine how functions and variables can be accessed outside of the class by other classes or programs. You will also see a function that includes the `inline` keyword, but that is declared outside of the class declaration. This is known as an `inline` function and is used with small functions to request that the compiler replace calls to a function with the function definition wherever the function is called in a program. Close the **RetirementPlanner.h** source file.
5. Open the **RetirementPlanner.cpp** file. This file contains the actual definitions for the functions declared in the RetirementPlanner.h header file. Figure 5-2 shows a portion of the file. Notice that the file imports the RetirementPlanner.h file using an #include statement, but that the header filename is enclosed in quotation marks instead of brackets. Also notice that each function definition is preceded by RetirementPlanner and the scope resolution operator (::). RetirementPlanner is the name of the class itself. You use the class name and the scope resolution operator to define a function as being part of a particular class.

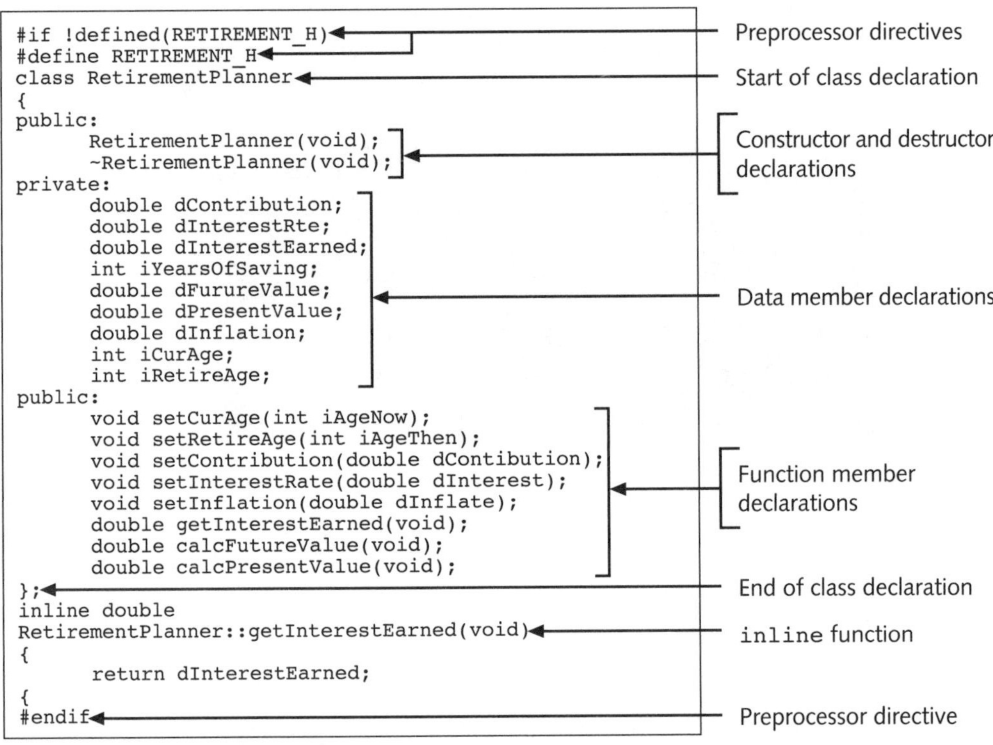

```
#if !defined(RETIREMENT_H)
#define RETIREMENT_H
class RetirementPlanner
{
public:
      RetirementPlanner(void);
      ~RetirementPlanner(void);
private:
      double dContribution;
      double dInterestRte;
      double dInterestEarned;
      int iYearsOfSaving;
      double dFurureValue;
      double dPresentValue;
      double dInflation;
      int iCurAge;
      int iRetireAge;
public:
      void setCurAge(int iAgeNow);
      void setRetireAge(int iAgeThen);
      void setContribution(double dContibution);
      void setInterestRate(double dInterest);
      void setInflation(double dInflate);
      double getInterestEarned(void);
      double calcFutureValue(void);
      double calcPresentValue(void);
};
inline double
RetirementPlanner::getInterestEarned(void)
{
      return dInterestEarned;
{
#endif
```


Figure 5-1 RetirementPlanner.h

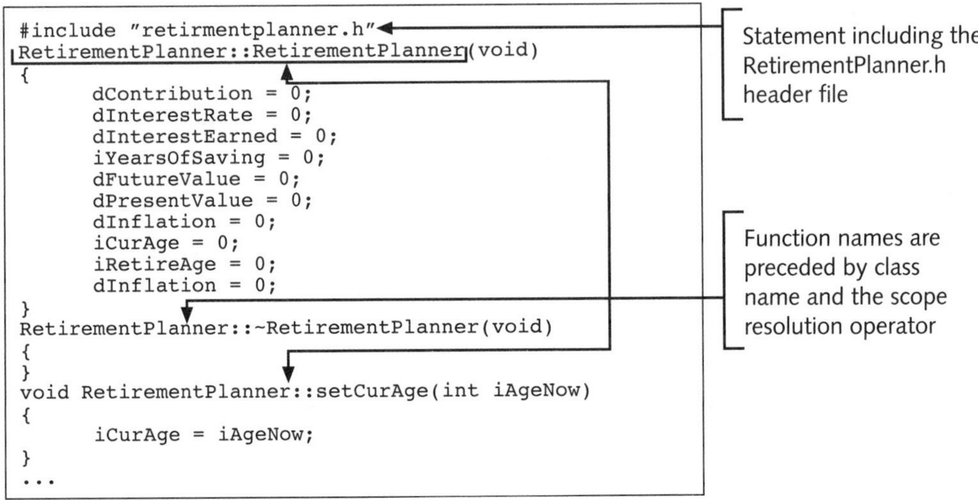

```
#include "retirmentplanner.h"
RetirementPlanner::RetirementPlanner(void)
{
      dContribution = 0;
      dInterestRate = 0;
      dInterestEarned = 0;
      iYearsOfSaving = 0;
      dFutureValue = 0;
      dPresentValue = 0;
      dInflation = 0;
      iCurAge = 0;
      iRetireAge = 0;
      dInflation = 0;
}
RetirementPlanner::~RetirementPlanner(void)
{
}
void RetirementPlanner::setCurAge(int iAgeNow)
{
      iCurAge = iAgeNow;
}
...
```


Figure 5-2 RetirementPlanner.cpp

6. Build and execute the Retirement Planner program. Then enter values for each of the variables to calculate retirement savings. Figure 5-3 shows how the program appears in the console window after entering some values.

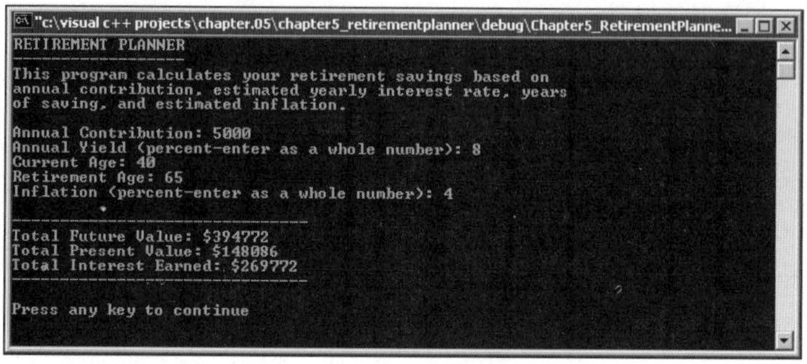

```
"c:\visual c++ projects\chapter.05\chapter5_retirementplanner\debug\Chapter5_RetirementPlanne...
RETIREMENT PLANNER
------------------
This program calculates your retirement savings based on
annual contribution, estimated yearly interest rate, years
of saving, and estimated inflation.

Annual Contribution: 5000
Annual Yield (percent-enter as a whole number): 8
Current Age: 40
Retirement Age: 65
Inflation (percent-enter as a whole number): 4
-------------------------------------------------------
Total Future Value: $394772
Total Present Value: $148086
Total Interest Earned: $269772
-------------------------------------------------------

Press any key to continue
```

Figure 5-3 Retirement Planner console window

7. Press any key to close the Retirement Planner program window.
8. Close the RetirementPlanner project by selecting Close Solution from the File menu.

OBJECT-ORIENTED PROGRAMMING AND CLASSES

Classes form the basis of object-oriented programming. Object-oriented programming is a way of designing and accessing code. The pieces of the programming puzzle—data types, variables, control structures, functions, and so on—are the same as in any other type of programming. What differs is how you assemble the puzzle. You first learned about classes in Chapter 1, "Introduction to Programming and Visual C++," in very general terms. In this chapter, you will learn about classes in detail.

Classes

Classes were defined in Chapter 1 as structures that contain code, methods, attributes, and other information. Now that you are familiar with the basics of a C++ program, let's refine this definition. In C++ programming, **classes** are data structures that contain variables along with functions for manipulating the variables. The functions and variables defined in a class are called **class members**. Class variables are referred to as **data members** or **member variables**, whereas class functions are referred to as **member functions** or **function members**. Functions that are not part of a class are referred to as **global functions**. To use the variables and functions in a class, you declare an object from that class. When you declare an object from a class, you are said to be **instantiating** an object. When you work with a class object, member functions are often referred to as methods, and data members are often referred to as properties.

Classes themselves are also referred to as user-defined data types or programmer-defined data types. These terms can be somewhat misleading, however, because they do not accurately reflect the fact that classes can contain member functions. Additionally, classes usually contain multiple data members of different data types, so calling a class a data type becomes even more confusing.

One reason that classes are referred to as user-defined data types or programmer-defined data types is that you can work with a class as a single unit, or *object*, in the same way you work with a variable. In fact, C++ programmers use the terms *variable* and *object* interchangeably. The term *object-oriented programming* comes from the fact that you can bundle variables and functions together and use the result as a single unit (a *variable* or *object*). What this means will become clearer to you as you progress through this text. For now, think of a hand-held calculator as an example. A calculator could be considered an object of a Calculation class. You access all of the Calculation class functions (such as addition and subtraction) and its data members (operands that represent the numbers you are calculating) through your calculator object. You never actually work with the Calculation class yourself, only with an object of the class (your calculator).

But why do you need to work with a collection of related variables and functions as a single object? Why not simply call each individual variable and function as necessary, without using all of this class business? The truth is you are not required to work with classes; you can create much of the same functionality without classes as you can by using classes. Some simple types of Visual C++ programs you write will probably not need to be created with classes. Classes help make complex programs easier to manage, however, by logically grouping related functions and data and by allowing you to refer to that grouping as a single object. Another reason for using classes is to hide information that users of a class do not need to access or know about. Information hiding helps minimize the amount of information that needs to pass in and out of an object, which helps increase program speed and efficiency. Classes also make it much easier to reuse code or distribute your code to others for use in their programs. (You will learn how to create your own classes and include them in your programs shortly.) Without a way to package variables and functions in classes and include those classes in a new program, you would need to copy and paste each segment of code you wanted to reuse (functions, variables, and so on) into any new program.

An additional reason to use classes is that instances of objects inherit their characteristics, such as class members, from the class upon which they are based. This inheritance allows you to build new classes based on existing classes without having to rewrite the code contained in the existing classes. You will learn more about inheritance in Chapter 7, "Object Manipulation." For now, you should understand that an object has the same characteristics as its class.

There are two primary types of classes that you will work with in this text: classes declared with the `struct` keyword and classes declared with the `class` keyword. First, you will learn about classes declared with the `struct` keyword.

Creating Structures

So far you have worked with data types that store single values such as integers, floating-point numbers, and characters. You have also worked with arrays, which contain sets of data represented by a single variable name. One drawback to using arrays is that all elements in an array must be of the same data type. Suppose you have several pieces of related information that you want to be able to refer to as a single variable, similar to an array. An example may be the information related to a mortgage, including the property value (`int`), down payment (`double`), interest rate (`double`), terms (`short`), and a Boolean value indicating that the closing has been scheduled. You cannot use an array, however, because the individual pieces of information are of different data types. To store this type of information as a single variable, you use something called a structure. A **structure**, or **`struct`**, is an advanced, user-defined data type that uses a single variable name to store multiple pieces of related information. Remember that a user-defined data type is another way of referring to a class. This means that a structure is also a class. The individual pieces of information stored in a structure are called **elements**, **fields**, or **members**. You define a structure using the `struct` keyword and the following syntax:

```
struct structure_name {
   data_type field_name;
   data_type field_name;
   ...
} variable_name;
```

You might also see structures referred to as record structures or data structures.

The *structure_name* portion of the structure definition is the name of the new, user-defined data type. You can use any name you like for a structure, as long as you follow the same naming conventions that you use when declaring variables and functions. Within the structure's curly braces, you declare the data type and field names for each piece of information stored in the structure, the same way you declare a variable and its data type. The *variable_name* portion of the structure declaration is optional and allows you to create a variable based on the new structure when the structure is first declared. If you omit *variable_name*, then you can later declare a new variable in your code using the structure name as the data type. The following code declares a structure for the mortgage information, but does not assign a variable name at declaration because *variable_name* is omitted:

```
struct Mortgage {
     char szPropertyLocation[50];
       int iPropertyValue;
       double dDownPayment;
       double dInterest;
```

```
        short siTerms;
        bool bClosingScheduled;
    };
```

After creating the preceding structure, you declare a new variable of type mortgage using a statement similar to `Mortgage vacationHome;`. This statement instantiates a Mortgage object named vacationHome. Recall that the terms variable and object are used interchangeably. This means that a variable based on a structure is also an object. To access the fields inside a structure variable, you append a period to the variable name, followed by the field name, using the syntax ***`variable.field;`***. When you use a period to access an object's members, such as a structure's fields, the period is referred to as the **member selection operator**. You use the member selection operator to initialize or modify the value stored in an object field. For example, to assign or modify the value stored in a `double` field named dInterest in a Mortgage structure named vacationHome, you use a statement similar to `vacationHome.dInterest = .08;`.

The following code shows the same Mortgage structure definition followed by statements that declare a new Mortgage variable named vacationHome and assign values to the structure fields. Then the code shows statements that print the contents of each field:

```
#include <iostream>
#include <cstring>
using namespace std;
struct Mortgage {
     char szPropertyLocation[50];
       int iPropertyValue;
       double dDownPayment;
       double dInterest;
     short siTerms;
     bool bClosingScheduled;
};
void main() {
     Mortgage vacationHome;
     strcpy(vacationHome.szPropertyLocation,
       "Miami, Florida");
     vacationHome.iPropertyValue = 250000;
     vacationHome.dDownPayment = .2;
     vacationHome.dInterest = .08;
     vacationHome.siTerms = 30;
     vacationHome.bClosingScheduled = true;
     cout << vacationHome.szPropertyLocation << endl;
     cout << vacationHome.iPropertyValue << endl;
     cout << vacationHome.dDownPayment << endl;
     cout << vacationHome.dInterest << endl;
     cout << vacationHome.siTerms << endl;
     cout << vacationHome.bClosingScheduled << endl;
}
```

You are not allowed to assign values to the fields inside the structure definition itself. For example, the following code causes a compile error:

```
struct Mortgage {
     char szPropertyLocation[50] = "Miami, Florida";
       int iPropertyValue = 250000;
       double dDownPayment = .2;
       double dInterest = .08;
     short siTerms = 30;
     bool bClosingScheduled = true;
};
```

You can, however, use an initializer list to assign values to a structure's fields when you declare a variable of the structure's type. An **initializer list** is a series of values that are assigned to an object at declaration. To use an initializer list, you must enclose the values you want assigned to the structure's fields within braces, separated by commas, and in the order in which the fields are declared in the structure definition. For example, the following code contains the employee structure definition, followed by the declaration of the currentEmployee variable, which assigns initial values to the fields:

```
#include <iostream>
#include <cstring>
using namespace std;
struct Mortgage {
char szPropertyLocation[50];
  int iPropertyValue;
  double dDownPayment;
  double dInterest;
short siTerms;
bool bClosingScheduled;
};
void main() {
   Mortgage vacationHome = {"Miami, Florida", 250000,
         .2, .08, 30, true};
   ...
}
```

Initializer list

When using an initializer list to initialize a struct's members, you must list each value within the brackets in the order that each member is declared in the `struct` definition. If you do not, then the values you supply will be assigned to the wrong `struct` member. You will receive a compile error if you list more initialization values than there are members in the `struct`. If you do not supply enough initialization values, then the members you did not initialize will be assigned a value of zero.

Although you can use string class variables with structures, you cannot initialize a structure's string class variables using an initializer list. For this reason, any structure examples you see in this book will use C-style string variables instead of string class variables.

Note that structures are part of the C programming language. However, they are widely used in Windows programming; in fact, you will use structures extensively when you work with Windows programs later in this text. In order to familiarize you with defining structures, you will now create a simple console application that creates a structure named sportsCar, assigns values to a sportsCar variable, and then prints the variable's contents. The sportsCar structure will define fields of several different data types that will contain the specifications of a particular sports car.

To create a simple console application that creates the sportsCar structure, assigns values to a sportsCar variable, and then prints the variable's contents:

1. Create a new Win32 Project named **CarInfo** in the **Chapter.05** folder in your Visual C++ Projects folder. Be sure to clear the **Create directory for Solution** check box in the New Project dialog box. In the Application Settings tab of the Win32 Application Wizard dialog box, select **Console application** as the application type, click the **Empty project** check box, and then click the **Finish** button. Once the project is created, add a C++ source file named **CarInfo**.
2. Type the preprocessor directives shown in Figure 5-4, which gives the program access to the iostream and cstring libraries along with the using directive shown in Figure 5-4, which designates the std namespace. Also, type the opening header for the main() function.

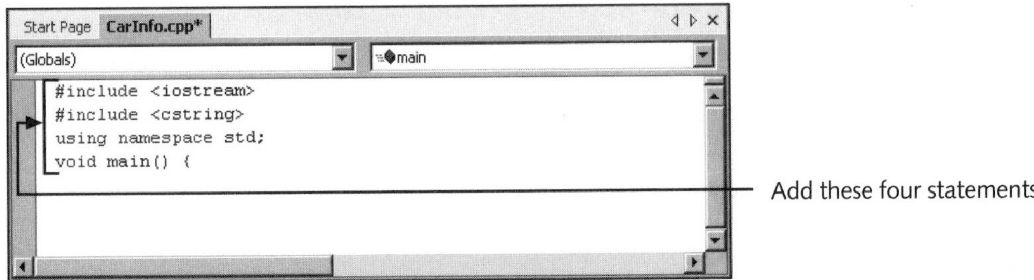

Figure 5-4 Opening statements added to CarInfo.cpp

3. In the main() function body, define the following sportsCar structure, as shown in Figure 5-5. Notice that the structure's fields are of different data types.
4. Type the statements shown in Figure 5-6, which declare a new sportsCar variable named myCar and assign values to the structure's fields.

Start Page CarInfo.cpp*

sportsCar

```
#include <iostream>
#include <cstring>
using namespace std;
void main() {
    struct sportsCar {
        char szMake[25];
        char szModel[25];
        long lYear;
        int iDoors;
        double dEngine;
    };
```

Add the sportsCar structure here

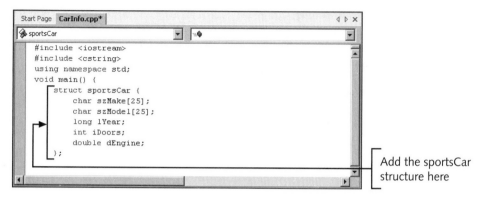

Figure 5-5 sportsCar `struct` added to the main() function

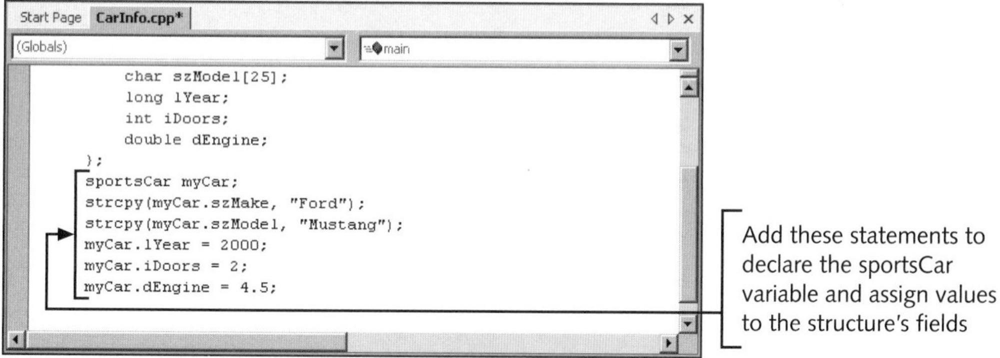

Figure 5-6 sportsCar variable declared and values assigned to the structure's fields

5. Finally, add the statements shown in Figure 5-7, which print the values assigned to the structure's fields. Also, type the main() function's closing brace.

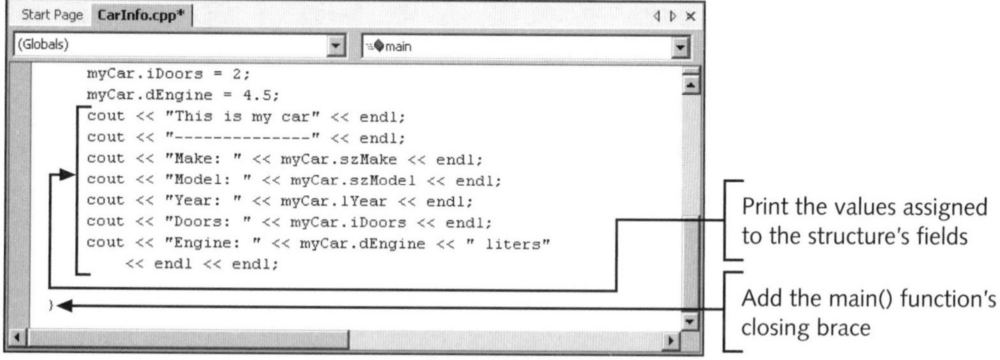

Figure 5-7 Output statements and the main()function's closing brace added to CarInfo.cpp

6. Build and execute the CarInfo program. Figure 5-8 shows the output.

```
"c:\visual c++ projects\chapter.05\carinfo\debug\CarInfo.exe"
This is my car
--------------
Make: Ford
Model: Mustang
Year: 2000
Doors: 2
Engine: 4.5 liters

Press any key to continue_
```

Figure 5-8 Output of the Car Info program

7. Press any key to close the command window.
8. Close the CarInfo project by selecting Close Solution from the File menu.

Creating Classes with the `class` Keyword

The most important type of class used in C++ programming is defined using the **`class`** keyword. For brevity, from this point forward classes defined with the **`class`** keyword will be referred to simply as classes. You define classes the same way you define structures, and you access a class's data members using the member selection operator. The following code shows an example of a class named Stocks:

```
class Stocks {
public:
  int iNumShares;
  double dPurchasePricePerShare;
  double dCurrentPricePerShare;
};
void main() {
  Stocks stockValue;
  stockValue.iNumShares = 500;
  stockValue.dPurchasePricePerShare = 10.785;
  stockValue.dCurrentPricePerShare = 6.5;
}
```

The differences between the preceding class and the structure example you saw earlier are the use of the **`class`** keyword and the **`public:`** label. The **`public:`** label determines default accessibility to a class's members. In fact, default accessibility is one of the only differences between structures and classes. For now, you should understand that the accessibility to a class's members is what allows you to hide information, such as data members, from users of your class. You will learn more about accessibility in the next section on information hiding.

Structures are left over from C programming. Classes are unique to C++ programming. In C programming, structures do not support encapsulation because C programming is primarily a procedural programming language, not object-oriented, as is C++. In C++ programming, however, structures do support encapsulation, making them virtually identical to classes. This means that you can substitute the `struct` keyword for any classes declared with the `class` keyword. However, most C++ programmers use the `class` keyword to clearly designate the programs they write as object-oriented C++ programs. Because you are studying C++, you will define your classes with the `class` keyword.

INFORMATION HIDING

One of the fundamental principals in object-oriented programming is the concept of information hiding. Information hiding gives an encapsulated object its black box capabilities so that users of a class can see only the members of the class that you allow them to see. Essentially, the principal of **information hiding** states that any class members that other programmers, sometimes called *clients*, do not need to access or know about should be hidden. Information hiding helps minimize the amount of information that needs to pass in and out of an object, which helps increase program speed and efficiency. Information hiding also reduces the complexity of the code that clients see, allowing them to concentrate on the task of integrating an object into their programs. For example, if a client wants to add to her Accounting program a Payroll object, she does not need to know the underlying details of the Payroll object's member functions, nor does she need to modify any local data members that are used by those functions. The client only needs to know which of the object's member functions to call and what data (if any) needs to be passed to those member functions.

Now consider information hiding on a larger scale. Professionally developed software packages are distributed in an encapsulated format, which means that the casual user—or even an advanced programmer—cannot see the underlying details of how the software is developed. Imagine what would happen if Microsoft distributed Excel without hiding the underlying programming details. Most users of the program would be bewildered if they accidentally opened the source files. Obviously, there is no reason why Microsoft would allow users to see the underlying details of Excel, because users do not need to understand how the underlying code performs the various types of spreadsheet calculations. Microsoft also has a critical interest in protecting proprietary information, as do you. The design and sale of software components is big business. You certainly do not want to spend a significant amount of time designing an outstanding software component, only to have an unscrupulous programmer steal the code and claim it as his or her own.

This same principal of information hiding needs to be applied in object-oriented programming. There are few reasons why clients of your classes need to know the underlying details of your code. Of course, you cannot hide *all* of the underlying code, or other programmers will never be able to integrate your class with their applications. But you need to hide most of it.

Information hiding on any scale also prevents other programmers from accidentally introducing a bug into a program by modifying a class's internal workings. Programmers are curious creatures and will often attempt to "improve" your code, no matter how well it is written. Before you distribute your classes to other programmers, your classes should be thoroughly tested and bug-free. With tested and bug-free classes, other programmers can focus on the more important task of integrating your code into their programs using the data members and member functions you designate.

To enable information hiding in your classes you must designate access specifiers for each of your class members. You must also place your class code into separate interface and implementation files. You will learn about these topics next.

Access Specifiers

The first step in hiding class information is to set access specifiers for class members. **Access specifiers** control a client's access to individual data members and member functions. There are four levels of access specifiers: `public`, `private`, `protected`, and `friend`. You will use the `public`, `private`, and `friend` access specifiers in this chapter. In Chapter 7, you will learn about the `protected` access specifier.

The **`public`** access specifier allows anyone to call a class's member function or to modify a data member. The **`private`** access specifier prevents clients from calling member functions or accessing data members and is one of the key elements in information hiding. `Private` access does not restrict a class's internal access to its own members; a class's member function can modify any private data member or call any `private` member function. `Private` access restricts clients from accessing class members. The `private` access specifier does not actually hide class member definitions; it only protects them. To hide class member definitions, you must separate classes into interface and implementation files, which you will learn about shortly.

Both `public` and `private` access specifiers have what is called **class scope**: Class members of both access types are accessible by any of a class's member functions. In contrast, variables declared inside a member function have local scope to the function only and are not available outside the function, even if the function is declared with the `public` access specifier.

You place access specifiers in a class definition on a single line followed by a colon, similar to a `switch` statement's `case` labels. An access specifier that is placed on a line by itself followed by a colon is called an **access label**. The access privilege of any particular access label is applied to any class members that follow, up to the next label. For example, the following code contains a `public` and a `private` access label. The `public` label declares two public data members, iNumShares and dPurchasePricePerShare, and the `private` label declares a single private data member, dCurrentPricePerShare.

```
class Stocks {
public:
   int iNumShares;
   double dPurchasePricePerShare;
private:
   double dCurrentPricePerShare;
};
```


Access labels can be repeated, although most programmers prefer to organize all of their **public** class members under a single public access label, and all of their **private** class members under a single **private** access label. However, the following code organization with its two **public** access labels is legal:

```
class Stocks {
public:
  int iNumShares;
private:
  double dCurrentPricePerShare;
public:
  double dPurchasePricePerShare;
};
```

It is common practice to list public class members first in order to clearly identify the parts of the class that can be accessed by clients.

The default access specifier for classes is **private**. If you exclude access specifiers from your class definition, then all class members in the definition are **private** by default. For example, because the following class definition does not include any access labels, the three data member definitions are **private** by default:

```
class Stocks {
    int iNumShares;
    double dPurchasePricePerShare;
    double dCurrentPricePerShare;
};
```

If you have some reason for making all of your class members **private**, you should include a **private** access label to make it clear how you intend for the class members to be used. Many programmers prefer to make all of their data members **private** to prevent clients from accidentally assigning the wrong value to a variable or from viewing the internal workings of their programs. Or, they simply want to prevent curious clients from modifying the various parts of their program. Even if you do not need to make it clear for yourself, you should include an access label in case other programmers need to modify your work.

Default class member access is one of the major differences between classes and structures in C++. Access to classes is `private` by default. Access to structures is `public` by default.

Even if you make all data members in a class `private`, you can still allow clients of your program to retrieve or modify the value of data members by using accessor functions. **Accessor functions** are `public` member functions that a client can call to retrieve or modify the value of a data member. Because accessor functions often begin with the words *get* or *set*, they are also referred to as get or set functions. Get functions retrieve data member values; set functions modify data member values. To allow a client to pass a value to your program that will be assigned to a `private` data member, you include arguments in a set function's header definition. You can then write code in the body of the set function that validates the data passed from the client, prior to assigning values to private data members. For example, if you write a class named Payroll that includes a private data member containing the current state income-tax rate, then you could write a public accessor function named getStateTaxRate() that allows clients to retrieve the variable's value. Similarly, you could write a setStateTaxRate() function that performs various types of validation on the data passed from the client (such as making sure the value is not null, is not greater than 100%, and so on) prior to assigning a value to the private state tax rate data member.

5

Interface and Implementation Files

Although the first step in information hiding is to assign `private` access specifiers to class members, private access specifiers only designate which class members a client is not allowed to call or change. `Private` access specifiers do not prevent clients from seeing class code. To prevent clients from seeing the details of how your code is written, you place your class's interface code and implementation code in separate files. The separation of classes into interface and implementation files is a fundamental C++ software development technique because it allows you to hide the details of how your classes are written and makes it easier to modify programs.

Interface code refers to the data member and member function declarations inside a class definition's braces. Interface code does not usually contain definitions for member functions, nor does it usually assign values to the data members. Declarations are statements that only declare data members without assigning a value to them, such as `double dCurrentPricePerShare;`, or function prototypes such as `double getTotalValue();`. You create interface code in a header file with an .h extension. The interface code should be the only part of your class that a client can see and access. In effect, the interface is the "front door" to your program.

Implementation code refers to a class's function definitions and any code that assigns values to a class's data members. In other words, implementation code contains the actual member functions themselves and assigns values to data members. You add implementation code to standard C++ source files with an extension of .cpp. You give the implementation code access to the interface code by importing the header file into the C++ source file using an #include directive, just as you would import a header file from the C++ run-time library. However, instead of placing the header filename within a set of angle brackets (as you would with a header file from the C++ run-time library), you must place the name of a custom class within a set of quotation marks and include the .h extension. For example, you give the Stocks class implementation file access to the Stocks class interface file by using the statement `#include "stocks.h"` (assuming that the Stocks class interface code is saved in a file named stocks.h).

If you are familiar with the Java programming language, then you know that Java files must use the same name, including letter case, as the class they contain. In C++, however, you are not required to name your interface or implementation files with the same name and letter case as the class name.

C++ source files are distributed in compiled format, whereas header files are distributed as plain text files. Thus, clients who use your code can see only the names of data members and member functions. Clients can use and access public class members, but they cannot see the details of how your code is written. Without this ability to hide implementation details, clients could easily get around restrictions you place on class members with the `private` access specifier by copying your code into a new class file, and changing `private` access specifiers to `public`.

If you are using classes only to make your own code more efficient and have no intention of distributing your classes to others, you can place both the declarations and definitions into the same file. However, this is not considered to be good programming practice, because the separation of interface and implementation is a fundamental C++ software development technique. Additionally, if you change your mind and decide to distribute your class to others, you would need to go back and separate the class into interface and implementation files.

Note that some of the examples of implementation files in this chapter include their own main() functions. Although you can add executable class code by including a main() function in an implementation file, you are not required to. For example, the RetirementPlanner.cpp implementation file will not include a main() function. Instead, the RetirementPlanner.cpp implementation file will be called by the CalcSavings.cpp file's main() function.

Modifying a Class

Hiding implementation details is reason enough for separating a class's interface from its implementation. But, another important reason for separating a class into interface and implementation files is to make it easier to modify a program at a later date. When you modify a class, interface code, such as class member declarations, should change the least.

The implementation code normally changes the most when you modify a class. This rule of thumb is not carved in stone because you may find it necessary to drastically modify your class's interface. But for the most part, the implementation is what will change.

No matter what changes you make to your implementation code, the changes will be invisible to clients if their only entry point into your code is the interface—provided that the interface stays the same. Designing your code so that modifications are made to the implementation code and not to the interface code means that if you make any drastic changes or improvements to your class, you only need to distribute a new .cpp file to your clients, not a new interface file. Be aware, however, that if you modify class member declarations or add new declarations to expand the program's functionality, you may also need to distribute a new header file.

If the public interface class members stay the same, then clients do not need to make any changes to *their* code in order to work with your modified class. For instance, consider the Payroll object discussed earlier. The Payroll object may contain a public function member named calcFederalTaxes() that calculates a paycheck's federal tax withholding based on income tax percentages published by the Internal Revenue Service. If the Internal Revenue Service changes any of the income tax percentages, then you will need to modify the private data members within the calcFederalTaxes() function. Clients, however, do not need to be concerned with these details; they will continue to call the public calcFederalTaxes() function as usual. For these types of changes, you would not need to distribute a new interface file to your clients. You would need to distribute only a new implementation file containing the modified calcFederalTaxes() function.

VISUAL C++ CLASS TOOLS

You can work with class header and source files using the Solution Explorer window, in the same manner that you work with C++ files that are not class-based. However, Visual C++ includes various tools that make it easier to work with the classes in your programs.

Although you have been working with the Code Editor window for some time now, it has a few additional class features that are worth examining. Figure 5-9 shows an example of the Retirement Planner project open in the Code Editor window. The Navigation `bar` at the top of the Code Editor window contains two combo boxes that you can use to navigate to a particular class or its members. The Types combo box at the left of the Navigation `bar` allows you to select a class name or *global*, which displays global declarations that are not associated with a particular class. The Members combo box at the right of the Navigation `bar` allows you to select a class member or global declaration, depending on what is selected in the Types combo box.

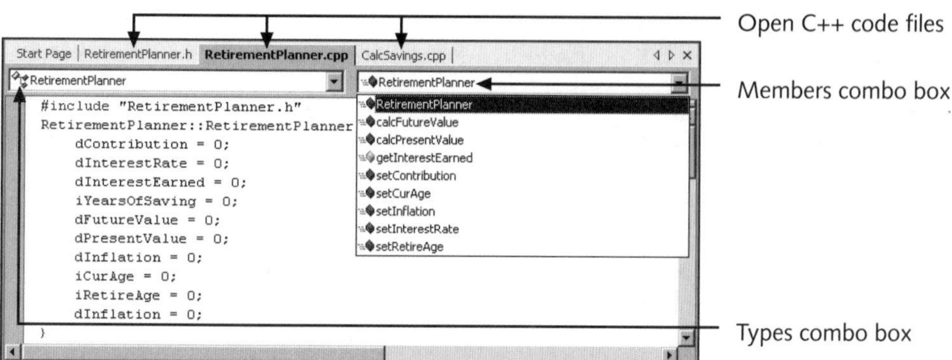

Figure 5-9 The Code Editor window with the contents of the Members como box displayed

Once your projects begin to include multiple files, you will find it helpful to use tabs at the top of the Code Editor window to navigate to an open file. In Figure 5-9 the tabs in the Code Editor window for each of the opened files are pointed out.

Another Visual C++ tool that you may find useful is the Object Browser window, which allows you to examine class members and other programming elements that are contained within objects that are used by your program. To manually display the Object Browser window point to the Other Windows submenu on the View menu and click Object Browser, or press Ctrl+Alt+J.

Class View

The **Class View window** displays project files according to their classes and is similar to the Solution Explorer window. However, whereas Solution Explorer displays a hierarchical list of all projects, folders, and files in the solution, Class View displays hierarchical lists of classes and the members they contain. You primarily use Class View to navigate through the declarations and definitions of class members. An icon represents each of the various items displayed in Class View.

In Class View, the icons that represent private class members include a symbol that looks like a padlock.

Double-clicking a data member's icon brings you to its declaration in the class header file. Double-clicking a member function's icon brings you to its definition in the class source file.

See the Class View and Object Browser Icons topic in the MSDN Library for a complete list of icons that appear in Class View.

You can also right-click a class member in ClassView and select from the shortcut menu one of the navigation or sorting commands listed in Figure 5-10.

Command	Description
Go To Definition	Opens the C++ file containing the member definition in the Code Editor window and places the insertion point in the definition statement
Go To Declaration	Opens the C++ file containing the member declaration in the Code Editor window and places the insertion point in the declaration statement
Browse Definition	Displays the selected class member in Object Browser
Quick Find Symbol	Searches for a symbol (which is an object, such as a class or its members) according to criteria you previously entered in the Find Symbol dialog box. You can open the Find Symbol dialog box by pointing to Find and Replace on the Edit menu and clicking Find Symbol, or by pressing Ctrl+Shift+Y.
Sort Alphabetically	Sorts the items displayed in Class View alphabetically
Sort By Type	Sorts the items displayed in Class View by data type
Sort By Access	Sorts the items displayed in Class View according to their access specifier (which you will study shortly)
Group By Type	Groups the items displayed in Class View by data type

Figure 5-10 Navigation and Sorting commands available in Class View

The shortcut menu in Class View also includes a copy command, which allows you to copy a member declaration, and a Properties command, which displays the Properties window for the selected member.

The commands appears on the shortcut menu in Class View will change, depending on the type of icon you select. The Go To Declaration command, for instance, is unavailable if you right-click a data member.

The Class View toolbar that appears at the top of the Class View window contains two buttons: Class View Sort By Type and New Folder. The Class View Sort By Type button displays the same sort commands that are listed in Figure 5-10. The New Folder button allows you to create "virtual folders" that you can use to organize the various items listed in the Class View window.

Code Wizards

As you start building more complex projects, you may find it somewhat tedious to add all of the necessary code for a specific C++ programming element. For instance, to add a single member function to a class, you need to declare the function prototype in the header file and define the function in a separate source file. If your function prototype and the header in your function definition do not match exactly, you will receive a compile error when you attempt to build the project. In order to make it easier to add code to your projects, Visual C++ includes **code wizards**, which automate the task of adding specific types of code to your projects. You have already worked with several code wizards, including the Add New Item command. Listed below are some additional code wizards that are designed specifically for classes:

- Add Class Wizard
- Add Function Wizard
- Add Variable Wizard

The Add Variable Wizard is of most use when working with MFC programs, so it will not be discussed until Chapter 10, "Microsoft Foundation Classes." The code wizards that will be examined in this chapter are the Add Class Wizard and Add Function Wizard.

Code wizards do not remove the need for you to understand how your code operates—they only assist you by adding the basic parts of each code element. It is still up to you to add the necessary code to give your program its functionality.

The Add Class Wizard

You can run the Add Class Wizard from anywhere in your project by selecting Add Class from the Project menu. Running the Add Class Wizard displays the Add Class dialog box shown in Figure 5-11.

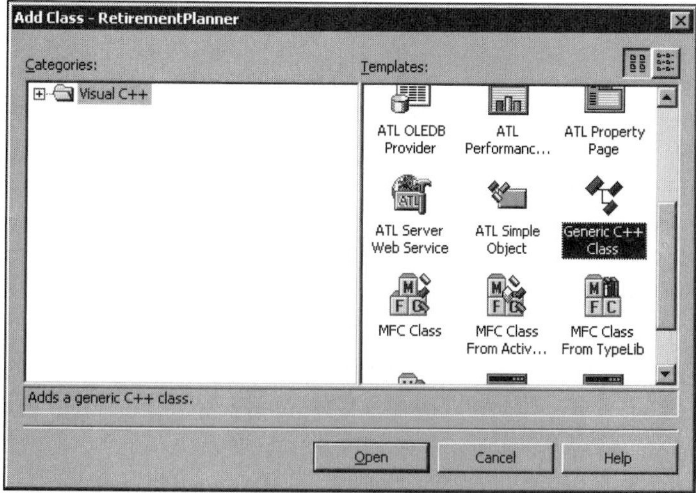

Figure 5-11 The Add Class dialog box

When you use the Add Class Wizard to add a class to a Visual C++ project, Visual C++ should be selected by default in the Categories pane. The Templates pane displays a list of the various types of classes that can be added with the Add Class code wizard. The Templates option you will use in the next few chapters will be the Generic C++ Class option, which adds to a project a regular C++ class (as opposed to an MFC class or other type of class). Once you select a class type in the Add Class Wizard dialog box and press the Open button, the class wizard for your selected option executes. When you select the Generic C++ Class option, for instance, the Generic C++ Class Wizard dialog box appears.

Figure 5-12 shows an example of the Generic C++ Class Wizard dialog box. You type the name of your new class in the Class name text box. As you type the class name, the Generic C++ Class Wizard uses the class name you type as the suggested name for the header and source files. Although you can change the names of the header and source files if you want, it is usually easier to use the class name as the name of its header and source files. You use the Base class text box to designate another class upon which to base the new class. The Access combo box determines the accessibility (`public`, `private`, and so on) that the new class will have to the members in its base class. The Virtual destructor check box creates a virtual destructor in the new class, which helps ensure that the correct destructor executes when objects of classes that are based on other classes are deleted. The Inline check box creates the class definition code in the same file (with an extension of .h) as the declaration code. Although creating a class's declaration and definition code in the same file may make it easier to manage your class, it removes the ability to use information-hiding techniques.

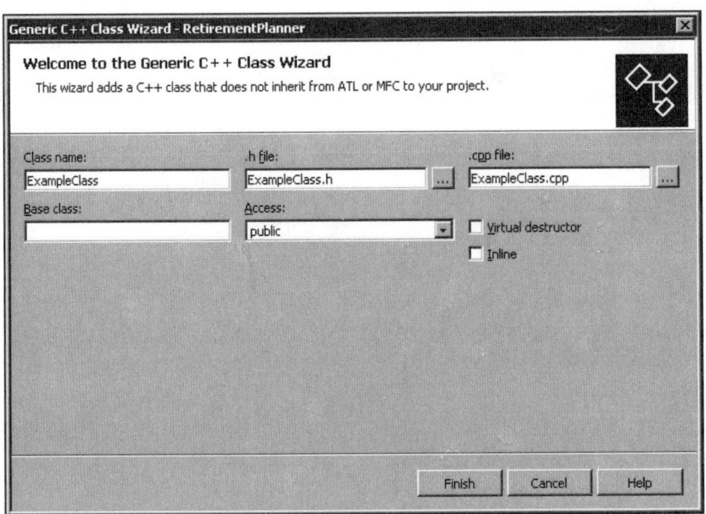

Figure 5-12 The Generic C++ Class Wizard dialog box

You will learn about base classes and destructors when you study inheritance techniques in Chapter 7.

Add Function Wizard

To run the Add Function Wizard, you click the Add Function command on the Project menu if you have a class icon selected in Class View. Alternately, you can right-click a class icon in Class View, and select the Add Function command from the Add submenu on the shortcut menu.

After you run the Add Function command, the Add Function Wizard dialog box appears, as shown in Figure 5-13. You enter the name of the new function (without the parentheses) in the Function name text box. As you build the function, its declaration is entered automatically into the Function signature text box at the bottom of the dialog box. You select a function's return type from the Return type combo box. To add a parameter, you select its type from the Parameter type combo box, type a name for the parameter in the Parameter name text box, and then click the Add button. The new parameter will appear in the Function signature text box at the bottom of the dialog box. You can then repeat the same steps to add additional parameters to the function. You can continue adding additional parameters, or remove a parameter by highlighting it in the Parameter list and clicking the Remove button. You select the function's access specifier from the Access combo box. The Static, Virtual, Pure, and Inline check boxes create advanced member function features that you will study later. The .cpp file box identifies the implementation file where the Add Function Wizard will create the function definition; by default, this is the .cpp file of the class to which the function is added.

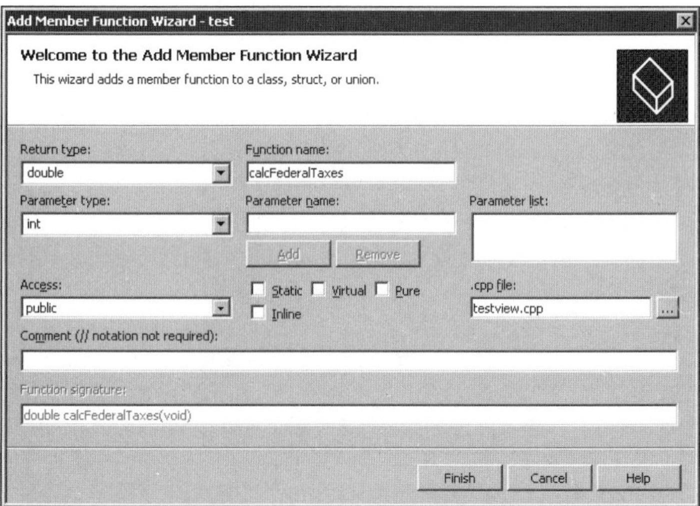

Figure 5-13 Add Member Function Wizard dialog box

In the Return type and Parameter type combo boxes, you can select a data type from the list or manually type an entry into the text portion of each combo box. You can also add a comment to the function using the Comment text box.

The function being added with the Add Function Wizard in Figure 5-13 does not include any parameters. However, notice that the definition in the Function signature text box contains the `void` keyword between the function's parentheses. A parameter value of `void` simply indicates that the function takes no parameters, and is equivalent to leaving the function's parentheses empty. The Add Function Wizard adds the `void` keyword to make it explicitly clear that the function does not take parameters. You can add the `void` keyword in the parameter list for any functions you manually create that do not accept parameters, although it is not necessary to do so. However, keep in mind that any functions you add to your project with the Add Function Wizard that do not include parameters *will* be created with the `void` keyword between the function's parentheses. For example, after clicking the Finish button in Figure 5-14, the Add Function Wizard creates the following function definition:


```
double Payroll::calcFederalTaxes(void)
{
return 0;
}
```

One last thing to note is that when you create a function that returns a value, the Add Function Wizard automatically adds a default return statement for you. For example, the preceding function is automatically created with a `return` statement of `return 0;`. You change this statement to whatever value you need to have returned from your function. The calcFederalTaxes() function, for instance, may return a `double` variable named dTaxResults. Therefore, you would change the `return 0;` statement to `return dTaxResults;`.

Next, you will begin working on the Retirement Planner program. First you will create the project, and then you will use the Add Class Wizard to add the RetirementPlanner class to the project. Shortly, you will use the Add Function Wizard to add member functions to the RetirementPlanner class.

To begin working on the Retirement Planner program:

1. Return to Visual C++.
2. Create a new Win32 Project named **RetirementPlanner** in the Chapter.05 folder in your Visual C++ Projects folder. Be sure to clear the **Create directory for Solution** check box in the New Project dialog box. In the Application Settings tab of the Win32 Application Wizard dialog box, select **Console application** as the application type, click the **Empty project** check box, and then click the **Finish** button.

3. Once the project is created, select **Add Class** from the **Project** menu to start the Add Class Wizard. The Add Class dialog box appears. If necessary, select Visual C++ in the Categories pane (it should be selected by default). The Templates pane displays a list of the various types of classes that can be added with the Add Class code wizard. Scroll through the list and select the **Generic C++ Class** option, then click the **Open** button.

4. After you click the Open button, the Generic C++ Class Wizard dialog box appears. Type **RetirementPlanner** in the Class name text box. Leave the Base class text box empty and the Access combo box set to its default setting of *public*. Make sure the Virtual destructor check box and Inline check boxes are cleared, and then click the **Finish** button. Figure 5-14 shows how the Generic C++ Class Wizard dialog box should appear before you select the Finish button.

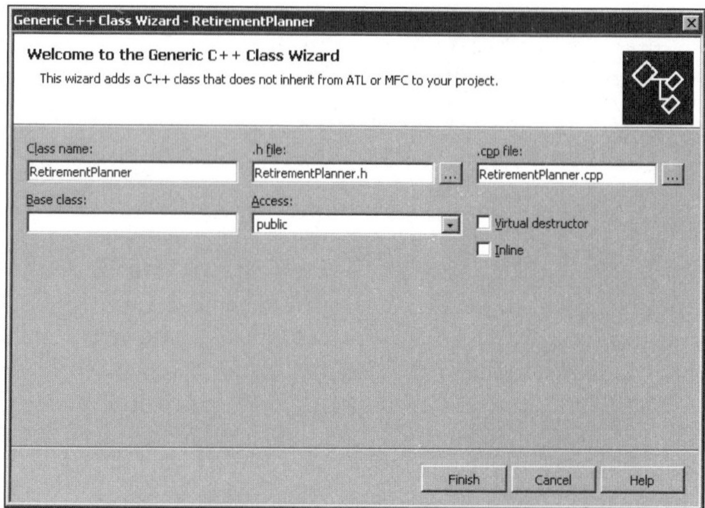

Figure 5-14 The Generic C++ Class Wizard dialog box when adding the RetirementPlanner class

5. After you click the Finish button, the Generic C++ Class Wizard creates the RetirementPlanner class header file (RetirementPlanner.h) and source file (RetirementPlanner.cpp). After the wizard finishes creating the files, the RetirementPlanner.h header file opens in the Code Editor. The first statement you see, `#pragma once`, is a preprocessor directive that prevents multiple instances of the same header file from being included when you compile the project. Multiple inclusion will be covered later in this chapter. The Generic C++ Class Wizard also creates the class declaration shown in Figure 5-15. The first statement within the `public` section of the class declaration is a constructor, which is a special function with the same name as its class that is called automatically when an object from a class is instantiated. The second

statement within the `public` section of the class declaration is a destructor, which is another special function with the same name as its class, but preceded by a tilde (~), that is called automatically when an object from a class is destroyed. You will learn about constructors later in this chapter. You will learn about destructors in Chapter 7.

6. In the Code Editor window, click the RetirementPlanner.cpp tab. Your Code Editor window should appear the same as Figure 5-16. You can see that the Generic C++ Class Wizard automatically added the `#include "RetirementPlanner.h"` statement to import the RetirementPlanner.h header file. Also, notice that the wizard added empty definitions for the RetirementPlanner constructor and destructor functions. For now, do not worry about what the constructor and destructor functions do or how they are set up. Simply familiarize yourself with the code that the Generic C++ Class Wizard adds for you automatically. You will learn how to add member functions to a class shortly.

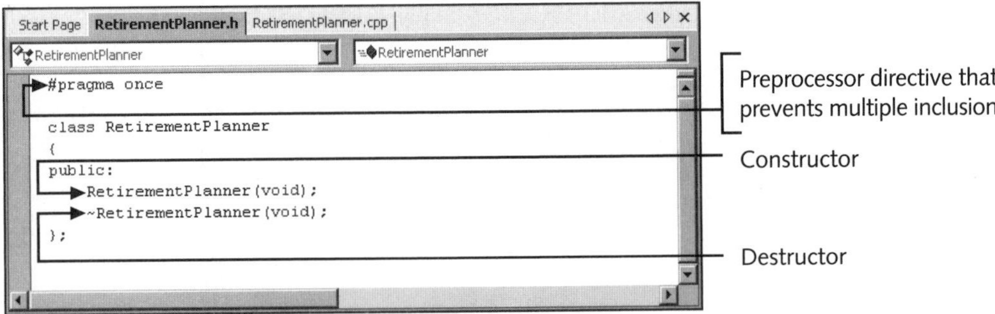

Figure 5-15 RetirementPlanner header file

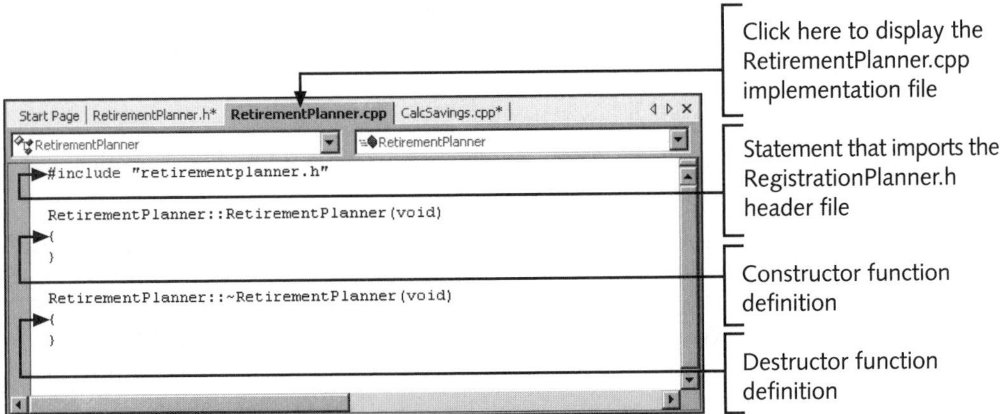

Figure 5-16 RetirementPlanner.cpp file in the Code Editor window

Next, you will add **private** labels to the RetirementPlanner.h file, along with some declarations for **private** data members.

To add **private** labels to the RetirementPlanner.h file, along with some declarations for **private** data members:

1. Return to the **RetirementPlanner.h** file in the Code Editor window.
2. Add the private label and private data members to the RetirementPlanner.h file as shown in Figure 5-17. Later you will add member function declarations to the public section that will modify and retrieve the data members declared in the private section.

Next you will start creating the CalcSavings.cpp file, which will contain the program's main() function. In the main() function, you will declare a RetirementPlanner object and use that object to access data members and member functions in the RetirementPlanner class.

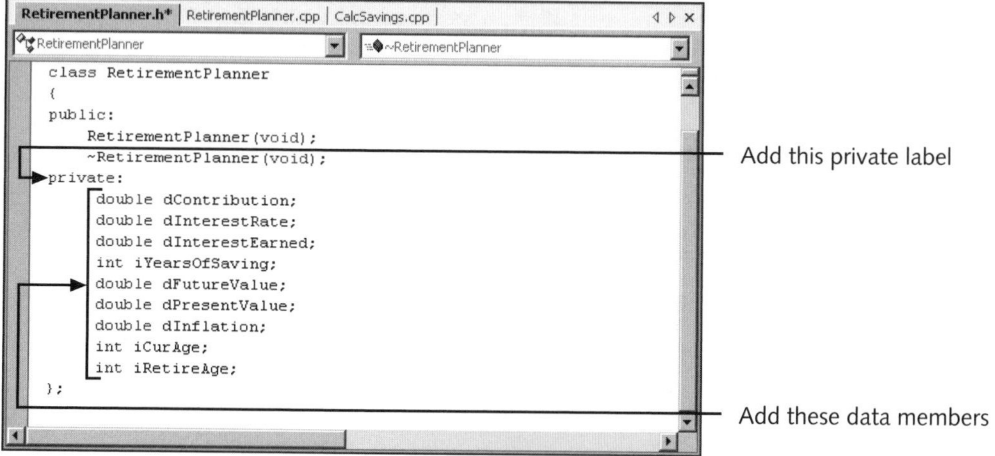

Figure 5-17 RetirementPlanner.h after adding private section and private data members

To start creating the CalcSavings.cpp file:

1. Add a new C++ source file, named **CalcSavings.cpp**, to the RetirementPlanner project.
2. Before you can instantiate an object of a class, you must first include the class's header file in your .cpp file, just as you would include any other header files you need in your program. With custom classes that you write yourself (as opposed to the run-time classes that are part of Visual C++), you must enclose the header filename within quotation marks instead of brackets, and include the file's .h extension. Type the statements shown in Figure 5-18 to include the iostream class and the RetirementPlanner class, along with the using directive that designates the std namespace.

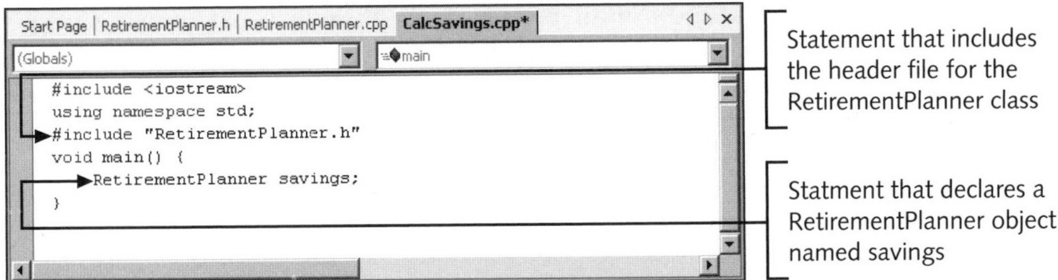

Figure 5-18 CalcSavings.cpp file after adding header files, a using statement, and a main() function

5

3. Also, as shown in Figure 5-18, add a main() function that includes a single statement that declares a RetirementPlanner object named savings.

PREVENTING MULTIPLE INCLUSION

Larger class-based programs are sometimes composed of multiple interface and implementation files. With larger programs, you need to ensure that you do not include multiple instances of the same header file when you compile the program, because multiple inclusions will make your program unnecessarily large. Multiple inclusions of the same header usually occur when you include one header in a second header, and then include the second header in an implementation file.

Visual C++ generates an error if you attempt to compile a program that includes multiple instances of the same header. To prevent multiple inclusions prior to compilation, the Generic C++ Class Wizard adds the `#pragma once` statement to a class header file. A **pragma** is a special preprocessing directive that can execute a number of different compiler instructions. The **once pragma** instructs the compiler to include a header file only once, no matter how many times it encounters an #include statement for that header in other C++ files in the project. If you examine the RetirementPlanner.h header in your Code Editor window, you will see that the `#pragma once` statement is the first line of code in the file.

You can view a list of pragma directives that C++ supports in the Pragma Directives topic in the MSDN Library.

Pragmas are compiler specific; you will not find the same pragmas supported in different C++ compilers. Visual C++, for instance, supports the pragma once directive. However, other C++ compilers consider the pragma once directive to be obsolete. To prevent multiple inclusion, these other compilers use the #define preprocessor directive with #if and #endif preprocessor directives in header files. You first learned how to use the #define preprocessor directive in Chapter 2, "C++ Programming Basics," to define a constant. The **#if** and **#endif preprocessor directives** determine which portions of a file to compile, depending on the result of a conditional expression. All statements located between the #if and #endif directives are compiled if the conditional expression evaluates to true. Each #if directive must include a closing #endif directive.

The #if and #endif preprocessor directives are similar to the `if` statements you learned how to use in Chapter 3 "Operators and Control Structures."

The following code shows the syntax for the #if and #endif preprocessor directives. Notice that unlike the conditional expression for standard `if` statements, the conditional expression for #if and #endif directives is not enclosed within parentheses.

```
#if conditional expression
    statements to compile;
#endif
```

To prevent multiple inclusions of header files, you use the #define directive to declare a constant representing a specific header file. Each time the compiler is asked to include that header file during the build process, it uses the defined constant expression with the #if directive to check if a specific header file's constant exists when you build a project. The **defined constant expression** returns a value of true if a particular identifier is defined or a value of false if it is not defined. The syntax for the defined constant expression is `#defined(`*`identifier`*`)`. To see if an identifier has *not* been defined, add the not operator (!) before the defined expression.

Common practice when defining a header file's constant is to use the header file's name in uppercase letters appended with _H. For example, the constant for the stocks.h header file is usually defined as STOCKS_H.

If a header file's constant has not been defined, statements between the #if and #endif directives define the constant, and any statements preceding the #endif directive are compiled. If a header file's constant has already been defined, however, all statements between the #if and #endif directives are skipped, preventing a multiple inclusion. Figure 5-19 shows how to add code to the header file that prevents multiple inclusions of the Stocks class.

```
#if !defined(STOCKS_H)
#define STOCKS_H
class Stocks {
private:
     int iNumShares;
     double dPurchasePricePerShare;
     double dCurrentPricePerShare;
};
#endif
```

Figure 5-19 Header file with preprocessor directives that prevent multiple inclusions

The once pragma is much easier to use than the #if and #endif directives. However, you should be familiar with how to use the #if and #endif directives to prevent multiple inclusion, especially if you ever work with a C++ compiler that does not support the once pragma. For practice, you will replace the once pragma in the RetirementPlanner header file with #if and #endif directives to prevent multiple inclusion in the RetirementPlanner class.

To replace the once pragma in the RetirementPlanner header file with #if and #endif directives to prevent multiple inclusion in the RetirementPlanner class:

1. Return to the RetirementPlanner.h header file in the Code Editor window.
2. Delete the once pragma statement, as shown in Figure 5-20.
3. Add the #if and #endif directives shown in Figure 5-21.

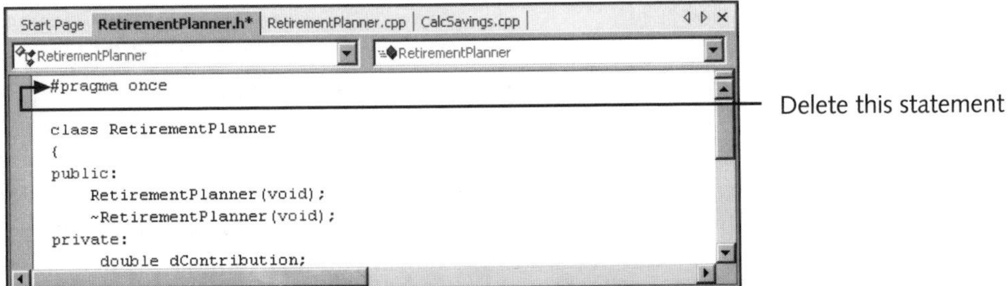

Figure 5-20 Delete the once pragma statement from the RetirementPlanner.h header file

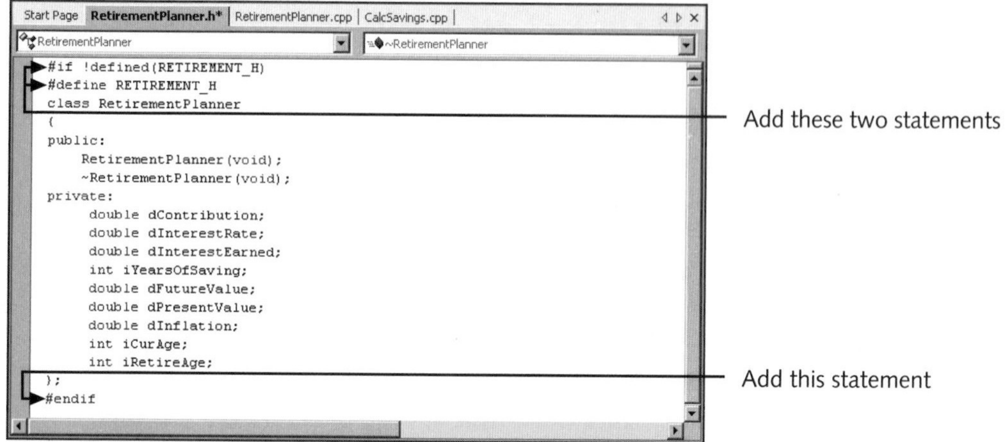

Figure 5-21 #if and #endif directives added to RetirementPlanner.h

MEMBER FUNCTIONS

Because member functions perform most of the work in a class, you will learn about the various techniques associated with them. As you saw earlier, you declare functions in an interface file, but define them in an implementation file. Member functions are usually declared as `public`, but they can also be declared as `private`. `Public` member functions can be called by anyone, whereas private member functions can be called only by other member functions in the same class.

You may wonder what good a `private` function member would be because a client of the program cannot access a `private` function. Suppose your program needs some sort of utility function that clients have no need to access. For example, your program may need to determine an employee's income tax bracket by calling a function named calcTaxBracket(). To use your program, the client does not need to access the calcTaxBracket() function. By making the calcTaxBracket() function private, you protect your program and add another level of information hiding.

In order for your class to identify which functions in an implementation file belong to it (as opposed to global function definitions), you precede the function name in the function definition header with the class name and the scope resolution operator (::). For example, to identify the getTotalValue() function in an implementation file as belonging to the Stocks class, the function definition header should read `double Stocks:: getTotalValue(int iShares, double dCurPrice){`. Figure 5-22 shows both the interface and implementation files for the Stocks class. The getTotalValue() function's prototype is declared in an interface file named stocks.h, whereas the getTotalValue() function definition is placed in an implementation file named stocks.cpp.

```
// stocks.h
class Stocks {
public:
     double getTotalValue(int iShares, double dCurPrice);
private:
     int iNumShares;
     double dCurrentPricePerShare;
     double dCurrentValue;
};
// stocks.cpp
#include "stocks.h"
#include <iostream>
using namespace std;
double Stocks::getTotalValue(int iShares, double dCurPrice){
     iNumShares = iShares;
     dCurrentPricePerShare = dCurPrice;
     dCurrentValue = iNumShares * dCurrentPricePerShare;
     return dCurrentValue;
}
void main() {
     Stocks stockPick;
     ...
}
```


Figure 5-22 Stocks class interface and implementation files

Even though the member functions of a class may be defined in an implementation file separate from the interface file, as long as the functions include the class's name and the scope resolution operator, they are considered to be part of the class definition. Just think of the declarations and definitions that compose your class as being spread across multiple files.

Next, you will use the Add Function Wizard to add member function declarations and definitions to the RetirementPlanner class. The RetirementPlanner class uses five functions for setting the values of private data members: setContribution(), setInterestRate(), setCurAge(), setRetireAge(), and setInflation(). Two other functions, calcFutureValue() and calcPresentValue(), perform the actual calculations that give the Retirement Planner program its functionality. The calcFutureValue() function returns the future value of an investment based on the amount invested each year, the yearly annual interest on the investment, and the number of years spent saving for retirement. The number of years spent saving for retirement is calculated by subtracting the age at which you started saving from the age at which you plan to retire. The calcPresentValue() function adjusts the future value of an investment for inflation. An accessor function, getInterestEarned(), returns the total amount of interest earned on retirement savings. The getInterestEarned() function is a typical *get* function that returns to the client the value of a `private` data member. Note that you will not learn how the functions perform the calculations because algebra is not the purpose of your studies. However, if you examine the formulas closely, you will see that they are structured using typical C++ operators.

To use the Add Function Wizard to add member function declarations and definitions to the RetirementPlanner class:

1. Open Class View by selecting **Class View** from the **View** menu, or by pressing **Ctrl+Shift+C**.
2. First, you will add the setCurAge() function. Click the RetirementPlanner icon once, and then select **Add Function** from the Project menu. Alternately, you can right-click the RetirementPlanner icon and select **Add Function** from the Add submenu on the shortcut menu. The Add Function Wizard dialog box appears.
3. In the Add Function Wizard dialog box, select a return type of **void** from the Return type combo box and enter **setCurAge** (without parentheses) in the Function name text box. Notice, as you build the function, that its declaration enters automatically into the Function signature text box at the bottom of the dialog box. The setCurAge() function includes a single int parameter named iAgeNow. To add this parameter, select **int** from the Parameter type combo box, type **iAgeNow** in the Parameter name text box, and then click the **Add** button. After you click the Add button, the new parameter appears in the Parameter list and in the Function signature text box. Leave the remainder of the dialog box options as they are. Because the iAgeNow function includes only a single parameter, you can click the **Finish** button. Figure 5-23 shows the Add Function Wizard dialog box as it should appear before you click the Finish button.
4. After you click the Finish button, the Add Function Wizard creates the setCurAge() function declaration in the interface file (RetirementPlanner.h) and also creates its function definition in the implementation file (RetirementPlanner.cpp). The Code Editor window opens to the new empty setCurAge() function definition in the implementation file. Add the statement show in Figure 5-24 that assigns the value of the iAgeNow parameter to the iCurAge data member.

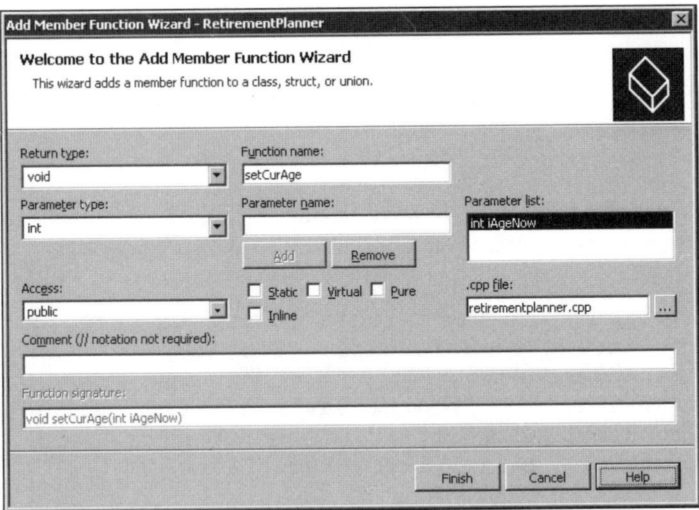

Figure 5-23 Adding the iAgeNow Function with the Add Member Function Wizard dialog box

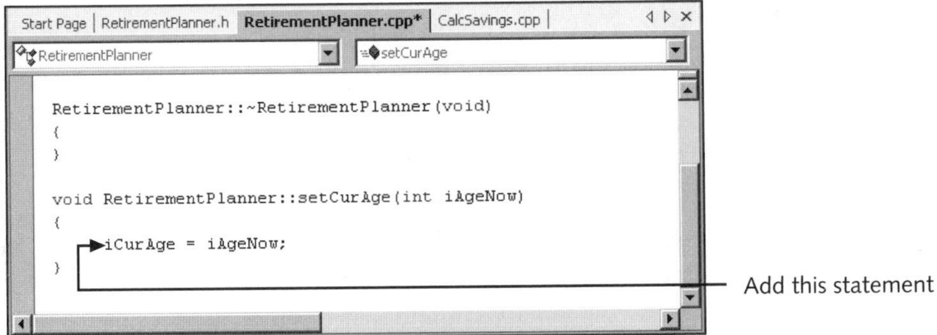

Figure 5-24 Assignment statement added to the setCurAge() member function

5. Use the Add Function Wizard to add the remainder of the set functions and getInterestEarned() member function, as follows:

```
void RetirementPlanner::setRetireAge(int iAgeThen) {
     iRetireAge = iAgeThen;
}
void RetirementPlanner::setContribution(
     double dContribute) {
     dContribution = dContribute;
}
void RetirementPlanner::setInterestRate(
     double dInterest) {
     dInterestRate = dInterest;
}
```

5

```
void RetirementPlanner::setInflation(double dInflate) {
   dInflation = dInflate;
}
double RetirementPlanner::getInterestEarned() {
   return dInterestEarned;
}
```

6. Finally, use the Add Function Wizard to add the following calcFutureValue() and calcPresentValue() member functions:

```
// calcFutureValue() function
double RetirementPlanner::calcFutureValue() {
  iYearsOfSaving = iRetireAge - iCurAge;
  dFutureValue = 0;
  for (int i=0; i < iYearsOfSaving; i++) {
      dFutureValue += 1;
      dFutureValue *= (1+(dInterestRate/100));
}
  dFutureValue *= dContribution;
  dInterestEarned = dFutureValue -
      (dContribution * iYearsOfSaving);
  return dFutureValue;
}
// calcPresentValue() function
double RetirementPlanner::calcPresentValue() {
  double dFutureValue = calcFutureValue();
  for(int i = 0; i < iYearsOfSaving; i++) {
      dFutureValue /= (1 + (dInflation/100));
      }
      dPresentValue = dFutureValue;
      return dPresentValue;
}
```

Once you create a member function, you execute it from your implementation file by appending the function name to the to the object name with the member selection operator, in the same manner that you access data members. Unlike data members, however, you must also place a set of parentheses after the function name, containing any arguments required by the function. For example, the first statement in the following code declares a Stocks object named stockPick. The second statement executes the getTotalValue() function, passing to it the number of stocks and the current price per share.

```
void main() {
    Stocks stockPick;
    stockPick.getTotalValue(100, 10.875);
}
```

Next you will add code to the CalcSavings.cpp file that accesses the RetirementPlanner class's functions. You will use cout statements to display instructions to users and cin statements to gather data. You will assign the data returned from the cin statements to variables, which you will then pass to the RetirementPlanner class's function members. Finally, you will calculate and display the results using the calcFutureValue(), calcPresentValue(), and getInterestEarned() functions.

To add code to the CalcSavings.cpp file that accesses the RetirementPlanner class's functions:

1. Open the **CalcSavings.cpp** file in the Code Editor window.
2. Add the statements shown in Figure 5-25. The statements declare variables that you will use to hold the values retrieved from the user with the cin statements. The variables will then be passed to the RetirementPlanner class member functions.

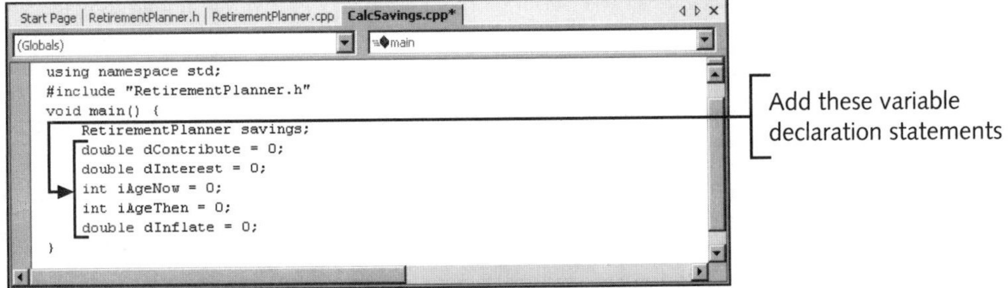

Figure 5-25 Variable declarations added to CalcSavings.cpp

3. Add the cout statements shown in Figure 5-26 that explain the program to the user.

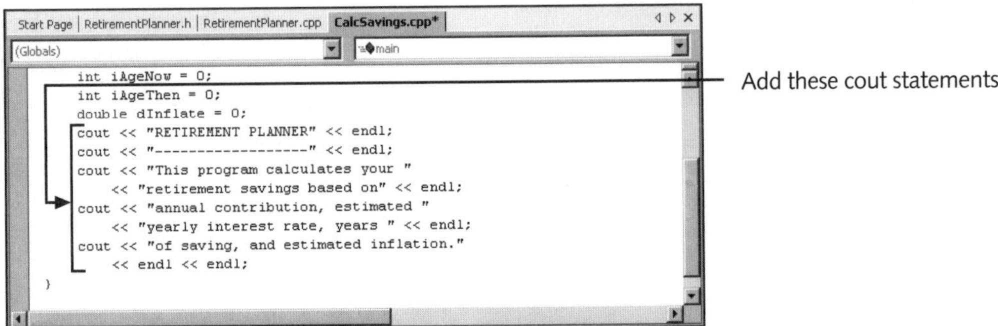

Figure 5-26 cout statements added to CalcSavings.cpp that explain the program to the user

4. Add the statements shown in Figure 5-27 that gather values from the user, assign the values to variables, and then pass the variables to the member functions.
5. Finally, add the statements shown in Figure 5-28, which display the calculated savings results to the user.

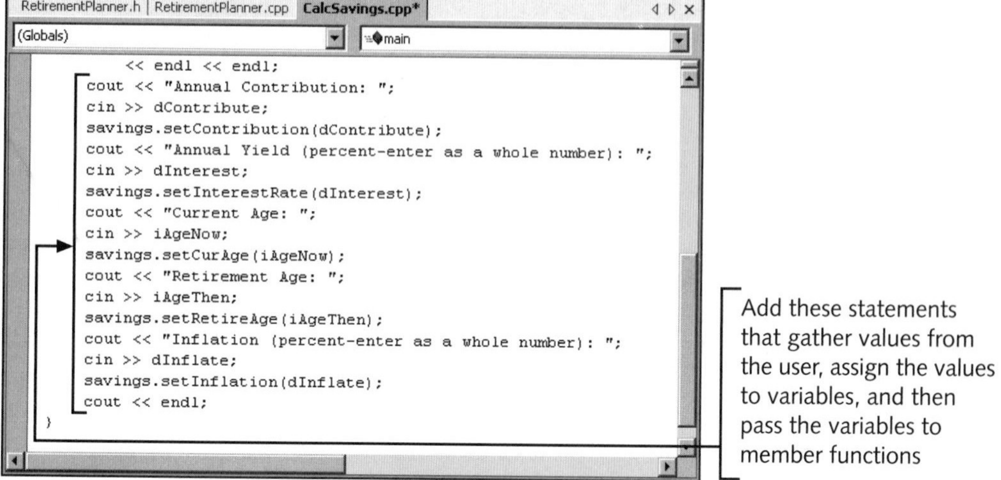

Figure 5-27 Input statements added to CalcSavings.cpp

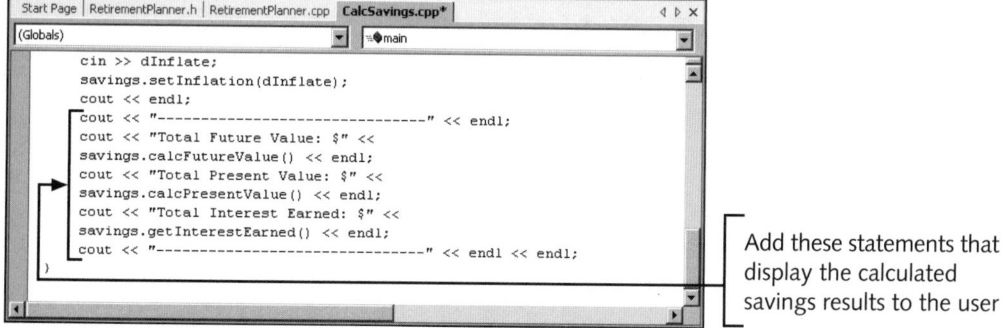

Figure 5-28 Statements added to CalcSavings.cpp that display the calculated savings results to the user

6. Build and execute the RetirementPlanner project. Then, test the program. When you enter percentages for either Annual Yield or Inflation, enter the numbers as whole numbers, without a decimal point. For example, to enter 10%, type *10*, not *.10*.

Inline Functions

Although member functions are usually defined in an implementation file, they can also be defined in an interface file. Functions defined inside the class body in an interface file are called **inline functions**. To conform to information-hiding techniques, only the shortest function definitions, such as accessor functions, should be added to the interface file. The following code shows an example of a `public` inline function definition in the Stocks class for a function member named getTotalValue(). The getTotalValue() function accepts two arguments from the client: the number of shares and the current price. The arguments are assigned to `private` data members, and then the price is calculated and returned.

```
class Stocks {
public:
  double getTotalValue(int iShares, double dCurPrice){
    iNumShares = iShares;
    dCurrentPricePerShare = dCurPrice;
    dCurrentValue = iNumShares * dCurrentPricePerShare;
    return dCurrentValue;
  }
private:
  int iNumShares;
  double dCurrentPricePerShare;
  double dCurrentValue;
};
```

Inline function

5

For functions that are not defined inside the class body, you can place the `inline` keyword at the start of a function header. An important point to remember is that you must place the function definition for a function declared with the `inline` keyword in the interface file—not the implementation file. For example, if the getTotalValue() function is defined within the Stocks interface file, but outside of the class body, you can mark it as an inline function by using the statement `inline double getTotalValue(int iShares, double dCurPrice);`.

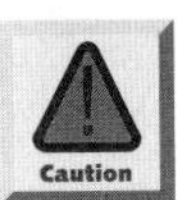

If you add the `inline` keyword to a function that is not declared within a class header file, you will receive a compile error.

When the compiler encounters either an inline function or a function declared with the `inline` keyword, it performs a cost/benefit analysis to determine whether replacing a function call with its function definition will increase the program's speed and performance. If the compiler's cost/benefit analysis determines that there will be no significant speed or performance gain by replacing a given function call with its function definition, then the inline function is executed as a normal function. Figure 5-29 illustrates how the compiler replaces a function call with its function definition.

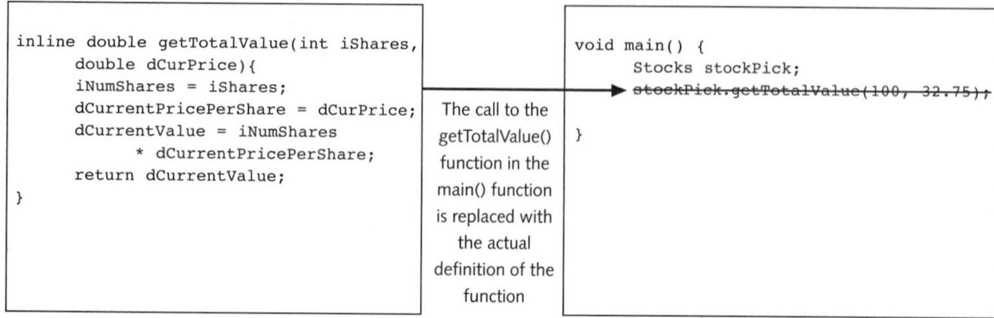
inline double getTotalValue(int iShares,
double dCurPrice){
iNumShares = iShares;
dCurrentPricePerShare = dCurPrice;
dCurrentValue = iNumShares
* dCurrentPricePerShare;
return dCurrentValue;
}
The call to the getTotalValue() function in the main() function is replaced with the actual definition of the function
void main() {
Stocks stockPick;
stockPick.getTotalValue(100, 32.75);
}

Figure 5-29 Compilation of a function marked with the `inline` keyword

Because they are declared in the interface file, `inline` functions do not take advantage of information hiding. If you want to hide a function definition, be sure not to define it as an `inline` function.

You can also use the `inline` keyword with global functions. As with member functions, however, the global functions you define as `inline` should be relatively small.

Next you will add the `inline` keyword to the getInterestEarned() function, which is small and stable enough that it can be defined as `inline`. You will also move the getInterestEarned() function definition to the header, or interface, file so that the program compiles correctly.

To define the getInterestEarned() function as `inline`:

1. Open the **RetirementPlanner.cpp** file in the Code Editor window.
2. Highlight the **getInterestEarned()** function definition and then cut it and place it on the Clipboard by selecting **Cut** from the Edit menu.
3. Open the **RetirementPlanner.h** file in the Code Editor window.
4. Paste the getInterestEarned() function definition after the class's closing brace and semicolon but above the #endif directive by selecting **Paste** from the Edit menu.
5. Modify the getInterestEarned() function definition so that it reads **`inline double RetirementPlanner:: getInterestEarned()`**. Your modified RetirementPlanner header file should look like Figure 5-30.

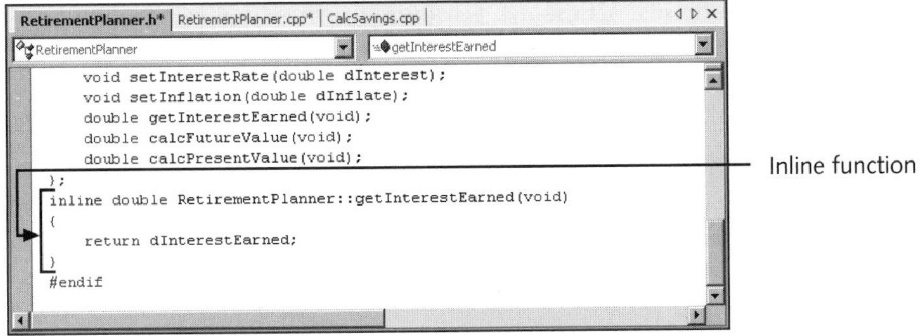

Figure 5-30 `Inline` function added to RetirementPlanner header

6. Rebuild and execute the RetirementPlanner project. The program should function the same as it did before you added the `inline` keyword to the getInterestEarned() function.

Constructor Functions

When you first instantiate an object from a class, you will often want to assign initial values to data members or perform other types of initialization tasks, such as calling a function member that may calculate and assign values to data members. In a C++ program that does not use classes, you simply assign an initial value to a variable in the main() function by using a statement such as `int ctCount = 1;`, or you call a custom function using a statement such as `double dInterest = calcInterest();`.

Although classes are "mini-programs," they do not include a main() function in which you can assign initial values to data members or call initialization functions. Instead, you use a constructor function. A **constructor function** is a special function with the same name as its class that is called automatically when an object from a class is instantiated. You define and declare constructor functions the same way you define other functions, although you do not include a `return` type because constructor functions do not return values. For example, the following `inline` constructor function for the Stocks class initializes the iNumShares, dCurrentPricePerShare, and dCurrentValue data members to zero:

```
class Stocks {
public:
Stocks() {
    iNumShares = 0;
    dCurrentPricePerShare = 0;
    dCurrentValue = 0;
};
private:
    int iNumShares;
    double dCurrentPricePerShare;
    double dCurrentValue;
};
```

Constructor function

You can also include just a function prototype in the interface file for the constructor function, and then create the function definition in the implementation file. The following code shows an example of how you implement the Stocks constructor function in an implementation file. It may look unusual, but when you define a constructor function in an implementation file, be sure to include the class name and scope resolution operator in order to identify the function as a class member.

```
Stocks::Stocks() {
     iNumShares = 0;
    dCurrentPricePerShare = 0;
    dCurrentValue = 0;
};
```

Class member functions, including constructor functions, can also assign default values to parameters in the function prototype. You assign the default parameter values in the prototype declaration for a member function in the interface file. You then create the member function definition as you normally would.

In Chapter 7 you will learn about some advanced constructor techniques, as well as how to use the opposite of a constructor, a *destructor*.

As you saw earlier, the Add Class Wizard automatically added an empty constructor function to the RetirementPlanner class for you. Next, you will modify the constructor so that it initializes all of the private data members to 0. Initializing private data members to 0 ensures that the calculations within the member functions have a value to work with in the event that a client fails to provide one of the values when executing any of the member functions.

To add a constructor to the RetirementPlanner class:

1. Return to the **RetirementPlanner.cpp** file in the Code Editor window.
2. Modify the constructor function definition so that it initializes the data members to 0, as shown in Figure 5-31.

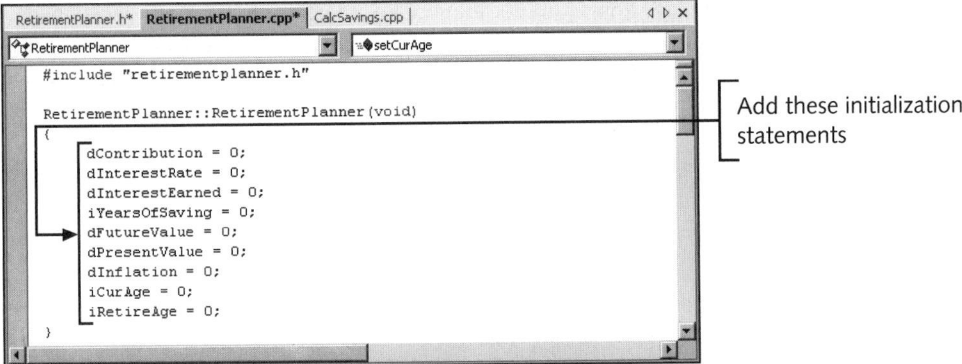

Figure 5-31 Constructor function definition modified so that it initializes the data members to 0

Be sure not to confuse the constructor function definition with the destructor function definition, which starts with a tilde (~).

3. Rebuild and execute the RetirementPlanner project. The program should work the same as it did before you added the constructor function.

`friend` Functions and Classes

When you use the `public` access modifier with a class member, the entire world has access to that class member. In contrast, only members of the same class can access `private` class members. What if you want to selectively allow access to class members, yet still maintain a level of information hiding? For example, another programmer in your department may have written a function in a separate program that needs to perform some calculations on your class's `private` data members. You could make the data members `public` (which removes information hiding), add the other programmer's function to your class (which may not make sense if the function is not useful to your class), or force the other programmer to use get methods to access the `private` data members (which could slow down his or her program). It would be easier to grant access to a class's `private` members only to a specific function or class. In these situations, the `friend` access modifier comes into play. The `friend` access modifier allows designated functions or classes to access a class's `private` members. Only a class itself can designate the function and class friends that can access its private members; external functions and classes cannot make themselves friends of a class. In other words, your class has to give `friend` access to external functions and classes. You declare a `friend` function by including the function's prototype in an interface file, preceded by the keyword `friend`.

You can place a `friend` declaration anywhere inside the class, except within a function definition. You can even place a `friend` declaration within the declarations for `public` and `private` class members. It is good practice, however, to keep all definitions for a specific type of access modifier together.

Here is a simple example that demonstrates how to declare a `friend` function. Assume that a computer manufacturer has a program with a class named Inventory that contains `private` data members that keep track of the company's inventory, along with accessor functions for each data member. (In a real-life application, the Inventory program would store inventory information in a database.) The Inventory class also contains a constructor that assigns some arbitrary values to each of the data members. (Again, in a real-life program, the number of units available for each item would normally be stored in and retrieved from a database.) You may also have an external function named checkInventory() that checks the number of units available for each item. The checkInventory() function compares the number of items available for each unit to a corresponding parameter that represents the number of items requested by a client. The function then returns a Boolean value indicating whether or not there is sufficient inventory to fulfill the order. Figure 5-32 shows the Inventory interface file and its implementation file. The class also includes a declaration for the checkInventory() function as a `friend` function. Although the checkInventory() function is defined in the class's implementation file, it is not part of the class because its header declaration does not include the name of the class and the scope resolution operator. The implementation file also declares a global Inventory variable named curOrder and a main() function, which, again, is not part of the class itself. The main() function calls the checkInventory() member function, passing to it arguments representing the number of items ordered by the customer. If the checkInventory() function in Figure 5-32 were not declared as a `friend` function, the statements would be illegal because they directly access the `private` data members of the Inventory class. Figure 5-33 shows the program's output.

```
// inventory.h
class Inventory {
private:
        int iDesktopComputers;
        int iNotebookComputers;
        int iLaserPrinters;
        friend bool checkInventory(int, int, int);
public:
        Inventory();
        void setDesktopComputers(int);
        int getDesktopComputers();
        void setNotebookComputers(int);
        int getNotebookComputers();
        void setPrinters(int);
        int getPrinters();
};
// inventory.cpp
#include "inventory.h"
#include <iostream>
using namespace std;
Inventory::Inventory() {
        iDesktopComputers = 250;
        iNotebookComputers = 150;
        iLaserPrinters = 125;

}
void Inventory::setDesktopComputers(int iUnits) {
        iDesktopComputers = iUnits;
}
int Inventory::getDesktopComputers() {
        return iDesktopComputers;
}
void Inventory::setNotebookComputers(int iUnits) {
        iNotebookComputers = iUnits;
}
int Inventory::getNotebookComputers() {
        return iNotebookComputers;
}
void Inventory::setPrinters(int iUnits) {
        iLaserPrinters = iUnits;
}
int Inventory::getPrinters() {
        return iLaserPrinters;
}
bool checkInventory(int, int , int , int);
Inventory curOrder;
void main() {
        bool bRetValue = checkInventory(50, 25, 10);
        if (bRetValue == true)
```

Figure 5-32 Inventory class declaring and defining a `friend` function

```
                cout << "We can fill the order." << endl;
        else
                cout << "We cannot fill the order." << endl;
}
bool checkInventory(int iDesktops, int iNotebooks,      ← friend function
        int iPrinters) {
        bool bFillOrder = true;
        if (curOrder.iDesktopComputers < iDesktops)
                bFillOrder = false;
        else if (curOrder.iNotebookComputers < iNotebooks)
                bFillOrder = false;
        else if (curOrder.iLaserPrinters < iPrinters)
                bFillOrder = false;
        return bFillOrder;
}
```

Figure 5-32 Inventory class declaring and defining a `friend` function (continued)

Figure 5-33 Output of Inventory program

The checkInventory() `friend` function is part of the Inventory implementation file in Figure 5-32 for simplicity. However, in reality the checkInventory() friend function would probably be part of another class or program. To designate all functions within another class as friends of the current class, you create a declaration in the current class, using the syntax **`friend class`** ***`name;`***, replacing *name* with the name of the class containing the functions you want to mark as friends. For example, assume that the checkInventory() function is really a member of a class named Fulfillment. To allow all the functions in a Fulfillment class to access the private members in the Inventory class, you would add the declaration **`friend class Fulfillment;`** to the Inventory class's interface file as follows:

```
class Inventory {
private:
   int iDesktopComputers;
   int iNotebookComputers;
   int iLaserPrinters;
   bool checkInventory(int, int, int
public:
   Inventory();
   void setDesktopComputers(int);
   int getDesktopComputers();
   void setNotebookComputers(int);
   int getNotebookComputers();
   void setPrinters(int);
   int getPrinters();
   friend class Fulfullment;◄── declaring a friend class
};
```


Chapter Summary

- The functions and variables defined in a class are called class members.
- Class variables are referred to as data members or member variables, whereas class functions are referred to as member functions or function members.
- When you declare an object from a class, you are said to be instantiating an object.
- A structure, or **struct**, is an advanced, user-defined data type that uses a single variable name to store multiple pieces of related information.
- When you use a period to access an object's members, such as a structure's fields, the period is referred to as the member selection operator.
- Most C++ programmers use the **class** keyword to clearly designate the programs they write as object-oriented C++ programs.
- The principal of information hiding states that any class members that other programmers, or clients, do not need to access or know about should be hidden.
- Access specifiers control a client's access to data members and member functions. There are four levels of access specifiers: **public**, **private**, **protected**, and **friend**.
- The separation of classes into separate interface and implementation files is considered to be a fundamental software development technique because it allows you to hide the details of how your classes are written and makes it easier to modify programs.
- The interface refers to the data member and function member declarations inside a class's braces.

- The implementation refers to a class's function definitions and any code that assigns values to a class's data members.
- The Class View window displays project files according to their classes.
- Code wizards automate the task of adding specific types of code to your projects.
- To prevent multiple inclusions prior to compilation, the generic C++ Class wizard adds the `#pragma once` statement to a class header file.
- The #if and #endif preprocessor directives determine which portions of a file to compile, depending on the result of a conditional expression.
- Even though the member functions of a class may be defined in separate files from the class declarations, as long as the function includes the class's name and the scope resolution operator, then it is considered to be part of the class definition.
- Member function definitions in an interface file are referred to as `inline` functions.
- A constructor function is a special function with the same name as its class that is called automatically when an object from a class is instantiated.

REVIEW QUESTIONS

1. Which of the following terms refers to class functions?
   a. member functions
   b. global functions
   c. user-defined data types
   d. programmer-defined data types
2. The term *object* is used interchangeably with the word(s).
   a. *function*
   b. *variable*
   c. *statement*
   d. *data type*
3. You define a structure using the ______________ keyword.
   a. `structure`
   b. `struct`
   c. `record`
   d. `data`

4. Which statement best describes how you store data types in a structure?
   a. All variables in a structure must be of the same data type.
   b. You must use all numeric data types or all character data types.
   c. You can use any mix of data types.
   d. Structures do not directly declare data types, only variable names that are later assigned a specific data type.
5. Which of the following is the correct syntax for declaring a variable named accountingInfo based on a structure named accounting?
   a. `accounting accountingInfo;`
   b. `currentEmployee accountingInfo;`
   c. `accountingInfo currentEmployee();`
   d. `accountingInfo = new currentEmployee();`
6. When you use a period to access an object's members, such as a structure's fields, the period is referred to as the ________________.
   a. object selector
   b. member selection operator
   c. field indicator
   d. structure operand
7. Examine the following structure declaration and determine why it will cause a compiler error:

```
struct accounting {
    int iPeriod = 2;
    long lFiscalYear = 2000;
    double dCurTaxRate = .15;
};
```

   a. The name of the structure must be followed by parentheses, the same as a function definition.
   b. You are only allowed to use a single data type within a structure definition.
   c. You are not allowed to assign values to the fields inside the structure definition itself.
   d. The structure must be declared using the `structure` keyword.
8. What is the accessibility of the data members in the following class?

```
class Boat {
    int iLength;
    double dEngineSize;
    char cClass;
}
```

a. public

b. private

c. friend

d. protected

9. What is the accessibility of the data members in the following structure?

```
struct Boat {
    int iLength;
    double dEngineSize;
    char cClass;
}
```

a. public

b. private

c. friend

d. protected

10. Which of the following elements is not considered part of a class's scope?

a. implementation files

b. interface files

c. constructor functions

d. a main() method

11. The ______________ window displays project files according to their classes and is similar to the Solution Explorer window.

a. Solution Explorer

b. Class View

c. Properties

d. Implementation

12. Which of the following code wizards is not designed specifically for working with classes?

a. Add New Item

b. Add Class

c. Add Member Function

d. Add Member Variable

13. When you use a code wizard to add a class to your project, which of the following statements is automatically added to prevent multiple header file inclusion?

a. `#pragma once`

b. `#pragma twice`

c. `#inclusion false`

d. `#ifincludeonce`

14. Which of the following preprocessor directives is used for preventing multiple header file inclusion?
    a. `#multiple`
    b. `#define...#!define`
    c. `#include...#stop_include`
    d. `#if` and `#endif`
15. Member functions that are defined within an interface file are referred to as ______________ functions.
    a. member
    b. inline
    c. embedded
    d. compiled
16. Which of the following keywords forces the compiler to replace calls to a function with the function definition wherever the function is called in a program?
    a. `include`
    b. `inline`
    c. `replace`
    d. `insert`
17. Which statement is the correct definition in an implementation file for the constructor function for a class named Boat, assuming that the construct function does not accept any arguments?
    a. `Boat () {`
    b. `Boat:Boat () {`
    c. `function Boat::Boat () {`
    d. `class Boat::Boat () {`
18. The ______________ access modifier allows designated functions or classes to access a class's hidden members.
    a. public
    b. private
    c. friend
    d. protected

PROGRAMMING EXERCISES

1. What is the difference between a class and a structure? How do the two class types differ between C and C++?
2. Rewrite the following structure as a class. Be sure to assign the same access to the data members as they have in the structure.

```
struct CourseInfo {
     double dTuition;
     int iCourseID;
     char cGrade;
}
```

3. To the main() function in the following code, add cout statements that print each of the carInfo object's data members.

```
struct Transportation {
     double dCarEngineSize;
     int iMotorcycleCCs;
     int iTruckNumberofAxels;
}
void main() {
     Transportation vehicleInfo;
     vehicleInfo.dCarEngineSize = 3.1;
     vehicleInfo.iMotorcycleCCs = 750;
     vehicleInfo.iTruckNumberofAxels = 6;
}
```

4. What is the difference between a class's interface file and its implementation file?
5. Recall that accessor functions, which assign values to and retrieve values from `private` data members, are often referred to as get and set functions. Write the appropriate implementation file for the following class declaration and create get and set functions so that they assign values to and retrieve values from the `private` data members.

```
#if !defined(MUTUALFUND_H)

#define MUTUALFUND_H

class MutualFund {
public:
     void setNumberOfShares(int iShares);
     void setAnnualYield(int iYield);
     int getNumberOfShares();
     double getAnnualYield();
private:
     int iNumberOfShares;
     double dAnnualYield;
}
#endif
```

6. Replace the code in the MutualFund interface file that prevents multiple inclusion with the correct pragma directive.
7. Write a main() function that sets, retrieves, and prints the values of the **private** data members in the MutualFund class.
8. Add a **friend** function named printDataMembers() to the MutualFund class that prints the values of the private data members in the MutualFund class.
9. Write the appropriate interface file for the following class implementation.

```
#include "DistanceConversion.h"
DistanceConversion:: DistanceConversion() {
     dMiles = 0;
     dKilometers = 0;
}
double DistanceConversion::milesToKilometers(
      double dMilesArg) {
     dMiles = dMilesArg;
     dKilometers = dMiles * 1.6;
     return dKilometers;
}
double DistanceConversion::kilometersToMiles(
     double dKiloArg) {
     dKilometers = dKiloArg;
     dMiles = dKilometers * .6;
     return dMiles;
}
```

10. Find two ways to modify the DistanceConversion class so that the member functions are compiled inline. Create separate versions of the class for each of your solutions.

Programming Projects

1. Create a Movies class that determines the cost of a ticket to a cinema, based on the moviegoer's age. Assume that the cost of a full-price ticket is $10. Gather the user's age using a cin statement, and then assign the age to a **private** data member. Next, use a **public** member function to determine the ticket price, based on the following schedule:

Age	Price
under 5	free
5 to 17	half-price
18 to 55	full-price
over 55	$2 off

After you determine the ticket price, print the cost to the screen.

2. Create a BaseballTeam class with appropriate data members such as team name, games won, games lost, and so on. Write appropriate get and set functions for each data member. Instantiate a number of BaseballTeam objects and assign appropriate values to each `private` data member using the set functions. Finally, use the get statements to retrieve and print the values in each `private` data member.
3. A painting company estimates the cost of its jobs based on materials and labor costs. The cost of materials is $.15 per square foot, and the cost of labor is $.25 per square foot. Write a Painting class that determines the cost of painting a house by allowing a prospective customer to enter the estimated number of feet they need to have painted. Store the number of feet in a `private` data member, along with get and set functions for setting and retrieving the value of the `private` data member. Use a separate member function for determining the cost of materials and the cost of labor. Also, include a function that calls the member functions for the materials and labor costs in order to calculate the total cost of the job. Store the total estimate in a `private` data member and print the estimate to the screen.
4. Create an Automobile class. Include `private` data members such as make, model, color, and engine, along with the appropriate get and set functions for setting and retrieving `private` data members. Use cin and cout statements to gather and display information.
5. Create a class-based temperature conversion program that converts Fahrenheit to Celsius and Celsius to Fahrenheit. To convert Fahrenheit to Celsius subtract 32 from the Fahrenheit temperature, then multiply the remainder by .55. To convert Celsius to Fahrenheit multiply the Celsius temperature by 1.8, then add 32. Use cin and cout statements to gather and display information.
6. A passenger train averages a speed of 50 mph. Each stop the train makes adds an additional five minutes to the train's schedule. Additionally, during bad weather the train can only average a speed of 30 mph. Write a Train class that allows a traveler to calculate how long it will take to reach his or her destination, based on speed, number of stops, and weather conditions. Use cin and cout statements to gather and display information. Save each piece of information you gather from the user in a `private` data member, and write the appropriate get and set functions for setting and retrieving each data member. Use a single `inline` function to calculate how long the traveler's trip will take, save the result in another `private` data member, and print the results to the screen.
7. Create a CompanyInfo class that includes `private` data members such as the company name, year incorporated, annual gross revenue, annual net revenue, and so on. Write set and get functions to store and retrieve values in the private data members. Also, create a `friend` function that calculates the company's operating costs by subtracting net revenue from gross revenue. Use cin and cout statements to gather and display information.

8. Create a Change class that calculates the correct amount of change to return when it performs a cash transaction. Allow the user (a cashier) to enter the cost of a transaction and the exact amount of money that the customer hands over to pay for the transaction. Use set and get functions to store and retrieve both amounts to and from `private` data members. Then use member functions to determine the largest amount of each denomination to return to the customer. Assume that the largest denomination a customer will give you is a $100 bill. Therefore, you will need to write member functions for $50, $20, $10, $5, and $1 bills, along with quarters, dimes, nickels, and pennies. For example, if the price of a transaction is $5.65 and the customer hands the cashier $10, the cashier should return $4.35 to the customer. Print your results to the screen using cout statements.
9. Create a BankAccount class that allows users to calculate the balance in a bank account. The user should be able to enter a starting balance, and then calculate how that balance changes when they make a deposit, withdraw money, or enter any accumulated interest. Add the appropriate data members and member functions to the BankAccount class that will enable this functionality. Also, add code to the class that ensures that the user does not overdraw his or her account. Be sure that the program adheres to the information-hiding techniques that were discussed in this chapter. Use cin and cout statements to gather and display information. You will need to use a decision-making structure that continually displays a menu from which the user can select commands to manage his or her account.

CHAPTER

6

MEMORY MANAGEMENT

In this chapter you will learn:

- How to work with pointers
- How to work with references
- How to use pointers and references with functions
- How to work with pointers and references to objects
- About advanced array techniques
- How to dynamically allocate memory

Memory feeds imagination.
Amy Tan

PREVIEW: THE FLORIST ORDER PROGRAM

On holidays such as Mothers' Day, many people send flowers as a gift to multiple recipients (their mother, wife, and grandmothers, for instance). When ordering flowers from a florist for an occasion such as Mothers' Day, it is usually easier to place a single order for all of the recipients instead of multiple orders. Although you may place a single order for multiple people, you still need to designate personal information for each recipient, such as her name, the type of flowers to send, and a personalized greeting. Many of these features present memory management problems when it comes to designing a C++ program. For instance, how can the C++ program create and work with a different class object for each of the recipients? What is the best way to store the types of flowers being sold along with their prices? To demonstrate memory management techniques, in this chapter you will create a simple ordering system that a florist might use to place multiple orders from a single client. Note that the Florist Order program you create is by no means a complete system in that it does not gather some of the important information a merchant would need to complete a business transaction. For example, the program does not gather addresses, payment information, and so. However, it does gather enough information to demonstrate some important memory management techniques.

To preview the Florist Order program:

1. Create a **Chapter.06** folder in your Visual C++ Projects folder.
2. Copy the **Chapter6_FloristOrder** folder from the Chapter.06 folder on your Data Disk to the Chapter.06 folder in your Visual C++ Projects folder. Then open the **FloristOrder** project in Visual C++.
3. The FloristOrder project contains two files: FloristOrder.h and FloristOrder.cpp. The FloristOrder.h file is a class interface file, whereas the FloristOrder.cpp file is a class implementation file. FloristOrder.cpp also contains a main() function. First, open FloristOrder.h in the Code Editor window and examine its contents. Notice that the pFlowerPrices member function has a return type of `double*`. The asterisk following the `double` data type identifies it as a pointer. A pointer is a special memory management tool that allows you to use one variable to point to the memory address of another variable. Also, notice the arVolumeDiscount[] array definition that includes two dimensions. Arrays with more than one dimension are called multidimensional arrays. The FloristOrder.h interface file is shown in Figure 6-1.

```
#pragma once
#include <iostream>
#include <string>
using namespace std;
class FloristOrder
{
public:
      FloristOrder(void);
      ~FloristOrder(void);
private:
      string sCustomerFirstName;
      string sCustomerLastName;
      int iItem;
      int iQuantity;
      string arFlowers[5];
      double arFlowerPrices[5];
      double* pFlowerPrices;
      double arVolumeDiscount[5][3];
...
```

Pointer data member

Multidimensional array

Figure 6-1 FloristOrder.h

4. Now open FloristOrder.cpp in your Code Editor window. First notice the statements in the constructor function that begin with `this->`. The code `this->` is a special pointer called a `this` pointer that identifies a member function or data member as being part of the current class. If you scroll through the file, you will see several other types of pointers being used, as indicated by declarations that contain an asterisk. Keep scrolling through the file until you find the modifyOrder() function prototype. Notice that an ampersand (&) follows the parameter. The ampersand identifies a variable as a reference variable, which is a type of an alias for another variable. Finally, locate the `FloristOrder* arFloristObjects = new`

`FloristOrder[iNumOrders];` statement in the main() function. This statement declares a pointer named arFloristObjects of the FloristOrder data type. The statement also uses the **new** operator to store the object on the heap, which is a special area of memory used for storing variables that you create dynamically at run time. Figure 6-2 shows some portions of the FloristOrder.cpp file.

```
#include "floristorder.h"
FloristOrder::FloristOrder(void)
{
      this->sCustomerFirstName = "";
      this->sCustomerLastName = "";
      this->iItem = 0;
      this->iQuantity = 0;
      this->arFlowers[0] = "Roses (per dozen)";
      this->arFlowers[1] = "Tulips (per dozen)";
      this->arFlowers[2] = "Carnations (per dozen)";
      this->arFlowers[3] = "Sunflowers (each)";
      this->arFlowers[4] = "Orchids (each)";
...
void modifyOrder(FloristOrder&);
void main() {
      cout << "FLOWER ORDERS" << endl;
      cout << "............." << endl;
      int iNumOrders;
      cout << "enter the  number of flower orders: ";
      cin >> iNumOrders;
      FloristOrder* arFloristObjects = new FloristOrder[iNumOrders];
```

This pointers

Reference parameter in the modifyOrder() function prototype

Declaring an object on the heap

Figure 6-2 FloristOrder.cpp

5. Build and execute the project. Test the program's functionality by creating multiple flower orders and entering information for each order. Figure 6-3 shows the output after running the program and entering some data.

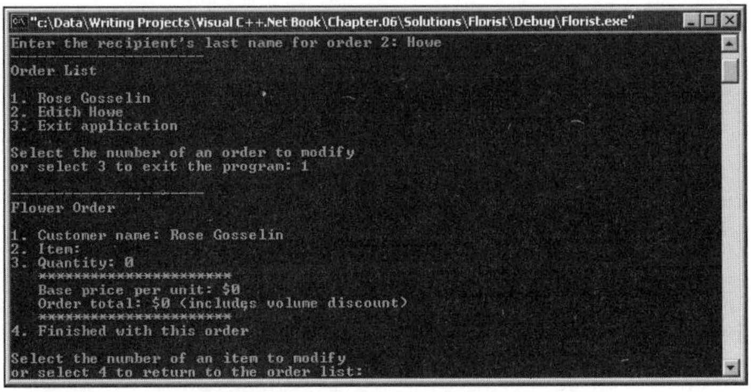

Figure 6-3 Output of the Florist Order program

6. When you are finished testing the program, follow the instructions on each screen to exit. When prompted, press **any key** to close the console window.

7. When you are finished examining the code and testing the program, close the FloristOrder project in Visual C++.

INTRODUCTION TO MEMORY MANAGEMENT

In order to work with advanced class techniques and with the Windows programs that you will create later in this text, you need to have a basic understanding of the mechanics of memory management. Managing memory involves manipulating the memory addresses where variables are stored. This gives you much greater control over your program and allows you to adjust memory requirements as necessary, which will increase the performance of your program. Nevertheless, memory management is one of the most challenging aspects of C++ programming. However, as you will learn in future chapters, Visual C++ automatically sets up many of the memory management aspects of the programs you will create. Therefore, this book does not delve too deeply into the theory behind, or reasons for, memory management. Yet, without at least a minimal understanding of what is going on in your code, you will never be able to fully master Visual C++ programming. This chapter is designed to help you gain that minimal understanding of memory management techniques.

Before beginning to learn memory management techniques, you need to create the basic structure of the Florist Order program.

To create the project and the FloristOrder class interface file:

1. Create a new Win32 Project named **FloristOrder** in the Chapter.06 folder in your Visual C++ Projects folder. Be sure to clear the **Create directory for Solution** check box in the New Project dialog box. In the Application Settings tab of the Win32 Application Wizard dialog box, select **Console application** as the application type, click the **Empty project** check box, and then click the **Finish** button.
2. Once the project is created, use the Add Class Wizard to add to the project a generic C++ class named **FloristOrder**. Leave the Base class text box, Access combo box, and Virtual destructor and Inline check boxes set to their default options.
3. After the `#pragma once` statement in the FloristOrder.h file, add the following statements to give the class access to the iostream class, string class, and standard namespace:

```
#include <iostream>
#include <string>
using namespace std;
```

4. As shown in Figure 6-4, add a private section that declares the data members you will need in the FloristOrder class.

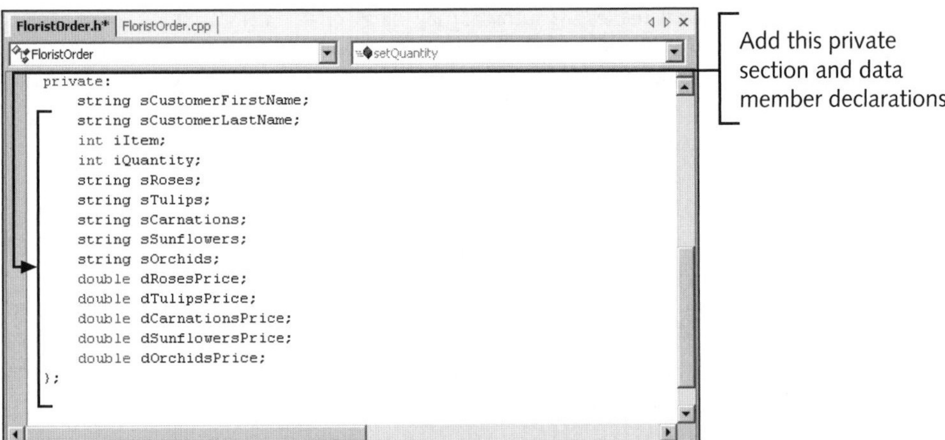

Figure 6-4 Private section added that declares the FloristOrder class data members

6

To add member functions to the FloristOrder class:

1. Open the **FloristOrder.cpp** file in the Code Editor window.
2. Modify the constructor as follows so it initializes the FloristOrder class data members. Because you do not know the customer's name, the sCustomerFirstName and sCustomerLastName fields are being assigned an initial value of an empty string. Similarly, the iItem and iQuantity data members are assigned an initial value of zero because you do not know in advance which item, or how many of it, a customer wants to purchase. The sRoses, sTulips, sCarnations, sSunflowers, and sOrchids data members are assigned text that describes each item, and the dRosesPrice, dTulipsPrice, dCarnationsPrice, dSunflowersPrice, and dOrchidsPrice data members are assigned the cost per unit of each item.

```
FloristOrder::FloristOrder() {
        sCustomerFirstName  = "";
        sCustomerLastName = "";
        iItem = 0;
        iQuantity = 0;
        sRoses = "Roses (per dozen)";
        sTulips = "Tulips (per dozen)";
        sCarnations = "Carnations (per dozen)";
        sSunflowers = "Sunflowers (each)";
        sOrchids = "Orchids (each)";
        dRosesPrice = 9.95;
        dTulipsPrice = 12.95;
        dCarnationsPrice = 7.95;
        dSunflowersPrice = 4.95;
        dOrchidsPrice = 8.95;
}
```

String class variables are automatically initialized to an empty string when you first declare them. Therefore, the initialization statements for the sCustomerFirstName and sCustomerLastName data members in the preceding code are unnecessary. However, it is good programming practice to always be sure that the data members and other variables in your programs are properly initialized.

3. Use the Add Function Wizard to add the following accessor functions that retrieve and modify the private data members of the FloristOrder class. Be sure to add each function as a public class member. Most of the functions are typical set and get functions. The getUnitPrice(), getOrderTotal(), and getFlowerType() functions are also get functions, but they use `switch` statements to evaluate an integer that is passed to them in order to determine what value to return.

Remember that to execute the Add Function Wizard, you must open Class View and expand the FloristOrder project. Then, you either click the FloristOrder class and select Add Function from the Project menu or right-click the FloristOrder class and select Add Function from the Add submenu on the shortcut menu.

```
void FloristOrder::setCustomerFirstName(string sName) {
   sCustomerFirstName = sName;
}
void FloristOrder::setCustomerLastName(string sName) {
   sCustomerLastName = sName;
}
void FloristOrder::setItem(int iSelectedItem) {
   iItem = iSelectedItem;
}
void FloristOrder::setQuantity(int iNumber) {
   iQuantity = iNumber;
}
string FloristOrder::getCustomerFirstName() {
   return sCustomerFirstName;
}
string FloristOrder::getCustomerLastName() {
   return sCustomerLastName;
}
int FloristOrder::getItem() {
   return iItem;
}
int FloristOrder::getQuantity() {
   return iQuantity;
}
```

```
double FloristOrder::getPricePerUnit() {
   switch (iItem) {
      case 1:
         return dRosesPrice;
      case 2:
         return dTulipsPrice;
      case 3:
         return dCarnationsPrice;
      case 4:
         return dSunflowersPrice;
      case 5:
         return dOrchidsPrice;
      default:
         return 0;
   }
}
double FloristOrder::getOrderTotal() {
   switch (iItem) {
      case 1:
         return iQuantity * dRosesPrice;
      case 2:
         return iQuantity * dTulipsPrice;
      case 3:
         return iQuantity * dCarnationsPrice;
      case 4:
         return iQuantity * dSunflowersPrice;
      case 5:
         return iQuantity * dOrchidsPrice;
      default:
         return 0;
   }
}
string FloristOrder::getFlowerType() {
   switch (iItem) {
      case 1:
         return sRoses;
      case 2:
         return sTulips;
      case 3:
         return sCarnations;
      case 4:
         return sSunflowers;
      case 5:
         return sOrchids;
      default:
         return "";
   }
}
```

4. Add the following prototypes for a custom function named showOrders() and a custom function named modifyOrder(). The showOrders() function is called from the main() function and displays a list of flower orders for the current customer. The modifyOrder() function is called from the showOrders() function and is used to modify the information in an individual flower order. Notice that both function prototypes declare a parameter of the FloristOrder type.

```
void showOrders(FloristOrder);
void modifyOrder(FloristOrder);
```

5. Add the main() function shown in Figure 6-5. The main() function instantiates a FloristOrder object named flowerOrder. For now, you will only work with a single flower order. Later in this chapter, you will learn how to instantiate multiple flower orders based on input from the user. The statements following the statement that instantiates the FloristOrder object assign values to the object's sCustomerFirstName and sCustomerLastName variables by calling the setCustomerFirstName() and setCustomerLastName() functions. The last statement calls the showOrders() function, passing to it the flowerOrder object you instantiated. Although this statement will work, it is not the most efficient method of passing an object to a function. You will return to this statement and improve it after you spend some time learning about pointers and references.

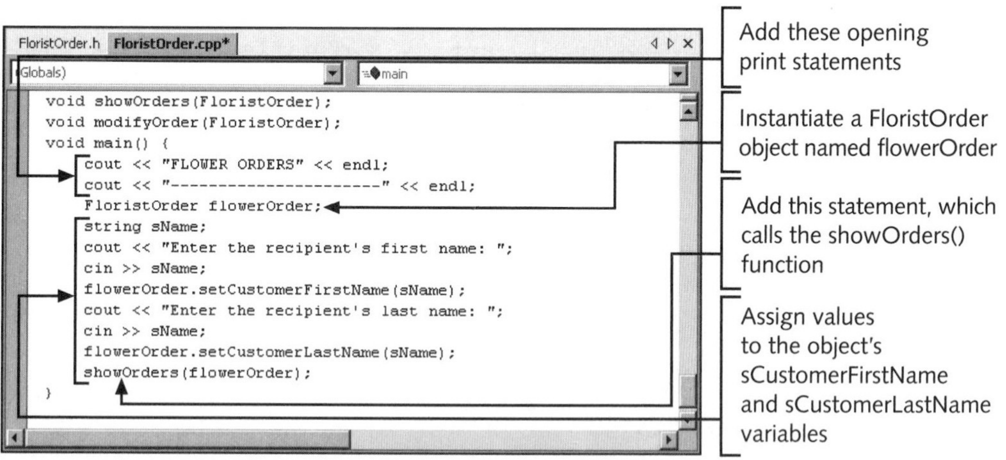

Figure 6-5 main() function added to FloristOrder.cpp

6. Finally, add the following empty definitions for the showOrders() and modifyOrder() functions. You will add code to each function shortly.

```
void showOrders(FloristOrder curOrder) {
}
void modifyOrder(FloristOrder curOrder) {
}
```

7. Build the project to make sure you entered the code correctly. If you receive any compile errors, fix them, and rebuild the project before continuing. Execute the program, and see if you can enter the first and last name for an order. Because you have not yet added code to the showOrders() and modifyOrder() functions, the program should end after you type the last name and press Enter, as shown in Figure 6-6.

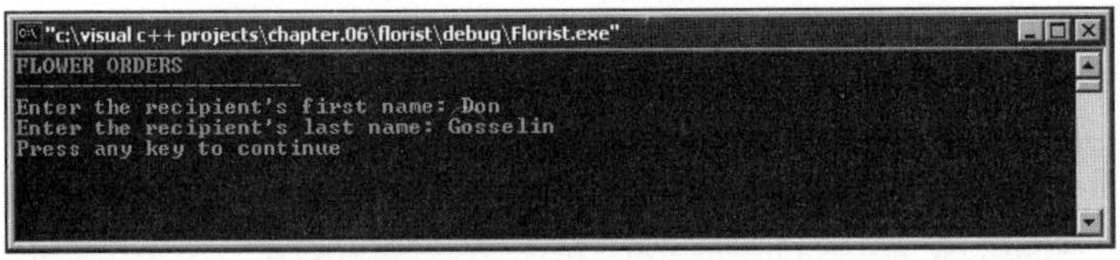

```
"c:\visual c++ projects\chapter.06\florist\debug\Florist.exe"
FLOWER ORDERS
------------
Enter the recipient's first name: Don
Enter the recipient's last name: Gosselin
Press any key to continue
```

Figure 6-6 Output of Florist Order program after creating the initial interface and implementation files

8. Press **any key** to close the console window.

POINTERS

One of the most commonly used memory management techniques in C++ is the pointer. A **pointer** is a special type of variable that stores the memory address of another variable. You use pointers to manipulate a variable and its contents through its memory address instead of through its variable name. Why do you use pointers? Why not just use a variable directly instead of using another variable that points to the original variable's memory address? Working with pointers confers many advantages, all related to the efficiency of your programs. But the most important advantage comes when you need to use functions to work with or modify large variables, such as an object or complex array.

What exactly is meant by "large variable"? Although it may contain a number as large as 1.7E308, a variable of the `double` data type is not considered particularly large because it will occupy only eight bytes, no matter what number it stores. Instead, when a large variable is referred to, class objects or complex arrays are being talked about. (Recall from the last chapter that programmers use the terms variables and objects interchangeably.) A class object may be very large if it contains dozens, or even hundreds, of data members and member functions. An array can also grow quite large if it contains hundreds of elements or is a multidimensional array. Although you will study multidimensional arrays later, for now you should understand that a multidimensional array consists of multiple indexes, which are comparable to rows in a table. As an example of a large variable, consider the currency conversion table shown in Figure 6-7.

	US Dollars	UK Pounds	French Francs	DMarks	Yen	Euros
US Dollars	1	1.448	7795	.1384	.008272	.9081
UK Pounds	.6905	1	.09557	.3206	.005712	.627
French Francs	7.224	10.46	1	3.354	.05976	6.56
DMarks	2.154	3.119	.2981	1	.01782	1.956
Yen	120.9	175.1	16.73	56.13	1	109.8
Euros	1.101	1.595	.1524	.5113	.009109	1

Figure 6-7 Currency conversion table

You can store the currency conversion table shown in Figure 6-7 in a multidimensional array as follows:

```
double arCurrencies[6][6] = {
   { 1, 1.448, 7795, .1384, .008272, .9081 },
   { .6905, 1, .09557, .3206, .005712, .627 },
   { 7.224, 10.46, 1, 3.354, .05976, 6.56 },
   { 2.154, 3.119, .2981, 1, .01782, 1.956 },
   { 120.9, 175.1, 16.73, 56.13, 1, 109.8 },
   { 1.101, 1.595, .1524, .5113, .009109, 1 } };
```

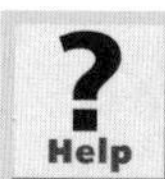

For now do not worry about how the multidimensional array is set up or how to work with it. You will learn about multidimensional arrays at the end of this chapter. Your goal for the moment is to understand how large a variable, such as a multidimensional array, can become.

Each set of values within its own set of braces is equivalent to a row in the table. The example shows only a few currency conversions due to space limitations. However, in reality, the table would consist of more than 150 rows, one for each of the world's currencies, along with an equal number of columns containing the rate for converting each individual currency to every other world currency. An array such as this would occupy a sizeable portion of memory.

As you know, you can pass primitive data types, such as double or int, to a function. You can also pass an object or an array to a function. However, when you pass an array to a function, you are really passing a pointer to the array. (You will learn why this occurs later in this chapter.) Again, keep in mind that, in reality, the currency array would be much larger and consist of more than 150 currencies, not just the six currencies shown in the example. Passing just a pointer to an array saves a signficant amount of memory over passing a copy of the array. This concept of passing a pointer to an array is illustrated in Figure 6-8.

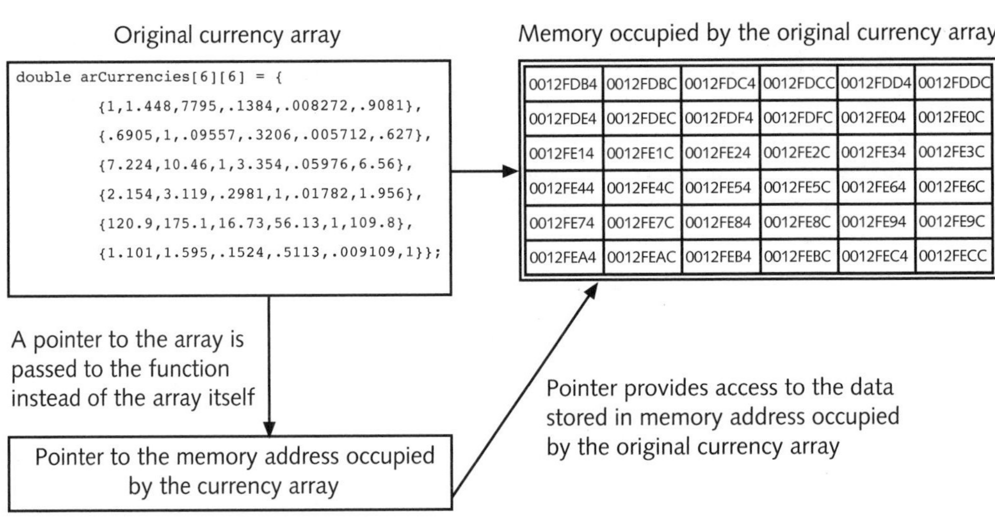
Original currency array
Memory occupied by the original currency array
double arCurrencies[6][6] = {
{1,1.448,7795,.1384,.008272,.9081},
{.6905,1,.09557,.3206,.005712,.627},
{7.224,10.46,1,3.354,.05976,6.56},
{2.154,3.119,.2981,1,.01782,1.956},
{120.9,175.1,16.73,56.13,1,109.8},
{1.101,1.595,.1524,.5113,.009109,1}};
0012FDB4 0012FDBC 0012FDC4 0012FDCC 0012FDD4 0012FDDC
0012FDE4 0012FDEC 0012FDF4 0012FDFC 0012FE04 0012FE0C
0012FE14 0012FE1C 0012FE24 0012FE2C 0012FE34 0012FE3C
0012FE44 0012FE4C 0012FE54 0012FE5C 0012FE64 0012FE6C
0012FE74 0012FE7C 0012FE84 0012FE8C 0012FE94 0012FE9C
0012FEA4 0012FEAC 0012FEB4 0012FEBC 0012FEC4 0012FECC
A pointer to the array is passed to the function instead of the array itself
Pointer provides access to the data stored in memory address occupied by the original currency array
Pointer to the memory address occupied by the currency array

Figure 6-8 Passing a pointer to the currency array

The memory addresses where the elements of an array are stored may differ on your computer, depending on the type of operating system you are using, how much memory you have installed, and how many applications you have running.

The more you progress through this chapter, the more you will understand the benefits of pointers and managing the memory that your application uses. Next, you need to learn the basics of how to use pointers.

Declaring and Initializing a Pointer

You declare a pointer with a data type, just as you declare ordinary variables. To declare a variable as a pointer, you place the **indirection operator (*)** after the data type or before the variable name. For example, both of the following statements declare pointer `int` variables. Notice that the pointer names, pFirstPointer and pSecondPointer, both begin with a *p*, which is Hungarian notation for a pointer variable.

```
int* pFirstPointer;
int *pSecondPointer;
```

Although both of the preceding statements correctly declare pointer variables, you should use the first syntax because that is the syntax used by Visual C++. You should be able to recognize the second statement, however, as being an equally correct method of declaring a pointer in C++.

The indirection operator gets its name because a pointer variable *indirectly* accesses a value through its memory address, whereas a regular variable *directly* accesses a stored value.

After you declare a pointer variable, you use the **address of (&)** operator to assign to the pointer variable the memory address of another variable. You place the address of operator in front of the variable whose address you want to assign to the pointer. For example, the first two statements in the following code declare a variable named dPrimeInterest and a pointer named pPrimeInterest. After declaring the pPrimeInterest pointer, the third statement uses the address of operator (&) to assign the dPrimeInterest variable's memory address to the pPrimeInterest pointer.

```
double dPrimeInterest;
double* pPrimeInterest;
pPrimeInterest = &dPrimeInterest;
```

In addition to using the address of operator (&) to assign a variable's memory address to a pointer, you can also assign the name of another pointer variable to a pointer. This type of statement assigns the memory address stored in the right pointer operand to the left pointer operand. For example, the following code declares one `double` variable named dPrimeInterest and two pointer variables: pPrimeInterest1 and pPrimeInterest2. The fourth statement assigns the memory address of the dPrimeInterest variable to the pPrimeInterest1 pointer. The last statement then assigns the memory address (of dPrimeInterest) stored in the pPrimeIntrerest1 variable to the dPrimeInterest2 pointer.

```
double dPrimeInterest;
double* pPrimeInterest1;
double* pPrimeInterest2;
pPrimeInterest1 = &dPrimeInterest;
pPrimeInterest2 = pPrimeInterest1;
```

You can also declare a pointer and assign to it a variable's memory address in the same statement, as follows:

```
double dPrimeInterest;
double* pPrimeInterest = &dPrimeInterest;
```

If you were to print the pPrimeInterest pointer variable to the screen using an output statement, you would see the memory address it stores. If you were to print the memory address of the dPrimeInterest variable (the variable, not the pointer variable) and precede it with the address of operator (&), you would see that the address stored in the pPrimeInterest pointer is the same as the address of the dPrimeInterest variable. The following code adds to the dPrimeInterest and pPrimeInterest declaration code cout statements that print the contents of the pPrimeInterest pointer and the address of the dPrimeInterest variable. If you were to execute the following code, you would see the output shown in Figure 6-9. Notice that the same memory address is printed twice, demonstrating that the pointer variable contains the memory address of the dPrimeInterest variable.

```
double dPrimeInterest;
double* pPrimeInterest = &dPrimeInterest;
cout << "The value stored in the pPrimeInterest "
   << "pointer is: " << pPrimeInterest << endl;
cout << "The memory address of the dPrimeInterest "
   << "variable is: " << &dPrimeInterest << endl;
```

```
"c:\visual c++ projects\chapter.06\pointers\debug\Pointers.exe"
The value stored in the pPrimeInterest pointer is: 0012FECC
The memory address of the dPrimeInterest variable is: 0012FECC
Press any key to continue
```

Figure 6-9 Output showing pPrimeInterest value and dPrimeInterest memory address

The memory addresses shown in Figure 6-9 may differ on your computer, depending on the type of operating system you are using, how much memory you have installed, and how many applications you have running.

Next, you will start building the showOrders() function. You will declare and initialize a pointer to one of the local variables in the showOrders() function. Note that there is little reason to use a pointer to a local variable if you do not intend to pass the variable to other functions. However, you are adding a local pointer to the showOrders() function so you can understand the basic mechanics of working with pointers.

To start building the showOrders() function:

1. Return to the FloristOrder.cpp file in your Code Editor window and locate the empty showOrders() function.
2. Add the variable and pointer declaration statements to the showOrders() function, as follows. The first statement declares an integer variable named iSelection, which will store an integer entered by the user that determines which flower order to modify. The second statement declares a pointer named pSelection that points to the iSelection variable

```
void showOrders(FloristOrder curOrder) {
        int iSelection;
        int* pSelection = &iSelection;
}
```

De-referencing a Pointer

Once you assign the memory address of a variable to a pointer, to access or modify the contents of the variable pointed to by the pointer, you precede a pointer name in an expression with the **de-reference (*)** operator. It is a little confusing that the de-reference operator (*) happens to be an asterisk, the same as the indirection operator. You can distinguish the two operator types by the fact that the indirection operator is used only when declaring a pointer, whereas the de-reference operator is used whenever you need to access or modify the contents of the address pointed to by a pointer.

For example, in the following code, the first statement declares the dPrimeInterest variable, and the second statement uses the indirection operator to assign the memory address of the dPrimeInterest variable to the pPrimeInterest pointer. The third statement uses the de-reference operator to store the value .08 in the memory address that is the target of the pPrimeInterest pointer. The third statement uses the de-reference operator again to print the value stored in the memory address that is the target of pPrimeInterest:

```
double dPrimeInterest = .07;
double* pPrimeInterest
   = &dPrimeInterest;  // indirection operator
*pPrimeInterest = .08; // de-reference operator
cout << *pPrimeInterest << endl; // de-reference operator
```

The de-reference operator gets its name because instead of returning the memory address stored by a pointer, it returns the value *referenced* by the pointer variable. Using the de-reference operator to return the value that is the target of a pointer variable is called *de-referencing* the pointer.

In the following code, which shows another example using the dPrimeInterest and pPrimeInterest variables, the fourth statement uses a standard assignment operation to assign the value .065 to the dPrimeInterest variable. The cout statement then prints the value of the dPrimeInterest variable to the screen. Then, the dPrimeInterest variable is assigned the value of .07, this time using the de-reference operator with the pPrimeInterest variable. The last statement prints the dPrimeInterest variable again, demonstrating that you can change the contents of a variable through a pointer to the variable's memory address without directly manipulating the original variable. Figure 6-10 shows the output.

```
double dPrimeInterest;
double* pPrimeInterest;  // indirection operator
pPrimeInterest = &dPrimeInterest;
dPrimeInterest = .065;
cout << "The value of dPrimeInterest is: "
  <<dPrimeInterest << endl;
*pPrimeInterest = .07;  // de-reference operator
cout << "The value of dPrimeInterest is: "
  << dPrimeInterest << endl;
cout << "The de-referenced value of pPrimeInterest is: "
  << *pPrimeInterest << endl; // de-reference operator
```

```
"c:\visual c++ projects\chapter.06\pointers\debug\Pointers.exe"
The value of dPrimeInterest is: 0.065
The value of dPrimeInterest is: 0.07
Press any key to continue
```

Figure 6-10 Output after assigning a new value using the de-reference operator

Next, you will add code to the showOrders() function that displays a menu of orders that a user can modify. The user can select a particular order by entering an integer value that represents that order. The integer value is assigned to the iSelection variable, but you access it through the pSelection pointer.

To add code to the showOrders() function that displays a menu of orders that a user can modify:

1. Return to the FloristOrder.cpp file in your Code Editor window.

2. Above the closing brace in the showOrders() function, add the following `do...while` loop. The `do...while` loop displays a menu of orders until the user presses the number 2, which ends the loop. This version of the program has a single object that is represented by the integer 1. If the user presses *2*, the `do...while` loop ends, which also ends the function. Notice that the cin statement and the `if` statement's conditional expression use the de-reference (*) operator with the pSelection pointer to reference the value of the iSelection variable. Also notice that the FloristOrder object named curOrder is being passed again, but this time to the modifyOrder() function. You will come back to this passing of the FloristOrder object shortly.

```
do {
   cout << "----------------------" << endl;
   cout << "Order List" << endl << endl;
   cout << "1. " << curOrder.getCustomerFirstName()
     << " " << curOrder.getCustomerLastName() << endl;
   cout << "2. " << "Exit application" << endl << endl;
   cout << "Select the number of an order to modify "
     << endl
     << "or select 2 to exit the program: ";
   cin >> *pSelection;
   cout << endl;
   if (*pSelection != 2)
     modifyOrder(curOrder);
} while (iSelection != 2);
```

3. Build and execute the Florist Order program. The Order List should appear after you enter a customer's first and last name. Because you have not yet added any code to the modifyOrder() function, pressing 1 only redisplays the Order List. However, you should be able to exit the application by pressing 2 Figure 6-11 shows the output.

4. Press **2** to exit the program. When prompted, press any key to close the console window.

6

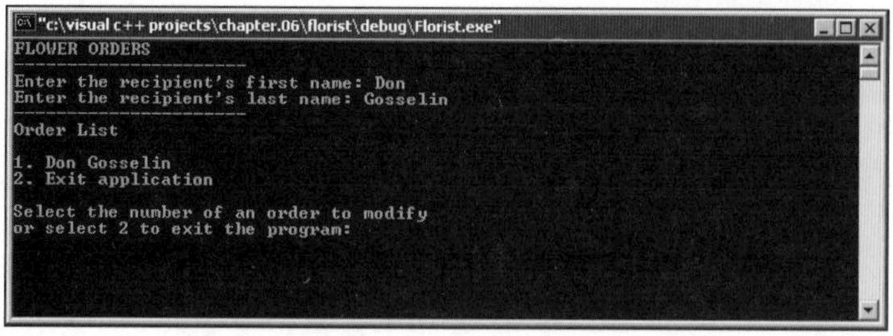

```
"c:\visual c++ projects\chapter.06\florist\debug\Florist.exe"
FLOWER ORDERS
Enter the recipient's first name: Don
Enter the recipient's last name: Gosselin
Order List
1. Don Gosselin
2. Exit application
Select the number of an order to modify
or select 2 to exit the program:
```

Figure 6-11 Output of the Florist Order program after adding code to the showOrders() function

REFERENCES

A **reference**, or **reference variable**, is an alias for an existing variable. Compared to pointer variables, references provide a streamlined way to pass large variables to and return large variables from a function. If you only intend to work with variables inside a local function, however, there is little reason to use references for variables, because it is easier to simply work with the variable itself. However, if you need to pass a large variable, such as an object, to a function, a reference provides a simplified alternative to using a pointer.

Declaring and Initializing a Reference

You create a reference by appending the address of operator (&) to the data type in a variable declaration and assigning an existing variable to the new variable name. The syntax for creating a reference is `data type& reference_name = variable_name;`. The following code creates a reference named rPrimeInterest that is an alias for the dPrimeInterest variable:

```
double dPrimeInterest;
double& rPrimeInterest = dPrimeInterest;
```

Notice that the pointer name, rPrimeInterest, begins with an r, which is Hungarian notation for a reference variable. When you first declare a reference, you must assign an existing variable to it or you will receive a compile error. The statement `double& rPrimeInterest;`, for instance, causes a compile error because no variable has been assigned to the rPrimeInterest reference. Additionally, once you declare and initialize a reference, there is no way to reassign it as an alias to another variable.

Once you create a reference, you can use it exactly as you would use a standard variable. You do not need to use any special operators to access or modify the original variable as you do with pointers. The following code shows how you can modify the dPrimeInterest variable through the rPrimeInterest reference. The last statement in the main() function also prints the contents of the dPrimeInterest variable through the rPrimeInterest reference. Figure 6-12 shows the output.

```
double dPrimeInterest;
double& rPrimeInterest = dPrimeInterest;
rPrimeInterest = .065;
cout << "The value of dPrimeInterest is: "
  <<dPrimeInterest << endl;
rPrimeInterest = .07;
cout << "The value of dPrimeInterest is: "
  <<dPrimeInterest << endl;
cout << "The value of rPrimeInterest is: "
  <<rPrimeInterest << endl;
```

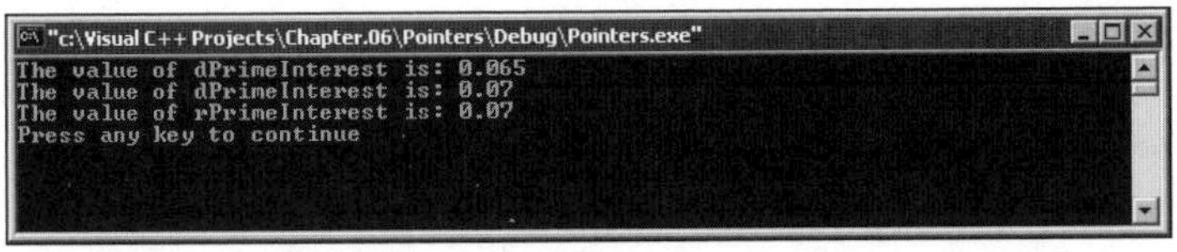

```
"c:\Visual C++ Projects\Chapter.06\Pointers\Debug\Pointers.exe"
The value of dPrimeInterest is: 0.065
The value of dPrimeInterest is: 0.07
The value of rPrimeInterest is: 0.07
Press any key to continue
```

Figure 6-12 Output after assigning new values through a reference

Next, you will modify the showOrders() function in the Florist Order program so that the iSelection variable is accessed through a reference instead of a pointer. As mentioned earlier, there is little reason to use references for variables if you only intend to work with the variables inside a local function, because it is easier to simply work with the variable itself. However, as with the pointer example, you are adding a local reference to the showOrders() function as an exercise to help understand the mechanics of working with references.

To modify the showOrders() function in the Florist Order program so that the iSelection variable is accessed through a reference instead of a pointer:

1. Return to the FloristOrder.cpp file in your Code Editor window.
2. As shown in the showOrders() function in Figure 6-13, modify the statement that declares the pSelection pointer so it instead declares a reference named rSelection, which references the iSelection variable. Also, in the `do...while` loop, modify the cin statement and the conditional expression in the `if` statement so that they access the contents of the iSelection variable through the rSelection variable instead of the pSelection pointer.

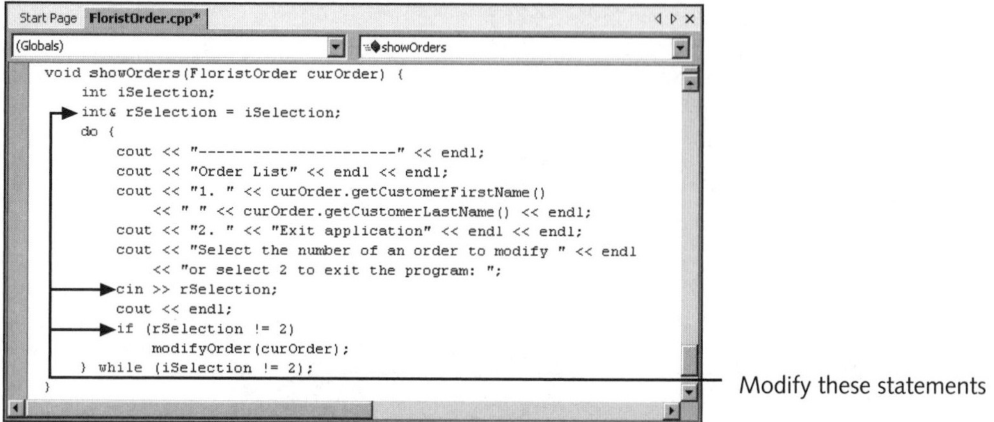

Figure 6-13 A reference added to the showOrders() function

3. Build and execute the project. The program should function the same as it did with the pSelection pointer variable.

References Compared to Pointers

At this point, you may be asking, "What is the difference between a pointer and a reference variable?" Although they appear similar on the surface, they are really two separate programming elements. A pointer stores the memory address of a variable, whereas a reference is an alias for a variable. In reality, a reference also stores the memory address of a variable, but it behaves like a variable. A reference can be easier to work with than a pointer because you do not have to use special operators to access the variable for which the reference is an alias. One of the most common times that a reference is used is when you need one function to work with a large variable that is declared in another function. Passing a reference to a called function eliminates the memory overhead associated with passing a copy of a large variable. You can pass a pointer, but then you would need to deal with the address of and de-reference operators.

One important reason why you would need to use a pointer instead of a reference is that a reference variable cannot be reassigned. In other words, you cannot declare a reference to be an alias for one object and then reassign it as the alias for another object. In contrast, you can use the address of (`&`) operator to reassign the memory address that is the target of a pointer. As an example, consider an Investment program that contains a pointer named pInvestment, which points to the memory address of an object representing an investment type. When a client uses the program, she may first select a stock investment, in which case the Investment program instantiates a Stock object and points the pInvestment pointer at the Stock object's memory address. However, the client may change her mind about the investment type and instead choose bonds. The Investment program would then instantiate a Bond object and reassign the Bond object's memory address to be the target of the pInvestment pointer. Although this scenario is legal with pointers, it is illegal with references.

A reference must always refer to an existing object.

Using Pointers and References with Functions

The examples discussed in the preceding sections demonstrate the basic mechanics of declaring, initializing, and working with pointers and references. However, all of the examples were presented within the context of the main() function. In other words, you only used each pointer and reference within the function where it was declared. Using pointers and references within the main() function allowed you to concentrate on the basic syntax for each element.

One of the most important reasons for working with pointers and references is to minimize the amount of memory required when passing arguments to a function. Next, you will learn about the three primary methods of passing arguments to a function: call-by-value, call-by-address, and call-by-reference.

Although the technique is not discussed in this book, you can also return pointers and references from functions. However, you need to be sure not to return a pointer or reference to a local variable because local variables cease to exist when the function that declares them ends. If you return a pointer or reference to a local variable and then attempt to modify the value of the variable through the returned pointer or reference, your program may not function correctly. This happens because the memory where the local variable was stored may be in use by another part of your program.

Call-by-Value

Recall that class objects are another form of variable. Class objects can be very large, and pointers allow you to reduce the amount of memory they require by eliminating the need to duplicate them when you need to have multiple functions work on the same variable. For example, you may need to pass a large variable to a function. Once the function receives the variable, it performs some sort of processing on it, and then returns the variable to the calling function. When you pass the variable itself, the program actually makes a copy of the variable to work with, which significantly increases the memory resources required by your program.

Passing a variable to a function is referred to as **calling-by-value** or **passing-by-value** because only the value of the variable is passed to the function instead of the variable itself. The important thing to remember when you pass a variable to a function by value is that the called function receives a *duplicate* of the value passed to it. Any change the called function makes to the duplicate value is *not* reflected in the original variable. Because a variable is essentially copied when you pass it by value, the call by value is most efficient when passing small variables of primitive data types. For example, you should pass primitive `int` or `double` variables by value because these types of variables occupy a relatively small amount of memory.

Figure 6-14 shows a simple example of how to use call-by-value. The program in the figure calculates the total carpeting cost for an office building. When the calcTotalCost() function is called, the dFeet variable is passed by value to the dSquareFeet parameter. The calcTotalCost() function then increases the dSquareFeet variable by 10% to account for waste material. However, because only its value was passed to the calcTotalCost() function, the dFeet variable still contains a value of 20000, as shown in Figure 6-15.

```
#include <iostream>
using namespace std;
double calcTotalCost(double dSquareFeet) {
        dSquareFeet *= 1.1;
        double dNumberOfFeet = dSquareFeet;
        double dPricePerFoot = 2.5;
        double dTotalCost = dNumberOfFeet * dPricePerFoot;
        cout << "Total square footage increased by 10% "
                << "to account for waste material." << endl;
        cout << "Your new square footage is: "
                << dSquareFeet << endl;
        return dTotalCost;
}
void main() {
        cout << "Enter the number of square feet to carpet: ";
        double dFeet;
        cin >> dFeet;
        cout << "Your total carpeting cost will be: $"
                << calcTotalCost(dFeet) << endl;
        cout << "The value of the dFeet variable is: "
                << dFeet << endl;
}
```

The value of the dFeet argument is *copied* to the dSquareFeet parameter because the calcTotalCost() function is called by value

Figure 6-14 Program that uses call-by-value to execute a function

```
"c:\Visual C++ Projects\Chapter.06\Carpets\Debug\Carpets.exe"
Enter the number of square feet to carpet: 20000
Total square footage increased by 10% to account for waste material.
Your new square footage is: 22000
Your total carpeting cost will be: $55000
The value of the dFeet variable is: 20000
Press any key to continue
```

Figure 6-15 Output of the call-by-value program

Next, you will add code to the modifyOrder() function that gives the program much of its functionality. You are adding functionality to the modifyOrder() function at this point because several of the statements you add call member functions of the FloristOrder class by value.

To add code to the modifyOrder() function:

1. Return to the FloristOrder.cpp file in your Code Editor window.
2. In the modifyOrder() function, add the following declarations for the iSelection variable, rSelection reference variable, and sName variable. (You are creating another rSelection reference variable in order to be consistent with the showOrders() function.) You will use the sName variable to temporarily

store a customer's first and last names before they are assigned to their corresponding data members in the FloristOrder class.

```
int iSelection;
int& rSelection = iSelection;
string sName;
```

3. After the reference variable declaration statement, start a `do...while` loop that displays a menu of items that can be changed for each order, similar to the `do...while` loop in the showOrders() function. Also add the output statements that create the menu of items that can be selected. The output statements call accessor functions in the FloristOrder class in order to list the details of the order. With the exception of the first and last name, the values retrieved for new orders will come from the initial values you assigned to each data member in the class constructor. Notice that with this `do...while` loop, the user needs to press *4* to exit the loop.

```
do {
   cout << "----------------------" << endl;
   cout << "Flower Order" << endl << endl;
   cout << "1. Customer name: "
        << curOrder.getCustomerFirstName()
        << " " << curOrder.getCustomerLastName() << endl;
   cout << "2. Item: " << curOrder.getFlowerType()
        << endl;
   cout << "3. Quantity: " << curOrder.getQuantity()
        << endl;
   cout << "    **********************" << endl;
   cout << "    Base price per unit: $"
        << curOrder.getPricePerUnit() << endl;
   cout << "    Order total: $"
        << curOrder.getOrderTotal() << endl;
   cout << "    **********************" << endl;
   cout << "4. Finished with this order "
        << endl << endl;
   cout << "Select the number of an item to modify "
        << endl
        << "or select 4 to return to the order list: ";
   cin >> rSelection;
   cout << endl;
```

4. Add the opening header for a `switch` statement `switch (rSelection) {`. The `switch` statement will evaluate the integer assigned to the iSelection variable and then execute the appropriate case label.

5. Press **Enter** and add the first case label, which modifies the order's first and last name:

```
case 1:
   cout << "Enter the recipient's first name: ";
   cin >> sName;
```

6

```
        rCurOrder.setCustomerFirstName(sName);
        cout << "Enter the recipient's last name: ";
        cin >> sName;
        rCurOrder.setCustomerLastName(sName);
        break;
```

6. Add a case label that allows users to select a different type of flower. Note that the setItem() accessor function simply assigns an integer value, 1 through 5, to the iItem data member in order to identify the type of flower selected for the order.

```
    case 2:
        int iSelectedItem;
        cout << "1. Roses (per dozen), $9.95" << endl;
        cout << "2. Tulips (per dozen), $12.95" << endl;
        cout << "3. Carnations (per dozen), $7.95" << endl;
        cout << "4. Sunflowers (each), $4.95" << endl;
        cout << "5. Orchids (each), $8.95" << endl;
        cout << "Select the type of flowers: ";
        cin >> iSelectedItem;
        curOrder.setItem(iSelectedItem);
        break;
```

7. Add a case label that sets the number of items the user wants to purchase:

```
    case 3:
        int iNumber;
        cout << "Enter the number of items: ";
        cin >> iNumber;
        curOrder.setQuantity(iNumber);
        break;
```

8. Add a default case label that simply reiterates the loop in the event the user pressed a key other than 1 through 4:

```
    default:
            continue;
```

9. Finally, add the closing brace for the `switch` statement and the closing portion of the `do...while` loop:

```
            }
    } while (iSelection != 4);
```

10. Build and execute the project. Enter a first and last name for the order. When the Order List menu appears, select **1** to modify the order. In the Flower Order menu, enter an item and a quantity. The price per unit and order total sections of the menu should be updated automatically as you make your selections. Figure 6-16 shows an example of the Flower Order menu after a user selects an item and quantity.

```
"c:\visual c++ projects\chapter.06\florist\debug\Florist.exe"
3. Quantity: 0
   **********************
   Price per unit: $4.95
   Order total: $0
   **********************
4. Finished with this order

Select the number of an item to modify
or select 4 to return to the order list: 3

Enter the number of items: 5
------------------------
Flower Order

1. Customer name: Don Gosselin
2. Item: Sunflowers (each)
3. Quantity: 5
   **********************
   Price per unit: $4.95
   Order total: $24.75
   **********************
4. Finished with this order

Select the number of an item to modify
or select 4 to return to the order list:
```


Figure 6-16 Florist Order program after adding code to the modifyOrder() function

11. When you are finished entering information for the order, press **4** to exit the Flower Order menu and then press **2** to exit the Order List menu. When prompted, press any key to close the console window.

Call-by-Address

Calling-by-value is most efficient for small variables of primitive data types, such as an `int` or `double` variable. However, for large objects, a more efficient method is to pass only the memory address of the variable, using a pointer variable. Passing a pointer to a function is referred to as **calling-by-address** or **passing-by-address** because only the memory address of the variable is passed to the function instead of the value of the variable. Using a pointer parameter, the function can manipulate the original variable, avoiding the costly memory overhead required to pass a large variable to and return a large variable from a function.

Some experts on C++ programming do not recognize the term *call-by-address* and instead feel that passing a pointer to a function is really a call-by-value or call-by-reference. This book (and other C++ books) uses the term call-by-address to make it specifically clear that you are passing a memory address, and not a value or reference, to a function.

As an example of calling-by-address, consider an object named q1Budget that is instantiated from a class named BudgetAnalys, which may contain methods and properties for calculating a company's budget. Suppose you instantiate the q1Budget object in your program's main() function, but you want a global function named costAnalysis() to perform some additional calculations on the q1Budget object to determine if the first quarter budget meets your company's budgetary guidelines. An object of the BudgetAnalysis class may become quite large if you assign sizeable amounts of data to its properties. Passing the q1Budget object by value could take up an unnecessarily large amount of memory because the object would be copied to the costAnalysis() function. Instead, you create a pointer to the q1Budget object's memory address and then pass the pointer to the costAnalysis() function. The costAnalysis() function can then use the pointer to indirectly manipulate the original q1Budget object through its memory address. In other words, the variable is never duplicated; any changes you make through a pointer that is passed by address *will be* reflected in the original object. Calling-by-address copies a variable's memory address to another pointer in the called function, so your program may contain multiple pointers to the same memory address. However, multiple pointers to the same memory address will usually take up less memory than a duplicated object. Figure 6-17 illustrates how the q1Budget object is indirectly accessed through pointers in the main() and costAnalysis() functions.

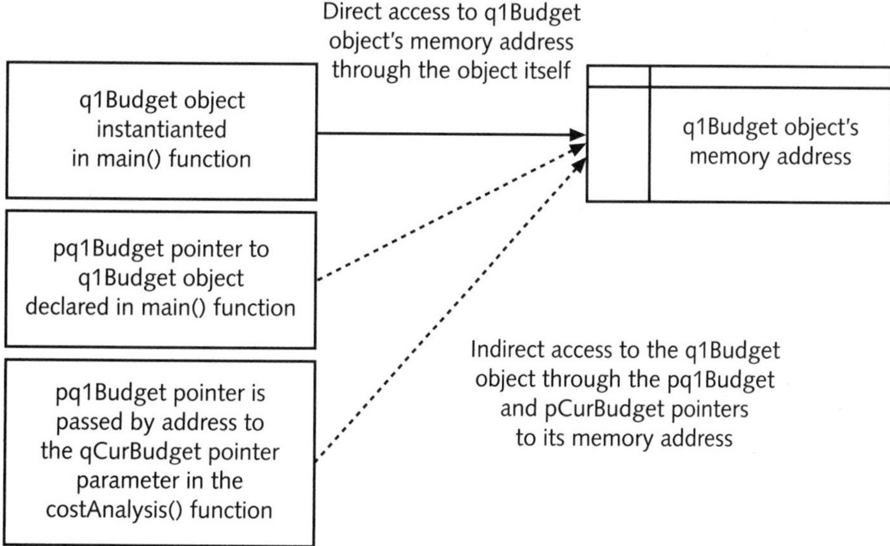

Figure 6-17 Pointers to the q1Budget object's memory address

The definition for a function you want to call-by-address must declare a pointer parameter of the object type you want to pass. For example, consider the Carpet Cost program. In order to pass the address of the dFeet variable to the calcTotalCost() function, you must use a function definition similar to the following. Notice that the function parameter declares a `double` pointer named pSquareFeet, using the same syntax that you use to declare a pointer in the body of a function.

```
double calcTotalCost(double* pSquareFeet) {
    statements;
}
```

To pass a pointer as an argument when you call a function, simply include the pointer name without any operators, as you would when passing a variable by value. Alternately, you can pass the address of the variable itself using the address of (&) operator. Using either method, the pass-by-address mechanism automatically handles the task of assigning to the pointer parameter the memory address of the passed pointer. For example, to call the calcTotalCost() function and pass to it the memory address of the dFeet variable, you use the statement `calcTotalCost(&dFeet);`. Figure 6-18 shows a complete example of the dFeet variable's address being passed from the main() method to the calcTotalCost() function, where it is assigned to the pSquareFeet pointer parameter.

```
#include <iostream>
using namespace std;
double calcTotalCost(double* pSquareFeet) {
        *pSquareFeet *= 1.1;
        double dNumberOfFeet = *pSquareFeet;
        double dPricePerFoot = 2.5;
        double dTotalCost = dNumberOfFeet * dPricePerFoot;
        cout << "Total square footage increased by 10% "
                << "to account for waste material." << endl;
        cout << "Your new square footage is: "
                << *pSquareFeet << endl;
        return dTotalCost;
}
void main() {
        cout << "Enter the number of square feet to carpet: ";
        double dFeet;
        cin >> dFeet;
        cout << "Your total carpeting cost will be: $"
                << calcTotalCost(&dFeet) << endl;
        cout << "The value of the dFeet variable is: "
                << dFeet << endl;
}
```

The value of the dFeet argument is passed by address to the pSquareFeet pointer parameter since the calcTotalCost() function is called by address

Figure 6-18 Program that uses call-by-address to execute a function

Notice in Figure 6-18 that the pSquareFeet pointer is being de-referenced before its value is increased by 10%. This means that the value of the dFeet variable (the target of the pSquareFeet pointer) in the main() function is being modified. When the statement in the calcTotalCost() function that prints the value of the pSquareFeet pointer executes, it will print the value that is assigned to the dFeet variable because the pSquareFeet pointer points to the dFeet variable. Figure 6-19 shows an example of the output.

```
"c:\Visual C++ Projects\Chapter.06\Carpets\Debug\Carpets.exe"
Enter the number of square feet to carpet: 20000
Total square footage increased by 10% to account for waste material.
Your new square footage is: 22000
Your total carpeting cost will be: $55000
The value of the dFeet variable is: 22000
Press any key to continue
```

Figure 6-19 Output of the call-by-address program

You may have already noticed that in the Florist Order program, the `showOrders(flowerOrder);` statement in the main() function and the `modifyOrder(curOrder);` statement in the showOrders() function both pass the FloristOrder object by value. You probably will not notice any sort of memory issues with such a small program. However, good programming practice dictates that objects should be passed-by-address. In addition, later you will be creating multiple FloristOrder class objects, at which point you may begin to see some performance issues due to the duplicate objects. Therefore, you will modify the objects so they are not passed-by-value.

First, you will modify the **showOrders(flowerOrder);** statement in the main() function so it is passed-by-address.

To modify the **showOrders(flowerOrder);** statement in the main() function so the FloristOrder object is passed-by-address:

1. Return to the FloristOrder.cpp file in your Code Editor window.
2. Modify the main() function, as shown in Figure 6-20.

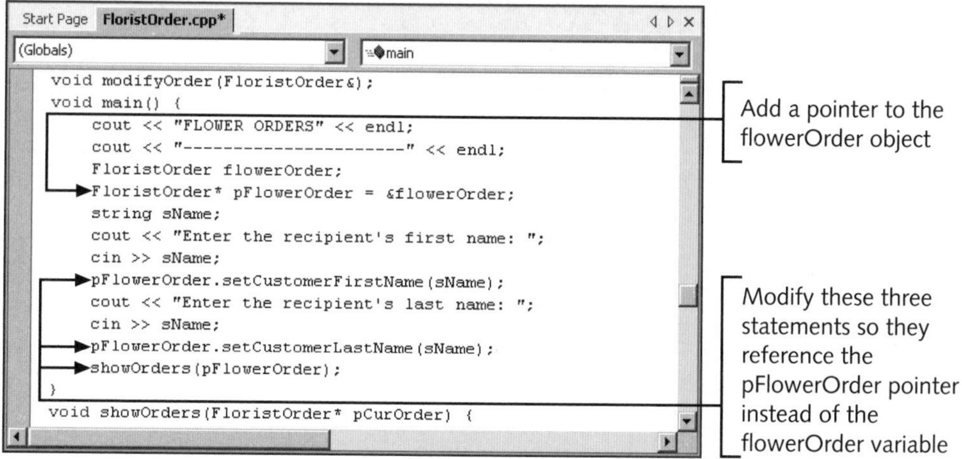

Figure 6-20 main() function modified so the FloristOrder object is passed-by-address

3. Locate the showOrders() function prototype and modify its parameter from a FloristOrder object to a pointer to a FloristOrder object by adding an indirection operator (*) after the FloristOrder parameter type. The modified statement should read **showOrders(FloristOrder*);**.
4. Also locate the showOrders() function definition and modify its parameter from a FloristOrder object to a pointer to a FloristOrder object by adding an indirection operator (*) after the FloristOrder parameter type. Also rename the parameter from curOrder to pCurOrder. The modified function definition should read **void showOrders(FloristOrder* pCurOrder) {**.
5. As shown in Figure 6-21, in the showOrders() function, modify the three statements that use the curOrder variable so they instead use the pCurOrder pointer variable.

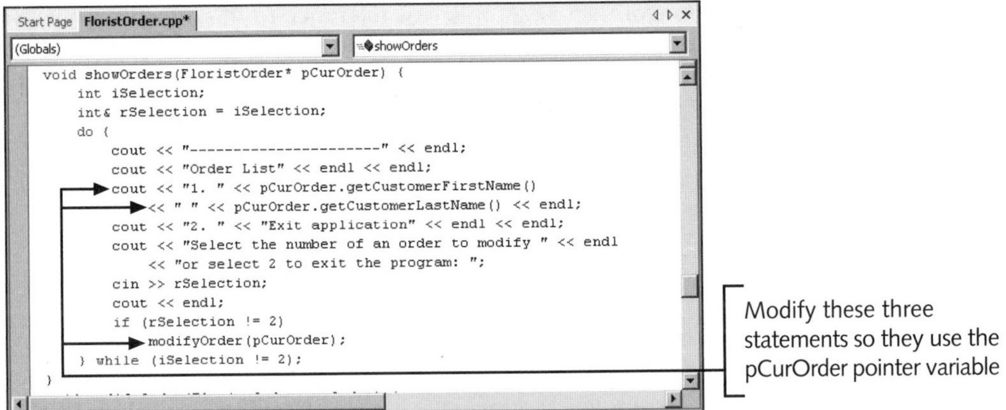

Figure 6-21 Statement in showOrders() function modified to use the pCurOrder pointer variable

6

Before you can build and execute the Florist Order program, you need to learn how to use the indirect member selection operator to allow the pointer object to access the class members. The indirect member selection operator will be discussed shortly.

Call-by-Reference

As mentioned earlier, one of the most common times to use a reference is when you need one function to work with a large variable that is declared in another function. As with pointers, you must pass a reference to the function that needs it. Passing a reference variable to a function is referred to as **calling-by-reference** or **passing-by-reference** because only a reference is passed to the function instead of the value itself. Just as with pointers, a function can manipulate an original variable through a passed reference, avoiding the costly memory overhead required by passing a large variable to, and returning a large variable from, a function.

The definition for a function you want to call-by-reference must declare a reference parameter of the object type you want to pass. For example, consider again the Carpet Cost program. In order to pass to the calcTotalCost() function a reference to the dFeet variable, you must use a function definition similar to the following. Notice that the function parameter uses the address of operator (&) to declare a `double` reference named rSquareFeet. This is the same syntax that you use to declare a reference in the body of a function.

```
double calcTotalCost(double& rSquareFeet) {
   statements;
}
```

To pass a reference as an argument when you call a function, simply include either the variable name or the name of a reference to the variable, without any operators. For example, to call the calcTotalCost() function and pass to it a reference to the dFeet variable, you use either `calcTotalCost(rFeet);` or `calcTotalCost(dFeet);`.

Figure 6-22 shows a complete example of a reference to the dFeet variable being passed from the main() method to the calcTotalCost() function, where it is assigned to the rSquareFeet reference parameter. When the calcTotalCost() function modifies the value assigned to the rSquareFeet reference, it is really modifying the dFeet variable in the main() method because rSquareFeet is simply an alias for the dFeet variable. The output from the program is the same as Figure 6-19.

```
#include <iostream>
using namespace std;
double calcTotalCost(double& rSquareFeet) {
        rSquareFeet *= 1.1;
        double dNumberOfFeet = rSquareFeet;
        double dPricePerFoot = 2.5;
        double dTotalCost = dNumberOfFeet * dPricePerFoot;
        cout << "Total square footage increased by 10% "
                << "to account for waste material." << endl;
        cout << "Your new square footage is: "
                << rSquareFeet << endl;
        return dTotalCost;
}
void main() {
        cout << "Enter the number of square feet to carpet: ";
        double dFeet;
        cin >> dFeet;
        cout << "Your total carpeting cost will be: $"
                << calcTotalCost(dFeet) << endl;
        cout << "The value of the dFeet variable is: "
                << dFeet << endl;
}
```

A reference to the dFeet argument is passed to the rSquareFeet reference parameter because the calcTotalCost() function is called by reference

Figure 6-22 Program that uses call-by-reference to execute a function

The original `modifyOrder(curOrder);` statement you added to the showOrders() function passes the FloristOrder object (curOrder) by value. As with the `showOrders(flowerOrder);` statement in the main() function, you probably will not notice any sort of memory issues with such a small program. You could change the modifyOrder(curOrder) statement so the FloristOrder object is passed by address. However, for practice you will modify it so the FloristOrder object is passed by reference.

To modify the `modifyOrder(curOrder);` statement in the showOrders() function so the FloristOrder object is passed-by-reference:

1. Return to the FloristOrder.cpp file in your Code Editor window.
2. Locate the modifyOrder() function prototype and modify its parameter from a FloristOrder object to a reference to a FloristOrder object by adding an address of operator (&) after the FloristOrder parameter type. The modified statement should read **`modifyOrder(FloristOrder&);`**.
3. Locate the modifyOrder() function definition and modify its parameter from a FloristOrder object to a reference to a FloristOrder object by adding an address of operator (&) after the FloristOrder parameter type. Also rename the parameter from curOrder to rCurOrder. The modified function definition should read **`void modifyOrder(FloristOrder& rCurOrder) {`**.

4. Modify each of the statements in the modifyOrder() function that use the curOrder variable by changing the variable to rCurOrder. You should change 10 statements in all.

5. Because the main() function's flowerOrder pointer was passed to the showOrders() function as a pointer (named pCurOrder), you need to de-reference it before passing it as a reference to the modifyOrder() function. As shown in Figure 6-23, add the de-reference operator (*) to the statement in the showOrders() function that calls the modifyOrder() function

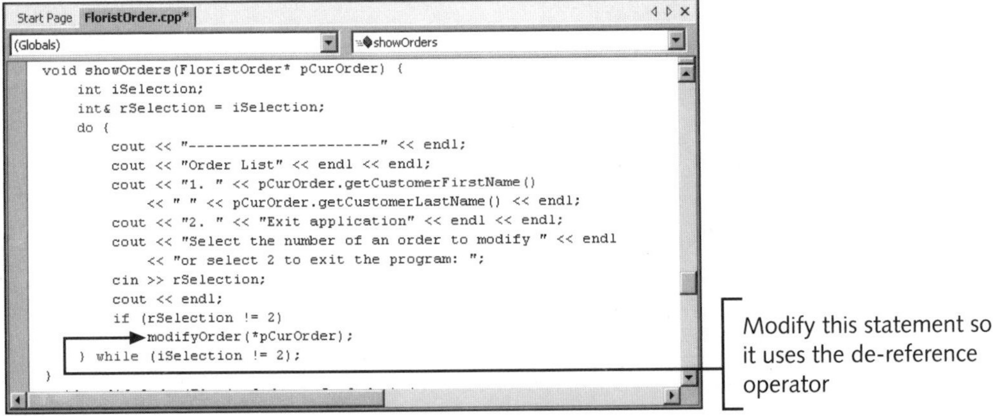

Figure 6-23 De-reference operator added to the statement in the showOrders() function that calls the modifyOrders() function

6. Do not build the project yet because you still need to add the indirect member selection operator to the statements that access class members through a pointer. You will study the indirect member selection operator next.

WORKING WITH POINTERS AND REFERENCES TO OBJECTS

As you know, you use the member selection operator (.) to access class members through an object instance. However, to access class members through a pointer to an object, you must use the **indirect member selection operator (->)**. Figure 6-24 shows an example of how to access a class's data members through a pointer. A pointer named pStock is declared for the stockPick object. Notice that the setNumShares() and setPricePerShare() member functions are accessed by using indirect member selection operators. The pStock pointer is then passed-by-address to the totalValue() function, which calculates the current stock price.

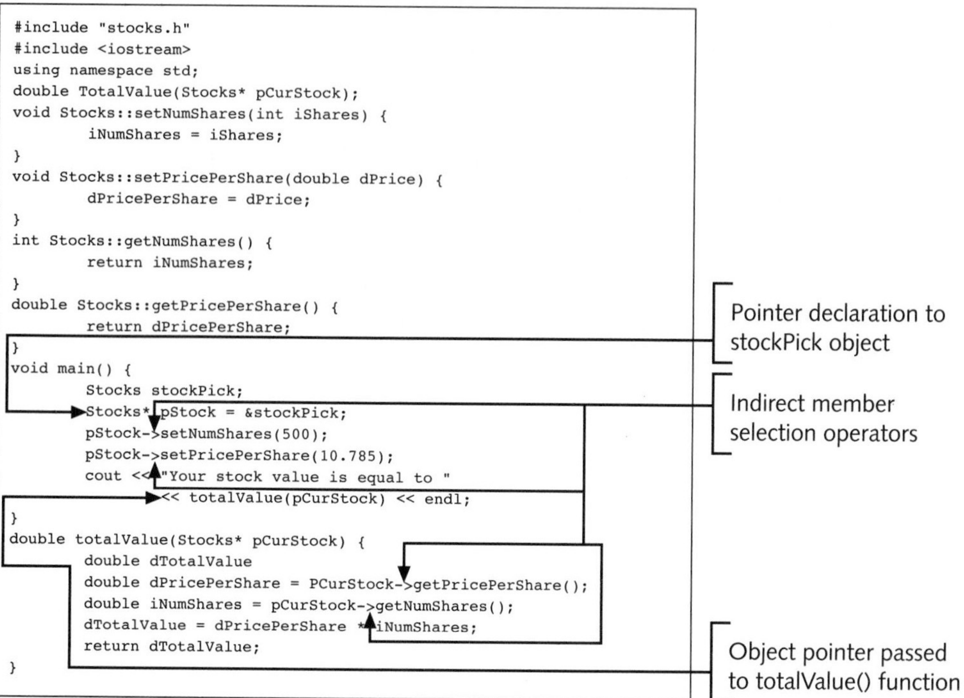

```
#include "stocks.h"
#include <iostream>
using namespace std;
double TotalValue(Stocks* pCurStock);
void Stocks::setNumShares(int iShares) {
        iNumShares = iShares;
}
void Stocks::setPricePerShare(double dPrice) {
        dPricePerShare = dPrice;
}
int Stocks::getNumShares() {
        return iNumShares;
}
double Stocks::getPricePerShare() {
        return dPricePerShare;
}
void main() {
        Stocks stockPick;
        Stocks* pStock = &stockPick;
        pStock->setNumShares(500);
        pStock->setPricePerShare(10.785);
        cout << "Your stock value is equal to "
        << totalValue(pCurStock) << endl;
}
double totalValue(Stocks* pCurStock) {
        double dTotalValue
        double dPricePerShare = PCurStock->getPricePerShare();
        double iNumShares = pCurStock->getNumShares();
        dTotalValue = dPricePerShare * iNumShares;
        return dTotalValue;
}
```


Figure 6-24 Program that declares and passes an object pointer

The totalValue() function in Figure 6-26 is not a member function of the Stocks class. Rather, it is a global function that is available to the entire program. If the totalValue() function were a member function of the Stocks class, there would be no need to pass to it a pointer to the Stocks object that is declared in the main() function.

You set references to class objects the same way you set references to other types of variables. Figure 6-25 shows a modified version of the Stocks program in 6-24. This time it uses a reference to the stockPick object, rStock, which is passed to the totalValue() function instead of a pointer. The argument in the totalValue() function definition has also been changed to a reference to a Stocks object instead of a pointer to a Stocks object.

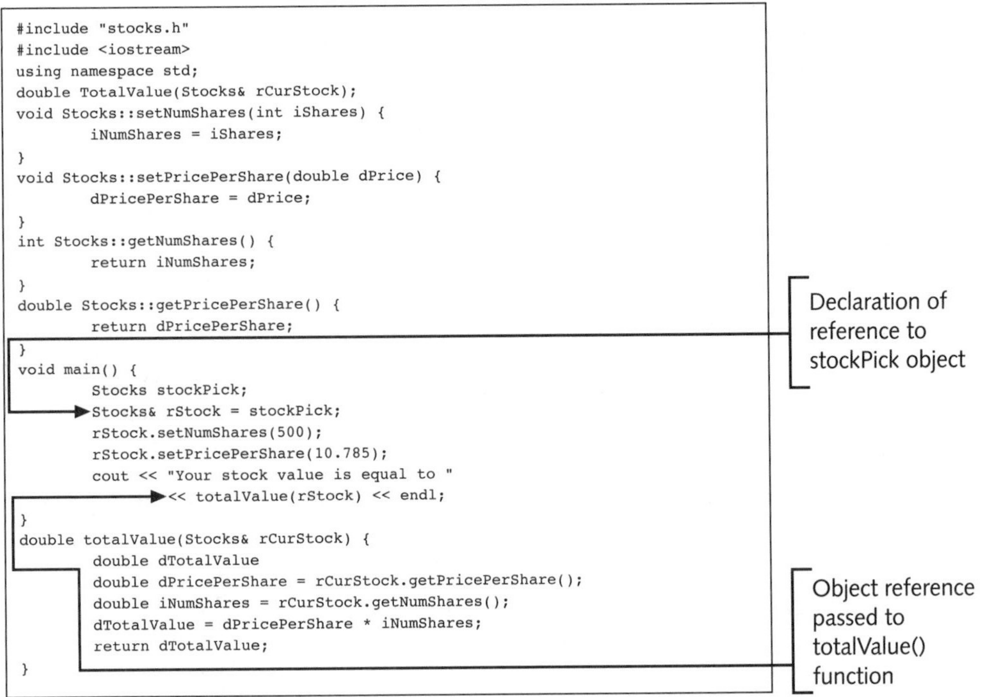
```
#include "stocks.h"
#include <iostream>
using namespace std;
double TotalValue(Stocks& rCurStock);
void Stocks::setNumShares(int iShares) {
        iNumShares = iShares;
}
void Stocks::setPricePerShare(double dPrice) {
        dPricePerShare = dPrice;
}
int Stocks::getNumShares() {
        return iNumShares;
}
double Stocks::getPricePerShare() {
        return dPricePerShare;
}
void main() {
        Stocks stockPick;
        Stocks& rStock = stockPick;
        rStock.setNumShares(500);
        rStock.setPricePerShare(10.785);
        cout << "Your stock value is equal to "
             << totalValue(rStock) << endl;
}
double totalValue(Stocks& rCurStock) {
        double dTotalValue
        double dPricePerShare = rCurStock.getPricePerShare();
        double iNumShares = rCurStock.getNumShares();
        dTotalValue = dPricePerShare * iNumShares;
        return dTotalValue;
}
```


Figure 6-25 Program that declares and passes an object reference

Next, you will modify the main() and showOrders() functions so that they can access the FloristOrder object class members through the FloristOrder pointer.

To modify the main() and showOrders() functions so that they can access the FloristOrder object class members through the FloristOrder pointer:

1. Return to the FloristOrder.cpp file in your Code Editor window.
2. As shown in Figure 6-26, modify the two accessor functions in the main() method so they use indirect member selection operators.
3. As shown in Figure 6-27, modify the two statements in the showOrders() function that reference the FloristOrder pointer so they use the indirect member selection operator.
4. Build and execute the project. The program should function normally.

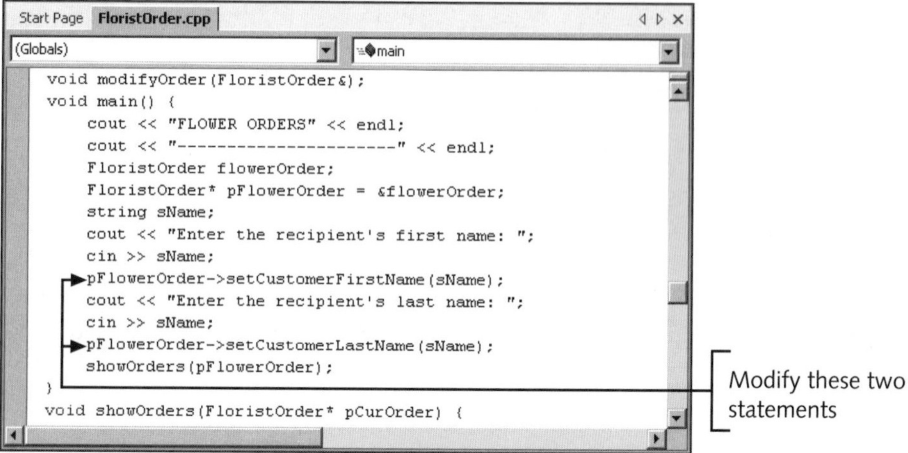

Figure 6-26 Accessor functions in the main() method modified to use indirect member selection operators

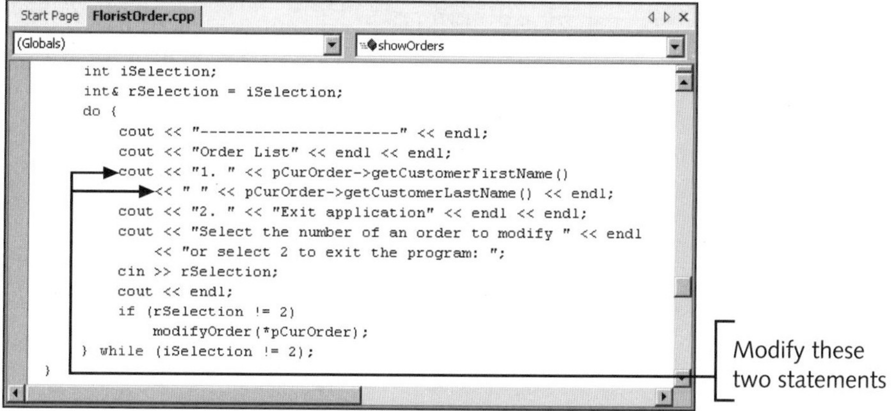

Figure 6-27 Statements in showOrders() modified to use indirect member selection operators

The `this` Pointer

With some types of programs, you may need to instantiate multiple objects based on the same class. For example, if you are calculating stock values with the Stocks object, you may instantiate a new Stocks object for each stock in your investment portfolio. Remember that because objects are encapsulated, each object contains its own copies of a class's members. When your program calls a member function of a class, the compiler knows which object instance called the function through the `this` pointer. The **`this`** pointer identifies the object instance that called a function. C++ uses the `this` pointer to be sure that a member function uses the correct set of data members for a given object.

By default, the this pointer is implied, meaning that a member function automatically knows that the this pointer points to the calling object. Therefore, it is not usually necessary to use the this pointer with your data members. The this pointer is, however, occasionally used to return a pointer to the current object. For this reason, you should be able to identify the this pointer if you encounter it.

The following code shows an example of the implementations for the Stock class member functions you saw earlier. Each data member is referenced using the this pointer with the indirect member selection operator:

```
void Stocks::setNumShares(int iShares) {
   this->iNumShares = iShares;
}
void Stocks::setPricePerShare(double dPrice) {
   this->dPricePerShare = dPrice;
}
int Stocks::getNumShares() {
   return this->iNumShares;
}
double Stocks::getPricePerShare() {
   return this->dPricePerShare;
}
```


Because the this pointer is implied by default, the following implementations for the Stock class member functions are equally correct:

```
void Stocks::setNumShares(int iShares) {
   iNumShares = iShares;
}
void Stocks::setPricePerShare(double dPrice) {
   dPricePerShare = dPrice;
}
int Stocks::getNumShares() {
   return iNumShares;
}
double Stocks::getPricePerShare() {
   return dPricePerShare;
}
```

You will not use this pointers in this book because they are implied by default. However, you should be able to recognize any this pointers that you encounter. As practice you will add this pointers to the FloristOrder class's constructor function.

To add this pointers to the FloristOrder class constructor function:

1. Return to the FloristOrder.cpp file in your Code Editor window and locate the FloristOrder class constructor function.
2. As shown in the following code, add this pointers to all of the data members in the constructor function.

```
FloristOrder::FloristOrder() {
```

```
        this->sCustomerFirstName  = "";
        this->sCustomerLastName = "";
        this->iItem = 0;
        this->iQuantity = 0;
        this->sRoses = "Roses (per dozen)";
        this->sTulips = "Tulips (per dozen)";
        this->sCarnations = "Carnations (per dozen)";
        this->sSunflowers = "Sunflowers (each)";
        this->sOrchids = "Orchids (each)";
        this->dRosesPrice = 9.95;
        this->dTulipsPrice = 12.95;
        this->dCarnationsPrice = 7.95;
        this->dSunflowersPrice = 4.95;
        this->dOrchidsPrice = 8.95;
}
```

3. Build and execute the project. The program should function normally.

ADVANCED ARRAY TECHNIQUES

In Chapter 2, you learned that an array is an advanced data type that contains a set of data of the same data type, represented by a single variable name. More technically, an array is a set of consecutive memory locations used to store data that can be accessed by a single variable name. Before learning how to work with advanced arrays, it is a good idea to be sure you understand how to work with simple or basic arrays.

Each element of an array represents one of the array's memory locations, and you access each element through its index number. The number of elements in an array is referred to as its dimension, and the numbering of elements within an array starts with an index number of 0 (zero). You should be familiar with the following code, which declares an array named arInterestRates[] of the `double` data type, designates that it contains five elements, and then assigns values to each of the five elements:

```
double arInterestRates[5];
arInterestRates[0] = .65;
arInterestRates[1] = .675;
arInterestRates[2] = .7;
arInterestRates[3] = .725;
arInterestRates[4] = .775;
```

You can also initialize an array's elements when you first declare the array using the following syntax:

```
double arInterestRates[5] =
   {.065, .675, .07, .0725, .075};
```

If you do not include enough elements when you initialize an array at declaration, the remaining elements are initialized with a value of zero.

If you include too many elements when you initialize an array at declaration, a compiler error occurs.

Figure 6-28 illustrates how the elements of the arInterestRates[] array are stored in memory using some sample memory addresses. Each element is stored in its own memory address, similar to the way primitive variables are stored in their own memory addresses.

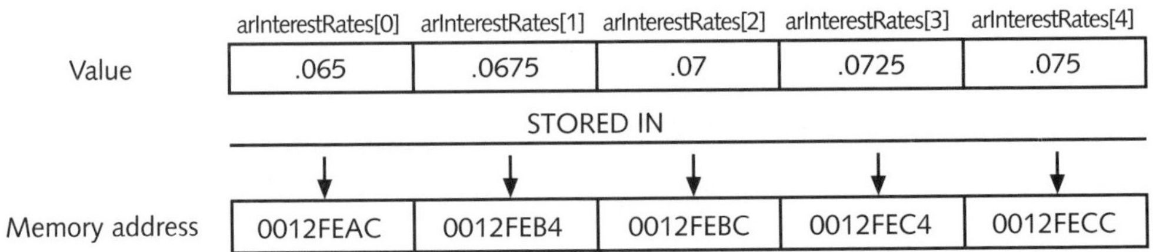

Figure 6-28 Examples of memory addresses occupied by the elements of the arInterestRates[] array

Once you have assigned a value to an array element, you can change it later just as you can change other variables in a program. To change the last element in the arInterestRates[] array from *.075* to *.08*, you include the statement `arInterestRates[4] = .08;` in your code. You can also use an element in an array the same way you use other types of variables. For example, the following code prints the values contained in the five elements of the arInterestRates[] array:

```
cout << arInterestRates[0] << endl; // prints A
cout << arInterestRates[1] << endl; // prints B
cout << arInterestRates[2] << endl; // prints C
cout << arInterestRates[3] << endl; // prints D
cout << arInterestRates[4] << endl; // prints F
```

To access all the elements of an array, it is easier to use a repetition statement, such as a `for` loop. The following code also prints the values contained in the five elements of the arInterestRates[] array. However, instead of printing each value using a separate output statement, the `for` statement loops through the array and prints each value using a single output statement.

```
for (int ctCount = 0; ctCount < 5; ++ctCount) {
   cout << arInterestRates[ctCount] << endl;
}
```

You also use a repetition statement to search for a value in an array element. The following code uses a modified version of the preceding `for` loop. However, the `for` loop also contains an `if` statement that checks if an element of the array contains an interest rate of 7%. If the interest rate is found, the text *interest rate found* is printed.

```
for (int ctCount = 0; ctCount < 5; ++ctCount) {
   if (arInterestRates[ctCount] == .07) {
            cout << "Interest rate found" << endl;
            break;
   }
}
```

Now you can begin to learn about some advanced array techniques, including the following:

- Pointers and arrays
- Pointer arithmetic
- Multidimensional arrays
- Character arrays
- Arrays of objects

Advanced arrays may seem somewhat unrelated to the memory management topics that have been covered so far. However, several advanced array techniques require knowledge of the memory management techniques that you studied earlier. For instance, you cannot study arrays of pointers until you know what a pointer is. As you progress through this section, you should begin to recognize the importance of understanding memory management issues when working with advanced array techniques.

As with other data types, you can use an array as a data member in a class. You may have noticed that the prices for each of the flowers in the FloristOrder class are stored as separate data members. A more efficient technique is to store each of the prices in an array data member, which you will do next.

To store the flower prices in an array data member:

1. Open the **FloristOrder.h** file in your Code Editor window and locate the five declarations for the price data members in the private section.
2. Replace the price data members with one double array, as shown in Figure 6-29.

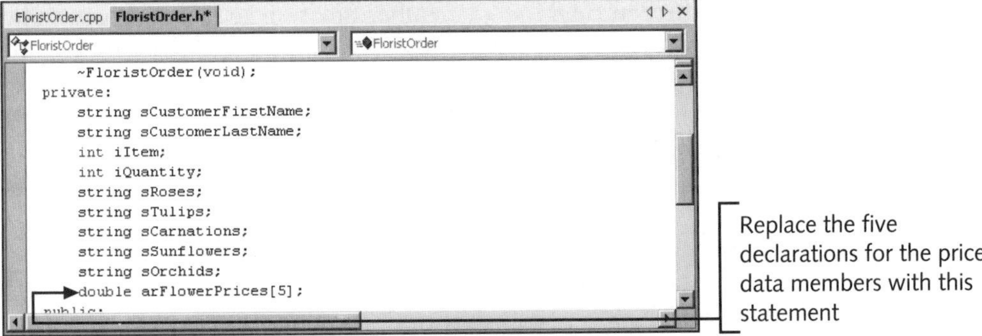

Figure 6-29 Double array declaration added to FloristOrder.h

3. Next, open the **FloristOrder.cpp** file in your Code Editor window and locate the FloristOrder class constructor function.
4. Modify the statements that initialize the old price data members so they instead initialize each flower type's corresponding element in the arFlowerPrices[] array as follows:

```
this->arFlowerPrices[0] = 9.95;
this->arFlowerPrices[1] = 12.95;
this->arFlowerPrices[2] = 7.95;
this->arFlowerPrices[3] = 4.95;
this->arFlowerPrices[4] = 8.95;
```

5. Modify the getPricePerUnit() member function so that it returns the values stored in the arFlowerPrices[] array instead of the values stored in the old price variables. The modified function should appear as shown in Figure 6-30.

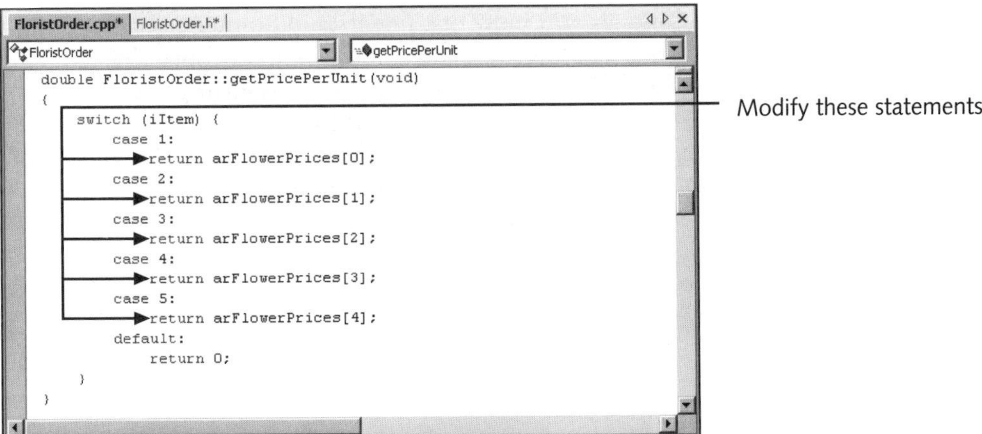

Figure 6-30 Modified getPricePerUnit() member function

6. Modify the getOrderTotal() member function so that returned values are multiplied by values in the arFlowerPrices[] array. The modified function should appear as shown in Figure 6-31.

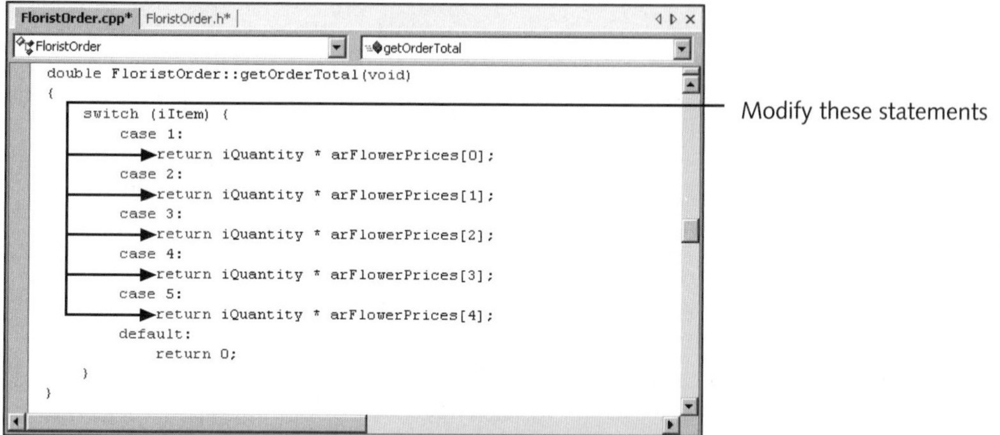

Figure 6-31 Modified getOrderTotal() member function

7. Build and execute the project. The program should function normally.

Pointers and Arrays

One of the first concepts you need to understand when working with advanced array techniques is that an array name is actually a pointer that points to the memory address of the first element in the array. This is one of the main reasons why you are learning advanced array techniques in a chapter on memory management. To understand advanced array techniques you must first understand pointers, because an array name is really a pointer. Understanding how to use the pointer aspects of arrays allows you greater control over them because you can more easily manipulate the values stored in each array element through its memory address. For instance, the name of the arInterestRates[] array is really a pointer that points to the memory address of the array's first element, arInterestRates[0], as illustrated in Figure 6-32.

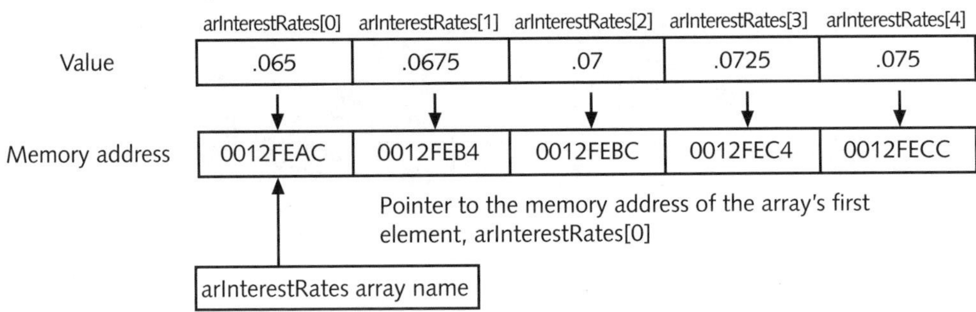

Figure 6-32 The name of the arInterestRates[] array pointing to the memory address of the array's first element

6

Although you do not need to declare an array name as a pointer using the indirection operator (*), it is in fact a pointer. Normally, to access the value of specific element you enclose an element's index number in brackets at the end of an array name. If you use the array name in code without any brackets or an element number, your code will receive the memory address to which the array name points–which is the memory address of the array's first element. For example, the statement `cout << arInterestRates << endl;` prints *0012FEAC* (assuming that is the memory address where the first element of the arInterestRate[] array is stored). You can use the address of operator (&) to access the memory addresses of the other elements in an array. Figure 6-33 shows a program that prints the memory addresses of the arInterestRates[] array. Notice that the first output statement, which prints the memory address pointed to by the arInterestRates array name, prints the same value as the memory address of the first element in the arInterestRates[] array. Figure 6-34 shows the output.

```
#include <iostream>
#include <string>
using namespace std;
void main() {
   double arInterestRates[5] = {.65, .675, .7, .725, .775};
   cout << "The memory address pointed to by arInterestRates is "
            << arInterestRates << endl;
   cout << "The memory address that stores arInterestRate[0] is "
            << &arInterestRates[0] << endl;
   cout << "The memory address that stores arInterestRate[1] is "
            << &arInterestRates[1] << endl;
   cout << "The memory address that stores arInterestRate[2] is "
            << &arInterestRates[2] << endl;
   cout << "The memory address that stores arInterestRate[3] is "
            << &arInterestRates[3] << endl;
   cout << "The memory address that stores arInterestRate[4] is "
            << &arInterestRates[4] << endl;
}
```

Figure 6-33 Program that prints the arInterestRates[] array's memory addresses

```
"c:\Visual C++ Projects\Chapter.06\Pointers\Debug\Pointers.exe"
The memory address pointed to by arInterestRates is 0012FEAC
The memory address that stores arInterestRate[0] is 0012FEAC
The memory address that stores arInterestRate[1] is 0012FEB4
The memory address that stores arInterestRate[2] is 0012FEBC
The memory address that stores arInterestRate[3] is 0012FEC4
The memory address that stores arInterestRate[4] is 0012FECC
Press any key to continue
```

Figure 6-34 Output of program that prints the arInterestRates[] array's memory addresses

Recall that you can assign the name of one pointer variable to another, which actually assigns the memory address stored in the right pointer operand to the left pointer operand. Because the name of an array is actually a pointer, you can assign it to another pointer, provided they are of the same data type. The arInterestRates[] array, for instance, is of the `double` data type. The following code instantiates a new pointer of the `double` data type named pInterestRates and assigns to it the arInterestRates array name. Notice that the statement does not use the address of (&) operator to assign the memory address of the arInterestRates array to the pInterestRates pointer. Because arInterestRates is already a pointer, the statement simply assigns its contents (the memory address of the array's first element) to the pInterestRates pointer.

```
double arInterestRates[5] = {.65, .675, .7, .725, .775};
double* pInterestRates;
pInterestRates = arInterestRates;
```

You can then use the pInterestRates pointer to access the elements in the arInterestRates[] array. For example, each of the following statements return the value stored in the second element of the arInterestRates[] array:

```
cout << arInterestRates[1] << endl;
cout << pInterestRates[1] << endl;
```

Although you can assign the memory address of an array name to another pointer, you cannot assign the memory address of a pointer to an array name. Array names are **constant pointers**; no change can be made to the value they store after they are declared and initialized. The following statements are illegal:

```
double arInterestRates[5] = {.65, .675, .7, .725, .775};
double* pInterestRates;
arInterestRates = pInterestRates;
```

If you want to assign to a pointer the memory address where an individual element of an array is stored, you must use the address of (&) operator. You must also place the appropriate index number in brackets at the end of the array name. You can then use the de-reference operator (*) to access the value stored in the memory address that is the target of the pointer. For example, the following code declares a pointer named pCurInterestRate and assigns to it the memory address of the second element in the arInterestRates[] array. After the memory address of the second element of the arInterestRates[] array is assigned to the pCurInterestRate pointer, an output statement uses the de-reference operator to print the value stored in the element.

```
double* pCurInterestRate = &arInterestRates[1];
cout << *pCurInterestRate << endl;
```

Next, you will add to the Florist Order program an array pointer named pFlowerPrices that points to the arFlowerPrices[] array.

To add to the Florist Order program an array pointer named pFlowerPrices that points to the arFlowerPrices[] array:

1. Open the **FloristOrder.h** file in your Code Editor window.
2. Declare a pointer named pFlowerPrices of the `double` data type immediately after the `double arFlowerPrices[5];` array declaration in the private section, as follows:

   ```
   double* pFlowerPrices;
   ```

3. Open the **FloristOrder.cpp** file in your Code Editor window and locate the FloristOrder class constructor function.
4. Immediately above the constructor function's closing brace, initialize the pFlowerPrices pointer so that it points to the arFlowerPrices[] array, as follows. You will use the pFlowerPrices pointer shortly to access the elements of the arFlowerPrices[] array using pointer arithmetic.

   ```
   pFlowerPrices = arFlowerPrices;
   ```

6

Pointer Arithmetic

Using pointers to elements of an array provides an alternate method of accessing, manipulating, and navigating the array. With **pointer arithmetic**, you can use addition and subtraction to change the element number that is the target of a pointer. The main benefit of pointer arithmetic is that it allows you to easily change the element number that is the target of a pointer.

Do not confuse pointer arithmetic with standard arithmetic; pointer arithmetic changes only the array element number that is the target of a pointer.

The following code declares a pointer named pCurInterestRate that points to the memory address of the second element in the arInterestRates[] array. To change the pCurInterestRate pointer so that it points to the third element in the arInterestRates[] array, you can use the statement `pCurInterestRate += 1;`. The following code shows how to declare the pCurInterestRate pointer, assign to it the memory address of the second element in the arInterestRates[] array, and then use pointer arithmetic to change the target of the pCurInterestRate pointer to the fourth element in the arInterestRates[] array. Notice that the pointer arithmetic increases the value of the pCurInterestRate pointer by two this time.

```
double arInterestRates[5] = {.65, .675, .7, .725, .775};
double* pCurInterestRate = &arInterestRates[1];
cout << *pCurInterestRate << endl;
pCurInterestRate = pCurInterestRate + 2;
cout << *pCurInterestRate << endl;
```

If you were to execute the preceding code, it would output the values 0.675 and 0.725.

You can also use the increment (++) and decrement (--) operators along with the += and -= assignment operators to perform pointer arithmetic.

Next, you will modify the getPricePerUnit() function in the Florist Order program so that the elements of the arFlowerPrices[] array are accessed using pointer arithmetic.

To modify the getPricePerUnit() function in the Florist Order program so that the elements of the arFlowerPrices[] array are accessed using pointer arithmetic:

1. Return to the FloristOrder.cpp file in your Code Editor window and locate the getPricePerUnit() member function.
2. Modify the getPricePerUnit() member function as shown in Figure 6-35. Add the `pFlowerPrices = arFlowerPrices;` statement to reset the pFlowerPrices pointer to point to the first element in the arFlowerPrices[] array each time the getPricePerUnit() function is called. Also, modify the case labels in the `switch` statement so that the elements in the arFlowerPrices[] array are returned using pointer arithmetic.

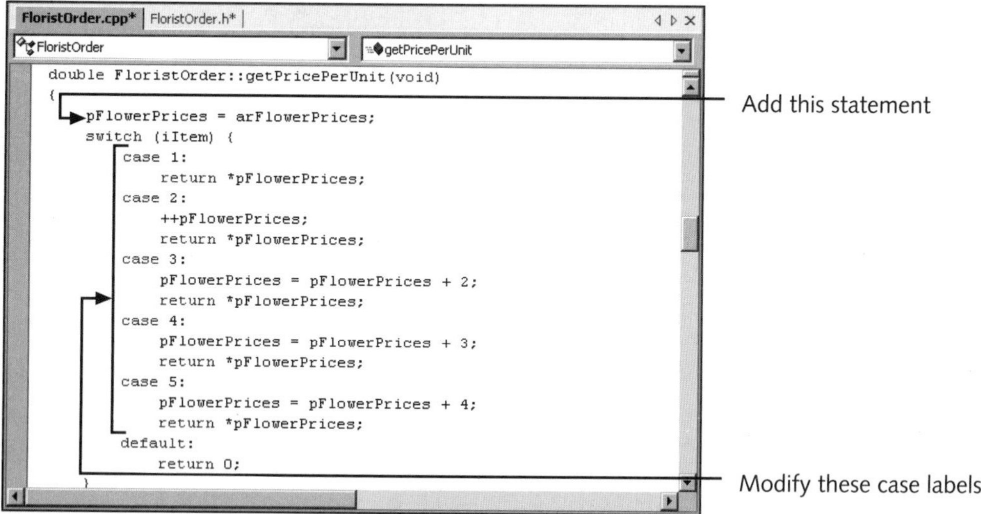

Figure 6-35 getPricePerUnit() member function modified to use pointer arithmetic

3. Build and execute the project. The program should function normally.

Remember that because an array name is a constant pointer, you cannot modify its contents, which is a memory address. Therefore, a pointer arithmetic statement that attempts to change the memory address of an element pointed to by the array name, such as `arInterestRates = pCurInterestRate + 1;`, is illegal. However, you can use pointer arithmetic with the array name to modify the value stored in the memory address of an array element. To modify the value of an array element using the array name and pointer arithmetic, you must use the de-reference (*) operator and place the pointer arithmetic portion of the statement in parentheses. For example, to modify the value of the third element in the arInterestRates[] array to 8% using the array name and pointer arithmetic, you use the statement `*(arInterestRates + 2) = .8;`. You must use parentheses for the order or precedence to be interpreted correctly. If you did not use parentheses, you would be adding two to the value of the first element in the arInterestRates array instead of using pointer arithmetic to point to the third element in the array.

When you use pointer arithmetic, C++ assumes that the pointer you are using points to an array. However, C++ does not check for the beginning or end of the array's dimensions. When you use pointer arithmetic, if you increase the array element to an index number that exceeds the dimensions of the array or decrease the array element to an index number that is less than zero, your program may cause a run-time error or return incorrect results.

Be aware that pointer arithmetic does not simply increase the integer that represents the index of an array element. Rather, pointer arithmetic changes the memory address being pointed to according to the size of the array's data type. Recall that an array's elements are stored in consecutive memory addresses. Also, recall that each data type consists of a certain number of bytes. For example, a `double` data type consists of eight bytes. Therefore, the elements in an array of the `double` data type are stored in consecutive eight-byte memory locations. When you use pointer arithmetic to increase a `double` array pointer by one, you are really increasing the memory address that is stored in the pointer by eight bytes. Similarly, if you use pointer arithmetic to increase a `double` array pointer by two, you are really increasing the memory address that is stored in the pointer by sixteen bytes. With arrays of other data types, pointer arithmetic increases the memory address stored in an array pointer according to the size of the type. Integer data types, for instance, consist of four bytes. Therefore, using pointer arithmetic to increase an `int` array pointer by one increases the memory address that is stored in the pointer by four bytes. Figure 6-36 illustrates the process of using pointer arithmetic to increase the pCurInterestRate pointer by one. The first statement declares the pCurInterestRate pointer and assigns to it the address of the first element in the arInterestRates[] array. The second statement then uses pointer arithmetic to increase the pCurInterestRate pointer by one. Notice that each memory address occupies eight bytes–the size of the `double` data type.

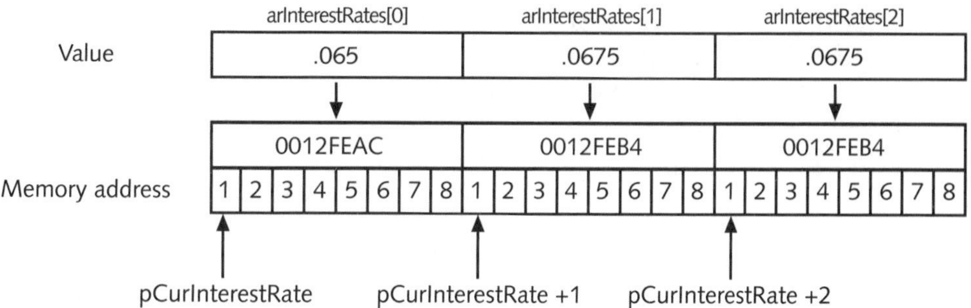

Figure 6-36 Using pointer arithmetic to increase a double array pointer by one

Multidimensional Arrays

The arrays you have created so far are known as one-dimensional arrays because they have consisted of a single index. You can also create **multidimensional arrays**, which consist of multiple indexes. To understand how a multidimensional array works, first consider a one-dimensional array that contains federal tax withholding amounts. For the tax year 2001, the IRS assesses a different base tax amount depending on whether you are single, married, married filing jointly, married filing separately, or the head of a household. The amount of the base tax also depends on whether your taxable income is more than one amount but less than another amount, according to a series of published tax tables. The IRS also charges an additional percentage of any income over a certain amount.

For example, if you are single and your taxable income is at least $26,250 but less than $63,550, then your base tax will be $3,637.50. You will also be charged 27% of any amount you earned over $26,250. You could create a single-dimensional array that stores these tax rates as follows:

```
double arTaxTable[6] = {26250, 63550, 3637.5, .27};
```

Figure 6-40 illustrates how the arTaxTable[] array appears in a table format.

Taxable Income		Base Tax	Tax Rate
At least	Less than		
26250	63550	3637.5	.27

Figure 6-37 arTaxTable[] array

A single-dimensional array works fine if you only need to store a single income bracket. However, the IRS tax tables contain six rows, one for each level of income. Figure 6-38, for instance, shows the IRS tax tables for the taxable income brackets for a single taxpayer.

Taxable Income		Base Tax	Tax Rate
At least	Less than		
0	6000	0	.1
6000	26250	600	.15
26250	63550	3637.5	.27
63550	132600	13708.5	.3
132600	288350	34423.5	.35
288350	999999*	88936	38.6

* There is no limit to the amount of income you can earn in this tax bracket. However, the table includes a value of 999999 in order to have something to place in the multidimensional array you will create shortly.

Figure 6-38 arTaxTable[] array with multiple rows

You could store each row in Figure 6-37 in its own array, but that is inefficient. A better choice is to create a multidimensional array. You create a multidimensional array by including more than one index when you declare the array. Each index should be declared in its own set of brackets. A multidimensional array that contains two indexes is referred to as a **two-dimensional array**. The first index in the declaration of a two-dimensional array determines the number of rows in the array, and the second index determines the number of columns. For example, you use the following code to declare a multidimensional array for the arTaxTable[] array shown in Figure 6-37. The first index in the array declaration uses a dimension of six for the number of rows, and the second index uses a dimension of four for the number of columns.

```
double arTaxTable[6][4] = {
        { 0, 6000, 0, .1 },
        { 6000, 26250, 600, .15 },
        { 26250, 63550, 3637.5, .27 },
        { 63550, 132600, 13708.5, .3 },
        { 132600, 288350, 34423.5, .35 },
        { 288350, 999999, 88936, 38.6 },
};
```

Notice how the preceding array is initialized. In addition to the curly braces that define the initializer list, each row in the array is contained within its own set of nested braces, and the rows are separated by commas.

The table in Figure 6-39 shows the index number for the element in the array where each value is stored.

Income and Tax Amounts

Income Levels		0	1	2	3
	0	0	6000	0	.1
	1	6000	26250	600	.15
	2	26250	63550	3637.5	.27
	3	63550	132600	13708.5	.3
	4	132600	288350	34423.5	.35
	5	288350	999999	88936	38.6

Figure 6-39 Elements in the two-dimensional arTaxTable[] array

If you do not want to initialize a multidimensional array at declaration, you can initialize individual elements later by using both indexes with the array name. For example, to initialize or modify the value stored at the intersection of the second row and the fourth column to 7000, you use the statement `arTaxTable[1][3] = .15;`. You use the same syntax to retrieve the value stored in a specific location in a multidimensional table. The statement `cout << arTaxTable[1][3] << endl;` prints the value stored at the intersection of the second row and the fourth column.

Figure 6-40 shows a simple program that returns a single taxpayer's federal income tax from the arTaxTable[] array, based on his or her taxable income. Figure 6-41 shows the output after entering some data.

```
#include <iostream>
using namespace std;
void main() {
   double arTaxTable[6][4] = {
                        { 0, 6000, 0, .1 },
                        { 6000, 26250, 600, .15 },
                        { 26250, 63550, 3637.5, .27 },
                        { 63550, 132600, 13708.5, .3 },
                        { 132600, 288350, 34423.5, .35 },
                        { 288350, 999999, 88936, 38.6 },
   };
   double dIncome = 0;
   double dBaseTax = 0;
   double dSuppTax = 0;
   cout << "Estimated 2001 Tax Liability" << endl;
   cout << "for a Single Taxpayer" << endl;
   cout << "----------------------------" << endl;
   cout << "Enter your taxable income: ";
   cin >> dIncome;
   cout << endl;

   if (dIncome < arTaxTable[0][1]) {
            dBaseTax = arTaxTable[0][2];
            dSuppTax = (dIncome - arTaxTable[0][0]) * arTaxTable[0][3];
   }

   else if (dIncome < arTaxTable[1][1]) {
               dBaseTax = arTaxTable[1][2];
               dSuppTax = (dIncome - arTaxTable[1][0]) * arTaxTable[1][3];
   }
   else if (dIncome < arTaxTable[2][1]) {
               dBaseTax = arTaxTable[2][2];
               dSuppTax = (dIncome - arTaxTable[2][0]) * arTaxTable[2][3];
   }
   else if (dIncome < arTaxTable[3][1]) {
               dBaseTax = arTaxTable[3][2];
               dSuppTax = (dIncome - arTaxTable[3][0]) * arTaxTable[3][3];
   }
   else if (dIncome < arTaxTable[4][1]) {
               dBaseTax = arTaxTable[4][2];
               dSuppTax = (dIncome - arTaxTable[4][0]) * arTaxTable[4][3];
   }
   else if (dIncome < arTaxTable[5][1]) {
               dBaseTax = arTaxTable[5][2];
               dSuppTax = (dIncome - arTaxTable[5][0]) * arTaxTable[5][3];
   }
   cout << "Your total Federal income tax is $"
               << dBaseTax + dSuppTax << endl;
}
```

Figure 6-40 Taxable income program

Figure 6-41 Output of the taxable income program

Multidimensional arrays are not limited to two dimensions. You can include as many indexes as you need when you declare the array. However, the more dimensions you use, the more complex, and more limited in use, the array becomes. Beginning programmers rarely need to use arrays larger than two dimensions, so this book will not spend much time discussing how to program with them. Nevertheless, you should understand that the concepts for working with multidimensional arrays of three or more dimensions are more or less the same as the concepts for working with two-dimensional arrays. As an example of a multidimensional array of more than two dimensions, consider an array that stores quarterly sales figures by state for a company's five-person sales force. For this type of an array, you would need three indexes. The first index would consist of 50 elements for the states. The second index would consist of five elements, one for each salesperson. The third index would consist of four elements, one for each quarter in the year. You can think of such an array as containing fifty tables, with each table containing a row for each salesperson and a column for each quarter. Figure 6-42 shows how the Alaska table might appear for the first year.

Quarters of the year index

Salesperson index	0	1	2	3
0	874	76	98	890
1	656	133	64	354
2	465	668	897	64
3	31	132	651	46
4	654	124	126	456

Figure 6-42 The Alaska table of the three-dimensional arSales[] array

To initialize a three-dimensional array, you need to include a separate nested initializer list, separated by commas, for each of the rows represented by the first index. The following code shows how to initialize the first two states in the three dimensional arSales[] array:

```
int arSales[50][5][4] = {
            { // initializer list for Alaska
                     { 874, 76, 98, 890 },
                     { 656, 133, 64, 354 },
                     { 465, 668, 897, 64 },
                     { 31, 132, 651, 46 },
                     { 654, 124, 126, 456 }
            },
            {  // initializer list for Alabama
                     { 31, 132, 651, 46 },
```

```
                        { 874, 76, 98, 890 },
                        { 465, 668, 987, 64 },
                        { 654, 124, 126, 566 },
                        { 546, 133, 64, 354 }
                },
                // initializer lists for other states
        };
```

To refer to an element in a three-dimensional array, be sure to use all three indexes with the array name. For instance, to print the Alabama (element number 1) sales figures for the third salesperson (element number 2) in the fourth quarter of the year (element number 3), use the statement **`cout << arSales[1][2][3] << endl;`**.

6

Next, you will add a multidimensional array to the Florist Order program that will store unit prices for each type of flower according to a volume discount. Each type of flower will have three levels of prices, depending on the number of units sold: 1–5, 6–10, and 11 or more units. For example, roses by the dozen will sell for $9.95 for 1 to 5 units sold, $8.95 for 5 to 10 units sold, and $7.95 for 11 or more units sold. Figure 6-43 shows a breakdown of the price discounts for each type of flower.

	1-5 units	6-10 units	+10 units
Roses (per dozen)	9.95	8.95	7.95
Tulips (per dozen)	12.95	10.50	9.25
Carnations (per dozen)	7.95	6.40	5.20
Sunflowers	4.95	3.50	2.25
Orchids	8.95	8.25	7.80

Figure 6-43 Volume discounts for flower sales

To add a multidimensional array to the Florist Order program that will store unit prices for each type of flower according to a volume discount:

1. Open the **FloristOrder.h** file in your Code Editor window and declare a multidimensional array named arVolumeDiscount[] at the end of the private section using the statement **`double arVolumeDiscount[5][3];`**. The arVolumeDiscount[] array consists of five rows (one for each type of flower sold) and three columns (one for each level of price discounting for each type of flower).

2. Open the **FloristOrder.cpp** file in your Code Editor window and locate the FloristOrder class constructor function.

3. At the end of the constructor function, add the following statements that initialize the arVolumeDiscount[] multidimensional array:

```
// Roses
arVolumeDiscount[0][0] = 9.95;
arVolumeDiscount[0][1] = 8.95;
arVolumeDiscount[0][2] = 7.95;
// Tulips
arVolumeDiscount[1][0] = 12.95;
arVolumeDiscount[1][1] = 10.5;
arVolumeDiscount[1][2] = 9.25;
// Carnations
arVolumeDiscount[2][0] = 7.95;
arVolumeDiscount[2][1] = 6.4;
arVolumeDiscount[2][2] = 5.2;
// Sunflowers
arVolumeDiscount[3][0] = 4.95;
arVolumeDiscount[3][1] = 3.5;
arVolumeDiscount[3][2] = 2.25;
// Orchids
arVolumeDiscount[4][0] = 8.95;
arVolumeDiscount[4][1] = 8.25;
arVolumeDiscount[4][2] = 7.8;
```

Recall that with classes, you declare a data member in the interface file, but initialize it in the constructor function in the implementation file. Because you can only use an initializer list with an array when you first declare it, you must use the assignment operator in the class constructor function to initialize each array element.

4. Locate the getOrderTotal() function. Above the `switch` statement, add the code shown in Figure 6-44 that performs a check to see how many units are being purchased and assigns the correct element number to the local iPriceLevel variable.

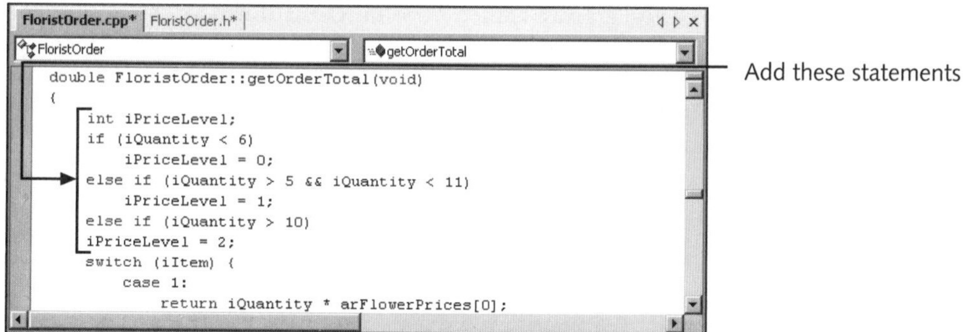

Figure 6-44 New statements added to getOrderTotal()

5. Modify the **switch** statement in the getOrderTotal() function so that it references the arVolumeDiscount[] array instead of the arFlowerPrices[] array. Also, use the iPriceLevel variable as the second index in the multidimensional array reference. The completed **switch** statement should appear as follows:

```
switch (iItem) {
   case 1:
     return iQuantity * arVolumeDiscount[0][iPriceLevel];
   case 2:
     return iQuantity * arVolumeDiscount[1][iPriceLevel];
   case 3:
     return iQuantity * arVolumeDiscount[2][iPriceLevel];
   case 4:
     return iQuantity * arVolumeDiscount[3][iPriceLevel];
   case 5:
     return iQuantity * arVolumeDiscount[4][iPriceLevel];
   default:
      return 0;
}
```


6. Finally, change the statement in the modifyOrders() function shown in Figure 6-45 to make it clear that the price includes a volume discount.

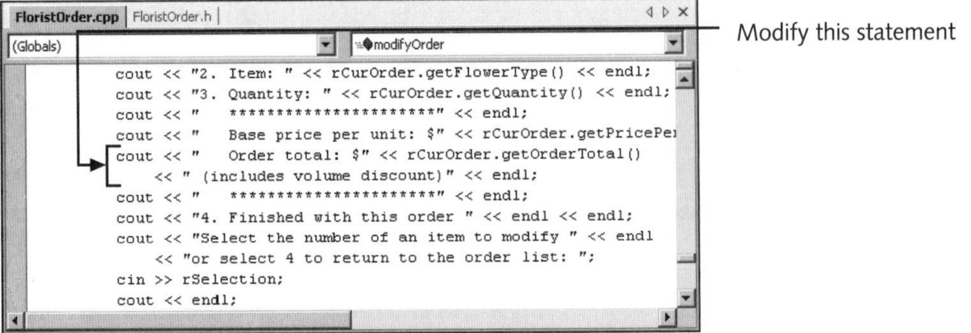

Figure 6-45 Modified statement in modifyOrders()

7. Build and execute the program. Test the program to see if it correctly discounts the purchase based on the number of units sold. Figure 6-46 shows the output after purchasing eight sunflowers.

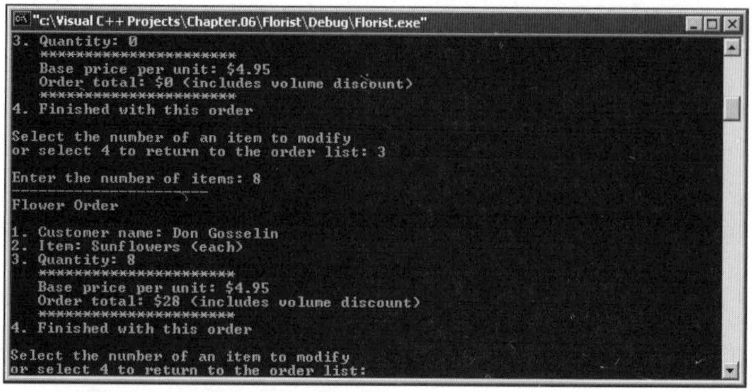

```
"c:\Visual C++ Projects\Chapter.06\Florist\Debug\Florist.exe"
3. Quantity: 0
   **********************
   Base price per unit: $4.95
   Order total: $0 (includes volume discount)
   **********************
4. Finished with this order

Select the number of an item to modify
or select 4 to return to the order list: 3

Enter the number of items: 8

Flower Order

1. Customer name: Don Gosselin
2. Item: Sunflowers (each)
3. Quantity: 8
   **********************
   Base price per unit: $4.95
   Order total: $28 (includes volume discount)
   **********************
4. Finished with this order

Select the number of an item to modify
or select 4 to return to the order list:
```

Figure 6-46 Output of Florist Order program after adding a multidimensional array

Character Arrays

When you create a `char` variable using a statement similar to `char szString[10];`, you are really creating an array of `char` elements. Each character in the string you assign to the `char` variable is stored in an element of the array. For example, the statement `char szHello[6];` creates a `char` array named szHello that can contain up to six characters. If you then assign the string *Hello* to the szHello variable, each character in *Hello* is assigned to a consecutive element in the szHello array, as illustrated in Figure 6-47. Notice that the last element in the array is occupied by the null character (\0).

szHello[0]	szHello[1]	szHello[2]	szHello[3]	szHello[4]	szHello[5]
H	e	l	l	o	\0

Figure 6-47 Memory locations occupied by the elements of the szHello[] character array

You can access the individual elements in a character array the same way that you access elements in arrays of other data types. For example, to print the first letter of the szHello variable, *H*, you use the statement `cout << szHello[0] << endl;`. If you need to manipulate the string contained within a character array, you must use one of the string functions contained in the cstring header file. (You learned about string functions in Chapter 3.)

So far, you have used two basic methods to define a character array. The first method declares the maximum number of elements in the array when it is first defined. If you do not initialize the array at declaration, then you must use the strcpy() function of the cstring class to assign it a value, as in the following example:

```
char szString[10];
strcpy(szString, "Hello");
```

Remember that with the preceding syntax, if you do not make the destination char variable large enough, then you will either lose data when you call the strcpy() or strcat() functions, or you will receive an error when you attempt to run the program.

The second method, shown below, does not require that you specify the maximum number of elements when you declare a char array. However, you must initialize the char array when you declare it so that C++ knows how many elements to create for the character array.

```
char szString[] = "Hello";
```


An easier method of creating a string variable is to use a char* pointer as in the following code. You can assign any string you want to the variable without having to declare the maximum number of characters.

```
char* szProgramming = "Visual C++";
```

Although char* is a pointer, it is common practice to prefix char* variable names with sz, which is Hungarian notation for a string of characters, terminated by a null character.

Once you create a char* pointer variable, you can use it in much the same way that you use a string class variable. Unlike other types of pointers, you do not need to use the address of or de-reference operators to access and modify the contents of a char* pointer variable. You also do not need to use any of the functions of the String object in order to modify the contents of a char* pointer after its initial declaration. You can simply assign a new value to a char* pointer whenever necessary, the same as you would assign a new value to a numeric data variable such as int or double. The following code shows an example of how you can use a char* pointer variable in a program:

```
char* myDog = "Golden Retriever";
cout << szMyDog << endl;
szMyDog = "Irish Setter";
cout << szMyDog << endl;
```

As you can see from the preceding example, the char* pointer does not follow the same rules as other pointers: You do not need to use the address of (&) operator when declaring the pointer. You also do not need the de-reference operator (*) when assigning a new value to the memory address targeted by the pointer. This is true because any string literal, such as "Golden Retriever," is actually a pointer to a character array; the character array being itself. Whenever you use a string literal in your program, C++ stores that string somewhere in memory. Whenever the compiler encounters the string literal, it treats the string itself as a pointer to its own first character (which is the first element in the character array). In other words, the "Golden Retriever" string literal is really two things: a character array and a pointer to the memory address of the character array's first element, which is the character *G*. All this means is that you can use a statement such as `char* szMyDog = "Golden Retriever";` to initialize a `char*` pointer variable, without using the address of (`&`) operator. Recall from the earlier discussion that you can assign the value of one pointer (which is a memory address) to another pointer, provided that they are of the same data type. Because "Golden Retriever" is a pointer, the statement `char* szMyDog = "Golden Retriever";` is only assigning the value of one pointer (the memory address of the first element in the Golden Retriever character array) to the `szMyDog char*` pointer variable.

Working with a `char*` pointer is very similar to working with a string class variable. However, you will probably find it easier to continue working with the string class. Nevertheless, character arrays and `char*` pointers are widely used, and you should be able to recognize and work with them if necessary.

Multidimensional Character Arrays

When you declare a multidimensional array of strings, the first index in the array declaration determines the number of rows, and the second index determines the maximum number of characters to store. The following code declares a multidimensional array to store the names of a hospital's medical departments. Although the largest department name consists of 14 characters, the code declares 15 characters, including one to hold the null character.

```
char arDepartments[10][15] = {"Anesthesia", "Biology",
                              "Neurology", "Oncology",
                              "Ophthalmology", "Otolaryngology,
                              "Pediatrics", "Psychiatry",
                              "Pulmonary", "Radiology" };
```

To return the entire name of one string in a multidimensional character array, you simply reference the first index number with the array name. For example, to print the third string ("Neurology ") in the arDepartments[] array, you would use the statement `cout << arDepartments[2] << endl;`. To return a single character in a multidimensional character array, you need to reference both index numbers with the array name. The statement `cout << arDepartments[0][1] << endl;` returns the second letter, *n*, in the first string, *Anesthesia.*

Just as the flower prices were originally stored in separate variables, the names of each type of flower are also stored in separate variables. A more efficient storage technique is to store each of the flower names in a multidimensional character array, which you will do next. Currently, the name of each type of flower is stored in a string variable. By the end of this section, you will end up with the flower names stored in an array of string class objects, which means you will eventually go back to using string class variables. However, for practice, you will now store the string variables in a multidimensional character array.

To store each of the flower names in a multidimensional character array:

1. Open the FloristOrder.h file in your Code Editor window. In the private section, locate the five declarations for the string class data members that store the names of the flower types.
2. Replace the five string class data members with a single multidimensional character array, as shown in Figure 6-48. The array will consist of five rows, one for each of the flower types, and each row will be capable of storing up to 25 characters.

6

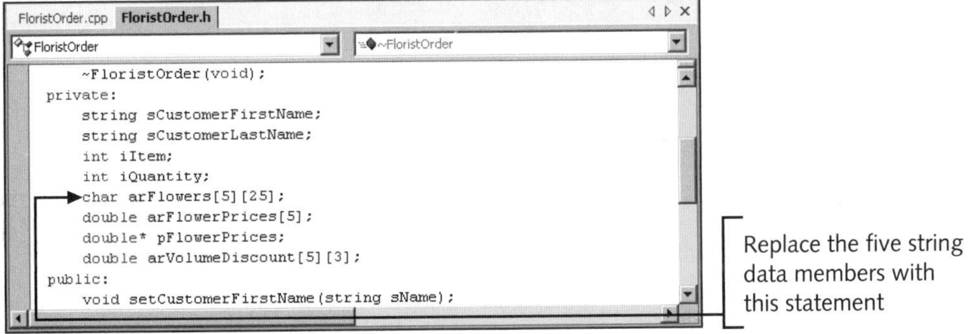

Figure 6-48 Multidimensional character array declaration added to FloristOrder.h

3. Next, open the FloristOrder.cpp file in your Code Editor window and locate the FloristOrder class constructor function.
4. Modify the statements that initialize the old `char` data members with each flower type so they instead initialize each flower type according to its corresponding element in the `arFlowers[]` array. The modified statements should appear as follows:

```
strcpy(this->arFlowers[0], "Roses (per dozen)");
strcpy(this->arFlowers[1], "Tulips (per dozen)");
strcpy(this->arFlowers[2], "Carnations (per dozen)");
strcpy(this->arFlowers[3], "Sunflowers (each)");
strcpy(this->arFlowers[4], "Orchids (each)");
```

Recall from Chapter 3 that the string functions for character arrays are contained in the cstring header file. Also recall that the same functions are also available in the string header file. Because you have already included the string header file in the FloristOrder class's interface file, you already have access to the functions you need such as strcpy(). Therefore, you do not need to include the cstring header file.

5. As shown in Figure 6-49, modify the getFlowerType() member function so that it returns the values stored in the arFlowers[] array instead of the old string class variables.

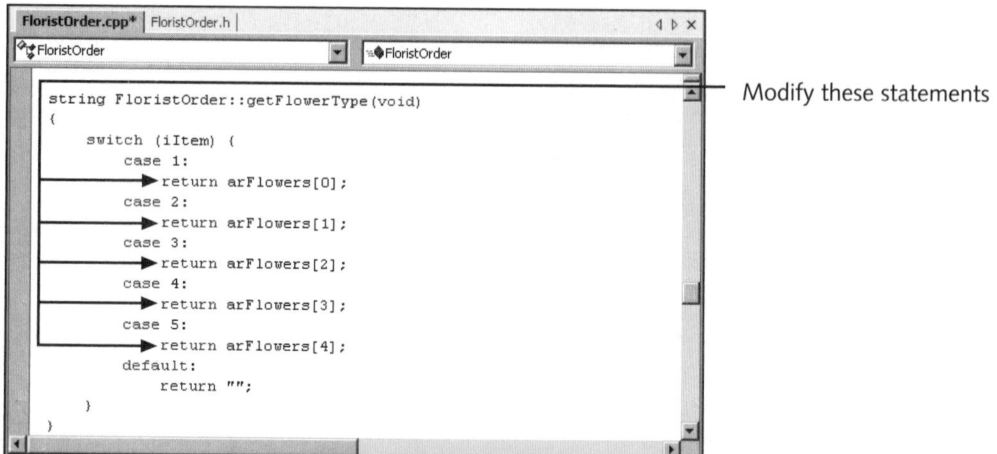


```
string FloristOrder::getFlowerType(void)
{
    switch (iItem) {
        case 1:
            return arFlowers[0];
        case 2:
            return arFlowers[1];
        case 3:
            return arFlowers[2];
        case 4:
            return arFlowers[3];
        case 5:
            return arFlowers[4];
        default:
            return "";
    }
}
```

Figure 6-49 getFlowerType() member function modified so that it returns the values stored in the arFlowers[] array

Notice that the getFlowerType() function is returning character arrays instead of string class variables. This is legal because the string class automatically handles the conversion of character arrays to string class objects.

6. Build and execute the project. The program should function normally.

The only problem with using a multidimensional character array is that for the second index number, you need to declare the maximum number of characters that the largest string in the array will hold. Each character that is stored in memory occupies approximately one byte of storage. When you declare a multidimensional character array, the maximum number of bytes is reserved for each string in the array, even if the string does not need that many characters. For instance, the arDepartments[] multidimensional character array reserves 15 bytes for each string, even though the *Otolaryngology* string is the only one that needs that many bytes. A total of 150 bytes is being reserved for the arDepartments[] multidimensional character array. Examine the layout of the multidimensional arDepartments[] array in Figure 6-50. Each gray square in the figure represents a wasted block of memory, for a total of 40 wasted bytes. 27%—almost a third—of the memory reserved for the arDepartments[] array is wasted.

Characters

Strings	0	1	2	3	4	5	6	7	8	9	10	11	12	13	14
0	A	n	e	s	T	h	e	s	I	A	\0				
1	B	i	o	l	o	g	y	\0							
2	N	e	u	r	o	l	o	g	Y	\0					
3	O	n	c	o	l	o	g	y	\0						
4	O	p	h	t	h	a	l	m	O	L	o	g	y	\0	
5	O	t	o	l	a	r	y	n	G	O	l	o	g	y	\0
6	P	e	d	i	a	t	r	i	C	S	\0				
7	P	s	y	c	h	i	a	t	R	Y	\0				
8	P	u	l	m	o	n	a	r	Y	\0					
9	R	a	d	i	o	l	o	g	Y	\0					

Figure 6-50 Multidimensional arDepartments[] array

Although 40 wasted bytes are not that significant, imagine the program on a much larger scale. Instead of 10 strings, what if the arDepartments[] array contained 10,000 strings, possibly containing the names of hospital employees. If the same 27% of the allocated memory space were wasted, the result would be approximately 40,500 wasted bytes. Although this is still not a huge amount of wasted space, it should start to give you an idea of how poor use of memory resources can cause programs to be inefficient.

Arrays of `Char*` Pointers

A more memory-efficient method of working with character strings than storing them in a multidimensional array is storing them in an array of `char*` pointers. Declaring an array of `char*` pointers stores only the pointers in the array. Each of the stored pointers in turn points to a character array. Each `char*` pointer reserves only enough memory to store the literal string that is passed to it. This means that no memory is wasted, as occurs with a multidimensional character array. To declare and initialize an array of `char*` pointers, use the syntax `char* name[] = {"string 1", "string 2", ...};`. The following code creates an array of pointers named arDepts[] for the hospital department names:

```
char* arDepts[] = {"Anesthesia", "Biology", "Neurology",
      "Oncology", "Ophthalmology", "Otolaryngology",
      "Pediatrics", "Psychiatry", "Pulmonary", "Radiology"
      };
```

6

You can access the value pointed to by a pointer element in an array of pointers by appending a set of brackets and the element's index number to the array name, the same as when you access standard array elements. For example, to print the fifth element (Ophthalmology) in the arDepts[] array, you use the statement `cout << arDepts[4] << endl;`.

Figure 6-51 shows an example of the memory spaces occupied by the pointers in the arDepts[] pointers array. Each pointer in the array reserves only the number of bytes needed to store all of the characters in its string, plus the null character. There are no wasted bytes, as there were in the multidimensional character array that stored the same hospital department names.

Characters

Strings	0	1	2	3	4	5	6	7	8	9	10	11	12	13	14		
arDepts[0]	A	N	e	s	t	h	e	s	l	a	\0	11 bytes					
arDepts[1]	B	i	o	L	o	g	y	\0	8 bytes								
arDepts[2]	N	e	u	r	o	l	o	g	Y	\0	10 bytes						
arDepts[3]	O	n	c	o	l	o	g	y	\0	9 bytes							
arDepts[4]	O	p	h	T	h	a	l	m	O	L	o	g	y	\0	14 bytes		
arDepts[5]	O	t	o	L	a	r	y	n	G	o	l	o	g	y	\0	15 bytes	
arDepts[6]	P	e	d	l	a	t	r	i	c	s	\0	11 bytes					
arDepts[7]	P	s	y	c	h	i	a	t	r	y	\0	11 bytes					
arDepts[8]	P	u	l	m	o	n	a	r	Y	\0	10 bytes						
arDepts[9]	R	A	d	l	o	l	o	g	Y	\0	10 bytes						

Figure 6-51 Memory spaces occupied by the arDepts[] array

Figure 6-50 shows only the memory spaces occupied by the character arrays that are pointed to by the pointers stored in the arDepts[] array. If you add the occupied memory spaces, you can see that even with this simple example, the arDepts[] array occupies only 109 bytes, which is approximately 25% smaller than the number of bytes occupied by the multidimensional character array, which occupied 150 bytes. You can imagine the memory that you would save if your program contained many more character strings consisting of much greater numbers of characters than are stored for the hospital department names. Even the small amount of savings demonstrated by the arDepts[] array underscores the importance of understanding and applying good memory management techniques in C++.

Each pointer stored in an array of `char*` pointers occupies 4 bytes. This means that the pointers stored in the arDepts[] array occupy a total of 40 bytes of memory. If you add the 40 bytes occupied by the pointers to the 109 bytes occupied by the character strings in the arDepts[] array, you will see that the memory savings over a multidimensional character array is insignificant—only one byte. However, for much larger arrays of `char*` pointers, the space occupied by each `char*` pointer is usually worth the extra memory savings you gain over using a multidimensional character array.

Next, you will modify the arFlowers[]array in the FloristOrder class so that it stores an array of pointers instead of a multidimensional character array.

To modify the arFlowers[]array in the FloristOrder class so that it stores an array of pointers instead of a multidimensional character array:

1. Open the FloristOrder.h file in your Code Editor window. In the private section, locate the declaration for the arFlowers[] multidimensional character array.
2. Add an indirection operator (*) to the end of the `char` data type and delete the second dimension. The new arFlowers[] declaration should read as follows: **`char* arFlowers[5];`**.
3. Open the FloristOrder.cpp file in your Code Editor window and locate the FloristOrder class constructor function.
4. Modify the initialization statements for the arFlowers[] array so the values are assigned directly to each array element instead of using strcpy() functions. The modified code should appear as follows:

```
this->arFlowers[0] = "Roses (per dozen)";
this->arFlowers[1] = "Tulips (per dozen)";
this->arFlowers[2] = "Carnations (per dozen)";
this->arFlowers[3] = "Sunflowers (each)";
this->arFlowers[4] = "Orchids (each)";
```

5. Build and execute the project. The program should function normally.

Arrays of Objects

Just as you can create arrays of primitive data types such as `int` and `double`, you can create an array of objects. One benefit of an array of objects is that it allows you to easily manage objects in your program that are of the same data type.

When you create an array of primitive data types, you can use an initializer list at declaration to initialize each element because each element will only contain one piece of data. However, with an array of objects, you must declare the array in one statement and then use additional statements to access the class members of each object according to its element number in the array. For example, the following code declares an array named arStocks consisting of three Stocks class objects, and then calls the class member functions for each of the array objects. Notice that the array name and element number are being used, along with the member selection operator and member function call.

```
Stocks arStocks[3];
// First stock
arStocks[0].setNumShares(100);
arStocks[0].setPricePerShare(67.5);
// Second stock
arStocks[0].setNumShares(200);
arStocks[0].setPricePerShare(48.25);
// Second stock
arStocks[0].setNumShares(300);
arStocks[0].setPricePerShare(73.75);
```

Although string class variables are really class objects, they act like primitive data types. This means that you can use an initialization list with arrays of string class objects. For example, the following code shows an example of the arDepts[] array, but this time using the string class:

```
string arDepts[] = {"Anesthesia", "Biology", "Neurology",
   "Oncology", "Ophthalmology", "Otolaryngology",
   "Pediatrics", "Psychiatry", "Pulmonary", "Radiology" };
```

However, when you use an array of string class objects as a data member, you must initialize it in the constructor function, just like other types of data members. The following code shows how to initialize each individual element in the arDepts[] array:

```
string arDepts[10];
arDepts[0] = "Anesthesia";
arDepts[1] = "Biology";
arDepts[2] = "Neurology";
arDepts[3] = "Oncology";
arDepts[4] = "Ophthalmology";
arDepts[5] = "Otolaryngology";
arDepts[6] = "Pediatrics";
arDepts[7] = "Psychiatry";
arDepts[8] = "Pulmonary";
arDepts[9] = "Radiology";
```

Next, you will modify the arFlowers[]array in the FloristOrder class a final time so it stores an array of string class objects instead of pointers.

To modify the arFlowers[]array in the FloristOrder class so that it stores an array of string class objects instead of pointers:

1. Open the FloristOrder.h file in your Code Editor window. In the private section, locate the declaration for the arFlowers[]array of char* pointers.
2. Modify the array declaration so it is of the string class data type instead of a char* pointer as follows: **`string arFlowers[5];`**.
3. Build and execute the project. The program should function normally.

Arrays and Functions

Just as you can pass primitive data types and class objects to a function, you can also pass an array. However, recall that an array name is really a pointer that points to the memory address of the first element in the array. When you pass an array to a function, you are really passing a pointer to the array. For this reason, arrays are one of the only data types that cannot be passed-by-value. Any changes you make to the array parameter inside the function will be reflected in the original array. An **array parameter** is a formal parameter that you define as part of a function definition. An **array argument** is an array that you pass to an array parameter in a call to a function. The memory address of the first element in the array argument is assigned to the array parameter defined in the function.

You define an array parameter using a data type and an empty set of brackets ([]) in the prototype and definition for a function that includes an array parameter. The empty set of brackets ([]) in a parameter definition notifies C++ that the parameter is an array parameter. For example, the following function prototype statement defines a double array parameter:

```
void yearEndBonus(double arSalaries[]);
```

Recall from Chapter 2 that you can optionally include the name of a parameter in its function prototype. For example, you can declare a function named calcNumbers() that accepts three `double` parameters using either of the following function definitions:

```
void calcNumbers(double, double, double);
void calcNumbers(double dFirstNum, double dSecondNum,
double dThirdNum);
```

With array parameters, however, you *must* include the parameter name and empty brackets in the function definition in order to notify C++ that the parameter is an array parameter. This means that you cannot use the following statement as the prototype to define the yearEndBonus() function with an array parameter:

```
void yearEndBonus(double);
```

When you call a function that includes an array parameter, do not include the brackets with the name of the passed array argument. For instance, to call the yearEndBonus() function and pass to it an array argument named arCurSalaries[], you use the following statement:

```
yearEndBonus(arCurSalaries);
```

When you pass an array argument to an array parameter, as in the preceding example, C++ simply assigns to the array parameter a pointer to the memory address of the first element in the array argument. However, because the array parameter definition does not include the number of array elements, the function has no way of knowing how large the array is. Therefore, for functions that include array parameters, you should also pass an integer value containing the number of elements in the passed array argument.

For example, the function prototype for the yearEndBonus() function could be `void yearEndBonus(double arSalaries[], int);`. You would then call the function using a statement similar to `yearEndBonus(arCurSalaries, iCount);` (assuming that iCount contains the number of elements in the arCurSalaries[] array).

Figure 6-52 shows an example of a program that includes the yearEndBonus() function with an array parameter. The yearEndBonus() function increases by 10% the value of each element in the passed array. Notice that after the values of each array element are modified in the yearEndBonus() function, they are printed from the main() function, demonstrating that passing an array argument actually passes a pointer to an array, not the array itself. Figure 6-53 shows the output.

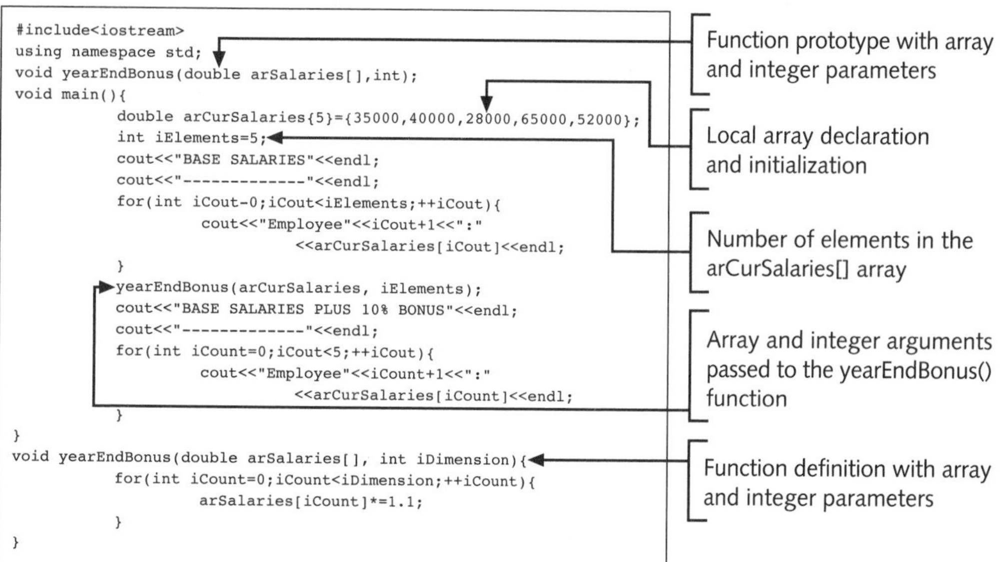

```
#include<iostream>
using namespace std;
void yearEndBonus(double arSalaries[],int);
void main(){
        double arCurSalaries{5}={35000,40000,28000,65000,52000};
        int iElements=5;
        cout<<"BASE SALARIES"<<endl;
        cout<<"-------------"<<endl;
        for(int iCout-0;iCout<iElements;++iCout){
                cout<<"Employee"<<iCout+1<<":"
                        <<arCurSalaries[iCout]<<endl;
        }
        yearEndBonus(arCurSalaries, iElements);
        cout<<"BASE SALARIES PLUS 10% BONUS"<<endl;
        cout<<"-------------"<<endl;
        for(int iCount=0;iCout<5;++iCout){
                cout<<"Employee"<<iCount+1<<":"
                        <<arCurSalaries[iCount]<<endl;
        }
}
void yearEndBonus(double arSalaries[], int iDimension){
        for(int iCount=0;iCount<iDimension;++iCount){
                arSalaries[iCount]*=1.1;
        }
}
```


Figure 6-52 Bonus program

```
"c:\visual c++ projects\chapter.06\bonus\debug\Bonus.exe"
BASE SALARIES
-------------
Employee1: 35000
Employee2: 40000
Employee3: 28000
Employee4: 65000
Employee5: 52000
BASE SALARIES PLUS 10% BONUS
-------------
Employee1: 38500
Employee2: 44000
Employee3: 30800
Employee4: 71500
Employee5: 57200
Press any key to continue
```

Figure 6-53 Output of Bonus program

DYNAMIC MEMORY ALLOCATION

The local variables, such as `int iCount;`, and pointers, such as `int* iCount;`, you have seen so far are created in an area of memory known as the stack. The **stack** is a region of memory where applications can store data such as local variables, function calls, and parameter information. Recall that local variables have automatic storage duration, which means that they exist only during the lifetime of the command block (such as a function) that contains them. With automatic storage duration, C++ automatically adds local variables to and removes local variables from the stack. Programmers have no control over the stack; C++ automatically handles placing data on and removing data from the stack. For many situations, storing data on the stack is the best way of managing memory because C++ handles memory allocation and de-allocation for you.

6

There will be cases, however, in which you will want to have greater control over the allocation and de-allocation of the memory used by your program. For example, you may write a program that needs to allocate memory to a variable, but you will not know the variable's data type or the value it will store until run time. For your program to be able to reserve the correct amount of memory on the stack, you need to know the variable's data type at compile time. To allocate variables at run time, you use an area of memory known as the heap. The **heap**, or the **free store**, is an area of memory that is available to an application for storing data whose existence and size are not known until run time. To add and remove variables to and from the heap, you use the `new` and `delete` keywords. Adding and removing variables with the `new` and `delete` keywords at run time is referred to as **dynamic memory allocation**.

The new Keyword

The **new** keyword creates a variable on the heap and returns a pointer to the variable's heap memory address. The syntax for using the `new` keyword is *`pointer`* `= new` *`data_type`*`;`. For example, to declare an `int` pointer named pPointer that points to a heap variable, you use the following statements:

```
int* pPointer;
pPointer = new int;
```

You can also combine the pPointer declaration with the statement that calls the `new` keyword as follows:

```
int* pPointer = new int;
```

Once you allocate a heap variable, you refer to it in your code the same way you refer to other pointer variables. For example, the following statements declare a new `double` heap variable named pPrimeInterest and assign to it the value .065. The first cout statement then prints the value of the dPrimeInterest variable (.065) and the second cout statement prints its memory address.

```
double* pPrimeInterest = new double;
*pPrimeInterest = .065;
out << *pPrimeInterest << endl;
cout << &pPrimeInterest << endl;
```

You declare character arrays on the heap using the following syntax:

```
char* varName = new char[elements];
```

To store an array on the heap, you need to use the syntax `type* pointer_name = new type[elements];`. For example, the following statement creates on the heap a single-dimensional `int` array named arInvestments consisting of 10 elements:

```
int* arInvestments = new int[10];
```

To create a multidimensional array on the heap, include all of the array's indexes after the data type. If you want to create the arInvestments array as a two dimensional array, with each index containing 10 elements, you would use the following statement:

```
int* arInvestments = new int[10][10];
```

When working with dynamic data members in a class, you must first declare a pointer data member in the class's interface file. Then, you use the pointer name in the class constructor to allocate space on the heap. For instance, the following statements declare pointer data members of various types in a class's interface file.

private:

```
double* pDoubleNumber;
int* pIntNumber;
string* pString Variable;
```

To declare space on the heap for the preceding pointer data members, you use statements similar to the following in the class constructor:

```
pDoubleNumber = new double;
pIntNumber = new int;
pStringVariable = new string;
```

Normally, there is little need to declare a single primitive variable on the heap if you know its data type at compile time. In the preceding example, for instance, you should store the pDoubleNumber, pIntNumber, and pStringVariable data members on the stack because you already know their data types. In contrast, one of the most common uses of dynamic memory allocation is to create an array when you do not know how many elements the array will require until run time. For instance, you may have a class that creates at run time an array of investment names, based on the number of investments entered by a user. In this case, you would declare a string class pointer in the interface file using a statement similar to `string* pInvestmentNames;`. You could then declare the array on the heap in a parameterized constructor that receives a parameter with the number of investments. You will learn about parameterized constructors in the next chapter. For now you should understand that a parameterized constructor allows you to pass arguments to a class at object declaration. For instance, the following code is a parameterized constructor for a class named Investments that accepts a single int variable named iNumInvestments. The statement in the function definition that allocates space on the heap for a dynamic array of string class objects uses the iNumInvestments variable to allocate the correct number of elements.

```
Investments::Investments(int iNumInvestments) {
   pInvestmentNames = new string[iNumInvestments];
}
```

Similarly, you can create a dynamic double array that stores the amount of each investment. You use the statement `double* pInvestementAmounts;` in the interface file. You then add a statement to the parameterized constructor that allocates the correct amount of elements on the heap for the dynamic double array, as follows:


```
Investments::Investments(int iNumInvestments) {
  pInvestmentNames = new string[iNumInvestments];
  pInvestmentAmounts = new double[iNumInvestment];
}
```

The main() function in the Florist Order program currently instantiates a single FloristOrder object and then passes the object to the showOrders() function. However, this technique significantly reduces the Florist Order program's usefulness because you can create only a single order when you run the program. A better technique is to allow the user to tell the program how many orders he or she wants to make. Then, the program will dynamically create an array of FloristOrder objects, one for each of the customer's orders. Next, you will modify the main() function so it dynamically creates an array of FloristOrder objects.

To modify the main() function so it dynamically creates an array of FloristOrder objects:

1. Return to the FloristOrder.cpp file in your Code Editor window and locate the main() function.
2. Replace the `FloristOrder flowerOrder;` statement with the statements shown Figure 6-54, which gather the number of objects to create from the user and assign the number to the iNumOrders variable. Add a statement that uses the iNumOrders variable to dynamically create an array of FloristOrder objects on the heap. Also, modify the `FloristOrder* pFlowerOrder = &flowerOrder;` so that the pFlowerOrder pointer points to the new arFloristObjects[] array.

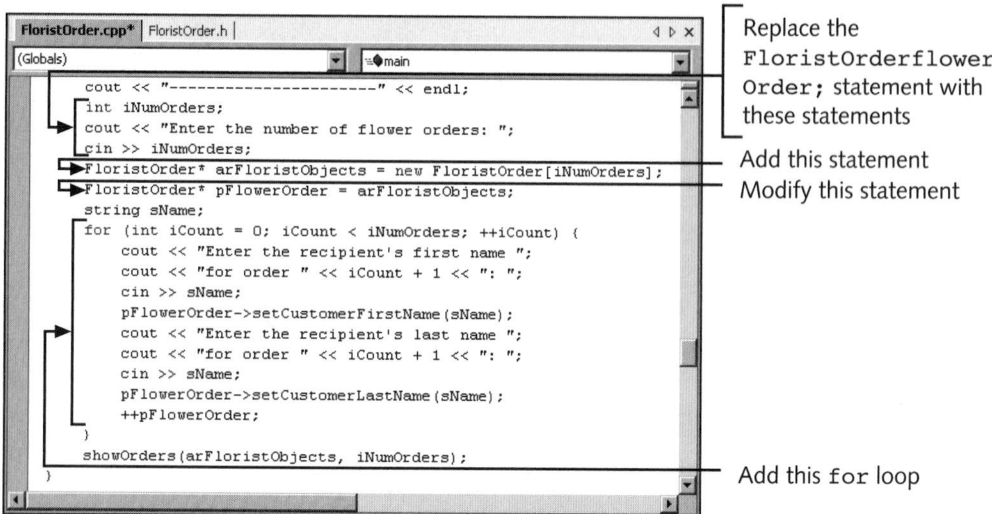

Figure 6-54 Statements added to the main() function that dynamically create an array of FloristOrder objects

3. As shown in Figure 6-54, add a **for** loop which gathers the first and last name for each object. Notice that the pFlowerOrder pointer is being used to make it easier to access the values in the arFloristObjects[] array. Also notice that the pFlowerOrder pointer is incremented using pointer arithmetic.

Next, you will modify the showOrders() function so that the arFloristObjects[] array is passed to it instead of the pFlowerOrder pointer.

To modify the showOrders() function so that the arFloristObjects[] array is passed to it instead of the pFlowerOrder pointer:

1. Return to the FloristOrder.cpp file in the Code Editor window and locate the showOrders() function prototype.
2. Modify the showOrders() function prototype's parameter list so that it accepts a FloristOrder array and an integer value to hold the number of elements assigned to the array: **void showOrders(FloristOrder curOrder[], int);**.
3. Locate the showOrders() function definition and modify its parameter list to match the function prototype: **void showOrders(FloristOrder curOrder[], int iNumOrders) {**.
4. Modify the last statement in the main() function that calls the showOrders() function, as shown in Figure 6-55

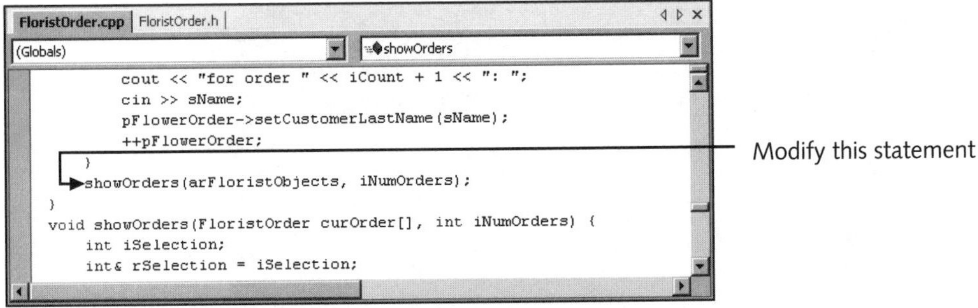

Figure 6-55 Modified call to the showOrders() function

5. Modify the showOrders() function's **do...while** loop as follows so that it builds a menu of orders by looping through the elements of the arFloristObjects[] array using the pCurOrder pointer.

```
do {
   cout << "----------------------" << endl;
   cout << "Order List" << endl << endl;
   int ctCount = 0;
   while (ctCount < iNumOrders) {
      cout << ctCount + 1 << ". "
         << curOrder[ctCount].getCustomerFirstName()
            << " "
         << curOrder[ctCount].getCustomerLastName()
            << endl;
      ++ctCount
   }
   cout << ctCount + 1 << ". "
           << "Exit application" << endl << endl;
   cout << "Select the number of an order to modify "
           << endl << "or select " << ctCount + 1
           << " to exit the program: ";
   cin >> rSelection;
   cout << endl;
   if (rSelection != iNumOrders + 1)
           modifyOrder(curOrder[rSelection - 1]);
} while (iSelection != iNumOrders + 1);
```

6. Rebuild and execute the program. When the program runs, test it by entering a multiple number of flower orders. Enter first and last names for each order and test your ability to select different items (flowers, price, and quantity) for each order. Figure 6-56 shows the output after creating three orders.

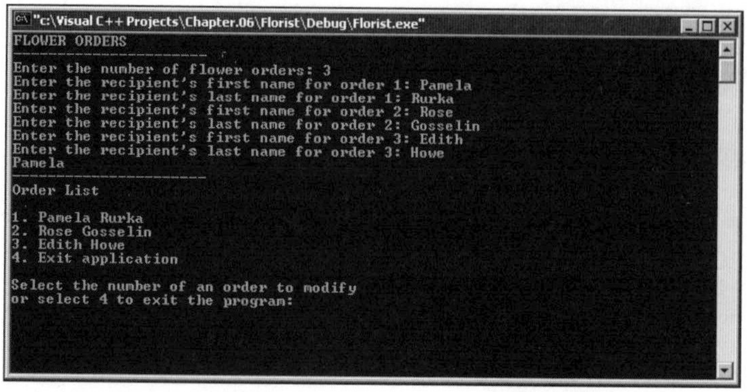

```
"c:\Visual C++ Projects\Chapter.06\Florist\Debug\Florist.exe"
FLOWER ORDERS
-------------------------
Enter the number of flower orders: 3
Enter the recipient's first name for order 1: Pamela
Enter the recipient's last name for order 1: Rurka
Enter the recipient's first name for order 2: Rose
Enter the recipient's last name for order 2: Gosselin
Enter the recipient's first name for order 3: Edith
Enter the recipient's last name for order 3: Howe
Pamela
-------------------------
Order List

1. Pamela Rurka
2. Rose Gosselin
3. Edith Howe
4. Exit application

Select the number of an order to modify
or select 4 to exit the program:
```

Figure 6-56 Florist Order program with multiple orders

The `delete` Keyword

Once you are through working with heap memory, you need to free it so that other parts of your program can use it. You use the **`delete`** keyword to de-allocate memory that has been reserved on the heap. The syntax for calling the `delete` keyword is `delete pointer_name;`. For example, to delete the heap memory pointed to by the pPrimeInterest pointer, you use the statement `delete pPrimeInterest;`.

It is important to understand that the `delete` keyword does not delete the pointer itself. Rather, it deletes the contents of the heap memory address pointed to by a pointer variable. You can reuse the pointer itself after calling the `delete` keyword. The pointer still exists and points to the same heap memory address that it did before you called the `delete` keyword. For example, the following code declares the pPrimeInterest pointer on the heap and assigns to it a value of .065. Then, the `delete` keyword deletes the heap address that stores the value of .065. Finally, a new value is added to the heap address. If you examine the output in Figure 6-57, you will see that after the `delete` statement executes, the pPrimeInterest pointer still points to the same memory address.

```
double* pPrimeInterest = new double;
*pPrimeInterest = .065;
cout << "The value of pPrimeInterest is: "
   << *pPrimeInterest << endl;
cout << "The memory address of pPrimeInterest is: "
   << &pPrimeInterest << endl;
delete pPrimeInterest;
*pPrimeInterest = .070;
cout << "The value of pPrimeInterest is: "
   << *pPrimeInterest << endl;
cout << "The memory address of pPrimeInterest is: "
     << &pPrimeInterest << endl;
```

```
"c:\Visual C++ Projects\Chapter.06\Pointers\Debug\Pointers.exe"
The value of pPrimeInterest is: 0.065
The memory address of pPrimeInterest is: 0012FED4
The value of pPrimeInterest is: 0.07
The memory address of pPrimeInterest is: 0012FED4
Press any key to continue
```

Figure 6-57 Output of program with heap variables

There is only so much heap memory available to an application. If you fail to delete heap variables, your program may experience something called a memory leak. A **memory leak** is a condition in which a system's memory is not released after it is used (in other words, it "leaks out" of the heap). If you have a program that continually creates heap variables without deleting them, you will eventually run out of heap memory, causing your program to crash.

Deleting the contents of an array stored on the heap requires a slightly different syntax. You must append opening and closing brackets to the `delete` keyword using the syntax `delete[] array_name;`. For example, the following statement deletes the heap memory that stores the array pointed to by the arInvestments pointer:

```
delete[] arInvestments;
```

The preceding method of deleting an array stored on the heap is valid for both single-dimensional and multidimensional arrays.

Next, you will add a statement to the Florist Order program that releases the heap memory used by the arFloristObjects array in the main() function.

To add a statement to the Florist Order program that releases the heap memory used by the arFloristObjects array in the main() function:

1. Return to the FloristOrder.cpp file in your Code Editor window and locate the main() function.
2. Add the statement **`delete[] arFloristObjects;`**, as shown in Figure 6-58, to delete the arFloristObjects heap variable.

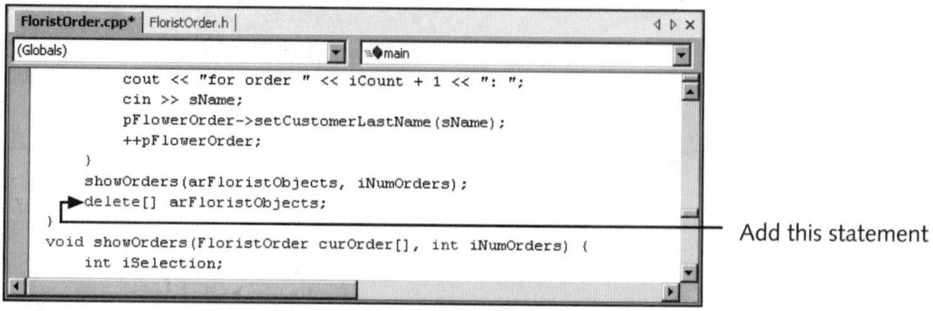

```
FloristOrder.cpp* | FloristOrder.h |
(Globals)                              main
            cout << "for order " << iCount + 1 << ": ";
            cin >> sName;
            pFlowerOrder->setCustomerLastName(sName);
            ++pFlowerOrder;
        }
        showOrders(arFloristObjects, iNumOrders);
        delete[] arFloristObjects;
    }
    void showOrders(FloristOrder curOrder[], int iNumOrders) {
        int iSelection;
```

Add this statement

Figure 6-58 Statement added that deletes the arFloristObjects heap variable

3. Build and execute the project. The program should function normally.

Chapter Summary

- A pointer is a special type of variable that stores the memory address of another variable.
- A reference, or reference variable, is an alias for an existing variable.
- Passing a variable to a function is referred to as calling-by-value or passing-by-value because only the value of the variable is passed to the function instead of the variable itself.
- Passing a pointer to a function is referred to as calling-by-address or passing-by-address because only the memory address of the variable is passed to the function instead of the value of the variable.
- Passing a reference variable to a function is referred to as calling-by-reference or passing-by-reference because only the reference variable is passed to the function instead of the value itself.
- When declaring and using pointers and references to class objects, follow the same rules as you would when declaring and using pointers and references to variables of primitive data types.
- You must use the indirect member selection operator (->) to access class members through a pointer to an object either on the stack or on the heap.
- The `this` pointer identifies the object instance that called a function.
- An array name is actually a pointer that points to the memory address of the first element in the array.
- With pointer arithmetic, you can use addition and subtraction to change the element number that is the target of a pointer.
- Multidimensional arrays consist of multiple indexes.

- An alternate method to declaring the number of elements in a character array using brackets is to use a `char*` pointer, which automatically allocates the correct number of elements to the character array.
- Passing an array to a function really passes a pointer to the array.
- The stack is a region of memory where applications can store data such as local variables, function calls, and parameter information.
- The heap, or the free store, is an area of memory that is available to an application for storing data whose existence and size are not known until run time.
- Adding variables to the heap with the `new` keyword and removing variables from the heap with the `delete` keyword at run time is referred to as dynamic memory allocation.
- The `new` keyword creates a variable on the heap and returns the variable's heap memory address.
- You use the `delete` keyword to de-allocate memory that has been reserved on the heap.

REVIEW QUESTIONS

1. You can create a pointer using the syntax *`type* pointer;`* or ________________.
   a. *`type *pointer`*;
   b. *`*type pointer`*;
   c. *`type pointer*`*;
   d. *`type& pointer`*;
2. Which operator do you use to assign to the pointer variable the memory address of another variable?
   a. &
   b. *
   c. %
   d. =
3. Which operator do you use to access or modify the contents of the variable pointed to by the pointer?
   a. &
   b. *
   c. %
   d. =

4. Which of the following correctly declares a reference named rBucks that is an alias for a variable named iDollars, assuming that the iDollars variable already exists?
   a. `int& rBucks = iDollars;`
   b. `int rBucks& = iDollars;`
   c. `int rBucks = &iDollars;`
   d. `int& rBucks;`
      `rBucks = iDollars;`
5. What is the correct syntax for printing the value of the iDollars variable through the rBucks reference variable?
   a. `cout << rBucks << endl;`
   b. `cout << *rBucks << endl;`
   c. `cout << rBucks* << endl;`
   d. `cout << &rBucks << endl;`
      `rBucks = iDollars;`
6. If you have a variable named rPrecipitation that references a variable named iRainfall, how do you reassign the rRainfall variable so it references another variable named iSnowfall?
   a. `int rPrecipitation& = iSnowfall;`
   b. `int rPrecipitation = &iSnowfall;`
   c. `int rPrecipitation& = *Snowfall;`
   d. You cannot reassign a reference variable.
7. Passing a copy of a variable to a function is referred to as ________________?
   a. call-by-value
   b. call-by-address
   c. call-by-reference
   d. call-by-copy
8. Passing the memory address of a variable to a function is referred to as ________________?
   a. call-by-value
   b. call-by-address
   c. call-by-reference
   d. call-by-memory
9. Passing a reference variable to a function is referred to as ________________?
   a. call-by-value
   b. call-by-address

c. call-by-reference

d. call-by-variable

10. Which operator do you use to access class members through a pointer to an object?

a. .

b. -

c. >

d. ->

11. How else can you write the statement `this->iLength = 10;` in a member function, assuming that the iLength variable is a data member of the same class?

a. `this.iLength = 10;`

b. `class.iLength = 10;`

c. `self.iLength = 10;`

d. `iLength = 10;`

12. Array names are referred to as ________________ because no change can be made to the value they store after they are declared and initialized.

a. constant pointers

b. constant references

c. aliases

d. fixed memory variables

13. You can assign the memory address of the first element in an array named arCurrencies[] to a pointer named pCurrencies using the statement `pCurrencies = &arCurrencies[0];` or the statement ________________.

a. `pCurrencies = arCurrencies;`

b. `pCurrencies = &arCurrencies;`

c. `pCurrencies = arCurrencies[0];`

d. `pCurrencies - 1= arCurrencies;`

14. Which of the following statements correctly assigns 200 to the third element in an int array named arCurrencies?

a. `(arCurrencies + 2) = 200;`

b. `*arCurrencies + 2 = 200;`

c. `(*arCurrencies) + 2 = 200;`

d. `*(arCurrencies + 2) = 200;`

15. Which of the following statements correctly declares an `int` multidimensional array named arAgeGroups[], with the first dimension containing 10 elements, the second dimension containing 20 elements, and the third dimension containing 15 elements?

    a. `int arAgeGroups[10, 20, 15];`

    b. `int arAgeGroups[10][20][15];`

    c. `int arAgeGroups[10 : 20 : 15];`

    d. `int arAgeGroups = [10][20][15];`

16. If you have a seven-character `char` variable named szCity that contains the value Boston, which of the following statements returns just the first letter, *B*?

    a. `cout << szCity << endl;`

    b. `cout << szCity(1) << endl;`

    c. `cout << szCity[1] << endl;`

    d. `cout << szCity[0] << endl;`

17. Which of the following is the correct syntax for assigning a string to a `char*` pointer named szCaliforniaCapital?

    a. `*szCaliforniaCapital = "Sacramento";`

    b. `char* szCaliforniaCapital[25] = "Sacramento";`

    c. `char* szCaliforniaCapital = "Sacramento";`

    d. `char szCaliforniaCapital = "Sacramento";`

18. What is the correct syntax for declaring a multidimensional character array named arFootbalTeams that contains 10 rows and 30 columns?

    a. `char arFootbalTeams = [10], [30];`

    b. `char[10][30] arFootballTeams;`

    c. `char arFootballTeams[10][30];`

    d. `char arFootballTeams, [10], [30];`

19. What is the correct syntax for declaring an array of `char*` pointers named arTropicalFish that contains 50 rows, with the largest entry consisting of 40 characters?

    a. `char arTropicalFish;`

    b. `char* arTropicalFish;`

    c. `char[50][40] arTropicalFish;`

    d. `char arTropicalFish[50][40];`

20. What is the correct syntax for declaring an array of string objects named arCountryNames that will contain up to 100 entries, with the largest entry consisting of 50 characters?
    a. `string arCountryNames;`
    b. `string* arCountryNames;`
    c. `string[100][50] arCountryNames;`
    d. `string arCountryNames [100][50];`
21. How is an array passed to a function?
    a. by value
    b. by address
    c. by reference
    d. You cannot pass an array to a function
22. When you declare a standard variable using a statement similar to `int iCount = 0;`, where in memory is the variable stored?
    a. stack
    b. heap
    c. free store
    d. iostream
23. Which of the following statements is the correct syntax for declaring a variable on the heap?
    a. `double dPrice = new double;`
    b. `double* dPrice = new double;`
    c. `double* dPrice = double;`
    d. `*double dPrice = new double;`
24. Which keyword do you use to remove a variable from the heap?
    a. `remove`
    b. `delete`
    c. `kill`
    d. `purge`

25. Which of the following statements declares a Boat object named sailBoat on the stack with a pointer to the sailBoat object?
    a. `Boat sailBoat;`
       `Boat* pSailBoat = &sailBoat;`
    b. `Boat sailBoat;`
       `Boat* pSailBoat = sailBoat;`
    c. `Boat sailBoat;`
       `Boat pSailBoat = &sailBoat;`
    d. `Boat sailBoat;`
       `Boat pSailBoat = sailBoat;`
26. Which of the following statements declares a Boat object named sailBoat and a reference to the Sailboat object?
    a. `Boat sailBoat;`
       `Boat& rSailBoat = *sailBoat;`
    b. `Boat sailBoat;`
       `Boat rSailBoat = &sailBoat;`
    c. `Boat sailBoat;`
       `Boat& rSailBoat = sailBoat;`
    d. `Boat sailBoat;`
       `Boat* rSailBoat = &sailBoat;`

PROGRAMMING EXERCISES

1. Declare a pointer to the dRadius variable in the following code. Use the pointer to print the memory address and the value of the dRadius variable.

```
#include <iostream>
using namespace std;
void main() {
 double dRadius = 1.75;
}
```

2. Declare a reference to the iDistance variable in the following code. Use the reference to print the value of the iDistance variable.

```
#include <iostream>
using namespace std;
void main() {
  int iDistance = 300;
}
```

3. Modify the following code so that the dTemp variable is passed by address to the convertToCelsius() function.

```
#include <iostream>
using namespace std;
void convertToCelsius(double);
void main() {
  double dTemp = 55;
  convertToCelsius(dTemp);
}
void convertToCelsius(double dTemp) {
  double dResult = (dTemp - 32) * .55;
  cout <<
   "The temperature you entered as Fahrenheit is
   equal to "
          << dResult << " in Celsius" << endl;
}
```


4. Modify the following code so that the dTemp variable is passed by reference to the convertToFahrenheit() function.

```
#include <iostream>
using namespace std;
void convertToFahrenheit(double);
void main() {
  double dTemp = 0;
  convertToFahrenheit(dTemp);
}
void convertToFahrenheit(double dTemp) {
  double dResult = (dTemp * 1.8) + 32;
  cout <<
   "The temperature you entered as Celsius is equal to "
   << dResult << " in Fahrenheit" << endl;
}
```

5. Create a program that uses a pointer to fill an integer array of 20 elements with the number 1, and then uses a `for` loop to print the value of each element.
6. Modify the program you created in Exercise 5 so that it uses pointer arithmetic to assign the values to the integer array and print them.
7. Create a multidimensional character array that stores the seven days of the week.
8. Create an array of `char*` pointers that stores the 12 months of the year.
9. Create an array of string objects that stores the four seasons of the year.

10. Modify the `for` loop in the following program so that it uses the array name and pointer arithmetic to print the contents of the array.

```
#include <iostream>
using namespace std;
void main() {
  int iPrimes[10] = {1, 2, 3, 5, 7, 9, 11, 13, 17, 19 };
  for(int iCount=0; iCount < 10; iCount ++)
            cout <<iPrimes[iCount] << endl;
  }
}
```

11. Add a pointer named dPrimes to the iPrimes[] array to the program in Exercise 13. Use the dPrimes pointer instead of the array name in the `for` loop to print the contents of the array.

12. Create a multidimensional `double` array named arBoxes containing three rows and three columns. The three rows will represent a small box, a medium box, and a large box. The three columns will represent the length, width, and depth of each box. After declaring and initializing the array, write a `for` loop that prints the volume (length * width * depth) of each box. Create the array using the dimensions shown in the following table.

	Length	Width	Depth
Small box	12	10	2.5
Medium box	30	20	4
Large box	60	40	11.5

13. When you pass an array to a function by value, the memory address that stores the array's first element is passed to the function instead of the array itself. Explain why this occurs.

14. Replace the statement in the following code that declares and assigns the stack variable named iDistance with a statement that stores the value 300 on the heap. Also, add a statement that prints the value of the heap variable and another statement that removes it from the heap.

```
#include <iostream>
using namespace std;
void main() {
  int iDistance = 300;
}
```

PROGRAMMING PROJECTS

1. Write a simple program that allows users to enter three integers. Store each integer in a variable and create a pointer to each integer. Print the values of each variable by de-referencing the pointer. Also, display the memory address of each variable using the address of operator.
2. Write a simple program that allows users to enter a single integer. After the user enters the number, display it using a reference. Add a looping statement that repeatedly prompts the user to enter *y* to modify the number or *n* to exit. If the user presses *y*, allow him or her to enter a new number, but modify it through the reference to the number.
3. Write a program that includes a function named sumNumbers(). The sumNumbers() function should include two int pointers: pFirstNum and pSecondNum. Include a single statement in the sumNumbers() function that prints the sum of the two int variables that are the target of the pFirstNum and pSecondNum variables. In the program's main() function, declare two integer variables: iFirstNum and iSecondNum. Call the sumNumbers() function from the main() function and pass to it the memory address of the iFirstNum and iSecondNum int variables *without declaring pointer variables in the main() function.*
4. Modify the program you created in Exercise 3 so it uses references instead of pointers.
5. Write a main() function that declares a double array named arRetail[] that contains five elements. Assign to the arRetail[] array the following values: 99.5, 78.65, 32.40, 59.95, and 12.75. Write a custom function named discount() that accepts a one-dimension array. The discount() function should not return a value. Within the body of the discount() function, reduce by 10% the values of the array that are passed to it. Call the discount() function from the main() function and pass to it the arRetail[] array. Print the values of the arRetail[] array before and after the call to the discount() function.
6. Write a program that includes a function named swapValues() that accepts two `int` pointer parameters: pNum1 and pNum2. Write code in the body of the function that swaps the values stored in the memory addresses that are the target of the pNum1 and pNum2 pointer parameters. Within the main() function, create two `int` variables named iFirstNum and iSecondNum. Assign the iFirstNum variable a value of 100 and assign the iSecondNum variable a value of 200. Create pointers named pFirstNum and pSecondNum that point to the memory addresses of the iFirstNum and iSecondNum variables. Call the swapValues() function and pass to it the pFirstNum and pSecondNum pointers. Print the values assigned to the iFirstNum and iSecondNum variables before you call the swapValues() function After the call to the swapValues() function, print the values of the iFirstNum and iSecondNum variables to see if the swapValues() function worked.

7. Instead of giving gifts during the holiday season, many businesses donate money to charitable organization for each of their clients. Write a program similar to the Florist Order program that creates a dynamic array of objects for a specified number of donations that a business would like to make. Allow the business to enter a predefined spending limit for all of the donations combined. Create a menu listing the clients who the donations will be made for and include a line that states how much money is left to donate. Create a separate menu that allows you to select a specific charity for a client, along with the amount of money to donate for the client. Save the project as Donations.

CHAPTER

7

OBJECT MANIPULATION

In this chapter you will learn:

- About default constructors
- How to create parameterized constructors
- How to work with initialization lists
- How to create copy constructors
- How to work with destructors
- How to overload operators
- About static class members
- About constant objects

Goto, n.: A programming tool that exists to allow structured programmers to complain about unstructured programmers.

Ray Simard

PREVIEW: THE BUILDING ESTIMATOR PROGRAM

The Building Estimator program is a console application that calculates the cost of building a home for three separate customers. The program allows users to select a home style, the number of bedrooms, and the number of bathrooms. It then calculates the estimated cost of building the home, based on preset amounts. The Building Estimator program is a fairly simple example of the type of program that building contractors and architects might use to estimate the cost of building an entire housing development. Although the program allows you to estimate costs for only three customers, it provides a sufficient demonstration of the object manipulation techniques discussed in this chapter.

To preview the Building Estimator program:

1. Create a **Chapter.07** folder in your Visual C++ Projects folder.
2. Copy the **Chapter7_BuildingEstimator** folder from the Chapter.07 folder on your Data Disk to the Chapter.07 folder in your Visual C++ Projects folder. Then open the **BuildingEstimator** project in Visual C++.

3. The Estimator project contains two files: Estimator.h and Estimator.cpp. You should recognize these files as the interface and implementation files for a class. Open the **Estimator.h** file in the Code Editor window. Notice some of the unfamiliar declarations. A parameterized constructor allows a client to pass initialization values to a class during object instantiation. A destructor cleans up any heap resources when an object of the class is deleted. A copy constructor is called when a new object is created by copying an existing object. An overloaded operator is used to designate an alternate function for an operator. Static data members store values that are accessible by all instantiated objects of a class, and static member functions return the value of a static data member. Notice that the getCustomerName() function, which is a simple get function, contains the keyword `const` at the end of its declaration. Using the keyword `const` at the end of a get function that does not modify data members is a good programming technique that makes your programs more reliable. Figure 7-1 highlights declarations for each of these elements. Close the **Estimator.h** interface file.

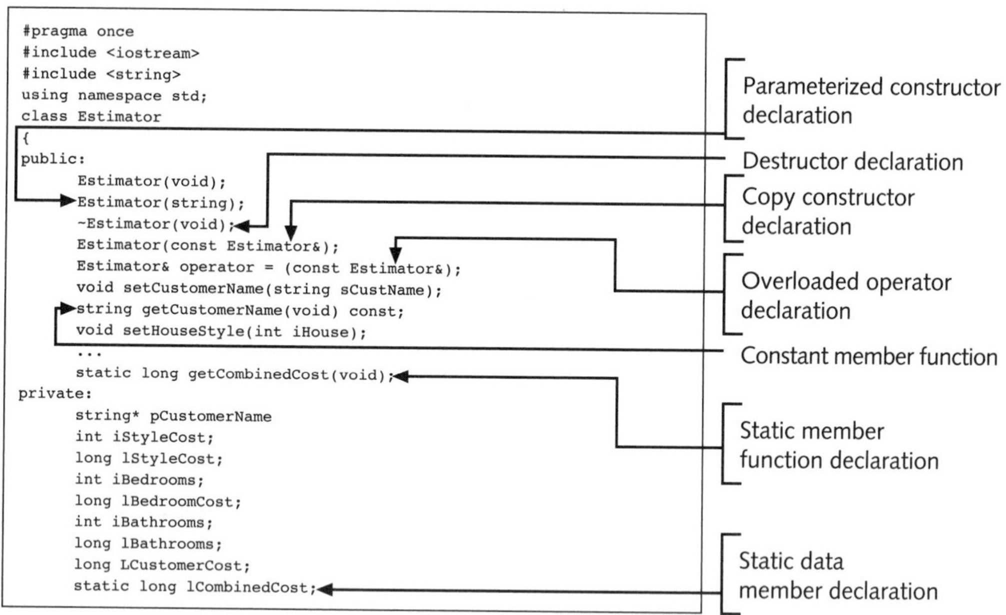

Figure 7-1 Estimator.h

4. Open the **Estimator.cpp** implementation file. Estimator.cpp is a fairly long file containing various C++ code segments that you should recognize. Figure 7-2 shows the class member definitions whose declarations were called out in Figure 7-1. Notice that the static data member is initialized at the global level.

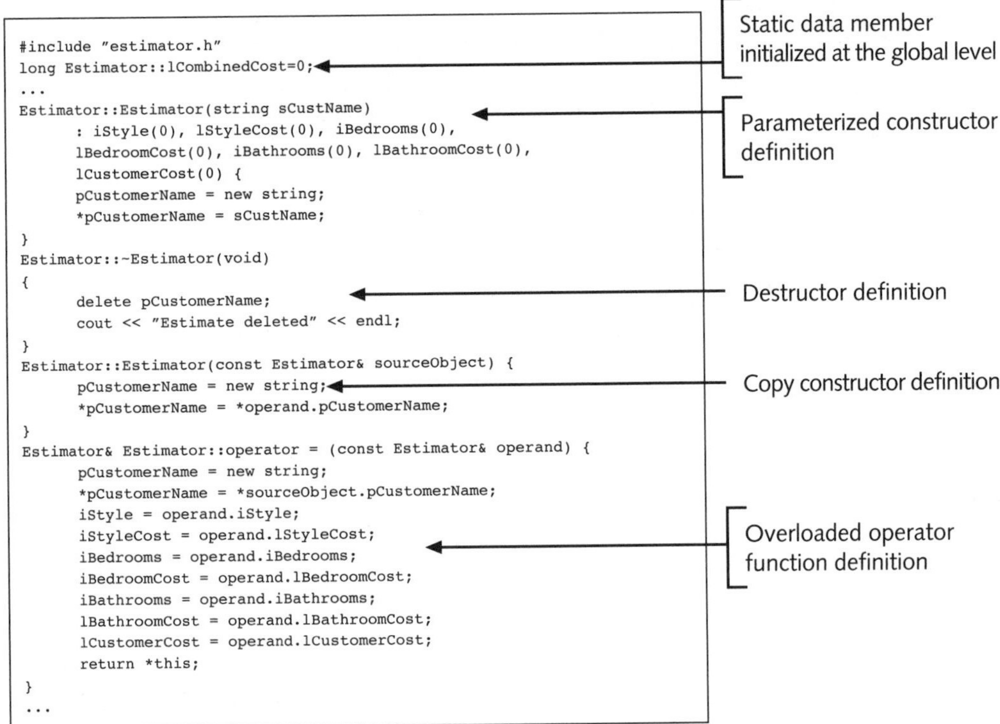

```
#include "estimator.h"
long Estimator::lCombinedCost=0;
...
Estimator::Estimator(string sCustName)
      : iStyle(0), lStyleCost(0), iBedrooms(0),
      lBedroomCost(0), iBathrooms(0), lBathroomCost(0),
      lCustomerCost(0) {
      pCustomerName = new string;
      *pCustomerName = sCustName;
}
Estimator::~Estimator(void)
{
      delete pCustomerName;
      cout << "Estimate deleted" << endl;
}
Estimator::Estimator(const Estimator& sourceObject) {
      pCustomerName = new string;
      *pCustomerName = *operand.pCustomerName;
}
Estimator& Estimator::operator = (const Estimator& operand) {
      pCustomerName = new string;
      *pCustomerName = *sourceObject.pCustomerName;
      iStyle = operand.iStyle;
      iStyleCost = operand.lStyleCost;
      iBedrooms = operand.iBedrooms;
      iBedroomCost = operand.lBedroomCost;
      iBathrooms = operand.iBathrooms;
      lBathroomCost = operand.lBathroomCost;
      lCustomerCost = operand.lCustomerCost;
      return *this;
}
...
```


Figure 7-2 Estimator.cpp

5. Build and execute the Building Estimator program. Enter values for each of the variables that are used to calculate building estimates. Figure 7-3 shows the output from a completed version of the Building Estimator program after entering some data for the first customer.

Be sure to enter only integers when the program prompts you for numeric values. The basic functionality of the program is fairly simple in order to allow you to concentrate on the class techniques presented in this chapter. The program does not include any error checking or ways of validating user input. Therefore, if you try to crash the program, you will probably succeed.

6. Press any key to close the Building Estimator program window.
7. Select **Close Solution** from the File menu to close the BuildingEstimator solution.

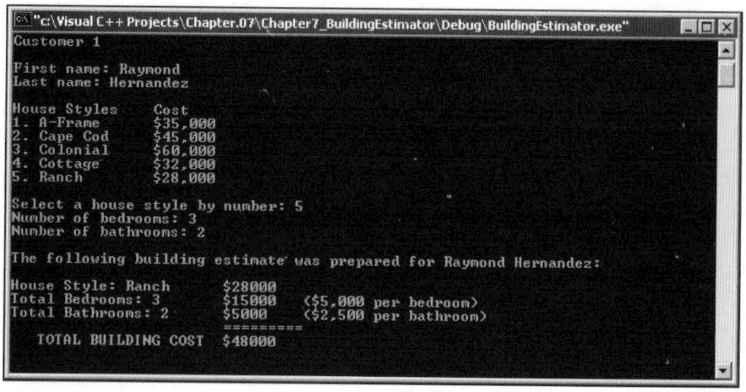

```
"c:\Visual C++ Projects\Chapter.07\Chapter7_BuildingEstimator\Debug\BuildingEstimator.exe"
Customer 1

First name: Raymond
Last name: Hernandez

House Styles    Cost
1. A-Frame      $35,000
2. Cape Cod     $45,000
3. Colonial     $60,000
4. Cottage      $32,000
5. Ranch        $28,000

Select a house style by number: 5
Number of bedrooms: 3
Number of bathrooms: 2

The following building estimate was prepared for Raymond Hernandez:

House Style: Ranch      $28000
Total Bedrooms: 3       $15000    ($5,000 per bedroom)
Total Bathrooms: 2      $5000     ($2,500 per bathroom)
                        =========
   TOTAL BUILDING COST  $48000
```

Figure 7-3 Output of Building Estimator program

INTRODUCTION

In Chapter 5 you learned about object-oriented programming techniques and basic class concepts. This chapter continues the discussion of class concepts by introducing various techniques for manipulating objects.

Classes are a fundamental, yet complex, feature of C++, and the topics in this chapter cover more advanced aspects of classes. As you work through this chapter, remember that your ultimate goal is creating Visual C++ programs using Microsoft Foundation Classes, not creating C++ programs that use standard classes. Although class concepts theory is invaluable in helping you understand advanced programming concepts and progressing further in computer science, this chapter mainly focuses on *how* to use some advanced class concepts in your programs. Having a basic understanding of how to implement the topics presented in this chapter will enable you to work with Microsoft Foundation Classes, which make use of advanced class features.

ADVANCED CONSTRUCTORS

In Chapter 5, the subject of constructors was touched on in order to provide a mechanism for initializing data members. Constructors, however, can do more than initialize data members. They can execute member functions and perform other types of initialization routines that a class may require when it first starts. The following constructor techniques will be discussed:

- Default constructor
- Parameterized constructors
- Initialization lists
- Copy constructor

First, you will learn about the default constructor.

Default Constructor

The **default constructor** does not include parameters, and is called for any declared objects of its class to which you do not pass arguments. But, before diving into default constructors, let's review what you already know about constructor functions. You define and declare constructor functions the same way you define other functions, although you do not include a `return` type because constructor functions do not return values. For example, in Figure 7-4 the constructor function for the Payroll class initializes the dFedTax and dStateTax data members, which are respectively assigned a federal tax rate of 28% and a state tax rate of 5%. The constructor function prototype is declared in the interface file, and the constructor function itself is declared in the implementation file.

7

```
// Payroll.h
#pragma once
#include <iostream>
using namespace std;
class Payroll {
public:
      Payroll();
      void setFedTax(double);
private:
      double dFedTax;
      double dStateTax;
};
// Payroll.cpp
#include" Payroll.h"
Payroll::Payroll() {
      dFedTax = .28;
      dStateTax = .05;
}
void Payroll::setFedTax(double dTax) {
      dFedTax = dTax;
}
```

Constructor function declaration

Constructor function definition

Figure 7-4 Constructor function for the Payroll class

The constructor function in Figure 7-4 is an example of a default constructor. You instantiate an object based on a default constructor function using the syntax ***`classname object_name;`***. For example, to declare an object named currentEmployee using the Payroll object's default constructor function, you use the statement `Payroll currentEmployee;`.

In addition to initializing data members and executing member functions, default constructors perform various types of behind-the-scenes class maintenance. For this reason, if you do not declare and define one in your code, Visual C++ automatically supplies a default constructor. Good programming technique dictates, however, that you should always create a default constructor for your class, even if you do not need to write your own default constructor to initialize data members and perform other initialization tasks.

You need to supply a default constructor because once you create a parameterized constructor, the Visual C++-supplied default constructor is no longer available. A parameterized constructor allows a client to pass initialization values to your class during object instantiation. If you create a parameterized constructor for your class but not a default constructor, a client will receive a compile error if he or she attempts to instantiate an object based on your class using the default constructor. Figure 7-5 shows an example of the Payroll class that contains a single parameterized constructor that accepts federal and state income tax percentages. The statement in the main() function is illegal because it attempts to instantiate an object using the missing default constructor.

```
// Payroll.h
#pragma once
#include <iostream>
using namespace std;
class Payroll {
public:
     Payroll(double, double);
     void setFedTax(double);
private:
     double dFedTax;
     double dStateTax;
};
// Payroll.cpp
#include" Payroll.h"
Payroll::Payroll(double dFed, double dState) {
     dFedTax =.28;
     dStateTax =.05;
}
void Payroll::setFedTax(double dTax) {
     dFedTax = dTax;
}
void main() {
     Payroll currentEmployee;
     ...
}
```


Figure 7-5 Payroll class missing default constructor function

For now, do not worry about the syntax of the parameterized constructor function in Figure 7-5. Parameterized constructors will be discussed shortly.

If you do not need the default constructor, simply leave the function body empty. For example, to include an empty default constructor for the Payroll class, include the statement `Payroll();` in the interface file and the following definition in the implementation file:

```
Payroll::Payroll(){
// empty function body
}
```

Figure 7-6 shows a corrected version of the Payroll class with an empty default constructor function.

```
// Payroll.h
#pragma once
#include <iostream>
using namespace std;
class Payroll {
public:
      Payroll();
      Payroll(double, double);
      void setFedTax(double);
private:
      double dFedTax;
      double dStateTax;
};
// Payroll.cpp
#include" Payroll.h"
Payroll::Payroll() {
      // empty function body
}
Payroll::Payroll(double dFed, double dState) {
      dFedTax =.28;
      dStateTax =.05;
}
void Payroll::setFedTax(double dTax) {
      dFedTax = dTax;
}
void main() {
      Payroll currentEmployee;
      ...
}
```

Empty default constructor function

Figure 7-6 Payroll class after adding empty default constructor function

Next you will start creating the Building Estimator program.

To create the Estimator.h interface file:

1. Create a new Win32 Project named **BuildingEstimator** in the **Chapter.07** folder in your Visual C++ Projects folder. Be sure to clear the **Create directory for Solution** check box in the New Project dialog box. In the Application Settings tab of the Win32 Application Wizard dialog box, select **Console application** as the application type, click the **Empty project** check box, and then click the **Finish** button.
2. Use Class Wizard to add a new class named **Estimator** to the Building Estimator project by selecting **Add Class** from the **Project** menu.
3. In the Estimator.h file, add the following statements after the `#pragma once` statement to give the class access to the iostream class, string class, and the standard namespace:

```
#include <iostream>
#include <string>
using namespace std;
```

4. Add to the end of the public declaration section the following statements that declare various functions for setting and retrieving data members in the Estimator class. For example, the setCustomerName() function sets the customer name in the sCustomerName variable (which you will create next)

using a string parameter. You retrieve the value in the sCustomerName variable using the getCustomerName() member function.

```
void setCustomerName(string);
string getCustomerName(void);
void setHouseStyle(int);
string getHouseStyle(void);
long getStyleCost(void);
void setBedrooms(int);
int getBedrooms(void);
long getBedroomCost(void);
void setBathrooms(int);
int getBathrooms(void);
long getBathroomCost(void);
long calcCustomerCost(void);
long getCustomerCost(void);
```

5. Next, add the following `private` declaration section and `private` data members. Each of these data members stores a specific piece of information that relates to a customer's estimate. For example, the iStyle variable contains an integer representing the selected building style. Notice that the pCustomerName variable, which stores the customer name in a string class variable, is declared as a pointer. You will instantiate the pCustomerName pointer variable on the heap in the class constructor function.

```
private:
        string* pCustomerName;
        int iStyle;
        long lStyleCost;
        int iBedrooms;
        long lBedroomCost;
        int iBathrooms;
        long lBathroomCost;
        long lCustomerCost;
```

The allocation and deallocation of memory is automatically managed for any string class variables that you declare on the stack. For this reason, there is no good reason to declare a single string class variable on the heap, although you would want to declare a dynamic array of string class objects on the heap. However, the pCustomerName string class variable is declared on the heap in order to demonstrate some of the object manipulation techniques that are presented in this chapter.

Next, you will create the Estimator.cpp implementation file. Included on your Data Disk is a file named EstimatorFunctionDefinitions.cpp that you can use to copy the function definitions to your project so you do not have to spend too much time typing. If you do not have access to a Data Disk, then type the program as shown in the figures in the following steps.

To create the function definitions in the Estimator.cpp implementation file:

1. Open the **Estimator.cpp** file in the Code Editor window.
2. As shown in Figure 7-7, add statements to the constructor function so it initializes the `class` data members. Notice that the pCustomerName variable is instantiated on the heap.

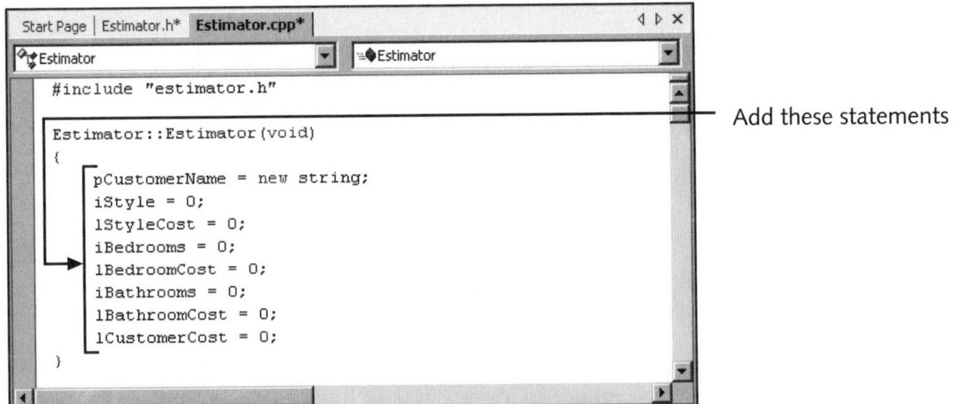

Figure 7-7 Modified constructor function in the Estimator class

3. Open the **EstimatorFunctionDefinitions.cpp** file on your Data Disk by selecting the **File** command on the **Open** submenu of the **File** menu. Copy the entire contents of the file by selecting the **Select All** command from the **Edit** menu, and then by selecting the **Copy** command from the **Edit** menu. Close the **EstimatorFunctionDefinitions.cpp** file by selecting the **Close** command from the **File** menu.
4. Open the **Estimator.cpp** file in the Code Editor window and paste the function definitions after the destructor function definition by selecting the **Paste** command from the **Edit** menu. Figure 7-8 shows the definitions for the set and get functions.

```
void Estimator::setCustomerName(string sCustName)
{
       *pCustomerName = sCustName;
}
string Estimator::getCustomerName(void)
{
    return *pCustomerName;
}
void Estimator::setHouseStyle(int iHouse)
{
       iStyle = iHouse;
       switch (iHouse) {
               case 1: // A-Frame
                          lStyleCost = 35000;
                          break;
               case 2: // Cape Cod
                          lStyleCost = 45000;
                          break;
               case 3: // Colonial
                          lStyleCost = 60000;
                          break;
               case 4: // Cottage
                          lStyleCost = 32000;
                          break;
               case 5: // Ranch
                          lStyleCost = 28000;
                          break;
               default:
                          lStyleCost = 0;
       }
}
long Estimator::getStyleCost(void)
{
       return lStyleCost;
}
string Estimator::getHouseStyle(void) const
{
        string sStyle;
        switch (iStyle){
                case 1: //A-Frame
                     sStyle = "A-Frame";
                     break;
                case 2: //Cape Cod
                     sStyle = "Cape Cod";
                     break;
                case 3: //Colonial
                     sStyle = "Colonial";
                     break;
                case 4: //Cottage
                     sStyle = "Cottage";
                     break;
                case 5: //Ranch
                     sStyle = "Ranch";
                     break;
                default:
                     sStyle = "";
                     break;
        }
        return sStyle;
}
void Estimator::setBedrooms(int iBeds)
```

Figure 7-8 Estimator class member function definitions

```
{
    iBedrooms = iBeds;
    lBedroomCost = 5000 * iBeds;
}
int Estimator::getBedrooms(void)
{
    return iBedrooms;
}
long Estimator::getBedroomCost(void)
{
    return lBedroomCost;
}
void Estimator::setBathrooms(int iBaths)
{
    iBathrooms = iBaths;
    lBathroomCost = 2500 * iBaths;
}
int Estimator::getBathrooms(void)
{
    return iBathrooms;
}
long Estimator::getBathroomCost(void)
{
    return lBathroomCost;
}
long Estimator::calcCustomerCost(void)
{
    lCustomerCost = lStyleCost + lBedroomCost + lBathroomCost;
    return lCustomerCost;
}
long Estimator::getCustomerCost(void)
{
    return lCustomerCost;
}
```

Figure 7-8 Estimator class member function definitions (continued)

5. Scroll down in the file until you see the getCustomerCost() member function definition shown in Figure 7-9. You will see two global function prototypes and a global variable declaration, followed by the main() function. The first global function, curCustomerName() (located directly below the main() function), is used for building the global sName variable with the client's first and last names after the names are received from the user via the cin statement. The second global function, curCustomerEstimate(), uses cin statements to gather building preferences from the user. You pass to the curCustomerEstimate() function a reference to the currently instantiated object. The Estimator class's members are then called through the object reference. The curCustomerEstimate() function may be intimidating at first. Actually, it is mostly composed of cout statements for displaying information from the user. (Several of the cout statements include \t escape characters to better format the output to the screen.)

```
void curCustomerName();
void curCustomerEstimate(Estimator&);
string sName;
void main() {
       cout << "New Home Building Estimator " << endl;
       cout << "--------------------------------" << endl << endl;
       cout << "Customer 1" << endl << endl;
       curCustomerName();
       Estimator customer1;
       customer1.setCustomerName(sName);
       curCustomerEstimate(customer1);
}
void curCustomerName(){
       string sInput;
       cout << "First name: ";
       cin >> sInput;
       sName = sInput;
       sName += " ";
       cout << "Last name: ";
       cin >> sInput;
       sName += sInput;
       cout << endl;
}
void curCustomerEstimate(Estimator& curCustomer){
       int iInput;
       cout << "House Styles \tCost" << endl;
       cout << "1. A-Frame \t$35,000" << endl;
       cout << "2. Cape Cod \t$45,000" << endl;
       cout << "3. Colonial \t$60,000" << endl;
       cout << "4. Cottage \t$32,000" << endl;
       cout << "5. Ranch \t$28,000" << endl << endl;
       cout << "Select a house style by number: ";
       cin >> iInput;
       curCustomer.setHouseStyle(iInput);
       cout << "Number of bedrooms: ";
       cin >> iInput;
       curCustomer.setBedrooms(iInput);
       cout << "Number of bathrooms: ";
       cin >> iInput;
       curCustomer.setBathrooms(iInput);
       cout << endl;
       cout << "The following building estimate was prepared for "
              << curCustomer.getCustomerName() << ":"
              << endl << endl;
       cout << "House Style: " << curCustomer.getHouseStyle()
              << "\t$" << curCustomer.getStyleCost() << endl;
       cout << "Total Bedrooms: " << curCustomer.getBedrooms()
              << "\t$" << curCustomer.getBedroomCost()
              << "\t ($5,000 per bedroom)" << endl;
       cout << "Total Bathrooms: " << curCustomer.getBathrooms()
              << "\t$" << curCustomer.getBathroomCost()
              << "\t ($2,500 per bathroom)" << endl;
       cout << "\t\t\t=========" << endl;
       cout << "TOTAL BUILDING COST\t$"
              << curCustomer.calcCustomerCost() << endl;
       cout << endl; cout << endl;
}
```

Figure 7-9 Estimator program's main() and global functions

6. Build and execute the project. Enter a customer's first and last name, and select the style house and the number of bedrooms and bathrooms. After entering the required information, the total estimate for the customer's house appears. After the program finishes executing, press any key to return to Visual C++.

Parameterized Constructors

As was mentioned earlier, a parameterized constructor allows a client to pass initialization values to your class during object instantiation. The constructor function in Figure 7-4 assigns default values to the dFedTax and dStateTax data members. Instead of assigning default values, you can allow a client to pass in the values for these data members by designing the constructor function with parameters, as shown in Figure 7-5. First, you include a function prototype such as `Payroll(double, double);` in the interface file. Then, you write the constructor function definition in the implementation file as follows:

```
Payroll::Payroll(double dFed, double dState) {
  dFedTax = dFed;
  dStateTax = dState;
}
```

7

Because you should always keep your data members private, the Payroll() constructor function in the preceding code assigns the parameters passed by the client to the private dFedTax and dStateTax data members.

Overloaded Functions

Any type of C++ function, whether a global function or member function, can be overloaded. An **overloaded function** refers to multiple functions within a program that share the same name, but that accept different parameters. Each version of an overloaded function must accept different parameters or you will receive a compiler error. You overload functions when you want to execute a different set of statements depending on the parameters and data types that are passed to the function. For example, you may have a function named downPayment() that calculates the down payment required for purchasing a home. You may have one version of the downPayment() function that accepts a single parameter consisting of the purchase price. Statements within the body of the downPayment() function assume that the down payment will be 10% and calculate the amount accordingly. The following code shows an example of the downPayment() function that accepts a single parameter:

```
double downPayment(double dPrice) {
  double dPercentDown = .1;
  return dPrice * dPercentDown;
}
```

You can overload the downPayment() function so that a second version of the function will be called if you supply a second parameter consisting of the percent that the function should use to calculate the down payment. The following code shows the overloaded downPayment() function that accepts two parameters:

```
double downPayment(double dPrice, double dPercent) {
  double dPercentDown = dPercent;
  return dPrice * dPercentDown;
}
```

C++ knows which version of the overloaded downPayment() function to execute and responds to the parameters that you pass to the function. For example, if you execute the statement `downPayment(185000);`, then Visual C++ calls the overloaded downPayment() function that accepts only a single parameter. If you execute the statement `downPayment(185000,.2);`, however, then Visual C++ calls the overloaded downPayment() function that accepts two parameters.

Overloaded Constructor Functions

Constructor functions can be overloaded, just like other functions. This means that you can instantiate different versions of a class, depending on the supplied parameters. Because constructors are called automatically when an object is instantiated, you only need to supply the correct number of arguments in order to call the correct overloaded constructor function. To instantiate an object based on a class constructor that accepts parameters, you append parentheses and the necessary parameters to the variable name when you instantiate the object. For example, if a constructor function for the Payroll class accepts a double parameter, then you can instantiate an object based on that constructor function using a statement similar to `Payroll currentEmployee(.12);`.

Remember that you do not include parentheses in the object declaration if you want the object to call the default constructor. Instead, you simply use a statement such as `Payroll currentEmployee;`. If you attempt to use parentheses when you instantiate an object based on a default constructor, you will receive a compile error when the compiler encounters a statement that attempts to use that object. For example, the statement `Payroll currentEmployee();` is incorrect.

To instantiate an object on the heap using a parameterized constructor, you append parentheses and the necessary parameters to the class name in the right operand. For example, the statement `Payroll* currentEmployee=new Payroll(.12);` declares a Payroll object on the heap and passes to it a single floating-point parameter. Note that you are not limited to instantiating objects using parameterized constructors; you can also call the default constructor by leaving the parentheses in the class name in the right operand empty, as in the statement `Payroll* currentEmployee=new Payroll();`.

Being able to overload a constructor function allows you to instantiate an object in multiple ways. For example, a client using the Payroll class, which calculates an employee's net pay, may live in a state that has no state income tax. For states without an income tax, clients would not have a value to pass into the dStateTax data member. To avoid this problem, you could rewrite the class so that it does not require state tax information. But the rewritten class would be useless to clients who live in states that have an income tax. A better solution is to overload the constructor by adding a function that accepts only a federal income tax parameter. Figure 7-10 shows a modified version of the Payroll class with two parameterized constructor functions: one for states that have a state income tax and one for states that do not have a state income tax. The first statement in the main()

function instantiates an object named employeeFL, for an employee in Florida, where there is no state income tax. The second statement in the main() function instantiates an object named employeeMA, for an employee in Massachusetts, where there is a 5.6% state income tax. Notice that the class also includes a default constructor function. This default constructor function assigns default values to the data members in the event that a client fails to call one of the parameterized constructor functions.

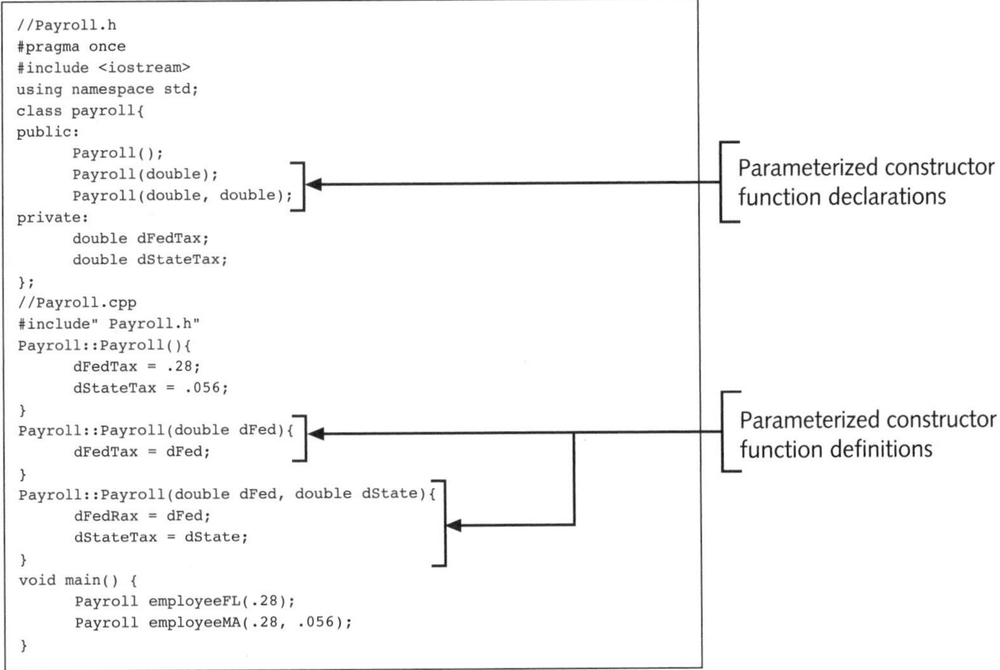

```
//Payroll.h
#pragma once
#include <iostream>
using namespace std;
class payroll{
public:
      Payroll();
      Payroll(double);
      Payroll(double, double);
private:
      double dFedTax;
      double dStateTax;
};
//Payroll.cpp
#include" Payroll.h"
Payroll::Payroll(){
      dFedTax = .28;
      dStateTax = .056;
}
Payroll::Payroll(double dFed){
      dFedTax = dFed;
}
Payroll::Payroll(double dFed, double dState){
      dFedRax = dFed;
      dStateTax = dState;
}
void main() {
      Payroll employeeFL(.28);
      Payroll employeeMA(.28, .056);
}
```


Figure 7-10 Parameterized constructor functions

Next you will add to the Building Estimator program a parameterized constructor for the customer's name.

Note that you can add constructors to a class using the Add Function Wizard, the same as you can with other member functions. However, in this chapter, you will manually add each constructor function in order to better understand the mechanics of how constructors operator.

To add a parameterized constructor for the customer's name to the Building Estimator program:

1. Open the **Estimator.h** file in the Code Editor window.
2. Add a member function declaration for the parameterized constructor after the default constructor, as shown in Figure 7-11.

3. Next, open the **Estimator.cpp** file in the Code Editor window. As shown in Figure 7-12, add the parameterized constructor function definition immediately after the default constructor function definition. The first statement creates the pCustomerName pointer variable on the heap, and the second statement copies the value of the sCustName parameter variable to the memory address that is the target of the pCustomerName pointer. The rest of the statements initialize the class's other data members.

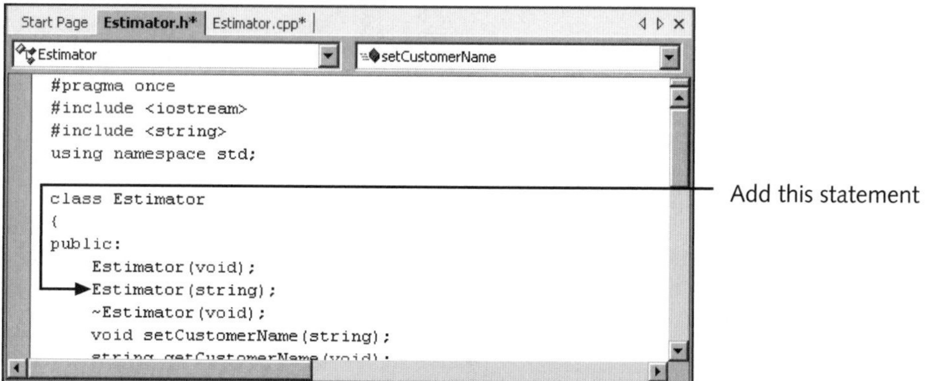

Figure 7-11 Parameterized constructor declaration added to Estimator.h

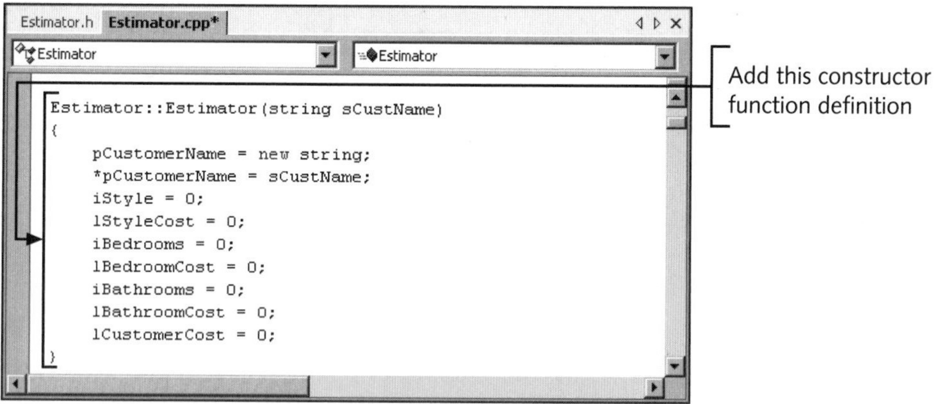

Figure 7-12 Parameterized constructor definition added to Estimator.cpp

4. As shown in Figure 7-13, modify the statements in the main() function that instantiate a new Estimator object so that the customer's name is passed as a parameter rather than assigned through the setCustomerName() function. Be sure to delete the `Estimator customer1;` and `customer1.setCustomerName(sName);` statements.

5. Rebuild and execute the program. The program should function the same as it did when you first built it.

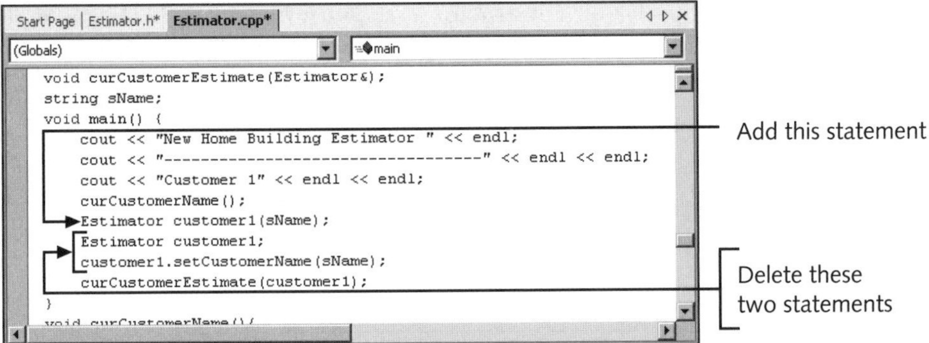

Start Page | Estimator.h* Estimator.cpp*
(Globals)
main
void curCustomerEstimate(Estimator&);
string sName;
void main() {
cout << "New Home Building Estimator " << endl;
cout << "--------------------------------" << endl << endl;
cout << "Customer 1" << endl << endl;
curCustomerName();
Estimator customer1(sName);
Estimator customer1;
customer1.setCustomerName(sName);
curCustomerEstimate(customer1);
}
Add this statement
Delete these two statements

Figure 7-13 main() function modified to instantiate a parameterized Estimator object

7

Initialization Lists

Initialization lists, or **member initialization lists**, are another way of assigning initial values to a class's data members. An initialization list is placed after a function header's closing parentheses, but before the function's opening curly brace. You start an initialization list with a single colon, followed by assignment statements separated by commas. The assignment statements in an initialization list must be in functional notation. **Functional notation** is another way of assigning a value to a variable, using the syntax `variable_name(value);`. For example, instead of using the statement `ctCount=10;` to assign an integer of 10 to a variable named ctCount, you can use the functional notation statement `ctCount(10);`.

Consider the following simple constructor that assigns parameter values to the Payroll class's dFedTax and dStateTax data members.

```
Payroll::Payroll(double dFed, double dState){
  dFedTax = dFed;
  dStateTax = dState;
}
```

Instead of using the preceding code to assign the parameter values to the data members, you can use the following initialization list:

```
Payroll::Payroll(double dFed, double dState)
  :dFedTax(dFed), dStateTax(dState){
}
```

Next, you will convert the Estimator class's constructor functions so that the numeric data members are initialized through initialization lists.

To convert the Estimator class's constructor functions so that the numeric data members are initialized through initialization lists:

1. Return to the **Estimator.cpp** file in the Code Editor window.

2. Modify the default constructor as shown in Figure 7-14. However, leave the initialization statement for the pCustomerName variable as it is.

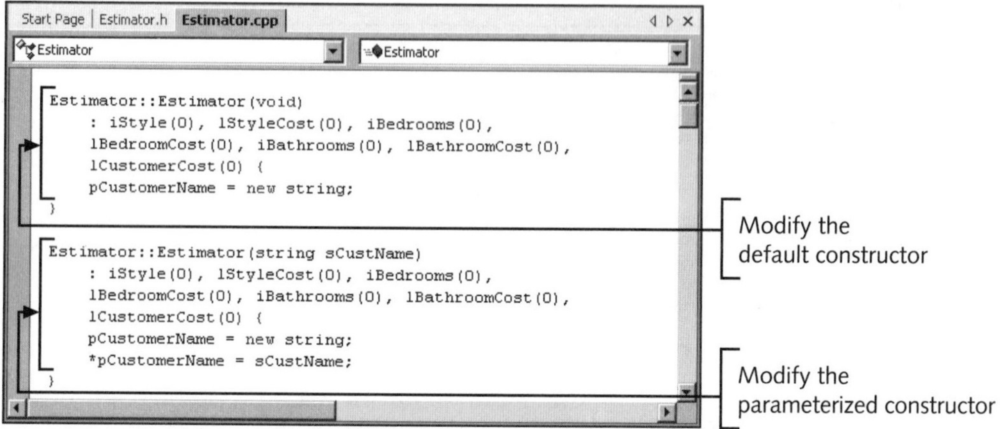

Figure 7-14 Constructors modified to include initialization lists

3. Also, as shown in Figure 7-14, modify the parameterized constructor so that it includes an initialization list, but leave the initialization statements for the pCustomerName variable as they are.
4. Build and execute the program. You should notice no changes in functionality.

Initialization lists can make more efficient use of memory because they do not require additional statements within the body of a constructor. The functional notation required by initialization lists, however, can be confusing because it resembles function calls. Therefore, except for the preceding exercise, you will continue to use standard assignment statements within the body of constructor functions for classes you create throughout the rest of this book. As you create larger and more complex programs, and become more comfortable with C++, you may want to experiment with initialization lists to see if they make your programs run more efficiently.

Copy Constructor

There will be times when you want to instantiate a new object based on an existing object. For example, you may have a class named Registration that is used for registering students in training classes. The Registration class may contain data members for the student's name, Social Security number, and so on, along with a data member representing the course for which the student is registering. Essentially, each object represents a single student enrollment into a single course. If a student registers for a second course, you do not necessarily want to go through the process of adding the student's vital statistics to a new object's data members. Instead, it is easier to make a copy of the existing object and only change the course to the new course for which the student wants to register.

There are two ways to create a new object from an existing object. You can use either the syntax `class new_object = existing_object;` or the syntax `class new_object(old_object);`. The first syntax declares a new object of the designated class and assigns to it the existing object. To use the first syntax to copy an existing Registration object named firstCourse to a new Registration object named secondCourse, you use the statement `Registration secondCourse = firstCourse;`.

The second syntax for copying an object resembles the syntax for instantiating an object based on a parameterized constructor. Instead of passing a variable or literal value, however, you pass an object. Recall from Chapter 5 that an object is actually a type of variable. Because you can pass a variable to a function, you can pass an object as well. Both syntax examples execute the default copy constructor, which you will learn about shortly. To use the second syntax to copy an existing Registration object named firstCourse to a new Registration object named secondCourse, you use the statement `Registration secondCourse(firstCourse);`.

7

Regardless of which syntax you use to copy an object, it is important to understand that *no default constructor executes for the new object*. Instead, C++ uses a copy constructor to exactly copy each of the first object's data members into the second object's data members in an operation known as **memberwise copying**. A **copy constructor** is a special constructor that is called when a new object is instantiated from an old object. Just as C++ supplies a default constructor if you fail to write one yourself, it also supplies a **default copy constructor** that automatically copies the members of the original object to the new object. Figure 7-15 shows how data members are copied with the default copy constructor, using the Registration class as an example.

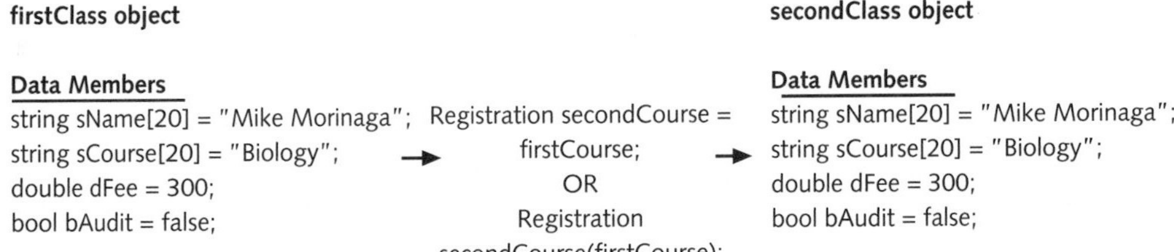
firstClass object
Data Members
string sName[20] = "Mike Morinaga";
string sCourse[20] = "Biology";
double dFee = 300;
bool bAudit = false;
Registration secondCourse =
firstCourse;
OR
Registration
secondCourse(firstCourse);
secondClass object
Data Members
string sName[20] = "Mike Morinaga";
string sCourse[20] = "Biology";
double dFee = 300;
bool bAudit = false;

Figure 7-15 Memberwise copying with the default copy constructor

A default copy constructor executes only when you initialize a new object based on an existing object, and not when you assign one existing object to another existing object. Initialization differs from assignment because initialization creates something new, whereas assignment assigns a new value to an object that already exists. For example, the default copy constructor is invoked for the statement `Registration secondCourse = firstCourse;` because a new object is actually being initialized, based on the old object. In contrast, the first two statements in the following code each perform object instantiations, executing the class's default constructor, not the copy constructor. The third statement only assigns the firstCourse object to the existing secondCourse object; it does not instantiate anything. The third statement does *not* execute the default copy constructor, or any other constructor for that matter.

```
Registration firstCourse;
Registration secondCourse;
secondCourse = firstCourse; // simple assignment statement
```

Later in this chapter you will learn how to overload the assignment operator in order to call the copy constructor during the assignment of one object to another.

The default copy constructor is sufficient for most purposes. It is not sufficient, however, when you need to use pointers to dynamically allocate memory. The memberwise copy operation that is performed by the default copy constructor exactly copies all members of an existing object to a new object, including memory addresses stored in pointers. The memberwise copy operation does not copy the information in the memory address, only the memory address itself. If you use the default copy constructor to create a new object from an existing object that is based on a class containing pointers, the new object and the existing object will contain pointers to the same memory addresses. When new and existing objects contain pointers to the same memory addresses, multiple objects in your program will share the same information. Objects that attempt to store and access information in the same memory address can cause chaos in your program. Figure 7-16 illustrates this scenario by showing how two string* pointers share the same memory address after you create a new Registration object by copying an existing Registration object.

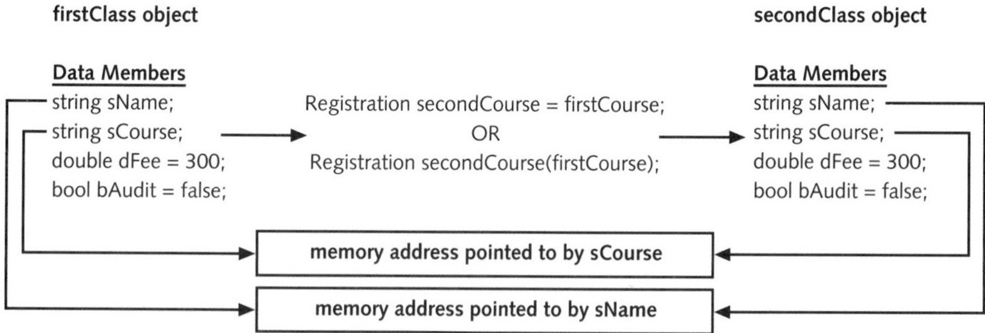
firstClass object
Data Members
string sName;
string sCourse;
double dFee = 300;
bool bAudit = false;
Registration secondCourse = firstCourse;
OR
Registration secondCourse(firstCourse);
secondClass object
Data Members
string sName;
string sCourse;
double dFee = 300;
bool bAudit = false;
memory address pointed to by sCourse
memory address pointed to by sName

Figure 7-16 Objects with pointers to the same memory address

As an example of copied objects that contain pointers to the same memory address, examine the modified Stocks class in Figure 7-17. The interface file declares a string pointer named pStockName that will point to the address of a string containing the stock's name. The constructor function accepts a single parameter representing the name of a stock, and then dynamically allocates memory for the pStockName. The value of the stock name parameter is then copied to the address pointed to by the pStockName pointer. The class also includes methods for getting and setting data members, along with a method for calculating the total value of a stock. The program's main() function instantiates a new Stocks object named stockPick1, passing to the constructor function the value *Cisco*. Then a new Stocks object named stockPick2 is copied from the stockPick1 object. The program then attempts to assign a new value of *Lucent* to the stock name of the stockPick1 object using the setStockName() function. Because both the stockPick1 and stockPick2 objects contain pointers to the same memory address for the stock name, the value of *Cisco* is overwritten by *Lucent*. Figure 7-18 shows the output.

```
//Stocks.h
#pragma once
#include <iostream>
#include <string>
using namespace std;
class Stocks {
public:
     Stocks(string);
     void setStockName(string);
     string getStockName();
     void setNumShares(int);
     int getNumShares();
     void setPricePerShare(double);
     double getPricePerShare();
     double calcTotalValue();
private:
     string* pStockName;
     int iNumShares;
     double dCurrentValue;
     double dPricePerShare;
};
//Stocks.cpp
#include "stocks.h"
Stocks::Stocks(string sName) {
     pStockName = new string;
     *pStockName = sName;
}
void Stocks::setNumShares(int iShares){
     iNumShares = iShares;
}
int Stocks::getNumShares(){
     return iNumShares;
}
void Stocks::setPricePerShare(double dPrice) {
     dPricePerShare = dPrice;
}
double Stocks::getPricePerShare() {
     return dPricePerShare;
}
void Stocks::setStockName(string sName){
     *pStockName = sName;
}
string Stocks::getStockName() {
     return *pStockName;
}
double Stocks::calcTotalValue() {
     dCurrentValue = iNumShares*dPricePerShare;
     return dCurrentValue;
}
```

Figure 7-17 Stocks class program with objects containing pointers to the same memory address

```
void main() {
     Stocks stockPick1("Cisco");
     stockPick1.setNumShares(100);
     stockPick1.setPricePerShare(68.875);
     Stocks stockPick2(stockPick1);
     stockPick2.setStockName("Lucent");
     stockPick2.setNumShares(200);
     stockPick2.setPricePerShare(59.5);
     cout << "The current value of your stock in "
          << stockPick1.getStockName() << " is $"
          << stockPick1.calcTotalValue()
          << "." << endl;
     cout << "The current value of your stock in "
          << stockPick2.getStockName() << " is $"
          << stockPick2.calcTotalValue()
          << "." << endl;
}
```

New object created by copying an existing object

Figure 7-17 Stocks class program with objects containing pointers to the same memory address (continued)

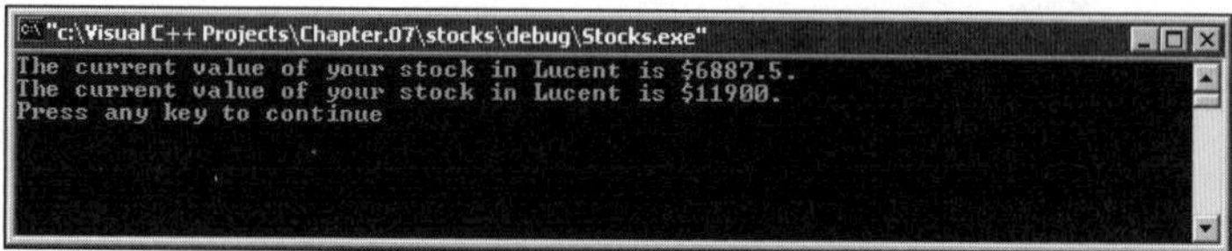

Figure 7-18 Output of Stocks class program with objects containing pointers to the same memory address

The Stocks class in Figure 7-17 does not include a default constructor so that you can focus on the use of the copy constructor. Remember that it is good programming practice, however, to always include a default copy constructor in your classes.

To prevent copied objects in your program from sharing pointers to the same memory address, you must write your own copy constructor. Copy constructors are identical to standard constructors, except they must accept a single call-by-reference parameter to an object preceded by the `const` keyword to indicate to the compiler that the original object is not to be modified in any way. The syntax for a copy constructor declaration is *`class_name(const class_name& object_name);`*. The call-by-reference object parameter in a copy constructor represents the object being copied. When an object reference parameter in a member function is preceded by the `const` keyword, the parameter is referred to as a **constant parameter**. You use a constant parameter in a copy constructor to assign values to a new object's data members. Once an object has been passed by reference to a function, you can refer to its data members by using the parameter name and the member selection operator.

Constant parameters are not restricted to use with copy constructors; you can use them with any object reference in a member function. The use of constant parameters in a member function is considered good programming practice because they clearly indicate which objects should not be modified by a member function. You can almost think of constant parameters as a "reminder" in the event that you forget that an object should not be modified. If you accidentally attempt to modify a constant parameter in a member function, you will receive a compile error.

The following code shows an example of a constructor function for the Stocks class that dynamically allocates new memory for the stock name for any new Stocks objects created by copying an existing object. Like the code in the constructor function, memory is dynamically allocated for the pStockName pointer. Because you do not yet know the name of the new stock, however, the old name is copied to the new memory address using the statement `*pStockName = *sourceStock.pStockName;`. Notice that both operands in the statement use the de-reference operator to copy the value that is the target of the original pointer to the memory address that is the target of the new pointer. This ensures that each name will be stored in its own memory address where you can safely manipulate it without affecting the data members of the other object.

```
// Stocks.h
...
Stocks(const Stocks&); // copy constructor declaration
...
// Stocks.cpp
Stocks::Stocks(const Stocks& sourceStock) {
  pStockName = new string;
  *pStockName = *sourceStock.pStockName;
}
```

Figure 7-19 shows a new version of the Stocks class with a copy constructor, and Figure 7-20 shows the program's output.

```
//Stocks.h
#pragma once
#include <iostream>
#include <string>
using namespace std;
class Stocks {
public:
     Stocks(string);
     Stocks(const Stocks&);
     void setStockName(string);
     string getStockName();
     void setNumShares(int);
     int getNumShares();
     void setPricePerShare(double);
```

Copy constructor declaration

Figure 7-19 Stocks class program with objects containing pointers to the same memory address

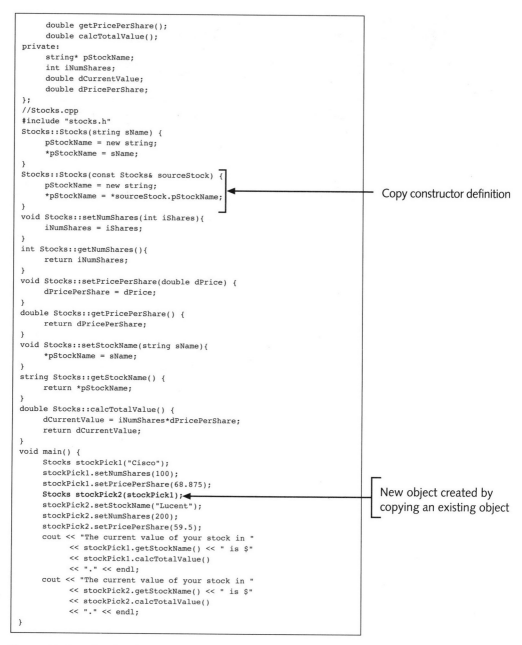

```
     double getPricePerShare();
     double calcTotalValue();
private:
     string* pStockName;
     int iNumShares;
     double dCurrentValue;
     double dPricePerShare;
};
//Stocks.cpp
#include "stocks.h"
Stocks::Stocks(string sName) {
     pStockName = new string;
     *pStockName = sName;
}
Stocks::Stocks(const Stocks& sourceStock) {
     pStockName = new string;
     *pStockName = *sourceStock.pStockName;
}
void Stocks::setNumShares(int iShares){
     iNumShares = iShares;
}
int Stocks::getNumShares(){
     return iNumShares;
}
void Stocks::setPricePerShare(double dPrice) {
     dPricePerShare = dPrice;
}
double Stocks::getPricePerShare() {
     return dPricePerShare;
}
void Stocks::setStockName(string sName){
     *pStockName = sName;
}
string Stocks::getStockName() {
     return *pStockName;
}
double Stocks::calcTotalValue() {
     dCurrentValue = iNumShares*dPricePerShare;
     return dCurrentValue;
}
void main() {
     Stocks stockPick1("Cisco");
     stockPick1.setNumShares(100);
     stockPick1.setPricePerShare(68.875);
     Stocks stockPick2(stockPick1);
     stockPick2.setStockName("Lucent");
     stockPick2.setNumShares(200);
     stockPick2.setPricePerShare(59.5);
     cout << "The current value of your stock in "
          << stockPick1.getStockName() << " is $"
          << stockPick1.calcTotalValue()
          << "." << endl;
     cout << "The current value of your stock in "
          << stockPick2.getStockName() << " is $"
          << stockPick2.calcTotalValue()
          << "." << endl;
}
```

Copy constructor definition

New object created by copying an existing object

Figure 7-19 Stocks class program with objects containing pointers to the same memory address (continued)

```
"c:\Visual C++ Projects\Chapter.07\stocks\debug\Stocks.exe"
The current value of your stock in Cisco is $6887.5.
The current value of your stock in Lucent is $11900.
Press any key to continue
```

Figure 7-20 Output of Stocks class program with a copy constructor

Next, you will instantiate a second object in the Building Estimator program by copying the first object.

To instantiate a second object in the Building Estimator program by copying the first object:

1. Return to the **Estimator.cpp** file in the Code Editor window.
2. Add to the end of the main() function the following code, which instantiates a new Estimator object named customer2 by copying the customer1 object. The curCustomerName() global function is called to gather the second customer's name into the sName global variable, which is then passed to the setCustomerName() member function. Finally, the curCustomerEstimate() function is called to collect the building information for the second customer.

```
cout << "Customer 2" << endl << endl;
Estimator customer2(customer1);
curCustomerName();
customer2.setCustomerName(sName);
curCustomerEstimate(customer2);
```

3. To the end of the main() function, add the following statements, which print each customer's name and estimate to the screen:

```
cout << "Customer, Estimate" << endl;
cout << "------------------" << endl;
cout << customer1.getCustomerName() << ", $"
     << customer1.getCustomerCost() << endl;
cout << customer2.getCustomerName() << ", $"
     << customer2.getCustomerCost() << endl;
```

4. Build and execute the program. Notice that when the customer names are printed at the end, the second customer's name prints twice. Because you have not yet added a copy constructor, calling the setCustomerName() member function in Step 2 overwrites the first customer's name because both objects' pCustomerName data members point to the same memory address. Figure 7-21 shows the output after adding some sample names.

7

```
"c:\Visual C++ Projects\Chapter.07\BuildingEstimator\Debug\BuildingEstimator.exe"
House Styles     Cost
1. A-Frame       $35,000
2. Cape Cod      $45,000
3. Colonial      $60,000
4. Cottage       $32,000
5. Ranch         $28,000

Select a house style by number: 3
Number of bedrooms: 4
Number of bathrooms: 2

The following building estimate was prepared for Erica Miller:

House Style: Colonial    $60000
Total Bedrooms: 4        $20000    ($5,000 per bedroom)
Total Bathrooms: 2       $5000     ($2,500 per bathroom)
                         =========
TOTAL BUILDING COST      $85000

Customer, Estimate
------------------
Erica Miller, $48000
Erica Miller, $85000
Press any key to continue
```

Figure 7-21 Output of Building Estimator program before adding a copy constructor

Because the Building Estimator program includes a data member (pCustomerName) for which memory is dynamically allocated, you also need to add a copy constructor.

To add a copy constructor to the Building Estimator program:

1. Open the **Estimator.h** file in the Code Editor window.
2. After the destructor declaration, add a declaration for the copy constructor as shown in Figure 7-22.

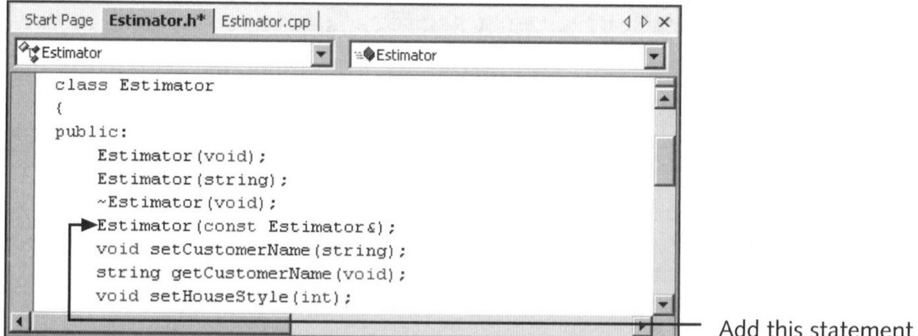

Figure 7-22 Copy constuctor declaration added to Estimator.h

3. Open the **Estimator.cpp** file in the Code Editor window.
4. Add the following copy constructor function definition after the destructor definition. Notice that the statements are identical to the statements in the parameterized constructor function that dynamically allocates memory to the pCustomerName data member.

```
Estimator::Estimator(const Estimator& sourceObject) {
        pCustomerName = new string;
        *pCustomerName = *sourceObject.pCustomerName;
}
```

5. Rebuild and execute the project. The pCustomerName data members for both objects should now be assigned and printed properly, as shown in Figure 7-23.

```
"c:\Visual C++ Projects\Chapter.07\BuildingEstimator\Debug\BuildingEstimator.exe"
House Styles    Cost
1. A-Frame      $35,000
2. Cape Cod     $45,000
3. Colonial     $60,000
4. Cottage      $32,000
5. Ranch        $28,000

Select a house style by number: 3
Number of bedrooms: 4
Number of bathrooms: 2

The following building estimate was prepared for Erica Miller:

House Style: Colonial   $60000
Total Bedrooms: 4       $20000   ($5,000 per bedroom)
Total Bathrooms: 2      $5000    ($2,500 per bathroom)
                        =========
TOTAL BUILDING COST     $85000

Customer, Estimate
------------------
Raymond Hernandez, $48000
Erica Miller, $85000
Press any key to continue
```

Figure 7-23 Output of Building Estimator program after adding a copy constructor

DESTRUCTORS

Just as a default constructor is called when a class object is first instantiated, a default destructor is called when the object is destroyed. A **default destructor** cleans up any resources allocated to an object once the object is destroyed. The default destructor is sufficient for most classes, except when you have allocated memory on the heap. Recall that variables you declare on the heap using the `new` operator must be manually removed with the `delete` operator. Even though an object might be destroyed, any variables declared on the heap would still exist, taking up valuable memory resources unless you were to manually destroy them. To delete any heap variables declared by your class, you must write your own destructor function.

Deleting heap variables is not the only task that destructor functions perform. You can also use destructor functions to complete any pending tasks or perform other types of system cleanup before an object is destroyed.

You create a destructor function using the name of the class, the same as a constructor function, preceded by a tilde (~). Destructor functions cannot be overloaded or accept parameters. Therefore, you can write only one destructor function for any given class. As with constructor functions, destructor functions are not defined with a data type because they do not return values. Figure 7-24 shows an example of a destructor declaration and definition for the Stocks class.

```
// Stocks.h
class Stocks {
public:
     Stocks(string);
     ~Stocks();
...
};
// Stocks.cpp
Stocks::~Stocks() {
     // destructor statements;
};
```

Destructor declaration

Destructor definition

Figure 7-24 Destructor declaration and definition for the Stocks class

A destructor is commonly called in two ways: (1) when a stack object loses scope because the function in which it is declared ends or (2) when a heap object is destroyed with the delete operator. Examine the modified version of the Stocks.cpp file in Figure 7-25. The main() function declares two Stocks objects, one on the stack and one on the heap. The constructor for the class declares a heap variable to contain the name of the stock. Because you have declared two Stocks objects, two string class heap variables will be created. To delete the string class heap variables, a destructor has been added that uses the statement `delete pStockName;`. So you can see when the destructor is called, the destructor includes a cout statement that prints *Destructor called*. Figure 7-26 shows the output.

```
// Stocks.cpp
#include "stocks.h"
Stocks::Stocks(string sName) {
     pStockName = new string;
     *pStockName = sName;
}
Stocks::~Stocks() {
     delete pStockName;
     cout << "Destructor called" << endl;
}
Stocks::Stocks(const Stocks& sourceStock) {
     pStockName = new string;
     *pStockName =  *sourceStock.pStockName;
}
void Stocks::setNumShares(int iShares) {
     iNumShares = iShares;
}
int Stocks::getNumShares(){
     return iNumShares;
}
void Stocks::setPricePerShare(double dPrice) {
     dPricePerShare = dPrice;
}
double Stocks::getPricePerShare() {
     return dPricePerShare;
}
void Stocks::setStockName(string sName){
     *pStockName = sName;
}
```

Destructor deleting the heap variable

Figure 7-25 Stocks class with a destructor

```
string Stocks::getStockName() {
     return *pStockName;
}
double Stocks::calcTotalValue() {
     dCurrentValue = iNumShares*dPricePerShare;
     return dCurrentValue;
}
void main() {
     Stocks stockPick1("Cisco");
     stockPick1.setNumShares(100);
     stockPick1.setPricePerShare(68.875);
     Stocks* stockPick2 = new Stocks("Lucent");
     stockPick2->setNumShares(200);
     stockPick2->setPricePerShare(59.5);
     cout << "The current value of your stock in "
          << stockPick1.getStockName() << " is $"
          << stockPick1.calcTotalValue()
          << "." << endl;
     cout << "The current value of your stock in "
          << stockPick2->getStockName() << " is $"
          << stockPick2->calcTotalValue()
          << "." << endl;
}
```

Variable created on the stack

Variable created on the heap

Figure 7-25 Stocks class with a destructor (continued)

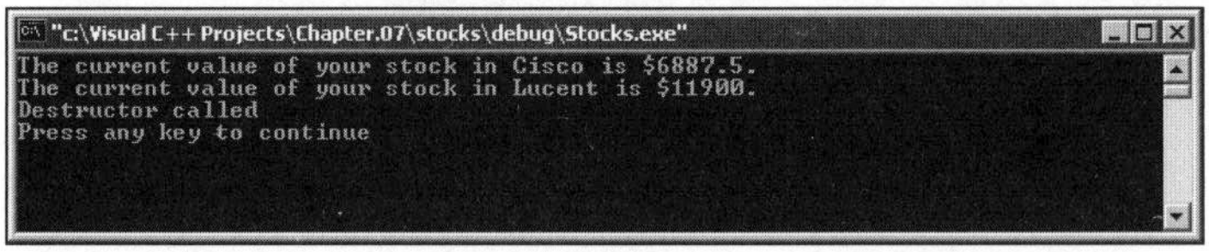

```
"c:\Visual C++ Projects\Chapter.07\stocks\debug\Stocks.exe"
The current value of your stock in Cisco is $6887.5.
The current value of your stock in Lucent is $11900.
Destructor called
Press any key to continue
```

Figure 7-26 Output of Stocks class with a destructor

Notice in Figure 7-25 that the destructor function is called only once. The stockPick1 object calls the destructor function when it is destroyed by the main() function going out of scope. The stockPick2 object does not call the destructor function because it is declared on the heap and must be deleted manually. To delete the stockPick2 object manually, add the statement `delete stockPick2;` to the main() function, as shown in Figure 7-27. Figure 7-28 shows the output.

```
//Stocks.cpp
void main() {
     Stocks stockPick1("Cisco");
     stockPick1.setNumShares(100);
     stockPick1.setPricePerShare(68.875);
     Stocks* stockPick2 = new Stocks("Lucent");
     stockPick2->setNumShares(200);
     stockPick2->setPricePerShare(59.5);
     cout << "The current value of your stock in "
          << stockPick1.getStockName() << " is $"
          << stockPick1.calcTotalValue()
          << "." << endl;
     cout << "The current value of your stock in "
          << stockPick2->getStockName() << " is $"
          << stockPick2->calcTotalValue()
          << "." << endl;
     delete stockPick2;
}
```


Figure 7-27 Stock class main() function after adding a delete statement

```
"c:\Visual C++ Projects\Chapter.07\stocks\debug\Stocks.exe"
The current value of your stock in Cisco is $6887.5.
The current value of your stock in Lucent is $11900.
Destructor called
Destructor called
Press any key to continue
```

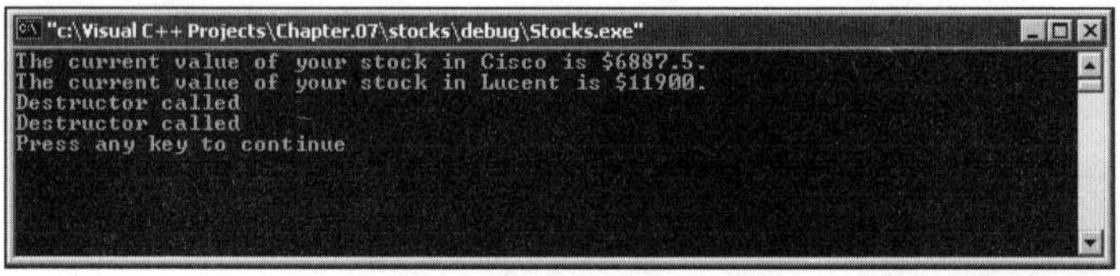

Figure 7-28 Output of Stocks class main() function after adding a delete statement

The Estimator class creates the pCustomerName data members on the heap. Therefore, you will add statements to a destructor function to delete them. You will also instantiate another Estimator object on the heap to represent a third customer. The third Estimator object instantiated on the heap will demonstrate how the destructor function is called when a heap object is deleted. The two other Estimator objects, which are instantiated on the stack, will demonstrate how the destructor function is called when an object goes out of scope.

To add statements to the destructor function and a heap object to the Estimator class:

1. Return to the **Estimator.cpp** file in the Code Editor window and locate the destructor function definition.

2. Add to the destructor function definition the two statements shown in Figure 7-29. The first statement deletes the pCustomerName data member, and the second statement prints the text *Estimate deleted* to the screen. Because pCustomerName is an array, brackets are appended to the `delete` keyword.

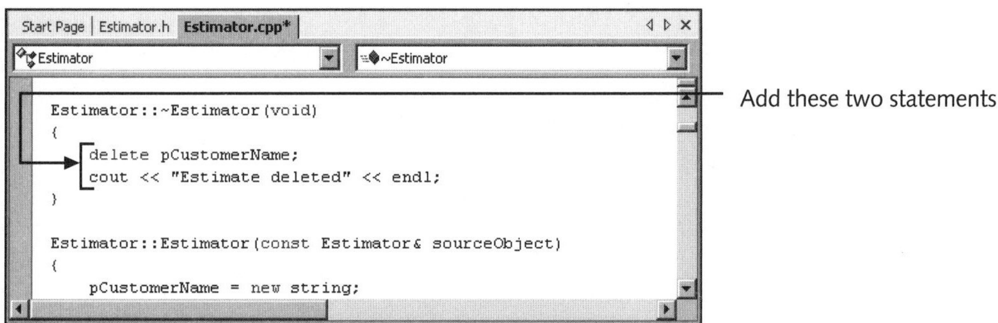

Figure 7-29 Statements added to the destructor function definition

3. Finally, modify the main() function as shown in Figure 7-30 so that a third object is instantiated. Unlike the other two objects, this third object is instantiated on the heap. The final statement deletes the heap object, which calls the destructor function.

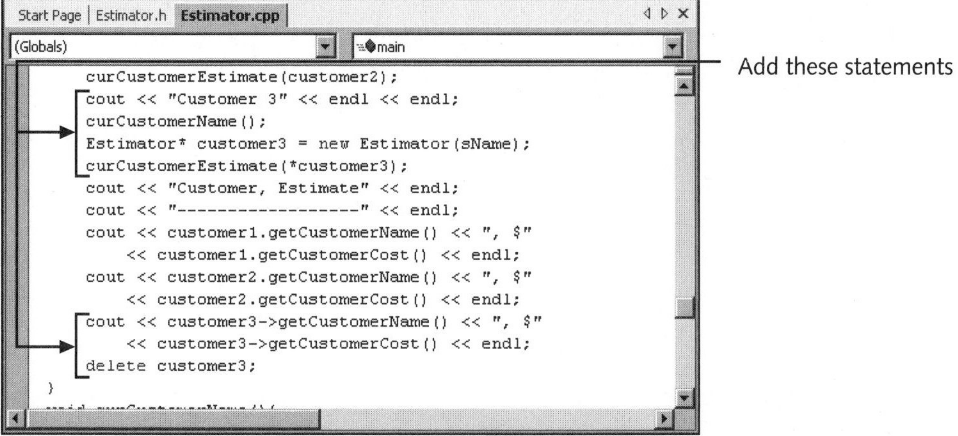

Figure 7-30 main() function modified to instantiate a third object

Notice that because you are accessing the customer3 object through a pointer, you must use the indirect member selection operator (->) instead of the member selection operator (.) to access its member functions.

4. Rebuild and execute the program. After entering data for all three customers, *Estimate deleted* should print three times, once for each object that was destroyed.

OPERATOR OVERLOADING

In C++, operators, such as the addition operator, are really internal C++ functions. For example, for the addition operator, the left and right operands are being passed as arguments to the internal addition operator *function,* which performs the actual addition operation. Because operators are really functions, you can overload them just as you can overload other types of functions. **Operator overloading** refers to the creation of multiple versions of C++ operators that perform special tasks required by a class in which an overloaded operator function is defined. You overload an operator when you want the operator to perform different operations, depending on the situation. For example, the default operation of the increment operator is to increase an operand by a value of 1. In stock trading, it is common to buy shares in blocks of 100. When you work with a Stocks class, you can overload the increment operator so that it increases a value by 100 only when used with objects of the Stocks class. The original implementation of the increment operator that increases values by 1 still functions when used with variables that are not objects of the Stocks class. You will see an example of how to overload the increment operator for the Stocks class later in this section. As another example, you may want to overload the carat operator (^) in one of your classes so that it returns the result of a number raised by a certain power. After writing the appropriate statements in an overloaded operator function for the ^ operator, you could use statements similar to the following to raise the value of a variable by a given power. Because the iNumber variable in the following code is assigned a value of 10, the value assigned to the iResult variable is 100000, which is the result of 10 raised to the fifth power.

```
int iNumber = 10;
int iResult = iNumber ^ 5;
```

You can overload almost any C++ operator, with the exception of the operators listed in Figure 7-31.

Operator	Name
.	Member selection
.*	Pointer-to-member selection
::	Scope resolution
? :	Conditional
#	Preprocessor symbol
##	Preprocessor symbol

Figure 7-31 C++ operators that cannot be overloaded

You create an overloaded operator function as either a class member function or a friend function of a class. The following operators must be overloaded as member functions:

- = assignment
- -> indirect member selection operator
- () function call
- [] subscript

There are no other special rules as to whether you create overloaded operator functions as member functions or friend functions. You are also not required to create an overloaded operator function as either a member function or a friend function. Overloaded operator functions can simply be created as global functions within your program. It is common practice, however, to create an overloaded operator function as either a member function or a friend function because overloaded operator functions usually need access to a class's `private` data members.

Overloaded operator functions defined as member functions and overloaded operator functions defined as global functions or friend functions have different parameter requirements. For example, if you overload the addition operator as a member function, then you need to include only a single parameter. However, if you overload the addition operator as either a global function or a friend function, then you need to include two parameters. The syntax used in this chapter is for overloaded operator functions defined as member functions.

To see a list of rules for creating overloaded functions, search in the index of the MSDN Library for the Operator Overloading topic, and then select the General Rules subtopic.

An overloaded binary operator function executes if the data types for each operand within a statement match the data types in the overloaded operator function's parameter list. At least one of the overloaded operator function's parameters must be of a class type. For unary operators that you overload as member functions, the operand to which you are applying the overloaded operator must be an object of the class that overloads the operator. If you use an overloaded operator in your program, but do not include the correct data types or class types for each operand in your statement, then the operator's default operation is performed. For example, you might overload the multiplication operator (*) to perform some special operation required by your class, provided that the left operand is of the Stocks data type and the right operand is of the `double` data type. However, if a statement in your program uses the multiplication operator, but does not include a Stocks data type as the left operand and a `double` data type as the right operand, then the default operation, multiplication, is performed.

Each type of operator (binary, unary, comparison, and so on) requires a slightly different type of function definition in order to overload an operator. Once you understand how to overload binary and unary operators, you should be able to figure out on your own how to overload other types of operators.

Overloading Binary Operators

A binary operator requires an operand before the operator and an operand after the operator. The multiplication sign (*) in the statement `iResult = 2 * 3;` is an example of a binary operator. Suppose in the Payroll class you want to create two overloaded operator functions for the binary addition operator +. Suppose also that you have instantiated three Payroll objects, ytdPay, firstWeekJan, and secondWeekJan, and that you have assigned values to their data members. The first overloaded addition operator function will add the dNetPay data members of two Payroll objects and assign the result to the dNetPay data member of a third Payroll object. The second overloaded addition operator function will add a `double` value to the dNetPay data member of one Payroll object and assign the result to the dNetPay data member of another Payroll object. After writing the overloaded operator functions, you will be able to use the addition operator in the following three ways:

```
// standard addition operation
int iNum = 20 + 30;
// adds the dNetPay data members of two Payroll objects
// and assigns the result to the dNetPay data member
// of a third object
ytdPay = firstWeekJan + secondWeekJan;
// adds a double value to the dNetPay data member
// of a Payroll object
ytdPay = ytdPay + 1000.00;
```

To overload a binary operator as a member function, you use the following overloaded function syntax:

```
type class:: operator binary_operator (const class&
     rightOperand) {
}
```

An overloaded operator function is defined with a type, just like other functions. The *`operator`* keyword designates a function definition as an overloaded operator function. The preceding syntax represents a binary overloaded operator, such as the addition operator. When you write a binary operator function, a temporary object representing the *left* operand of the unary statement is instantiated each time you call the function. The parameter in the parameter list represents the *right* operand. Recall that the `this` pointer identifies the object instance that called a function. In the case of an overloaded binary operator function, the `this` pointer refers to the temporary object instance created by the function itself. Because the `this` pointer is implied, you can refer to the temporary object's data members directly.

Good programming practice dictates that when using an object as a parameter you should use a reference to the class to prevent it from being copied by value. Additionally, you should declare each object parameter in an overloaded operator function as a constant parameter in order to ensure that the function does not modify the original object.

In the following example, the overloaded addition operator function will essentially build a new Payroll object and assign to its dNetPay data member the combined values of the two object operand's dNetPay data members. The new object is then returned to the statement that calls it. Because you are returning a Payroll object, the function is defined to `return` a data type of Payroll. Recall that classes are really user-defined data types. Because classes are actually data types, you can use them as a function's `return` value. The first statement in the function body instantiates a new Payroll object named ytdPay. The second statement uses the standard addition operator to add the values of the dNetPay data members of the leftOperand object reference (through the `this` pointer that represents a temporary instance of the left operand) and the rightOperand object reference parameter and assign the result to the dNetPay data member of the ytdPay object. Finally, the third statement returns the ytdPay object. To overload the addition operator + in the Payroll class, with each operand being of a Payroll object, you use the following code:

7

```
Payroll Payroll::operator + (const Payroll& amount) {
  Payroll ytdPay;
  ytdPay.dNetPay = this->dNetPay + amount.dNetPay;
  return ytdPay;
}
```

To execute the preceding overloaded operator, you use a statement similar to `ytdPay = firstWeekJan + secondWeekJan;`. Note that you do not append the data members to each operand because the overloaded operator function needs to receive a reference to an object, not a data member.

The right operand parameter in an overloaded binary operator function does not necessarily need to be of the same class as the left operand; it can also be of another data type. For example, you use the following function definition if you want the right operand in the preceding example to be of the `double` data type:

```
friend Payroll operator + (const double dAmount) {
  Payroll ytdPay;
  ytdPay.dNetPay = this->dNetPay + dAmount;
  return ytdPay;
}
```

The preceding overloaded operator may be used with the Payroll class if you want to add a holiday bonus or other type of additional compensation to the dNetPay data member of the ytdPay object. To execute the preceding overloaded operator and add a bonus of $1000 to the dNetPay data member of the ytdPay object, you would use a statement similar to the following:

```
ytdPay = ytdPay + 1000.00;
```

The following statement, however, would not execute the overloaded operator because the left and right operands are not of the correct data type. The left operand should be of the Payroll data type and the right operand should be of the double data type.

```
ytdPay = 1000.00 + ytdPay;
```

Figure 7-32 shows a completed version of the Payroll class with two overloaded addition operators. Figure 7-33 shows the output.

```
// Payroll.h
#pragma once
#include <iostream>
using namespace std;
class Payroll{
public:
     Payroll();
     Payroll(double);
     Payroll(double, double);
     double calcNetPay(double, double);
     double getNetPay();
     Payroll operator + (const Payroll&);
     Payroll operator + (const double);
private:
     double dFedTax;
     double dStateTax;
     double dNetPay;
};
// Payroll.cpp
#include "Payroll.h"
Payroll::Payroll(){
     dFedTax = .28;
     dStateTax = .05;
}
Payroll::Payroll(double dFed){
     dFedTax = dFed;
}
Payroll::Payroll(double dFed, double dState){
     dFedTax = dFed;
     dStateTax = dState;
}
double Payroll::calcNetPay(double dPay,double dHours) {
     double dGrossPay = dPay * dHours;
     double dCurFedTaxes = dGrossPay * dFedTax;
     double dCurStateTaxes = dGrossPay * dStateTax;
     dNetPay = dGrossPay - (dCurFedTaxes + dCurStateTaxes);
     return dNetPay;
}
double Payroll::getNetPay() {
     return dNetPay;
}
Payroll Payroll::operator + (const Payroll& amount) {
     Payroll ytdPay;
     ytdPay.dNetPay = this->dNetPay + amount.dNetPay;
     return ytdPay;
}
Payroll Payroll::operator + (const double dAmount){
     Payroll ytdPay;
     ytdPay.dNetPay = this->dNetPay + dAmount;
     return ytdPay;
}
```

Overloaded addition operator declarations

Overloaded addition operator definitions

Figure 7-32 Payroll class with two overloaded addition operators

```
void main(){
     Payroll firstWeekJan;
     Payroll secondWeekJan;
     Payroll ytdPay;
     cout << "Net pay for the 1st week in January is $";
     cout << firstWeekJan.calcNetPay(25.5,40) << endl;
     cout << "Net pay for the 2nd week in January is $";
     cout << secondWeekJan.calcNetPay(25.5,37.5) << endl;
     ytdPay = firstWeekJan + secondWeekJan;
     cout << "Year-to-date net pay is $";
     cout << ytdPay.getNetPay() << endl;
     ytdPay = ytdPay + 1000.00;
     cout << "Year-to-date net pay with bonuses is $";
     cout << ytdPay.getNetPay() << endl;
}
```

Statement that calls overloaded addition operator with two Payroll object parameters

Statement that calls overloaded addition operator with one Payroll object parameter and one double value parameter

Figure 7-32 Payroll class with two overloaded addition operators (continued)


```
"c:\Visual C++ Projects\Chapter.07\Payroll\Debug\Payroll.exe"
Net pay for the 1st week in January is $683.4
Net pay for the 2nd week in January is $640.688
Year-to-date net pay is $1324.09
Year-to-date net pay with bonuses is $2324.09
Press any key to continue
```

Figure 7-33 Output of Payroll class with two overloaded addition operators

Overloading Unary Operators

A unary operator requires a single operand either before or after the operator. For example, the increment operator (++), an arithmetic operator, is used for increasing an operand by a value of 1. If you have a variable named myNumber that contains the value 100, then the statement `++iMyNumber;` changes the value of the myNumber variable to 101. When you overload a unary operator as a member function, you declare the operator's overloaded function with a class *reference* data type instead of a `class` data type. You also do not include any parameters in the function definition. When you write a unary operator function, a temporary object representing the operand of the unary statement is instantiated each time you call the function. Instead of returning an entire object from the function, you return just the value of this temporary object using the `this` pointer.

The syntax for an overloaded unary operator function is as follows:

```
class& operator unary_operator () {
  statements;
  return *this;
}
```

The unary operators that you can overload are listed in Figure 7-34. Note that when overloading of increment and decrement operators is discussed in this section, only an explanation of how to overload the prefix forms of these operators is offered.

Overloading postfix increment and decrement operators requires some special coding techniques, which are too advanced for your purposes.

Operator	Description
!	Logical NOT
&	Address of
~	One's complement
*	Pointer de-reference
+	Unary plus
++	Increment
-	Unary negation
--	Decrement

Figure 7-34 Unary operators that can be overloaded

To see how to overload a unary operator, consider overloading the increment operator (++) in the Stocks class so that it increases the number of shares of a particular Stocks object by 100, instead of by the default value of 1. The default increment operator will still function if used with any type of variable other than a Stocks object. When used with the Stocks object, however, the increment operator will increase the iNumShares data member by a value of 100. The overloaded function definition for the increment operator that increases a Stocks object operand by a value of 100 is as follows:

```
Stocks& Stocks::operator ++ () {
  this->iNumShares += 100;
  return *this;
};
```

The preceding function requires only two statements: one statement to increment the iNumShares data member by 100 and another statement to return the value of the current object.

Figure 7-35 contains an abbreviated version of the Stocks program you have seen throughout this chapter, including the overloaded increment operator. Figure 7-36 shows the output.

```
//Stocks.h
#pragma once
#include <iostream>
#include <string>
using namespace std;
class Stocks {
public:
     Stocks(string);
     ~Stocks();
     Stocks(const Stocks&);
     Stocks& operator ++ ();
...
};
//Stocks.cpp
#include "stocks.h"
...
Stocks& Stocks::operator ++ () {
     this->iNumShares += 100;
     return *this;
};
...
void main() {
     Stocks stockPick1("Cisco");
     stockPick1.setNumShares(100);
     stockPick1.setPricePerShare(68.875);
     cout << "The value of your stock in "
           << stockPick1.getStockName() << " is $"
           << stockPick1.calcTotalValue() << "." << endl;
     ++stockPick1;
     cout << "After purchasing 100 additional shares, " << endl
           << "the value of your stock in "
           << stockPick1.getStockName() << " is $"
           << stockPick1.calcTotalValue()
           << "." << endl;
}
```

Overloaded increment operator declaration

Overloaded increment operator definition

Figure 7-35 Stock class with and overloaded increment operator

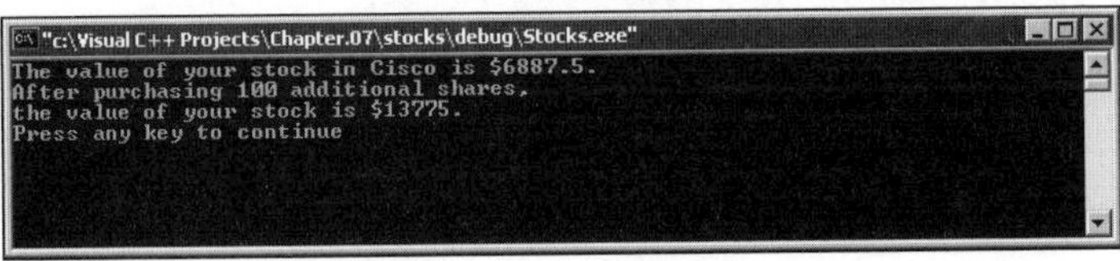

Figure 7-36 Output of Stocks class with an overloaded increment operator

Overloading the Assignment Operator

Next, you will overload the assignment operator so that it can be used to assign the data members of one object to the data members of another object of the same class. The overloaded operator examples you have seen in this section have instantiated new objects of a particular class, assigned values to the new object's data members, and then returned the object itself to the calling statement.

The syntax for overloading the assignment operator is similar to the syntax for overloading a unary operator in that you declare the assignment operator's overloaded function with a class *reference* data type instead of a `class` data type. However, you must also include a parameter that represents the right operand. A temporary object representing the left operand of the assignment statement is instantiated each time you call the function.

To overload the assignment operator in the Estimator class:

1. Open the **Estimator.h** file in the Code Editor window.
2. Add the following overloaded assignment operator function declaration after the copy constructor declaration.

```
Estimator& operator = (const Estimator&);
```

Remember that the assignment operator must be created as a member function, not as a friend function or a global function.

3. Open the **Estimator.cpp** file in the Code Editor window.
4. Add the following definition for the overloaded assignment operator after the copy constructor definition. Notice that the data members of the operand object are being assigned to the overloaded assignment operator function's temporary Estimator object. A reference to the temporary object is then returned using the `return*this;` statement.

```
Estimator& Estimator::operator = (const Estimator&
        operand) {
        pCustomerName = new string;
        *pCustomerName = *operand.pCustomerName;
        iStyle = operand.iStyle;
        lStyleCost = operand.lStyleCost;
        iBedrooms = operand.iBedrooms;
        lBedroomCost = operand.lBedroomCost;
        iBathrooms = operand.iBathrooms;
        lBathroomCost = operand.lBathroomCost;
        lCustomerCost = operand.lCustomerCost;
        return *this;
}
```

5. In the main() function, replace the statement `Estimator customer2 (customer1);` with the two statements shown in Figure 7-37 that demonstrate the overloaded assignment operator.

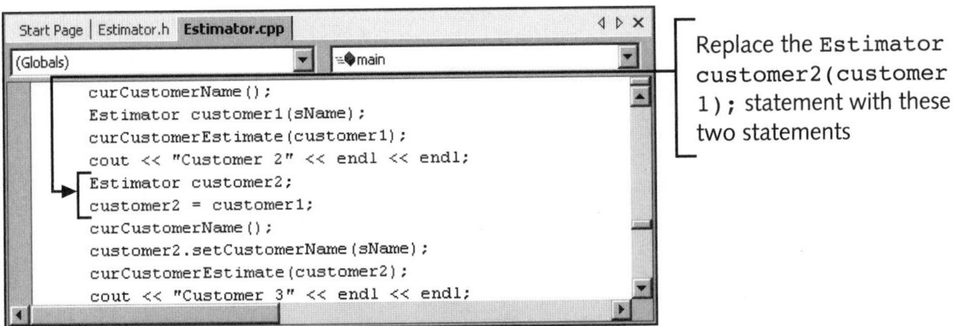
Start Page | Estimator.h | Estimator.cpp
(Globals)
main
curCustomerName();
Estimator customer1(sName);
curCustomerEstimate(customer1);
cout << "Customer 2" << endl << endl;
Estimator customer2;
customer2 = customer1;
curCustomerName();
customer2.setCustomerName(sName);
curCustomerEstimate(customer2);
cout << "Customer 3" << endl << endl;
Replace the Estimator customer2(customer1); statement with these two statements

Figure 7-37 main() function modified to use the overloaded assignment operator

6. Rebuild and execute the program. Although you should not see any difference in the way the program functions, you can see how useful overloading the assignment operator can be.

7

STATIC CLASS MEMBERS

When you first studied variables in Chapter 2, you learned how to use the `static` keyword when declaring a variable. When used with a local variable declaration, the `static` keyword changes the variable's storage duration to permanent. A local variable declared with the `static` keyword is *not* destroyed after its function or command block finishes executing. Instead, a static variable exists for the lifetime of the program.

You can also use the `static` keyword when declaring class members. `Static` class members, however, are somewhat different from `static` variables. When you declare a class member to be `static`, only one copy of that class member is created during a program's execution, regardless of how many objects of the class you instantiate. In contrast, each class object receives its own individual copies of non-static class members. Figure 7-38 illustrates the concept of `static` and non-static data members with the Payroll class by making the dFedTax and dStateTax data members `static`. It is much more efficient to make dFedTax and dStateTax `static` data members. The values of these data members will be exactly the same for all Payroll objects. Having them be non-static class members would create unnecessary duplication of information.

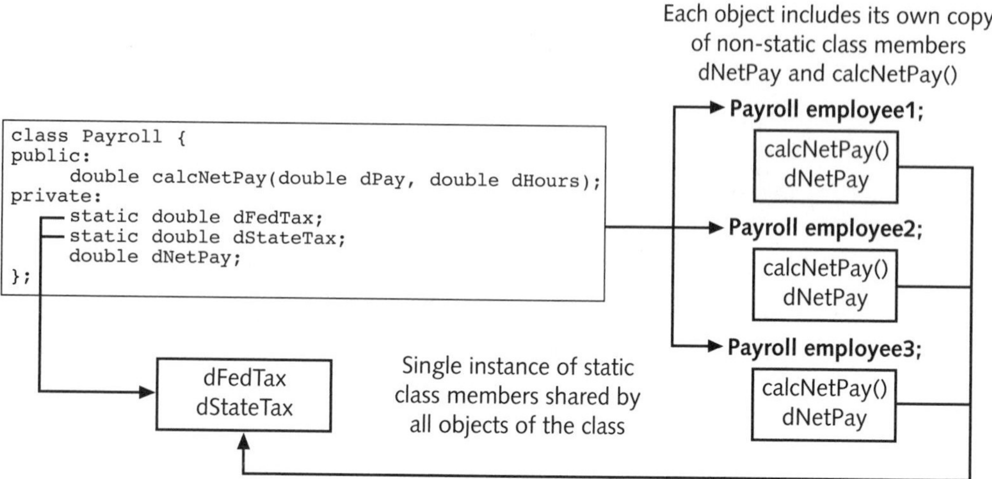

Figure 7-38 Multiple class objects with static and non-static data members

Next, you will learn about `static` data members and `static` member functions.

Static Data Members

You declare a `static` data member in your implementation file using the syntax `static` *`typename`*`;`, similar to the way you define a `static` variable. `Static` data members are bound by access specifiers, the same as non-static data members. This means that `public static` data members are accessible by anyone, whereas `private static` data members are available only to other functions in the class or to friend functions. When a program executes, each instantiated object can access the `static` data member, just as it would access non-static data members.

What happens if you want to assign an initial value to a `static` data member? You could use a statement in the class constructor, although doing so will reset a `static` variable's value to its initial value each time a new object of the class is instantiated. Instead, to assign an initial value to a `static` data member, you add a global statement to the implementation file using the syntax *`type class::variable=value;`*. Initializing a `static` data member at the global level ensures that it is only initialized when a program first executes—not each time you instantiate a new object. The type portion of the statement indicates the variable's data type as declared in the interface file. The *class*::*variable* portions of the statement are the class name, scope resolution operator, and the name of the variable (as declared in the interface file). Notice that even though the `static` data member's initialization statement is similar to the data member declaration in the interface file, it does not include the `static` keyword.

As an example of declaring and initializing a `static` data member, consider one of the most common uses of `static` data members: counting the number of a class's instantiated objects. To declare in the Stocks class a **static** data member named iStockCount, you add the statement **static int iStockCount;** to the interface file. Because a **static** data member is not associated with any particular object, you cannot initialize it in any constructor functions or the variable would be reinitialized each time you instantiated a new object of the class. To initialize the iStockCount data member to 0 (zero), you add to the implementation file the statement **int Stocks::iStockCount = 0;** at a global level, outside of any function definitions. To increment the iStockCount static data member by 1 each time a new Stocks object is instantiated, you add a statement to the constructor function similar to **++iStockCount;**. In order for the value stored in iStockCount to be valid, however, you must add code to the destructor function that decrements the iStockCount variable each time a Stocks object is destroyed. Figure 7-39 contains an example of the Stocks class, with the iStockCount **static** data member. Statements in the constructor and destructor increment and decrement the iStockCount variable each time a new Stocks object is created or destroyed. Figure 7-40 shows the program's output.

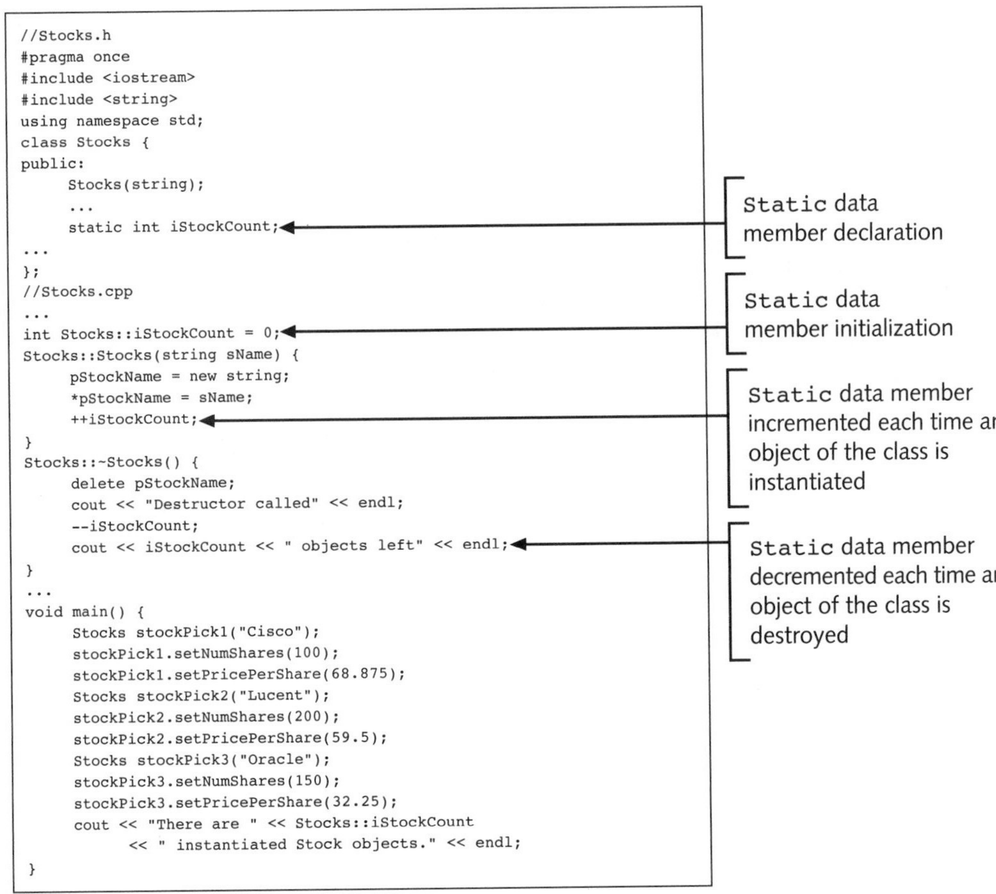

//Stocks.h
#pragma once
#include <iostream>
#include <string>
using namespace std;
class Stocks {
public:
Stocks(string);
...
static int iStockCount;
...
};
//Stocks.cpp
...
int Stocks::iStockCount = 0;
Stocks::Stocks(string sName) {
pStockName = new string;
*pStockName = sName;
++iStockCount;
}
Stocks::~Stocks() {
delete pStockName;
cout << "Destructor called" << endl;
--iStockCount;
cout << iStockCount << " objects left" << endl;
}
...
void main() {
Stocks stockPick1("Cisco");
stockPick1.setNumShares(100);
stockPick1.setPricePerShare(68.875);
Stocks stockPick2("Lucent");
stockPick2.setNumShares(200);
stockPick2.setPricePerShare(59.5);
Stocks stockPick3("Oracle");
stockPick3.setNumShares(150);
stockPick3.setPricePerShare(32.25);
cout << "There are " << Stocks::iStockCount
<< " instantiated Stock objects." << endl;
}
Static data member declaration
Static data member initialization
Static data member incremented each time an object of the class is instantiated
Static data member decremented each time an object of the class is destroyed

Figure 7-39 Stock class with a static data member that counts the number of a class's instantiated objects

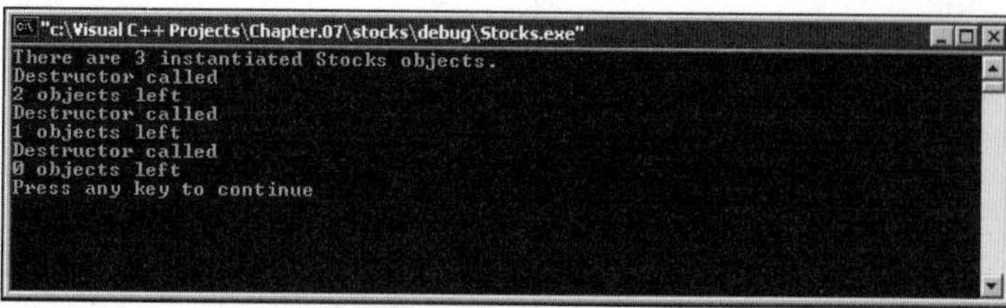

Figure 7-40 Output of Stocks class with a static data member that counts the number of a class's instantiated objects

In a member function, you can refer to a `static` data member directly, the same as you refer to other data members directly. For example, to assign a value of 10 to the iStockCount variable from inside one of the Stocks class's member functions, you simply use the statement `iStockCount=10;`. To refer to a `static` data member from outside a member function, you precede the variable name with the name of the class and the scope resolution operator. For example, to assign a value of 10 to the iStockCount `static` data member from within a main() function, you use the statement `Stocks::iStockCount=10;`.

You can refer to a `static` data member by appending its name and the member selection operator to *any* instantiated object of the same class, using syntax such as `stockPick.iStockCount`. By using the class name and the scope resolution operator instead of any instantiated object of the class, however, you more clearly identify the data member as `static`. Clearly identifying data members as `static` makes working with a program easier when you have not worked with it in a long time or when another programmer needs to modify your application.

As another example, consider a `static` Stocks `class` data member named dPortfolioValue that keeps track of the total value of all instantiated stocks. Instead of updating the dPortfolioValue data member in each object's constructor function, you update it each time the calcTotalValue() member function is called. Figure 7-41 shows an example of the Stocks `class` program with the dPortfolioValue `static` data member. The dPortfolioValue `static` data member is assigned an initial value of 0 (zero) in the implementation file. The main() method in the implementation file now instantiates three Stocks objects: stockPick1, stockPick2, and stockPick3. As the calcTotalValue() function executes for each object, stockPick1's value returns as 1087.50, stockPick2's value returns as 12850, and stockPick3's value returns as 1750. Each time the calcTotalValue() function executes, it increments the dPortfolioValue `static` data member by the value of each stockPick object. The dPortfolioValue `static` data member's total value of 23625 prints after the program calculates the value of each individual stock. (Note that the code that declared and modified the iStockCount data member from the previous example has been removed for simplicity.) Figure 7-42 shows the program's output.

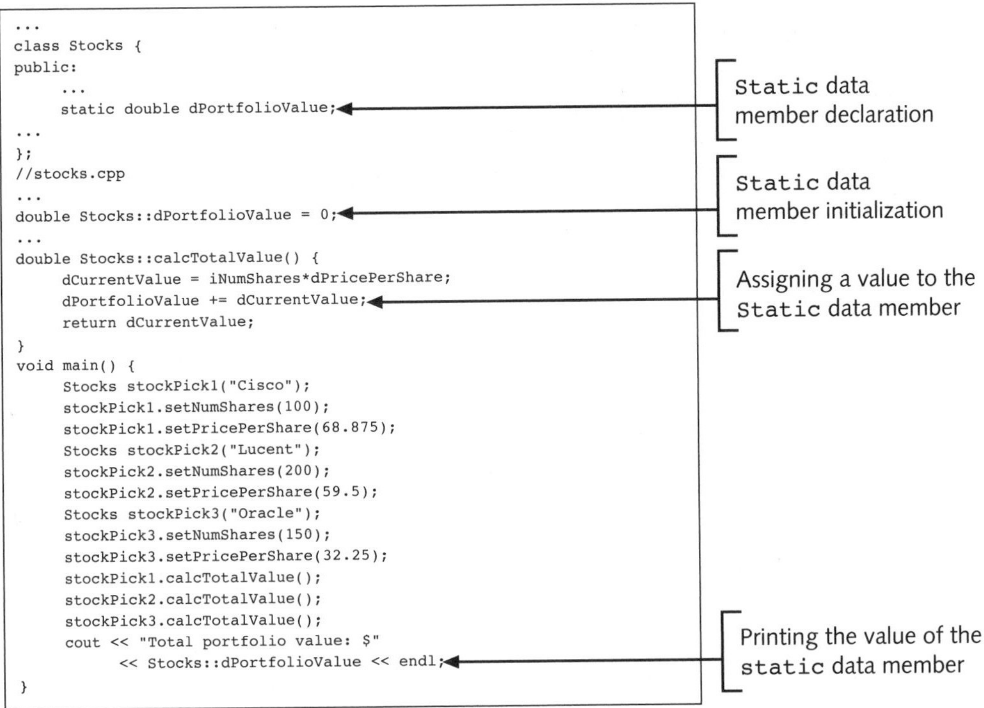

```
...
class Stocks {
public:
     ...
     static double dPortfolioValue;
...
};
//stocks.cpp
...
double Stocks::dPortfolioValue = 0;
...
double Stocks::calcTotalValue() {
     dCurrentValue = iNumShares*dPricePerShare;
     dPortfolioValue += dCurrentValue;
     return dCurrentValue;
}
void main() {
     Stocks stockPick1("Cisco");
     stockPick1.setNumShares(100);
     stockPick1.setPricePerShare(68.875);
     Stocks stockPick2("Lucent");
     stockPick2.setNumShares(200);
     stockPick2.setPricePerShare(59.5);
     Stocks stockPick3("Oracle");
     stockPick3.setNumShares(150);
     stockPick3.setPricePerShare(32.25);
     stockPick1.calcTotalValue();
     stockPick2.calcTotalValue();
     stockPick3.calcTotalValue();
     cout << "Total portfolio value: $"
          << Stocks::dPortfolioValue << endl;
}
```


Figure 7-41 Stock class with a static data member that keeps track of the total value of all instantiated stocks

Figure 7-42 Output of Stocks class with a static data member that keeps track of the total value of all instantiated stocks

Next, you will add to the Estimator class a `static` data member that stores the combined total of each customer's estimate.

To add to the Estimator class a `static` data member that stores the combined total of each customer's estimate:

1. Open the **Estimator.h** file in the Code Editor window.
2. Add the declaration **`static long lCombinedCost;`** to the end of the private declaration section.
3. Open the **Estimator.cpp** file in the Code Editor window.

4. Initialize the lCombinedCost `static` data member,as shown in Figure 7-43. Be sure to add the initialization statement at the global level, outside of any function definitions so that the `static` data member, is not reinitialized each time you instantiate a new object.

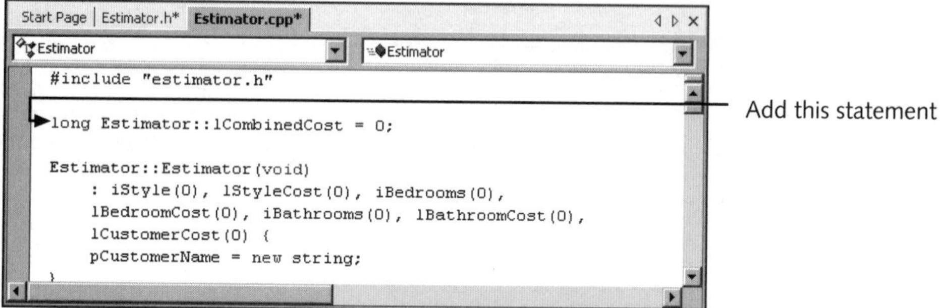

Figure 7-43 Static data member initialized in Estimator.cpp

5. The calcCustomerCost() member function calculates the building cost estimate for each customer. Modify the function by adding the statement shown in Figure 7-44 so that each customer cost is added to the lCombinedCost `static` data member.

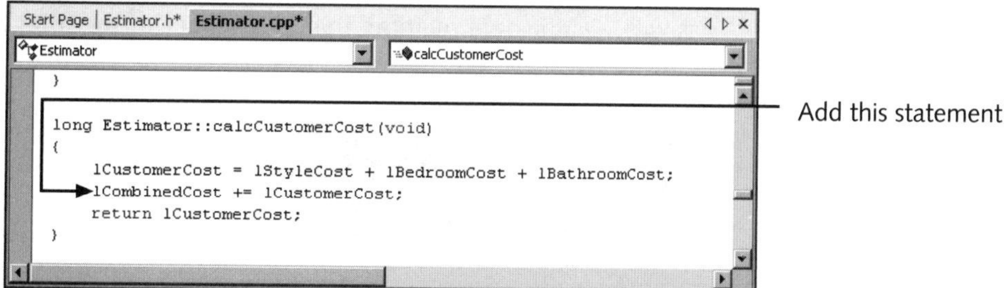

Figure 7-44 calcCustomerCost() function modified to use the static data member

To access the lCombinedCost `static` data member, you will use a `static` member function, which you will study next.

`Static` Member functions

Static member functions are useful for accessing `static` data members. Like `static` data members, they can be accessed independently of any individual class objects. This is useful when you need to retrieve the contents of a `static` data member that is declared as `private`, such as when you need to find out the current number of a class's instantiated objects. `Static` member functions are somewhat limited because they can only access other `static` class members or functions and variables located outside of the class.

You declare a **static** member function similar to the way you declare a **static** data member by preceding the function declaration in the interface file with the **static** keyword. You do not include the **static** keyword, however, in the function definition in the implementation file.

Like **static** data members, you need to call a **static** member function's name only from inside another member function of the same class. If you use a **static** member function outside of the same class, you precede its name with the class name and scope resolution operator, or you append the function name to an existing object of the class using the member selection operator. For example, to access a function without using an instantiated object, you call a **static** function named getPortfolioValue() of the Stocks class using the statement `Stocks::getPortfolioValue();`. Alternately, if you have an instantiated object of the Stocks class (stockPick, for example), then you can use the statement `stockPick.getPortfolioValue();`.

You can execute **static** member functions even if no objects of a class are instantiated. Therefore, you can use a **static** member function to check the value of a **static** data member, even if no objects of the class exist. For example, you may write code that uses a **static** member function with a **static** counter data member that automatically exits the program once a user closes the last object of a class.

One use of **static** member functions is to access **private static** data members. Recall that many programmers prefer to hide all of a class's data members. If you decide to hide your **static** data members, you can access them with a **static** member function. Note that you are not allowed to use the **const** keyword with a **static** member function, even if the member function does not modify any data members.

Next, you will add to the Estimator class a **static** member function that returns the value of the **static lCombinedCost** data member.

To add to the Estimator class a **static** member function that returns the value of the **static lCombinedCost** data member:

1. Open **Class View** and use the Add Function Wizard to add the following member function to the Estimator class. Click the **Static** check box in the Add Member Function Wizard dialog box to create the getCombinedCost() member function as **static**. Remember that the Add Function Wizard returns a value of zero by default; you need to modify the function with your own return value.

```
long Estimator::getCombinedCost() {
        return lCombinedCost;
}
```

2. Add to the main() function the statements shown in Figure 7-45. The statements call the **static** getCombinedCost() member function, which returns the value of the **lCombinedCost static** data member.

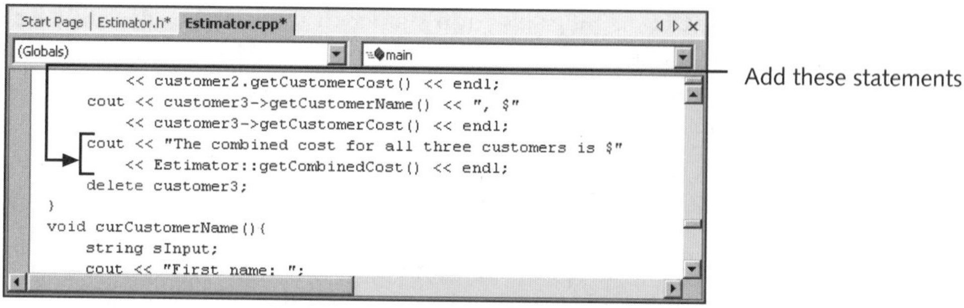
Start Page | Estimator.h* | Estimator.cpp*
(Globals)
main
<< customer2.getCustomerCost() << endl;
cout << customer3->getCustomerName() << ", $"
<< customer3->getCustomerCost() << endl;
cout << "The combined cost for all three customers is $"
<< Estimator::getCombinedCost() << endl;
delete customer3;
}
void curCustomerName(){
string sInput;
cout << "First name: ";
Add these statements

Figure 7-45 Statements added to main() which call the static getCombinedCost() member function

3. Rebuild and execute the program. After entering data for all three customers, your screen should appear similar to Figure 7-46.

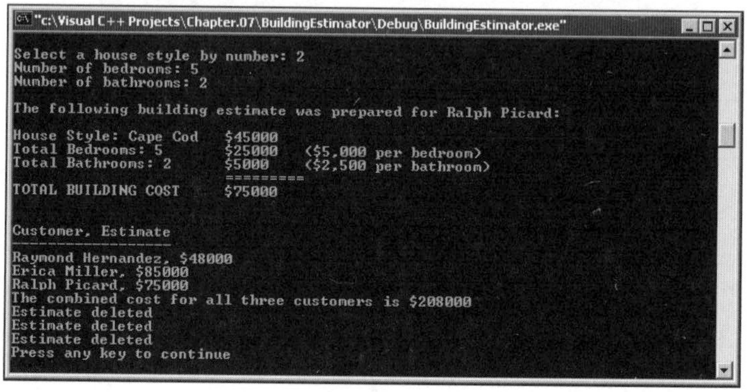
"c:\Visual C++ Projects\Chapter.07\BuildingEstimator\Debug\BuildingEstimator.exe"
Select a house style by number: 2
Number of bedrooms: 5
Number of bathrooms: 2
The following building estimate was prepared for Ralph Picard:
House Style: Cape Cod $45000
Total Bedrooms: 5 $25000 ($5,000 per bedroom)
Total Bathrooms: 2 $5000 ($2,500 per bathroom)
=========
TOTAL BUILDING COST $75000
Customer, Estimate
Raymond Hernandez, $48000
Erica Miller, $85000
Ralph Picard, $75000
The combined cost for all three customers is $208000
Estimate deleted
Estimate deleted
Estimate deleted
Press any key to continue

Figure 7-46 Output of final version of Building Estimator program

Constant Objects

If you have any type of variable in a program that does not change, you should always use the `const` keyword to declare the variable as a constant. Constants are an important aspect of good programming technique because they prevent clients (or you) from modifying data that should not change. Because objects are also variables, they too can be declared as constants. As with other types of data, however, you only declare an object as constant if it does not change. For example, you may have a class that instantiates an object representing the current date. If you will not need to modify any of the object's data members, then you should declare the object as constant. To declare an object as constant, place the `const` keyword in front of the object declaration. For example, to declare a constant object named currentDate from a class named Date using the default constructor, you use the statement `const Date currentDate;`.

Constant data members in a class cannot be assigned values using a standard assignment statement within the body of a member function. Instead, you must use an initialization list to assign initial values to these types of data members. Consider the Payroll class again. Assume that it may be more efficient to use constants for the dFedTax and dStateTax data members. The following code shows how to declare the dFedTax and dStateTax data members as constants in the interface file and how to initialize their values using an initialization list in the default constructor:

```
//Payroll.h
#pragma once
#include <iostream>
using namespace std;
class Payroll {
public:
   Payroll();
private:
   const double dFedTax;
   const double dStateTax;
};
// Payroll.cpp
#include "Payroll.h"
Payroll::Payroll()
  :dFedTax(.28), dStateTax(.05) {
};
```

Constant data member declarations

Constant data member initialization

In contrast, the following code raises several compile errors because constants must be initialized in an initialization list:

```
//Payroll.h
#pragma once
#include <iostream>
using namespace std;
classPayroll {
public:
   Payroll();
private:
   const doubledFedTax;
   const doubledStateTax;
};
// Payroll.cpp
#include "Payroll.h"
Payroll::Payroll() {
   dFedTax = .28; // illegal
   dStateTax = .05; // illegal
};
```

Another good programming technique is to always use the **const** keyword to declare get functions that do not modify data members as constant functions. The **const** keyword makes your programs more reliable by ensuring that functions that are *not* supposed to modify data *cannot* modify data. To declare a function as constant, you add the **const** keyword after a function's parentheses in both the function declaration and its definition. For example, in the last chapter you saw a function named getStateTax() that only returns the current state tax rate stored in the dStateTax data member. Because the getStateTax() function does not modify any data, it should be a constant function. The following code shows the declaration and definition for a constant version of the getStateTax() function. Notice that the **const** keyword has been added after the function's parentheses.

```
// Payroll.h
double getStateTax(Payroll*) const;
// Payroll.cpp
double Payroll::getStateTax(Payroll* pStateTax) const {
  return pStateTax->dStateTax;
}
```

Next, you will define the Estimator class's get functions as constant.

To define the Estimator class's get functions as constant:

1. Open the **Estimator.h** file in the Code Editor window.
2. In the public section, add the **const** keyword after each of the get function's parentheses. The following code shows the function declarations that you need to modify, along with where you need to place the **const** keyword:

   ```
   string getCustomerName(void) const;
   string getHouseStyle(void) const;
   long getStyleCost(void) const;
   int getBedrooms(void) const;
   long getBedroomCost(void) const;
   int getBathrooms(void) const;
   long getBathroomCost(void) const;
   long getCustomerCost(void) const;
   ```

3. Open the **Estimator.cpp** file in the Code Editor window.
4. In each of the get function definitions corresponding to the function declarations you modified in Step 2, add the **const** keyword after each of the function's parentheses.
5. Rebuild and execute the program. The program should function the same as it did in the previous set of steps.

Chapter Summary

- The default constructor is the constructor that does not include any parameters and that is called for any declared objects of its class to which you do not pass arguments.
- An overloaded function refers to multiple functions within a program that share the same name, but that accept different parameters.
- Constructor functions can accept parameters that a client can use to pass initialization values to your class.
- Initialization lists, or member initialization lists, are another way of assigning initial values to a class's data members.
- A copy constructor is a special constructor that is called when a new object is instantiated from an old object.
- A default destructor cleans up any resources allocated to an object once the object is destroyed.
- Operator overloading refers to the creation of multiple versions of C++ operators that perform special tasks required by the class in which an overloaded operator function is defined.
- When you declare a class member to be static, only one copy of that class member is created during a program's execution, regardless of how many objects of the class you instantiate.
- A good programming technique is to always use the `const` keyword to declare get functions that do not modify data members as constant functions.

Review Questions

1. Which is the correct syntax for declaring a stack object of the Students class using the default constructor?
   a. `Students curStudent;`
   b. `Students curStudent();`
   c. `Students curStudent = new Students;`
   d. `Students curStudent = new Students();`
2. How many parameters can you include in a default constructor?
   a. 0
   b. 1
   c. 2
   d. 5

3. Which of the following statements is true of an overloaded function?
   a. Each version of an overloaded function must accept different parameters.
   b. Each version of an overloaded function must accept identical parameters.
   c. The parameters accepted by the different versions of an overloaded function make no difference, provided that each version contains different sets of statements in its function body.
   d. Overloaded functions cannot accept parameters.
4. What happens if you write a parameterized constructor for the Students class, but not a default constructor, and you attempt to instantiate a new object of the class using the default constructor?
   a. The compiler automatically supplies a default constructor.
   b. The compiler converts the statement into a format that can be used with a parameterized constructor.
   c. You will receive a compiler error because the automatically supplied default constructor is no longer available.
   d. The compiler prompts you to enter the appropriate value for the parameterized constructor.
5. How can you initialize constant data members?
   a. within the body of parameterized constructor functions
   b. within the body of default constructor functions
   c. using initialization lists
   d. within the parameter list of a member function declaration
6. You can create a new Students object named newStudent by copying the existing curStudent object using the statement `Students newStudent = curStudent;` or by using the statement ________.
   a. `newStudent=curStudent;`
   b. `curStudent=newStudent;`
   c. `Students newStudent(curStudent);`
   d. `Students curStudent(newStudent);`
7. When you create a new object by copying an existing object, data members of the original object are automatically copied to the new object using ________.
   a. the default constructor
   b. the default copy constructor
   c. a parameterized constructor
   d. the default destructor

8. When should you write your own copy constructor function?
   a. when you declare an object on the stack
   b. when your project includes friend functions
   c. if you have multiple classes in a project
   d. when you need to use pointers to dynamically allocate memory
9. When an object reference parameter in a member function is preceded by the `const` keyword, the parameter is referred to as a ________________.
   a. dynamic variable
   b. constant parameter
   c. `static` data member
   d. dynamic parameter
10. A ________________ cleans up any resources allocated to an object once the object is destroyed.
    a. parameterized destructor
    b. copy constructor
    c. system administrator
    d. default destructor
11. A destructor is called when a stack object loses scope, when the function in which it is declared ends, or ________________.
    a. when a heap object is destroyed with the delete operator
    b. when you call the kill operator
    c. when you manually remove the object from the stack by calling the ~stack() function
    d. when you explicitly call the destructor function
12. Which is the correct destructor function declaration for the Students class?
    a. `Students~();`
    b. `~Students();`
    c. `!Students();`
    d. `*Students();`
13. Which of the following operators must be overloaded as a member function?
    a. ->
    b. +
    c. &
    d. !

14. What is the correct syntax for overloading a binary operator?
    a. `type binary_operator (const class& rightOperand) { }`
    b. `operator binary_operator (const class& leftOperand) { }`
    c. `type operator binary_operator (const class rightOperand) { }`
    d. `type operator binary_operator (const class& rightOperand) { }`
15. When you overload a unary operator as a member function, you declare the operator's overloaded function with a ______________ data type.
    a. class pointer
    b. class reference
    c. class object
    d. It depends on the operator.
16. What is the correct function declaration for overloading the assignment operator in the Students class?
    a. `Students* operator = (const Students* operand);`
    b. `Students & operator = (const Students& operand);`
    c. `Students operator = (const Students operand);`
    d. `Students operator = (const Students& operand);`
17. To instruct a class to create only one copy of a class member, regardless of how many objects of that class you instantiate, you precede the class member declaration with the keyword ______________.
    a. `fixed`
    b. `single`
    c. `permanent`
    d. `static`
18. What is the correct syntax for declaring a constant object named astronomyClass from a class named Syllabus?
    a. `const Syllabus astronomyClass;`
    b. `Syllabus const astronomyClass;`
    c. `Syllabus astronomyClass const;`
    d. `astronomyClass const Syllabus;`
19. When do you declare a class's member functions as constant?
    a. if the function is a static data member
    b. whenever the function operates on a `static` data member
    c. for set functions that modify data
    d. for get functions that do not modify data

20. Which of the following is the correct declaration for a constant function named returnGPA() that returns an `int` value?
    a. `int returnGPA(int) const;`
    b. `int const returnGPA(int);`
    c. `const int returnGPA(int);`
    d. `int returnGPA(const int);`

PROGRAMMING EXERCISES

1. Write an empty default constructor function definition for a class named Bicycle.
2. Overload the following function so it also includes a parameter for a person's age. The overloaded function with two parameters should print the person's age in addition to the person's name.

```
void person(string);
void main() {
  person("Don");
}
void person (string sName) {
  cout << "Your name is " << sName << endl;
}
```

3. Write the appropriate copy constructor for the following class:

```
// Auto.h
#pragma once
#include <iostream>
#include <string>
using namespace std;
class Auto {
public:
  Auto (string, double);
  void setCarMake(string);
  string getCarMake();
  void setCarEngine(double);
  double getCarEngine();
private:
  string* pCarMake;
  double dCarEngineSize;
};
  //Auto.ccp
#include "Auto.h"
Auto::Auto(string sMake, double dEngine) {
  pCarMake = new string;
  *pCarMake = sMake;
  dCarEngineSize = dEngine;
}
void Auto::setCarMake(string sMake) {
```

```
    *pCarMake = sMake;
  }
  string Auto::getCarMake() {
    return *pCarMake;
  }
  void Auto::setCarEngine(double dEngine) {
    dCarEngineSize  = dEngine;
  }
  double Auto::getCarEngine() {
    return dCarEngineSize;
  }
  void main() {
    Auto oldCar("Ford", 351);
    Auto newCar(oldCar);
    newCar.setCarMake("Chevy");
    newCar.setCarEngine(3.1);
    cout << oldCar.getCarMake() << endl;
    cout << oldCar.getCarEngine() << endl;
    cout << newCar.getCarMake() << endl;
    cout << newCar.getCarEngine() << endl;
  }
```

4. Explain the difference between a constructor and destructor. What names must you use for each function type?
5. Add an appropriate destructor to the class in Exercise 3.
6. Add an appropriate destructor to the following class. (*Hint*: be sure to notice that the dynamically allocated string variables are stored in a character array–not a string class variable.)

```
// schedule.h
#pragma once
#include <iostream>
#include <string>
using namespace std;
class Schedule {
public:
  Schedule(void);
  void setCurrentDay(char*);
  char* getCurrentDay(void);
  void setCurrentMonth(char*);
  char* getCurrentMonth(void);
private:
  char* szCurDay;
  char* szCurMonth;
};
// schedule.cpp
#include "schedule.h"
Schedule::Schedule(void) {
```

```
    szCurDay = new char[25];
    szCurMonth = new char[25];
  }
  void Schedule::setCurrentDay(char* szDay) {
    szCurDay = szDay;
  }
  char* Schedule::getCurrentDay(void) {
    return szCurDay;
  }
  void Schedule::setCurrentMonth(char* szMonth)  {
    szCurMonth = szMonth;
  }
  char* Schedule::getCurrentMonth(void) {
    return szCurMonth;
  }
  void main() {
    Schedule curSchedule;
    curSchedule.setCurrentDay("Tuesday");
    curSchedule.setCurrentMonth("August");
    cout << "The current day is "
            << curSchedule.getCurrentDay() << endl;
    cout << "The current month is "
            << curSchedule.getCurrentMonth() << endl;
  }
```


7. When you write an overloaded assignment operator, there is the possibility that a client will attempt to assign an existing object to itself. For example, if you have a Students object named curStudent, the statement `curStudent = curStudent;` will attempt to assign the same object to itself. Rewrite the following overloaded assignment operator so that it checks whether the temporary object created when you call the overloaded assignment operator function is the same as the object parameter. If they are the same, simply return the current object instead of reassigning new values to the temporary object. (*Hint*: you will need to use a decision-making structure and the `this` reference.)

```
MutualFund& MutualFund::operator = (const MutualFund& oper
and) {
  pFundName = new string;
  *pFundName = *operand.pFundName;
  iFundShares = operand.iFundShares;
  return *this;
}
```

PROGRAMMING PROJECTS

1. Create an Auction class that contains data members appropriate for an auction, including itemName, highBidder, lowBidder, and reserve price. Store the itemName, highBidder, and lowBidder fields as heap variables. Instantiate an Auction object on the heap. Allow two people to play an "auction game" using a console application. Once one of the bidders meets the reserve price, end the auction and print the high bidder's name to the screen. Also, write a destructor function that cleans up the heap variables and prints AUCTION CLOSED once the reserve price is reached.
2. Create a CompanyInfo class that includes `private` data members such as the company name, year incorporated, annual gross revenue, annual net revenue, and so on. Use a parameterized constructor to obtain the company name. Write set and get functions to store and retrieve values in the `private` data members. Copy the original object into a subsidiary company object and create an appropriate copy constructor function. Use `static` data members to store the combined gross revenue for both companies. Output each company's information in a console application, using a `static` member function to retrieve the `static` combined gross revenue data member. Be sure to include a destructor.
3. Overload the subtraction operator for the Stocks class so that one class's number of shares is subtracted from another class's number of shares.
4. Create an Investment class that includes the appropriate data members for various types of investments. Write appropriate get and set functions for each data member. Also include a data member that holds the investment's total value. Use a parameterized constructor to receive the name of each investment in a `string*` pointer. Be sure to include a destructor to clean up the heap when each object is destroyed. Also include a `static` data member and a `static` member function that calculates the total worth of an investment portfolio by adding together the total value of data members for each instantiated object. Add the Investment class to a console application, and then instantiate an Investment object and initialize its data. Create two additional Investment objects by copying the original object. You will need to write a copy constructor for when you duplicate objects. Retrieve and print the data members for each object. Also print the contents of the `static` data member using a statement similar to "Your investments are worth a total of $100,000."
5. Earlier in this chapter, it was mentioned that you may want to overload the carat operator ^ in one of your classes so that it returns the result of a number raised by a certain power. If you are unfamiliar with this mathematical concept, raising a number by a certain power, or exponential notation, refers to when you multiply a number by itself a given number of times. For instance, 10 multiplied by 10 results in a value of 100, and is referred to as 10 to the second power. The equation 10 * 10 * 10 results in a value of 1000 and is referred to as 10 to the third power. Write an Exponent class that overloads the ^ operator so it can be used to perform exponential notation. For instance, if you use the statement `int iResult = 10^3;`, the iResult variable should be assigned a value of 1000.

CHAPTER

8

INHERITANCE

In this chapter you will learn:

- About base classes and derived classes
- About access specifiers and inheritance
- How to override base class member functions
- About constructors and destructors in derived classes
- About polymorphism and how to use virtual functions and virtual destructors
- How to create abstract classes

The loftier the building, the deeper must the foundation be laid.

Thomas Kempis

PREVIEW: THE CONVERSION CENTER PROGRAM

One of the most important features of C++ is the ability of one class to use the member functions and data members of another class through a process known as inheritance. Although inheritance is an important feature of C++ (or any object-oriented programming language), it is a critical feature of Microsoft Foundation Classes. You *must* use inheritance techniques in order to work with Microsoft Foundation Classes later in this book, so it is vital that you understand the concepts presented in this chapter.

To study the inheritance techniques presented in this chapter, you will work on a Conversion Center program that performs temperature, distance, and household measurement conversions. You will work with four classes to perform the conversions: Conversion, Temperature, Distance, and Household.

To preview the Conversion Center program:

1. Create a **Chapter.08** folder in your Visual C++ Projects folder.
2. Copy the **Chapter8_ConversionCenter** folder from the Chapter.08 folder on your Data Disk to the Chapter.08 folder in your Visual C++ Projects folder. Then open the **ConversionCenter** project in Visual C++.
3. Open the Conversion class interface file, **Conversion.h**, in the Code Editor window. The Conversion class is a base class file on which the other class files in the program are based. The file contains two unfamiliar elements: function declaration statements that begin with the `virtual` keyword, and the protected access specifier. Notice that one function declaration statement beginning with the `virtual` keyword includes `=0` at the end of the statement. This type of function is known as a pure virtual function and is used when you need to force a new class that inherits the characteristics of your class in order to provide its own implementation of a given function. The Conversion interface file is shown in Figure 8-1.

```
#pragma once
#include <iostream>
#include <string>
using namespace std;
class Conversion {
public:
	Conversion(void);
	virtual ~Conversion(void);
	double getResult(void) const;
	virtual void setResult(double) = 0;
	string getConversionType(void) const;
protected:
	string sCurConversion;
	double dResultAmount;
};
```

Virtual function declaration

Protected access specifier

Figure 8-1 Conversion interface file

4. Open the **Conversion.cpp** implementation file and examine its contents. It contains some standard function definitions, including definitions for the functions that were declared with the virtual keyword.
5. The other three classes on your Data Disk, Temperature, Distance, and Household, are standard classes that perform different types of data conversion operations. Open the Temperature.h file. Above the class declaration is a #include statement that makes the Conversion class available to the Temperature class. The class declaration itself also includes the code `: public Conversion`, which allows the Temperature class to inherit the characteristics of the Conversion class. The Temperature.h file is shown in Figure 8-2. The other class interface files contain similar statements. You can examine them on your own.

```
#pragma once
#include "Conversion.h"
class Temperature : public Conversion {
public:
        Temperature(void);
        ~Temperature(void);
        void convertToCelsius(double);
        void convertToFahrenheit(double);
        void setResult(double);
};
```

Modifier that allows the Temperature class to inherit the characteristics of the Conversion class

Figure 8-2 Temperature.h

6. Finally, open the Temperature class's implementation file, Temperature.cpp, in the Code Editor window, and examine its contents. The function definitions are fairly straightforward. Notice that the file contains a definition for the virtual function that was declared in the Conversion interface file.
7. Build and execute the Conversion Center program, and then test the calculations. Figure 8-3 shows the output for a completed version of the Conversion Center program after performing a distance conversion.

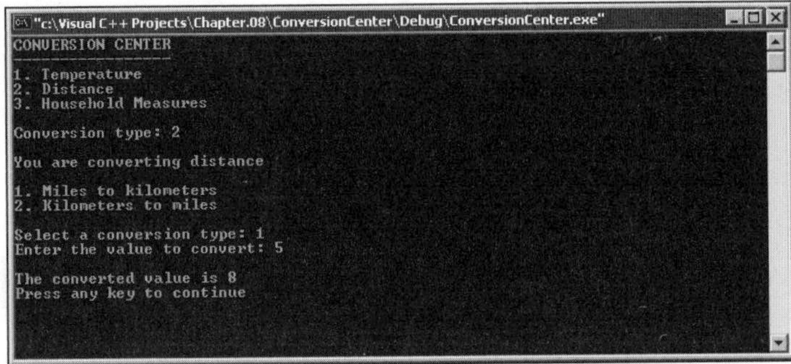

"c:\Visual C++ Projects\Chapter.08\ConversionCenter\Debug\ConversionCenter.exe"
CONVERSION CENTER
1. Temperature
2. Distance
3. Household Measures
Conversion type: 2
You are converting distance
1. Miles to kilometers
2. Kilometers to miles
Select a conversion type: 1
Enter the value to convert: 5
The converted value is 8
Press any key to continue

Figure 8-3 Output of the Conversion Center program

8. Press any key to close the Conversion Center program window.
9. Select **Close Solution** from the File menu to close the Conversion Center solution.

Basic Inheritance

In the previous two chapters, you studied how to create classes and use them as objects in C++ programs. You learned only how to create and manipulate individual classes, one at a time. There will be times, however, when you have a particular class that does not quite contain all of the class members you need in your program. Nonetheless, the class contains *some* member functions and data members that exactly match the requirements of your program. One option is to recreate all of the original class's functionality—provided you have access to the implementation file—and add any additional class members you need. Another option is to use inheritance to give a new class access to the original class's class members and create only the new class members you need in your program. **Inheritance** is the ability of one class to take on the characteristics of another class.

To explore the topic of inheritance, you will examine a program for allocating grant money that might be written for a School of Anthropology at a college or university. The school administration might need to keep track of grant money that is allocated to each anthropologist for his or her research. In the Grant Allocation program, a basic Anthropology class, such as the class shown in Figure 8-4, handles much of the program's functionality, such as recording the name of each anthropologist and the countries where research will take place, calculating the amount of grant money each anthropologist needs, and so on. Notice that the Anthropology class declares a dynamic array of string class objects that stores the names of countries in which anthropologists conduct their research. The default constructor (`Anthropology(void);`) and the single parameter constructor (`Anthropology(string);`) each instantiate the string class object array with a default number of three elements. The two-parameter constructor (`Anthropology(string, int);`) allows you to enter a different number of elements for the dynamic array in case an anthropologist is doing research in a different number of countries.

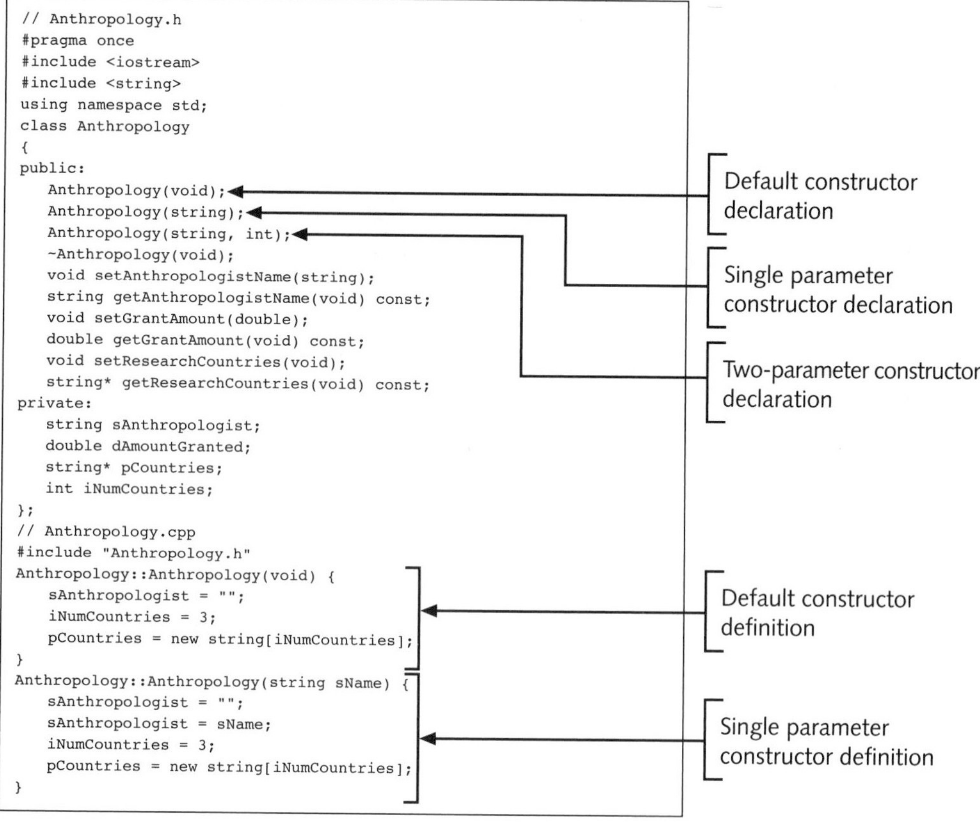

```
// Anthropology.h
#pragma once
#include <iostream>
#include <string>
using namespace std;
class Anthropology
{
public:
   Anthropology(void);
   Anthropology(string);
   Anthropology(string, int);
   ~Anthropology(void);
   void setAnthropologistName(string);
   string getAnthropologistName(void) const;
   void setGrantAmount(double);
   double getGrantAmount(void) const;
   void setResearchCountries(void);
   string* getResearchCountries(void) const;
private:
   string sAnthropologist;
   double dAmountGranted;
   string* pCountries;
   int iNumCountries;
};
// Anthropology.cpp
#include "Anthropology.h"
Anthropology::Anthropology(void) {
   sAnthropologist = "";
   iNumCountries = 3;
   pCountries = new string[iNumCountries];
}
Anthropology::Anthropology(string sName) {
   sAnthropologist = "";
   sAnthropologist = sName;
   iNumCountries = 3;
   pCountries = new string[iNumCountries];
}
```


Figure 8-4 Anthropology class

```
Anthropology::Anthropology(string sName, int iCountries) {
        sAnthropologist = "";
        sAnthropologist = sName;
        iNumCountries = iCountries;
        pCountries = new string[iNumCountries];
}
Anthropology::~Anthropology(void) {
        delete [] pCountries;
}
void Anthropology::setAnthropologistName(string sName) {
        sAnthropologist = sName;
}
string Anthropology::getAnthropologistName(void) const {
     return sAnthropologist;
}
void Anthropology::setGrantAmount(double dGrantAmount) {
     dAmountGranted = dGrantAmount;
}
double Anthropology::getGrantAmount(void) const {
     return dAmountGranted;
}
void Anthropology::setResearchCountries(void) {
        for (int iCount = 0; iCount < iNumCountries; ++iCount) {
                 cout << "Research country " << iCount + 1 << ": ";
                 cin >> pCountries[iCount];
        }
}
string* Anthropology::getResearchCountries(void) const {
        return pCountries;
}
```


Figure 8-4 Anthropology class (continued)

The School of Anthropology is divided into two departments, Physical Anthropology and Cultural Anthropology. (Physical anthropology deals with the physical study of humans and related species such as apes; cultural anthropology deals with cultural aspects of human beings such as language and archaeology.) Each department head wants the Grant Allocation program to record information that is specific to his or her discipline. Rather than write separate, unrelated classes for each department that duplicate the functionality of the Anthropology class, you can write classes that inherit the characteristics of the Anthropology class. Then, to each new class, you can add member functions and data members that are specific to that department. For example, a new Physical class may be created for the Physical Anthropology Department, and a Cultural class may be created for the Cultural Anthropology Department. The Physical class needs to store a data member for the amount of grant money reserved for primate care. The Cultural class needs to store data members for the amount of grant money allocated for two separate purposes: the purchase of Egyptian antiquities, and cassette tapes to record speech patterns. Assuming that each class will inherit the members of the Anthropology class, you would need only the class declarations and definitions shown in Figures 8-5 and 8-6. Note that these two classes do not yet inherit the characteristics of the Anthropology class. How to implement inheritance will be discussed in the next section.

```
// Physical.h
#pragma once
class Physical {
public:
   Physical(void);
   ~Physical(void);
   void setPrimateCare(double);
   double getPrimateCare(void) const;
private:
   double dPrimateCare;
};
// Physical.cpp
#include "Physical.h"
Physical::Physical(void) {
   dPrimateCare = 0;
}
Physical::~Physical(void) {
}
void Physical::setPrimateCare(double dCost) {
   dPrimateCare = dCost;
}
double Physical::getPrimateCare(void) const {
   return dPrimateCare;
}
```

Figure 8-5 Physical class

```
// Cultural.h
#pragma once
class Cultural {
public:
   Cultural(void);
   ~Cultural(void);
   void setAntiquitiesCost(double);
   double getAntiquitiesCost(void) const;
   void setCassettesCost(double);
   double getCassettesCost(void) const;
private:
   double dAntiquitiesCost;
   double dCassettesCost;
};
// Cultural.cpp
#include "Cultural.h"
Cultural::Cultural(void) {
   dAntiquitiesCost = 0;
   dCassettesCost = 0;
}
Cultural::~Cultural(void) {
}
void Cultural::setAntiquitiesCost(double dCost) {
   dAntiquitiesCost = dCost;
}
double Cultural::getAntiquitiesCost(void) const {
   return dAntiquitiesCost;
}
void Cultural::setCassettesCost(double dCost) {
   dCassettesCost = dCost;
}
double Cultural::getCassettesCost(void) const {
   return dCassettesCost;
}
```

Figure 8-6 Cultural class

Next, you will start creating the Conversion Center program. The three types of conversions, temperature, distance, and household measurements, require slightly different types of functions. They share some common features, however, that can be inherited from a main Conversion class. For example, the Conversion class contains member functions such as getResult() and setResult(), which are used to set and retrieve the results of a dResultAmount data member. These member functions and the dResultAmount data member can be inherited by the Temperature, Distance, and Household classes. Another data member that can be inherited is sCurConversion, which contains a string describing the current type of conversion. Included on your Data Disk are basic versions of the four interface files and the four implementation files used in the Conversion Center program. You can add these files to your project so you do not have to spend too much time typing. If you do not have access to a Data Disk, then type the program as shown in the figures in the following steps. First, you will create the interface files, which contain standard declarations for the various member functions and data members required by each class.

To create the Conversion Center program's interface files:

1. Return to Visual C++.
2. Create a new empty Win32 console application project named **ConversionCenter**. Save the project in the **Chapter.08** folder in your Visual C++ Projects folder.
3. Copy the **Conversion.h**, **Temperature.h**, **Distance.h**, **Household.h**, **Conversion.cpp**, **Temperature.cpp**, **Distance.cpp**, **Household.cpp**, and **main.cpp** files from your Data Disk to the ConversionCenter folder in the Chapter.08 folder in your Visual C++ Projects folder.
4. Add the **Conversion.h**, **Temperature.h**, **Distance.h**, and **Household.h** interface files to the ConversionCenter project using the **Add Existing Item** command on the **Project** menu. If you do not have access to a Data Disk, then create new header files by entering the code for each of the interface files, as shown in Figures 8-7 to 8-10.

```
#pragma once
#include <iostream>
#include <string>
using namespace std;
class Conversion {
public:
      Conversion(void);
      ~Conversion(void);
      double getResult(void) const;
      void setResult(double);
      string getConversionType(void) const;
private:
      string sCurConversion;
      double dResultAmount;
};
```

Figure 8-7 Conversion.h

```
#pragma once
class Temperature {
public:
	Temperature(void);
	~Temperature(void);
	void convertToCelsius(double);
	void convertToFahrenheit(double);
};
```

Figure 8-8 Temperature.h

```
#pragma once
class Distance {
public:
	Distance(void);
	~Distance(void);
	void convertToMiles(double);
	void convertToKilometers(double);
};
```

Figure 8-9 Distance.h

```
#pragma once
class Household {
public:
	Household(void);
	~Household(void);
	void teaspoonsToTablespoons(double);
	void tablespoonsToTeaspoons(double);
	void cupsToQuarts(double);
	void quartsToCups(double);
};
```

Figure 8-10 Household.h

Next, you will create the implementation files.

To add the implementation files to the Conversion Center program:

1. Add the **Conversion.cpp**, **Temperature.cpp**, **Distance.cpp**, and **Household.cpp** implementation files to the ConversionCenter project using the **Add Existing Item** command on the **Project** menu. If you do not have access to a Data Disk, then create new implementation files by entering the code for each of the files shown in Figures 8-11 to 8-14.

```
#include "Conversion.h"
Conversion::Conversion(void) {
      sCurConversion = "";
      dResultAmount = 0;
}
Conversion::~Conversion(void) {
}
string Conversion::getConversionType(void) const {
      return sCurConversion;
}
void Conversion::setResult(double dAmount) {
      dResultAmount = dAmount;
}
double Conversion::getResult(void) const {
      return dResultAmount;
}
```

Figure 8-11 Conversion.cpp


```
#include "Temperature.h"
Temperature::Temperature(void) {
      sCurConversion = "temperature";
}
Temperature::~Temperature(void) {
}
void Temperature::convertToCelsius(double dTemperature) {
      dResultAmount = dTemperature - 32 * .55;
      setResult(dResultAmount);
}
void Temperature::convertToFahrenheit(double dTemperature) {
      dResultAmount = dTemperature * 1.8 + 32;
      setResult(dResultAmount);
}
```

Figure 8-12 Temperature.cpp

```
#include "Distance.h"
Distance::Distance(void) {
      sCurConversion = "distance";
}
Distance::~Distance(void) {
}
void Distance::convertToMiles(double dKilometers) {
      dResultAmount = dKilometers * .6;
      setResult(dResultAmount);
}
void Distance::convertToKilometers(double dMiles) {
      dResultAmount = dMiles * 1.6;
      setResult(dResultAmount);
}
```

Figure 8-13 Distance.cpp

```
#include "Household.h"
Household::Household(void) {
        sCurConversion = "household";
}
Household::~Household(void) {
}
void Household::teaspoonsToTablespoons(double dMeasure) {
        dResultAmount = dMeasure * .33;
        setResult(dResultAmount);
}
void Household::tablespoonsToTeaspoons(double dMeasure) {
        dResultAmount = dMeasure * 3;
        setResult(dResultAmount);
}
void Household::cupsToQuarts(double dMeasure) {
        dResultAmount = dMeasure * .25;
        setResult(dResultAmount);
}
void Household::quartsToCups(double dMeasure) {
        dResultAmount = dMeasure * 4;
        setResult(dResultAmount);
}
```

Figure 8-14 Household.cpp

Base Classes and Derived Classes

When you write a new class that inherits the characteristics of another class, you are said to be **deriving** or **subclassing** a class. An inherited class is referred to as the **base class**, and the class that inherits a base class is referred to as a **derived class**. A class that inherits the characteristics of a base class is also said to be **extending** the base class, because you often *extend* the class by adding your own class members.

Professional programmers, as well as other books on C++, use several other terms to describe base classes and derived classes. Base classes are also called parent classes, ancestor classes, or superclasses. Derived classes are also called child classes, descendent classes, or subclasses. This book, however, uses the terms base class and derived class.

When a class is derived from a base class, the derived class inherits all of the base class's data members and all of its member functions, with the exception of the following member functions:

- Constructor functions
- Copy constructor functions
- Destructor functions
- Friend functions
- Overloaded assignment operator (=) functions

A derived class must provide its own implementations of these functions. Note that even though a derived class does not inherit constructor, copy constructor, destructor, friend, or overloaded assignment operator functions from a base class, a base class's constructor and destructor functions still execute when you instantiate or destroy an object of a derived class that extends the base class. You will further explore this topic later in this chapter.

Figure 8-15 shows the hierarchy of the Physical and Cultural classes when they are derived from the Anthropology base class. Both the Physical and Cultural derived classes inherit the class members of the Anthropology base class. Each derived class also includes its own unique class members. A derived class's members are not available to the base class or to other classes that are derived from the same base class. They are available only to the derived class itself or to other derived classes to which it may be a base class.

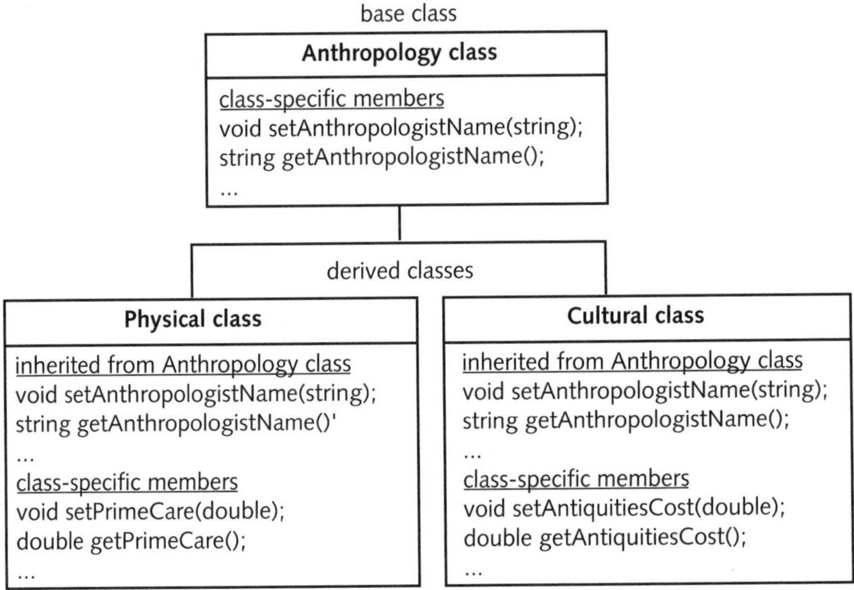

Figure 8-15 Base class and derived classes

You derive a class by including the base class in the derived class's interface file with a #include preprocessor directive. You must also append a colon to the header declaration statement in the interface file, followed by an access modifier and the name of the base class. The access modifiers and base class names following the colon in a class's header declaration statement are known as the **base list**. To modify the interface file for the Cultural class so that it inherits the characteristics of the Anthropology class, you modify the class header declaration statement as follows:

```
class Cultural : public Anthropology
{
public:
    Cultural(void);
    ...
```

By including multiple access modifiers and base class names separated by commas in the base list, you can add multiple inheritance to your programs. Multiple inheritance, however, is an advanced topic that you will learn about later.

Once you extend a base class, you can access its class members directly through objects instantiated from the derived class. For example, the following main() function declares a Physical object named currentGrant and then calls several member functions. If you refer back to Figure 8-5, you will see that the Physical class does not include setAnthropologistName() or getAnthropologistName() member functions. Even so, once you extend the Anthropology class in the Physical class, the Physical class has access to these member functions because they are inherited from the Anthropology class.

```
void main() {
     Physical currentGrant;
     currentGrant.setAnthropologistName("Richard Leakey");
     cout << currentGrant.getAnthropologistName() << endl;
}
```

Derived classes themselves can serve as base classes for other derived classes. When you build a series of base classes and derived classes, the chain of inherited classes is known as a **class hierarchy**. Generally, most class hierarchies have an "is a(n)" or "kind of" relationship. For example, the Physical class "is an" Anthropology class. Consider a larger class hierarchy. Within Anthropology, the field of cultural anthropology is further divided into three major subfields: archaeology (the study of a past culture through its material remains), linguistics (the study of languages), and ethnology (the study of cultures). As with the Physical Anthropology and Cultural Anthropology departments, the heads of each subdepartment might also want to record unique information in the Grant Allocation program for their specific subfields. For example, the Archaeology subdepartment might want to record in which country an archaeologist is digging, the Linguistics subdepartment might want to record the name of a linguist's primary language of study, and the Ethnology department might want to record which culture an ethnologist is studying. You can derive each of these subfields as classes in the Anthropology class hierarchy for the Grant Allocation program. Each new class, each representing a subfield, "is a" Cultural class, which "is an" Anthropology class. The more detailed Anthropology class hierarchy is shown in Figure 8-16.

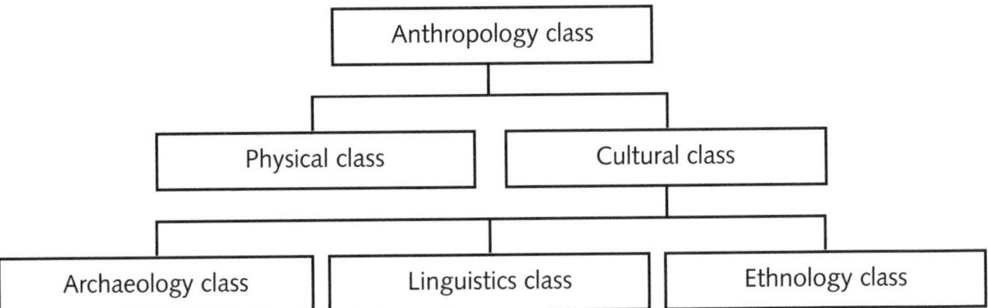

Figure 8-16 Anthropology class hierarchy

Another type of class relationship is a "has a relationship." In a "has a(n)" relationship, a class does not inherit the characteristics of another class. Rather, the class simply contains, or "has an," object of the class. For instance, you have frequently used the string class in your class-based programs. Your classes did not *derive* from the string class with an "is a(n)" relationship. Instead, your classes *included* the string class, with a "has a(n)" relationship. The BuildingEstimator class you created in Chapter 7, for instance, "has a" string class included in its declaration. Understanding the difference between an "is a(n)" relationship or a "has a(n)" relationship will help you determine whether to derive your new class from an existing class, or to simply include an instance of the existing class in your new class. You should only derive a new class from a base class if there is a clear hierarchical relationship between the classes.

The Physical and Cultural classes that derive from the Anthropology class are good examples of classes that should have an "is a(n)" relationship. You should not, however, derive the Physical or Cultural classes from a class such as the string class. Although it is possible to derive the Physical or Cultural classes from the string class, which would allow both classes to inherit all the public and protected members of the string class, doing so makes no sense. In contrast, you may want to write your own custom class named AdvancedStrings that performs advanced string manipulation functions. In this case, it would make sense to derive the AdvancedStrings class from the string class because you would want the new class to inherit much of the functionality contained within the string class.

Each class in a class hierarchy cumulatively inherits the class members of all classes that precede it in the hierarchy chain. For example, in the class hierarchy shown in Figure 8-16, the Cultural class inherits the class members of the Anthropology class. The Archaeology, Linguistics, and Ethnology classes that derive from the Cultural class inherit the class members of the Cultural class, as well as the class members of the Anthropology class. A class that directly precedes another class in a class hierarchy and that is included in the derived class's base list is called the **direct base class**. A class that does not directly precede a class in a class hierarchy and therefore is not included in the class's base list is called an **indirect base class**. In Figure 8-16, the Cultural class is the direct base class of the Archaeology, Linguistics, and Ethnology classes. The Anthropology class is the indirect base class for those classes.

Next, you will modify the Temperature, Distance, and Household classes so that they derive from the Conversion base class.

To modify the Temperature, Distance, and Household classes so that they derive from the Conversion base class:

1. Modify the Temperature.h file as follows:

```
#pragma once
#include "Conversion.h"
class Temperature : public Conversion {
public:
     Temperature(void);
...
};
```

2. Modify the Distance.h file as follows:

```
#pragma once
#include "Conversion.h"
class Distance : public Conversion {
public:
     Distance(void);
...
};
```

3. Modify the Household.h file as follows:

```
#pragma once
#include "Conversion.h"
class Household : public Conversion {
public:
     Household(void);
...
};
```

If you use the Generic C++ Class Wizard to add a new class to your project, you can use the Base class text box and the Access combo box in the Generic C++ Class Wizard dialog box to define a base class from which to derive the new class.

Next, you will add to the Conversion Center program a new C++ source file, named main.cpp, that imports all three of the derived classes. The main.cpp file also includes the program's main() function and uses numerous cout and cin statements to communicate with the user. Note that you do not need to import the Conversion base class because it is already imported by the three derived classes.

To add a new C++ source file named main.cpp to the Conversion Center program:

1. Add to the ConversionCenter project the **main.cpp** file that you copied earlier to the ConversionCenter folder in the Chapter.08 folder in your Visual C++

Projects folder. If you do not have access to a Data Disk, then create a new main.cpp file and enter the code for the file as shown in Figure 8-17. The #include statements import the Temperature, Distance, and Household classes. The first part of the main() function prompts the user to enter a number representing the type of conversion he or she wants to perform: Temperature, Distance, or Household Measures. Then an `if` statement is called that instantiates the correct object based on the user's selection. Within the `if` statement are additional `if` statements that narrow the user's conversion choices. Other than the somewhat lengthy cout and cin statements, the only tasks that the main() function performs are to find out which conversion the user wants to perform, gather a number from the user and store it in the dValue variable, and pass the dValue variable to the appropriate class's member function. If you examine the .cpp files, you will see that the derived class objects are calling several member functions that are defined in the Conversion base class, including the getResult() and getConversionType() member functions.


```
#include "Temperature.h"
#include "Distance.h"
#include "Household.h"
void main() {
	int iSelection;
	double dValue;
	cout << "CONVERSION CENTER" << endl;
	cout << "-----------------" << endl;
	cout << "1. Temperature" << endl;
	cout << "2. Distance" << endl;
	cout << "3. Household Measures" << endl << endl;
	cout << "Conversion type: ";
	cin >> iSelection;
	cout << endl;
	if (iSelection == 1) {
	   Temperature temp;
	   cout << "You are converting " << temp.getConversionType() << endl << endl;
	   cout << "1. Celsius to Fahrenheit" << endl;
	   cout << "2. Fahrenheit to Celsius" << endl << endl;
	   cout << "Select a conversion type: ";
	   cin >> iSelection;
	   cout << "Enter the value to convert: ";
	   cin >> dValue;
	   cout << endl;
	   if (iSelection == 1) {
			temp.convertToFahrenheit(dValue);
			cout << "The converted value is " << temp.getResult() << endl;
	   }
	   else if (iSelection == 2) {
			temp.convertToCelsius(dValue);
			cout << "The converted value is " << temp.getResult() << endl;
	   }
	   else
			cout << "You did not select a correct number!" << endl;
	}
```

Figure 8-17 main.cpp

```
        else if (iSelection == 2) {
        Distance distance;
        cout << "You are converting " << distance.getConversionType() << endl;
        cout << endl;
        cout << "1. Miles to kilometers" << endl;
        cout << "2. Kilometers to miles" << endl << endl;
        cout << "Select a conversion type: ";
        cin >> iSelection;
        cout << "Enter the value to convert: ";
        cin >> dValue;
        cout << endl;
        if (iSelection == 1) {
                distance.convertToKilometers(dValue);
                cout << "The converted value is " << distance.getResult() << endl;
        }
                else if (iSelection == 2) {
                        distance.convertToMiles(dValue);
                        cout << "The converted value is " << distance.getResult() << endl;
                }
                else
                        cout << "You did not select a correct number!" << endl;
        }
        else if (iSelection == 3) {
                Household measure;
                cout << "You are converting " << measure.getConversionType() << endl;
                cout << endl;
                cout << "1. Teaspoons to tablespoons" << endl;
                cout << "2. Tablespoons to teaspoons" << endl;
                cout << "3. Cups to quarts" << endl;
                cout << "4. Quarts to cups" << endl << endl;
                cout << "Select a conversion type: ";
                cin >> iSelection;
                cout << "Enter the value to convert: ";
                cin >> dValue;
                cout << endl;
                if (iSelection == 1) {
                        measure.teaspoonsToTablespoons(dValue);
                        cout << "The converted value is " << measure.getResult() << endl;
                }
                else if (iSelection == 2) {
                        measure.tablespoonsToTeaspoons(dValue);
                        cout << "The converted value is " << measure.getResult() << endl;
                }
                else if (iSelection == 3) {
                        measure.cupsToQuarts(dValue);
                        cout << "The converted value is " << measure.getResult() << endl;
                }
                else if (iSelection == 4) {
                        measure.quartsToCups(dValue);
                        cout << "The converted value is " << measure.getResult() << endl;
                }
                else
                        cout << "You did not select a correct number!" << endl;
        }
        else
                cout << "You did not select a correct number!" << endl;
}
```

Figure 8-17 main.cpp (continued)

Notice that although the main.cpp file uses cout statements, it does not include the iostream class or the standard namespace. You do not need to add these statements because the main.cpp file already inherits them from the Conversion.h file through the Distance.h, Household.h, and Temperature.h files.

2. Build the **ConversionCenter** project. You should receive a number of compile errors that are the result of the derived classes not having access to the base class's private members. Next you will learn how to fix this problem by using protected access specifiers.

Access Specifiers and Inheritance

Even though a derived class inherits the class members of a base class, the base class's members are still bound by its access specifiers. Private class members in the base class can be accessed only by the base class's member functions. The private class members of a base class are instantiated with an object of the derived class—you just do not have access to them. For example, the sAnthropologist data member in the Anthropology class is private. If you write the following member function in the Cultural class, which attempts to directly modify the sAnthropologist data member, you will receive a compile error.

```
void Cultural::setAnthropologistName(string sName) {
  sAnthropologist = sName;
}
```


Instead, to access the sAnthropologist data member you must call the Anthropologist class's setAnthropologistName() member function, which is public. Alternately, you can declare the sAnthropologist data member with the `protected` access specifier. The **protected access specifier** restricts class member access to the class itself, to member functions in classes derived from the class, or to friend functions and friend classes. You declare class members as `protected` in an interface file in the same fashion that you declare `public` and `private` class members: by placing the `protected` access specifier on a line by itself followed by a colon, followed by the class members. The following code shows a modified version of the Anthropology class's interface file in which the `private` access modifier has been changed to `protected`. A member function in the Cultural class that attempts to directly modify the sAnthropologist data member will function correctly because the Cultural class is a derived class of the Anthropology class and the sAnthropologist data member is now declared as `protected`.

```
class Anthropology {
public:
     Anthropology(void);
     Anthropology(string);
     ...
protected:
     string sAnthropologist;
     double dAmountGranted;
...
};
```

The access specifier included in a class header declaration's base list is another important facet of inheritance. You saw that a `public` access modifier was used when the base list was first introduced.

```
class Cultural : public Anthropology
{
public:
     Cultural(void);
     ...
```

Using a `public` access modifier in the base list gives the derived class public access to each of the base class's `public` members. Using a `protected` access modifier in the base list gives the derived class protected access to each of the base class's `public` members. In other words, only member functions in the derived class will have access to the base class's `public` members. If you use the `private` access modifier in the base list, then the base class's `public` members become `private`. In this case, the derived class will not be able to access any members of the base class. There are few compelling reasons to use a `private` or `protected` modifier to hide a base class's `public` members from clients of a derived class, so you should normally use the `public` access specifier in the base list.

Although you should always use an access specifier in the base list, you are not required to. Remember, however, that a class's default access is private. If you fail to include an access specifier in the base list, your base class's `public` members become `private` to clients of your derived class. For example, the following Cultural class header declaration, which extends the Anthropology class, hides the Anthropology class's `public` data members from clients of the Cultural class:

```
class Cultural : Anthropology
{
public:
     Cultural(void);
     ...
```

Next, you will modify the Conversion.h interface file's `private` class members so that they become `protected` class members:

To modify the Conversion.h interface file's class members so that they become protected instead of public:

1. Open the **Conversion.h** file in the Code Editor window.
2. Change the `private` access specifier to `protected`, as shown in Figure 8-18:
3. Rebuild the **ConversionCenter** project and execute the program. You should now be able to call any of the conversion routines.

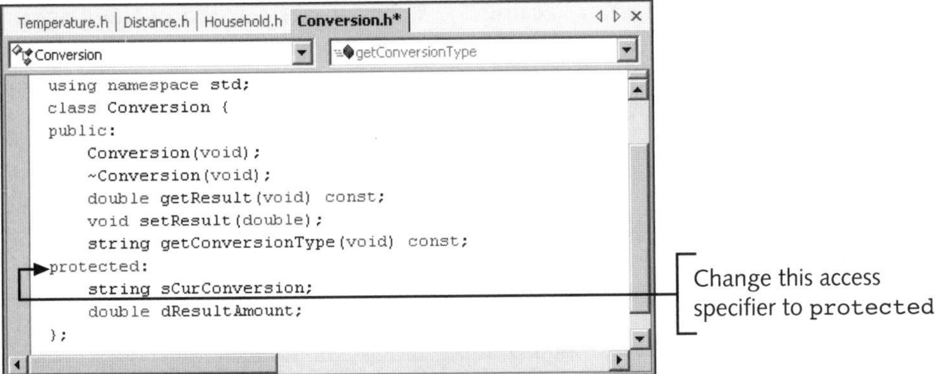
Temperature.h | Distance.h | Household.h | Conversion.h*
Conversion
getConversionType
using namespace std;
class Conversion {
public:
Conversion(void);
~Conversion(void);
double getResult(void) const;
void setResult(double);
string getConversionType(void) const;
protected:
string sCurConversion;
double dResultAmount;
};
Change this access specifier to protected

Figure 8-18 Private access specifier in Conversion.h changed to protected

Overriding Base Class Member Functions

Derived classes are not required to use a base class's member functions. You can write a more suitable version of a member function for a derived class when necessary. Writing a member function in a derived class to replace a base class member function is called **function overriding**. As an example of when you would override a function, consider a base class named Expenses that includes a function named calcExpenses(). The calcExpenses() function in the base class calculates the total expenses that an employee incurs in a monthly period. However, you may derive a class named TravelExpenses from the Expenses base class that only needs to calculate an employee's monthly travel expenses, not his or her total monthly expenses. In this case, you would implement in the derived TravelExpenses class your own version of the calcExpenses() function that calculates just travel expenses.

Caution

You cannot override a data member.

In order to override a base class function, the derived member function declaration must exactly match the base class member function declaration, including the function name, return type, and parameter list. However, the statements in the body of each function definition can be entirely different. If the derived class member function declaration does not match the base class member function declaration, overriding does not occur; you simply create a new member function in the derived class. For example, the following code shows setGrantAmount() function declarations in both the Anthropology class and in the Cultural class. The Cultural class version of the function definition *does not* override the

Anthropology class version because the Cultural class version of the function returns a **double** value while the Anthropology class version does not return a value:

```
// Anthropology.h
...
void setGrantAmount(double);
...
// Cultural.h
...
double setGrantAmount(double);
```

The difference between function overriding and function overloading can be somewhat confusing. Essentially, function overriding allows you to create new behavior for a base class member function. Function overloading allows you to create multiple versions of the same function (possibly with different behavior) with different parameter lists. Figure 8-19 shows an example of overriding the setGrantAmount() member function in the Physical class derived from the Anthropology class. The setGrantAmount() member function in the Anthropology class simply assigns the value passed to the **double** parameter to the dAmountGranted data member. The Physical Anthropology department, however, automatically assigns 25% of all grant amounts to a dPrimateFund data member that ensures enough grant money is reserved for the care of primates being studied. The overridden setGrantAmount() member function in the Physical class performs the necessary calculations to deduct 25% from the grant money and assign it to the dPrimateFund data member. Of that grant money, 75% is then assigned to the dAmountGranted data member.

```
// BASE CLASS
// Anthropology.h
...
public:
...
     void setGrantAmount(double);
...
// Anthropology.cpp
void Anthropology::setGrantAmount(double dGrantAmount) {
     dAmountGranted = dGrantAmount;
}
// DERIVED CLASS
// Physical.h
...
public:
...
     void setGrantAmount(double);   <-- Overridden function declaration
...
// Physical.cpp
void Physical::setGrantAmount(double dGrantAmount) {   <-- Overridden function definition
     dPrimateCare = dGrantAmount * .25;
     dAmountGranted = dGrantAmount * .75;
}
```

Figure 8-19 Overridden member function in a derived class

You can also override overloaded functions in a class definition. If you override an overloaded function, however, you need to create a separate function definition in the derived class for each version of the overloaded function.

If you instantiate both a base class object and a derived class object on the stack, the compiler will know which version of an overridden function to call for each stack object. If a stack object of the base class calls the function, then the base class version of the function executes. If a stack object of the derived class calls the function, then the derived class's version of the function executes.

However, if you use pointers to class objects, the compiler may not automatically know which version of an overridden function to execute. If you anticipate that clients of your class hierarchy will use pointers to objects of your base and derived classes, then you need to declare any overridden functions as virtual. You will learn about virtual functions later in this chapter in the section on polymorphism.

There may be times when you want a derived class object to call a base class version of an overridden function. To force a derived class object to use the base class version of an overridden function, you precede the function name with the base class name and the scope resolution operator using the syntax ***`object.base_class::function();`***. Figure 8-20 shows an example of a main() function that instantiates three objects: one object of the Anthropology class, and two objects of the Physical class. All three objects call the setGrantAmount() function and pass to it a grant amount of 10,000. When the Anthropology class object, grant1, calls the setGrantAmount() member function, the Anthropology base class version of the function executes. When the first Physical class object, grant2, calls the setGrantAmount() member function, the derived Physical class version of the function executes. The second Physical object, grant3, calls the base class version of the setGrantAmount() member function using the Anthropology class name and the scope resolution operator. Because the first Physical object, grant2, is the only object to call the overridden function, it is the only object to assign an amount of 7,500 to the dAmountGranted data member. The other two objects assign the full grant amount of 10,000 to the dAmountGranted data member because they called the Anthropology base class version of the overridden function. The output shown in Figure 8-21 shows that each object called the correct version of the function.

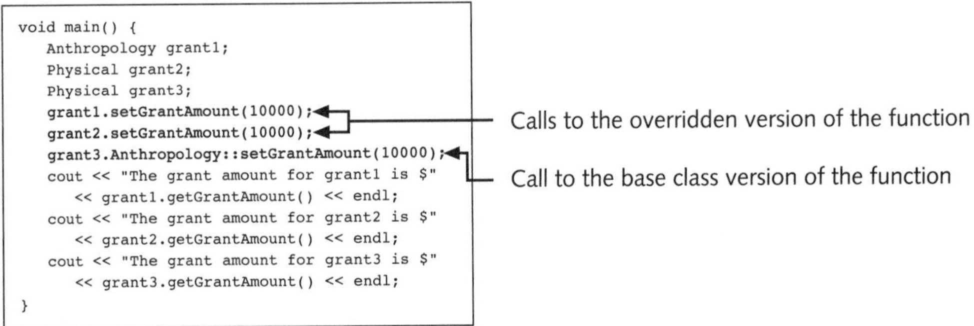

```
void main() {
   Anthropology grant1;
   Physical grant2;
   Physical grant3;
   grant1.setGrantAmount(10000);
   grant2.setGrantAmount(10000);
   grant3.Anthropology::setGrantAmount(10000);
   cout << "The grant amount for grant1 is $"
      << grant1.getGrantAmount() << endl;
   cout << "The grant amount for grant2 is $"
      << grant2.getGrantAmount() << endl;
   cout << "The grant amount for grant3 is $"
      << grant3.getGrantAmount() << endl;
}
```


Figure 8-20 Calling the base class and overridden versions of an inherited function

```
"c:\Visual C++ Projects\Chapter.08\Anthropology\Debug\Anthropology.exe"
The grant amount for grant1 is $10000
The grant amount for grant2 is $75000
The grant amount for grant3 is $10000
Press any key to continue
```

Figure 8-21 Output of program that calls the base class and overridden versions of an inherited function

Next, you will override the setResult() function in each of the Conversion Center program's derived classes. You do not actually need to override the setResult() function, because each of the derived classes does not need a unique implementation of the function. You are overriding the function for practice.

To override the setResult() function in each of the Conversion Center program's derived classes:

1. Open the **Conversion.h** interface file in the Code Editor window.
2. Copy the **setResult()** function declaration statement.
3. Open the **Temperature.h** interface file in the Code Editor window and paste the setResult() function declaration statement into the public section, as shown in Figure 8-22.

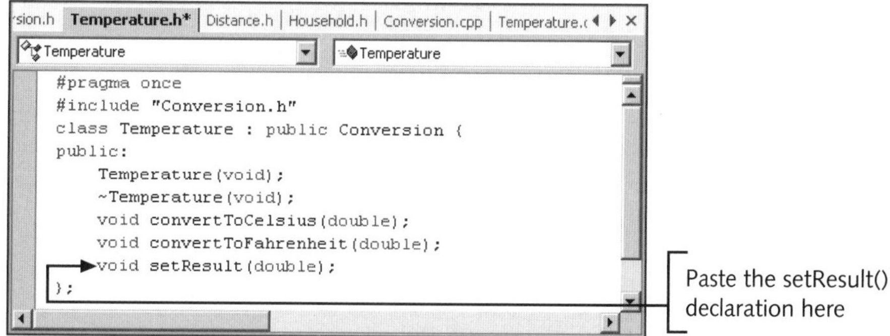

sion.h Temperature.h* Distance.h Household.h Conversion.cpp Temperature.c
Temperature
Temperature
#pragma once
#include "Conversion.h"
class Temperature : public Conversion {
public:
Temperature(void);
~Temperature(void);
void convertToCelsius(double);
void convertToFahrenheit(double);
void setResult(double);
};
Paste the setResult() declaration here

Figure 8-22 setResult() function declaration pasted into Temperature.h

4. Open the **Distance.h** interface file in the Code Editor window and paste the setResult() function declaration statement at the end of the public section, as you did for the Temperature class.
5. Open the **Household.h** interface file in the Code Editor window and paste the setResult() function declaration statement at the end of the public section, as you did for the Temperature and Distance classes.
6. Next, open the **Conversion.cpp** file in the Code Editor window and copy the setResult() function definition.

7. Open the **Temperature.cpp** file in the Code Editor and paste the setResult() function definition after the destructor. After you paste the function, be sure to change the Conversion class reference preceding the scope resolution operator to Temperature, as shown in Figure 8-23.
8. Open the **Distance.cpp** file in the Code Editor and paste the setResult() function definition after the destructor, as you did for the Temperature class. After you paste the function, be sure to change the Conversion class reference preceding the scope resolution operator to Distance.
9. Open the **Household.cpp** file in the Code Editor and paste the setResult() function definition after the destructor, as you did for the Temperature and Distance classes. After you paste the function, be sure to change the Conversion class reference preceding the scope resolution operator to Household.

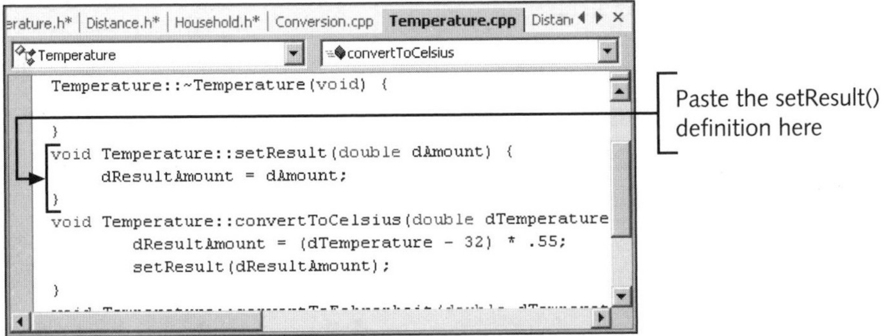

Figure 8-23 setResult() function definition added to Temperature.cpp

10. Rebuild the project and execute the program. The program should function the same as before you overrode the setResult() function.

CONSTRUCTORS AND DESTRUCTORS IN DERIVED CLASSES

When you derive one class from another class, you can think of any instantiated objects of the derived class as having two portions: the base class portion and the derived class portion. During the instantiating process, the base class portion of the object is instantiated, and then the derived class portion of the object is instantiated. Two constructors execute for a single derived class object: the base class constructor and the derived class constructor. Earlier you learned that a derived class does not inherit a base class's constructor or destructor. This is true, but it does not mean that the base class's constructor and destructor do not execute. In fact, every constructor in a class hierarchy for classes above a specific derived class execute when you instantiate an object based on the derived class. If the currently instantiated object has three base classes above it in a class hierarchy, then four constructors execute, one for each of the three base classes and one for the current derived class. Just as each constructor in a class hierarchy executes when a derived class object is instantiated, each destructor in a class hierarchy executes when a derived class object goes out of scope or is destroyed.

When a derived class object instantiates, constructors begin executing at the top of the class hierarchy. First, the base class constructor executes, then any indirect base class's constructors execute. Finally, the derived class's constructor executes. When an object is destroyed, class destructors are executed in the reverse order. First, the derived class's destructor is called, then the destructors for any indirect base classes, and finally, the destructor for the base class. Figure 8-24 illustrates this process using a class hierarchy with four levels.

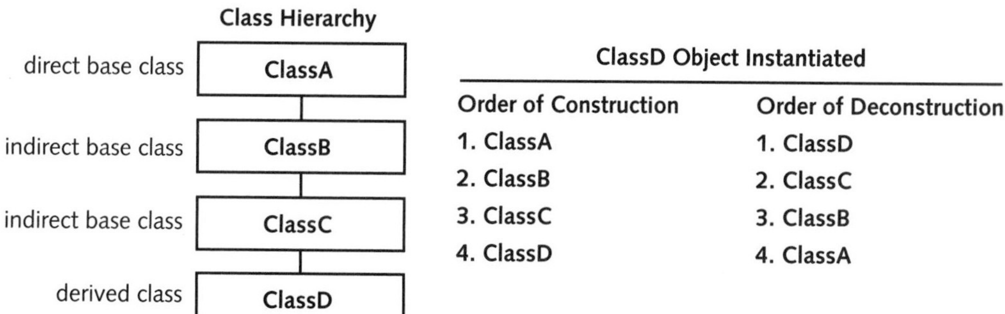

Figure 8-24 Execution of constructors and destructors in a class hierarchy

The order of construction makes sense, because it allows base classes to perform any initialization on class members that may be used by derived classes. And the order of destruction ensures that any base class members required by derived classes are not destroyed until all objects of any derived classes are destroyed. For example, the Anthropology base class constructors allocate memory on the heap for the pCountries pointer, which stores the names of countries where research will take place. Derived classes of the Anthropology base class can then use the inherited setResearchCountries() and getResearchCountries() member functions to store and retrieve the names of research countries. If a derived class's constructor were called before the Anthropology base class constructor, then the derived class could conceivably try to call the setResearchCountries() member function before space is allocated on the heap for the pCountries pointer, causing an error. Similarly, if the Anthropology base class destructor were called and deleted the pCountries pointer before a derived class's destructor was called, the derived class could try to store or retrieve the value pointed to by the pCountries pointer, again causing an error.

Figure 8-25 shows modified versions of the constructors and destructors for the Anthropology base class and the derived Physical class, along with a main() function, that demonstrate the order of execution for the constructors and destructors. Output statements have been added to each constructor and destructor that print a line of text describing when each function is called. Figure 8-26 shows the output when you execute the default constructor from the main() function.

```
// Anthropology.cpp
...
Anthropology::Anthropology(void) {
      sAnthropologist = "";
      iNumCountries = 3;
      pCountries = new string[iNumCountries];
      cout << "Base class constructor called."   << endl;
}
Anthropology::Anthropology(string sName) {
      sAnthropologist = "";
      sAnthropologist = sName;
      iNumCountries = 3;
      pCountries = new string[iNumCountries];
      cout << "Base class constructor called."   << endl;
}
Anthropology::Anthropology(string sName, int iCountries) {
      sAnthropologist = "";
      sAnthropologist = sName;
      iNumCountries = iCountries;
      pCountries = new string[iNumCountries];
      cout << "Base class constructor called."   << endl;
}
Anthropology::~Anthropology(void) {
      delete [] pCountries;
      cout << "Base class destructor called."   << endl;
}
...
// Physical.cpp
...
Physical::Physical(void) {
     dPrimateCare = 0;
     cout << "Derived class constructor called." << endl;
}
Physical::~Physical(void) {
     cout << "Derived class destructor called." << endl;
}
...
void main() {
      Physical grant1;
      grant1.setAnthropologistName("Richard Leakey");
      grant1.setResearchCountries();
      cout << "The anthropologist's name is "
            << grant1.getAnthropologistName() << endl;
      string* pCountries = grant1.getResearchCountries();
      for (int iCount = 0; iCount < 3; ++iCount) {
            cout << "Research country " << iCount + 1 << ": ";
            cout << pCountries[iCount] << endl;
      }
}
```

Figure 8-25 Order of construction and destruction for the Anthropology base class and the derived Physical class

8

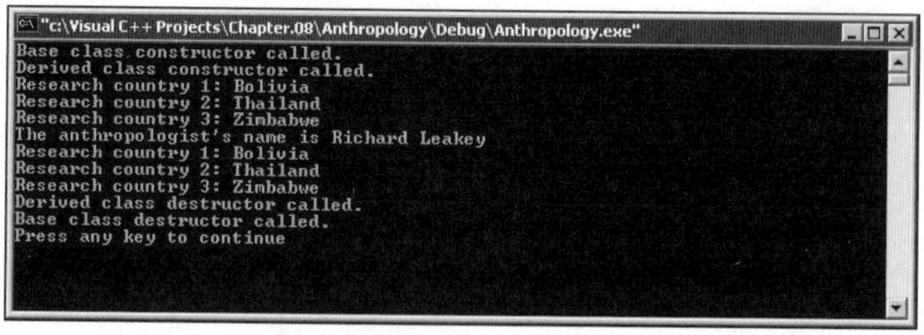

```
"c:\Visual C++ Projects\Chapter.08\Anthropology\Debug\Anthropology.exe"
Base class constructor called.
Derived class constructor called.
Research country 1: Bolivia
Research country 2: Thailand
Research country 3: Zimbabwe
The anthropologist's name is Richard Leakey
Research country 1: Bolivia
Research country 2: Thailand
Research country 3: Zimbabwe
Derived class destructor called.
Base class destructor called.
Press any key to continue
```

Figure 8-26 Output showing the order of construction and destruction for the Anthropology base class and derived Physical class

Parameterized Base Class Constructors

Notice that the main() function in Figure 8-25 executes the default constructor for both the Anthropology class and the Physical class because the statement that instantiates the Physical object, grant1, does not include parentheses or parameters. There will be times, however, when you will need to execute a base class's parameterized constructor instead of its default constructor. For instance, you may want to pass the anthropologist's name to the single parameter constructor at object instantiation. Or, rather than using three as the default number of elements in the string class array, you may want to use a different number by calling the two-parameter base class constructor when you first instantiate the grant1 object. You execute a base class's parameterized constructor using an initializer list in a derived class's parameterized constructor. The two-parameter constructor for the Anthropology base class, for instance, accepts a text string parameter containing an anthropologist's name and an integer representing the number of research countries. You create a parameterized constructor for the Physical class that also accepts a text string parameter containing an anthropologist's name and an integer representing the number of research countries, and you include an initializer list that passes the parameters to the Anthropology class's two-parameter constructor. This forces the Anthropology class's two-parameter constructor to execute instead of its default constructor.

Figure 8-27 shows a parameterized Physical class constructor with an initializer list that calls the Anthropology class's two-parameter constructor, along with a modified main() function. Notice that the parameters are not used in the body of the Physical class constructor; they are only passed to the base class parameterized constructor. The output of the modified program is shown in Figure 8-28.

```
// Physical.cpp
...
Physical::Physical(string sName, int iCountries)
        : Anthropology(sName, iCountries) {
        dPrimateCare = 0;
        cout << "Derived class constructor called."   << endl;
}
...
void main() {
        int iNumCountries = 2;
        Physical grant1("Richard Leakey", iNumCountries);
        grant1.setResearchCountries();
        string* pCountries = grant1.getResearchCountries();
        cout << grant1.getAnthropologistName()
                << "'s research countries: ";
        for (int iCount = 0; iCount < iNumCountries; ++iCount) {
                cout << pCountries[iCount];
                if (iCount != iNumCountries-1)
                        cout << ", ";
        }
        cout << endl;
}
```

Parameterized derived class constructor passing arguments to the base class parameterized constructor

Call to the parameterized constructors

Figure 8-27 Physical class constructor with an initializer list

```
"c:\Visual C++ Projects\Chapter.08\Anthropology\Debug\Anthropology.exe"
Base class constructor called.
Derived class constructor called.
Research country 1: Angola
Research country 2: Belize
Richard Leakey's research countries: Angola, Belize
Derived class destructor called.
Base class destructor called.
Press any key to continue
```

Figure 8-28 Output of Physical class constructor with an initializer list

Base Class Copy Constructors

When you create a new derived class object by copying an existing derived class object, if the base class constructor allocates memory on the heap, you need to call a base class copy constructor. You do this to ensure that the new derived class object and the existing class object do not contain pointers to the same memory addresses. You call a base class copy constructor using an initializer list with the derived class copy constructor, the same as when you call a parameterized base class constructor. The main() function in Figure 8-29 creates a new Physical object named grant2 by copying the existing grant1 object. The Physical derived class's copy constructor includes an initializer list that passes the derived copy constructor's object parameter to the Anthropology class copy constructor. Notice that in this case the derived class's copy constructor only serves to pass the object parameter to the Anthropology class copy constructor (although it also prints some text to the screen saying it was called). If you execute the Grant Allocation program with the code in Figure 8-29, you will see the output in Figure 8-30. Notice that the class constructors are called for the grant1 object and that the copy constructors are called for the grant2 object.

```
// Anthropology.cpp
...
Anthropology::Anthropology(const Anthropology& sourceObject) {
      iNumCountries = sourceObject.iNumCountries;
      pCountries = new string[iNumCountries];
      cout << "Base class copy constructor called." << endl;
}
...
// Physical.cpp
...
Physical::Physical(const Physical& sourceObject)
    : Anthropology(sourceObject) {
    cout << "Derived class copy constructor called." << endl;
}
...
void main() {
      int iNumCountries = 2;
      Physical grant1("Richard Leakey", iNumCountries);
      grant1.setResearchCountries();
      string* pCountries = grant1.getResearchCountries();
      cout << grant1.getAnthropologistName()
            << "'s research countries: ";
      for (int iCount = 0; iCount < iNumCountries; ++iCount) {
            cout << pCountries[iCount];
            if (iCount != iNumCountries-1)
                  cout << ", ";
      }
      cout << endl;
      Physical grant2(grant1);
      grant2.setAnthropologistName("Dianne Fossey");
      grant2.setResearchCountries();
      pCountries = grant2.getResearchCountries();
      cout << grant2.getAnthropologistName()
            << "'s research countries: ";
      for (int iCount = 0; iCount < iNumCountries; ++iCount) {
            cout << pCountries[iCount];
            if (iCount != iNumCountries-1)
                  cout << ", ";
      }
      cout << endl;
}
```

Base class copy constructor

Derived class copy constructor

Statement that creates a new Physical object by copying an existing one

Figure 8-29 Calling a base class copy constructor

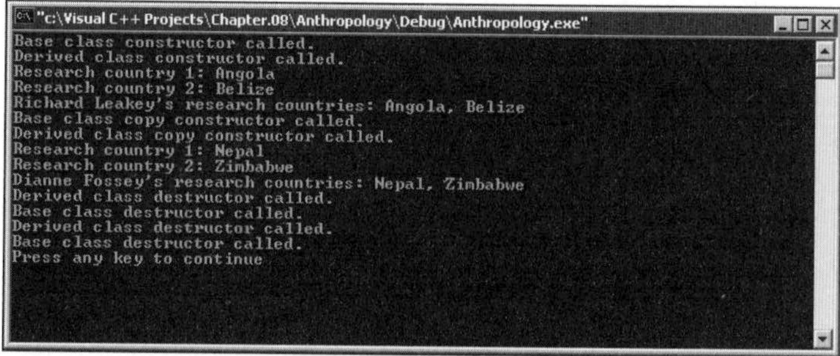

Figure 8-30 Output for Anthropology base class and Physical derived class after adding copy constructors

POLYMORPHISM

As you learned earlier, member functions in a base class can be overridden by derived classes. Thus, you will have multiple versions of the same function available to your program. The ability to override base member functions in derived classes is called **polymorphism**, which means "many forms." As a more general object-oriented programming term, polymorphism refers to a programming language's ability to process objects differently depending on their data type.

When declaring objects with overridden functions on the stack, you do not need to worry about polymorphism because the compiler can figure out which overridden function object to execute based on the class type of each object. When you use pointers to objects, however, the compiler can become confused by the class type of an object and call the wrong version of an overridden function. Recall that an object of a derived class "is an" object of its base class. For this reason, a pointer to an object of a base class can also point to an object of a derived class. It does not work the other way: a pointer of a derived class cannot point to a base class object. As an example, look at the overridden setGrantAmount() member function again. In the following code, a Physical class object is declared on the stack using the default constructor. Then, an Anthropology pointer is declared and assigned the address of the Physical class object. Finally, the overridden setGrantAmount()member function is called.


```
void main() {
     Physical aGrant("Richard Leakey");
     Anthropology* pGrant = &aGrant;
     pGrant->setGrantAmount(10000);
     cout << "The grant amount for "
          << pGrant->getAnthropologistName()
          << " is $" << pGrant->getGrantAmount() << endl;
}
```

In the preceding code, how does the compiler know which version of the overridden setGrantAmount()function to execute? Should it execute the base class version of the function, because that is the data type of the pointer, or should it execute the derived class version, because that is the data type of the object being pointed to? Unfortunately, the incorrect Anthropology class version of the function executes, which does not reserve 25% of the grant amount to the Physical class's dPrimateCare data member. If you were to execute the code, the output statement in the console window would read *The grant amount for Richard Leakey is $10000* instead of correctly reading *The grant amount for Richard Leakey is $7500.*

The problem with the preceding code is that the decision about which class's version of the function to execute is decided at compile time, when you first build the project. The compiler uses the base class version of the function, not the inherited class that the object points to, because the base class version of the function is the only thing it sees during the compilation process. Deciding which class members to use at compile-time is called **early binding**. With polymorphism, however, you want decisions about which class members to use to be made at run time, based on an object's class type. Deciding which class members to use at run time is called **dynamic binding**, or **run-time binding**. To enable dynamic binding, you declare an overridden member function as virtual.

Virtual Functions

There will be times when you know that a function you implement in your base class will need to be overridden in any derived classes. For example, the calcExpenses() function in the Expenses class that you learned about earlier will probably always need to be overridden to create a version of the function tailored to the needs of any derived classes. In order to be sure that the compiler knows which version of a function to execute, the base class version or a derived class version, you declare the base class version as `virtual`. A **virtual function** instructs the compiler to decide at run time which version of an overridden function to call. In other words, a `virtual` function ensures that the compiler knows which version of a function to execute. To declare an overridden function as `virtual`, you add the `virtual` keyword at the beginning of the member function declaration in the base class. You do not need to add the `virtual` keyword to the base class function definition or the derived class function declaration or definition. Figure 8-31 shows a modified version of the Grant Allocation program. This time the base class declaration of the overridden function includes the `virtual` keyword. Now when you execute the main() function with the heap objects, the correct derived class version of the overridden function is called. Figure 8-32 shows the output.

```
// BASE CLASS
// Anthropology.h
...
public:
...
   virtual void setGrantAmount(double);
...
// Anthropology.cpp
void Anthropology::setGrantAmount(double dGrantAmount) {
   dAmountGranted = dGrantAmount;
}
// DERIVED CLASS
// Physical.h
...
public:
...
   void setGrantAmount(double);
...
// Physical.cpp
void Physical::setGrantAmount(double dGrantAmount) {
   dPrimateCare = dGrantAmount * .25;
   dAmountGranted = dGrantAmount * .75;
}
...
void main() {
   Physical aGrant("Richard Leakey");
   Anthropology* pGrant = &aGrant;
   pGrant->setGrantAmount(10000);
   cout << "The grant amount for "
        << pGrant->getAnthropologistName()
        << " is $" << pGrant->getGrantAmount() << endl;
}
```

Virtual function declaration

Virtual function definition

Figure 8-31 Grant Allocation program with a `virtual` overridden member function

```
"c:\Visual C++ Projects\Chapter.08\Anthropology\Debug\Anthropology.exe"
Base class constructor called.
Derived class constructor called.
The grant amount for Richard Leakey is $7500
Derived class destructor called.
Base class destructor called.
Press any key to continue
```

Figure 8-32 Output of Grant Allocation program with a virtual overridden member function

Next, you will modify the object declarations in the main.cpp file so that the objects are instantiated on the heap. So that the correct overridden version of the setResult() function executes, you will modify the setResult() function declaration in the Conversion class so that it is virtual.

To instantiate the class objects in the main.cpp on the heap and to modify the overridden setResult() function in the Conversion class so that it is virtual:

1. Open the **main.cpp** file in the Code Editor window.
2. Modify the `if` statement that instantiates the Temperature object so that it is instantiated on the heap, as shown in Figure 8-33. Be sure to change the member selection operators to indirect member selection operators.

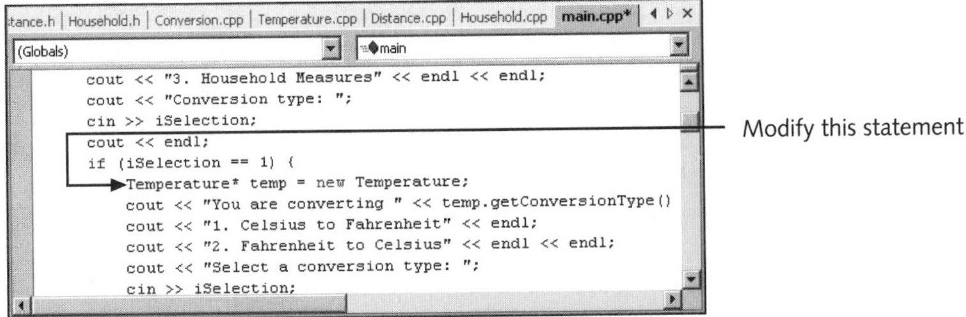
tance.h | Household.h | Conversion.cpp | Temperature.cpp | Distance.cpp | Household.cpp main.cpp*
(Globals)
main
cout << "3. Household Measures" << endl << endl;
cout << "Conversion type: ";
cin >> iSelection;
cout << endl;
if (iSelection == 1) {
Temperature* temp = new Temperature;
cout << "You are converting " << temp.getConversionType()
cout << "1. Celsius to Fahrenheit" << endl;
cout << "2. Fahrenheit to Celsius" << endl << endl;
cout << "Select a conversion type: ";
cin >> iSelection;
Modify this statement

Figure 8-33 main() function modified so the Temperature object instantiated on the heap

3. As shown in Figure 8-34, add a statement to the end of the `if` block that deletes the temp heap object.

8

```
tance.h | Household.h | Conversion.cpp | Temperature.cpp | Distance.cpp | Household.cpp | main.cpp*
(Globals)                                    main
            temp.convertToCelsius(dValue);
        else {
            cout << "You did not select a correct number!" << endl
            exit(1);
        }
        cout << "The converted value is " << temp.getResult() << e
        delete temp;
    }
    else if (iSelection == 2) {
        Distance distance;
        cout << "You are converting " << distance.getConversionTyp
```

Add this statement

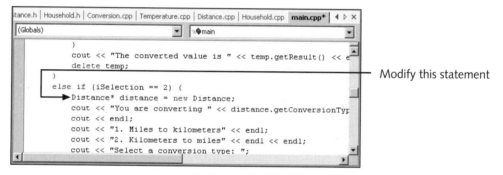

Figure 8-34 Statement added that delete the temp heap object

4. Modify the `if` statement that instantiates the Distance object so that it is instantiated on the heap, as shown in Figure 8-35. Be sure to change the member selection operators to indirect member selection operators

```
tance.h | Household.h | Conversion.cpp | Temperature.cpp | Distance.cpp | Household.cpp | main.cpp*
(Globals)                                    main
        }
        cout << "The converted value is " << temp.getResult() << e
        delete temp;
    }
    else if (iSelection == 2) {
        Distance* distance = new Distance;
        cout << "You are converting " << distance.getConversionTyp
        cout << endl;
        cout << "1. Miles to kilometers" << endl;
        cout << "2. Kilometers to miles" << endl << endl;
        cout << "Select a conversion type: ";
```

Modify this statement

Figure 8-35 main() function modified so the Distance object instantiated on the heap

5. As shown in Figure 8-36, add a statement to the end of the `if` block that deletes the distance heap object.

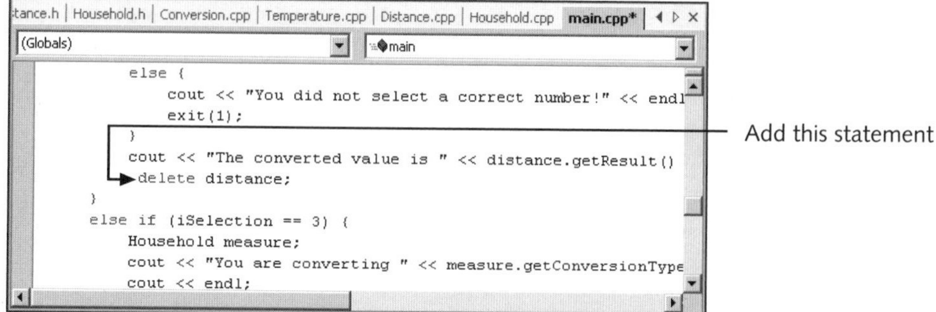

Figure 8-36 Statement added that deletes the distance heap object

6. Modify the `if` statement that instantiates the Household object so that it is instantiated on the heap, as shown in Figure 8-37. Be sure to change the member selection operators to indirect member selection operators.

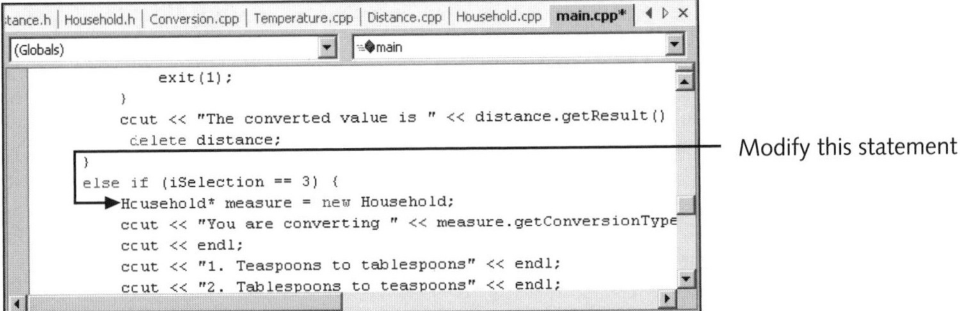

Figure 8-37 main() function modified so Household object is instantiated on the heap

7. As shown in Figure 8-38, add a statement to the end of the `if` block that deletes the measure heap object.

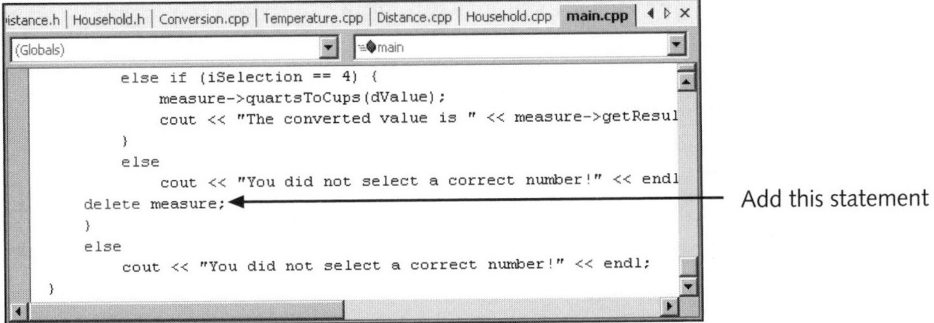

Figure 8-38 Statement added that deletes the measure heap object

8. Open the **Conversion.h** file in the Code Editor window.
9. Add the `virtual` keyword to the start of the setResult() function declaration, as shown in Figure 8-39:
10. Rebuild and execute the program. The program should execute normally.

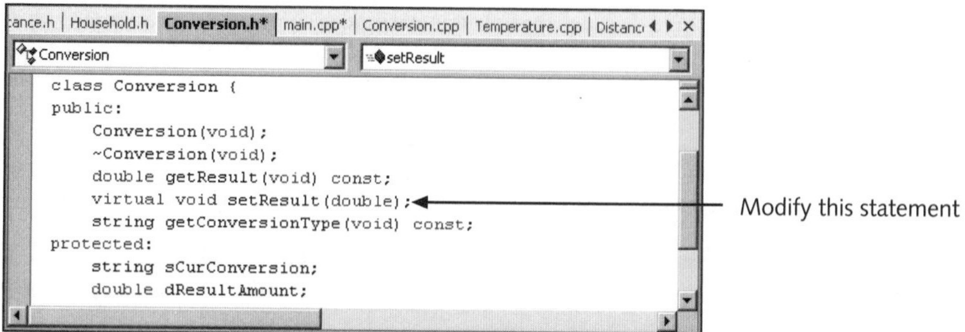

ance.h | Household.h | Conversion.h* | main.cpp* | Conversion.cpp | Temperature.cpp | Distanc
Conversion
setResult
class Conversion {
public:
Conversion(void);
~Conversion(void);
double getResult(void) const;
virtual void setResult(double);
string getConversionType(void) const;
protected:
string sCurConversion;
double dResultAmount;
Modify this statement

Figure 8-39 `virtual` keyword added to the start of the setResult() function declaration in the Conversion class

Virtual Destructors

As mentioned earlier, a base class pointer can point to an object of a derived class. Why would you use a base class pointer to point to a derived class object? Why not just create a pointer of the correct derived class type? Well, you may not know which derived class type to use until run time. Therefore, it is easier to create a more generic pointer of the base class type that can point to multiple derived class types. Consider a Shape base class from which multiple other classes derive, such as a Rectangle class, a Square class, and a Circle class. Clients using the Shape class hierarchy may allow users of their program to select a specific shape to be drawn on screen. Because a client cannot know what shape a user will select, he or she may use a Shape pointer to point to an object that corresponds to the selected shape.

As with overridden functions, when you use a base class pointer to point to a derived class, the compiler will not know at compile time which destructor to call: the pointer class type or the class type of the object pointed to. By default, the compiler will use early binding and call only the base class destructor. However, with a base class pointer that points to a derived class, you need to call the destructor for both classes. To force the compiler to use dynamic binding with a destructor, you use the `virtual` keyword with the base class destructor declaration, the same as for `virtual` functions. A **`virtual` destructor** instructs the compiler to decide at run time which destructor, or multiple destructors, to call. You do not need to add the `virtual` keyword to the base class destructor definition or the derived class destructor declaration or definition. Figure 8-40 shows a modified version of the Grant Allocation program's main() function that executes the setGrantAmount() member function. In this version, an Anthropology pointer is declared and points to a Physical object. The figure also shows the destructors for both the Anthropology class and the Physical class. Notice there is a problem in the output in Figure 8-41: The destructor is called only once.

```
// BASE CLASS
// Anthropology.h
...
public:
...
   ~Anthropology(void);
...
// Anthropology.cpp
Anthropology::~Anthropology(void) {
   delete sCountries;
   cout << "Base class destructor called." << endl;
}
// DERIVED CLASS
// Physical.h
...
public:
...
   ~Physical(void);
...
// Physical.cpp
void Physical::setGrantAmount(double dGrantAmount) {
   dPrimateCare = dGrantAmount * .25;
   dAmountGranted = dGrantAmount * .75;
}
Physical::~Physical(void) {
   cout << "Derived class destructor called." << endl;
}
...
void main() {
   Anthropology* aGrant = new Physical("Richard Leakey");
   aGrant->setGrantAmount(10000);
   cout << "The grant amount for "
      << aGrant->getAnthropologistName()
      << " is $" << aGrant->getGrantAmount() << endl;
   delete aGrant;
}
```

Base pointer pointing to a derived class object

Deleting the base class pointer

Figure 8-40 Grant Allocation program with an Anthropology pointer to a Physical object

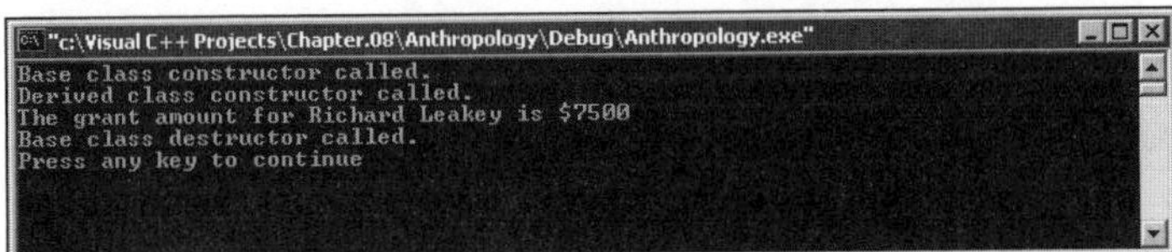

Figure 8-41 Output of Grant Allocation program with an Anthropology pointer to a Physical object

In order to correct the problem and call the destructors for both the base class and the derived class, add the `virtual` keyword to just the base class function declaration as follows:

```
// Anthropology.h
...
public:
...
     virtual ~Anthropology(void);
...
```

Now when you execute the program, both the base class destructor and the derived class destructor execute, as shown in the output in Figure 8-42.

```
"c:\Visual C++ Projects\Chapter.08\Anthropology\Debug\Anthropology.exe"
Base class constructor called.
Derived class constructor called.
The grant amount for Richard Leakey is $7500
Derived class destructor called.
Base class destructor called.
Press any key to continue
```

Figure 8-42 Output of Grant Allocation program with an Anthropology pointer to a Physical object after adding a `virtual` destructor

Tip

When you use the Add Class Wizard to add a class to a project, you can create the class with a virtual destructor by clicking the Virtual destructor check box in the Class Wizard dialog box.

You will not have any problems with the destructor for the Conversion Center program because the object declarations in the main.cpp file of the Conversion Center program do not use base class pointers to point to derived class objects. It is possible, however, that a client of the Conversion Center program may need to use a Conversion pointer to point to an object of one of the derived classes. For this reason, you will add the `virtual` keyword to the Conversion base class destructor.

To add the `virtual` keyword to the Conversion base class destructor:

1. Open the **Conversion.h** file in the Code Editor window.
2. Add the `virtual` keyword to the destructor declaration statement as shown in Figure 8-43:

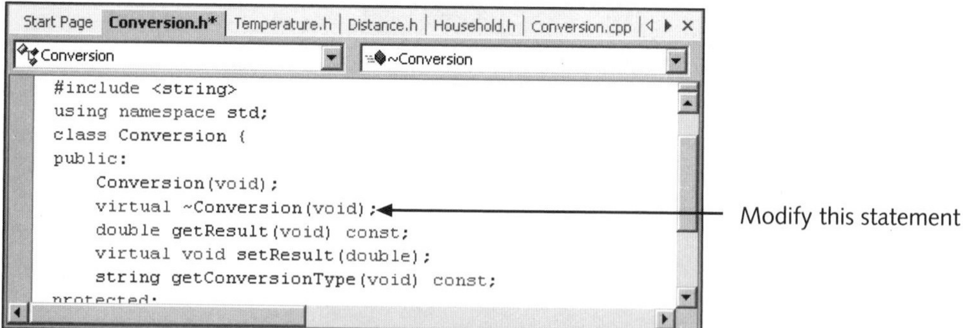
Start Page
Conversion.h*
Temperature.h
Distance.h
Household.h
Conversion.cpp
Conversion
~Conversion
#include <string>
using namespace std;
class Conversion {
public:
Conversion(void);
virtual ~Conversion(void);
double getResult(void) const;
virtual void setResult(double);
string getConversionType(void) const;
Modify this statement

Figure 8-43 `virtual` keyword added to the Conversion class destructor declaration statement

3. Rebuild and execute the program. The program should execute normally.

Abstract Classes

You may have a base class in a class hierarchy that exists only as a template from which other classes are derived. For example, you may have a generic Aviation class from which you want to derive other types of aviation classes such as Airplanes or Helicopters. Or, the base class may contain members that you want to make sure are implemented only in other derived classes, almost as a set of guidelines that derived classes of your base class should follow. Clients should not be able to instantiate objects from these types of classes, only use them as a basis from which to derive other classes. Classes from which you cannot instantiate an object and that serve only to enforce a design protocol for derived classes are called **abstract classes**.

You create an abstract class by including one or more pure `virtual` functions in the class definition. A **pure `virtual` function** is a member function that is declared in an abstract class, but defined in a derived class. You declare a function as `virtual` by including `=0` at the end of the function declaration statement in an abstract class. For example, to declare as a pure `virtual` function, a function named calcTravelCosts() that returns a double value, you use the statement `virtual double calcTravelCosts() = 0;`. As with function overriding, you must be sure that the return value and parameter list of a derived class's definition of a pure `virtual` function exactly match the return value and parameter list of the pure `virtual` function declaration in the abstract class.

8

Abstract classes can also include standard member functions that derived classes can use or override as necessary. A class derived from an abstract base class, however, must provide a definition for all of the abstract class's pure virtual functions or the derived class itself will also be an abstract class.

Why would you use an abstract class? Consider the Cultural class discussed earlier that represents the Cultural Anthropology department of the School of Anthropology. The Cultural class in the Anthropology class hierarchy could be used as a base class to derive three "subdepartment" classes: Archaeology, Linguistics, and Ethnology, as illustrated in Figure 8-44.

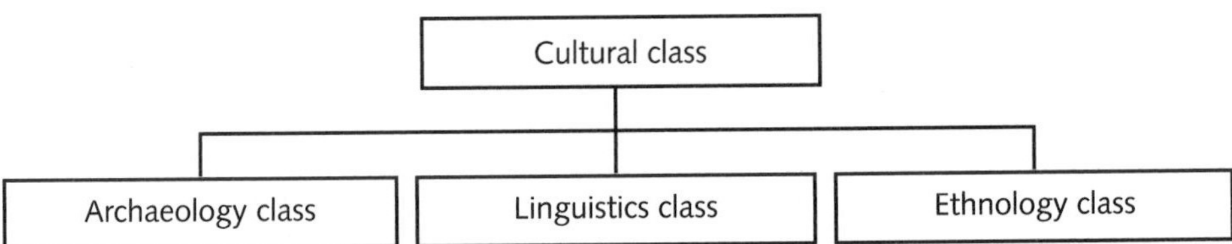

Figure 8-44 Cultural class hierarchy

Suppose that as you are designing the Cultural class, you learn that another programmer has been hired to write the Archaeology, Linguistics, and Ethnology classes. The head of the Cultural Archaeology department wants each of the subdepartments to record the miscellaneous expenses associated with a particular grant. Each department has different types of expenses due to the differences in its fields of study, so you cannot write a single function that can be used by all three departments. You want to make sure that the new programmer writes a unique definition of the setExpenses() member function for each subdepartment. Therefore, you make the Cultural class abstract by writing a pure declaration for the setExpenses() function.

Figure 8-45 shows the interface file for an abstract Cultural class containing two pure virtual functions: calcTravelCosts() and setExpenses(). Notice that both pure virtual function declarations end with `=0`. A definition file for the Cultural class is not shown because it would not contain definitions for the pure virtual functions. Instead, the pure virtual functions are defined in the Archaeology, Linguistics, and Ethnology classes that derive from the Cultural class.

```
#pragma once
#include "Anthropology.h"
class Cultural : public Anthropology {
public:
   Cultural(void);
   ~Cultural(void);
       virtual double calcTravelCosts(void) = 0;
       virtual double setExpenses(void) = 0;
   void setAntiquitiesCost(double);
   double getAntiquitiesCost(void) const;
   void setCassettesCost(double);
   double getCassettesCost(void) const;
private:
   double dAntiquitiesCost;
   double dCassettesCost;
};
```

Pure `virtual` function declarations

Figure 8-45 Cultural class interface file with pure `virtual` functions

The one function in the Conversion Center program that should be defined in all derived classes is the setResult() function. In fact, because the Conversion class does not perform any calculations itself, no object should be instantiated from it. Therefore, you will make it into an abstract class. Because you have already added setResult() function definitions to each of the derived classes, you can easily turn the Conversion class into an abstract class.

To turn the Conversion class into an abstract class by modifying the setResult() function into a pure virtual function:

1. Return to the **Conversion.h** file in the Code Editor window.
2. Convert the setResult() function into a pure `virtual` function by adding `=0` to the end of the setResult() function definition as shown in Figure 8-46:
3. Open the **Conversion.cpp** file in the Code Editor window.
4. Delete the setResult() function definition because pure `virtual` functions cannot be defined in a base class.
5. Rebuild and execute the program. The program should execute normally.

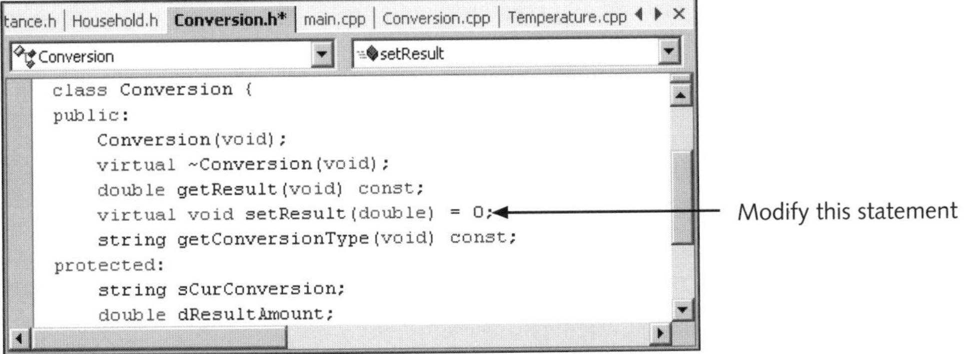
tance.h | Household.h | Conversion.h* | main.cpp | Conversion.cpp | Temperature.cpp
Conversion
setResult
class Conversion {
public:
Conversion(void);
virtual ~Conversion(void);
double getResult(void) const;
virtual void setResult(double) = 0;
string getConversionType(void) const;
protected:
string sCurConversion;
double dResultAmount;
Modify this statement

Figure 8-46 setResult() function in Conversion class converted to a pure `virtual` function

8

Chapter Summary

- Inheritance refers to the ability of one class to take on the characteristics of another class.
- An inherited class is called the base class, and the class that inherits a base class is called a derived class.
- A derived class must provide its own implementations of constructor, copy constructor, destructor, friend, and overloaded assignment operator functions.
- You derive a class by including the base class in the derived class's interface file with an #include statement. You must also append a colon to the header declaration statement in the interface file, followed by an access modifier and the name of the base class.
- The access modifiers and base class names following the colon in a class's header declaration statement are called the base list.
- When you build a series of base classes and derived classes, the chain of inherited classes is known as a class hierarchy.
- A class that directly precedes another class in a class hierarchy, and that is included in the derived class's base list, is called the direct base class.
- A class that does not directly precede a class in a class hierarchy, and therefore is not included in the class's base list, is called an indirect base class.
- The `protected` access modifier restricts class member access to the class itself, to member functions in classes derived from the class, or to friend functions and friend classes.
- Writing a member function in a derived class to replace a base class member function is called function overriding.

- You execute a base class's parameterized constructor using an initializer list in a derived class's parameterized constructor.
- You call a base class copy constructor using an initializer list with the derived class copy constructor.
- The ability to override base member functions in derived classes is referred to as polymorphism, which means "many forms."
- A virtual function instructs the compiler to decide at run time which version of an overridden function to call.
- A virtual destructor instructs the compiler to decide at run time which destructor, or multiple destructors, to call.
- Classes from which you cannot create an object and that only serve to enforce a design protocol for derived classes are called abstract classes.

Review Questions

1. A class that inherits the characteristics of a base class is also said to ________________ the base class.
   a. evolve
   b. extend
   c. transform
   d. override
2. Which of the following terms does not refer to a base class?
   a. superclass
   b. subclass
   c. ancestor
   d. parent
3. Which of the following types of functions does a derived class inherit?
   a. member functions
   b. constructor functions
   c. destructors functions
   d. friend functions

4. The access modifiers and base class names following the colon in a class's header declaration statement is(are) known as ________________.

   a. access specifiers

   b. inheritance specifiers

   c. the class list

   d. the base list

5. The Students class includes a member function named getStudentID(). Assuming the Freshman class derives from the Students class, which of the following is the correct syntax for calling the getStudentID() member function from a Freshman object named curStudent?

   a. `curStudent.Student.getStudentID();`

   b. `curStudent.Student(getStudentID());`

   c. `curStudent.getStudentID();`

   d. `curStudent.getStudentID(Student);`

6. When you build a series of base classes and derived classes, the chain of inherited classes is known as a class hierarchy or a(n) ________________.

   a. inheritance chain

   b. abstract data structure

   c. base pyramid

   d. object model

7. What is the name of the relationship between a derived class and a base class?

   a. "is a(n)"

   b. "has a(n)"

   c. "was a(n)"

   d. "from a(n)"

8. What is the name of the relationship when one class *includes* a reference to another class?

   a. "is a(n)"

   b. "has a(n)"

   c. "was a(n)"

   d. "from a(n)"

9. How would you describe the Undergraduate class in relation to its derived classes in the following class hierarchy?

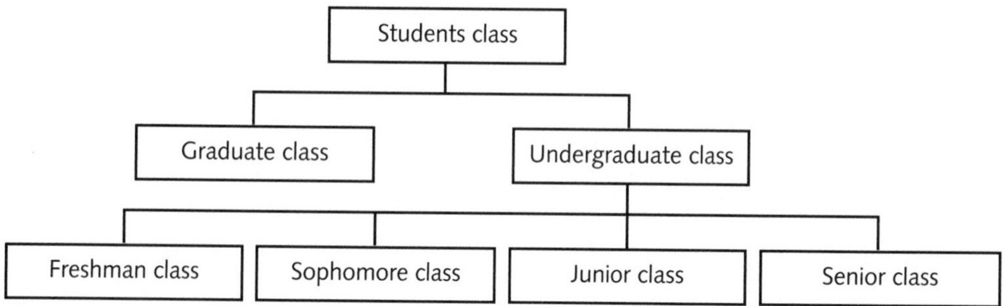

   a. base class
   b. indirect base class
   c. derived class
   d. subclass

10. Which of the following does not have access to a base class's protected members?
   a. classes derived from the base class
   b. friend functions of the base class
   c. friend classes of the base class
   d. global functions

11. What access does the Sophomore class have to the Students class in the following class declaration?

```
class Sophomore : Students
  {
  ...
  }
```

   a. private
   b. public
   c. protected
   d. friend

12. What is the correct syntax to force an Undergraduate object named curStudent to use the Students base class version of the overridden getStudentID() function?
   a. `curStudent.Students::getStudentID();`
   b. `curStudent.Students(getStudentID());`
   c. `Students.curStudent::getStudentID();`
   d. `curStudent.Students.getStudentID();`

13. The ability to override base member functions in derived classes is referred to as ________________.
    a. multiplicity
    b. polymorphism
    c. inheritance
    d. derivation
14. Deciding at compile time which class members to use is referred to as ________________.
    a. early binding
    b. dynamic binding
    c. precompilation
    d. pseudo-binding
15. Deciding at run time which class members to use is referred to as ________________, or run-time binding.
    a. early binding
    b. dynamic binding
    c. postcompilation
    d. pseudo-binding
16. When do you need to use `virtual` overridden functions and destructors?
    a. when a base class pointer points to a derived class object
    b. when a derived class pointer points to a base class object
    c. whenever you instantiate an object on the stack
    d. whenever you instantiate an object on the heap
17. Where do you add the `virtual` keyword when declaring functions as `virtual`?
    a. in the base class function declaration
    b. in the base class function declaration and definition
    c. in the base class function declaration and definition, and in the derived class function declaration
    d. in the base class function declaration and definition, and in the derived class function declaration and definition
18. Which of the following declares the void setCarName() function as a pure `virtual` function?
    a. `pure virtual void setCarName();`
    b. `virtual void setCarName();`
    c. `void setCarName() = 0;`
    d. `virtual void setCarName() = 0;`

19. What type of class includes pure virtual functions?
    a. base class
    b. indirect base class
    c. abstract class
    d. derived class

PROGRAMMING EXERCISES

1. Write a parameterized constructor for the derived Residential class that calls the following parameterized RealEstate base class constructor. The body of the parameterized Residential class constructor should be empty.

```
// RealEstate class parameterized constructor
RealEstate::RealEstate(string sName) {
  sCustomerName = sName;
}
```

2. Explain the difference between function overriding and function overloading.
3. What is the difference between early binding and dynamic binding?
4. Explain when you would need to declare functions and destructors as `virtual`.
5. Explain why the following code causes a compile error:

```
class Inventory {
public:
  virtual void setVolumeDiscount() = 0;
protected:
  double dDiscount;
};
class Wholesale : public Inventory {
public:
  void setVolumeDiscount();
};
void main() {
  Inventory westernDistributor;
  westernDistributor.setVolumeDiscount();
}
```

6. Describe why you would create an abstract base class.

PROGRAMMING PROJECTS

1. Create a console application project that includes a Loan base class. Add three `private` data members to the Loan class: a `float` variable named fLoanAmount that stores the amount of the loan, a `double` variable named dPercentageRate that stores the annual percentage rate, and an `int` variable named iTermYears that stores the number of years to repay the loan. Initialize the data members to zero in the default constructor. Also, write accessor functions in the Loan base class for each of the data members. Each set function should receive a single parameter that is passed by the user. Derive two classes from the Loan class: MortgageLoan and AutoLoan. In the program's main() function, instantiate an object of each of the derived classes, prompt the user for the values to assign to the fLoanAmount, dPercentageRate, and iTermYears data members of each object, and then call the base class set functions. Use the base class get functions to retrieve and print the values stored for each object.

2. Modify the access specifier for the `private` data members in the Loan class you created in Project 1 so they are `protected`. In the MortgageLoan derived class, override the set function that stores a value in the iTermYears data member. In the overridden function body, add code that checks if the passed value is greater than 30 years. If the value is greater than 30, print a message to the user that the maximum term for a mortgage loan is 30 years, and prompt them to enter a new value. Override the same function in the AutoLoan derived class and use the same code, but make the term a maximum of five years. Also, in the AutoLoan derived class, override the set function that stores a value in the fLoanAmount data member. Add code that checks if the loan amount is greater than $100,000. If it is, print a message to the user that they have exceeded the maximum loan amount and allow them to enter a different value.

3. Create a console application project that includes a Seafood base class. Add to the Seafood base class a `protected double` data member named dLobsterPrice, which will store the wholesale price per pound for lobster. Write an accessor function named getLobsterPrice()in the base class for the dLobsterPrice data member. In the base class constructor function, initialize the dLobsterPrice data member to 8.8. Derive a class named SeafoodWholesale from the Seafood base class. Override the getLobsterPrice() function in the SeafoodWholesale class. In the body of the overridden function, return the value stored in the dLobsterPrice data member, but increase it by 15%. For instance, the return value in the function should be `return dLobsterPrice * 1.15;`. In the program's main() function, instantiate a SeafoodWholesale object named wholesaleLobster. Use the wholesaleLobster object to call the base class version of the getLobsterPrice() function to print a statement similar to *The base price of lobster is $8.8 per pound.* Also call the overridden getLobsterPrice() function to print a statement similar to *The wholesale price of lobster is $10.12 per pound.*

8

4. Add another derived class named SeafoodRetail to the program you created in Project 3, but derive the class from the SeafoodWholesale class–not the Seafood class. This means that the SeafoodWholesale class will be the direct base class of the SeafoodRetail class, while the Seafood class will be an indirect base class. Override the getLobsterPrice() function in the SeafoodRetail class. In the body of the overridden function, return the value stored in the dLobsterPrice data member, but increase it by 30%. Replace the SeafoodWholesale object named wholesaleLobster in the main() function with a SeafoodRetail object named retailLobster. Use the retailLobster object to call the indirect base class and base class versions of the getLobsterPrice() function in order to print the statements *The base price of lobster is $8.8 per pound.* and *The wholesale price of lobster is $10.12 per pound.* Add a final statement that calls the SeafoodRetail class's derived version of the getLobsterPrice() function to print a statement similar to *The retail price of lobster is $11.44 per pound.*
5. Create a base class named Olympics and add a statement to the constructor that prints *The Olympics begin.* Derive a class named SwimmingEvents from the Olympics base class and add a statement to the constructor that prints *The swimming events begin.* Then, derive a class named FreestyleEvent from the SwimmingEvents class and add a statement to the constructor that prints *The freestyle swimming event begins.* Next, add output statements to the Olympics class destructor that print *The Olympics end*, an output statement to the SwimmingEvents destructor that prints *The swimming events end*, and an output statement to the FreestyleEvent that prints *The freestyle swimming event ends.* Finally, add a single statement to the program's main() function that instantiates a FreestyleEvent object named olympicEvent and execute the program. You should see the six statements print to the screen. Note that it is actually poor programming practice to use output statements in constructors and destructors. Output statements are used here, however, in order for you to better understand the execution sequence of constructors and destructors.
6. Create a base class named HotelRates that includes a single `protected double` data member named dRoomRate. Write two accessor functions named setRoomRate() and getRoomRate() that store values to and retrieve values from the dRoomRate data member. The set function should receive a single parameter that is passed by the user. Assign the dRoomRate data member a value of zero in the default constructor. Also create a parameterized constructor for the HotelRates class that assigns a value to the dRoomRate data member at object instantiation. Derive two classes from the HotelRates class, named JuniorSuite and ExecutiveSuite. Create parameterized constructors for each class that call the parameterized base class constructor. In the program's main() function, instantiate a JuniorSuite object named room1, passing to the parameterized constructor a value of 110. Also, instantiate an ExecutiveSuite object named room2, passing to the parameterized constructor a value of 160. Call the getRoomRate() function for each of the objects to print the regular cost of each type of room. Then, use the setRoomRate() function to decrease the dRoomRate data member by a 10% corporate discount. Finally, call the getRoomRate() function again to print each room rate after subtracting the 10% corporate discount.

7. Create a Tailor class that includes a single **protected double** data member named dDressPrice. Write two accessor functions named setDressPrice() and getDressPrice() that store values to and retrieve values from the pDressPrice data member. Do not include any parameters in the setDressPrice() function declaration. In the setDressPrice() function definition, assign a value of 500 to the dDressPrice variable. Derive a class named FormalDress from the Tailor class and override the setDressPrice() function. In the overridden setDressPrice() function, assign a value of 1000 to the dDressPrice data member. Derive another class named WeddingDress, but this time, derive it from the FormalDress class. Override the setDressPrice() function in the WeddingDress class and assign a value of 2500 to the dDressPrice data member. In the program's main() function, Next, create a Tailor object named pCustomDress on the heap. Call the customDress object's setDressPrice() and getDressPrice() functions in order to set and display the cost of a basic custom dress. Instantiate a FormalDress object named evening and a WeddingDress object named marriage. Assign to the pCustomDress heap object the address of the FormalDress object named evening. Then use the pCustomDress object to call the setDressPrice() function and the getDressPrice() function to display the dress's cost. Next, assign to the pCustomDress heap object the address of the WeddingDress object named marriage, and call the setDressPrice() and getDressPrice() functions again. When you execute the program, the cost of a basic custom dress is incorrectly displayed for both the FormalDress and WeddingDress objects. How can you fix the problem?

8. In this exercise, you will create a Shapes class program that dynamically displays either a rectangle, a circle, or a triangle from a derived class, depending on a user's selection. Because you are limited by what you can do with a console application, you cannot write code that dynamically changes the size of each shape. Rather, you will simply draw the appropriate shape when the user requests it.

   a. Create a Shapes class and add a virtual function named drawShape(). Do not include any statements in the drawShape() function definition.

   b. Derive a Rectangle class from the Shapes class. Override the drawShape() function and include the following statements in the function definition to draw a rectangle that is 10 asterisks high by 15 asterisks wide.

```
cout << "* * * * * * * * * * * * * * *" << endl;
cout << "* * * * * * * * * * * * * * *" << endl;
cout << "* * * * * * * * * * * * * * *" << endl;
cout << "* * * * * * * * * * * * * * *" << endl;
cout << "* * * * * * * * * * * * * * *" << endl;
cout << "* * * * * * * * * * * * * * *" << endl;
cout << "* * * * * * * * * * * * * * *" << endl;
cout << "* * * * * * * * * * * * * * *" << endl;
cout << "* * * * * * * * * * * * * * *" << endl;
cout << "* * * * * * * * * * * * * * *" << endl;
```

c. Derive a Circle class from the Shapes class. Override the drawShape() function and include the following statements in the function definition to draw a circle with a radius of eight asterisks.

```
cout << "            * * * *" << endl;
cout << "         * * * * * * *" << endl;
cout << "      * * * * * * * * * *" << endl;
cout << "    * * * * * * * * * * * *" << endl;
cout << "   * * * * * * * * * * * * *" << endl;
cout << "  * * * * * * * * * * * * * *" << endl;
cout << " * * * * * * * * * * * * * * *" << endl;
cout << " * * * * * * * * * * * * * * *" << endl;
cout << " * * * * * * * * * * * * * * *" << endl;
cout << " * * * * * * * * * * * * * * *" << endl;
cout << " * * * * * * * * * * * * * * *" << endl;
cout << "  * * * * * * * * * * * * * *" << endl;
cout << "   * * * * * * * * * * * * *" << endl;
cout << "    * * * * * * * * * * * *" << endl;
cout << "      * * * * * * * * * *" << endl;
cout << "         * * * * * * *" << endl;
cout << "            * * * *" << endl;
```

d. Derive a RightTriangle class from the Shapes class. Override the drawShape() function and include the following statements in the function definition to draw a right triangle with a height of 15 asterisks and a base of 15 asterisks.

```
cout << "*" << endl;
cout << "* *" << endl;
cout << "* * *" << endl;
cout << "* * * *" << endl;
cout << "* * * * *" << endl;
cout << "* * * * * *" << endl;
cout << "* * * * * * *" << endl;
cout << "* * * * * * * *" << endl;
cout << "* * * * * * * * *" << endl;
cout << "* * * * * * * * * *" << endl;
cout << "* * * * * * * * * * *" << endl;
cout << "* * * * * * * * * * * *" << endl;
cout << "* * * * * * * * * * * * *" << endl;
cout << "* * * * * * * * * * * * * *" << endl;
cout << "* * * * * * * * * * * * * * *" << endl;
```

e. In the program's main() function, instantiate a Shapes class pointer. Then, create a looping statement that displays a menu allowing users to pick the type of shape they want to display. When the user picks a shape, instantiate a new object of that shape's class and assign it to the Shapes class pointer. Use the Shapes class pointer to call the getShapeType() and drawShape() functions. Be sure to delete the curShapes pointer at the end of the main() function.

f. Modify the Shapes class so it is an abstract base class.

CHAPTER

9

INTRODUCTION TO WINDOWS PROGRAMMING

In this chapter you will learn:

- About Windows programming with Visual C++
- About Windows architecture
- About the Windows API
- How to create a WinMain() function
- About events and messages

The danger from computers is not that they will eventually get as smart as men, but that we will meanwhile agree to meet them halfway.

Bernard Avishai

PREVIEW: INTRODUCTION TO WINDOWS PROGRAMMING

The next step toward mastering Visual C++ programming is to understand the basics of Windows programming. Creating a Windows program is quite a bit different from creating console applications, because you need to write code that your application can use to communicate with the Windows operating system itself. In order to write a Windows application, you need to understand the basics of Windows architecture and how to work with the Windows API, which your program uses to communicate with the Windows operating system. Additionally, you will need to know how to work with events and messages, which Windows uses to inform your application that it needs to perform some sort of task. To help you understand the basics of Windows programming, in this chapter you will create a Windows calculator program that performs basic arithmetic calculations.

To preview the calculator program:

1. Create a **Chapter.09** folder in your Visual C++ Projects folder.
2. Copy the **Chapter9_Calculator** folder from the Chapter.09 folder on your Data Disk to the Chapter.09 folder in your Visual C++ Projects folder. Then, open the **Chapter9_Calculator** project in Visual C++.
3. Open the **Calculator.cpp** file in the Code Editor window and examine the code. You will notice that the code looks quite a bit different from the C++ programs you have created so far. There are several new data types, which you have not learned about yet, and there is no main() function, as you would find in a console application. Instead, there is a WinMain() function, which is the entry point for all Windows applications. In Windows programming, the WinMain() function is used primarily for setting up and displaying new windows. Much of a program's functionality actually executes in a special function called the window procedure. At the end of the WinMain() function is a special `while` loop that is used for handling the application's events and messages. Scroll to the end of the file to see the calculator program's window procedure, which is a function named MainWndProc(). Figure 9-1 shows portions of the Calculator.cpp file.

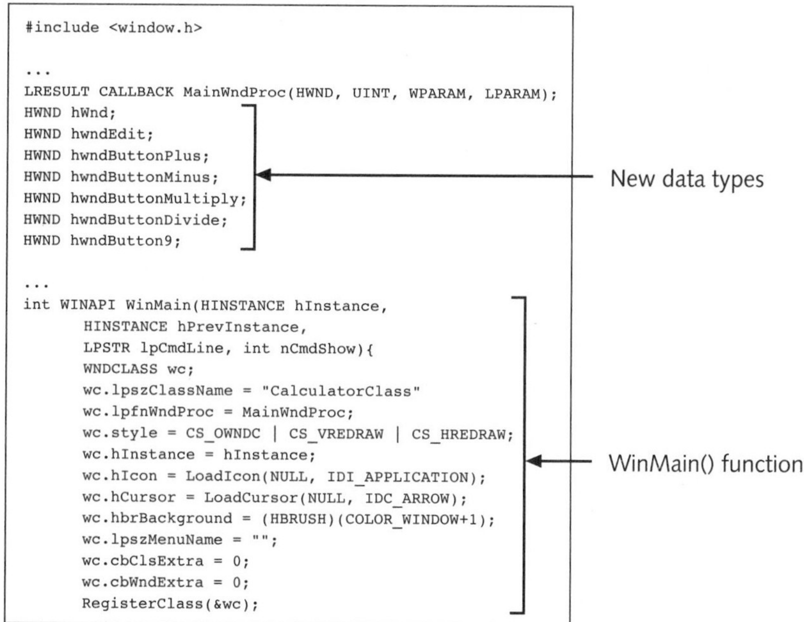

```
#include <window.h>

...
LRESULT CALLBACK MainWndProc(HWND, UINT, WPARAM, LPARAM);
HWND hWnd;
HWND hwndEdit;
HWND hwndButtonPlus;
HWND hwndButtonMinus;
HWND hwndButtonMultiply;
HWND hwndButtonDivide;
HWND hwndButton9;

...
int WINAPI WinMain(HINSTANCE hInstance,
      HINSTANCE hPrevInstance,
      LPSTR lpCmdLine, int nCmdShow){
      WNDCLASS wc;
      wc.lpszClassName = "CalculatorClass"
      wc.lpfnWndProc = MainWndProc;
      wc.style = CS_OWNDC | CS_VREDRAW | CS_HREDRAW;
      wc.hInstance = hInstance;
      wc.hIcon = LoadIcon(NULL, IDI_APPLICATION);
      wc.hCursor = LoadCursor(NULL, IDC_ARROW);
      wc.hbrBackground = (HBRUSH)(COLOR_WINDOW+1);
      wc.lpszMenuName = "";
      wc.cbClsExtra = 0;
      wc.cbWndExtra = 0;
      RegisterClass(&wc);
```


Figure 9-1 Calculator.cpp

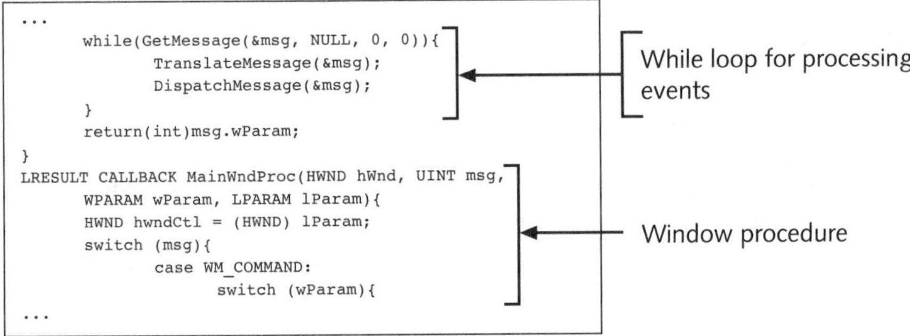

...
while(GetMessage(&msg, NULL, 0, 0)){
TranslateMessage(&msg);
DispatchMessage(&msg);
}
return(int)msg.wParam;
}
LRESULT CALLBACK MainWndProc(HWND hWnd, UINT msg,
WPARAM wParam, LPARAM lParam){
HWND hwndCtl = (HWND) lParam;
switch (msg){
case WM_COMMAND:
switch (wParam){
...
While loop for processing events
Window procedure

Figure 9-1 Calculator.cpp (continued)

4. Build and execute the Calculator program, and then test the calculations. Figure 9-2 shows the calculator window that the program generates. The window is similar to other types of windows you will find in the Windows operating system environment.

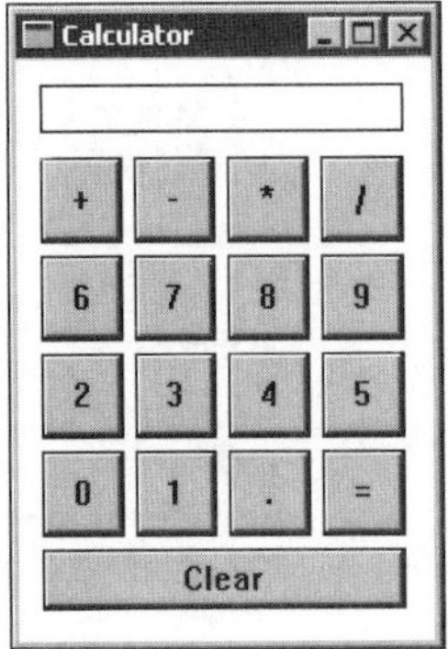

Figure 9-2 The Calculator program

5. Click the **Close button** to close the Calculator program window.

6. Select **Close Solution** from the File menu to close the solution.

WINDOWS PROGRAMMING WITH VISUAL C++

At this point in the text, you begin create Windows programs that use a graphical user interface instead of the command-line interfaces found in console applications. The ability to create Windows programs is one of the most important aspects of the Visual C++ environment. Of course, there are plenty of reasons why you may need to create command-line interfaces with console applications, but creating Windows programs is what Visual C++ is really all about.

There are two ways to create Windows programs in Visual C++: with C or C++ and the Windows application programming interface, or with C++ and Microsoft Foundation Classes. This chapter discusses how to create Windows programs with C or C++ and the Windows application programming interface. An **application programming interface**, or **API**, is a library of methods and code that allows programmers to access the features and functionality of an application or operating system. The **Windows API** allows you to write programs for Windows operating systems. The Windows API is the foundation for creating all Windows programs using *any* type of programming language, such as Visual Basic, Fortran, Pascal, as well as C or C++. The Windows API is really a very large collection of code written in the C programming language. Windows operating systems themselves are actually written mostly in the C programming language. You create Windows programs by combining code written in a source programming language with calls to the Windows API. Figure 9-3 illustrates this concept.

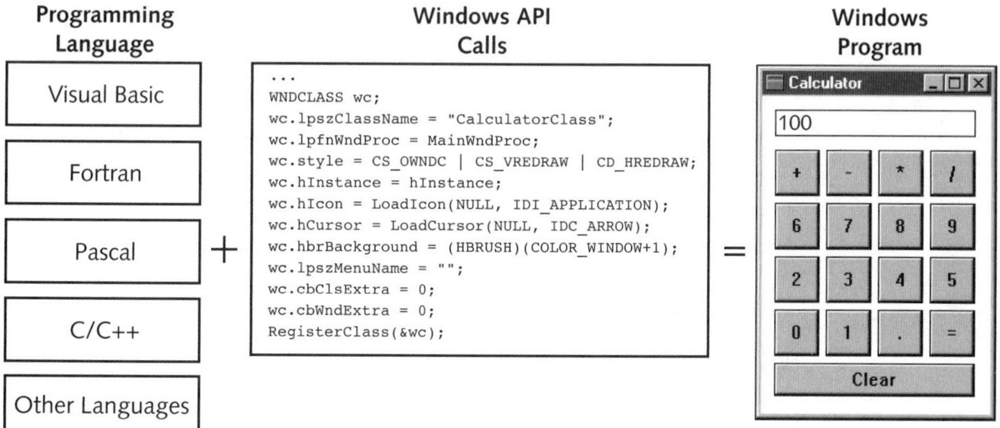

Figure 9-3 Building a Windows program

Mastering Windows API programming involves a steep learning curve. Not only must you thoroughly understand C programming, but you must also learn how to choose from the literally thousands of functions (as well as other types of code elements, such as constants) that make up the Windows API. Some experts on the subject claim that true mastery over the Windows API requires a year or more of study. Do not be alarmed, however. In this chapter, you will learn only the basics you need to get started. Even though you are studying only the basics, keep in mind that mastery over the Windows API will significantly improve your ability to create professional quality Windows programs. Additionally, the more you know about Windows API programming, the better you will be at working with Microsoft Foundation Classes because they are based on the Windows API.

Although you can create Windows programs using C++ and the Windows API, with Visual C++ the preferred method of creating Windows programs is to use C++ with the

Microsoft Foundation Classes. Microsoft Foundation Classes assist C++ programmers in writing Windows programs by hiding much of the underlying details of the C code that makes up the Windows API. The Microsoft Foundation Classes also organize Windows API code so that it can be accessed using object-oriented programming techniques. You will learn about and work with object-oriented programming in the next chapter and throughout the remainder of this book.

This is the only chapter in which you will directly create Windows applications using C++ and the Windows API. If the Microsoft Foundation Classes make the task of writing Windows programs with Visual C++ much easier, why bother to spend time learning how to create Windows API applications? The answer is because Microsoft Foundation Classes programming is built on Windows API programming. In this chapter you will learn key Windows programming concepts that are vital to your success in working with Microsoft Foundation Classes programming. This chapter presents fundamental information on how Windows programs are designed, and this information will help you when you tackle the Microsoft Foundation Classes and throughout your programming career.

You should already be more than familiar with the graphical user interface of Windows environments. A **graphical user interface**, or GUI, is a graphically based environment that you use to interact with applications. Some components that are common to most GUI environments include menus, icons to represent files and applications, a desktop, and the ability to interact with the environment by using a mouse. In a nutshell, Windows programs do not run in console windows, but exist as separate floating windows in the Windows environment. Windows programs include Minimize, Maximize, and Close buttons, along with title bars containing descriptive text. Many Windows programs also include menu bars, toolbars, scroll bars, and other elements, and they are often resizable. The types of Windows programs can range from the simple calculator program you will create in this chapter to large applications such as Visual C++. To help you clearly understand what a Windows program is, you will now create and examine a simple Windows API program. You will not actually write the code that creates the program. Instead, you will allow Visual C++ to create the code for you.

To create a simple Windows API program:

1. Return to Visual C++.
2. Create a new empty Win32 project named **SimpleApp**. Save the project in the **Chapter.09** folder in your Visual C++ Projects folder. In the Application Settings tab of the Win32 Application Wizard dialog box, leave Application type set to the default **Windows application** setting, and make sure the Empty project check box is cleared, as shown in Figure 9-4.
3. Click the **Finish** button to open the new project in the IDE.
4. Open the **SimpleApp.cpp** file in the Code Editor and examine the code. The program contains various Windows data types, a special WinMain() function named _tWinMain(), and a window procedure, similar to the calculator program you saw in the preview.

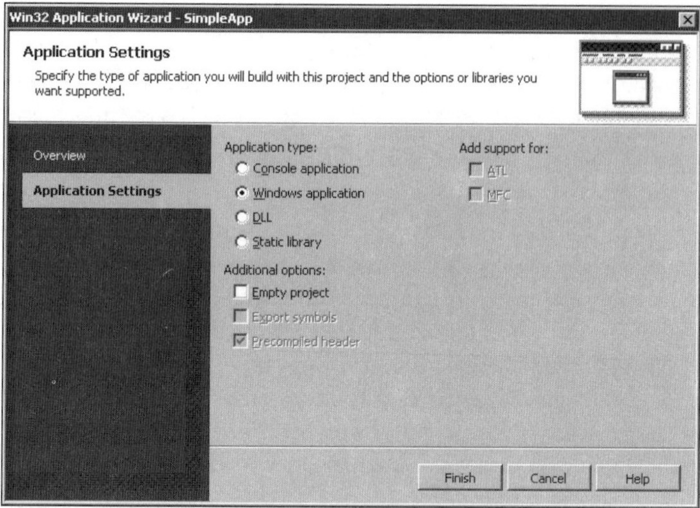

Figure 9-4 Application Settings tab of the Win32 Application Wizard dialog box

5. Next, build and execute the program. Figure 9-5 shows how the application window should appear. The figure also identifies standard Windows elements.

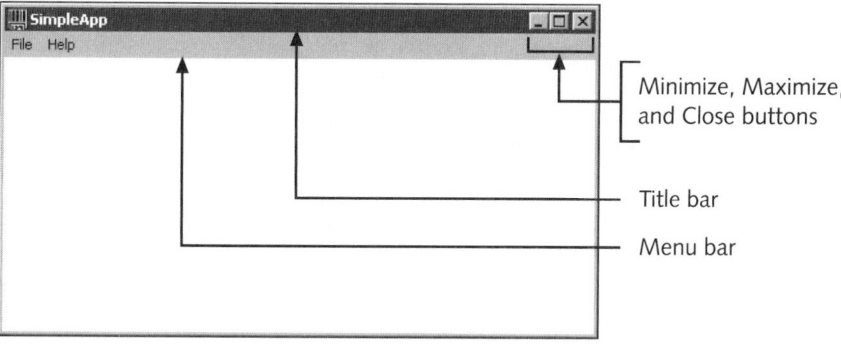

Figure 9-5 SimpleApp application window

6. Close the **SimpleApp** application window by selecting **Exit** from the **File** menu or by clicking the **Close** button in the title bar.

7. Select **Close Solution** from the File menu to close the solution.

Windows Architecture

Before getting into the specifics of how Windows API programs are constructed, it helps to understand the basics of Windows architecture. You have probably heard the term "bit" many times, as in 16-bit, 32-bit, and so on. The term **bit** refers to a binary number of 0 or 1. (Recall from Chapter 1, that machine languages are written entirely in 0s and 1s.) Computers are classified according to how many bits can be transmitted simultaneously into the microprocessor, or CPU. The **bus**, or **data bus**, refers to the electronic path that the bits travel into the microprocessor. You can think of the data bus as the number of roads leading into a microprocessor. The wider the data bus, the more information (bits) can be sent simultaneously to the microprocessor, and the faster a program runs. The actual speed with which information is processed also depends on several other factors, including the microprocessor architecture (80386, i486, Pentium, and so on) and the megahertz at which the microprocessor operates. The 80386 and i486 microprocessors have 32-bit wide data buses, whereas the Pentium family of microprocessors has 64-bit wide data buses. Figure 9-6 illustrates bits being transmitted along the data bus into a microprocessor.

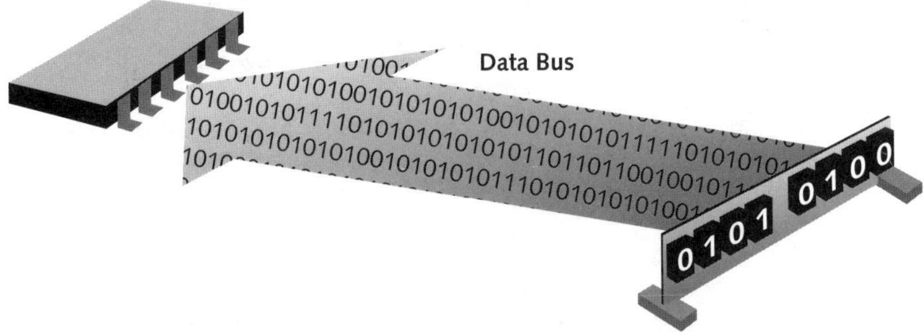

Figure 9-6 A data bus

There are Windows operating systems specifically designed to work with each width of data bus: 16-bit, 32-bit, and 64-bit. The older (and essentially obsolete) Windows 3.1 operates at 16 bits. Windows NT, Windows 95, Windows 98, and Windows CE are 32-bit operating systems. At the time of this writing, Windows 2000 and Windows XP are the only 64-bit Windows operating systems. The number of bits in a data bus that an operating system can access simultaneously depends on the operating system or application that is accessing the microprocessor. Windows 3.1 can operate on 80386, i486, and Pentium microprocessors, but can use only 16 bits of each data bus, even though the 80386 and i486 microprocessors are 32-bits wide and the Pentium microprocessor is 64-bits wide. Similarly, Windows NT can operate on 64-bit Pentium computers, but can take advantage of only 32 bits of the data bus. Windows 2000 and Windows XP, however, can take advantage of all 64 bits of a Pentium microprocessor, making them run faster than 16-bit and 32-bit Windows operating systems.

A separate Windows API exists for each generation of Windows operating systems. The Windows API for Windows 3.1 was originally called the Win API, but is now usually referred to as the Win16 API to avoid confusion with later versions of the Windows API.

All 32-bit Windows operating systems share the same Windows API, known as the Win32 API. Because Windows NT, Windows 95, Windows 98, and Windows CE share the same

Windows API, you can write one application using the Win32 API that can run on all three versions of the operating system. There are some exceptions to this rule in that functionality unique to one operating system is not necessarily available to another operating system. For example, Windows NT contains advanced network security features that are not available on other 32-bit Windows platforms. However, with the exception of operating system-specific features, such as Windows NT security, you can be assured that Win32 applications will run successfully on all Win32 operating systems.

One of the problems with the different generations of Windows operating systems is that applications written specifically for one generation will not usually work with earlier Windows operating systems. For example, if you write a true 32-bit Windows application, then that application will not run on the 16-bit Windows 3.1 operating system. A major goal in the development of Windows 2000 was that applications written for 64-bit Windows operating systems would also be able to run on 32-bit Windows operating systems. To accomplish this goal, Microsoft made the Win64 API almost identical to the Win32 API, but with some important changes to data types that allow 64-bit applications to run on 32-bit Windows operating systems. Because of the similarities between the two APIs, this text uses the term *Windows API* to refer to both the Win32 and Win64 APIs.

THE WINDOWS API

A C++ program can access the Windows API by importing the `windows.h` header file, which is included as part of the Visual Studio development environment. The **`windows.h`** header file includes all of the functions, variables, and other programming elements that make up the Windows API. You import the `windows.h` header file into your program using the #include statement, just as you would any other header file.

The `windows.h` header file is also included as part of the Microsoft Platform Software Development Kit (SDK), or Platform SDK. The Platform SDK contains header files, sample code, tools, and information for building applications using the Windows API. The Platform SDK was previously known as the Win32 SDK. However, to allow developers to create one set of code that runs on both Win32 and Win64 platforms, the Win32 SDK was redesigned to support both the older Win32 platform and the current Win64 platform. It was then renamed to the Platform SDK. You can download the Platform SDK from www.microsoft.com/msdownload/platformsdk/sdkupdate/home.htm.

If you would like to learn more about Windows API programming, the Platform SDK is the best place to start. You can also find extensive information on Windows API programming in the MSDN Library.

The Windows API defines its own data types in the `windows.h` header file. You can identify Windows data types by their uppercase letters. For example, the `char` data type definition in the Windows API is written as CHAR. Some of the Windows API data types, such as **CHAR**, **INT**, and **BOOL**, are identical to their C or C++ language counterparts. Many other Windows API data types have no equivalents in C or C++. You will not see the Windows API data types listed here because there are literally hundreds of them. The Windows API data types used in this chapter will be explained as you encounter them. If you would like to see a list of all the Windows API data types, you can find them in the MSDN Library.

The Windows API includes hundreds of data types so that it can control the information passed to it from source programming languages (such as C, C++, Visual Basic, and so on), and correctly execute a program on different types of computers. One category of Windows API data types you will use in this chapter are pointer data types. Unlike C and C++, the Windows API includes data types that are used only to declare pointers. A **pointer data type** declares the type and name of a Windows API pointer. In comparison, you declare C and C++ pointers using standard variable data types, such as `int` and `char`. Most Windows API pointer data types begin with a prefix of *P* or *LP* (*P* stands for *P*ointer and *LP* stands for *L*ong *P*ointer).

Another category of Windows API data types you will use in this chapter are handle data types. A **handle** is used to access an object that has been loaded into memory. A handle is essentially the same thing as a C++ pointer. Windows API programming, however, uses the term *handles* instead of *pointers* because you typically use a handle to control and manipulate a window (in other words, you use a handle to "handle a window"). Handle data types begin with a prefix of *H*. You already understand that all Windows applications are contained within their own window. An important concept to grasp, however, as you start creating Windows API programs is that all individual controls (such as buttons) and user interface components are also windows, each requiring its own handle. For example, the buttons and edit box in the calculator program you saw in the preview are all considered to be their own windows. Each of these components is a child window within the parent window of the calculator program. A **child window** always appears within the area defined by a parent window. A **parent window** is a primary application window containing one or more child windows. Figure 9-7 uses the calculator program to illustrate the concept of parent and child windows.

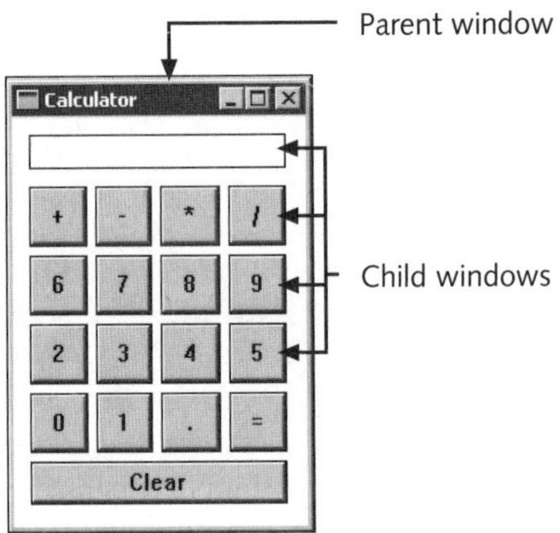

Figure 9-7 Parent and child windows

Next, you will start creating the calculator program by creating a new project and importing the `windows.h` header file.

To start creating the calculator program:

1. Create a new Win32 project named **Calculator**. Save the project in the **Chapter.09** folder in your Visual C++ Projects folder. In the Application Settings tab of the Win32 Application Wizard dialog box, leave Application type set to the default **Windows application** setting, but select the Empty project check box. Once the project is created, add a C++ source file named **Calculator**.
2. Type the preprocessor directive that gives the program access to the windows.h header file: **`#include <windows.h>`**.
3. Save the **Calculator.cpp** file by selecting **Save Calculator.cpp** from the **File** menu. You will return to the Calculator.cpp file later.

THE WINMAIN() FUNCTION

Just as the main() function is the starting point for any C++ program, the **WinMain() function** is the starting point for any Windows API program. The syntax for the WinMain() function definition is as follows:

```
int WINAPI WinMain(  HINSTANCE hInstance,
           HINSTANCE hPrevInstance,
           LPSTR lpCmdLine,
           int nCmdShow ) {
 statements;
}
```

The parameters in the preceding WinMain() function definition are written on separate lines for clarity.

The WinMain() function declaration must be declared with type `int`. The WINAPI portion of the function declaration is a Windows API data type that is required in all Windows API functions. Each of the WinMain() function's four parameters is declared using Windows API data types. The first and second parameters are of the HINSTANCE data type, which represents a handle to a window instance. An **instance** is a particular copy of a window, program, or other type of object that happens to be running. You can execute most Windows programs multiple times and have several copies of the same program running simultaneously. Each of these copies is considered to be an instance of the program. Figure 9-8 demonstrates the concept of instances by showing multiple running copies of the game Minesweeper (which is installed with most versions of Windows). Each copy of Minesweeper is an instance of the application.

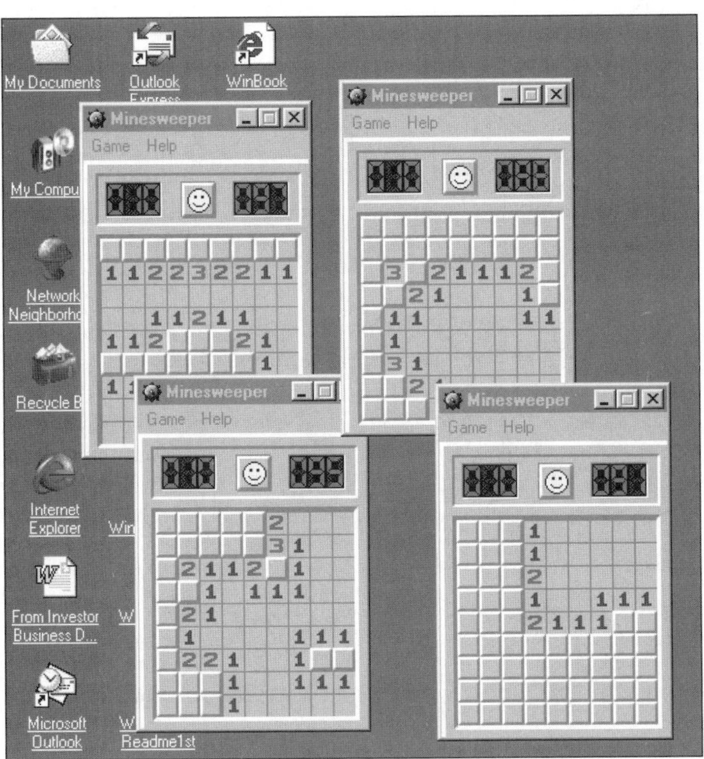

Figure 9-8 Multiple instances of Minesweeper

The first HINSTANCE parameter, named hInstance, is the handle that represents the current instance of the program's parent window. The second HINSTANCE parameter, named hPrevInstance, represents a previously created instance of the program. The hPrevInstance parameter is left over from 16-bit Windows 3.1, when a program needed to be aware of other instances of itself in order to avoid memory conflicts and other system problems. 32-bit and 64-bit Windows operating systems do not have the same memory conflicts as Windows 3.1 and therefore do not use the hPrevInstance parameter.

The third parameter, named lpCmdLine, is of the `LPSTR` data type, which is a pointer to a string. The lpCmdLine parameter points to the command line string that executes the program. For example, if you execute the calculator program from a directory named MyProjects on your C: drive, then the lpCmdLine parameter will contain the string `c:\MyProjects\calculator.exe`. The lpCmdLine parameter is often used for gathering additional pieces of information entered at the command line or that might be part of a Windows shortcut. For example, a Windows program may require the user to enter a password at the command line. For password-protected programs, you can extract the password from the lpCmdLine parameter for validation purposes.

The last parameter, named nCmdShow, is of the `int` data type. The nCmdShow parameter returns a constant representing the window's startup mode (minimized, maximized, and so on). Window constants begin with the prefix SW_, followed by a description of the window mode. For example, SW_NORMAL indicates the window is to open normally, and SW_MAXIMIZE indicates that the window is to open maximized. Typically, the window constant is passed by the operating system from a selection made in a Windows shortcut. Your program then checks the value and determines how to display the program's window.

The names assigned to each of the WinMain() function's parameters are arbitrary. You can use any name you like, provided you follow the standard C++ rules for naming identifiers. Many Windows API programmers, however, routinely use the names hInstance, hPrevInstance, lpCmdLine, and nCmdShow to identify these parameters.

Next, you will add a WinMain() function definition to the calculator program.

To add a WinMain() function definition to the calculator program:

1. Return to the **Calculator** project in Visual C++. If necessary, open the **Calculator.cpp** file in the Code Editor window.
2. After the preprocessor directive, add the WinMain() function shown in Figure 9-9.

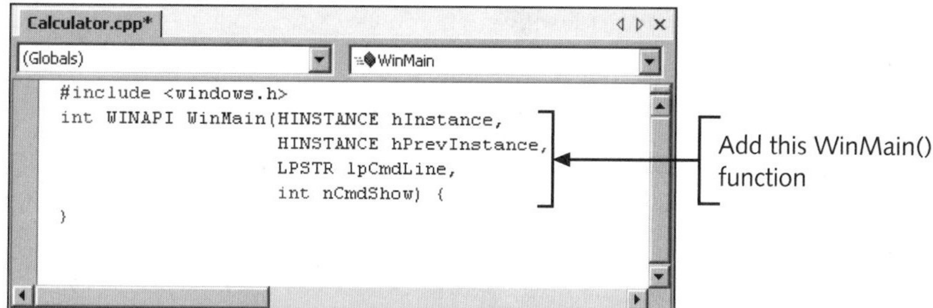

Figure 9-9 WinMain() function added to Calculator.cpp

One of the most important tasks performed by the WinMain() function (other than being an entry point for all Windows applications) is the creation and instantiation of windows. The steps involved in creating and instantiating windows are as follows:

1. Define the window class by creating an object of the WNDCLASS structure, and notify Windows of the new class using the RegisterClass() method
2. Create the program's main (parent) window, along with any child windows, using the CreateWindow() method
3. Display the program using the ShowWindow() method

You will now examine each of these steps in detail.

Defining the Window Class

To create and display a window, you must first define and register its window class. The **window class** defines the characteristics of a program's main window. Some examples of characteristics include the style of window and what type of icon will be used to represent the window. Do not confuse the term *window class* with the C++ classes you learned about in previous chapters. A window class refers only to the information used to create a window. The classes you learned about in the previous chapters are a separate topic that are the basis of object-oriented programming.

The predefined **WNDCLASS structure** is used for defining the characteristics of a window class. The following code shows the WNDCLASS structure definition. Notice that all but two of the fields are of Windows API data types. You will not actually see the WNDCLASS structure definition in your program because it is already defined in the `windows.h` header file. However, you will instantiate an object based on the WNDCLASS structure.

9

```
struct _WNDCLASS {
   UINT     style;
   WNDPROC  lpfnWndProc;
   int      cbClsExtra;
   int      cbWndExtra;
   HANDLE   hInstance;
   HICON    hIcon;
   HCURSOR  hCursor;
   HBRUSH   hbrBackground;
   LPCTSTR  lpszMenuName;
   LPCTSTR  lpszClassName;
};
```

Each of the fields in the WNDCLASS structure determines various characteristics of a window. Figure 9-10 lists the WNDCLASS structure fields with a description of what the field controls.

Field	Description
style	The window class style
lpfnWndProc	Pointer to the window procedure
cbClsExtra	The number of extra bytes to allocate following the window class structure
cbWndExtra	The number of extra bytes to allocate following the window class instance

Figure 9-10 WNDCLASS structure fields

Field	Description
hInstance	The handle to the instance containing the window procedure (lpfnWndProc) for the window class
hIcon	A handle to the program icon resource, which is displayed whenever the program is minimized
hCursor	A handle to a cursor resource
hbrBackground	A handle to the class background brush
lpszMenuName	A pointer to a null-terminated string containing the menu resource for the window class
lpszClassName	A pointer to a null-terminated string representing the window class name

Figure 9-10 WNDCLASS structure fields (continued)

Most of the WNDCLASS structure's fields are fairly advanced—too advanced for your brief study of Windows API programming in this chapter. Therefore, this book will not go into detail on most of them. The appropriate values for each field will be listed for you in the examples and exercises you encounter in this chapter.

You do need to understand two fields: the hInstance and the lpfnWndProc fields. The hInstance field contains the handle to the current program, so you assign to the hInstance field the hInstance argument of the WinMain() class. You will use a statement similar to `wc.hInstance = hInstance;`, which may be a little bit confusing. Just remember that you are assigning the value of the hInstance *argument* to the hInstance *field*.

The lpfnWndProc field contains a pointer to the name of a special function known as the window procedure that will handle messages. For now, you will assign the value *MainWndProc* to the lpfnWndProc field. You will learn about messages and create the window procedure later in this chapter. Note that although the value *MainWndProc* represents the name of a function, you do not include the function's parentheses when assigning the value to the field.

If you would like more information on the fields in the WNDCLASS structure, search for the WNDCLASS topic in the MSDN Library.

Figure 9-11 shows how to declare a new variable named wc, based on the WNDCLASS structure. Again, do not worry about understanding the values assigned to the fields, except for the lpfnWndProc and hInstance fields. The lpfnWndProc field is assigned the function named MainWndProc, and the hInstance field is assigned the hInstance parameter of the WinMain() function. The hInstance parameter in the WinMain() function declaration and the statements that assign values to the lpfnWndProc and hInstance fields in the body of the function are highlighted in bold so that you can quickly locate them.

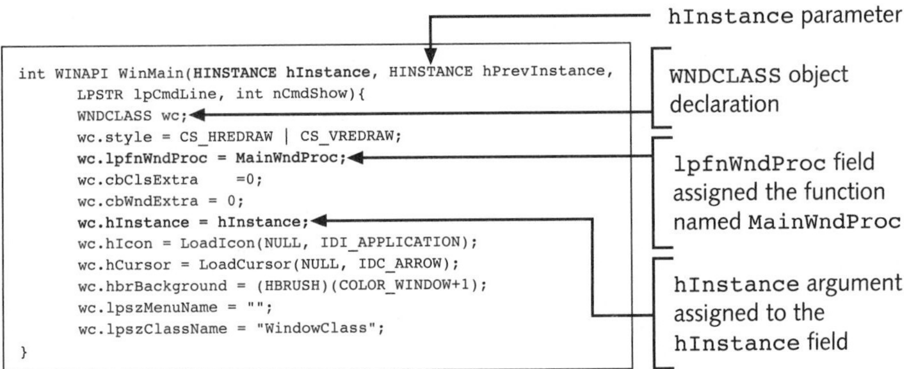

```
int WINAPI WinMain(HINSTANCE hInstance, HINSTANCE hPrevInstance,
       LPSTR lpCmdLine, int nCmdShow){
       WNDCLASS wc;
       wc.style = CS_HREDRAW | CS_VREDRAW;
       wc.lpfnWndProc = MainWndProc;
       wc.cbClsExtra    =0;
       wc.cbWndExtra = 0;
       wc.hInstance = hInstance;
       wc.hIcon = LoadIcon(NULL, IDI_APPLICATION);
       wc.hCursor = LoadCursor(NULL, IDC_ARROW);
       wc.hbrBackground = (HBRUSH)(COLOR_WINDOW+1);
       wc.lpszMenuName = "";
       wc.lpszClassName = "WindowClass";
}
```


Figure 9-11 Declaring a new variable based on the WNDCLASS structure

Next, you will define the calculator program's window class.

To define the calculator program's window class:

1. Return to the Calculator.cpp file in the Code Editor window.
2. As shown in Figure 9-12, declare a variable named wc, based on the WNDCLASS structure, and assign values to the window class fields:

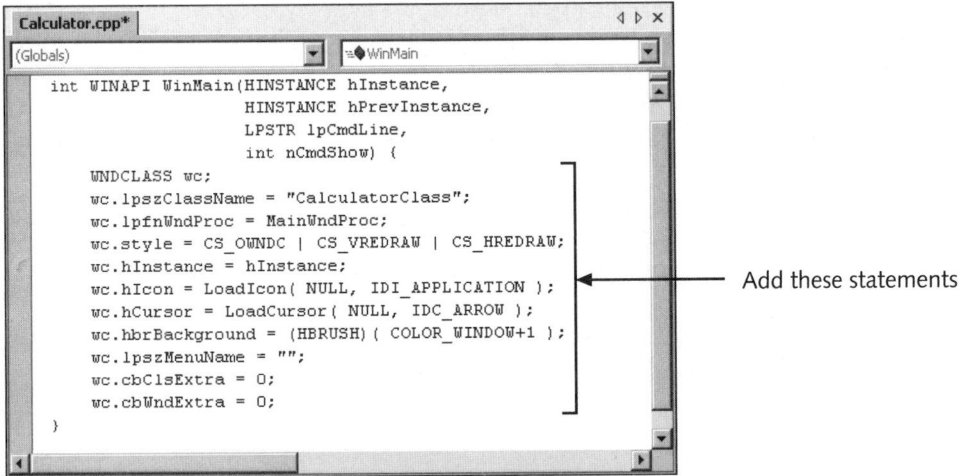

```
int WINAPI WinMain(HINSTANCE hInstance,
                   HINSTANCE hPrevInstance,
                   LPSTR lpCmdLine,
                   int nCmdShow) {
    WNDCLASS wc;
    wc.lpszClassName = "CalculatorClass";
    wc.lpfnWndProc = MainWndProc;
    wc.style = CS_OWNDC | CS_VREDRAW | CS_HREDRAW;
    wc.hInstance = hInstance;
    wc.hIcon = LoadIcon( NULL, IDI_APPLICATION );
    wc.hCursor = LoadCursor( NULL, IDC_ARROW );
    wc.hbrBackground = (HBRUSH)( COLOR_WINDOW+1 );
    wc.lpszMenuName = "";
    wc.cbClsExtra = 0;
    wc.cbWndExtra = 0;
}
```


Figure 9-12 WNDCLASS variable declared in WinMain() and values assigned to its window class fields

Once you have defined the WNDCLASS structure, you need to use the **RegisterClass() function**, which informs the operating system about the newly defined window class. The RegisterClass() function accepts a single variable consisting of the address of the WNDCLASS structure you defined. For example, the statement `RegisterClass(&wc);` registers the wc object from the preceding example by using the address operator (&) to pass its address to the operating system.

Next, you will register the calculator program's window class.

To register the calculator program's window class:

1. Add the statement shown in Figure 9-13 above the WinMain() function's closing brace to register the wc window class.

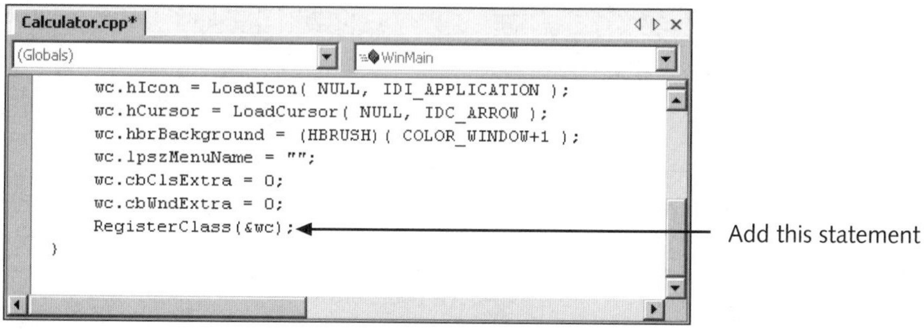

```
Calculator.cpp*
(Globals)                    WinMain
        wc.hIcon = LoadIcon( NULL, IDI_APPLICATION );
        wc.hCursor = LoadCursor( NULL, IDC_ARROW );
        wc.hbrBackground = (HBRUSH) ( COLOR_WINDOW+1 );
        wc.lpszMenuName = "";
        wc.cbClsExtra = 0;
        wc.cbWndExtra = 0;
        RegisterClass(&wc);   <---- Add this statement
    }
```

Figure 9-13 wc window class registration statement added to the WinMain() function

Creating New Windows

The WNDCLASS structure and RegisterClass() function only define the characteristics of a window; they do not actually create and display the window. After declaring a WNDCLASS structure and calling the RegisterClass() function, you must call the CreateWindow() function to create a new window based on the window class. The **CreateWindow() function** creates a new window based on several parameters, including window class, size, position, and style. The value returned from the CreateWindow() function is a handle to the newly created window, which you assign to a variable of the HWND data type. You can then use the handle to refer to and control the window. The following code shows the CreateWindow() function syntax. The data types for each parameter are shown in comments.

```
handle = CreateWindow(
  lpClassName,   // LPCTSTR
  lpWindowName,  // LPCTSTR
  dwStyle,       // DWORD
  x,             // int
  y,             // int
  nWidth,        // int
  nHeight,       // int
  hWndParent,    // HWND
  hMenu,         // HMENU
  hInstance,     // HINSTANCE
  lpParam        // LPVOID
  );
```

All windows must be created using their own CreateWindow() functions. For example, in the calculator program, you must create the main program window with a CreateWindow() function, and then use separate CreateWindow() functions for each of the program's controls.

To understand how to use the CreateWindow() function, you need to understand each of the function's parameters. Note that not all of the parameters are required. When parameters are not required, you use a value NULL as a placeholder to maintain the CreateWindow() function's parameter order. As with other Windows API code in this chapter, do not expect to become an expert based on the examples included here; remember there is a steep learning curve to the Windows API. Your goal here is trying to develop a general understanding of how the CreateWindow() function operates.

lpClassName

The **lpClassName parameter** is a pointer to a text string representing the name of the class upon which you want to base the new window. You can assign to the lpClassName parameter either the name of the window class you created with the WNDCLASS structure and RegisterClass() function, or a predefined control class. **Predefined control classes** represent standard types of window controls such as buttons, edit boxes, and scroll bars. You will use several predefined control classes in the calculator program. Figure 9-14 lists the predefined control classes that can be assigned to the lpClassName parameter.

Name	Description
BUTTON	A command button such as an OK or Cancel button
COMBOBOX	An edit box (text box) that also contains a list of selectable choices
EDIT	A single-line text box
LISTBOX	A list of selectable choices
MDICLIENT	A Multiple Document Interface (MDI) client window (you will learn about MDI programs in later chapters)
RichEdit	A Rich Edit version 1.0 control that allows users to enter and edit text with character and paragraph formatting
RICHEDIT_CLASS	A Rich Edit version 2.0 control that allows users to enter and edit text with character and paragraph formatting
SCROLLBAR	Scroll bars that are used for navigating within a parent window
STATIC	A static text label used for providing information or describing parts of a parent window

Figure 9-14 Predefined control classes

lpWindowName

The **lpWindowName parameter** is a pointer to a text string containing a name for the window. If the window being created contains a title bar, then the value pointed to by the lpWindowName parameter is used as the title bar text. If the window is a control such as a button or a check box, the lpWindowName parameter specifies the text of the control. For example, if you pass the text *Click Me* to the lpWindowName parameter for a button, then *Click Me* appears as the text on the button's face.

dwStyle

The **dwStyle parameter** determines the specific window styles that will be applied to the new window. Figure 9-15 lists the values that can be passed to the dwStyle parameter. Note that you can quickly identify window styles because they are prefixed with `WS_`.

Style	Description
`WS_BORDER`	Includes a thin-line border for the window
`WS_CAPTION`	Includes a title bar for the window
`WS_CHILD` or `WS_CHILDWINDOW`	Creates a child window
`WS_CLIPCHILDREN`	When drawing occurs within the parent window, excludes the areas occupied by child windows
`WS_CLIPSIBLINGS`	When drawing occurs within a child window, excludes any overlapping areas of other child windows
`WS_DISABLED`	Initially disables window
`WS_DLGFRAME`	Includes a border style for a window, similar to a dialog box window
`WS_GROUP`	Determines the first control within a group of controls
`WS_HSCROLL`	Includes a horizontal scroll bar with the window
`WS_MAXIMIZE`	Initially maximizes a window
`WS_MAXIMIZEBOX`	Includes a maximize box for a window
`WS_MINIMIZE`	Initially minimizes a window
`WS_MINIMIZEBOX`	Includes a minimize box for a window
`WS_OVERLAPPED` or `WS_TILED`	Creates an overlapped window, which includes a title and a border
`WS_OVERLAPPEDWINDOW` or `WS_TILEDWINDOW`	Creates an overlapped window with the WS_OVERLAPPED, WS_CAPTION, WS_SYSMENU, WS_THICKFRAME, WS_MINIMIZEBOX, and WS_MAXIMIZEBOX styles
`WS_POPUP`	Creates a pop-up window
`WS_POPUPWINDOW`	Creates a pop-up window with WS_BORDER, WS_POPUP, and WS_SYSMENU styles
`WS_SIZEBOX` or `WS_THICKFRAME`	Includes a sizeable border for a window
`WS_SYSMENU`	Includes a window menu in the title bar for a window
`WS_TABSTOP`	Enables a control to receive keyboard focus when the user presses the Tab key
`WS_VISIBLE`	Makes a window initially visible
`WS_VSCROLL`	Includes a vertical scroll bar for a window

Figure 9-15 Window styles

The Window styles listed in Figure 9-15 are generic styles that can be applied to any of the predefined control classes. However, several of the predefined control classes can be formatted with additional window styles. For example, you can use the BS_CHECKBOX style with the BUTTON predefined control class to create a button control in the style of a check box. See the MSDN Library for more information.

You can pass multiple window styles to the dwStyle property by separating them with a pipe |. For example, to create a window that includes both minimize and maximize boxes, you pass both values to the dwStyle parameter using the format: `WS_MINIMIZEBOX | WS_MAXIMIZEBOX`.

x, y, nWidth, and nHeight

The **x** and **y** parameters represent the starting position of a window's upper-left corner. The **nWidth** and **nHeight** parameters represent the window's lower-right corner. When the nWidth and nHeight parameters are based on the starting positions of the x and y parameters, all four parameters together determine the window's size. Note that for parent windows, the x, y, nWidth, and nHeight positions are measured from the upper-left corner of the monitor. For child windows, the four parameters are measured from the upper-left corner of the parent window.

9

A window's position and size are measured in pixels. Remember, a **pixel** (short for picture element) represents a single point on a computer screen. The number of pixels available depends on a computer monitor's resolution—640 columns by 480 rows of pixels on a VGA monitor, and 1,024 columns by 768 rows of pixels on a Super VGA monitor. You reference a window's pixels with x-axis and y-axis coordinates, beginning in the upper-left corner of the screen at an x-axis position of 0 and a y-axis position of 0. Pixel measurements are usually written in the format *x, y,* which means that the starting point in the upper-left corner of the screen is written as position 0, 0. As you move right from the upper-left corner of the screen along the x-axis, or down along the y-axis, the pixel measurements increase. Therefore, a pixel position that is 100 pixels to the right along the x-axis and 200 pixels down on the y-axis is written as 100, 200.

Figure 9-16 shows an example of the pixel positions for a simple parent window containing a button, which is a child window. It also shows the pixel positions for the button, relative to the parent window.

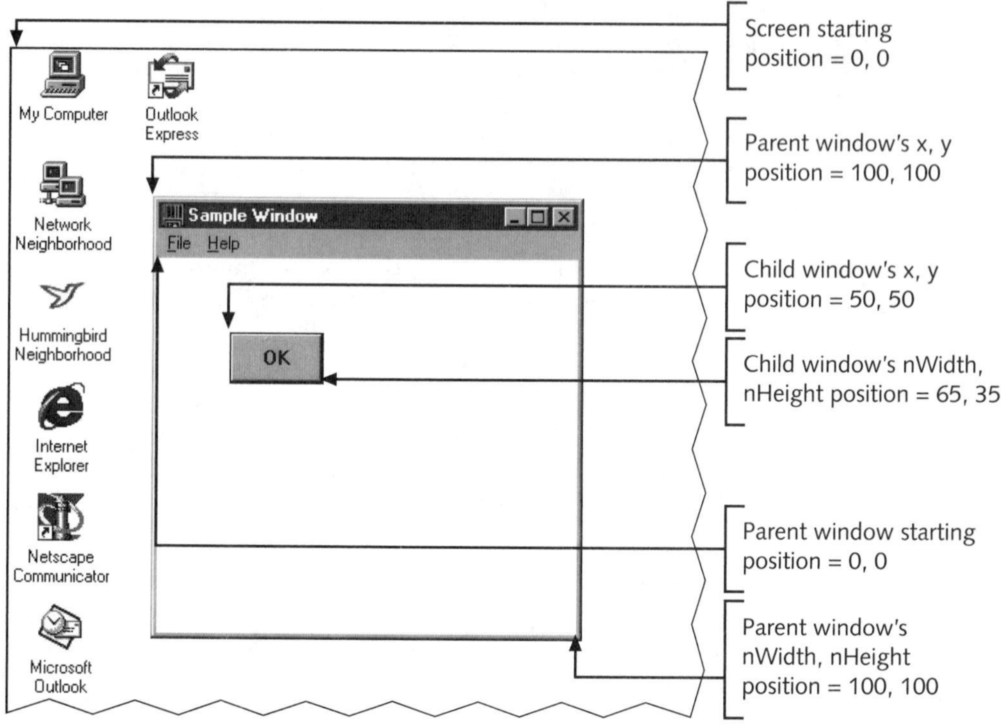

Figure 9-16 Pixel positions

You can use the value CW_USEDEFAULT with the x and nWidth parameters. When CW_USEDEFAULT is used with the x parameter, the system sets the window to the default position and ignores the y parameter. When CW_USEDEFAULT is used with the nWidth parameter, the system sets the window to the default size and ignores the nHeight parameter. CW_USEDEFAULT is valid only for overlapped windows. If you use CW_USEDEFAULT with a pop-up or child window's x parameter, both the x and y parameters are set to 0, which sets the window's starting position to the upper-left corner of the screen. Similarly, if you use CW_USEDEFAULT with a pop-up or child window's nWidth parameter, both the nWidth and nHeight parameters are set to 0.

hWndParent

The **hWndParent parameter** specifies a handle to a parent window and tells the system the correct window within which a child window should be created. If the window is a top-level parent window (such as the calculator program's main window), set the hWndParent parameter to NULL. Setting the hWndParent parameter to NULL informs the system that the window is a parent window and should be created directly on the screen instead of within the context of a parent window. For child windows, you set the hWndParent parameter to the handle of the parent window. For example, suppose you have a parent window that you created with its own CreateWindow() function and assigned to a handle named hMainWindow. In the child window's CreateWindow() function, you use hMainWindow for the hWndParent parameter to specify the child window's parent.

hMenu

The **hMenu parameter** specifies a handle to a menu. You will set this value to NULL because you do not need to work with menus in the calculator program.

hInstance

The **hInstance parameter** informs the system in which application instance the window should be created. In most cases, you use the HINSTANCE argument declared in the WinMain() function declaration. For example, if you declared in the WinMain() function declaration an HINSTANCE argument of hMyProgram, then you assign hMyProgram to the hInstance parameter to inform the system that you want the window created in the application designated by the hMyProgram instance handle.

lpParam

The **lpParam parameter** points to either a value passed through the CREATESTRUCT structure or to a CLIENTCREATESTRUCT structure. This is a somewhat advanced parameter that you will not use in the calculator program, so you will set its value to NULL.

The following code shows a complete example of a CreateWindow() function whose return value is assigned to a handle named hSampleWnd. The lpClassName parameter is assigned a class named WindowClass and the lpWindowName parameter is assigned the text *Sample Window*. The dwStyle parameter is passed a single style, WS_OVERLAPPEDWINDOW. Because the x and hWidth parameters are assigned CW_USEDEFAULT, the y and hHeight parameters are assigned values of NULL. The window being created is a parent window, so hWndParent is assigned a value of NULL instead of the handle to another window. The hMenu parameter is also NULL, because the window will not include a menu. Finally, the hInstance parameter is assigned an application handle named hCurInstance and lpParam is assigned a value of NULL.

```
HWND hSampleWnd;
hSampleWnd = CreateWindow(
    "WindowClass",
    "Sample Window",
    WS_OVERLAPPEDWINDOW,
    CW_USEDEFAULT,
    NULL,
    CW_USEDEFAULT,
    NULL,
    NULL,
    NULL,
    hCurInstance,
    NULL
    );
```

Next, you will create the windows that make up the calculator program, including the main calculator window and the individual controls that make up the calculator program's interface.

To create the windows that make up the calculator program:

1. As shown in Figure 9-17, add the declarations that create variables based on the HWND data type:

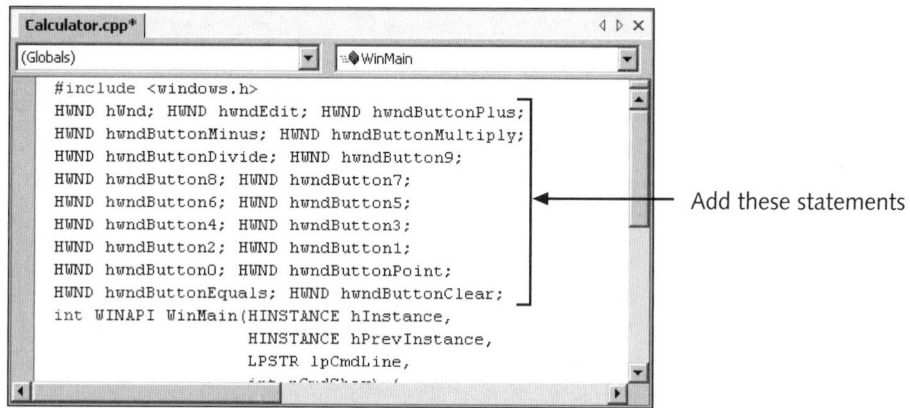

Figure 9-17 Declarations added to Calculator.cpp that create variables based on the HWND data type

2. Insert a new line above the WinMain() function's closing brace, and type the following statement to create the main calculator window and assign it to the hWnd handle. Notice that the lpClassName parameter is assigned a value of CalculatorClass, which is the name you assigned to the window class earlier in the WinMain() function. Also notice that the hWndParent parameter is assigned a value of null because this is the top-level parent window.

```
hWnd = CreateWindow("CalculatorClass", "Calculator",
WS_OVERLAPPEDWINDOW, CW_USEDEFAULT, CW_USEDE-
FAULT, 185, 265, NULL, NULL, hInstance, NULL);
```

3. Press **Enter** and add the following statement to create the calculator's edit box and assign it to the hwndEdit handle. The lpClassName parameter is assigned the predefined EDIT control class, and the hWndParent parameter is assigned a value of hWnd to identify that window as the edit box's parent window.

```
hwndEdit = CreateWindow("EDIT", NULL, WS_VISIBLE |
WS_CHILD | WS_BORDER | ES_LEFT, 10, 10, 155, 20, hWnd,
NULL, hInstance, NULL);
```

4. Press **Enter** again and add the statements to create the calculator's buttons. Each button is assigned to an appropriately named handle, such as hwndButtonPlus for the plus button. The lpClassName parameters are assigned the predefined BUTTON control class, and the hWndParent

parameter is assigned a value of hWnd to identify that window as each button's parent window. If you prefer not to type all of the code, you can copy it from the Chapter9_Calculator.cpp file in the Chapter9_Calculator folder in the Chapter.09 folder in your Visual C++ Projects folder.

```
hwndButtonPlus = CreateWindow( "BUTTON", "+",
WS_VISIBLE | WS_CHILD | BS_DEFPUSHBUTTON, 10, 40, 35, 35,
hWnd, NULL, hInstance, NULL);
hwndButtonMinus = CreateWindow( "BUTTON", "-",
WS_VISIBLE | WS_CHILD | BS_DEFPUSHBUTTON, 50, 40, 35, 35,
hWnd, NULL, hInstance, NULL);
hwndButtonMultiply = CreateWindow( "BUTTON", "*",
WS_VISIBLE | WS_CHILD | BS_DEFPUSHBUTTON, 90, 40, 35, 35,
hWnd, NULL, hInstance, NULL);
hwndButtonDivide = CreateWindow( "BUTTON", "/",
WS_VISIBLE | WS_CHILD | BS_DEFPUSHBUTTON, 130, 40, 35, 35,
hWnd, NULL, hInstance, NULL);
hwndButton6 = CreateWindow( "BUTTON", "6", WS_VISIBLE |
WS_CHILD | BS_DEFPUSHBUTTON, 10, 80, 35, 35, hWnd, NULL,
hInstance, NULL);
hwndButton7 = CreateWindow( "BUTTON", "7", WS_VISIBLE |
WS_CHILD | BS_DEFPUSHBUTTON, 50, 80, 35, 35, hWnd, NULL,
hInstance, NULL);
hwndButton8 = CreateWindow( "BUTTON", "8", WS_VISIBLE |
WS_CHILD | BS_DEFPUSHBUTTON, 90, 80, 35, 35, hWnd, NULL,
hInstance, NULL);
hwndButton9 = CreateWindow( "BUTTON", "9", WS_VISIBLE |
WS_CHILD | BS_DEFPUSHBUTTON, 130, 80, 35, 35, hWnd, NULL,
hInstance, NULL);
hwndButton2 = CreateWindow( "BUTTON", "2", WS_VISIBLE |
WS_CHILD | BS_DEFPUSHBUTTON, 10, 120, 35, 35, hWnd, NULL,
hInstance, NULL);
hwndButton3 = CreateWindow( "BUTTON", "3", WS_VISIBLE |
WS_CHILD | BS_DEFPUSHBUTTON, 50, 120, 35, 35, hWnd, NULL,
hInstance, NULL);
hwndButton4 = CreateWindow( "BUTTON", "4", WS_VISIBLE |
WS_CHILD | BS_DEFPUSHBUTTON, 90, 120, 35, 35, hWnd, NULL,
hInstance, NULL);
hwndButton5 = CreateWindow( "BUTTON", "5", WS_VISIBLE |
WS_CHILD | BS_DEFPUSHBUTTON, 130, 120, 35, 35, hWnd,
NULL, hInstance, NULL);
hwndButton0 = CreateWindow( "BUTTON", "0", WS_VISIBLE |
WS_CHILD | BS_DEFPUSHBUTTON, 10, 160, 35, 35, hWnd, NULL,
hInstance, NULL);
hwndButton1 = CreateWindow( "BUTTON", "1", WS_VISIBLE |
WS_CHILD | BS_DEFPUSHBUTTON, 50, 160, 35, 35, hWnd, NULL,
hInstance, NULL);
hwndButtonPoint = CreateWindow( "BUTTON", ".",
WS_VISIBLE | WS_CHILD | BS_DEFPUSHBUTTON, 90, 160, 35,
35, hWnd, NULL, hInstance, NULL);
```

```
hwndButtonEquals = CreateWindow( "BUTTON", "=",
WS_VISIBLE | WS_CHILD | BS_DEFPUSHBUT-
TON, 130, 160, 35, 35, hWnd, NULL, hInstance, NULL);
hwndButtonClear = CreateWindow( "BUTTON", "Clear",
WS_VISIBLE | WS_CHILD | BS_DEFPUSHBUTTON, 10, 200, 155,
25, hWnd, NULL, hInstance, NULL);
```

5. Save the Calculator.cpp file by selecting **Save Calculator.cpp** from the **File** menu.

Displaying New Windows

The final step in creating a new window is to display it. The CreateWindow() function does not actually display a window; it only creates a new window in memory. The **ShowWindow() function** displays a window onscreen that was created with the CreateWindow() function. The ShowWindow()function accepts two arguments: the handle to a window and the nCmdShow argument that was passed to the WinMain() function. (As you may recall, the nCmdShow argument specifies the startup mode for the window: minimized, maximized, and so on.) For example, to display the window assigned to the hSampleWnd handle, you use the statement `ShowWindow(hSampleWnd, nCmdShow);`. When you first execute a Windows program, you only need to use the ShowWindow() function to display the program's main parent window because child windows are displayed automatically when the parent window is displayed.

Next, you will add a single ShowWindow() function to the calculator program.

To add a ShowWindow() function to the calculator program:

1. As shown in Figure 9-18, insert a new line above the WinMain() function's closing brace and type `ShowWindow(hWnd, nCmdShow);`. Although the code that creates and displays the calculator program's windows is now complete, you cannot run the program just yet. First, you need to learn about events and messages.

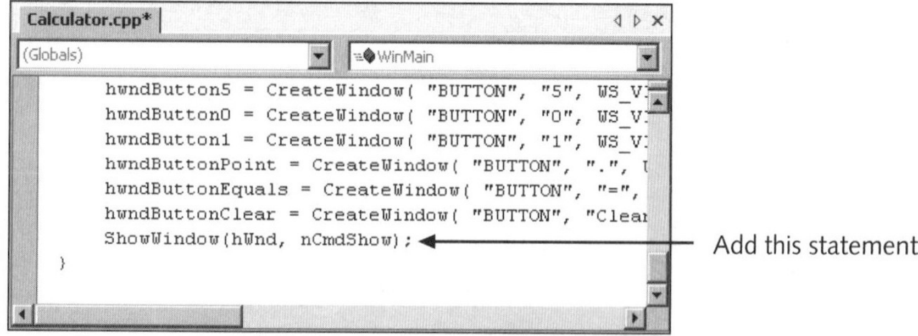

Figure 9-18 ShowWindow() function added to Calculator.cpp

EVENTS AND MESSAGES

One of the most powerful aspects of Windows programs is that they are driven by events. An **event** is a specific circumstance that is monitored by Windows. Some of the most common events are actions that users take, such as clicking a button in a Windows application. Other types of events occur behind the scenes and do not involve user interaction. For example, when one window that was obscured by another window becomes visible again, an event occurs that causes Windows to redraw the newly visible portions of the previously obscured window. A common use of events is to add interactivity between your Windows program and its users. The calculator program, for instance, uses button click events to execute the appropriate code segments that give the program its functionality.

When an event occurs, Windows sends a message to the program associated with the event. A **message** is a set of information about a particular event, such as where and when the event occurred. You refer to messages in code by using predefined Windows constants beginning with a prefix of WM_ (*WM* stands for Windows Messaging). One of the more commonly used messages is the **WM_COMMAND message**, which is generated for events involving menus and buttons, such as when a user clicks a button. There are literally hundreds of Windows messages. You will be introduced to the messages used in this chapter as necessary. Figure 9-19 illustrates the concept of how Windows generates a message when a user clicks a button in an application.

9

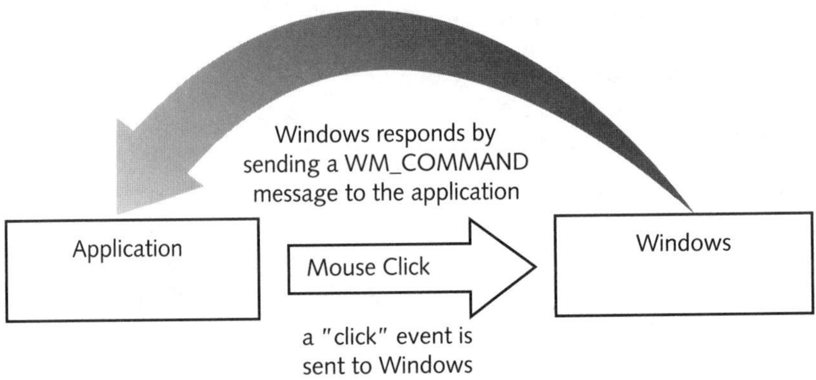
Windows responds by
sending a WM_COMMAND
message to the application
Application
Mouse Click
Windows
a "click" event is
sent to Windows

Figure 9-19 Processing of an event

Tip

You can find a complete listing of Windows messages in the MSDN Library.

Every 32-bit Windows application has its own **message queue** where messages are placed until they are processed by the application. To process a message in an application's message queue, you must perform the following two steps:

1. Write a message loop that retrieves messages from the queue and sends them to the window procedure.
2. Add code to the window procedure code that performs an appropriate action depending on the generated event.

Figure 9-20 illustrates how these two steps work.

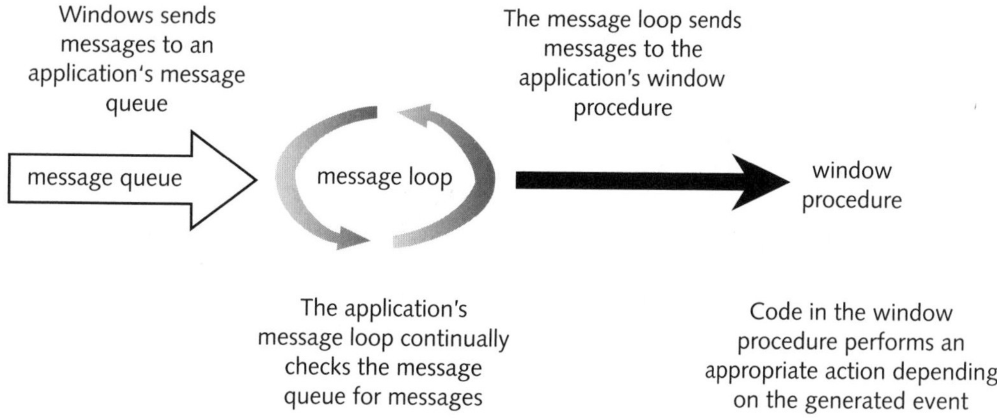

Figure 9-20 Processing of the message queue

Message Loops

Windows applications need a way of checking the message queue for new messages. A **message loop** continually checks the queue for new messages, and then sends any new messages found to the window procedure. You place a message loop inside a WinMain() function so that it starts running (and checking for messages) when the program first executes. Message loops usually use a `while` statement, along with an MSG structure variable and the GetMessage(), TranslateMessage(), and DispatchMessage() Windows API functions. The **MSG structure** contains information about the current message in the application's message queue. The following code is a typical example of a message loop created with a `while` statement that you would place inside a WinMain() function. The first statement in the following code declares a variable of the MSG structure type in order to access the current message information:

```
MSG msg;
while(GetMessage(&msg, NULL, 0, 0 )) {
   TranslateMessage(&msg);
   DispatchMessage(&msg);
}
return (int) msg.wParam;
```

The **GetMessage() function** retrieves messages from an application's message queue and is called as the `while` loop's conditional expression. Note that you can include any type of a statement within a conditional expression, so long as it returns a Boolean value of true or false. You pass to the GetMessage() function the address of the MSG variable, along with several other parameters, which you will not learn about in detail. It is important for you to understand what keeps the `while` loop iterating. Remember that a looping statement, such as a `while` statement, will continue to iterate as long as its conditional expression evaluates to true. The GetMessage() function returns a value of true for all messages except for one, the WM_QUIT message. The **WM_QUIT message** is generated when an application closes, such as when a user clicks the main application window's close icon. Because WM_QUIT returns a value of false, the message loop ends, which also ends the program. Note that when there are no messages in the message queue, the message loop will continue looping until a new message is generated.

The body of the `while` loop contains the TranslateMessage() and the DispatchMessage() functions. The **TranslateMessage() function** converts keyboard messages into a format Windows can understand. The **DispatchMessage() function** sends messages to the window procedure for processing.

9

How does the DispatchMessage() function know which function to send a message to? Recall that when you defined the window class, you defined a lpfnWndProc field with a pointer to the name of the window procedure that will handle messages. The function name you assigned to the lpfnWndProc field in the example and in the calculator program was MainWndProc. (You will create the MainWndProc() window procedure in the next section.) The following code contains a partial listing of the window class definition for the example you created earlier, with the lpfnWndProc field highlighted.

```
WNDCLASS wc;
wc.style = CS_HREDRAW | CS_VREDRAW;
wc.lpfnWndProc = MainWndProc;
wc.cbClsExtra  = 0;
wc.cbWndExtra = 0;
...
}
```

For an application to close properly, the WinMain() function's return statement should return the wParam field of the MSG structure. When the WM_QUIT message executes, the wParam field of the MSG structure contains an exit code that should be returned to Windows as the `return` value from the WinMain() function.

Next, you will add a message loop to the calculator program.

To add a message loop to the calculator program:

1. As shown in Figure 9-21, declare the MSG variable and add the `while` structure for the message loop at the end of the WinMain() function. Also, add the statement `return (int) msg.wParam;`, which returns to the operating system the value of the MSG structure's wParam field after casting it to the `int` data type.

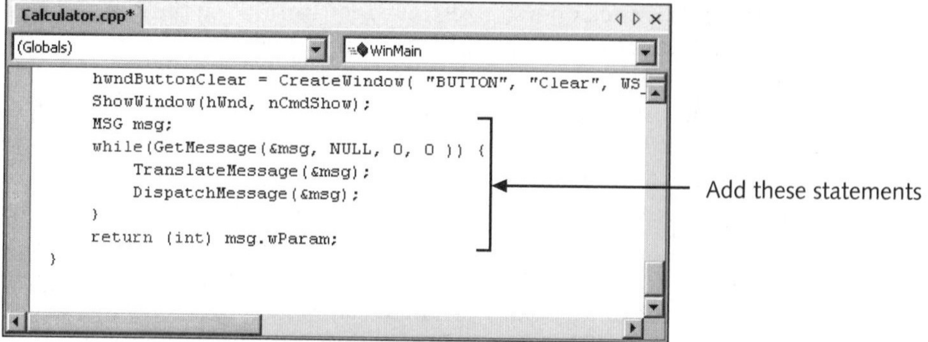

Figure 9-21 Message loop added to Calculator.cpp

Window Procedures

A **window procedure**, or **windproc**, is a special function that processes any messages received by an application. You may also see window procedures referred to as *callback functions* because they give Windows a way of "calling back" your application once it generates an event and message. Essentially, your application "calls" Windows by generating an event, and Windows "calls back" your application and gives it the message in the message queue. The message loop then forwards the message to the window procedure that Windows is trying to reach (or "call back"). You can really think of the window procedure as the heart of a Windows API program because that is where the majority of the program's functionality resides. Figure 9-22 illustrates the concept of a callback function, using an expanded version of the message queue figure you saw earlier.

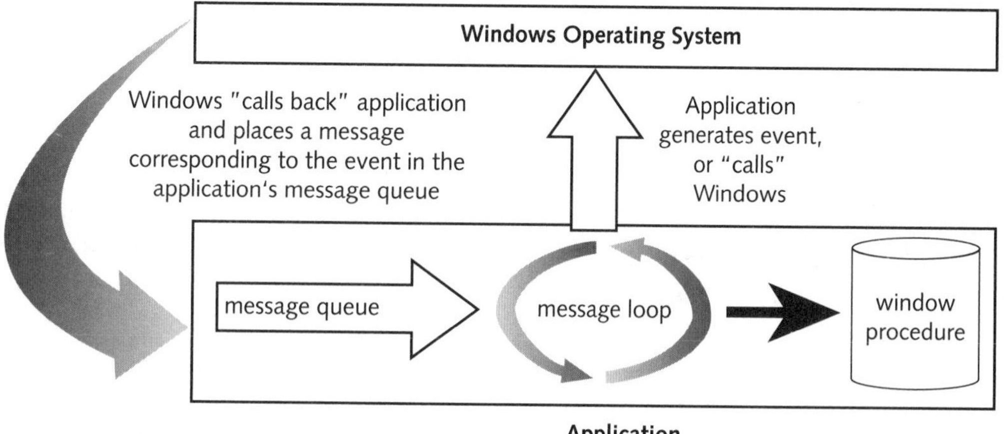

Figure 9-22 Callback function

The following code is a typical function declaration for a window procedure named MainWndProc(). The function declaration declares a `return` type of LRESULT and includes the CALLBACK data type to designate it as a callback function. The hWnd parameter represents a handle to the application window that generated the message. The msg parameter is an identifier representing the current message. The wParam and lParam parameters both contain additional pieces of information about the current message.

```
LRESULT CALLBACK WINAPI MainWndProc(
  HWND hWnd,
  UINT msg,
  WPARAM wParam,
  LPARAM lParam){
  // statements
}
```

Next, you will add a window procedure to the calculator program.

To add a window procedure to the calculator program:

1. First, as shown in Figure 9-23, insert a new line after the `#include <windows.h>` statement and type the function prototype for the window procedure:

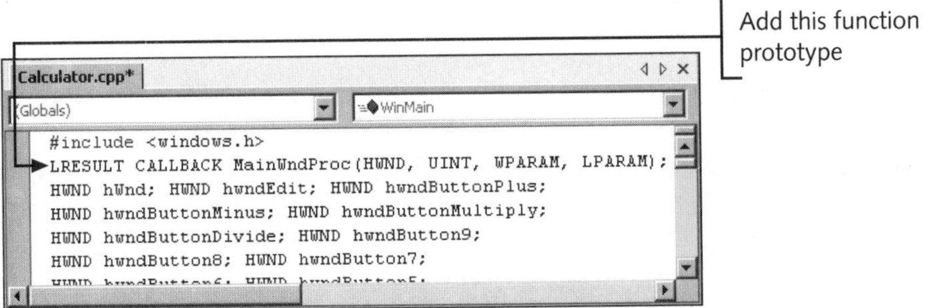

Figure 9-23 Function prototype for the window procedure added to Calculator.cpp

2. Now add the function definition for the window procedure after the WinMain() function's closing brace, as shown in Figure 9-24. The function contains a single `return` statement, which returns a value of 0 to indicate that any calls to the window procedure executed normally.

The primary purpose of a window procedure is to execute the appropriate code, or handler, for a specific message. A **handler** is a segment of code within a window procedure that executes for a specific message. You use a `switch` structure to determine the type of message contained in the msg parameter of the window procedure's function definition. `Case` labels within the `switch` statement contain the handlers or call the appropriate handler functions for each message.

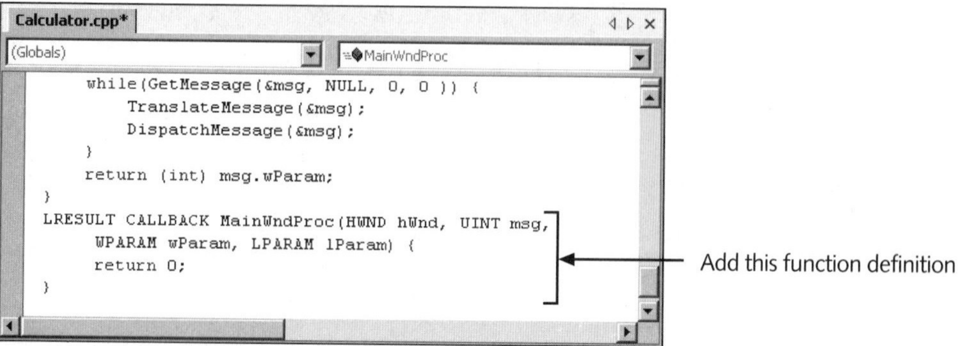
Calculator.cpp*
(Globals)
MainWndProc
while(GetMessage(&msg, NULL, 0, 0)) {
TranslateMessage(&msg);
DispatchMessage(&msg);
}
return (int) msg.wParam;
}
LRESULT CALLBACK MainWndProc(HWND hWnd, UINT msg,
WPARAM wParam, LPARAM lParam) {
return 0;
}
Add this function definition

Figure 9-24 Function definition for the window procedure added to Calculator.cpp

The following code contains a `switch` structure that evaluates the contents of the msg parameter.

```
    switch(msg) {
    case WM_COMMAND:
      ...
      break;
    case WM_DESTROY:
      PostQuitMessage(0);
      return 0;
default:
      return DefWindowProc(hWnd, msg, wParam, lParam);
}
```

The preceding code contains `case` labels for two messages: WM_COMMAND and WM_DESTROY. As mentioned previously, WM_COMMAND is generated for events involving menus and buttons. The **WM_DESTROY message** is generated when a window is being destroyed. The handler for the WM_DESTROY message needs to call the PostQuitMessage() function, which generates the WM_QUIT message that tells the message loop to end the program. If you do not include in the window procedure a WM_DESTROY message that calls the PostQuitMessage() function to generate a WM_QUIT message (and perform any other processing before the application's windows are destroyed), then the application will not close properly.

Notice the `default` label in the `switch` statement. The `switch` statement in window procedures must include a default label that calls the Windows API DefWindowProc() function (Def WindowProc stands for *Default Window Procedure*), to which you pass the four parameters that were received by the window procedure itself (hWnd, msg, wParam, lParam). The **DefWindowProc() function** calls the default window procedure for any message for which you do not provide a handler. In other words, if you do not provide handlers for a message, the DefWindowProc() function hands the message back to Windows. It is important to understand that although there are hundreds of Windows messages, you are not required to write handlers for each one. As mentioned previously, Windows processes many types of events behind the scenes—some of which are aimed directly at your application.

However, you only need to write code that responds to the events for which your program needs to take specific action, such as to perform the calculation when the equal sign button is pressed in the calculator program (generating a WM_COMMAND message). Windows first checks to see if you have written a handler for a specific message. If you have written a handler for a specific message, then Windows uses it to process the message. If not, the DefWindowProc() function sends the message to Windows, which performs its own default processing.

You may be wondering what the default processing is for many types of events, such as the WM_COMMAND message generated for a button click. In some cases, Windows does nothing by default. For example, if you fail to write code that handles a button click, then when a user clicks a button in your program, Windows performs its own default processing—which is to do nothing.

Next, you will add a `switch` statement to the window procedure. The `switch` statement for the calculator program requires a WM_COMMAND message handler, a WM_DESTROY message handler, and a default label that calls the default window procedure.

To add a `switch` statement to the window procedure:

1. As shown in Figure 9-25, insert a new line above the window procedure's `return` statement and type the `switch` statement and the `case` label for the WM_COMMAND message.

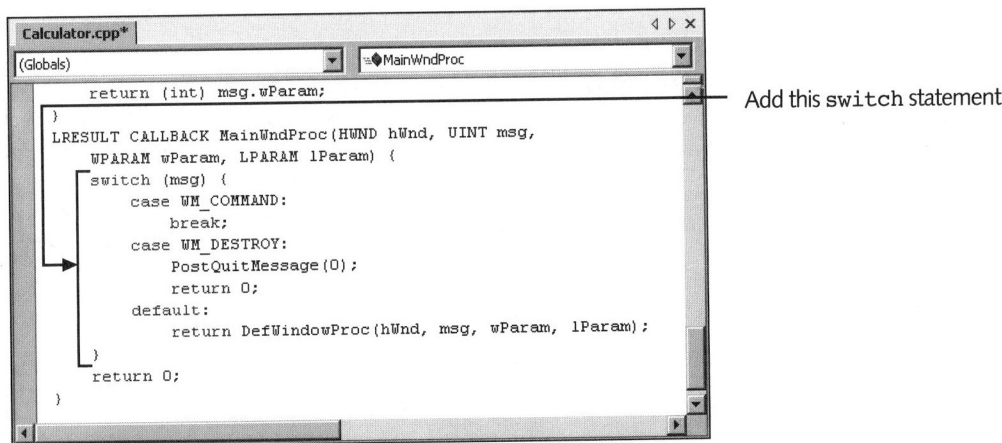

Figure 9-25 `switch` statement added to the window procedure

2. Build and execute the **Calculator** program. Figure 9-26 shows how the application window appears. Although you can click the buttons in the program, nothing will happen because you still need to add code to the WM_COMMAND handler. In the next section you will add the final code to the WM_COMMAND handler.

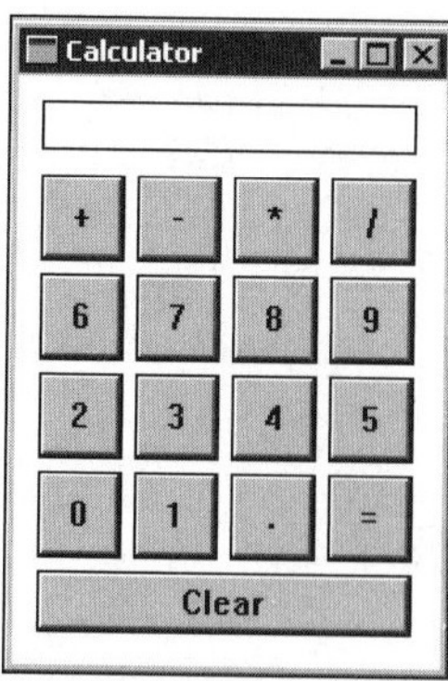

Figure 9-26 Calculator application window

3. Close the **Calculator** window.

For the calculator program, you are using the WM_COMMAND message to notify the program when one of the calculator buttons is clicked once. However, there are numerous events associated with buttons, not just single-click events. For example, the double-click event is another commonly used button event. You can identify a specific event using the wParam parameter that is passed to the window procedure. For button events, the wParam parameter contains notification codes that identify specific button event types. For example, when a button is double-clicked the wParam parameter will contain the value BN_DBLCLK. Similarly, when a button is clicked once, the wParam parameter will contain the value BN_CLICKED.

Check the MSDN Library for a complete listing of button events.

Next, you will add to the handler for the WM_COMMAND message a `switch` statement that evaluates the wParam parameter.

To add a `switch` statement for the WM_COMMAND message:

1. Above the `break` statement in the `case` label for the WM_COMMAND message, add the `switch` statement shown in Figure 9-27.

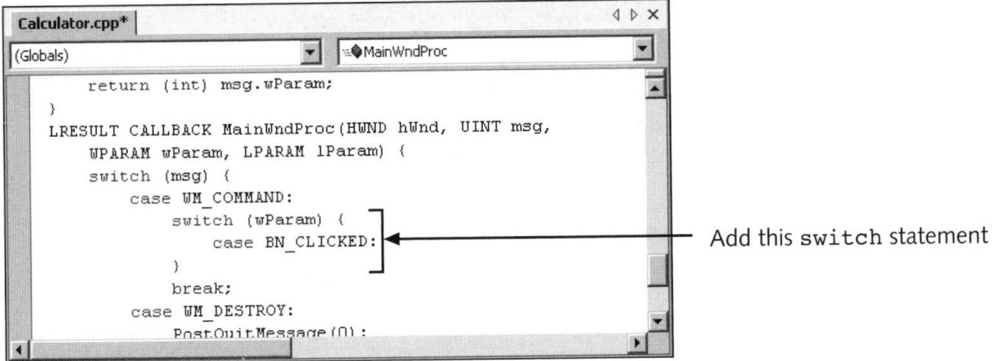

Calculator.cpp*
(Globals)
MainWndProc
return (int) msg.wParam;
}
LRESULT CALLBACK MainWndProc(HWND hWnd, UINT msg,
WPARAM wParam, LPARAM lParam) {
switch (msg) {
case WM_COMMAND:
switch (wParam) {
case BN_CLICKED:
}
break;
case WM_DESTROY:
Add this switch statement

Figure 9-27 `switch` statement added for the WM_COMMAND message

Because you are only checking for BN_CLICKED events in the calculator program, you could use an `if` statement instead of a `switch` statement. Most Windows API programs use a `switch` statement, however, when checking for notification codes because they usually use multiple types of WM_COMMAND events. Although the calculator program uses only one WM_COMMAND event, you are using a `switch` statement because programs you create in real life will probably use multiple WM_COMMAND events. Additionally, using a `switch` statement makes it easier to add support for other types of WM_COMMAND events in the future.

9

COMPLETING THE CALCULATOR PROGRAM

To complete the calculator program, you need to understand how to calculate numbers in C++. The functionality of the program is not very complex and does calculations with only two numbers (operands) using a single operator (+, -, *, or /). For example, the program can calculate 1 + 2, or 10 / 5, or 15 * 14, and so on. To perform the calculation, you will capture the three parts of an equation in three separate variables: one for the left operand, one for the operator, and one for the right operand. The calculation will use two functions: setNumbers() and runCalculation(). You will learn about each function in turn.

The calculator program requires several string manipulation functions in order to set and retrieve the values that will appear in the edit box. Therefore, before creating the setNumbers() and runCalculation() functions, you need to add a preprocessor directive that gives the program access to the cstring header file. Note that the program uses character arrays instead of string class variables because the program uses several data conversion routines that only work with character arrays.

You also need to add variable declarations to the calculator program that are necessary to perform the calculations, along with function prototypes for the setNumbers() and runCalculation() functions.

To add a preprocessor directive, variable declarations, and a function prototype to the Calculator program:

1. As shown in Figure 9-28, type the preprocessor directive for the cstring header file and declare the std namespace. Also add the following two function prototype declarations for the setNumbers() and runCalculation() function.

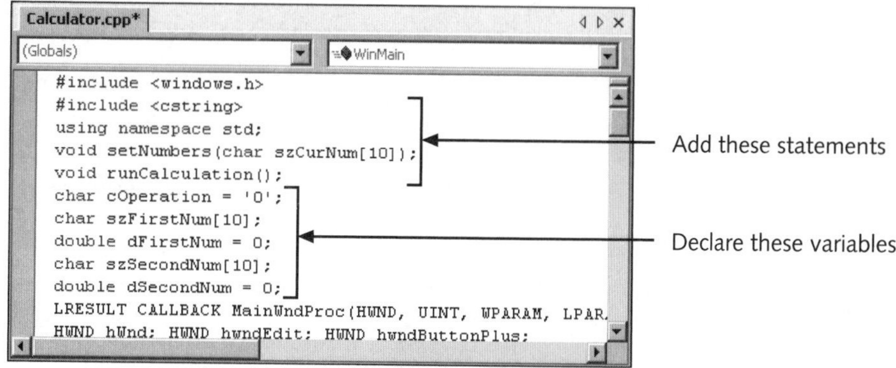

Figure 9-28 Preprocessor directive, variable declarations, and a function prototype added to Calculator.cpp

2. Also, as shown in Figure 9-28, declare the variables after the `void runCalculation();` statement. The first variable will determine the type of operation being performed (addition, subtraction, multiplication, or division). The next two variables are a `char` variable and a `double` variable for the left operand in the equation. The last two variables are a `char` variable and a `double` variable for the right operand in the equation. The `char` variable will temporarily store the numbers when you display them and retrieve them in the edit box, and the `double` variables will be used to perform the actual calculations.

Next, you will learn about the setNumbers() function.

Setting the Calculation Variables

The setNumbers() function displays the operands in the calculator's edit box. You cannot place the contents of number variables into the edit box because an edit box accepts only text. For this reason, in the last set of steps you declared two global variables for each operand: one as a `char` data type and the other as a `double` data type. The setNumbers() function uses the `char` version of each operand variable. In the runCalculation() function you will convert the values in the `char` variables to numeric values, copy the numeric values into the `double` data type versions of the operand variables, and then carry out the calculation.

To determine which value to display in the edit box, you need to be able to determine which button was clicked. You will do this by comparing each button's window handle to the handle that was passed to the window procedure's lParam parameter. First, you must convert the value contained in the lParam parameter from text to a handle by casting the lParam parameter to the HWND data type using the following statement:

```
HWND hwndCtl = (HWND) lParam;
```

After adding the preceding statement to the program you can use `if` statements to compare the hwndCtl handle to the handles for each of the buttons to see which one generated the click event.

Next, you will add to the window procedure a statement to declare the hwndCtl handle. You will also add statements for each of the numeric buttons to the BN_CLICKED label that call the setNumbers() function when a particular button is clicked and pass to it the value represented by the button.

To add code to the window procedure that compares the handle in the lParam parameter to each numeric button handle:

9

1. As shown in Figure 9-29, add the statement that declares a new window handle variable named hwndCtl.

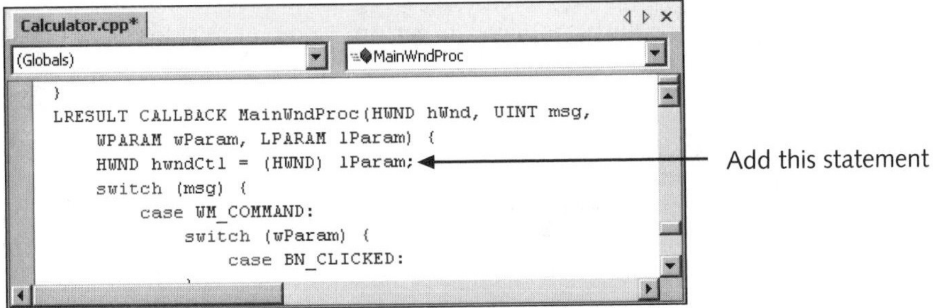

Figure 9-29 New window handle variable declared in the window procedure

2. Next, add to the BN_CLICKED case label the following `if...else` block. Each `if` statement compares the value of the hwndCtl handle to each button's handle. If a match is found, then the setNumbers() function is called and is passed a text string with the appropriate value for each button. For example, if the hwndCtl handle matches the hwndButton1 handle (the button for the number 1), then a value of "1" is passed to the setNumbers() function using the statement `setNumbers("1");`.

```
case BN_CLICKED:
if (hwndCtl == hwndButton1)
    setNumbers("1");
else if (hwndCtl == hwndButton2)
    setNumbers("2");
else if (hwndCtl == hwndButton3)
    setNumbers("3");
else if (hwndCtl == hwndButton4)
    setNumbers("4");
else if (hwndCtl == hwndButton5)
    setNumbers("5");
else if (hwndCtl == hwndButton6)
    setNumbers("6");
else if (hwndCtl == hwndButton7)
    setNumbers("7");
else if (hwndCtl == hwndButton8)
    setNumbers("8");
else if (hwndCtl == hwndButton9)
    setNumbers("9");
else if (hwndCtl == hwndButton0)
    setNumbers("0");
else if (hwndCtl == hwndButtonPoint)
    setNumbers(".");
```

Next, you will create the setNumbers() function. Figure 9-30 shows how the function is set up.

```
void setNumbers(char szCurNum[10]){
      if (cOperation == '0') {
          strcat(szFirstNum, szCurNum);
          SetWindowText(hwndEdit, szFirstNum);
      }
      else {
          strcat(szSecondNum, szCurNum);
          SetWindowText(hwndEdit, szSecondNum);
      }
}
```

Figure 9-30 setNumbers() function

The value passed to the function is assigned to a character array variable named szCurNum that consists of a single element.You must use a character array instead of a single `char` variable because the value passed to the function is a string, even though you are passing only a single character. Because a null character is appended to the single character when it is passed to the setNumbers() function, the passed information becomes a string instead of a single character.

The `if` statement checks the value of the cOperation variable. If its value is equal to 0, the initially assigned value, then the user is currently building the left operand and the `if` block's statements execute. If the value is not equal to 0, then the user is currently building the right operand and the `else` block's statements execute. (If cOperation does not contain a value of 0, then it will contain a value of +, -, *, or /.) Both the `if` and `else` clauses build the value displayed in the edit box by using the strcat() function to add the value of the szCurNum variable to either the szFirstNum or szSecondNum variables. Recall that the strcat() function is used for combining the contents of one string with another.

Following the strcat() statement is a statement that executes the SetWindowText() function. The **SetWindowText() function** is a Windows API function that changes either the value displayed in a control or the title text for windows that are not controls. The syntax for the SetWindowText() function is `SetWindowText(`*`handle, text`*`);`. You will pass to the SetWindowText() function the handle of the edit control (hwndEdit) along with either the szFirstNum or szSecondNum variable, depending on whether the `if` or `else` clause is executing.

To create the setNumbers() function:

1. After the closing brace for the window procedure, add the setNumbers() function, as shown in Figure 9-31.

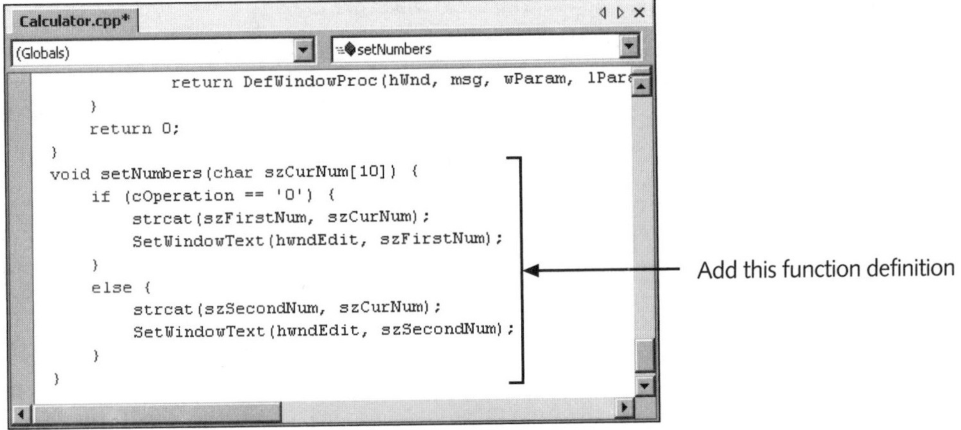

Figure 9-31 setNumbers() function added to Calculator.cpp

The final step in setting the calculation variables is to add handlers that determine the type of operation being performed: addition, subtraction, multiplication, or division. When any of these buttons is clicked, the program will assign its associated value (+, -, *, or /) to the cOperation variable.

Additionally, the left operand value currently displayed in the edit box will be assigned to the `double` data type version of the variable. However, you cannot directly assign a text value to a numeric value. Instead you must use a data conversion routine. The data conversion routine you will use is the **atof() function** in the stdlib.h header, which converts strings to floating-point numbers. Note that you do not need to include the stdlib.h header into your programs because it is already included when you declare the std namespace with the statement `using namespace std;`. The syntax for the atof() function is `variable = atof(string);`.

See the MSDN Library for a list of other data conversion routines.

To add handlers that determine the type of operation being performed:

1. Modify the `case BN_CLICKED:` label in the MainWndProc() function by adding the `else...if` statements shown in Figure 9-32 for the operator variables. The conditional expressions check if the hwndCtl handle is equal to the handle for each operation. Within each `else...if` block, the first statement assigns the appropriate value to the cOperation variable, while the second statement uses the atof() function to assign the value of the szFirstNum variable to the dFirstNum variable.

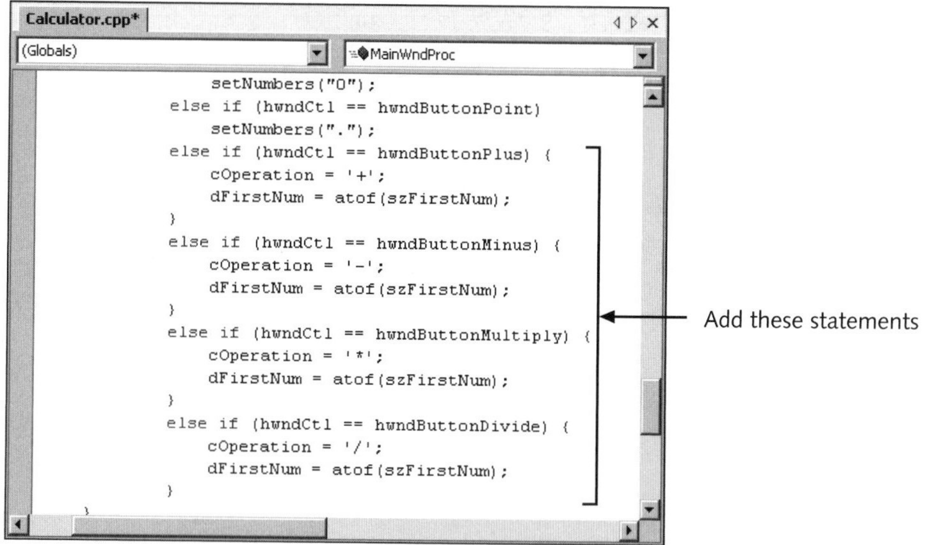

Figure 9-32 Handlers added that determine the type of operation being performed

Adding the Calculation Code

The calculation is performed when the equal sign button is clicked, which assigns the value of the second operand to the dSecondNum variable and executes the runCalculation() function. The runCalculation() function contains the code that actually performs the calculation. First, you will add handler code for the equal sign button. You will also add handler code that resets the program's variables to their default values when the Clear button is clicked.

To add handler code for the equal sign button and Clear button:

1. After the `else...if` statement that compares the hwndCtl handle to the division button handle, add the `else...if` statement for the equal sign button, as shown in Figure 9-33. The conditional expression checks whether the hwndCtl handle is equal to the hwndButtonEquals handle. Within the `else...if` block, the first statement uses the atof() function to assign the value of the szSecondNum variable to the dSecondNum variable, while the second statement calls the runCalculation() function.

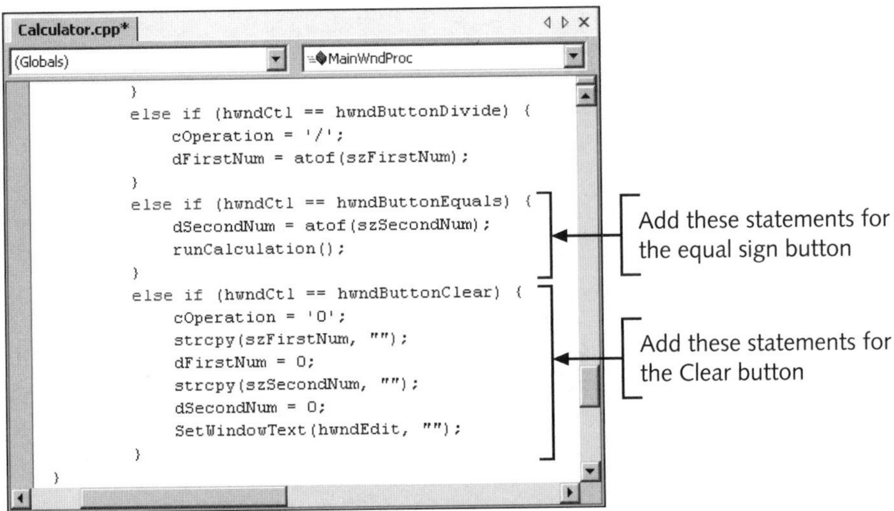

Figure 9-33 Handler code added for the equal sign button and Clear button

2. Also as shown in Figure 9-33, add the last `else...if` statement, which resets the program's variables to their original values when the Clear button is clicked.

The last step, before you can use the calculator program, is to create the runCalculation() function. The runCalculation() function will examine the contents of the cOperation variable, and then perform the appropriate calculations. For example, if the cOperation variable is equal to +, then the dFirstNum and dSecondNum variables will be added. Once the result is calculated, it will be converted to a string using the _gcvt()function. The **_gcvt() function** is a data conversion function in the stdlib.h header that converts floating-point values to string values. The syntax for the _gcvt() function is `_gcvt(floating-point value, digits, char array);`. The digits portion of the function determines the number of digits to convert from the floating-point value to the string value. Number of digits does not mean the number of decimal places, but the number of characters that compose the number. For example, the number 10.8765 is the equivalent of seven digits. You will use a value of 10, which should be sufficient for most simple calculations.

To create the runCalculation() function:

1. After the closing brace for the setNumbers() function, add the runCalculation() function header:

```
void runCalculation() {
```

2. Press **Enter** and add the following two variable declarations. The dResult variable will contain the result of the numeric calculation, and the szResult variable will contain the result after it has been converted using the _gcvt() function.

```
double dResult = 0;
char szResult[25];
```

3. After the second variable declaration, add the following `if...else` block, which evaluates the cOperation variable and then performs the appropriate calculation:

```
if (cOperation == '+') {
        dResult = dFirstNum + dSecondNum;
}
else if (cOperation == '-') {
        dResult = dFirstNum - dSecondNum;
}
else if (cOperation == '*') {
        dResult = dFirstNum * dSecondNum;
}
else if (cOperation == '/') {
        dResult = dFirstNum / dSecondNum;
}
```

4. Insert a new line after the closing brace for the last `else...if` clause and add the following two statements. The first statement uses the _gcvt() function to assign the value of dResult variable to the szResult variable. The second statement uses the SetWindowText() function to place the results of the calculation in the edit box.

```
_gcvt(dResult, 10, szResult);
SetWindowText(hwndEdit, szResult);
```

5. Press **Enter** and add the following statements that reset the variables to their default values:

```
cOperation = '0';
strcpy(szFirstNum, szResult);
dFirstNum = 0;
strcpy(szSecondNum, "");
dSecondNum = 0;
```

6. Press **Enter** again and add the function's closing brace: `}`.

7. Build, execute, and test the program. If you have problems building the project, or if the calculations do not perform correctly, then compare your code to the Chapter9_Calculator.cpp file on your Data Disk.

CHAPTER SUMMARY

- The Windows API allows you to write programs for Windows operating systems.
- Computers are classified according to how many bits they can transmit simultaneously into the microprocessor, or CPU. The bus, or data bus, refers to the electronic path that the bits travel into the microprocessor.
- A separate Windows API exists for each generation of Windows operating systems.
- The `windows.h` header file includes all of the functions, variables, and other programming elements that make up the Windows API.
- A child window always appears within the area defined by a parent window.
- A parent window is a primary application window containing one or more child windows.
- The WinMain() function is the starting point for any Windows API program.
- The window class defines the characteristics of a program's main window.
- The predefined WNDCLASS structure is used for defining the characteristics of a window class.
- The RegisterClass() function informs the operating system about a newly defined window class.
- The CreateWindow() function creates a new window based on several parameters, including window class, size, position, and style.
- The ShowWindow() function displays a window onscreen that was created with the CreateWindow() function.
- An event is a specific circumstance that is monitored by Windows.
- A message is a set of information about a particular event, such as where and when the event occurred.
- Every 32-bit Windows application has its own message queue where messages are placed until they are processed by the application.
- A window procedure, or windproc, is a special function that processes any messages received by an application.

9

Review Questions

1. Which of the following best describes how Windows programs are created?
   a. You can only write Windows programs using standard C programming syntax.
   b. You create Windows programs by combining code written in a source programming language with calls to the Windows API.
   c. You can only write Windows programs using standard C++ programming syntax with calls to the Windows API.
   d. Visual C++ is the only current programming environment capable of writing Windows programs because it allows programmers to combine C and C++ syntax.
2. When operating on a 64-bit Pentium computer, Windows NT can operate at ________________.
   a. 16 bits
   b. 32 bits
   c. 64 bits
   d. 128 bits
3. What is the name of the API that is shared by all 32-bit Windows operating systems?
   a. Win32 SDK
   b. Platform SDK
   c. Win API
   d. Win32 API
4. Support for programming in the Windows API is defined ________________.
   a. in the `windows.h` header file
   b. in Visual C++
   c. in the Win API
   d. automatically by each Windows operating system
5. Which of the following statements is true?
   a. The Windows API uses the exact same data types as Visual C++.
   b. The Windows API defines its own data types.
   c. The Windows API does not use data types.
   d. The Windows API only uses C data types.

6. A handle ________________.
   a. refers to the Windows API version to which a program conforms
   b. is another way of referring to a Windows program's executable file
   c. is the area of the screen where an application window is drawn
   d. is used to refer to a resource or object that has been loaded into memory
7. All individual controls and user interface components in a Windows API program, such as buttons and edit boxes, are also ________________.
   a. handles
   b. windows
   c. programs
   d. variables
8. Which of the following statements is true about parent and child windows?
   a. Child windows are generated by the Windows operating system itself, while parent windows are created by applications written in C++ that make calls to the Windows API.
   b. Parent windows are generated by the Windows operating system itself, while child windows are created by applications written in C++ that make calls to the Windows API.
   c. Parent windows are larger than 100 * 100 pixels, while child windows are smaller than 100 * 100 pixels.
   d. A parent window is a primary application window containing one ore more child windows.
9. A(n) ________________ is a particular copy of a window or other type of object that happens to be running.
   a. representation
   b. depiction
   c. instance
   d. object
10. The ________________ structure is used for defining the characteristics of a window class.
    a. WINDOWCLASS
    b. WNDCLASS
    c. WCLASS
    d. WDCLASS

11. The ______________ parameter of the CreateWindow() function determines whether the new window is based on a custom window class definition or a predefined window class.
    a. lpClassName
    b. lpWindowName
    c. hWndParent
    d. hInstance
12. What should you assign to the hWndParent parameter of the CreateWindow() function for a top-level window?
    a. ""
    b. HINSTANCE
    c. hInstance
    d. NULL
13. To position a window in the default position, you set the x parameter of the CreateWindow() function to ______________.
    a. USEDEFAULT
    b. DEFAULT
    c. CW_USEDEFAULT
    d. CW_DEFAULT
14. What must you do in order to display a new window after creating it with the CreateWindow() function?
    a. add a message loop
    b. write the window procedure
    c. call the ShowWindow() function
    d. Nothing. The window appears automatically.
15. The ______________ message is generated for events involving menus and buttons, such as when a button is clicked by a user.
    a. WM_COMMAND
    b. WM_EXECUTE
    c. WM_SELECT
    d. WM_CLICK

16. Which function retrieves messages from the message queue?
    a. GetMessage()
    b. RetrieveMessage()
    c. NextMessage()
    d. Message()
17. The ______________ function converts keyboard messages into a format Windows can understand.
    a. ConvertMessage()
    b. TranslateMessage()
    c. EncodeMessage()
    d. DecipherMessage()
18. What does the DispatchMessage() function do?
    a. cancels any message that cannot be converted into a format Windows can understand
    b. returns a notification message to the Windows operating system
    c. executes the appropriate handler
    d. sends messages to the window procedure for processing
19. A window procedure is also referred to as ______________.
    a. the program entry point
    b. a callback function
    c. the WinMain() procedure
    d. a message structure
20. The case label for the WM_DESTROY message should call the ______________ function, which generates the WM_QUIT message that tells the message loop to end the program.
    a. MessageLoop()
    b. MessageQueue()
    c. Destroy()
    d. PostQuitMessage()
21. Which function must be included in the default label of a window procedure's `switch` statement in order to return messages that are not handled by your window procedure to the Windows operating system for processing?
    a. DefWindowProc()
    b. WindowProc()
    c. WindowHandler()
    d. RetWindows()

22. The ______________ function is a Windows API function that changes either the value displayed in a control or the title text for windows that are not controls.
    a. WindowText()
    b. SetWindowText()
    c. WindowValue()
    d. SetValue()

PROGRAMMING EXERCISES

1. Explain the differences between 16-bit, 32-bit, and 64-bit Windows operating systems. Also, identify which Windows operating systems are designed to work with each width of data bus.
2. Explain why the Windows API defines its own data types.
3. Explain the difference between handles and pointers.
4. Explain the relationship between parent and child windows.
5. Write the syntax for the WinMain() function and explain the use of each of its parameters. Do not include any statements in the body of the function definition.
6. Create a WinMain() function and declare a window class variable named wc, based on the WNDCLASS structure. Then, use Figure 9-34 to assign values to the fields in the wc variable:

Field	Value
Style	CS_HREDRAW I CS_VREDRAW
lpfnWndProc	MainWndProc
cbClsExtra	0
cbWndExtra	0
hInstance	hInstance
hIcon	LoadIcon(NULL, IDI_APPLICATION)
hCursor	LoadCursor(NULL, IDC_ARROW)
hbrBackground	(HBRUSH)(COLOR_WINDOW+1)
lpszMenuName	" "
lpszClassName	"ExampleClass"

Figure 9-34 Values to assign to the fields in the wc structure

7. Add a statement to the WinMain() function you created in Exercise 6 that informs the operating system about the newly defined window class.
8. Write the CreateWindow() function to create a main window using the parameters shown in Figure 9-35. Assign the handle returned from the CreateWindow() function to a variable named hCurWnd.

Parameter	Value
lpClassName	CustomClass
lpWindowName	"Custom Class"
dwStyle	WS_OVERLAPPEDWINDOW
X	CW_USEDEFAULT
Y	CW_USEDEFAULT
nWidth	100
nHeight	100
hWndParent	NULL
hMenu	NULL
hInstance	hCurInstance
lpParam	NULL

Figure 9-35 CreateWindow() function values for a main window

9. Write the CreateWindow() function to create an edit box window using the parameters shown in Figure 9-36. Assign the handle returned from the CreateWindow() function to a variable named hEditWnd.

Parameter	Value
lpClassName	EDIT
lpWindowName	NULL
dwStyle	WS_VISIBLE | WS_CHILD | WS_BORDER | ES_LEFT
X	20
Y	20
nWidth	150
nHeight	20
hWndParent	hCurWnd
hMenu	NULL
hInstance	hCurInstance
lpParam	NULL

Figure 9-36 CreateWindow() function values for an edit box window

10. Write the CreateWindow() function to create a button class window using the parameters shown in Figure 9-37. Assign the handle returned from the CreateWindow() function to a variable named hButtonWnd.

Parameter	Value
lpClassName	BUTTON
lpWindowName	"OK"
dwStyle	WS_VISIBLE | WS_CHILD | BS_DEFPUSHBUTTON
X	10
Y	10
nWidth	35
nHeight	35
hWndParent	hCurWnd
hMenu	NULL
hInstance	hCurInstance
lpParam	NULL

Figure 9-37 CreateWindow() function values for a button class window

11. Write the statement that displays a window onscreen that was created with the CreateWindow() function. Use a window handle named hCurWnd.
12. Write a typical message loop that you would add to a WinMain() function. Be sure to declare a MSG variable and a return statement.
13. Write a typical window procedure that you would add to a Windows API program. Include a `switch` statement with labels for the WM_COMMAND and WM_DESTROY messages. Also include a default label. You do not need to add any custom code to the WM_COMMAND label, but be sure to add the necessary statements to the WM_DESTROY and default labels.
14. Add a `switch` statement to the window procedure you wrote in Exercise 13 that checks for BN_CLICKED events. Do not worry about adding custom code for any BN_CLICKED events; just correctly write the `switch` statement and add it to the correct location in the window procedure.

Programming Projects

1. The STATIC predefined control class creates a window that displays a simple static text label, which is used for providing information or describing parts of a parent window. You pass the text you want displayed in a static window to the lpWindowName parameter of the CreateWindow() function. Create a simple Win32 Application project with a parent window that contains a single static window that prints the text *Hello World!*
2. Create a Win32 Application project that contains three separate static windows within the main parent window. The first static window should display the city where you live, the second static window should display the state or province where you live, and the third static window should display the country where you live.

3. Create five different Win32 Application projects. Within each project, use five different visual styles from Figure 9-15, such as WS_BORDER, when creating the application's parent window. Each project's main window should include at least one style attribute that is not included in the other projects. Use a static window to describe styles used in the parent window. For example, if an application includes a minimize button, then a static window should contain the text *This window includes a minimize button*. Save the projects as Style1, Style2, Style3, Style4, and Style5 in the Chapter.09 folder in your Visual C++ Projects folder.
4. Create a Win32 Application that allows users to play a simple guessing game. In the game, users try to guess a number between 0 and 100. Assign the correct number and the user's guess to variables. Set up an edit box for users to input the number they are guessing. Also create a button named Guess. Use a static window to provide instructions to users and to inform them if they guessed the number correctly.
5. Create a Win32 Application that calculates an employee's weekly gross salary, withholding tax (which is 15% of gross pay), and net pay, based on the number of hours worked and hourly wage. Compute any hours over 40 as time and a half. Use the appropriate decision structures to create the program. Display the weekly gross pay, withholding tax, and net pay in static windows.
6. Create a math quiz for a sixth grade class as a Win32 Application. Include five questions in the program's parent window, and store the answers to the quiz in global variables. Within the parent window, add a button named Score Quiz. When students click the Score Quiz button, determine if they have answered all the questions. If they have answered all the questions, score the quiz using the answers in the global variables and display the score in a static window. If they have not answered all the questions, display a message in the static window that instructs them to answer all of the questions before selecting the Score Quiz button.
7. Create a Win32 Application project with sections for each of your last three jobs. Include edit boxes listing the employer's name, your salary, and the number of years you worked there. Next, add four buttons: Highest Salary, Lowest Salary, Longest Employment, and Shortest Employment. Write handler code for each button that determines the appropriate value. After you click a button, display the result in a static window, along with the name of the associated employer.
8. Create a Win32 Application that determines the cost of carpeting a room, based on the room's dimensions and the cost per square foot of carpet. Include edit boxes in the program that allow users to enter the room's length and width in feet, along with an edit box in which they can enter the price per square foot of carpet. Also include a Calculate button that calculates the correct dimensions and total cost. Display the total cost in a static window using explanatory text and the variables. For example, "The total cost to carpet a room is $460."
9. Create a Win32 Application version of the Retirement Planner program you created in Chapter 5. Save the project as RetirementPlanner in the Chapter.09 folder in your Visual C++ Projects folder.

10. Use functions found in the math.h header file to create a more advanced version of the calculator program. Refer to the MSDN Library on the methods available in math.h that you can use in your calculator including the exp() (exponential value) function and the sqrt() (square root) function.

CHAPTER

10

MICROSOFT FOUNDATION CLASSES

In this chapter you will learn:

- About Microsoft Foundation Class programming
- How to write basic MFC programs
- How to work with resources
- About the CString class
- How to create dialog-based applications
- How to work with message maps
- How to build an application framework with the MFC Application Wizard

An apprentice carpenter may want only a hammer and saw, but a master craftsman employs many precision tools. Computer programming likewise requires sophisticated tools to cope with the complexity of real applications, and only practice with these tools will build skill in their use.

Robert L. Kruse, Data Structures and Program Design

PREVIEW: THE MFC CALCULATOR PROGRAM

In this chapter you will create a calculator program—the same calculator program you worked with in Chapter 9—as a Microsoft Foundation Class program. Creating the calculator program as both a Windows API program and a Microsoft Foundations Class program will help you understand how a Microsoft Foundation Class program compares to a standard Windows API program.

To preview the MFC Calculator program:

1. Create a **Chapter.10** folder in your Visual C++ Projects folder.
2. Copy the **Chapter10_Calculator** folder from the Chapter.10 folder on your Data Disk to the Chapter.10 folder in your Visual C++ Projects folder. Then open the **MFCCalculator** project in Visual C++.

3. Individually open the **CalcApp.h** and **Calculator.h** files in the Code Editor window. The CalcApp.h file represents an application class named CCalcApp, and the Calculator.h file represents a dialog window class named CCalculator. The extra *C* in front of the class names identifies the classes as Microsoft Foundation Classes. These files contain some fairly typical code that is found in most header files. In the class header declaration statements, you can see the Microsoft Foundation Classes from which both of these classes are derived; the CCalcApp class is derived from the CwinApp class, and the CCalculator class is derived from the CDialog class.
4. Next, open the **MFCCalculator.rc** file, which represents the visual portion of a dialog box window. This file opens the Resource View tab in the Solution Explorer window, which is used for managing the graphic components of a Microsoft Foundation Class program. In the Resource View tab, expand the Dialog folder and double-click the IDD_CALCULATOR icon. The Visual C++ Dialog Editor opens, which is used for graphically creating windows and other elements. You can see that the dialog box resembles the calculator you created in the last chapter. The CCalculator dialog window class manipulates the dialog box window.
5. Use Solution Explorer to open the CCalculator dialog window class's implementation file, **Calculator.cpp**, in the Code Editor window. You can see that the dialog window class contains a number of member function definitions and other standard elements found in classes. You will also see that the file includes two statements: `Begin_MESSAGE_MAP()` and `END_MESSAGE_MAP()`. These statements are called macros and declare a "message map" that will be added to the implementation file in order to process Windows messages. The statements between the two macros are used for processing Windows messages.
6. Next, open the **CalcApp.cpp** file. This class implementation file represents the application as a whole and is required by all Microsoft Foundation Class programs. An application class includes an InitInstance() function that is used for displaying the windows used in the program. An application class must also include a global statement that instantiates an object based on the application class itself. Figure 10-1 shows an example of the application class implementation file. You can see in the InitInstance() function that an object of the CCalculator dialog window class is instantiated. The DoModal() function is what actually displays the dialog box window.
7. Build and execute the **MFCCalculator** project, and then test the calculations. Figure 10-2 shows an example of the dialog box window that appears when you run the MFC Calculator program. The program should function the same as the calculator you created in the last chapter.
8. Click the **Close** button to close the Calculator program window, and then close the MFCCalculator project by selecting **Close Solution** from the File menu.

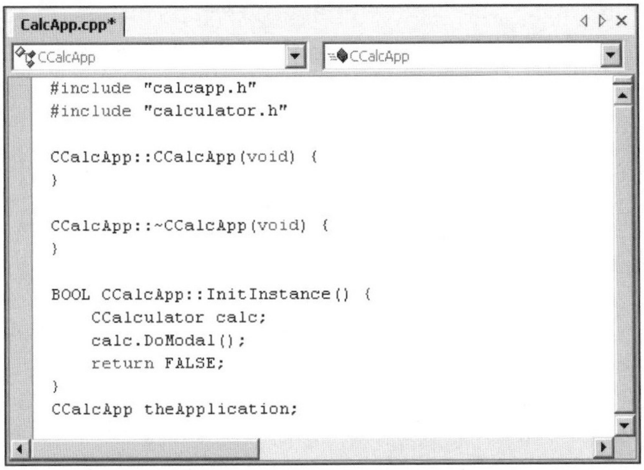

CalcApp.cpp*
CCalcApp
CCalcApp
#include "calcapp.h"
#include "calculator.h"
CCalcApp::CCalcApp(void) {
}
CCalcApp::~CCalcApp(void) {
}
BOOL CCalcApp::InitInstance() {
CCalculator calc;
calc.DoModal();
return FALSE;
}
CCalcApp theApplication;

Figure 10-1 Application class implementation file

MFC Calculator
0
+
-
*
/
6
7
8
9
2
3
4
5
0
1
.
=
Clear

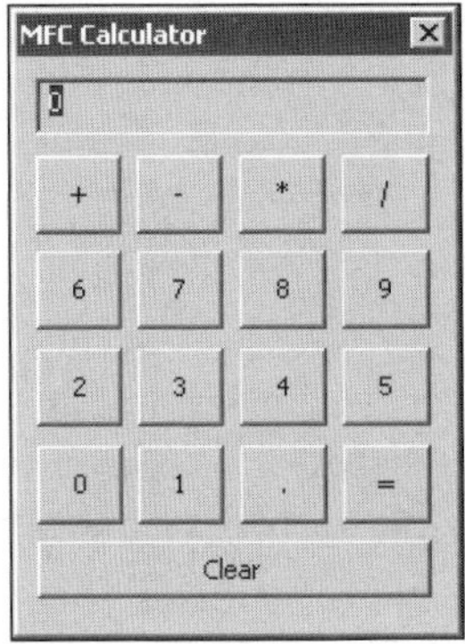

Figure 10-2 MFC calculator program window

MICROSOFT FOUNDATION CLASSES

Virtually all of the code and programming examples you have seen so far in this book have used standard C++ syntax that can be used with Visual C++ and with almost any other C++ compiler. This chapter begins by discussing Microsoft Foundation Class programming techniques. The **Microsoft Foundation Classes**, or MFC, is a class library that assists programmers in creating Windows-based applications. Perhaps two of the most important aspects of MFC programming are:

- MFC adds object-oriented programming capabilities to Windows API programming
- MFC encapsulates the Windows API into a logically organized class hierarchy

MFC programming is not exclusive to Microsoft Visual C++. Other C++ programming environments that support Microsoft Foundation Classes include Borland C++ Builder and Watcom C/C++.

One of Microsoft's main goals in designing MFC was to create a C++ object-oriented class library for building Windows API applications. Prior to MFC, programmers had to design their programs so that they conformed to the C language requirements of the Windows API. This means that they could not use the object-oriented capabilities of C++, which are not found in C. Recall from the last chapter that the Windows API consists of thousands of C functions and other types of code elements. To successfully program with the Windows API, you must know which of these functions to choose from, and you must also understand the fairly complex requirements for structuring a Windows program using a WinMain() function and a window procedure that processes messages. MFC assists C++ programmers in writing Windows programs by encapsulating into logically organized classes the C functions and other code that make up the Windows API. MFC classes also provide much of the functionality required by a Windows API program. The WinMain() function, for instance, is already written within an MFC class. By including or inheriting MFC classes in your program, you inherit the prewritten WinMain() function. When a Windows API program is written with MFC, Visual C++ automatically calls the inherited WinMain() function for you when your program executes. Your main responsibility when writing an MFC program is to derive your own classes from the MFC classes. Once you derive your classes from an MFC class, you then add code to give the program its functionality.

Visual C++ is designed to make writing MFC programs a relatively easy process. When you use Visual C++ to write an MFC program, you first use the MFC Application Wizard to walk you through the steps involved in creating an MFC application. After running MFC Application Wizard, Visual C++ provides something called the **Microsoft Foundation Class framework**, or MFC framework for short, which is basically a skeleton application created from MFC classes that you can use as a basis for your program. The MFC Application Wizard performs almost all of the rudimentary work associated with an MFC program for you, by setting up your classes so that they derive from the appropriate MFC classes, including the correct header files in the various C++ files, and performing various other tasks.

Your job as a programmer is to find the hooks in the MFC framework that you can use to give your program its functionality. A **hook** is a location in a program where a programmer can insert code that adds functionality. Visual C++ provides plenty of comments to help you find the hooks. For example, Figure 10-3 shows the window that is generated for a simple MFC framework created with the MFC Application Wizard.

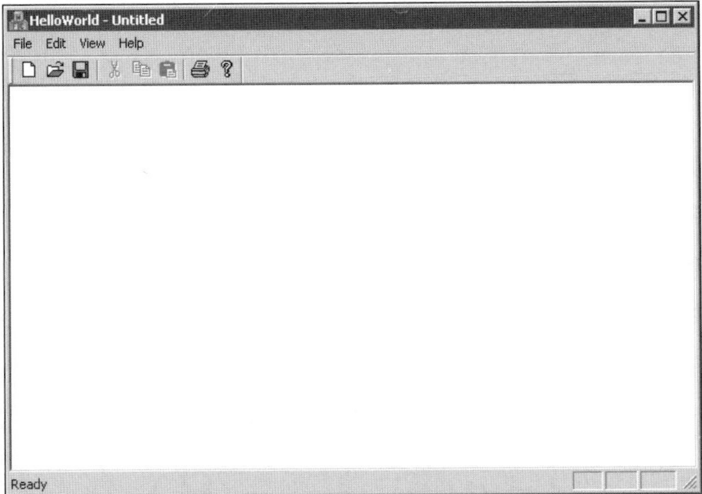

Figure 10-3 Window generated by a simple MFC framework

10

In order to understand just what a hook is, examine the following MFC OnDraw() function, which is used for adding graphical elements to a window. For now, do not worry about understanding exactly how the OnDraw() function works. Simply understand that the MFC framework includes places for you to add your own code that gives your program its functionality. To display the text *Hello World* in the window shown in Figure 10-3, you need to locate the OnDraw() function shown below:

```
void CHelloWorldView::OnDraw(CDC* /*pDC*/)
{
  CHelloWorldDoc* pDoc = GetDocument();
  ASSERT_VALID(pDoc);

  // TODO: add draw code for native data here
}
```

The hook in the preceding code is the // TODO: comment located above the function's closing brace. To output *Hello World* in the window, you remove the comments around the pDC pointer parameter in the function header and replace the // TODO: comment with a call to the TextOut() function, as shown in the following example. The TextOut() function graphically adds text to a window.

```
void CHelloWorldView::OnDraw(CDC* pDC)
{
  CHelloWorldDoc* pDoc = GetDocument();
  ASSERT_VALID(pDoc);
  pDC->TextOut(100, 100, "Hello World");
}
```

You will study both the OnDraw() and TextOut() functions later in this book.

Now, when you execute the program, the window will include *Hello World*, as shown in Figure 10-4.

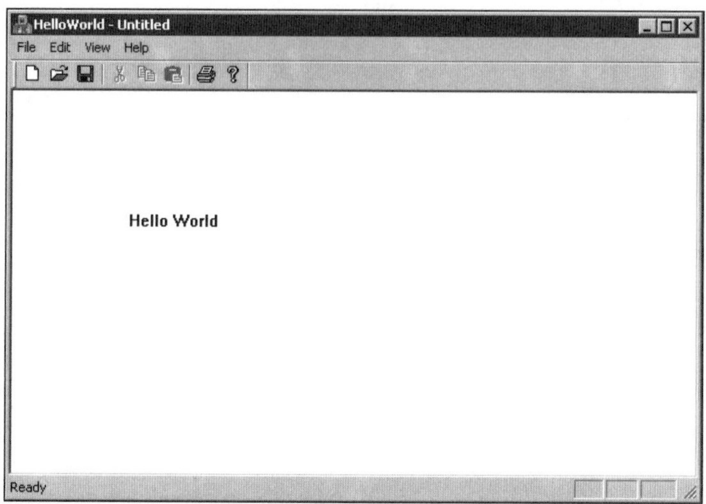

Figure 10-4 Window generated by a simple MFC framework after adding the TextOut() function

Finding the hooks in a MFC framework might seem like an easy task based on this example, but it is, unfortunately, not so simple. Although MFC programs are written using C++ and object-oriented programming techniques, they still ultimately end up as Windows API programs. You still need to use some special techniques for setting up your classes and source files and for working with MFC programs in general. If you do not know these techniques, you will be hopelessly lost when you try to find the hooks you need.

Even the simplest MFC program created with the MFC Application Wizard consists of at least eight separate files and dozens of lines of code. Many experienced C++ programmers have attempted to jump right into MFC programming by building a program with the MFC Application Wizard. Once they examine the large amounts of unfamiliar and confusing code, it is not uncommon for some programmers to simply abandon the new program, exit Visual C++, and vow never to work with MFC programs again. To avoid such a scenario, you will start by building your MFC Calculator program from scratch instead of by using the MFC Application Wizard. Building your MFC Calculator program from scratch will allow you to examine MFC programming techniques. At the end of this chapter, you will build an MFC program with the MFC Application Wizard and examine the MFC framework. At that point, you should have a fairly clear idea of what each piece of the program does.

As with traditional Windows API programming, MFC programming is a large topic. Even though the thousands of Windows API functions (and other code) are encapsulated in the MFC library, each of those functions still exists and needs to be understood before you can use it in your program. The MFC library is composed of over two hundred classes. The remainder of this text discusses the most basic Windows API programming techniques, which use only a handful of the MFC classes.

If you would like to continue your studies of MFC, the MSDN Library contains vast amounts of information. Numerous texts also exist that are devoted exclusively to the study of MFC programming. Remember as you study MFC programming, or any programming language for that matter, that programming is a large and complex topic. Few people exist who have memorized the entire language structure of large programming languages such as C++ and MFCs—although there are some. The majority of professional programmers have a solid understanding of only the basics of a particular programming language, and rely on excellent reference material when they encounter unfamiliar or rarely used topics. Do not feel that you must memorize or understand every programming topic associated with a particular language. Have a basic understanding, but most important, know where you can find the information you need.

Next, this chapter discusses the MFC class library, which is at the heart of MFC programming. Then, you will learn about MFC notation.

MFC Class Library

The MFC class library consists of two major sections:

- The MFC class hierarchy
- Global functions and macros

MFC Class Hierarchy

The simple class hierarchy examples you saw in Chapter 8 were relatively small. In contrast, the MFC class hierarchy is surprisingly large. The MFC class library contains over two hundred classes, so this book cannot list the entire hierarchy here. Figure 10-5, however, shows a partial listing of the class hierarchy, highlighting some of the more important classes.

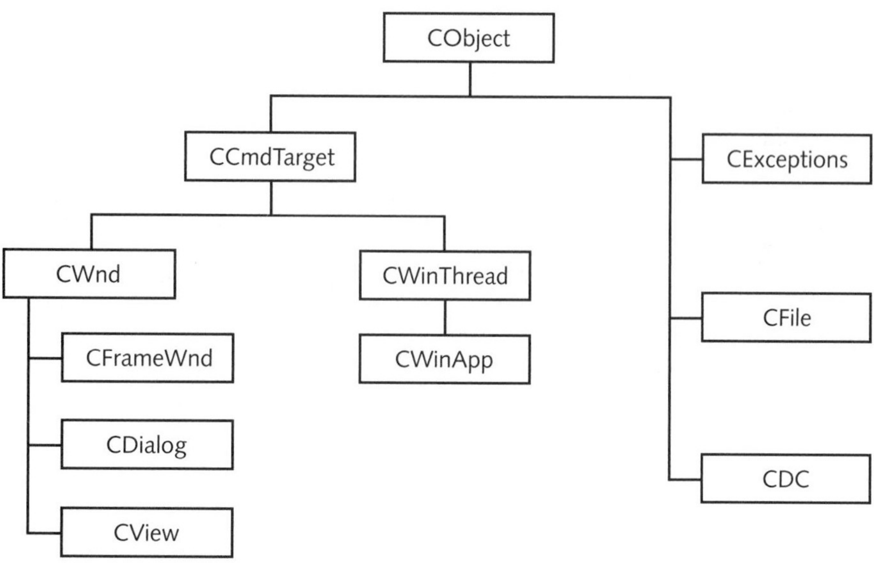

Figure 10-5 Partial listing of the MFC class hierarchy

You can find a complete listing of the MFC class hierarchy in the MSDN Library index by selecting the *hierarchy chart* subtopic in the MFC (Microsoft Application Classes) topic.

Most classes in the MFC class hierarchy derive from the **CObject base class**. You will indirectly work with members of the CObject class because its functionality is inherited by its derived classes. The CObject class includes members for writing data to disk files in a process known as serialization. You will use the CObject class later in this text to serialize data to disk files. For now you should understand that every MFC class inherits the functionality of the CObject base class.

The most important branch of the MFC class hierarchy is the **CCmdTarget class**, which encapsulates the messaging features of the Windows API. Derived from the CCmdTarget class are several other important classes including the CWinApp class and the CWnd class. One class derived from CCmdTarget that you will work with in this chapter is the CDialog class, which creates dialog boxes. Because CDialog is derived from CCmdTarget, CDialog inherits all of CCmdTarget's messaging features. This means that you can add events that generate messages to a dialog class. Later, you will learn how to add events and messages to a dialog class, and how to handle them in your program.

The **CWinApp class**, also known as the **application class**, is responsible for initializing, starting, running, and stopping an MFC windows application. When you run any type of MFC application, it is up to the application class to manage the execution of that application.

The **CWnd class** encapsulates the various Windows API functions, data types, and other code used for creating and instantiating windows. Derived from the CWnd class are more specialized types of window classes such as the **CFrameWnd class**, which creates a standard type of window known as a frame window, and the **CDialog class** for creating dialog boxes. You will learn about each of these classes throughout this chapter; and additional MFC classes in future chapters.

Global Functions

If a function is not a member of an MFC class, then it is a global function that is available to all MFC classes, regardless of their position in the MFC class hierarchy. All MFC global functions begin with a prefix of `Afx`. Although most of the MFC functions and variables you work with will be a member of a class, some will not. For example, one commonly used global function is the AfxMessageBox() function that displays a simple message box to the user. The basic syntax for the AfxMessageBox() function involves passing a single string argument containing the text you want to be displayed in the message box. For example, the statement `AfxMessageBox("Hello World");` displays a message box containing the text *Hello World*. Figure 10-6 shows an example of a message box created with the AfxMessageBox() function.

Figure 10-6 Message box

Normally, to display a simple message box, you would use the MessageBox() member function of the CWnd class, which is almost identical to the AfxMessageBox() function. (Recall that the CWnd class encapsulates the window functionality of the Windows API.) However, you cannot use a class's member function before an object of the class is instantiated. In some cases, you may need to use a message box before a CWnd class object is instantiated in your program. Because you cannot use a class's member function before an object of the class is instantiated, you must use a global function.

You can pass several other parameters to both the AfxMessageBox() function and the MessageBox() member function. These additional parameters determine the style of the message box and other attributes. For your studies, however, you will display only a simple text string to demonstrate functionality. If you would like more information on message box parameters, search for AfxMessageBox() and MessageBox() in the MSDN Library.

Macros

A programming element that is commonly used in MFC programming is a macro. A **macro** represents C++ code, constants, and other programming elements and is defined using the #define preprocessor directive. You will not actually create any macros in this chapter because the macros you need already exist in the MFC library. Even though you won't be creating macros, it helps to understand what they are when you use them.

The first thing you need to understand is that a macro in C++ is different from a macro you may see in other environments. End user applications such as Word and Excel allow you to record a set of steps you would like to execute later. For example, in Word, you can record the necessary steps to search for a specific text string, copy the text string, move it to a different location in the document, paste it into the new location, and then apply bold and underline formatting to the text. Word and Excel refer to these types of recorded steps as macros. However, a macro in C++ is a name that represents C++ code and other programming elements that you would like to execute simply by calling the macro name, similar to the way you call a function name. There are actually many similarities between macros and functions. Understanding when to use a macro and when to use a function, however, requires a more advanced understanding of C++ programming.

Essentially, during preprocessing, a macro name is replaced by the code and other programming elements that it represents. This process is similar to using the `inline` keyword to request that the compiler replace calls to a function with the function definition wherever in a program the function is called. One of the main differences between inline functions and macros is that in addition to functions, macros can represent other programming elements such as constants.

Macro names in the MFC library are in all uppercase letters. Two of the more common macros you will use are BEGIN_MESSAGE_MAP() and END_MESSAGE_MAP(), which are used for handling messages. Macros can accept parameters, just like functions, so they are followed by parentheses. Unlike functions, however, when you place a macro on a line in a C++ source file you do not use a semicolon. The following code shows an example of the BEGIN_MESSAGE_MAP() and END_MESSAGE_MAP() macros, along with the ON_COMMAND() macro.

```
BEGIN_MESSAGE_MAP(CHelloWorldApp, CWinApp)
  ON_COMMAND(ID_APP_ABOUT, OnAppAbout)
  // Standard file based document commands
  ON_COMMAND(ID_FILE_NEW, CWinApp::OnFileNew)
  ON_COMMAND(ID_FILE_OPEN, CWinApp::OnFileOpen)
  // Standard print setup command
  ON_COMMAND(ID_FILE_PRINT_SETUP,
   CWinApp::OnFilePrintSetup)
END_MESSAGE_MAP()
```

The preceding code is from a MFC framework that was created with the MFC Application Wizard. You will examine the parts of the code shortly in the Message Maps section.

MFC Notation

All MFC class names begin with *C*. Additionally, data members of MFC classes are prefixed with *m_*. Following the underscore character in an MFC data member name is a Hungarian notation character representing the data member's type. For example, m_hWnd and m_pMainWnd are both examples of MFC data members. The m_hWnd data member is a Windows API handle data type, and the m_pMainWnd data member is a Windows API pointer data type.

As you derive classes from the MFC classes, you should also begin your class names with a C and your data members with m_ in order to identify your program as an MFC program. In fact, the Add Class Wizard encourages you to use MFC notation when you add new classes to your project. For instance, in the past several chapters, you have used the Generic C++ Class Wizard to add classes to your projects. When you select Add Class from the Project menu, you can also select MFC Class from the Add Class dialog box to run the MFC Class Wizard, which walks you through the steps to create an MFC class. When you add a class using either the Generic C++ Class Wizard or the MFC Class Wizard, Visual C++ automatically assumes that your new class name will begin with a *C*. However, you do not normally use the *C* prefix for the filename. Therefore, Visual C++ strips the C prefix off the suggested class file name. Figure 10-7 shows an example of the MFC Class Wizard when you add an MFC class named CCalculator. Notice in the File Name box that the suggested name for the class file is *Calculator.cpp*, not *CCalculator.cpp*. If you want to include the *C* prefix in your class file name, then you can do so by clicking the ellipsis button (...) and adding *C* to the suggested file name. For the classes you create in this book, however, you will accept the file names suggested by Visual C++.

10

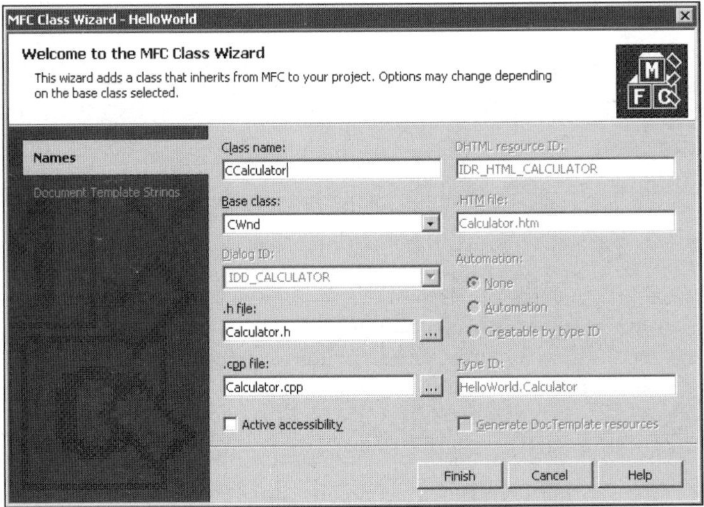

Figure 10-7 MFC Class Wizard

BASIC MFC PROGRAMS

You can easily create the MFC framework for an MFC program using the MFC Application Wizard. However, unless you understand the basic structure of an MFC program, the MFC framework created by the MFC Application Wizard will be of little use to you. Therefore, you need to examine the basic structure of an MFC program.

The classes that turn a standard C++ program into an MFC program derive from MFC classes. As you start deriving classes from the MFC classes, remember that the MFC classes are part of a class hierarchy, and, therefore, inherit various data members and member functions. Although you will override a few of the inherited functions, you will most often use a function's base class version along with inherited data members. And, keep in mind that you can always create standard classes to give your program its functionality.

By default, Win32 application projects do not support MFC programming. In order to enable MFC support in a Win32 application project, you must select the Use MFC in a Shared DLL setting in the Use of MFC combo box in the General category of the Property Pages dialog box. Next, you will start creating the MFC Calculator program based on a Win32 application project and modify the project so that it supports MFC.

To start creating the MFC Calculator program:

1. Return to Visual C++.
2. Create a new Win32 application project named **MFCCalculator**. Save the project in the **Chapter.10** folder in your Visual C++ Projects folders. In the Application Settings tab of the Win32 Application Wizard dialog box, leave Application type set to the default **Windows application** setting, but select the Empty project check box.
3. By default, Win32 Application projects do not support MFC programming. To change this, open the Property Pages dialog box by clicking the project icon in Solution Explorer, and then selecting **Properties** from the Project menu. Click the **General** category in the Project Property Pages dialog box, which is shown in Figure 10-8.
4. Select **Use MFC in a Shared DLL** in the Use of MFC combo box.
5. Click the **OK** button to close the Property Pages dialog box.

At their most basic level, all MFC programs require an application class and a window class. MFC programs also require message maps to handle Windows messages, but you will learn about that later. As you know, MFC is built on the Windows API, which runs on the Windows platform. Conceptually, you can think of the application class as being the MFC class that sits on top of the Windows API, while the window class sits on top of the application class. The structure of an MFC program and its application class and window class as they relate to the Windows API are illustrated in Figure 10-9.

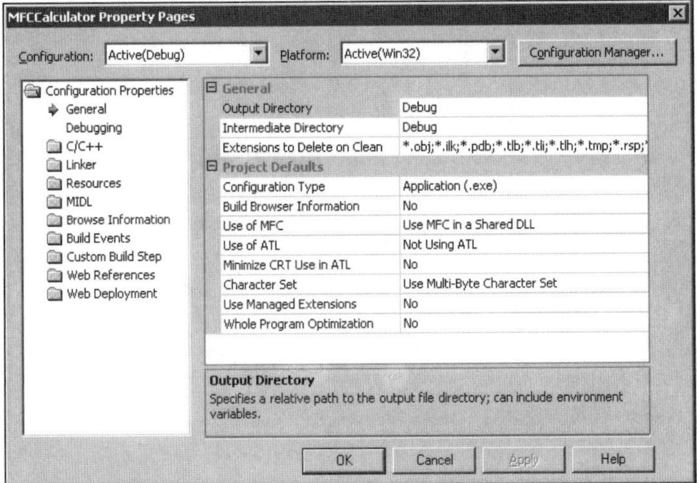

Figure 10-8 General category in the Project Property Pages dialog box

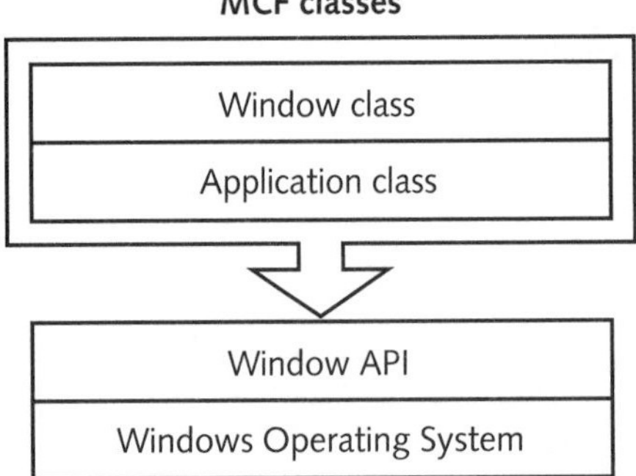

Figure 10-9 MFC application structure

First, you will examine the application class.

The Application Class

An application class is the starting point of any MFC application. You derive an application class from the CWinApp class. The application class object you instantiate in an MFC program represents the application as a whole. Through the application class object you can initialize, start, run, and stop the MFC application. The application class does not actually create anything visible that you can see. Rather, it is used for instantiating window class objects and displaying the windows they represent, in addition to other tasks such as initializing application variables.

When you derive an application object, you must:

- Override the virtual InitInstance() function
- Instantiate a global object of your application class

The InitInstance() function is called by the inherited WinMain() function each time a new instance of your MFC program starts. Remember that MFC provides the WinMain() function for you, and you do not need to write or override it. However, you must override the InitInstance() function in order to display your program's windows. The following code shows an InitInstance() function declaration. Notice that the InitInstance() function declaration is of the BOOL data type and that it includes the `virtual` keyword to instruct the compiler at run time which version of the overridden InitInstance() function to use. It returns a value of `TRUE` if the function is successful and a value of `FALSE` if it is unsuccessful.

```
virtual BOOL InitInstance();
```

What actually executes the WinMain() function, which calls the InitInstance() function in turn, is the instantiation of a global application class object. You can instantiate only one global application class object, and it is usually instantiated within the application class's implementation file. Figure 10-10 shows an example of a basic application class named CBasicApp.

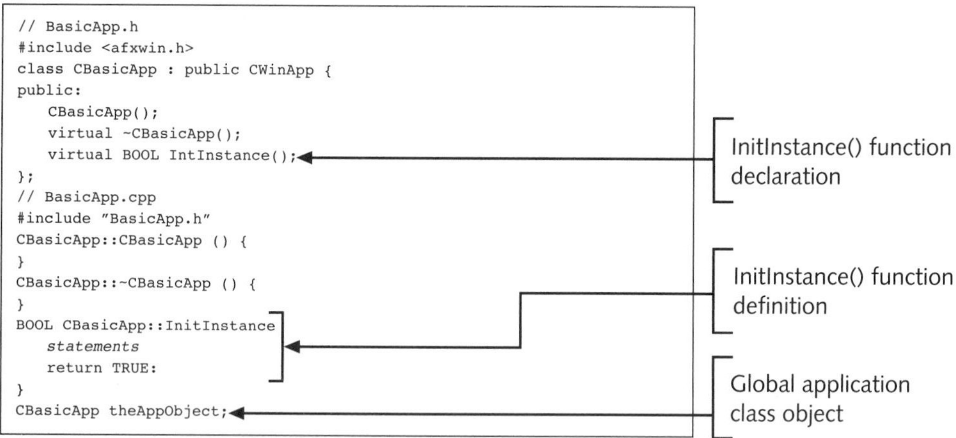

Figure 10-10 Basic application class

Next, you will create the application class for the MFC Calculator program. Because you cannot display any windows until you learn about the window class, you will place a global AfxMessageBox() function in the InitInstance() function in order to demonstrate when the application class executes.

Most of the MFC classes are defined in the afxwin.h file, so you must include that file in the header files of any classes you want to derive from MFC. If you use a Class Wizard to create a class that derives from an MFC class, the afxwin.h file is included automatically in the class's header file.

To create the application class for the MFC Calculator program:

1. Start the Generic C++ Class Wizard.

You may be wondering why you are running the Generic C++ Class Wizard instead of the MFC Class Wizard. The reason is that you can only run the MFC Class Wizard in a project that was created with the MFC Application Wizard. However, you can use the Generic C++ Class Wizard to add MFC classes to your project.

2. In the Generic C++ Class Wizard dialog box, type **CCalcApp** as the name of the class and derive the class from **CWinApp** using **public** access. Also, click the **Virtual destructor** check box.
3. Click the **Finish** button. Visual C++ creates two files, one called CalcApp.h and one called CalcApp.cpp. The CalcApp.h file opens in the Code Editor window.
4. Notice in the CalcApp.h file that the afxwin.h header file is already included. Add the InitInstance() function declaration, shown below, to the CalcApp.h header file:

```
#pragma once
#include "afxwin.h"
class CCalcApp  : public CWinApp {
public:
   CCalcApp(void);
   virtual ~CCalcApp(void);
   virtual BOOL InitInstance();
};
```

5. Next, open the **CalcApp.cpp** file in the Code Editor window and add the InitInstance() function after the destructor function, as shown in Figure 10-11. The InitInstance() function includes an AfxMessageBox() statement that displays a message box with the text *Application Started*.
6. Also as shown in Figure 10-11, add the statement `CCalcApp theApplication;` after the InitInstance() function's closing brace to instantiate the application object.
7. Build and execute the project. You should see a message box displaying the text *Application Started*.
8. Click the **OK** button to close the message box, which also stops the application.

10

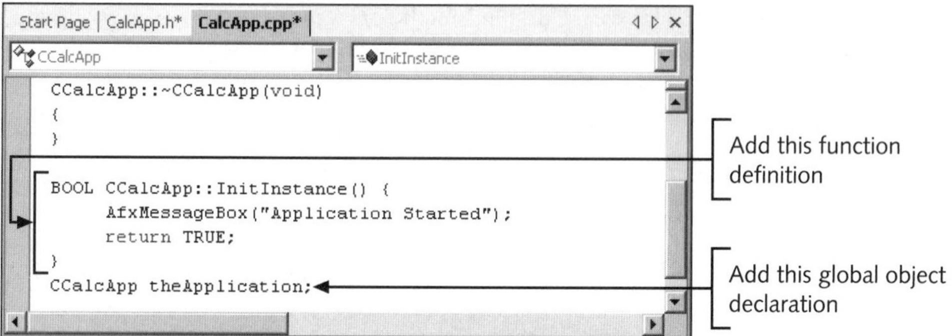

Figure 10-11 InitInstance() function definition and global application class object declaration added to CalcApp.cpp

The Window Class

The MFC classes that derive from the CWnd class are used for creating the different types of windows that are visible to the user. The class you will use in this section is the **CFrameWnd class**, which creates a simple window with a frame, title bar, control menu, and control buttons. These windows are called frame windows because they usually "frame" an application, acting as a primary window that includes other windows such as view windows, toolbars, and status bars. Almost all MFC programs include a window class derived from the CFrameWnd class, with the exception of dialog-based applications (which you will study next).

With a basic MFC program like the one you are creating, there is little you need to do with the window class other than create its class interface and implementation files and derive the class from the CFrameWnd class. With more complex window classes, you need to write the code that manages the layout of various child windows of the frame class and that processes messages for its child windows. One task that is required for all window classes is calling the inherited Create() function from the class constructor. The **Create() function** creates the window itself when an object of the window class is instantiated. The basic syntax for the Create() function is `Create(NULL, `*`title`*`);`. The first parameter of NULL, or 0, creates the window using default parameters, and the second parameter is a string that is used in the window's title bar. The Create() function also accepts additional parameters that determine the size, formatting, and position of the window. In fact, the Create() function is equivalent to the CreateWindow() function you studied in the last chapter and accepts many of the same parameters. For your basic MFC program, however, you only need to use the first two parameters of the Create() function. Figure 10-12 shows an example of a basic window class named CBasicFrameWnd derived from the CFrameWnd class.

```
// BasicFrameWnd.h
#include <afxwin.h>
class CBasicFrameWnd : public CFrameWnd {
public:
   CBasicFrameWnd();
   virtual ~CBasicFrameWnd();
};
// CBasicFrameWnd.cpp
#include "BasicFrameWnd.h"
CBasicFrameWnd::CBasicFrameWnd () {
   Create(NULL, "Basic MFC Program");   <-- Create() function
}
CBasicFrameWnd::~CBasicFrameWnd () {
}
```

Figure 10-12 Basic window class

As you recall from the last chapter, creating a window does not actually display it. In standard Windows API programming, you use the ShowWindow() function to display a window. MFC programming also uses a ShowWindow() function to display windows. It is important that you understand that in an MFC Program, the ShowWindow() function is *not* called from the window class. Instead, you call the ShowWindow() function from the application class's InitInstance() function using an instantiated object of the window class. For example, examine the following modified version of the CBasicApp class implementation file:


```
#include "BasicApp.h"
#include "BasicFrameWnd.h"
...
BOOL CBasicApp::InitInstance() {
  m_pMainWnd = new CBasicFrameWnd;
  m_pMainWnd->ShowWindow(m_nCmdShow);
  m_pMainWnd->UpdateWindow();
  return TRUE;
}
CBasicApp theAppObject; // global object
```

The preceding code includes the BasicFrameWnd.h header file in order to access the members in the window class. The first statement in the InitInstance() function instantiates a new CBasicFrameWnd object on the heap and assigns to it the pointer to the inherited m_pMainWnd data member (which is a pointer data type—note the *p* in the variable name). Notice that the InitInstance() function does not include a statement that deletes the m_pMainWnd object from the heap. You do not need to delete the m_pMainWnd pointer yourself because the inherited WinMain() function automatically deletes it.

The second statement in the InitInstance() function calls the ShowWindow() function, which displays the frame window that was created in the CBasicFrameWnd class. The MFC ShowWindow() function is virtually identical to the Windows API ShowWindow() function you studied in the last chapter, except that you do not pass to it a window handle. Instead, you pass only the inherited m_nCmdShow data member that is inherited from the CWinApp class. The m_nCmdShow data member is equivalent to the Windows API nCmdShow parameter, which represents the window's startup mode. The first time you call the ShowWindow() function in your MFC program you *must* pass to it the m_nCmdShow data member.

After a program's first call to ShowWindow(), you can use the function to manage a window's show state by passing a display constant. For example, if you want to programmatically maximize the window, you can pass to the ShowWindow() function the SW_MAXIMIZE constant using the statement `m_pMainWnd->ShowWindow(SW_MAXIMIZE);`. Look up the ShowWindow topic in the MSDN Library for a listing of other display constants.

The third statement in the InitInstance() function calls the UpdateWindow() function, which is used for updating the display in the window. The UpdateWindow() function is required by almost every MFC program, although it is not necessary for the basic MFC application you are creating. If you were to compile an MFC project that contained the CBasicApp class and the CBasicFrame class, and then execute the program, you would see the window shown in Figure 10-13.

Figure 10-13 Basic MFC program window

An important concept to understand is that m_pMainWnd object is not the window itself. All objects that display windows are not the windows themselves. The window is only a visual representation of the object. Closing a window does not delete the object. In fact, all of the object's data members will still be available in case you need to redisplay the window. The object is only destroyed when it is deleted by the inherited WinMain() function when the InitInstance() function goes out of scope.

Next, you will use the MFC Class Wizard to add a window class to the MFC Calculator program.

To add a window class to the MFC Calculator program:

1. Start the Generic C++ Class Wizard.
2. In the Generic C++ Class Wizard dialog box, type **CCalcFrame** as the name of the class and derive the class from **CFrameWnd** using **public** access. Also, click the **Virtual destructor** check box. Click the **Finish** button. Visual C++ creates two files called CalcFrame.h and CalcFrame.cpp.
3. Open the **CalcFrame.cpp** file in the Code Editor window and add a Create() function statement to the class constructor function as shown in Figure 10-14.

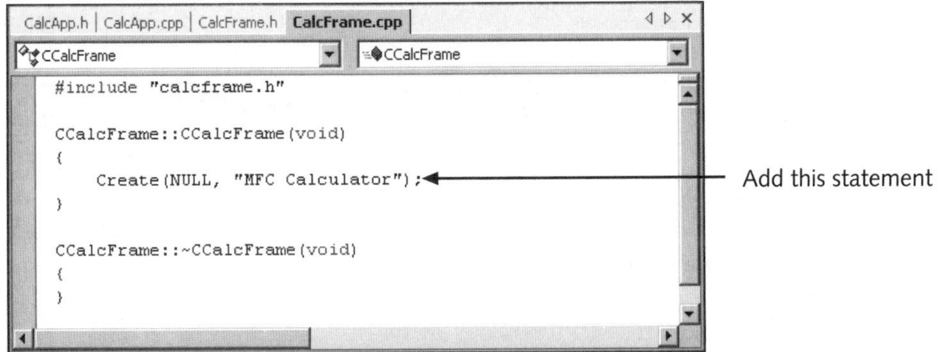

Figure 10-14 Create() function statement added to the CCalcFrame class constructor function

10

4. Open the **CalcApp.cpp** file and add `#include "CalcFrame.h"` after the `#include "CalcApp.h"` statement to give the application class access to the frame class.
5. Replace the AfxMessageBox() statement in the InitInstance() function with the three statements shown in Figure 10-15 that instantiate a new CCalcFrame object and then show and update the window.

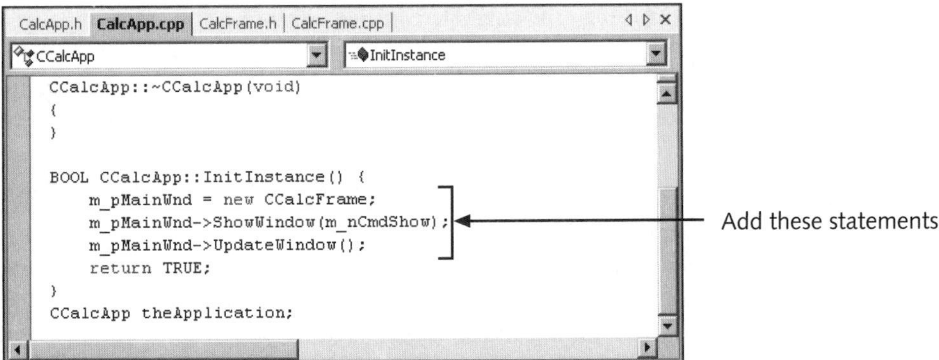

Figure 10-15 Statements added to the InitInstance() function that instantiate a new CCalcFrame object, and then show and update the window

6. Rebuild and execute the program. You should see a basic frame window, similar to Figure 10-13.
7. Close the frame window by clicking the **Close** button in the title bar.

RESOURCES

This chapter introduces new programming elements called resources that are exclusive to Windows API programming. A **resource** is a graphical user interface element or type of stored information that is used by a Windows application. Figure 10-16 lists the standard Windows API resources.

Resource	Description
Accelerator tables	Keyboard shortcut keys
Bitmaps	Icons and other image files
Cursors	Alternate mouse cursors that can be used in place of the standard Windows arrow cursor
Dialog boxes	Dialog boxes, such as Open and Save
HTML pages	Web page documents
Menus	Menus of commands contained in the Windows menu bar
String tables	IDs, values, and captions that are required by an application
Toolbar resources	Graphical elements that execute commands after being clicked by the mouse
Version information	Company and product identification, a product release number, and copyright and trademark notification

Figure 10-16 Standard Windows API resources

Resources are defined in special files called **resource scripts**. Resource scripts have an extension of .rc and are written in C preprocessor language. When you build a project, all of the project's resources are compiled into a file with an extension of .res. You refer to resources in an MFC program using a resource ID. A **resource ID** is an integer constant declared with the #define preprocessor directive and is used for programmatically referring to a resource. It is common practice to declare all resource constants in an interface file named resource.h in order to make it easier to reference them in your program. Visual C++ automatically creates a resource script when you run either the MFC Application Wizard or the Add Resource Wizard.

Although resource files are written in C preprocessor language, you do not actually need to write any code. Instead, you use a Visual C++ Resource editor. When a Visual C++ project includes resources, the Solution Explorer window includes a Resource View tab that allows you to quickly open a resource in a resource editor. You will learn about resource editors shortly.

Add Resource Wizard

You use the **Add Resource Wizard** to add new resources to an MFC project. You start the Add Resource Wizard by selecting the Add Resource command from the Project menu to display the Add Resource dialog box. Then, you select the resource you want to add from the Resource type list, and click the New button. You can also use the Import button to import an existing resource into your project, or use the Custom button to create a custom resource. Figure 10-17 shows an example of the Add Resource dialog box.

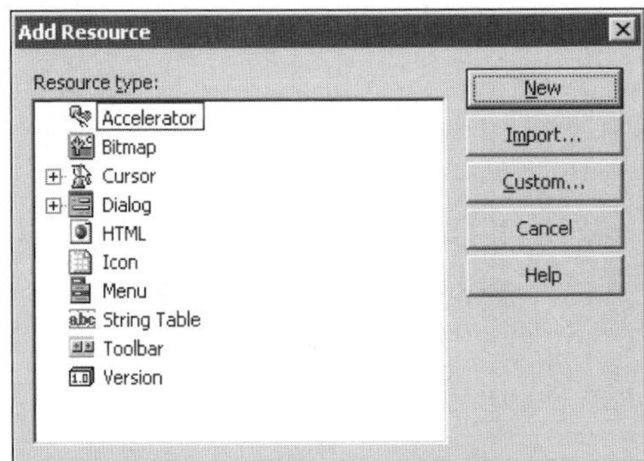

Figure 10-17 Add Resource dialog box

Resource Editors

Resource editors allow you to quickly create and modify resources in a graphical environment. You can still edit a resource file's C preprocessor code, although there is little reason to do so because Visual C++ does an excellent job of writing the code for you. As an example of a resource editor, consider the Dialog Editor, which you will use extensively in this chapter. Whenever you open the Dialog Editor, the Toolbox window also opens. The Toolbox window contains a number of tools that you can use to graphically draw the dialog box's controls. As you draw the controls, Visual C++ automatically writes the C preprocessor code for you. Figure 10-18 shows a simple dialog box in the Dialog Editor, and Figure 10-19 shows the C preprocessor code that represents the same dialog box. You can also see the Toolbox in Figure 10-18.

You can view and edit a resource's C preprocessor code by selecting File from the Open submenu on the File menu to display the Open File dialog box. In the Open File dialog box, select the resource file (with an extension of .rc), click the arrow to the right of the Open button and select the Open With command to display the Open With dialog box. In the Open With dialog box, select Source Code (Text) Editor (Default), and then click the Open button. The resource's C preprocessor code opens in the Code and Code Editor window.

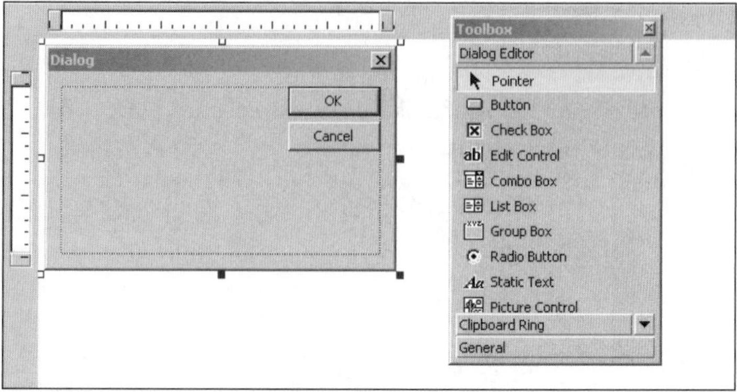

Figure 10-18 Dialog Editor

```
///////////////////////////////////////////////////////////////////////////////
//
// Dialog
//

IDD_DIALOG1 DIALOGEX 0, 0, 186, 95
STYLE DS_SETFONT | DS_MODALFRAME | DS_FIXEDSYS | WS_POPUP | WS_CAPTION |
    WS_SYSMENU
CAPTION "Dialog"
FONT 8, "MS Shell Dlg", 400, 0, 0x1
BEGIN
    DEFPUSHBUTTON   "OK",IDOK,129,7,50,14
    PUSHBUTTON      "Cancel",IDCANCEL,129,24,50,14
END
```

Figure 10-19 Dialog box C preprocessor code

You can manually open the Toolbox window by selecting Toolbox from the View menu.

Resource View

A project's resources appear in the Resource View tab in the Solution Explorer window. Resource View contains folders representing the different resource types. You can use Resource View to quickly open a resource in a resource editor. To view a particular resource in its editor, expand its resource folder and double-click the resource name. Figure 10-20 shows the IDE after expanding the Toolbar folder on the Resource View tab and double-clicking the IDR_MAINFRAME resource.

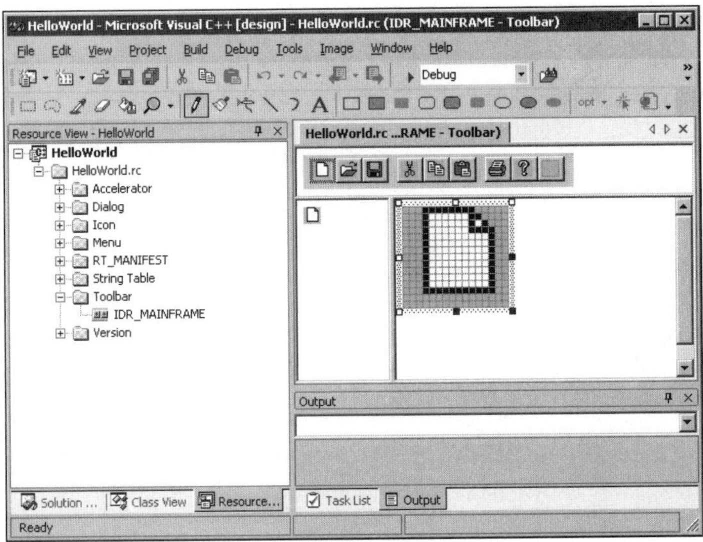

Figure 10-20 Resource View tab

Properties Window

The Properties window in Visual C++ (and other Visual Studio tools) is used for managing the properties of various elements in a project, including the properties of resources. Different types of resources have different properties available in their Properties window. For example, in the Dialog Box editor you use the Properties window to modify a button's resource ID, set the text that appears on the button's face (its caption), and set the style of the button. You display the Properties window by selecting Properties Window from the View menu. Figure 10-21 shows a portion of the Properties window for a button in the Dialog Box editor.

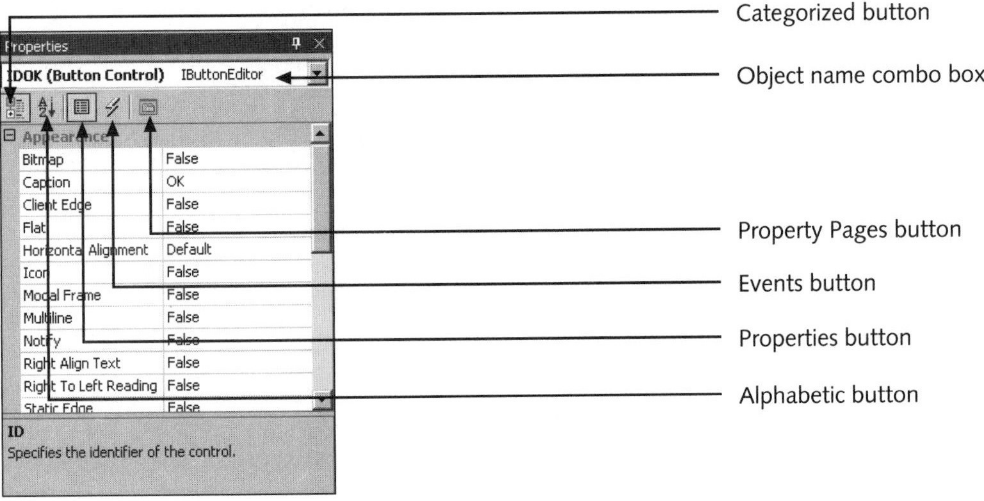

Figure 10-21 Properties window for a button in the Dialog Box editor

At the top of the Properties window is the Object name combo box, which displays the name of the currently selected object or objects. Below the Object name combo box is the Properties window toolbar, which includes the following buttons:

- A Categorized button, which displays all of an object's properties by category
- An Alphabetic button, which displays all of an object's properties alphabetically
- A Properties button, which displays an object's properties
- A Property Pages button, which displays the project's Property Pages dialog box

An Events button also appears for any selected objects that have associated events. Additional buttons will appear on the Properties window toolbar, depending on the selected object.

Visual C++ treats almost everything, including class members, as a property. If you need to make any changes to the basic declarations (function parameters, the data types of member variables, and so on) in your class, you have two choices. You can either make the changes manually in the header and source files, or you can use the Properties window. For example, Visual C++ treats the return type of a function as a property named *TypeString*. If you want to change a function member's return type, you can simply enter a new type for the TypeString property in the Properties window. After making the change and moving your cursor out of the TypeString property field, Visual C++ automatically changes the function's return type in both the header and source files.

In order to display a class member's properties in the Properties window, you must select the class member in Class View. Figure 10-22 shows a portion of the Properties window for the InitInstance() member function in the CCalculator class. Notice in Figure 10-22 that InitInstance() is selected in Class View.

The Properties window toolbar includes two additional buttons, Messages and Overrides, when one of the following conditions is true:

- When the Code Editor window is the active window in the IDE and it is opened to a class interface or implementation file
- When Class View is the active window in the ID, and you have selected a class icon in Class View

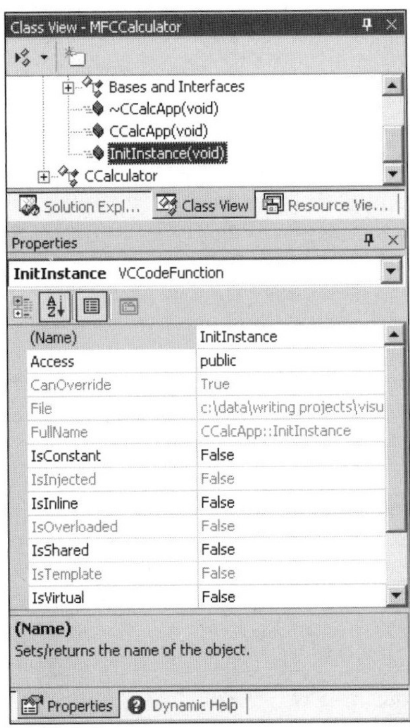

Figure 10-22 A member function in the Properties window

Clicking the Messages button lists the Windows messages that are associated with the class that is currently selected in Class View. You can use the Messages button to add or delete handler functions for messages that are available to the selected class. Clicking the Overrides button lists all of the virtual functions that are available to the selected class. You can use the Overrides button to override a virtual function in the selected class. The names of any virtual functions that your class already overrides are duplicated in each virtual function's value field in the Properties window. To override a particular virtual function, place the insertion point in the empty value field next to the function name, click the drop-down arrow to the right of the field, and then select the <Add> command that appears.

If you click the drop-down arrow in the value field of a virtual function in the Properties window, you will see two additional commands: a <Delete> command, which allows you to delete the overridden function, and an <Edit Code> command, which allows you to edit the overridden function.

THE CSTRING CLASS

An important MFC class that you need to know about because you will use it in the next section is the **CString class**, which is used for manipulating strings in MFC programs, and works in much the same was as the string class. You create a string variable with the CString class using a statement similar to `CString myString;`. You can also assign a string directly to the variable name using a statement such as `CString myString = "This is a text string.";`. There is no need to declare the number of characters you want to store or use as there is with a `char*` pointer. Once you have instantiated two CString variables, you can assign the contents of one variable to the other using the assignment operator, in the same way you use the assignment operator with numeric data types. The following code shows an example of how to assign the contents of one CString variable to another CString variable:

```
CString firstString = "This is a text string";
CString secondString;
secondString = firstString;
```

You can also use several operators with CString variables, including the concatination operator (+), the += assignment operator, and the == comparison operator. The following code combines a CString variable and a literal string and assigns the new value to another variable:

```
CString firstString = "San Francisco ";
CString newString;
newString = firstString + "is in California";
```

The combined value of the firstString variable and the string literal that is assigned to the newString variable is *San Francisco is in California*.

You can also use the += assignment operator to combine two strings. The following code combines the two text strings, but without using the newString variable:

```
CString firstString = "San Francisco ";
firstString += "is in California";
```

As with string class variables, the comparison operator is useful with CString variables to determine if they contain the same text. For example, the following code contains an `if` statement that compares the values of two CString variables. Because the variables do not contain the same string values, the message box in the `if` statement does not appear.

```
CString firstCity = "San Francisco";
CString secondCity = "Los Angeles";
if (firstCity == secondCity)
     AfxMessageBox("Same cities");
```

DIALOG-BASED APPLICATIONS

One of the more common types of windows used in Windows applications is the dialog box. A **dialog box** is a window that is used to display information or to gather information from users. The message box you have seen in this chapter is an example of a dialog box. Some standard Windows dialog boxes, which are shared by many different types of Windows applications, are called common dialog boxes, and they include the

Open and Save dialog boxes, Print dialog boxes, and Font dialog boxes. Figure 10-23 shows the Open dialog box that is shared by many Windows applications.

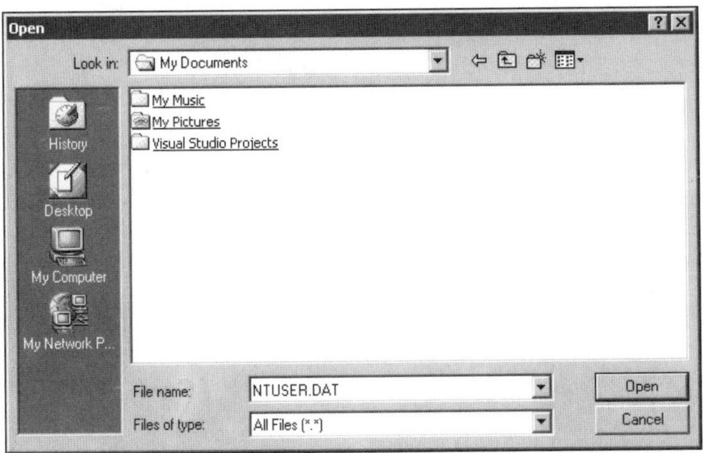

Figure 10-23 Open dialog box

10

Windows includes a common dialog box library from which you can choose common dialog boxes to include in your applications, regardless of the programming language you use. Using common dialog boxes ensures that the standard dialog box types used by all Windows applications are consistent from one Windows application to another. Also, using common dialog boxes means that you do not have to waste time creating your own versions of each dialog box type. In this chapter, you will learn how to create your own custom dialog boxes.

All dialog boxes—whether standard or custom—are created using two components: a dialog resource and a dialog class derived from the CDialog class. The dialog resource represents the visual aspect of the dialog box, and the dialog class provides programmatic access to the dialog box. The CDialog class is a window class because it derives from the CWnd class, the same as the CFrameWnd class does. Most dialog boxes are usually associated with a CFrameWnd class, or another class derived from CWnd. For example, an application that includes a frame window often calls various CDialog class windows in order to display information or to gather information from the user. However, you can also use a dialog box as an application's primary interface window. Applications that use a dialog box as their primary interface window are called **dialog-based applications**. The MFC Calculator program is a dialog-based application, as is the Calculator program that is installed with Windows operating systems.

In order for a class derived from CDialog to know which dialog box resource it is associated with, you must call a parameterized constructor for the CDialog base class and pass to it the `enum` variable that represents the dialog box resource ID. You call the parameterized CDialog constructor using an initializer list in the derived class's default constructor. For instance, you may have a class named CMainDlg that derives from CDialog and a dialog box resource with a resource ID of IDD_MAIN. In order to associate the CMainDlg class with the IDD_MAIN dialog box resource ID, you can write the following default constructor for the CMainDlg class, which uses an initializer list to pass the IDD_MAIN resource ID to the parameterized CDialog constructor:

```
CMainDlg::CMainDlg(void) : CDialog(IDD_MAIN){
}
```

Technically, the preceding syntax is all that a class derived from CDialog needs to know which dialog box resource it is associated with. However, in order for you to use several features of the IDE, including the Add Variable Wizard, you must pass to the CDialog base class a constant member variable that contains the dialog resource ID and that has been initialized within an `enum` data type declaration. An **enumerated**, or **`enum`**, type declaration allows you to create your own data type to which you can assign only a series of predefined constant integer values. You declare an enum type declaration using the syntax `enum type_name {value1, value2, value3, ...};`. The values between the braces are known as enumerators and are used for symbolically representing a value. Each enumerator receives an integer value, starting with 0 for the first enumerator. For example, to create an `enum` variable named Grades that contains descriptive constant enumerators for each of the standard letter grades from Failing through Excellent (F, D, C, B, and A), you use a declaration statement similar to the following:

```
enum Grades {Failing, Passing, Fair, Good, Excellent};
```

After declaring an `enum` type, you can then declare a variable in your code of the new type. For instance, to declare a variable named thisStudent of the Grades type, you use the statement `Grades thisStudent;`. Alternately, you can include a variable name within the `enum` type declaration itself using the following declaration statement:

```
enum Grades {Failing, Passing, Fair, Good, Excellent}
thisStudent;
```

The thisStudent variable can only be assigned one of the enumerators in the declaration list, which are Excellent, Good, Fair, Passing, and Failing. If you attempt to assign any other value to the thisStudent variable, you will receive a compile error. Note that each value represents only an integer value, starting with 0. For example, if you assign the value Passing to the thisStudent variable using the statement `thisStudent = Passing;`, the thisStudent variable is really being assigned a value of 1. Although each enumerator receives an integer value by default, starting with 0 for the first enumerator, you can also assign your own integer values to each enumerator in the `enum` type declaration. For instance, you can use the following statement to assign a value of 50 to the Excellent enumerator in the Grades `enum` type declaration:

```
enum Grades {Failing=50, Passing, Fair, Good, Excellent}
thisStudent;
```

Each enumerator in an **enum** type declaration is assigned the integer value of the preceding enumerator, plus one. This means that in the preceding code, the Passing enumerator is assigned a value of 51, Fair is assigned a value of 52, and so on. Therefore, with the Grades **enum** type declaration, you would probably want to explicitly assign a value to each enumerator, as follows:

```
enum Grades {Failing=50, Passing=60, Fair=70, Good=80,
Excellent=90} thisStudent;
```

Now that you understand the basics of **enum** type declarations, you can learn why you need to use them with a class derived from the CDialog base class. Recall that you can declare a constant in an interface file, but that you must initialize it in a constructor in the implementation file. Unfortunately, this means that you cannot pass the constant to a base class constructor using an initializer list in the constructor (as you must do with the CDialog class) because the initializer list executes before the constant is intialized in the body of the constructor. Now consider that each enumerator in an **enum** type declaration is really a constant integer variable. In order to declare and initialize a constant member variable inside a class interface file, some programmers, including Microsoft programmers, use a trick (or "hack" in programming parlance) with an **enum** type declaration. You can simply exclude the type name and variable name from an **enum** statement to declare and initialize any constant integer variables inside the statement's braces. For instance, to declare and initialize a constant integer variable named IDD and assign to it the integer value of the IDD_MAIN dialog resource ID, you add the following statement to the interface file of a class that derives from CDialog:

10

```
enum {IDD=IDD_MAIN};
```

You then pass the IDD constant integer variable instead of the IDD_MAIN resource ID to the parameterized CDialog constructor, using the initializer list in the CMainDlg class, as follows:

```
CMainDlg::CMainDlg(void) : CDialog(IDD) {
}
```

Next, you will add a dialog resource and a dialog class to the MFC Calculator program.

To add a dialog resource to the MFC Calculator project:

1. Select **Add Resource** from the Project menu to display the Add Resource dialog box. After the Add Resource dialog box opens, a resource script is automatically added to the project.
2. Click the **Dialog** resource type and click the **New** button. A new dialog resource with an OK button and Cancel button appears in the Dialog Editor.

3. With the dialog box selected in the Dialog Editor, select **Properties Window** from the View menu to display the properties window.
4. In the Properties window, locate the ID property (which represents the resource ID for the dialog resource) and change the default ID from IDD_DIALOG1 TO **IDD_CALCULATOR**. Also, locate the Caption property and change the dialog caption from Dialog to **MFC Calculator**.
5. Save the dialog resource by selecting **Save MFCCalculator.rc** from the File menu.
6. Close the Dialog Editor by clicking the **Close** button or by activating the Dialog Editor window and selecting **Close** from the File menu.

Now you will add IDD_CALCULATOR programmatic access to the dialog resource.

To add a dialog class that provides programmatic access to the dialog resource:

1. First, delete the **CalcFrame.h** and **CalcFrame.cpp** files from your project by selecting each file in the Solution Explorer window and pressing delete. You will no longer need these files because the MFC Calculator program will be dialog-based. Remember from Chapter 1 that deleting a file from the Solution Explorer window does not delete it from your hard drive. Therefore, you also need to open Windows Explorer and delete the files from your project folder. When you are through, return to Visual C++.

If you did not close the Dialog Editor in the preceding set of steps, be sure that it is not the active window before executing the next step. If the Dialog Editor is the active window when you run the Class Wizard, Visual C++ will automatically attempt to run the MFC Class Wizard. The MFC Class Wizard will not function because the MFC Calculator project is not an MFC project.

2. Start the Generic C++ Class Wizard. In the Generic C++ Class Wizard dialog box, type **CCalculator** as the name of the class and derive the class from **CDialog** using **`public`** access. Also, click the **Virtual destructor** check box. Click the **Finish** button. Visual C++ creates two files called Calculator.h and Calculator.cpp. The Calculator.h file opens in the Code Editor window.
3. As shown in Figure 10-24, add the statement `#include "resource.h"` to give the class access to the project's resource IDs. Also add an `enum` type declaration that defines an integer constant named IDD containing the value of the IDD_CALCULATOR resource.

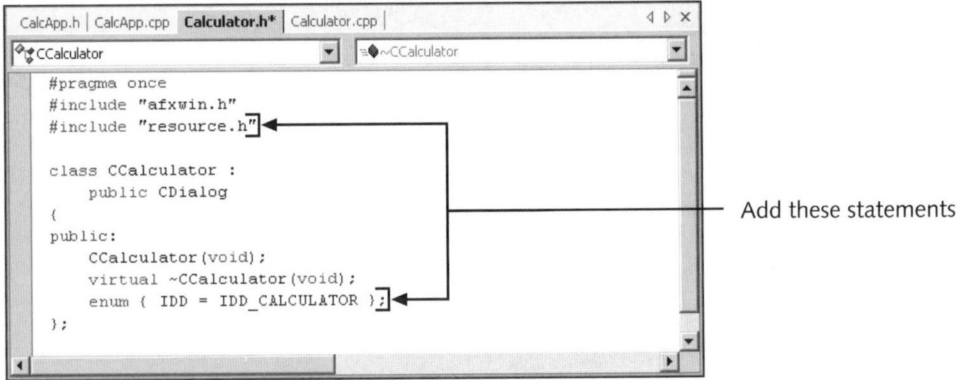

Figure 10-24 #include statements add to Calculator.h

4. Open the **Calculator.cpp** file in the Code Editor window and add an initializer list to the default constructor definition that passes the IDD integer constant to the parameterized CDialog constructor, as follows:

```
CCalculator::CCalculator(void) : CDialog(IDD)
{
}
```

10

Before you can add code that displays the dialog box, you need to understand the difference between modal and modeless dialog boxes.

Modal and Modeless Dialog Boxes

Modal dialog boxes require users to close or cancel the dialog box before they can continue working with an application. The message boxes you have worked with are examples of modal dialog boxes. Once a modal message box appears on your screen, you cannot access any other window in the application until you close the message box. Simple modal message boxes contain only a single OK button. More complex modal dialog boxes usually contain a Cancel button in addition to an OK button. For example, Figure 10-25 shows the modal Font dialog box for WordPad, a simple word-processing program supplied with Windows operating systems. Because the Font dialog box is modal, you cannot click the main WordPad window until you either select the desired font information and click the OK button, or close the dialog box by clicking the Cancel button.

The OK button in some types of modal dialog boxes may be a more descriptive button, depending on the dialog box's function. For example, the Open dialog box includes an Open button instead of an OK button, and the Save dialog box includes a Save button instead of an OK button.

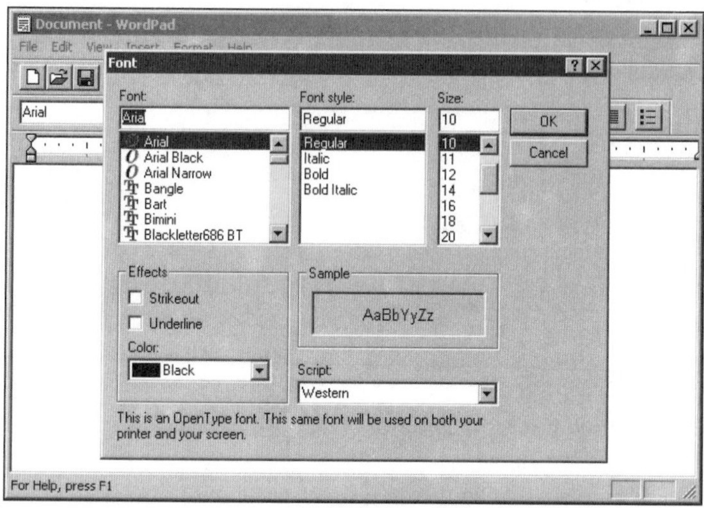

Figure 10-25 Modal Font dialog box in WordPad

In comparison to a modal dialog box, **modeless dialog boxes** do not need to be closed before you return to another window in the application. Modeless dialog boxes function more like frame windows and other types of primary application windows. For dialog-based applications like the MFC Calculator program, you can usually use either modeless or modal dialog boxes. If your dialog-based application uses other dialog boxes to gather information that is then used in the main dialog window, you would probably want your main dialog window to be modeless and any other dialog boxes that are called by the main dialog window to be modal.

Modeless dialog boxes require quite a bit more work than modal dialog boxes. Much of the behind-the-scenes work, such as closing and destroying the dialog window, is handled automatically with modal dialog boxes. With modeless dialog boxes, however, especially in dialog-based applications, you need to override several inherited member functions. Overriding the inherited member functions allows you to correctly close and destroy the dialog window. Additionally, overriding inherited member functions allows you to be sure that the dialog box functions correctly within the context of the application window. Because of these complexities, you will concentrate on working with modal dialog boxes.

If you would like to learn how to create modeless dialog boxes, search for *modeless dialog boxes* in the index of the MSDN Library.

Displaying Modal Dialog Boxes

You display a modal dialog box from an application's InitInstance() function, the same way you display a frame window. You instantiate an object of the dialog class and use the inherited **DoModal() function** to display the modal dialog box. By default, if a user clicks a button containing a resource ID of IDOK or IDCANCEL, the dialog box closes. The IDOK resource ID represents the OK button, and the IDCANCEL resource ID represents the Cancel button.

The DoModal() function returns an integer value representing the resource ID that caused the dialog box to close. You use these resource IDs in an `if` statement to take the appropriate action, depending on whether the user pressed the OK button or the Cancel button. For example, if your dialog box prompts the user for his or her name, then you would use the OK branch of the `if` statement to assign the name to a data member. By default, the IDCANCEL resource ID causes the dialog box to be destroyed. However, you may find it necessary to use the cancel branch of the `if` statement to make sure the user wants to close the dialog box or to save any unsaved data.

The following code shows an example of an application class's InitInstance() function that displays a modal dialog box based on a dialog class named CHelloWorldDlg. The DoModal() function returns the resource ID to an `int` variable named nResponse. The `if` statement then checks the value of nResponse and executes the appropriate code block. Notice that the InitInstance() function returns a value of FALSE. Because this is a dialog-based application, you return a value of FALSE from the InitInstance() function in order to exit the application.

```
BOOL CHelloWorldApp::InitInstance() {
   CHelloWorldDlg dlg;
   int nResponse = dlg.DoModal();
   if (nResponse == IDOK) {
       // OK button statements
   }
   else if (nResponse == IDCANCEL) {
       // Cancel button statements
   }
   return FALSE;
}
```

Next, you will add code to the MFC Calculator application class's InitInstance() function, that displays the MFC Calculator program's dialog box as a modal dialog box. Because the MFC Calculator program does not require OK and Cancel buttons, you will delete them from the dialog box. You can close the application by clicking the Close button or by pressing the Escape key. Also, because the dialog box will not include OK and Cancel buttons, there is no need to include the `if` statement. Thus, you can simply call the DoModal() function using a statement similar to `dlg.DoModal();`, without assigning the `return` value to an integer variable.

10

To add code to the MFC Calculator application class's InitInstance() function that displays the MFC Calculator program's dialog box as a modal dialog box:

1. Open the **IDD_CALCULATOR** resource in the Dialog Editor by clicking the **Resource View** tab, expanding the **Dialog** folder, and then double-clicking the **IDD_CALCULATOR** icon. Then delete the **OK** and **Cancel** buttons by clicking each button once and pressing **Delete**.
2. Open the **CalcApp.cpp** file in the Code Editor window.
3. As shown in Figure 10-26, modify the #include statement that includes the deleted CalcFrame.h file so that it includes the **Calculator.h** file instead.

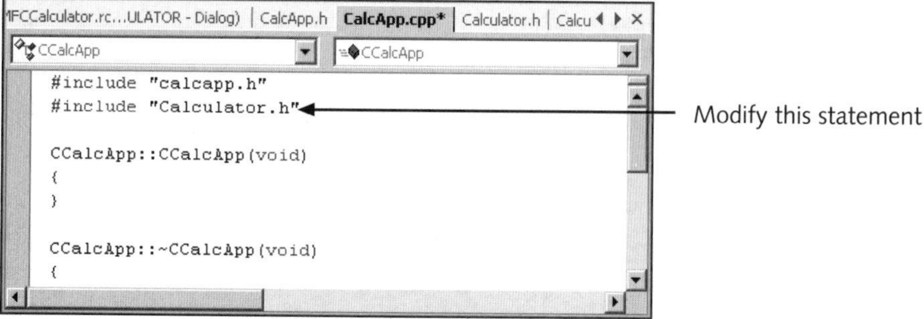

MFCCalculator.rc...ULATOR - Dialog) | CalcApp.h | CalcApp.cpp* | Calculator.h | Calcu
CCalcApp
CCalcApp
#include "calcapp.h"
#include "Calculator.h"
CCalcApp::CCalcApp(void)
{
}
CCalcApp::~CCalcApp(void)
{
Modify this statement

Figure 10-26 Modified #include statement in CalcApp.cpp

4. As shown in Figure 10-27, modify the InitInstance() function so that it declares a new Calculator object named *calc* and calls the DoModal() function. Be sure to delete the statements that instantiated the frame window and modify the `return` statement so that it returns a value of `FALSE`.

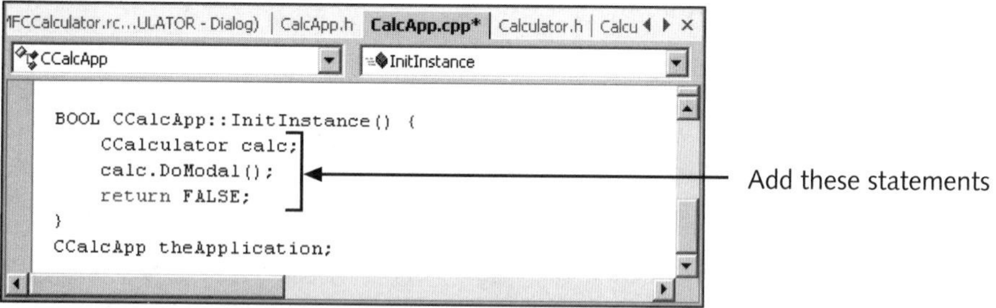

MFCCalculator.rc...ULATOR - Dialog) | CalcApp.h | CalcApp.cpp* | Calculator.h | Calcu
CCalcApp
InitInstance
BOOL CCalcApp::InitInstance() {
CCalculator calc;
calc.DoModal();
return FALSE;
}
CCalcApp theApplication;
Add these statements

Figure 10-27 Modified InitInstance() function

5. Build and execute the program. You should see the dialog box shown in Figure 10-28.

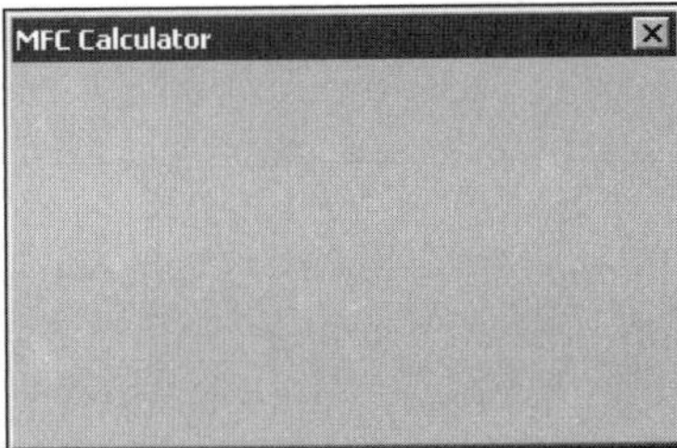

Figure 10-28 Dialog box created by MFC Calculator program

6. Close the dialog box by clicking the **Close** button in the title bar or by pressing **Escape**.

Working with Controls

Dialog boxes typically contain groups of controls through which a user interacts with an application. **Controls** are user interface items such as check boxes, command buttons, text boxes, and other objects. You add controls to a dialog box by using the Controls toolbar in the Dialog Editor. The ability to easily add controls is one of the greatest benefits of using dialog boxes. You can add controls as child windows to frame windows, and other windows, but not as easily as you can add them to dialog windows. With dialog windows, you use the Dialog Editor to draw the controls you need onto your dialog box; Visual C++ then enters the correct code in the program's resource script. Dialog windows are the only windows that you can create with a resource editor such as the Dialog Editor. With other types of windows, you need to manually add the code for each control.

You can add the following three types of controls to MFC programs:

- Windows common controls
- MFC controls
- ActiveX controls

Windows common controls are the standard controls, such as edit boxes, buttons, check boxes, and so on, you see in common dialog boxes. Windows common controls are actually provided by the Windows operating system itself, not by Visual C++ or MFC.

MFC controls are provided by MFC and are not part of the Windows operating system. There are three MFC controls: the Bitmap Button control, the Checklist Box control, and the Drag List Box control. The Bitmap Button control is similar to a standard command button except that it displays a bitmap image on its face. The Checklist Box control displays a list of items, such as filenames, that a user can check or uncheck. The Drag List Box control allows users to reorder lists of items, such as a filename list.

ActiveX is a technology that allows programming objects to be easily reused with any programming language that supports Microsoft's Component Object Model. The **Component Object Model**, or **COM**, is an architecture for cross-platform development of client/server applications. **ActiveX controls** are objects that are placed in Web pages or inside programs created with COM-enabled programming languages. ActiveX controls are very popular in Windows programming; you can literally find thousands of types of ActiveX controls in various places on the Web. MFC controls and ActiveX controls are somewhat advanced for your studies. Therefore, you will work with Windows common controls for the rest of this book.

Recall from the last chapter that individual controls are actually windows, the same as frame windows and dialog windows. Because controls are windows, they can be controlled programmatically using classes derived from the CWnd class. Figure 10-29 lists the Windows common controls, along with a description of each control and its associated MFC class.

Control	Description	MFC Class
animation	AVI video player	CAnimateCtrl
button	Command button	CButton
combo box	Combination edit box/list box	CComboBox
date and time picker	Date and time selection control	CDateTimeCtrl
edit box	Single line text box	CEdit
extended combo box	Combo box control that is capable of displaying images	CComboBoxEx
header	Button that appears above a column of text and controls the width of the displayed text	CHeaderCtrl
hotkey	Shortcut keys that allow users to quickly perform a task	CHotKeyCtrl
image list	Lists of icons or bitmaps	CImageList
list	Selectable list of text strings with icons	CListCtrl
list box	Selectable list of text strings	CListBox
month calendar	Monthly calendar control	CMonthCalCtrl
progress	Progress bar that tracks the completion of a task	CProgressCtrl

Figure 10-29 Windows common controls and MFC classes

Control	Description	MFC Class
rebar	Toolbar capable of containing control child windows	CRebarCtrl
rich edit	Multiline edit box with character formatting and paragraph	CRichEditCtrl
scroll bar	Control that scrolls the display of a dialog window	CScrollBar
slider	Selection bar with optional tick marks	CSliderCtrl
spin button	Increment or decrement a value	CSpinButtonCtrl
static-text	Explanatory text	CStatic
status bar	Informational control that appears at the bottom of an application window	CStatusBarCtrl
tab	Dialog box control that divides a dialog box into multiple sections	CTabCtrl
toolbar	List of commands represented by image buttons	CToolBarCtrl
tool tip	Pop-up window that describes a toolbar button	CToolTipCtrl
tree	Hierarchical list of items	CTreeCtrl

Figure 10-29 Windows common controls and MFC classes (continued)

You do not usually need to derive classes for individual controls placed on a dialog box. Remember that controls are usually placed as child windows within a dialog box parent window. Therefore, you can have the dialog box class manage the functionality for each individual control. For example, the controls in the MFC Calculator program you are creating do not need to be controlled using individual MFC classes. Instead, the dialog class will use messages generated by each control to execute the functions that give the program its functionality.

More complex types of controls must be controlled using an associated MFC class. For example, the status bar control is used for displaying various kinds of status information about an application. You will not find a status bar control on the Controls toolbar. Instead, you must use the CStatusBarCtrl class to declare a status bar object, and then use member functions of the CStatusBarCtrl class to format the display of the status bar and assign the various types of status information you want to see displayed. Any required class syntax for controls will be introduced as you encounter the controls in the text.

Before you start adding controls to the MFC Calculator program's dialog window, you need to think about some interface design issues. Professional programming departments are often separated into two groups: programmers who write code and programmers who design interfaces. Although there is some overlap between these two disciplines, programmers who specialize in interface design often have additional training in graphic design techniques. When trying to design an interface, you may find yourself growing frustrated because your controls may not line up perfectly, you may not be satisfied with your color choices, and so on. As you start designing visual interfaces, remember that you are studying only the basics. Your goal is to learn the essentials of MFC programming and make the MFC Calculator program function—not necessarily to win design awards. Be patient as you develop your interface design skills.

When you activate the Dialog Editor window, a new menu item, Format, appears to assist you in designing your dialog window. The Format menu contains various commands that will assist you in arranging, organizing, and spacing the controls placed on your dialog box. One very useful command that you will use in the next exercise is the Test Dialog command, which allows you to see a preview of your dialog box exactly as it will appear when you execute the application.

Next, you will add controls to the MFC Calculator program's dialog resource. You will create the text box using the Edit Box control and the calculator buttons using the Button control. Use the finished calculator shown in Figure 10-30 as a model for how your dialog box should appear.

Figure 10-30 MFC Calculator dialog box

To add controls to the MFC Calculator program's dialog resource:

1. Open the **IDD_CALCULATOR** resource in the Dialog Editor. As you adjust the placement and size of your dialog box and its controls in this exercise, occasionally select the Test Dialog command on the Format menu to see a preview of your dialog box that is exactly as it will appear when you execute the application.

2. The dialog window should appear with squares at its corners and sides that are used for resizing the window. You resize the window by pointing at one of these handles, holding your left mouse button, and dragging to the desired size. Resize your calculator window so that it matches Figure 10-30.

3. Next, add the Edit control. Click the **Edit Control** on the Control once and hold the pointer over the approximate location in the dialog window of the upper-left corner of the control. Still holding your left mouse button down, drag to the approximate location of the lower-right corner of the control, and then release the mouse button. The new Edit Control appears with the same sizing handles you saw around the dialog window. Use the sizing handles to adjust the size of the control, if necessary.
4. Click the **Edit Control** that you just added once and select **Properties Window** from the View menu to display the Properties window. Change the control's ID property from the default IDC_EDIT1 to **IDC_DISPLAY**.
5. The MFC Calculator program's functionality will be accessed through its buttons, so you do not want users to be able to click in the IDC_DISPLAY Edit Control and type numbers. Change the Read-Only property to **True**, which will prevent users from manually entering data into the Edit Control. Close the Properties window.
6. Next, add the calculator buttons using the Button control. You can also use sizing handles to adjust the size of a Button control after adding it to the dialog window.
7. Click each button once and select **Properties** from the View menu to display the Properties window. Change each button's Caption property to the captions shown in Figure 10-31. Also, change each button's ID property to the IDs shown in Figure 10-31.

Caption	Resource ID
+	IDC_PLUS
–	IDC_MINUS
*	IDC_MULTIPLY
/	IDC_DIVIDE
.	IDC_POINT
=	IDC_EQUALS
Clear	IDC_CLEAR
0	IDC_ZERO
1	IDC_ONE
2	IDC_TWO
3	IDC_THREE
4	IDC_FOUR
5	IDC_FIVE
6	IDC_SIX
7	IDC_SEVEN
8	IDC_EIGHT
9	IDC_NINE

Figure 10-31 Button captions and resource IDs

Dialog Data Exchange

To set and retrieve control values in an MFC application, you can use the same SetWindowText() and GetWindowText() Windows API functions that you learned about in Chapter 8. MFC provides a special mechanism, however, called **dialog data exchange**, or **DDX**, to handle the exchange of values between controls and variables. You do not need to call the SetWindowText() and GetWindowText() functions in an MFC program because DDX handles the exchange of information for you. A related mechanism called **dialog data validation**, or **DDV**, assists in the validation of data as it is exchanged between controls and variables.

Before you can use DDX or DDV, you must first override the DoDataExchange() function in the class derived from CDialog that is associated with your dialog resource ID. The DoDataExchange() function is a member of the CWnd class and manages the exchange and validation of dialog data. Once you override the DoDataExchange() function, you can then execute the AddVariable Wizard, which displays the Add Member Variable Wizard dialog box where you create a data member and associate it with a control's resource ID. In the Add Member Variable Wizard dialog box, you must select the Control variable check box to enable DDX and DDV. Figure 10-32 shows an example of the Add Member Variable Wizard dialog box with the Control variable check box selected.

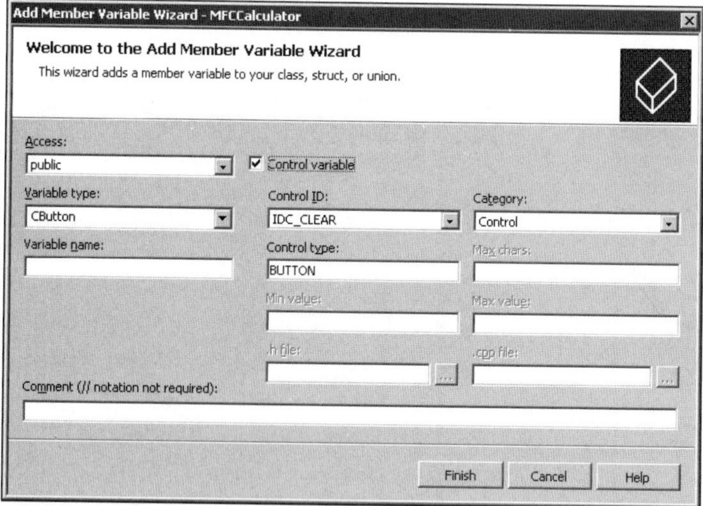

Figure 10-32 Add Member Variable Wizard dialog box with the Control variable check box selected

You associate a data member name with a control ID. For controls that can accept a value, such as an Edit Box control, you can select a category of either *Control* or *value*. If you select a category of *value*, then you can select the primitive data type of the data member using the Variable type combo box. The Max chars, Min value, and Max value text boxes enable the DDV mechanism and are available depending on the primitive data type selected for the data member. The Min value and Max value text boxes, for instance, are only available for numeric data types.

After you close the Add Member Variable Wizard dialog box, initialization statements for primitive data members are placed in the dialog class's constructor, and the appropriate DDX functions for setting the data member's value in the associated control are added to the DoDataExchange() function. The following code shows an example of the constructor and DoDataExchange() function for a dialog class named HelloWorldDlg. The constructor uses an initializer list to initialize a m_sHello data member using the _T() function, which is a special data mapping function for CString data types that assigns a text string to the m_sHello data member. Notice that the _T() function is called using functional notation. The only thing you need to do with the _T() function is change the text that it passes as an argument. The DoDataExchange() function contains a single statement that uses a function named DDX_Text() to initialize the IDC_EDIT1 control with the value assigned to the m_sHello data member.

```
CHelloWorldDlg::CHelloWorldDlg(void) : CDialog(IDD)
  , m_sHello(_T("")) {
}
void CHelloWorldDlg::DoDataExchange(CDataExchange* pDX)
{
  CDialog::DoDataExchange(pDX);
  DDX_Text(pDX, IDC_EDIT1, m_sHello);
}
```

10

When your MFC program is initialized, an inherited function named OnInitDialog() is called, which in turn calls the UpdateData() function. The UpdateData() function then calls the DoDataExchange() function. This is all done behind the scenes, but you should be aware of the process. The **UpdateData() function** either initializes dialog box controls using associated data members, or it copies the current control values back into the associated data members. The UpdateData() function calls the DoDataExchange() function when it is passed a value of `FALSE` by the OnInitDialog() function. When the user closes a modal dialog box by clicking the OK button, the UpdateData() function is called and passed a value of `TRUE`, which copies the control's current values into the associated data members.

You can also use the UpdateData() function to quickly assign a dialog box's control values to their associated data members. For example, if you want to use in your code the most recent value a user entered into an edit control named IDC_EDIT1, you first call the statement `UpdateData(TRUE);`, which copies the most recent control values to their associated data members.

Never call the DoDataExchange() function directly; always call it using the UpdateData() function.

Next, you will override the DoDataExchange() function and add a DDX data member to the MFC Calculator program. You will add a DDX data member only for the IDC_DISPLAY control because that is the only control for which you need to set and retrieve values.

To add a DDX data member to the MFC Calculator program:

1. Open either the **Calculator.h** file or the **Calculator.cpp** file in the Code Editor window. Then display the Properties window, click the **Overrides** button in the Properties window toolbar, and override the DoDataExchange() function.
2. Open the **IDD_CALCULATOR** dialog box in the Dialog Editor, click the **IDC_DISPLAY** control, and then select Add Variable from the Project menu to display the Add Member Variable Wizard dialog box. The Control variable check box is automatically selected because you had a control selected in the Dialog Editor before executing the Add Variable Wizard.
3. Select **Value** in the Category combo box.
4. If necessary, select **CString** in the Variable type combo box.
5. Type **m_sDisplay** in the Variable name text box.
6. Click the **Finish** button to close the Add Member Variable Wizard dialog box. The Calculator.cpp file opens in the Code Editor window.
7. Examine the constructor and DoDataExchange() functions in the Calculator.cpp file. The statement `m_sDisplay(_T(""))` has been added to the constructor's initializer list to initialize the m_sDisplay variable to zero. The statement `DDX_Text(pDX, IDC_DISPLAY, m_sDisplay);` has been added to the DoDataExchange() function to set the IDC_DISPLAY control's value to the value of m_sDisplay upon initialization. Change the `m_sDisplay(_T(""))` statement in the constructor's initializer list to `m_sDisplay(_T("0"))` so that an initial value of 0 is assigned to the IDC_DISPLAY control.

Message Maps

As with Windows API programs, in MFC programs, messages are raised for events that occur. In MFC programs, you do not need to create a window procedure to process messages. Instead, the MFC framework handles the processing of messages using message maps. The inherited Run() function of the CWinApp class automatically retrieves queued messages and sends each message to the appropriate window. Each individual window in an MFC application handles its own messages using a message map. A **message map** associates messages with message handler functions. All windows derived from CCmdTarget can include message maps. Because CWnd derives from CCmdTarget, any of the child class windows of CWnd can include their own message maps.

You add a message map to a window by first adding the DECLARE_MESSAGE_MAP() macro to the class interface file. Then, you must add a message map block to the class implementation file starting with the BEGIN_MESSAGE_MAP() macro and ending with the END_MESSAGE_MAP() macro. The BEGIN_MESSAGE_MAP() macro accepts two parameters: the class name for which the message map is defined, and the base class to search if the class for which the message map is defined does not include a handler function for the message. The following code shows the message map macros for a class named CMainDlg. Notice in the implementation file that the first parameter sent to the BEGIN_MESSAGE_MAP() macro is CMainDlg, which is the class name for which the message map is defined. The second parameter, CDialog, is CMainDlg's base class. The MFC framework searches the CDialog class if the CMainDlg class does not include a handler function for a message.

```
// MainDlg.h
class CMainDlg : public CDialog {
public:
...
    DECLARE_MESSAGE_MAP()
};

// MainDlg.cpp
...

BEGIN_MESSAGE_MAP(CMainDlg, CDialog)
END_MESSAGE_MAP()
```

If a class interface file includes a DECLARE_MESSAGE_MAP() macro, then its implementation file *must* include the BEGIN_MESSAGE_MAP() and END_MESSAGE_MAP() macros.

Inside the BEGIN_MESSAGE_MAP() and END_MESSAGE_MAP() macros you place other macros that represent messages you want a specific window to handle. One of the more common message macros you will use is the **ON_COMMAND macro**, which represents the events that are raised when a user selects a menu option or presses a shortcut key. The ON_COMMAND macro takes two parameters: a resource ID and the name of a message handler function. When the Run() function sends a message to the appropriate window, it also passes the resource ID of the element that raised the event. The message map then searches its list for a macro that matches the message type and that includes the correct resource ID as its first parameter. If the message map finds a matching macro, then it executes the function specified as the macro's second parameter.

The following code shows an example of a message map that includes two ON_COMMAND macros, one for a menu resource ID named ID_FILE_NEW (the New command on a File menu), and one for a resource ID named ID_FILE_OPEN (the Open command on a File menu). The ON_COMMAND macro for the ID_FILE_NEW resource executes a message handler named OnFileNew(), and the ON_COMMAND macro for the ID_FILE_OPEN resource executes a message handler named OnFileOpen(). Both message handlers are inherited functions that are being called directly from the CWinApp class. Notice that you do not include semicolons following a handler function's name.

```
BEGIN_MESSAGE_MAP(CExample, CDialog)
  ON_COMMAND(ID_FILE_NEW, CWinApp::OnFileNew)
  ON_COMMAND(ID_FILE_OPEN, CWinApp::OnFileOpen)
END_MESSAGE_MAP()
```

To give the MFC Calculator program its functionality, you will use the **BN_CLICKED macro**, which is raised for the BN_CLICKED event. The BN_CLICKED event occurs when a user clicks a button. Using a message map with the BN_CLICKED macro is much easier than the technique used in Windows API programming, in which you need to compare each button's window handle to the handle that was passed to the window procedure's lParam parameter.

You associate dialog controls with an event by using the Control Events button in each control's Properties window or by using the Event Handler Wizard. If you highlight a dialog control, such as a button, and then click the Control Events button in the Properties window, you will see a list of the events that are available for that control. Clicking the text box next to each event name displays an arrow you can click that lists a command that will add a suggested handler function name for that particular event. Figure 10-33 shows an example of the suggested handler function name for a button control's BN_CLICKED event.

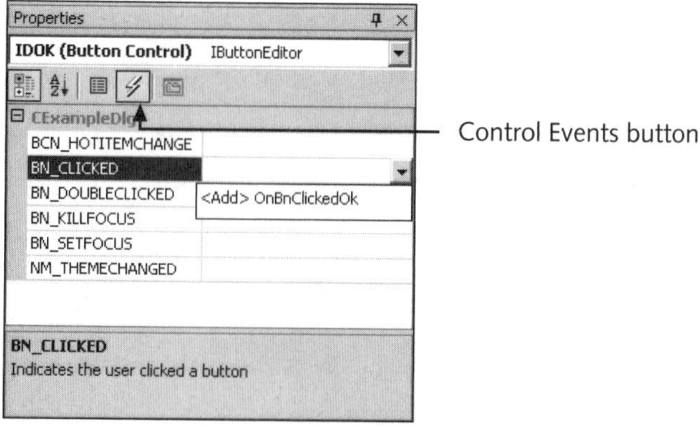

Figure 10-33 Control events for a button control in the Properties window

Selecting the command shown in Figure 10-33 creates the following event handler function:

```
void CExampleDlg::OnBnClickedOk()
{
  // TODO: Add your control notification handler code here
}
```

The **Event Handler Wizard** provides an automated way of associating a dialog control with an event. You use the Event Handler Wizard by highlighting a dialog control and then by selecting Add Event Handler from the Menu submenu on the Edit menu. The Event Handler Wizard allows you to select the message type from a list, assign a custom name to the event handler, and select the specific class to which you want to add the event handler. Figure 10-34 shows an example of the Event Handler Wizard dialog box.

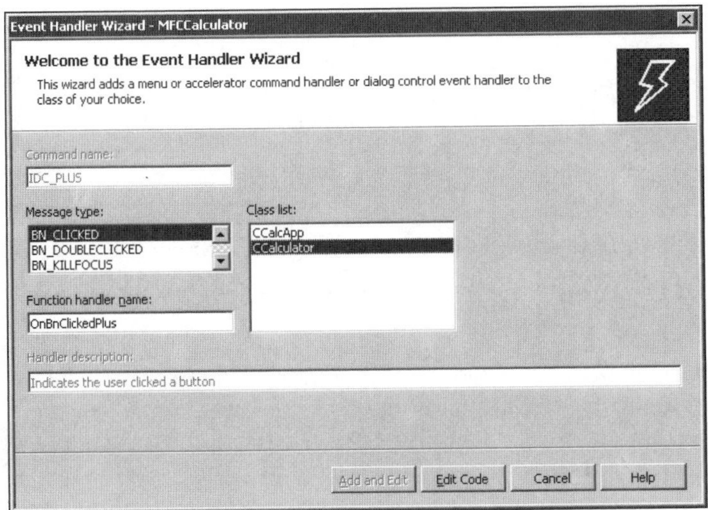

10

Figure 10-34 Event Handler Wizard dialog box

Another way to add an event handler function is to double-click a particular dialog control in Dialog Editor, which creates and opens a handler function for the control's default event in the project's dialog class. For example, the default event for a button control is the BN_CLICKED event. Double-clicking a button control in the Dialog Editor creates and opens a BN_CLICKED event handler function for the control.

Which method you use to add an event handler to your MFC programs is entirely up to you because each method performs the same task. However, using the Control Events button of the Properties window can be a little more confusing than the Event Handler Wizard. For this reason, you will use the Event Handler Wizard in this book to add event handlers to your MFC programs.

The Windows API version of the Calculator program also uses the global setNumbers() and runCalculation() functions to give the program its functionality. In the MFC program, you create these functions as member functions of the CCalculator class. Additionally, the global variables used by the setNumbers() and runCalculation() functions are created as data members of the CCalculator class. Message handler functions for each of the buttons execute the setNumbers() and runCalculation() functions and execute other required code. Another major change in the functions is that they now include UpdateData() functions to handle the exchange of data between the IDC_DISPLAY edit box and the m_sDisplay variable.

Note that with the MFC version of the Calculator program, you could have converted the char data members into CString data members. In order to concentrate on how to make the program work in MFC, however, you will leave the char variables as is.

To give the Calculator program its functionality, first you will add the required data members along with the setNumbers() and runCalculation() member functions.

To add the required data members along with the setNumbers() and runCalculation() member functions:

1. Open the **Calculator.h** file in the Code Editor window.
2. First add **`#include <cstring>`** after the `#include "resource.h"` statement.
3. As shown in Figure 10-35, add a new `private` section with data member declarations above the class's closing brace:

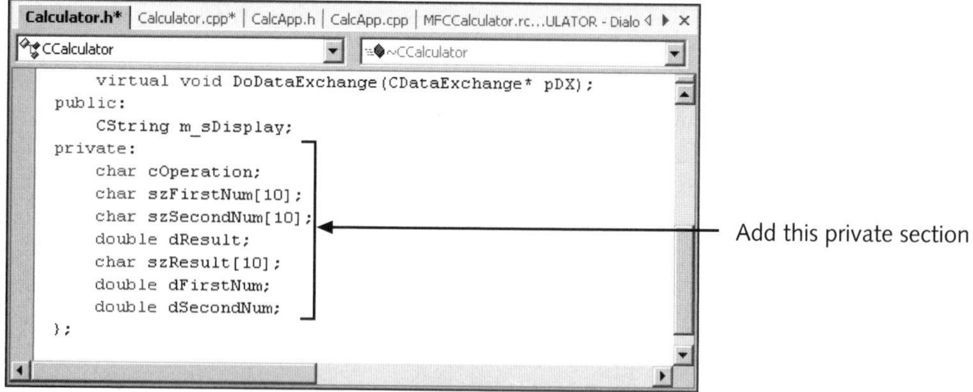


```
    virtual void DoDataExchange(CDataExchange* pDX);
public:
    CString m_sDisplay;
private:
    char cOperation;
    char szFirstNum[10];
    char szSecondNum[10];
    double dResult;
    char szResult[10];
    double dFirstNum;
    double dSecondNum;
};
```

Figure 10-35 New private section with data member declarations added to the CCalculator class

4. Add two member function declarations to the public section, as shown in Figure 10-36.

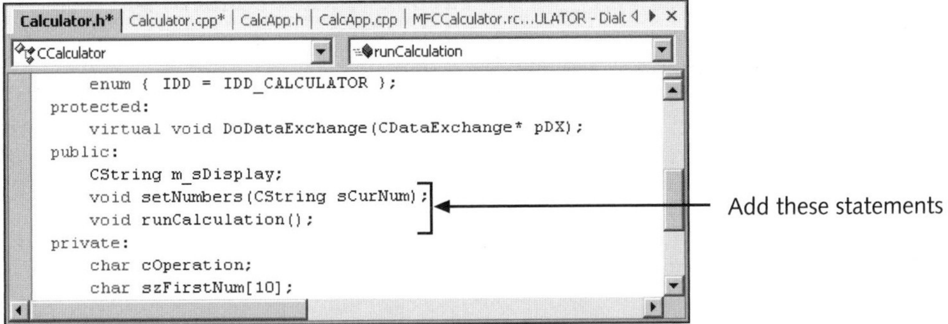

Figure 10-36 New member function declarations added to the section of the CCalculator class

5. Open the **Calculator.cpp** file in the Code Editor window and add to the end of the file the following setNumbers() function definition that builds the left and right operands. Notice that instead of including the SetWindowText() function, as you did in the Windows API program, this MFC version assigns the value of the current operand to the m_sDisplay variable, and then updates the display in the dialog box by passing a value of FALSE to the UpdateData() function.

```
void CCalculator::setNumbers(CString sCurNum)
{
    if(cOperation == '0') {
    strcat(szFirstNum, sCurNum);
    m_sDisplay = szFirstNum;
    }
    else {
    strcat(szSecondNum, sCurNum);
    m_sDisplay = szSecondNum;
    }
    UpdateData(FALSE);
}
```

6. Following the setNumbers() function definition, add the runCalculation() function definition that performs the calculation. This function is virtually identical to the function you created in the Windows API program, except that the dResult and szResult variables are now declared as data members. Also, instead of using the SetWindowText() function to update the display in the dialog box, the m_sDisplay variable is now used with the UpdateData() function.

10

```
void CCalculator::runCalculation()
{
    if (cOperation == '+') {
        dResult = dFirstNum + dSecondNum;
    }
    else if (cOperation == '-') {
        dResult = dFirstNum - dSecondNum;
    }
    else if (cOperation == '*') {
        dResult = dFirstNum * dSecondNum;
    }
    else if (cOperation == '/') {
        dResult = dFirstNum / dSecondNum;
    }
    _gcvt(dResult, 10, szResult);
    m_sDisplay = szResult;
    UpdateData(FALSE);
    cOperation = '0';
    strcpy(szFirstNum, "");
    dFirstNum = 0;
    strcpy(szSecondNum, "");
    dSecondNum = 0;
}
```

7. Finally, initialize the data members by modifying the CCalculator constructor function in the Calculator.cpp file, as shown in Figure 10-37.

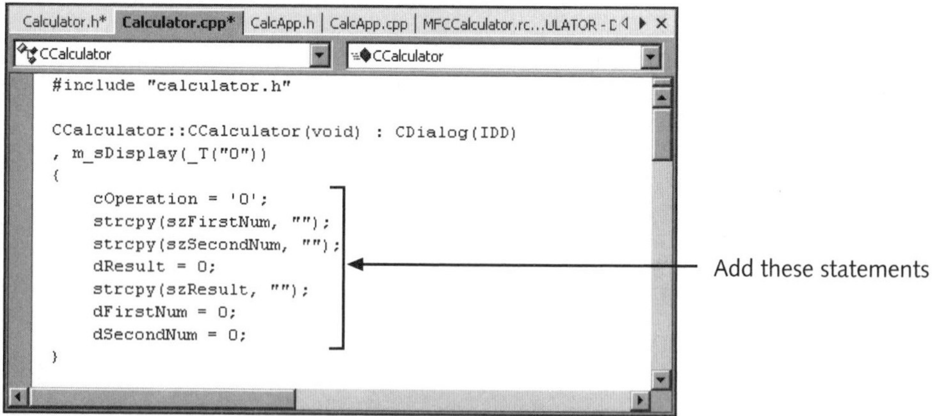

Figure 10-37 New data members initialized in the CCalculator constructor function

Next, you will use the Event Handler Wizard to add message handler functions for each button that execute the setNumbers() and runCalculation() functions and other required code. Note that you do not need to manually add the message map macros because the Event Handler Wizard will automatically add them for you if they do not already exist.

To add message handler functions for each button that execute the setNumbers() and runCalculation() functions and other required code:

1. Open the **IDD_CALCULATOR** dialog box in the Dialog Editor.
2. Click the **Clear** button and open the Event Handler Wizard by selecting **Add Event Handler** from the Menu submenu on the Edit menu. In the Event Handler Wizard dialog box, select **BN_CLICKED** from the Message type list and **CCalculator** in the Class list box. Accept the suggested function name of OnBnClickedClear, and then click the **Add and Edit** button. Visual C++ adds an event handler function named OnBnClickedClear() for the Clear button and opens to the function in the Calculator.cpp file. Replace the `// TODO` comment in the OnBnClickedClear() function with the following code, which appears in boldface, that resets each of the data members and sets the IDC_CLEAR control to a value of 0 by calling the UpdateData() function as follows:

```
void CCalculator::OnBnClickedClear()
{
    cOperation = '0';
    strcpy(szFirstNum, "");
    dFirstNum = 0;
    strcpy(szSecondNum, "");
    dSecondNum = 0;
    m_sDisplay  = "0";
    UpdateData(FALSE);
}
```

3. Repeat Steps 1 and 2 to add BN_CLICKED message handler functions for the rest of the buttons in the dialog window. After creating each message handler function, add the appropriate code to each function definition as follows:

```
void CCalculator::OnBnClickedPlus()
{
    cOperation = '+';
    dFirstNum = atof(szFirstNum);
}
void CCalculator::OnBnClickedMinus()
{
    cOperation = '-';
    dFirstNum = atof(szFirstNum);
}
void CCalculator::OnBnClickedMultiply()
{
    cOperation = '*';
    dFirstNum = atof(szFirstNum);
}
void CCalculator::OnBnClickedDivide()
```

10

```
{
   cOperation = '/';
   dFirstNum = atof(szFirstNum);
}
void CCalculator::OnBnClickedZero()
{
   setNumbers("0");
}
void CCalculator::OnBnClickedOne()
{
   setNumbers("1");
}
void CCalculator::OnBnClickedTwo()
{
   setNumbers("2");
}
void CCalculator::OnBnClickedThree()
{
   setNumbers("3");
}
void CCalculator::OnBnClickedFour()
{
   setNumbers("4");
}
void CCalculator::OnBnClickedFive()
{
   setNumbers("5");
}
void CCalculator::OnBnClickedSix()
{
   setNumbers("6");
}
void CCalculator::OnBnClickedSeven()
{
   setNumbers("7");
}
void CCalculator::OnBnClickedEight()
{
   setNumbers("8");
}
void CCalculator::OnBnClickedNine()
{
   setNumbers("9");
}
void CCalculator::OnBnClickedPoint()
{
   setNumbers(".");
}
void CCalculator::OnBnClickedEquals()
```

```
{
   dSecondNum = atof(szSecondNum);
   runCalculation();
}
```

4. Rebuild and execute the program, and then test the calculator to see if the calculations function correctly. Your program should function the same as the Windows API program you created in the last chapter.

5. Close the MFC Calculator window by clicking the **Close** icon in the title bar or by pressing **Escape**.

Building an Application Framework with the MFC Application Wizard

You have now examined several of the most important pieces of an MFC framework. Although there are other important aspects of the MFC framework that you still need to explore, at this point you should be able to understand the parts of a simple dialog-based application created with the MFC Application Wizard. Therefore, you will now use the MFC Application Wizard to create a dialog-based application so that you can examine the automatically generated code and classes. After all of the work you put into building the MFC Calculator program from scratch, you might wish that you had just skipped right to this section of the chapter! Remember, however, that in order to understand the MFC framework as a whole, you first need to understand its individual pieces.

After you create the dialog-based application using the MFC Application Wizard, you still might not recognize much of what you see in the MFC framework. However, much of the MFC framework code is automatically created when run the MFC Class Wizard, so you do not need to worry about it. Parts of the MFC framework that you will not recognize include error-checking functions, message handlers, and other code that you will examine in later chapters. Additionally, the syntax for some of the code may be a little more complex than the syntax introduced earlier in this chapter. For instance, in an MFC program created with the MFC Application Wizard, the DoModal() function returns a Windows API data type of INT_PTR instead of an `int` value. However, you should be able to recognize the application class, the window class, and the dialog resource file and class.

One important aspect of MFC programs that you will not find in the MFC Class Wizard-generated program is AfxWin.h include files. Instead, the StdAfx.h file manages the inclusion of AfxWin.h and other MFC headers. By allowing StdAfx.h to manage the inclusion of the required MFC header files, you never need to worry about making sure you have included AfxWin.h or any other MFC header into your classes.

To create a dialog-based application using the MFC Application Wizard:

1. Use the MFC Application Wizard to add a new project named **AppWizardExample** in the **Chapter.10** folder in your Visual C++ Projects folders.
2. The MFC Application Wizard executes and starts to walk you through the steps involved in creating an MFC program. Click the **Application Type** tab and select **Dialog based** from the application choices.
3. The next three tabs are unavailable because they do not apply to dialog-based applications, so skip ahead and click the **User Interface Features** tab, which allows you to select the features you want to include in your program. You will see two selected objects: the System menu check box and the About box check box. A System menu is a standard Windows component that appears as an icon in an application's title bar and includes commands such as the Minimize and Maximize commands. An About box is another standard Windows component that displays information about an application and is usually available from an application's Help menu. Leave the System menu check box and About box check box selected.
4. Click the **Advanced Features** tab and clear the **ActiveX controls** and **Common Controls Manifest** check boxes.
5. Click the **Generated Classes** tab, which displays the classes that the MFC Application Wizard will add to your new project. You can also change several items, including the class names and base classes. You will work with this tab in future chapters. Leave the default options as they are, and click the **Finish** button to create the project.
6. The project should immediately open to the Dialog Editor and display an automatically created dialog box. Before you do anything else, build the project and execute the program. The program will run and display the dialog box that appears in the Dialog Editor. The MFC Application Wizard did all the work for you by creating the application class, the dialog class, and the other code required by the program. Click **OK** or **Cancel** to close the program.
7. Now examine the source files listed in Solution Explorer. The AppWizardExample.cpp file is the application window, the AppWizardExample.rc file is the dialog resource file, and the AppWizardExampleDlg.cpp file is the dialog class for the dialog resource file. The stdAfx.cpp file is used by the StdAfx.h file to manage the inclusion of the required MFC header files.

8. Although you will not examine every file in detail, at least look at the application class files. First, open the application class header file, **AppWizardExample.h**, in the Code Editor window. You should recognize the code in this file, including the InitInstance() function declaration and the DECLARE_MESSAGE_MAP() macro.

9. Now open the **AppWizardExample.cpp** file in the Code Editor window. Although you may not be able to recognize all of the code and macros, you should be able to recognize most of it, including the message map declaration and the code within the InitInstance() function that instantiates and displays the dialog window. Also, notice the hooks within several of the functions (the comments that begin with // TODO).

Now that you understand the basics of how MFC programs function, in future chapters you will use the MFC Application Wizard to build new programs.

Chapter Summary

- The Microsoft Foundation Classes, or MFC, is a class library that helps programmers create Windows-based applications.
- Visual C++ provides the Microsoft Foundation Class framework, or MFC framework, for short, which is basically a skeleton application created from MFC classes that you can use as a basis for your program.
- A hook is a location in a program where a programmer can insert code that enhances functionality.
- The CWinApp class, also known as the application class, is responsible for initializing, starting, running, and stopping an MFC windows application.
- The CWnd class encapsulates the various Windows API functions, data types, and other code used for creating and instantiating windows.
- A macro represents C++ code, constants, and other programming elements and is defined using the #define preprocessor directive.
- An application class is the starting point of any MFC application.
- When you derive an application object, you must override the virtual InitInstance() function and instantiate a global object of your application class.
- The MFC classes that derive from the CWnd class are used for creating the different types of windows that are visible to the user.
- The Create() function creates the window itself when an object of the window class is instantiated.

- MFC programming uses a ShowWindow() function to display windows. You call the ShowWindow() function from the application class's InitInstance() function using an instantiated object of the window class.
- A resource is a graphical user interface element or type of stored information that is used by a Windows application.
- Resource editors allow you to quickly create and modify resources in a graphical environment.
- The Properties window in Visual C++ (and other Visual Studio tools) is used for managing the properties of various elements in a project, including the properties of resources.
- Applications that use a dialog box as their primary interface window are called dialog-based applications.
- Modal dialog boxes require users to close or cancel the dialog box before they can continue working with the application.
- Modeless dialog boxes do not need to be closed before returning to another window in the application.
- Controls are user interface items such as check boxes, command buttons, text boxes, and other objects. In Visual C++, you add controls to a dialog box using the Toolbox in the Dialog Editor.
- MFC provides a special mechanism called dialog data exchange, or DDX, to handle the exchange of values between controls and variables.
- A message map associates messages with message handler functions.
- Much of the MFC framework code is automatically created when you run the MFC Class Wizard.

Review Questions

1. A ______________ is a location in a program where a programmer can insert code that enhances functionality.
    a. block
    b. plug
    c. hook
    d. gap

2. Which of the following is a global MFC function?
   a. `Create();`
   b. `UpdateData();`
   c. `MessageBox();`
   d. `AfxMessageBox();`
3. A ______________ represents C++ code, constants, and other programming elements and is defined using the #define preprocessor directive.
   a. global function
   b. MFC data member
   c. macro
   d. script
4. MFC class names begin with ______________.
   a. MFC
   b. MF
   c. C
   d. W
5. MFC class data members are prefixed with ______________.
   a. mfc_
   b. m_
   c. mf_
   d. w_
6. Most of the MFC classes are defined in the ______________ file.
   a. mfcwin.h
   b. mfcclass.h
   c. afxwin.h
   d. mfcapi.h
7. Which is the correct declaration for the InitInstance() function?
   a. `virtual WND InitInstance();`
   b. `virtual BOOL InitInstance();`
   c. `virtual void InitInstance();`
   d. `virtual HWND InitInstance(CString);`

8. Where must you declare an application class object?
   a. at the global level of the application class
   b. inside the InitInstance() function
   c. in the application class constructor
   d. in the application interface file
9. Which function creates the window itself when an object of the window class is instantiated?
   a. Open()
   b. Initiate()
   c. Start()
   d. Create()
10. From where must you call the ShowWindow() function?
    a. the application class constructor
    b. the window class constructor
    c. the InitInstance() function
    d. the window class interface file
11. It is common practice to declare all resource constants in an interface file named ________________ in order to make it easier to reference them in your program.
    a. resource.rc
    b. resource.h
    c. recource.cpp
    d. recource.rs
12. What do you use to modify the resource ID, caption, and other settings of a resource?
    a. the MFC Application Wizard
    b. MFC Class Wizard
    c. the Solution Explorer window
    d. the Properties window
13. You create a dialog box using a dialog resource and ________________.
    a. the AfxMessageBox() function
    b. a window resource
    c. a dialog class derived from the CFrameWnd class
    d. a dialog class derived from the CDialog class

14. Applications that use a dialog box as their primary interface window are called ________________.
    a. dialog box programs
    b. message box programs
    c. dialog-based applications
    d. utility functions
15. ________________ dialog boxes require the user to close or cancel the dialog box before they can continue working with the application.
    a. Modal
    b. Modeless
    c. Primary
    d. Stateless
16. ________________ do not need to be closed before returning to another window in the application.
    a. Modal
    b. Modeless
    c. Primary
    d. Stateless
17. You display a dialog box window using the ________________ function.
    a. Dialog()
    b. ShowWindow()
    c. DoModal()
    d. ShowDialog()
18. Which mechanism does MFC provide to handle the exchange of values between controls and variables?
    a. Dialog Data Exchange
    b. Dialog Data Validation
    c. Data Extraction Protocol
    d. Control Value Exchange
19. What is the correct syntax to use with the UpdateData() function to transfer values from control data members to the dialog box controls?
    a. `UpdateData(TRUE);`
    b. `UpdateData(FALSE);`
    c. `UpdateData(SEND);`
    d. `UpdateData(RECEIVE);`

10

20. Which macro must you place in an interface file to declare a message map?
    a. DECLARE_MESSAGE_MAP()
    b. START_MESSAGE_MAP()
    c. MESSAGE_MAP()
    d. OPEN_MESSAGE_MAP()
21. The first parameter of the BEGIN_MESSAGE_MAP() macro designates the class name for which the message map is defined. What is the second parameter of the BEGIN_MESSAGE_MAP() macro?
    a. the base class from which the current class derives
    b. the function to execute for any messages the message map does not handle
    c. the base class to search if the class for which the message map is defined does not include a handler function for a message
    d. The BEGIN_MESSAGE_MAP() macro does not take a second parameter.
22. The ________________ file manages the inclusion of AfxWin.h and other MFC headers in an application created with the MFC Class Wizard.
    a. CCmdTarget.h
    b. CObject.h
    c. AfxMessage.h
    d. StdAfx.h

PROGRAMMING EXERCISES

1. Modify the following class so that it is an application class. Be sure to add the appropriate functions and declarations to the implementation file.

```
// RealEstate.h
class CRealEstateApp {
public:
   CRealEstateApp();
   virtual ~ CRealEstateApp();
};
// RealEstate.cpp
#include "RealEstate.h"
CRealEstate:: CRealEstate () {
}
CRealEstate::~CRealEstate () {
}
```

2. Modify the following class so that it is a window class that derives from CFrameWnd:

```
// RealEstateFrameWnd.h
class CRealEstateFrameWnd {
public:
   CRealEstateFrameWnd();
   virtual ~ CRealEstateFrameWnd();
};
// RealEstateFrameWnd.cpp
#include "RealEstateFrameWnd.h"
CRealEstateFrameWnd::CRealEstateFrameWnd() {
}
CRealEstateFrameWnd::~ CRealEstateFrameWnd () {
}
```

3. Modify the implementation file for the application class you created in Exercise 1 so that it displays a window from the window class you created in Exercise 2.

4. Add to the following InitInstance() function appropriate code that displays a modal dialog window based on a class named CTransportationDlg. Also include an `if` statement that checks whether the user clicked the OK button or the Cancel button. If the user clicks the OK button, display a message box with the text *You clicked OK*. If the user clicks the Cancel button, display a message box with the text *You clicked Cancel*.

```
BOOL CTransportationApp::InitInstance() {
}
```

5. Programs created with MFCs have an additional tool available, the TRACE macro, which can be used for tracing the value of variables as a program executes. Search the MSDN Library for information on the TRACE macro. How do you use the TRACE macro? MFC programs do not use console windows. Where is the output from the TRACE macro written to?

6. Another debugging tool that can be used with MFC programs is the ASSERT macro, which allows you to test the validity of an expression. Search the MSDN Library for information on the ASSERT macro. Why would you use the ASSERT macro in your programs? Describe a scenario in which you would use the ASSERT macro to test your program before releasing it.

7. The MFC TRACE macro and the ASSERT macro are only used for debugging purposes. What happens if you create a Win32 Release build of a project that includes these macros? Are they compiled with the release build? Search the MSDN Library for your answer.

Programming Projects

1. Create a modal dialog-based application project. In the main dialog resource, include a single OK button whose caption reads *Close Application*. Also, add a second dialog box resource to the project. The second dialog box should display the text *Are you sure you want to close the application?* Also include an OK button that closes the application, and a Cancel button that displays the main dialog window. When the user clicks the Close Application button in the main dialog window, display the second dialog window.
2. Create a dialog-based application that displays the names of state capitals. In the dialog box window include one Edit control and three Button controls. Change the caption of each Button control to the name of a state in your area of the country. When the user clicks a button, display that state's capital in the Edit control.
3. Create a dialog-based application to be used as a software development bug report. Use as many types of controls as you can, including Static Text, Edit, Button, and Check Box controls. Look in the MSDN Library for information on how to use individual control types. For example, you may include a Check Box control for the different types of software installed on a system. Format the Edit controls so that they are read-only, and only allow users to fill in values by selecting the various controls on the dialog box. Change each control's resource ID to a value that matches the purpose of each control. Once users finish filling out the bug report and click the OK button, display all of their entries in another dialog box window before closing the application.
4. Create a dialog-based application to be used for tracking, documenting, and managing the process of interviewing candidates for professional positions. Include Edit controls such as a candidate's name, business knowledge, and the interviewer's comments. Also, include other controls, such as Check Box and Radio Button, for recording information such as professional appearance and computer skills. Change each control's resource ID to a value that matches the purpose of each control. Once the interviewer completes the interview and clicks the OK button, display the candidate's information in another dialog box window before closing the application.
5. Create an MFC version of the Moving Estimator program you worked on in Chapter 4. Use a single dialog window for the application. Gather the service charges using six Edit controls: Distance in miles, Weight in pounds, # of flights of stairs, # of appliances, # of pianos, and Extra charges. Use an additional Edit control to display the total moving estimate. Make the Edit control containing the total moving estimate read-only so that users cannot directly enter information in it. Update the value in the moving estimate Edit control using the ON_EN_KILLFOCUS macro, which is raised when a control, such as an edit box, loses the "focus." When you click a control or press your Tab key to move to a

control, that control is said to have the focus. Focus refers to the control that is currently active in the window. When you click off the control or press your Tab key to move to another control, the original control is said to lose focus. The MFC version of Moving Estimator program should use the ON_EN_KILLFOCUS macro to recalculate the cost of the move each time a new number is entered into an edit box and that edit box loses focus.

6. Create an MFC version of the Retirement Planner program you created in Chapter 5. Use a single dialog window for the application. Gather the calculation figures using five Edit controls: Annual Contribution, Annual Yield, Current Age, Retirement Age, and Inflation. Also use three Button controls to calculate the values: Total Future Value, Total Present Value, and Total Interest Earned.
7. Create an MFC version of the Conversion Center program you created in Chapter 8. Use the main dialog window as a menu from which the user can select the type of conversion he or she wants to perform. Use separate dialog windows for each of the conversion types. Allow the user to perform multiple conversions within the same window. For example, for the temperature conversion, include a single Edit Box control where the user can enter the temperature he or she wants to convert. Also include two Button controls, one that converts from Celsius to Fahrenheit and another that converts from Fahrenheit to Celsius. Display the results in a read-only Edit Box control.

CHAPTER

11

WORKING WITH DOCUMENTS AND VIEWS

In this chapter you will learn:

- About documents and views
- About document interfaces
- How to work with the CView class
- How to work with the CDocument Class
- How to store data

The gates of hell are open night and day;
Smooth the descent, and easy is the way:
But to return, and view the cheerful skies,
In this the task and mighty labor lies.

Virgil's Aeneid

PREVIEW: THE INVOICE PROGRAM

In this chapter, you will work with an Invoice program to learn how to use documents with MFC programs. The Invoice program allows you to create individual invoices that you can save to a disk file, the same way you can save document or spreadsheet files from programs such as Word or Excel.

To preview the Invoice program:

1. Create a **Chapter.11** folder in your Visual C++ Projects folder.
2. Copy the **Chapter11_Invoice** folder from the Chapter.11 folder on your Data Disk to the Chapter.11 folder in your Visual C++ Projects folder, and then open the Invoice project in Visual C++.

3. Open Solution Explorer window and expand the Source Files folder, if necessary. The Invoice.cpp file is the implementation file for the program's application class, and the MainFrm.cpp file is the implementation file for the frame class. Notice the InvoiceDoc.cpp and InvoiceView.cpp files. These are the implementation files for the CInvoiceDoc and CInvoiceView classes that give the MFC program its ability to work with documents. The CInvoiceDoc class derives from the CDocument class and is used for managing and storing a document's data. The CInvoiceView class derives from the CView class and is used for displaying to a user the data that is managed and stored by the CInvoiceDoc class.
4. Open the **InvoiceDoc.cpp** file. If you scroll through the file, you will see some typical MFC functions. You will also see an OnNewDocument() function, a Serialize() function, and a DeleteContents() function. The OnNewDocument() function executes each time the user creates a new document. To reinitialize the data each time a new document is created, the OnNewDocument() function calls the DeleteContents() function, which reinitializes the class's data members. The Serialize() function is what actually writes a document's data to and reads a document's data from a disk file. Figure 11-1 shows the OnNewDocument(), Serialize(), and DeleteContents() functions.

```
BOOL CInvoiceDoc::OnNewDocument()
{
     DeleteContents();
     if (!CDocument::OnNewDocument())
          return FALSE;
     return TRUE;
}
void CInvoiceDoc::Serialize(CArchive& ar)
{
     if (ar.IsStoring())
     {
          ar << m_dAmount1; ar << m_dAmount2;
          ar << m_dAmount3; ar << m_sDescription2;
          ar << m_sDescription1; ar << m_sDescription3;
          ar << m_iQuantity1; ar << m_iQuantity2;
          ar << m_iQuantity3; ar << m_dRate1;
          ar << m_dRate2; ar << m_dRate3;
          ar << m_dTotal; ar << m_sDate;
          ar << m_sCustomer; ar << m_sInvoice;
          ar << m_sTerms;
     }
     else
     {
          ar >> m_dAmount1; ar >> m_dAmount2;
          ar >> m_dAmount3; ar >> m_sDescription2;
          ar >> m_sDescription1; ar >> m_sDescription3;
          ar >> m_iQuantity1; ar >> m_iQuantity2;
          ar >> m_iQuantity3; ar >> m_dRate1;
          ar >> m_dRate2; ar >> m_dRate3;
          ar >> m_dTotal; ar >> m_sDate;
          ar >> m_sCustomer; ar >> m_sInvoice;
          ar >> m_sTerms;
     }
}
void CInvoiceDoc::DeleteContents()
```

Figure 11-1 InvoiceDoc.cpp

```
{
     m_dAmount1 = 0.0; m_dAmount2 = 0.0;
     m_dAmount3 = 0.0;
     m_sDescription2 = _T("");
     m_sDescription1 = _T("");
     m_sDescription3 = _T("");
     m_iQuantity1 = 0; m_iQuantity2 = 0;
     m_iQuantity3 = 0; m_dRate1 = 0.0;
     m_dRate2 = 0.0; m_dRate3 = 0.0;
     m_dTotal = 0.0; m_sDate = _T("");
     m_sCustomer = _T(""); m_sInvoice = _T("");
     m_sTerms = _T("");
     CDocument::DeleteContents();
}
```

Figure 11-1 InvoiceDoc.cpp (continued)

5. Next, open the **InvoiceView.cpp** file. The CInvoiceView class displays a document's data, which is stored in the CInvoiceDoc class. If you scroll through the file, you will see a number of member functions that give the program its functionality, along with some typical MFC functions. You will also see an OnUpdate() function. The OnUpdate() function updates the display in the window if any of the data in the CInvoiceDoc changes. Notice that the statements in the function's body use a CInvoiceDoc class pointer (pDoc) to a function named GetDocument(). The GetDocument() function allows classes derived from CView to communicate with their associated classes that are derived from CDocument. Figure 11-2 shows the OnUpdate() function.


```
void CInvoiceView::OnUpdate(CView* pSender, LPARAM lHint,
CObject* pHint)
{
     CInvoiceDoc* pDoc = GetDocument();
     m_dAmount1 = pDoc->m_dAmount1;
     m_dAmount2 = pDoc->m_dAmount2;
     m_dAmount3 = pDoc->m_dAmount3;
     m_sDescription1 = pDoc->m_sDescription1;
     m_sDescription2 = pDoc->m_sDescription2;
     m_sDescription3 = pDoc->m_sDescription3;
     m_iQuantity1 = pDoc->m_iQuantity1;
     m_iQuantity2 = pDoc->m_iQuantity2;
     m_iQuantity3 = pDoc->m_iQuantity3;
     m_dRate1 = pDoc->m_dRate1;
     m_dRate2 = pDoc->m_dRate2;
     m_dRate3 = pDoc->m_dRate3;
     m_dTotal = pDoc->m_dTotal;
     m_sDate = pDoc->m_sDate;
     m_sCustomer = pDoc->m_sCustomer;
     m_sInvoice = pDoc->m_sInvoice;
     m_sTerms = pDoc->m_sTerms;
     UpdateData(FALSE);
}
```

Figure 11-2 OnUpdate() function

6. Build and execute the Invoice program. The program allows you to enter three lines of billing information. Enter some data in the document. After

you enter numbers into the Quantity and Rate edit boxes, the values in the Amount boxes and the TOTAL box are recalculated when each edit box loses focus. After entering data, select the **Save** command from the program's File menu. A typical Windows Save dialog box, which is a common dialog box, appears. Save the invoice as Invoice001 in the Chapter.11 folder in your Visual C++ projects folder, and then close the Invoice program.

7. Open the Invoice program again, and select the **Open** command on the File menu to reopen the invoice you just saved. Alternately, you can select the filename from the list of most recently opened files at the bottom of the File menu. Figure 11-3 shows an example of the Invoice program window.

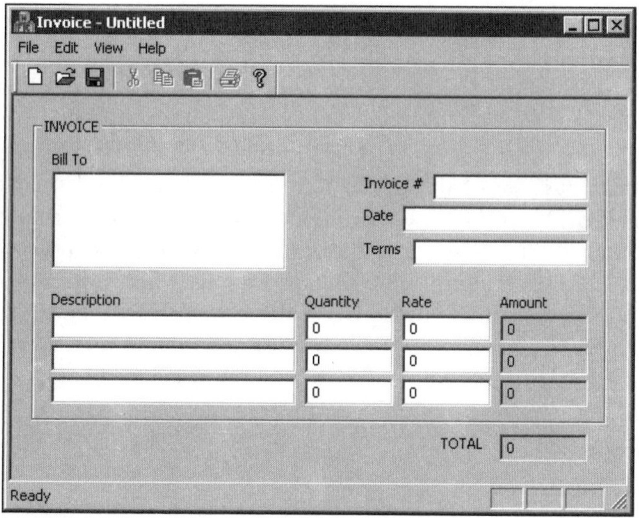

Figure 11-3 Invoice program window

8. Click the Close button to close the Invoice program window.

INTRODUCTION

So far, all of the projects you have created performed some sort of calculation or task that was applicable only to the current application session. For example, the console application-based Chemistry Quiz, Retirement Planner, Conversion Center, and Building Estimator programs gathered information from the user, returned a result, and then exited. Even the Windows-based Calculator and Moving Estimator programs simply returned a result to the user that existed only until the program closed.

A very important missing piece of the application puzzle is the ability to store data that you can retrieve later. The Chemistry Quiz, for instance, would be much more useful if you could store each student's test results. The Moving Estimator program would be much more valuable if you could save moving estimates for different customers. With the current application, you could enter information for one customer, calculate the results, write the information down on a piece of paper, and then reenter new information for another customer. But this is the Information Age—you should not need to manually write information on a piece of paper. Instead, you should be able to save that information to a computer's hard drive. As another example, consider the Invoice program you will create in this chapter. What good would the Invoice program be if you could not save the data you entered? Your only alternative would be to print a hard copy of each invoice that you would then store in a filing cabinet. If you had to store a hard copy, then you might as well use a typewriter to fill in a preprinted form, or even write your invoice information onto the preprinted form by hand. It is worth noting that not all applications need to have the ability to save different sets of data. For instance, you would not normally need to enter or save different sets of data for the simple Calculator programs you have created. However, the ability to enter and save different sets of data would certainly add to the functionality of other programs, such as the Chemistry Quiz and Moving Estimator programs.

The MFC applications you have worked with in the last two chapters have been dialog based in that dialog boxes control the entire functionality of the program. More powerful, and often more useful, MFC applications are usually document based. A **document** is a file that is associated with a particular application and that contains different sets of data depending on your program's functionality and each user's needs. Users can create their own documents within a document-based application that they can later reopen for viewing or editing. You have probably worked with many document-based applications. Microsoft Word and Excel are both document-based applications that you may have seen or worked with at one time or another. Documents do not necessarily need to be complex like the word-processing documents you use with Word or the spreadsheet documents you use with Excel. Instead, a document can consist of a simple set of data, such as the customer information you enter into the Moving Estimator program.

In this chapter, you will learn how to create document-based MFC applications that users can use to open and save their own files. Before you actually create a document-based application using the MFC Application Wizard, you need to understand the basics of documents and views.

Documents and Views

When you first learned how to work with MFC programming in Chapter 10, you briefly reviewed how to create a window class based on the CFrameWnd class, which creates a simple window with a frame, title bar, control menu, and control buttons. With the exception of dialog-based applications, almost all MFC programs include a window class derived from the CFrameWnd class. The windows displayed by classes that derive from the CFrameWnd class are referred to as frame windows. To refresh your memory on the

CFrameWnd class, Figure 11-4 shows a basic MFC program that includes an application class and a window class derived from the CFrameWnd class. The most significant parts of the window class are the class header declaration that derives the class from the CFrameWnd class, and the Create() function that creates the window itself when an object of the window class is instantiated. The window is then displayed by calling the ShowWindow() function from the application class's InitInstance() function using an instantiated object of the window class. Figure 11-5 shows the frame window displayed by the basic MFC application.

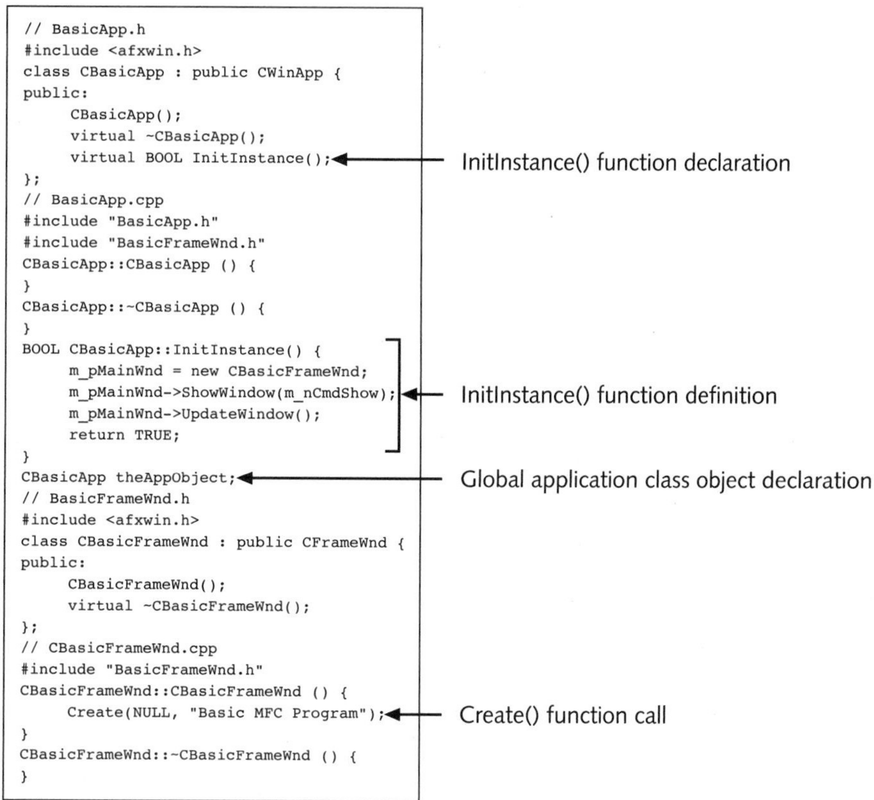

```
// BasicApp.h
#include <afxwin.h>
class CBasicApp : public CWinApp {
public:
     CBasicApp();
     virtual ~CBasicApp();
     virtual BOOL InitInstance();
};
// BasicApp.cpp
#include "BasicApp.h"
#include "BasicFrameWnd.h"
CBasicApp::CBasicApp () {
}
CBasicApp::~CBasicApp () {
}
BOOL CBasicApp::InitInstance() {
     m_pMainWnd = new CBasicFrameWnd;
     m_pMainWnd->ShowWindow(m_nCmdShow);
     m_pMainWnd->UpdateWindow();
     return TRUE;
}
CBasicApp theAppObject;
// BasicFrameWnd.h
#include <afxwin.h>
class CBasicFrameWnd : public CFrameWnd {
public:
     CBasicFrameWnd();
     virtual ~CBasicFrameWnd();
};
// CBasicFrameWnd.cpp
#include "BasicFrameWnd.h"
CBasicFrameWnd::CBasicFrameWnd () {
     Create(NULL, "Basic MFC Program");
}
CBasicFrameWnd::~CBasicFrameWnd () {
}
```


Figure 11-4 Basic MFC application with a frame window

There are many similarities in appearance between the dialog windows you have created and frame windows—remember that both the CDialog class and the CFrameWnd class derive from the CWnd class. However, you need to understand an important difference between dialog-based applications and applications based on the CFrameWnd class. Whereas a dialog-based application is used for creating applications that perform some sort of calculation or task that is applicable only to the current application session, applications based on the CFrameWnd class are document based. A **document-based application** allows users to read and write to documents that are associated with the application.

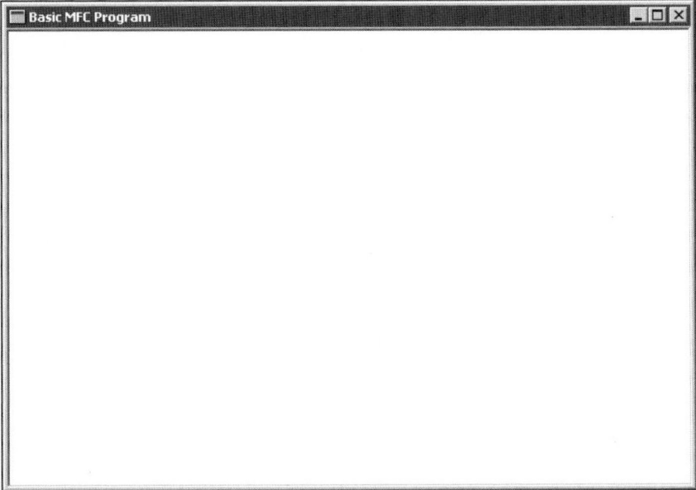

Figure 11-5 Basic MFC program window

Whereas dialog windows contain controls that are used for interacting with your program's functionality, a frame window provides a frame around one or more views of a document. To understand what this means, you need to understand the MFC document/view architecture. The **MFC document/view architecture** separates a program's data from the way that data is displayed and accessed by users. A program's data (the document) is *managed and stored* by a class derived from the **CDocument class**. How a document-based program's data is *displayed* to the user is controlled by one or more classes derived from the **CView class**. In simpler terms, CDocument manages and stores a program's data, while CView displays it. Although CDocument and CView are separate classes that do not derive from each other, the classes you derive from them will communicate with each other, as illustrated in Figure 11-6.

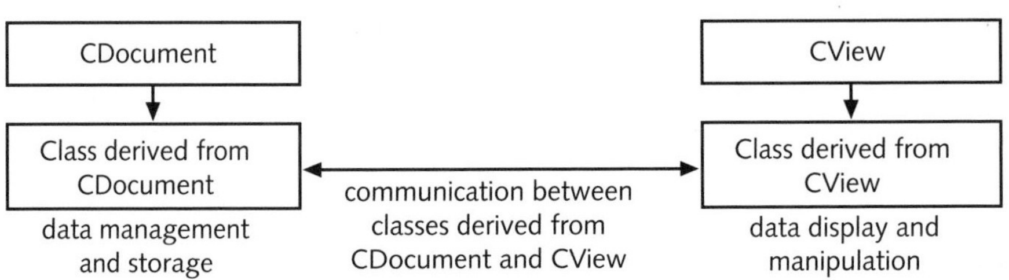

Figure 11-6 Relationship between CDocument and CView classes

CDocument and CView classes are added to an MFC program in addition to an application class derived from CWinApp, and a window class derived from CFrameWnd. Although Windows applications can include multiple CDocument classes, most include only a single CDocument class to contain the application's data.

With many types of Windows applications today, however, you can simultaneously view the same data in several different ways. Therefore, your MFC programs may include multiple CView classes for displaying and manipulating the data contained in a single CDocument class. Each view is just a different way of looking at the same data. Figure 11-7 illustrates the concept of multiple CView classes that display and manipulate the data contained in a single CDocument class.

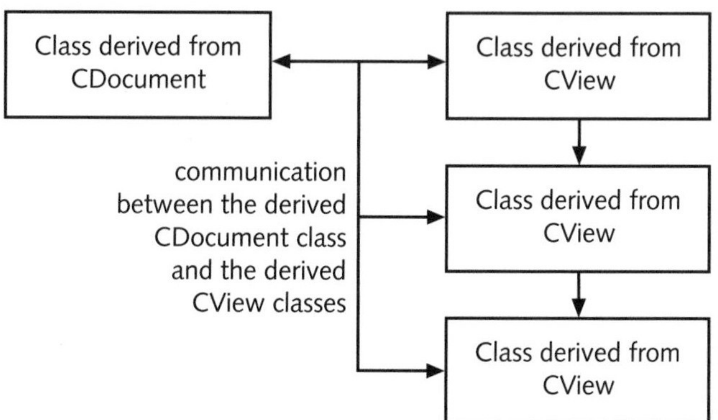

Figure 11-7 Relationship between CDocument class and multiple CView classes

Note that the data stored in a CDocument class can be displayed and manipulated by multiple CView classes. However, a CView class can display and manipulate only the data from a single CDocument class.

As an example of document/view architecture, consider Microsoft Excel, which is a typical Windows spreadsheet application that employs the document/view architecture. Although you will not be creating anything quite so ambitious, a spreadsheet application provides one of the best ways to illustrate the document/view architecture because it can present the same data in multiple formats. Modern spreadsheet programs allow you to enter data into a table (the spreadsheet) and then present the data as pie charts, bar charts, and so on. The Excel spreadsheet represents the *document* portion of the program, whereas each chart represents a *view*. Figure 11-8 shows an example of a simple Excel spreadsheet containing several charts that graphically display portions of the spreadsheet data.

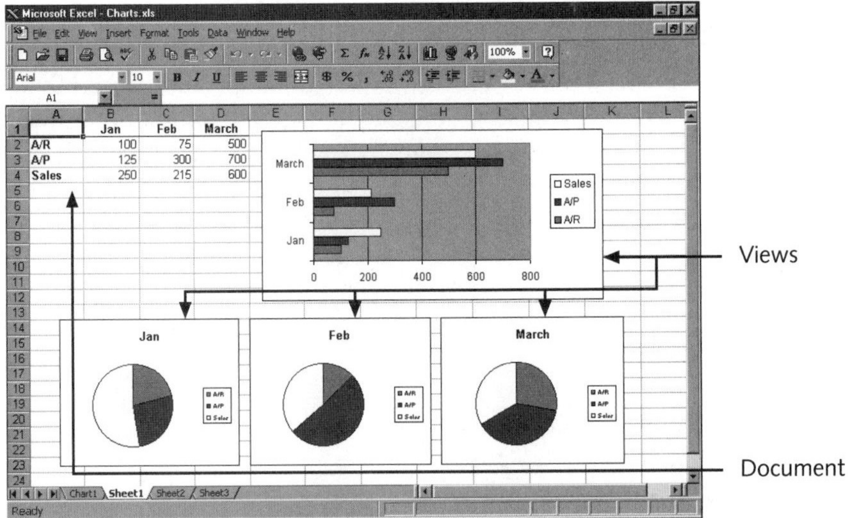

Figure 11-8 Excel "document" and "views"

You are not required to use document/view architecture in your document-based MFC programs; you can actually turn off document/view architecture support when you use the MFC Application Wizard to build a document-based application. However, by enabling document/view architecture, your document-based MFC applications automatically inherit a wide range of document functionality that allows you to read and write documents, use print and print preview functions, and perform other types of document-specific tasks. Automatically inheriting this functionality means you do not have to manually write much of the code that is required by document-based applications; Visual C++ generates the code for you. Document-based MFC programs that are created without document/view architecture do not automatically inherit document functionality. You can add these features by hand, although doing so can be a tedious task, especially for a beginner.

As you start examining the specifics of how to build a document-based application, keep in mind that you will use the MFC Application Wizard to generate much of the application. The code generated by the MFC Application Wizard is designed by some of the best software engineers in the world and can be somewhat complex. Because Visual C++ generates this code for you, you will not examine every single segment of code in detail. Instead, you will focus on learning to find the hooks in the generated code that you can use to build your own applications.

You should ultimately understand the code created by the MFC Application Wizard. The more you understand about the intricacies of MFC programming, the better your own programs will be.

DOCUMENT INTERFACES

Current Windows programming supports two models for document-based applications: single document interface and multiple document interface. The **single document interface**, or **SDI**, allows users to have only one document open at a time. The **multiple document interface**, or **MDI**, allows users to have multiple documents open at the same time. The Notepad text editor application that is part of Windows is an example of an SDI program. Examples of MDI applications include Word, Excel, and Visual C++. You can usually tell that an application is an MDI application if it includes a Window option in the menu bar. Figure 11-9 shows an example of the single document that is available in Notepad, and Figure 11-10 shows an example of Word with multiple documents open.

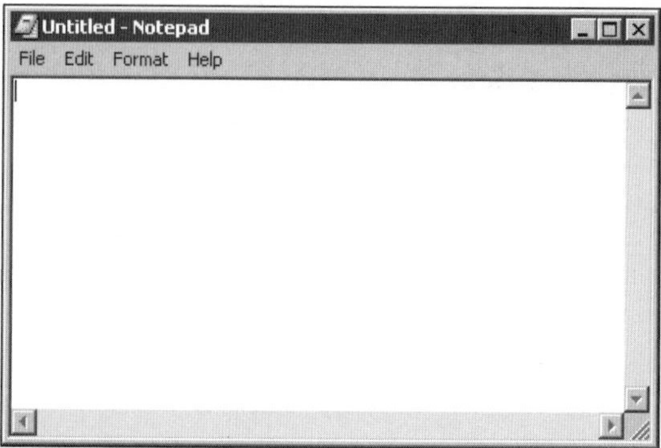

Figure 11-9 Notepad single document interface

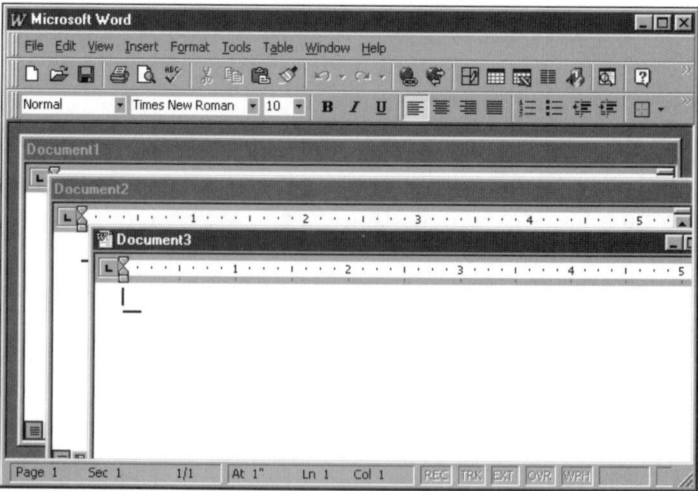

Figure 11-10 Word multiple document interface

Figure 11-10 shows the MDI interface for Word 97. Later editions of Word, such as Word 2000, also support the MDI interface. However, instead of being contained within the Word application window, each document appears in its own separate window.

In this book, the focus is on creating SDI applications because MDI applications are too difficult for new and intermediate users to learn. Once you develop your MFC skills a bit further, you may want to explore on your own how to create MDI applications.

THE CVIEW CLASS

Earlier you learned that a frame window provides a frame around one or more views of a document. You display a window created from a class derived from CView *within* a frame window. This means the CView window is a child of a frame window. The CView window completely covers the frame window's client area, but does not cover visual interface elements such as the title bar or scroll bars. Figure 11-11 illustrates this concept.

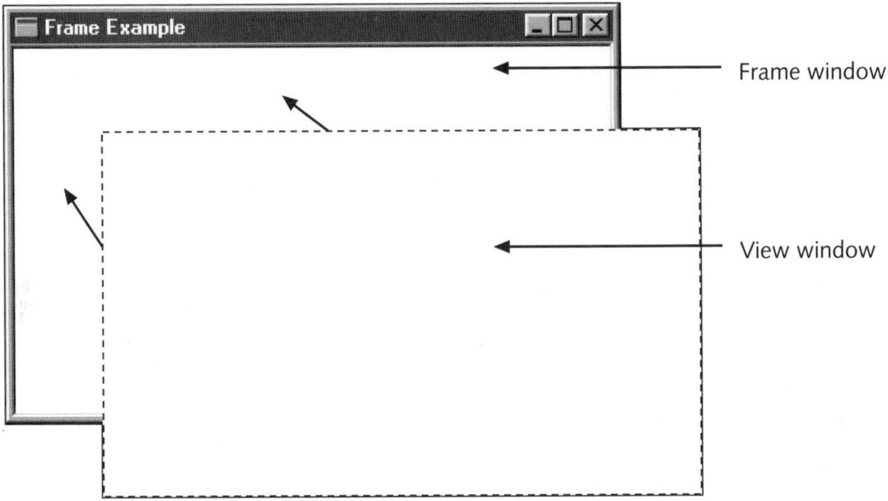

Figure 11-11 Frame window and view window

11

You may wonder why view windows are necessary at all. Why not just display document data and interface controls directly in the frame window? The answer is that using view windows allows you to display multiple views within the same window. If you want to show a different view of data and you only have a single frame window, then you need to replace the existing view with the view you want to see—you would not be able to see both views of the data simultaneously. With view windows, you can divide the frame's client area into different views, depending on the needs of your program. For example, you may have a program that tracks company sales by region. In one view of the program you can display the sales numbers for each region; in a second view you can display the same data graphically in a pie chart, as illustrated in Figure 11-12. You are working with the same data in both views—you are just choosing to display the data graphically in the second view.

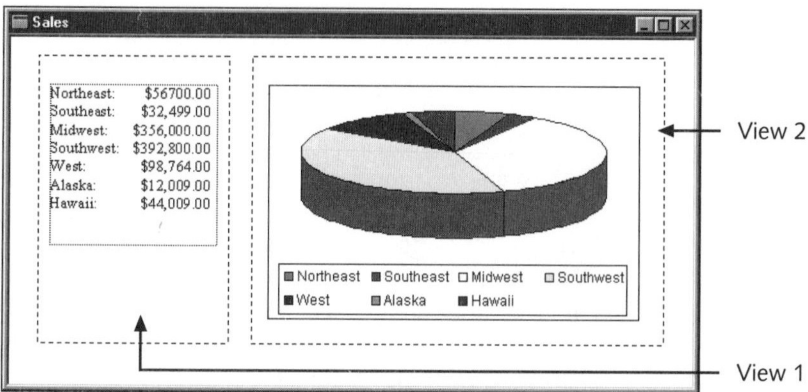

Figure 11-12 Multiple views in a frame window

Do not confuse a multiple document interface with multiple views of the same document. The multiple document interface allows you to open multiple, separate documents within the same program, while multiple views allow you to display multiple views of a single document.

In this chapter, you will not actually create projects with more than one view. You still need to understand, however, that the reason for using the document/view architecture is that it allows you to separate your program's data from how it is displayed. Multiple views allow you to display the same data in multiple formats if necessary.

CView Child Classes

When you create a document-based application, you can base your view class on CView or on one of the classes that derive from CView, which are described in Figure 11-13. The classes that derive from CView are used for creating more specialized view windows. In this chapter, you will use the CEditView and CListView classes.

Class	Description
CCtrlView	Creates view windows that use tree, list, and rich edit controls
CDaoRecordView	Displays DAO database records in dialog box controls
CEditView	Creates a simple text editor
CFormView	Creates a view window that is similar to a dialog box window and that can be edited in the Dialog Editor
CHTMLView	Displays HTML documents
CListView	Creates a view window that uses list controls
COLeDBRecordView	Displays OLE DB database records in dialog box controls
CRecordView	Displays database records in dialog box controls
CRichEditView	Creates a view window that uses rich edit controls
CScrollView	Provides scrolling support to view windows
CTreeView	Creates a view window that uses tree controls

Figure 11-13 CView child classes

Next, you will start creating a simple text editor SDI application based on the CEditView class.

To start creating a simple text editor SDI application based on the CEditView class:

1. Using the MFC Application Wizard, create a new project named **SimpleTextEditor**. Save the project in the **Chapter.11** folder in your Visual C++ Projects folder.
2. The MFC Application Wizard executes and starts to walk you through the steps involved in creating an MFC program. Click the Application Type tab and select **Single document** from the application choices as shown in Figure 11-14. Be sure to leave the **Document/View architecture support** check box selected and the other options in the tab set to their default settings. Then click the **Compound Document Support** tab.

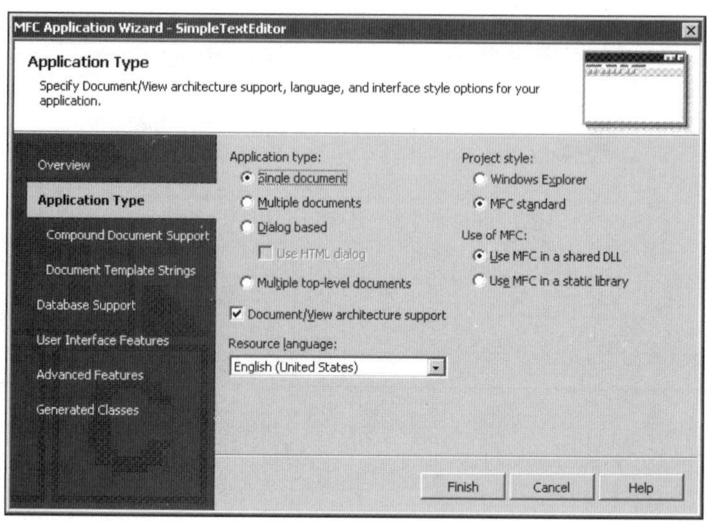

Figure 11-14 The Application Type tab of the MFC Application Wizard

3. In the Compound Document Support tab, you can select your project's compound document support options. A compound document contains data of different formats, such as graphics, sound files, video files, spreadsheets, and so on. Because you will not be using data in different formats, leave the compound document support option set to **None**. Additional options are available, depending on the type of compound document you select. Because you selected no compound document support, the additional options are not available to you. Figure 11-15 shows the Compound Document Support tab. Click the **Document Template Strings** tab to continue.

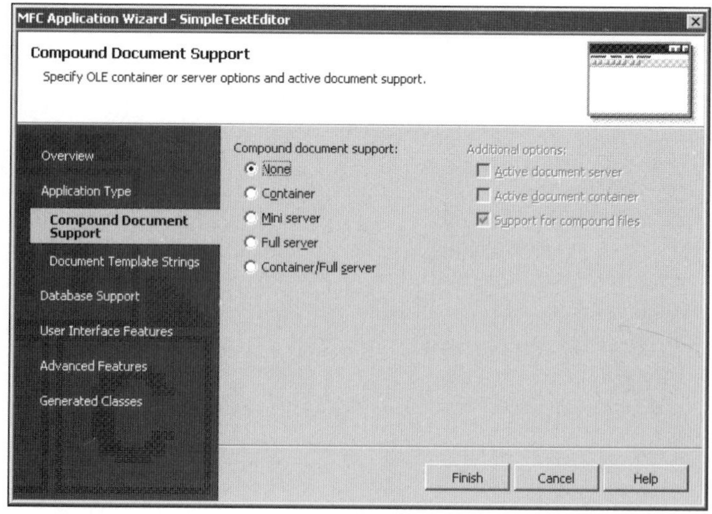

Figure 11-15 The Compound Document Support tab of the MFC Application Wizard

4. The Document Template Strings tab contains various text boxes for customizing the document settings in a document-based application, as shown in Figure 11-16. A description of each text box in the Document Template Strings tab is listed in Figure 11-17. Type **ste** (for *S*imple *T*ext *E*ditor) in the File extension box. Any files saved from the Text Editor program will be saved with an extension of .ste. Notice as you are typing the file extension that the Filter Name text box changes to reflect the new file extension. Modify the Main frame caption text box to read **Text Editor Program**. Leave the rest of the options as they are. Click the **Database Support** tab to continue.

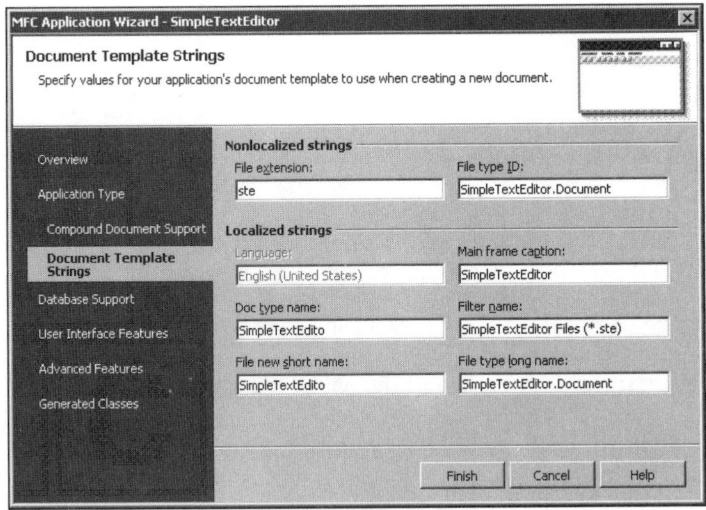

Figure 11-16 The Document Template Strings tab of the MFC Application Wizard

11

Text Box	Description
File extension	Designates a file extension to use with files created from your program
File type ID	Identifies the document type in the System Registry
Main frame	Sets the text that will appear in the application's main title bar caption
Doc type name	Designates the document type under which a file can be grouped
Filter name	Determines the file type and extension that appear in the Open and Save dialog boxes
File new name (short name)	Determines the name that will appear in the New dialog box if the application supports more than one file type
File type name (long name)	Designates the file type name in the System Registry and is used with an Automation server program as the Automation object's long filename

Figure 11-17 Text box descriptions in the Document Template Strings tab of the MFC Application Wizard

5. In the Database Support tab, leave the data support option set to **None** as shown in Figure 11-18, and then click the **User Interface Features** tab. Data support options are used for databases, which you will examine in the next chapter.

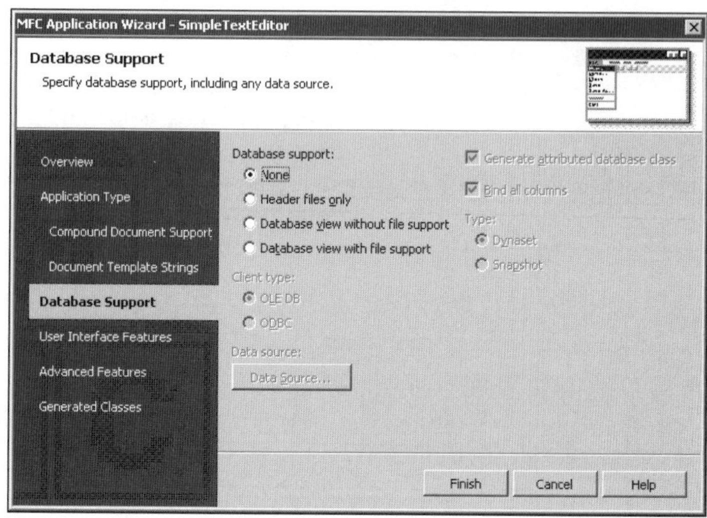

Figure 11-18 The Database Support tab of the MFC Application Wizard

6. The options in the User Interface Features tab are used for determining the style of the application window and are self-explanatory. For example, clicking the Maximize box check box adds a maximize box to the application window. Figure 11-19 shows an example of the User Interface Features tab. Leave the options in the User Interface Features tab as they are and click the **Advanced Features** tab.
7. In the Advanced Features tab, clear all of the selected check boxes, as shown in Figure 11-20. By default, the number of files displayed in a document-based application's most recently used file list is set to four, which is fine for the program you are creating. Click the **Generated Classes** tab to continue.

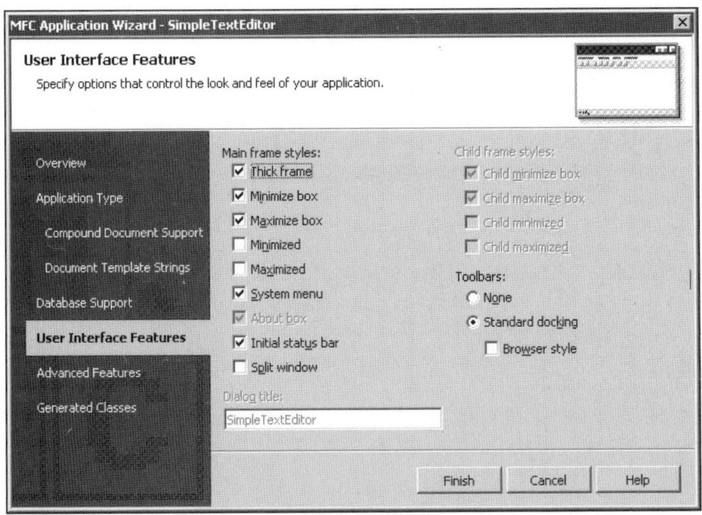

Figure 11-19 The User Interface Features tab of the MFC Application Wizard

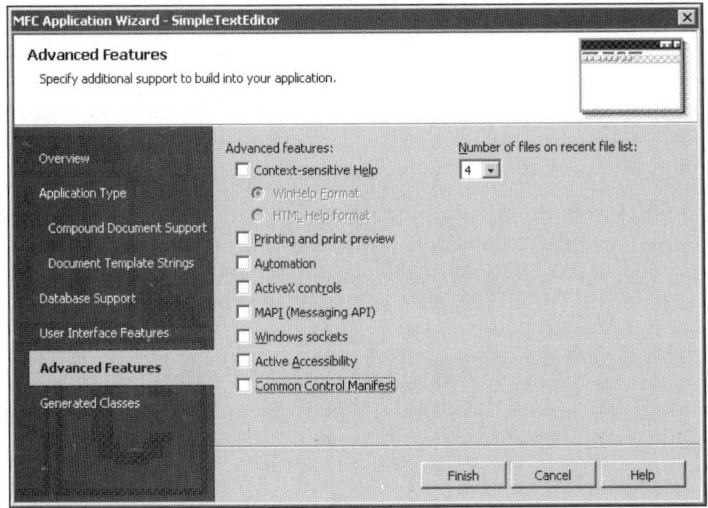

Figure 11-20 The Advanced Features tab of the MFC Application Wizard

8. The Generated Classes tab, shown in Figure 11-21, lists the names that will be assigned to each class in the Text Editor program. The Base class combo box also displays the child classes of the CView class upon which you can base the application. Select **CEditView** from the Base class combo box and then click the **Finish** button.

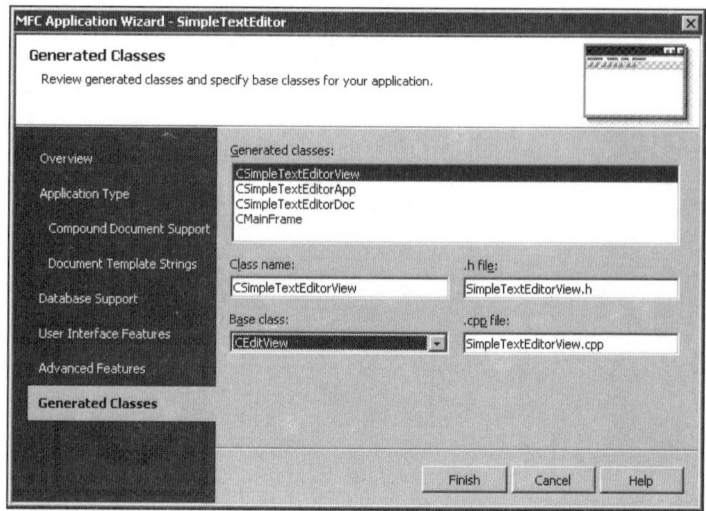

Figure 11-21 The Generated Classes tab of the MFC Application Wizard

Once the MFC Application Wizard finishes creating your program, open the Solution Explorer window and examine the files that were created. The MFC Application Wizard should have created two classes with which you are already familiar: an application class named CSimpleTextEditor and a frame class named CMainFrm. (As you look at the file names, remember that the naming convention in MFC programming is to exclude the *C* that precedes class names from the text filenames when they are saved. Therefore, SimpleTextEditor.cpp is the file containing the CSimpleTextEditor class definition.) Although the code in these classes is more complex than the basic MFC program you saw in Chapter 8, the classes still perform the same task of creating and instantiating the application and frame window of an MFC program. The MFC Application Wizard also creates a CView class named CSimpleTextEditorView that derives from CEditView and a CDocument class named CSimpleTextEditorDoc.

Open the SimpleTextEditorView.h file in your Code Editor window and examine the code. An example of the class declaration portion of the file is shown in Figure 11-22.

You should recognize the usual constructor, destructor, and DECLARE_MESSAGE_MAP declarations that are found in all CWnd-derived classes that are generated by the MFC Application Wizard. The class also includes declarations for the following functions: PreCreateWindow(), AssertValid(), and Dump(). The **PreCreateWindow() function** is called by the MFC framework before a frame window is created in order to specify the window's styles. This function applies the styles you specified in the User Interface Features tab of the MFC Application Wizard. The AssertValid() and Dump() functions are special diagnostic functions that are available to MFC programs. The AssertValid() function checks the validity of an object when it is created. The Dump() function "dumps" information about a program's objects to the Output window for diagnostic purposes. See the MSDN Library for detailed information on each of these functions.

```
// SimpleTextEditorView.h : interface of the CSimpleTextEditorView class
//

#pragma once
class CSimpleTextEditorView : public CEditView
{
protected: // create from serialization only
     CSimpleTextEditorView();
     DECLARE_DYNCREATE(CSimpleTextEditorView)

// Attributes
public:
     CSimpleTextEditorDoc* GetDocument() const;

// Operations
public:

// Overrides
     public:
virtual BOOL PreCreateWindow(CREATESTRUCT& cs);
protected:

// Implementation
public:
     virtual ~CSimpleTextEditorView();
#ifdef _DEBUG
     virtual void AssertValid() const;
     virtual void Dump(CDumpContext& dc) const;
#endif

protected:

// Generated message map functions
protected:
     DECLARE_MESSAGE_MAP()
};
#ifndef _DEBUG  // debug version in SimpleTextEditorView.cpp
inline CSimpleTextEditorDoc* CSimpleTextEditorView::GetDocument() const
   { return reinterpret_cast<CSimpleTextEditorDoc*>(m_pDocument); }
#endif
```

Figure 11-22 SimpleTextEditorView.h

The SimpleTextEditorView.h file also includes a macro named DECLARE_DYNCREATE() and an inline function named GetDocument(). The DECLARE_DYNCREATE() macro dynamically creates an object from data stored in a file. The GetDocument() function returns a pointer to the document associated with a view. You will learn more about the DECLARE_DYNCREATE() macro and GetDocument() function later in this chapter.

Next, you will build the Simple Text Editor program and examine its functionality.

To build the Simple Text Editor program and examine its functionality:

1. Build and execute the program. Even though you have not written any of your own code, the program is a complete and functional text-editing program.

11

2. Examine the program's menu and toolbars. All of the commands on both the menu bar and toolbar are functional. Enter some text into the document area, and then use the Cut, Copy, and Paste commands to manipulate the text. Open one of the menus and move your cursor over each command without selecting it. Notice that a description of each command appears in the status bar at the bottom of the program window. If you hold your mouse over a toolbar button, you will also see a ScreenTip for each button along with a more detailed description of each button in the status bar. The MFC Application Wizard automatically creates basic menu and toolbar commands for you. You will learn how to create and modify menus and toolbars in the next chapter. Figure 11-23 shows an example of the Simple Text Editor program window.

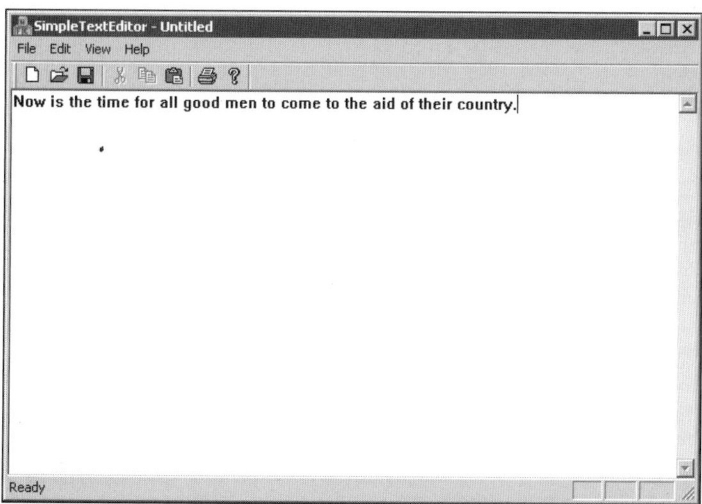

Figure 11-23 Simple Text Editor program window

3. Next, save the document by selecting **Save** from the File menu. Save the file as **text1** in the Chapter.11 folder in your Visual C++ Projects folder. After you save the file, select the **New** command from the File menu to create a new document. If you want to reopen the file you just saved, you can select **Open** from the File menu, or select the filename from the list of most recently opened files at the bottom of the File menu.

If you try to close the program without saving the document, you will see a message box prompting you to save the file, just as you see in most other document-based Windows applications.

4. Close the Simple Text Editor program window.

5. Select **Close Solution** from the File menu to close the SimpleTextEditor project.

The Simple Text Editor program requires no further programming on your part because the MFC Application Wizard automatically created most of its functionality. However, more advanced programs such as the Invoice program require that you add custom code. Next, you will start building the Invoice program.

To start creating the Invoice program:

1. Create a new project named **Invoice** using the MFC Application Wizard. Save the project in the **Chapter.11** folder in your Visual C++ Projects folder.
2. Click the Application Type tab and select **Single document** from the application choices. Be sure to leave the **Document/View architecture support** check box selected. You can skip the Compound Document Support tab because its default data support option of None is fine for our purposes. Click the **Document Template Strings** tab.
3. In the Document Template Strings tab, type **inv** in the File extension box. Any files saved from the Invoice program will be saved with an extension of .inv. Leave the rest of the options as they are in the Document Template Strings tab and click the **Database Support** tab.
4. In the Database Support tab, leave the Database support option set to **None**. The default settings in the User Interface Features tab are also fine for our purposes, so skip ahead and click the **Advanced Features** tab.
5. In the Advanced Features tab, clear all of the selected check boxes, but leave the most recently used file list set to four. Click the **Generated Classes** tab to continue.
6. In the Generated Classes tab, select **CFormView** from the Base class combo box, and then click the **Finish** button.
7. Because you cleared the Printing and print preview check box on the Advanced Features tab, you will receive a dialog box confirming that no printing support will be available for the CFormView class. Click the **Yes** button to continue.

11

Next, you will add controls to the Invoice program's view window, along with DDX data members for each control. Because they are so similar to dialog windows, you can use the dialog editor to add controls to a form view window. Figure 11-24 shows an example of how the controls in the window should be placed. You should already be familiar with the Edit Box controls. Two new controls that you have not yet added to a project are the Static Text control and the Group Box control. Static Text controls are simply unchanging text boxes that you use to add instructions and labels to your interface. Group Box controls are used for visually grouping other controls together in a window. Both types of controls are used only for enhancing the visual design of your windows. Do your best when designing the form, and be sure to check your work using the Test Dialog command on the Format menu.

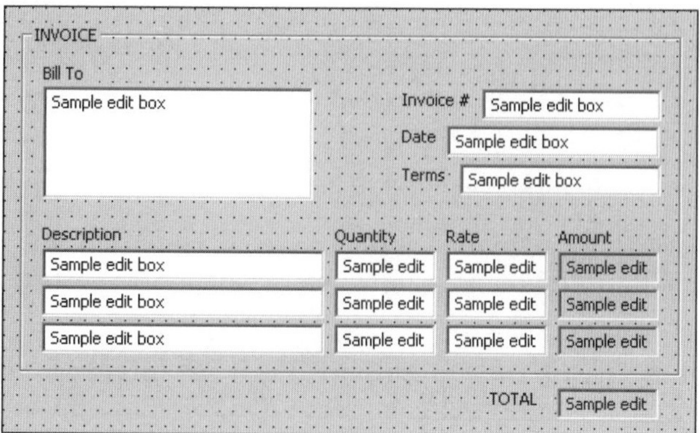

Figure 11-24 Invoice program controls

To add controls to the Invoice program's view window, along with DDX data members for each control:

1. Use Resource View to open the **IDD_INVOICE_FORM** dialog resource in the Dialog Editor. (The IDD_INVOICE_FORM resource ID is automatically assigned by the MFC Application Wizard.) Delete the Static Text control that reads *TODO: Place form controls on this dialog.* Then, add Static Text controls, Edit Box controls, and a Group Box control to the window, using the captions shown in Figure 11-24.
2. Open the **Properties** window for the **Bill To** edit box and change its resource ID to **IDC_CUSTOMER**. Be sure the Multiline and Want return properties are set to **True**.
3. Use the table shown in Figure 11-25 to modify the resource IDs for the rest of the Edit Box controls. Also, make the Amount boxes and TOTAL box read-only.

Edit Box Control	Resource ID
Invoice #	IDC_INVOICE
Date	IDC_DATE
Terms	IDC_TERMS
Description (first line)	IDC_DESCRIPTION1
Description (second line)	IDC_DESCRIPTION2
Description (third line)	IDC_DESCRIPTION3
Quantity (first line)	IDC_QUANTITY1
Quantity (second line)	IDC_QUANTITY2
Quantity (third line)	IDC_QUANTITY3

Figure 11-25 Button captions and resource IDs

Edit Box Control	Resource ID
Rate (first line)	IDC_RATE1
Rate (second line)	IDC_RATE2
Rate (third line)	IDC_RATE3
Amount (first line)	IDC_AMOUNT1
Amount (second line)	IDC_AMOUNT2
Amount (third line)	IDC_AMOUNT3
TOTAL	IDC_TOTAL

Figure 11-25 Button captions and resource IDs (continued)

4. When you are finished adding the controls to the dialog resource, use the Add Variable Wizard to add DDX data members to the CInvoiceView class for each of the controls using the variable names and data types shown in Figure 11-26. For example, for the IDC_CUSTOMER resource ID, click the IDC_CUSTOMER control and select the **Add Variable Wizard** from the Project menu. The Add Member Variable Wizard dialog box appears. In the Add Member Variable Wizard dialog box, type **m_sCustomer** in the Variable name text box. Next, select **Value** in the Category combo box. The option in the Variable type combo box should automatically change to CString. However, be sure to change the Variable type combo box to the `int` or `double` data type for the appropriate DDX data members listed in Figure 11-26.

In order to remove a DDX data member that you either entered incorrectly or no longer need, you must perform three tasks. First, you must delete the variable declaration from the class interface file. Next, you must delete the variable initialization statement in the initializer list of the class constructor definition. Finally, you must delete the associated DDX statement from the DoDataExchange() function definition.

Resource ID	Variable Name	Data Type
IDC_CUSTOMER	m_sCustomer	CString
IDC_INVOICE	m_sInvoice	CString
IDC_DATE	m_sDate	CString
IDC_TERMS	m_sTerms	CString
IDC_DESCRIPTION1	m_sDescription1	CString
IDC_DESCRIPTION2	m_sDescription2	CString
IDC_DESCRIPTION3	m_sDescription3	CString
IDC_QUANTITY1	m_iQuantity1	int

Figure 11-26 DDX data member names and types

Resource ID	Variable Name	Data Type
IDC_QUANTITY2	m_iQuantity2	int
IDC_QUANTITY3	m_iQuantity3	int
IDC_RATE1	m_dRate1	double
IDC_RATE2	m_dRate2	double
IDC_RATE3	m_dRate3	double
IDC_AMOUNT1	m_dAmount1	double
IDC_AMOUNT2	m_dAmount2	double
IDC_AMOUNT3	m_dAmount3	double
IDC_TOTAL	m_dTotal	double

Figure 11-26 DDX data member names and types (continued)

5. Build and execute the program. Although the program is displayed, you still need to add code to give it functionality.
6. Close the Invoice program window.

CView Member Functions

A view class is responsible for graphically displaying a document's data and for handling the manipulation of that data according to user requests. For example, if the document class contains a data member that contains a stock price, then it is up to the view class to display that stock price to the user. Additionally, if the user changes the displayed stock price and clicks a button named Update Stock, then it is also up to the view class to update that data in the document class.

The CView class contains various functions for displaying and manipulating data. The primary CView class member functions that you use to display and manipulate data are as follows:

- OnDraw()
- GetDocument()
- OnUpdate()

One of the most important functions in the CView class is the OnDraw() function, which is used to graphically display and print a document's data. For the Text Editor program, you did not need to worry about displaying the document's data because the display of a text file is handled automatically by the CEditView class. You also do not need to worry about the OnDraw() function for the Invoice program because the Invoice program is based on the CFormView class, which uses the Dialog Editor to create the user interface. Therefore, you will not learn about the OnDraw() function or several other important functions, including OnPrint(), until Chapter 12 in this book. Note that because the OnDraw() function is declared as a pure virtual function in the CView base class, you must override it in any classes that derive from CView.

The GetDocument() Function

The **GetDocument() function** returns a pointer to the document associated with a view. If you examine the header file for the CInvoiceView class, you will see that the GetDocument() function is declared in the public section and returns a pointer data type of the document class, CInvoiceDoc. A pointer to the document is automatically created in the inherited m_pDocument data member. Remember, you will never actually see the m_pDocument data member declared or defined in your document-based program because it has already been declared and defined in a base class.

The GetDocument() function returns a pointer to the m_pDocument data member that you can use anywhere in the view class when you need to access the document's data. For example, if you have a member function in the document class named setStockPrice() that modifies the value of a `double` data member, you can call that function from the view class using the following statement:

```
GetDocument()->setStockPrice(120.5);
```

Rather than calling the GetDocument() function directly, you can assign it to a pointer variable of your document class's type, and then call the pointer variable. Calling a function repeatedly is not as efficient as calling a function once. Therefore, if you know you will need to use a pointer to a document repeatedly in any given instance (such as within the body of a function), then it is usually more efficient to call the GetDocument() function once and assign its `return` value to a pointer variable. You can then use the pointer variable in place of the GetDocument() function. For example, the preceding call to the setStockPrice() function could also be accomplished using the following pDoc pointer:


```
CStocksDoc* pDoc = GetDocument();
pDoc->setStockPrice(120.5);
```

You will actually find two definitions of the GetDocument() function in your view classes: a debug version and a release build version. The debug version of the GetDocument() function is defined in the view class's implementation file and uses the ASSERT() macro and IsKindOf() function to verify the validity of the document pointer. The ASSERT() macro is used for identifying program errors during development, while the IsKindOf() function determines if an object belongs to a particular class or if it derives from a specific class. Once the pointer is verified, it is cast to your document class data type and returned. The following code is an example of the debug version of the GetDocument() function in the InvoiceView.cpp file:

```
CInvoiceDoc* CInvoiceView::GetDocument() const
// non-debug version is inline
{
  ASSERT(m_pDocument->IsKindOf(
     RUNTIME_CLASS(CInvoiceDoc)));
  return (CInvoiceDoc*)m_pDocument;
}
```

The release build version of the GetDocument() function is defined as an inline function in the view class interface file, within a pair of #ifndef and #endif preprocessor directives immediately following the class definition. The release build version does not include the ASSERT() macro or IsKindOf() function and simply returns the pointer to the m_pDocument data member after casting it to the document class data type, as follows:

```
#ifndef _DEBUG  // debug version in InvoiceView.cpp
inline CInvoiceDoc* CInvoiceView::GetDocument() const
   { return reinterpret_cast<CInvoiceDoc*>(m_pDocument); }
#endif
```

Using the #ifndef preprocessor directive is identical to using the #if preprocessor directive with the defined constant expression to determine which portions of a file to compile, depending on the result of a conditional expression. For example, the statement `#if !defined(STOCKS_H)` could also be written as `#ifndef STOCKS_H`. Using the #if preprocessor directive and the defined constant expression, however, is the preferred method. The MFC Application Wizard uses the #ifndef preprocessor directive to define the GetDocument() function in order to provide backward-compatibility with previous versions of C++.

Next, you will add message map functions to the CInvoiceView class along with an updateDataMembers() function. The message map functions will use the EN_CHANGE message. Each time the text in a control changes, its EN_CHANGE message map function calls the updateDataMembers() function. The first statement in the updateDataMembers() function will call the UpdateData() function to update the CInvoiceView class's DDX data members. For the Quantity and Rate controls, the updateDataMembers() function will calculate the Amount and Total control values. The updateDataMembers() function will also use the GetDocument() function to update the CInvoiceDoc class's data members from the CInvoiceView class's DDX data members.

To add message map functions to the CInvoiceView class along with an updateDataMembers() function:

1. In the Dialog Editor, use the Event Handler Wizard, located on the Menu submenu on the Edit menu, to add the following EN_CHANGE message map functions to the CInvoiceView class. The name of each message map function's resource ID is contained in a comment line above each function. For example, to add the OnEnChangeCustomer() message map function, first click the **IDC_CUSTOMER** control in the Dialog Editor, and then select **Add Event Handler** from the Menu submenu on the Edit menu to display the Event Handler Wizard dialog box. Select **EN_CHANGE** in the Message type list, make sure **CInvoiceView** is selected in the Class list box, and then click the **Add and Edit** button. The InvoiceView.cpp file opens to the OnEnChangeCustomer() handler function. Replace the `// TODO` comment with a call to the updateDataMembers() function. Repeat these steps for the rest of the message map functions.

```
// IDC_CUSTOMER
void CInvoiceView::OnEnChangeCustomer() {
     updateDataMembers();
}
// IDC_INVOICE
void CInvoiceView::OnEnChangeInvoice() {
     updateDataMembers();
}
// IDC_DATE
void CInvoiceView::OnEnChangeDate() {
     updateDataMembers();
}
// IDC_TERMS
void CInvoiceView::OnEnChangeTerms() {
     updateDataMembers();
}
// IDC_DESCRIPTION1
void CInvoiceView::OnEnChangeDescription1() {
     updateDataMembers();
}
// IDC_DESCRIPTION2
void CInvoiceView::OnEnChangeDescription2() {
     updateDataMembers();
}
// IDC_DESCRIPTION3
void CInvoiceView::OnEnChangeDescription3() {
     updateDataMembers();
}
// IDC_QUANTITY1
void CInvoiceView::OnEnChangeQuantity1() {
     updateDataMembers();
}
// IDC_QUANTITY2
void CInvoiceView::OnEnChangeQuantity2() {
     updateDataMembers();
}
// IDC_QUANTITY3
void CInvoiceView::OnEnChangeQuantity3() {
     updateDataMembers();
}
// IDC_RATE1
void CInvoiceView::OnEnChangeRate1() {
     updateDataMembers();
}
// IDC_RATE2
void CInvoiceView::OnEnChangeRate2() {
     updateDataMembers();
```

```
}
// IDC_RATE3
void CInvoiceView::OnEnChangeRate3() {
     updateDataMembers();
}
```

2. Next, use the Add Member Function Wizard to add to the CInvoiceView class the updateDataMembers() function. Create the function with a **`return`** type of **`void`** and **`Public`** access. Leave the Static, Virtual, Pure, and Inline check boxes cleared, and do not include any parameters. After the function is created, add the following statements that calculate the Amount and Total control values and update and transfer the values from the CInvoiceView class to the data members in the CInvoiceDoc class:

```
void CInvoiceView::updateDataMembers(void)
{
     UpdateData(TRUE);
     m_dAmount1 = m_iQuantity1 * m_dRate1;
     m_dAmount2 = m_iQuantity2 * m_dRate2;
     m_dAmount3 = m_iQuantity3 * m_dRate3;
     m_dTotal = m_dAmount1 + m_dAmount2 + m_dAmount3;
     UpdateData(FALSE);
     CInvoiceDoc* pDoc = GetDocument();
     pDoc->m_dAmount1 = m_dAmount1;
     pDoc->m_dAmount2 = m_dAmount2;
     pDoc->m_dAmount3 = m_dAmount3;
     pDoc->m_sDescription1 = m_sDescription1;
     pDoc->m_sDescription2 = m_sDescription2;
     pDoc->m_sDescription3 = m_sDescription3;
     pDoc->m_iQuantity1 = m_iQuantity1;
     pDoc->m_iQuantity2 = m_iQuantity2;
     pDoc->m_iQuantity3 = m_iQuantity3;
     pDoc->m_dRate1 = m_dRate1;
     pDoc->m_dRate2 = m_dRate2;
     pDoc->m_dRate3 = m_dRate3;
     pDoc->m_dTotal = m_dTotal;
     pDoc->m_sDate = m_sDate;
     pDoc->m_sCustomer = m_sCustomer;
     pDoc->m_sInvoice = m_sInvoice;
     pDoc->m_sTerms = m_sTerms;
}
```

The OnUpdate() Function

Another important CView member function is the OnUpdate() function. Each view class inherits an **OnUpdate() function** that is called each time the document class changes or whenever the document class executes an UpdateAllViews() function. The OnUpdate() function allows all of the view windows in an application to display the most current data. The **UpdateAllViews() function** is a member function of

CDocument and causes each view window's OnUpdate() function to execute in order to allow each view to display the most recent data. Passing a single value of NULL to the UpdateAllViews() function informs the system that all views in the program should be updated. Note that you execute the UpdateAllViews() function from a derived CDocument class, not a derived CView class.

The inherited default OnUpdate() function does not automatically update its view. You must write your own definition of the OnUpdate() function, which uses the GetDocument() function to retrieve the most recent data values from the document object and then display those values in the view window. For example, if you have a Stocks program that includes a view window named CStocksView that is based on CFormView, you could write the following OnUpdate() function to display the most recent values when the document window executes its UpdateAllViews() function. The code uses the CStocksDoc class's member functions to retrieve the most recent data member values, which are then assigned to DDX data members. The UpdateData() function then copies each DDX data member's value to its associated dialog control. The first statement in the body of the function instantiates a new pointer named pDoc and assigns to it the pointer that is returned from the GetDocument() function. The other statements use the new pDoc pointer to call member functions of the CStocksDoc class.

```
void CStocksView::OnUpdate(CView* pSender,
     LPARAM lHint, CObject* pHint) {
     CStocksDoc* pDoc = GetDocument();
     m_iNumShares = pDoc->getNumShares();
     m_dCurrentValue = pDoc->getCurrentValue();
     m_dPricePerShare = pDoc->getPricePerShare();
     UpdateData(FALSE);
}
```

11

Next, you will add an OnUpdate() function to the Invoice program's CView class. Each time the user creates a new document, the controls in the Invoice program's form need to be reset to their original values. In the next section, you will learn how to reset the document member's data values using the document class's inherited **OnNewDocument() function**, which is called when a user creates a new document. To display the reset values in the form, you must create an OnUpdate() function, which is called automatically after the OnNewDocument() function executes.

To add an OnUpdate() function to the Invoice program's CView class:

1. Open **InvoiceView.cpp** or **InvoiceView.h** in the Code Editor window. If necessary, display the **Properties** window, and then click the **Overrides** button.
2. Locate **OnUpdate** in the properties list and place the insertion point in its value field. Click the drop-down arrow to the right of the value field and select **<Add> OnUpdate**. The new function is created and your cursor moves to the function definition.

3. Modify the OnUpdate() function definition as follows to copy the values of the CInvoiceDoc class's data members to the CInvoiceView class's DDX data members. The last statement in the function passes a value of FALSE to the UpdateData() function to update the controls in the dialog window.

```
void CInvoiceView::OnUpdate(CView* /*pSender*/,
      LPARAM /*lHint*/, CObject* /*pHint*/) {
      UpdateData(TRUE);

      CInvoiceDoc* pDoc = GetDocument();
      m_dAmount1 = pDoc->m_dAmount1;
      m_dAmount2 = pDoc->m_dAmount2;
      m_dAmount3 = pDoc->m_dAmount3;
      m_sDescription1 = pDoc->m_sDescription1;
      m_sDescription2 = pDoc->m_sDescription2;
      m_sDescription3 = pDoc->m_sDescription3;
      m_iQuantity1 = pDoc->m_iQuantity1;
      m_iQuantity2 = pDoc->m_iQuantity2;
      m_iQuantity3 = pDoc->m_iQuantity3;
      m_dRate1 = pDoc->m_dRate1;
      m_dRate2 = pDoc->m_dRate2;
      m_dRate3 = pDoc->m_dRate3;
      m_dTotal = pDoc->m_dTotal;
      m_sDate = pDoc->m_sDate;
      m_sCustomer = pDoc->m_sCustomer;
      m_sInvoice = pDoc->m_sInvoice;
      m_sTerms = pDoc->m_sTerms;
      UpdateData(FALSE);
}
```

THE CDOCUMENT CLASS

One aspect of working with programs created with the MFC Application Wizard that is a little hard to get used to is that most of the work is already done for you. The Simple Text Editor program, for instance, is a complete and functioning program. To create a useful program, however, you still must do some work. For example, with more advanced programs such as the Invoice program, you need to do some additional coding because Visual C++ does not automatically know what type of data you want to read from and write to a file. Once the MFC Application Wizard creates your derived document class, you must perform the following tasks:

- Create data members to temporarily hold the data for the current document
- Override the CDocument class's member functions to customize the creating, loading, and saving mechanisms of the document/view architecture
- Override CDocument's Serialize() member function in order to read the document's data from and write the document's data to a file

In this section, you will learn how to create data members to temporarily hold the data for the current document and how to override some of the CDocument class's member functions to customize the creating, loading, and saving mechanisms of the document/view architecture. Later in the chapter, you will learn how to override CDocument's Serialize() member function in order to read the document's data from, and write the document's data to, a file. Keep in mind that data members stored in a CDocument-derived class and the inherited CDocument member functions are designed to work with the Serialize() member function in order to read information from, and write information to, a file.

CDocument Data Members

You create data members in the CDocument class by adding declarations for each data member to the interface file, the same way you create data members in other classes. You can then initialize each data member in the class constructor and use appropriate *set* and *get* member functions to manipulate each data member.

One of the main differences between CDocument and other types of classes is that you call the *set* and *get* member functions from the view class using the GetDocument() function. For example in the Stocks program, a view class would use the GetDocument() function to call a document class's setStockPrice() and getStockPrice() member functions in order to set and retrieve the values of a stock price data member using the following statements:


```
GetDocument()->setStockPrice(120.5);
GetDocument()->getStockPrice();
```

You must add data members to the Invoice program's derived CDocument class for each of the controls on the Invoice form. Next, you will add data members to the Invoice program's CInvoiceDoc class, which derives from CDocument. To keep things simple, you will use the same names for the CInvoiceDoc class that you used for the CInvoiceView class. Also, you will declare the data members as public so that they can be easily accessed from the CInvoiceView class.

To add data members to the Invoice program's CInvoiceDoc class:

1. Because you are using the same data member names for the CInvoiceView and CInvoiceDoc classes, the easiest way to add the data members to the CInvoiceDoc class is to copy the data member declarations from the CInvoiceView class. First, open **InvoiceView.h** in the Code Editor window. Locate the following data member declarations in the public section and copy them to the Clipboard. Note that the data members in your InvoiceView.h file may be in a different order from the ones shown below:

   ```
   CString m_sCustomer;
   CString m_sInvoice;
   CString m_sDate;
   CString m_sTerms;
   ```

```
CString m_sDescription1;
CString m_sDescription2;
CString m_sDescription3;
int m_iQuantity1;
int m_iQuantity2;
int m_iQuantity3;
double m_dRate1;
double m_dRate2;
double m_dRate3;
double m_dAmount1;
double m_dAmount2;
double m_dAmount3;
double m_dTotal;
```

2. Open the **InvoiceDoc.h** file in the Code Editor window and paste the data member declarations into the first public section.

CDocument Member Functions

Although many of the CDocument member functions are called automatically by the MFC framework, you can override each of the functions to customize how your application creates, loads, and saves documents. Figure 11-27 lists some of the functions that are inherited from the CDocument class.

Function	Description
DeleteContents()	Used to reinitialize a CDocument object's data members
OnCloseDocument()	Called by the MFC framework when the File Close command executes
OnNewDocument()	Called by the MFC framework when the File New command executes
OnOpenDocument()	Called by the MFC framework when the File Open command executes
OnSaveDocument()	Called by the MFC framework when the File Save command executes
Serialize()	Used for reading data from and writing data to a file
SetModifiedFlag()	Used to determine if a document has been modified since the last time it was saved
UpdateAllViews()	Causes each view window's OnUpdate() function to execute in order to allow each view to display the most recent data

Figure 11-27 Common CDocument member functions

The function names in Figure 11-27 that are preceded by *On* are called automatically by the MFC framework. For example, the OnOpenDocument() function is called automatically when the user selects the Open command from the File menu. Similarly, the OnSaveDocument() function is called when the user selects the Save or Save As commands from the File menu. If you want to perform any sort of special processing when one of these events occurs, you can override any of the functions in your derived

CDocument class. The only functions for which the MFC Application Wizard automatically provides overridden implementations are the OnNewDocument() and Serialize() functions, because the OnNewDocument() function is one of the most commonly overridden functions and the Serialize() function is necessary for reading data from, and writing data to, files.

Figure 11-28 shows the Invoice program's derived CDocument class, InvoiceDoc.h. Notice the overridden OnNewDocument() and Serialize() functions.

```
// InvoiceDoc.h : interface of the CInvoiceDoc class
//
#pragma once
class CInvoiceDoc : public CDocument
{
protected: // create from serialization only
        CInvoiceDoc();
        DECLARE_DYNCREATE(CInvoiceDoc)
// Attributes
public:
        CString m_sCustomer;
        CString m_sInvoice;
...
// Operations
public:
// Overrides
        public:
        virtual BOOL OnNewDocument();
        virtual void Serialize(CArchive& ar);

// Implementation
public:
        virtual ~CInvoiceDoc();
#ifdef _DEBUG
        virtual void AssertValid() const;
        virtual void Dump(CDumpContext& dc) const;
#endif
protected:
// Generated message map functions
protected:
        DECLARE_MESSAGE_MAP()
};
```

Figure 11-28 InvoiceDoc.h

When a user creates a new document in an SDI application, MFC reuses the same document object. This is not a problem in the Simple Text Editor program because the CEditView class automatically reinitializes the document object for you. With other types of programs, however, you need to override the DeleteContents() function to reinitialize the document object's data members each time a new document is created. For example, a user of the Invoice program may enter values into the program's fields, save the document, and then select New from the File menu. Because the program reuses the same document object, the values contained in the document class's data members will appear in the fields, unless you reinitialize the data members using the DeleteContents() function. You call the DeleteContents() function from the OnNewDocument() function. The following code shows an example (from the Invoice program) of the OnNewDocument() function definition that is created automatically by the MFC framework.

```
BOOL CStocksDoc::OnNewDocument()
{
  if (!CDocument::OnNewDocument())
       return FALSE;
  // TODO: add reinitialization code here
  // (SDI documents will reuse this document)
  return TRUE;
}
```

Notice in the preceding code the hooks that are provided for you in the form of comments. You replace the comments with any initialization code required by your program. For example, the following code shows the same OnNewDocument() function with the hook comments replaced by a call to the DeleteContents() function. The DeleteContents() function reinitializes the data members of the Stocks class to 0.

```
BOOL CStocksDoc::OnNewDocument()
{
  if (!CDocument::OnNewDocument())
       return FALSE;
  DeleteContents();
  return TRUE;
}
void CStocksDoc::DeleteContents()
{
     m_iNumShares = 0;
     m_dCurrentValue = 0;
     m_dPricePerShare = 0;
     CDocument::DeleteContents();
}
```

When you use the Overrides button in the Properties window to add the virtual DeleteContents() function to your derived CDocument class, the function definition that is created for you automatically includes a call to the CDocument base class's DeleteContents() function with the statement `CDocument::DeleteContents();`. Although the CDocument class's default implementation of the DeleteContents() function does nothing, it is included in the preceding code in order to help you recognize the DeleteContents() function that the Properties window creates for you. In your overridden implementations of the DeleteContents() function, you can safely delete the `CDocument::DeleteContents();` statement.

Next, you will override the DeleteContents() function in the CInvoiceDoc class.

To override the DeleteContents() function in the CInvoiceDoc class:

1. Open **InvoiceDoc.cpp** or **InvoiceDoc.h** in the Code Editor window. If necessary, display the **Properties** window.

2. Use the **Overrides** button in the **Properties** window to override the **DeleteContents()** function.

3. Add the following statements, which appear in boldface, to the DeleteContents() function to reinitialize the data members:

```
void CInvoiceDoc::DeleteContents() {

        m_dAmount1 = 0.0;
        m_dAmount2 = 0.0;
        m_dAmount3 = 0.0;
        m_sDescription2 = _T("");
        m_sDescription1 = _T("");
        m_sDescription3 = _T("");
        m_iQuantity1 = 0;
        m_iQuantity2 = 0;
        m_iQuantity3 = 0;
        m_dRate1 = 0.0;
        m_dRate2 = 0.0;
        m_dRate3 = 0.0;
        m_dTotal = 0.0;
        m_sDate = _T("");
        m_sCustomer = _T("");
        m_sInvoice = _T("");
        m_sTerms = _T("");
        CDocument::DeleteContents();
}
```

11

4. Finally, replace the comments in the OnNewDocument() function with a call to the new DeleteContents() function as shown in Figure 11-29.

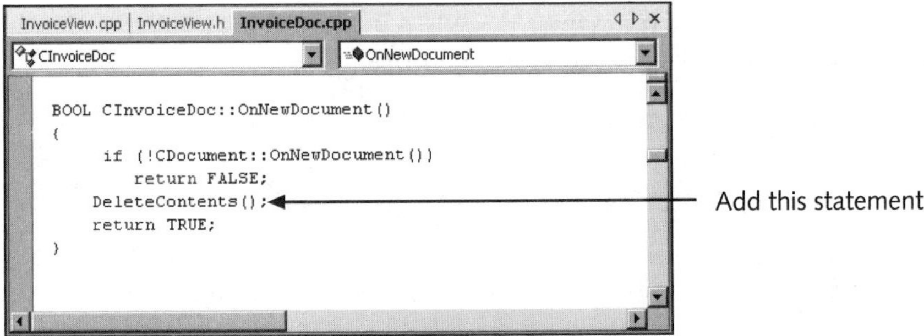
InvoiceView.cpp
InvoiceView.h
InvoiceDoc.cpp
CInvoiceDoc
OnNewDocument
BOOL CInvoiceDoc::OnNewDocument()
{
if (!CDocument::OnNewDocument())
return FALSE;
DeleteContents();
return TRUE;
}
Add this statement

Figure 11-29 Call to DeleteContents() added to OnNewDocument()

5. Rebuild and execute the program and test its functionality. Although you can enter data into each field, and have the amounts calculated correctly, you still need to add code that saves the data to a file.

6. Close the Invoice program window.

Two CDocument functions that you should call in almost every document-based application are the UpdateAllViews()and SetModifiedFlag() functions. As you learned earlier, the UpdateAllViews() function causes each view window's OnUpdate() function to execute in order to allow each view to display the most recent data. The **SetModifiedFlag() function** is used by the MFC framework to determine if a document has been modified since the last time it was saved. When you change a document's data, you pass to the SetModifiedFlag() function a value of TRUE to indicate that the document needs to be saved. If users attempt to close the document or open a new document without saving it, and the SetModifiedFlag() function has been called with a value of TRUE, they will receive a dialog box prompting them to save their changes. With the Simple Text Editor program, you do not need to call the SetModifiedFlag() when a user makes changes to a document because it is already called internally by the CEditView class. For other types of document-based programs, however, you need to call the SetModifiedFlag() manually. You should follow each SetModifiedFlag() call with a call to UpdateAllWindows(). For example, you may have a *set* function named setPricePerShare() in a CDocument class named CStocksDoc that sets the value of a data member named m_dPricePerShare. Once you assign a new value to the m_dPricePerShare data member, you call the SetModifiedFlag() and UpdateAllViews()functions, as follows:

```
void CStocksDoc::setPricePerShare(double dPrice) {
     m_dPricePerShare = dPrice;
     SetModifiedFlag(TRUE);
     UpdateAllViews(NULL);
}
```

Next, you will modify the Invoice program's OnNewDocument() function and add the SetModifiedFlag()and UpdateAllViews() functions to the updateDataMembers() function. Because the Invoice program includes only a single view, you do not actually need the UpdateAllViews() function. However, it is good practice to always include the UpdateAllViews() function anytime you change the data in a CView class in case you decide to add additional views to a program later.

To add the SetModifiedFlag() and UpdateAllViews()functions to the updateDataMembers() function:

1. Open the **InvoiceView.cpp** file in the Code Editor window.
2. Add the SetModifiedFlag() and UpdateAllViews() functions to the updateDataMembers() function, as shown in Figure 11-30.

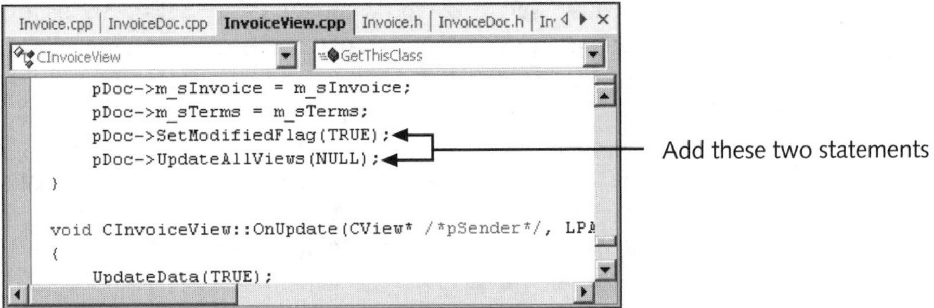
Invoice.cpp | InvoiceDoc.cpp | InvoiceView.cpp | Invoice.h | InvoiceDoc.h
CInvoiceView
GetThisClass
pDoc->m_sInvoice = m_sInvoice;
pDoc->m_sTerms = m_sTerms;
pDoc->SetModifiedFlag(TRUE);
pDoc->UpdateAllViews(NULL);
}
void CInvoiceView::OnUpdate(CView* /*pSender*/, LPA
{
UpdateData(TRUE);
Add these two statements

Figure 11-30 SetModifiedFlag() and UpdateAllViews() functions added to the updateDataMembers() function

3. Rebuild and execute the program. It should function the same as it did before adding the new statements to the updateDataMembers() function.
4. Close the Invoice program window.

STORING DATA

For a document-based application to be useful, you must be able to make the application's data persistent. **Persistence** refers to the ability for data to continue to exist after the program closes. The process of storing data to, and retrieving data from, a persistent storage medium is called **serialization**. (The process of retrieving data stored in a disk file is sometimes referred to as *deserialization*.) For your purposes, storage medium refers to disk files, although the term can also refer to other types of storage such as memory locations. With serialization, you store objects rather than just text or numbers. In this chapter, the objects you store will be the simple data member variables (which are objects) in the document classes.

Note

The data storage concepts discussed in this chapter apply only to MFC applications. Data storage for console applications is handled through the C++ iostream class library. To learn how to add data storage capabilities to console application programs, search the MSDN Library index for *iostream library*.

Although the behind-the-scenes mechanics that MFC uses to enable serialization is rather complex, you need to perform only a few tasks to save your documents to disk. The serialization capabilities in MFC programming are stored in the CObject class. You may recall from Chapter 10 that the CObject class is the base class for all MFC classes. Therefore, almost any MFC program can support serialization. In addition to deriving from the CObject class, basic serialized classes must also include the following:

- The DECLARE_SERIAL() macro
- An empty, default constructor
- An overridden Serialize() function

When you build a document-based MFC program with the MFC Application Wizard, the preceding requirements are automatically added to the document, view, and frame classes. The only thing you need to do is add code to the Serialize() function to store and retrieve data. The **Serialize() function** reads data from and writes data to a disk file.

Serialized classes also require the IMPLEMENT_SERIAL macro, which the MFC framework automatically provides for you. The **IMPLEMENT_SERIAL macro** defines the code and various functions needed by a serialized class. If you create a serialized MFC class without using the MFC framework, you must manually add the IMPLEMENT_SERIAL macro to your class implementation file. For more information, look for IMPLEMENT_SERIAL in the MSDN Library index.

In the Simple Text Editor program, serialization techniques are handled automatically by the CEditView class. For other types of document-based classes, such as classes created from CView, the MFC Application Wizard adds the following overridden Serialize() function to the derived CDocument class:

```
void CExampleDoc::Serialize(CArchive& ar)
{
        if (ar.IsStoring())
        {
                // TODO: add storing code here
        }
        else
        {
                // TODO: add loading code here
        }
}
```

Notice that the Serialize() method accepts as its argument a single reference named ar to a CArchive object. The **CArchive class** is used for writing data to and reading data from a storage medium. You can think of CArchive as an intermediary between your program and a disk file.

Now, examine the `if...else` structure in the Serialize() function's body. The Serialize() function is called in one of two circumstances: when the document is being saved or when it is being retrieved. The conditional statement in the `if` statement uses the CArchive class's IsStoring() function to see if the document is being saved. If the IsStoring() function returns true, then the `if` statement executes and stores the data. However, if the IsStoring() function returns false, then the `else` statement executes and retrieves the data.

To actually write to and read from a disk file, you use the CArchive object within the `if` and `else` structure's command blocks, along with the insertion operator (<<) and the extraction operator (>>) and the document class's data members. Recall that you used the insertion and extraction operators with console applications. However, instead of writing to the output stream and reading from the input stream, when used with serialization, the insertion and extraction operators write to and read from a CArchive object. The CArchive object internally handles the storage of data to, and retrieval of data from, the disk file. The CStocksDoc document class example you examined earlier in this chapter includes several data members. To write the CStocksDoc document class's data members to a disk file and read them from a disk file, you modify the Serialize() function as follows:

```
void CExampleDoc::Serialize(CArchive& ar)
{
     if (ar.IsStoring())
     {
          ar << m_iNumShares;
          ar << m_dCurrentValue;
          ar << m_dPricePerShare;
     }
     else
     {
          ar >> m_iNumShares;
          ar >> m_dCurrentValue;
          ar >> m_dPricePerShare;
     }
}
```

In the preceding code, the CArchive object and insertion operators in the `if` statement store the contents of the data members to a disk file. The CArchive object and extraction operators in the `else` statement read the objects from the disk file and assign them to the appropriate data member.

Next, you will modify the Invoice program's Serialize() function so the program can save documents to disk.

To modify the Invoice program's Serialize() function so the program can save documents to disk:

1. Open the **InvoiceDoc.cpp** file in the Code Editor window and locate the Serialize() function.
2. Add to the Serialize() function the following statements, which appear in boldface, that write the CInvoiceDoc class's data members to, and read them from, disk files.

```
void CInvoiceDoc::Serialize(CArchive& ar)
{
     if (ar.IsStoring())
     {
          ar << m_dAmount1;
          ar << m_dAmount2;
          ar << m_dAmount3;
          ar << m_sDescription2;
          ar << m_sDescription1;
          ar << m_sDescription3;
```

```
            ar << m_iQuantity1;
            ar << m_iQuantity2;
            ar << m_iQuantity3;
            ar << m_dRate1;
            ar << m_dRate2;
            ar << m_dRate3;
            ar << m_dTotal;
            ar << m_sDate;
            ar << m_sCustomer;
            ar << m_sInvoice;
            ar << m_sTerms;
        }
        else
        {
            ar >> m_dAmount1;
            ar >> m_dAmount2;
            ar >> m_dAmount3;
            ar >> m_sDescription2;
            ar >> m_sDescription1;
            ar >> m_sDescription3;
            ar >> m_iQuantity1;
            ar >> m_iQuantity2;
            ar >> m_iQuantity3;
            ar >> m_dRate1;
            ar >> m_dRate2;
            ar >> m_dRate3;
            ar >> m_dTotal;
            ar >> m_sDate;
            ar >> m_sCustomer;
            ar >> m_sInvoice;
            ar >> m_sTerms;
        }
}
```

3. Finally, rebuild and execute the Invoice program. Test the program to see if it functions properly by saving a document, by creating a new document, and then by reopening the document you saved.
4. When you are finished testing the program, close the Invoice program window.

CHAPTER SUMMARY

- A document is a file that is associated with a particular application and contains different sets of data, depending on your program's functionality and each user's needs.
- A program's data (the document) is managed and stored by a class derived from the CDocument class.

- A program's data is displayed to the user by one or more classes derived from the CView class.
- The data stored in a CDocument class can be displayed and manipulated by multiple CView classes. However, a CView class can only display and manipulate the data from a single CDocument class.
- The single document interface, or SDI, allows users to have only one document open at a time.
- The multiple document interface, or MDI, allows users to have multiple documents open at the same time.
- A view class is responsible for graphically displaying a document's data and for handling the manipulation of that data according to user requests.
- Each view class inherits an OnUpdate() function that is called each time the document class changes or whenever the document class executes an UpdateAllViews() function.
- The UpdateAllViews() function is a member function of CDocument and causes each view window's OnUpdate() function to execute in order to allow each view to display the most recent data.
- The OnNewDocument() function is called when a user creates a new document.
- When a user creates a new document in an SDI application, MFC reuses the same document object.
- You need to override the DeleteContents() function to reinitialize the document object's data members each time a new document is created. You call the DeleteContents() function from the OnNewDocument() function.
- Persistence refers to the ability for data to continue to exist after the program closes.
- The process of storing data to, and retrieving data from, a persistent storage medium is called serialization.
- The Serialize() function reads data from, and writes data to, a disk file.

REVIEW QUESTIONS

1. CDocument manages and stores a program's data, while CView ________________ it.

   a. archives

   b. files

   c. deletes

   d. displays

2. A CDocument class can be associated with ______________ CView classes.
   a. zero
   b. one
   c. two
   d. any number of
3. A CView class can be associated with ______________ CDocument classes.
   a. zero
   b. one
   c. two
   d. any number of
4. Which of the following statements is correct?
   a. You are required to use document/view architecture in your document-based MFC programs.
   b. You are not required to use document/view architecture in your document-based MFC programs.
   c. MFC programs created with the document/view architecture are of little value.
   d. Programs that are created with the document/view architecture do not automatically inherit the document functionality that allows you to read and write documents, use print and print preview functions, and perform other types of document-specific tasks.
5. Where do you display a class instantiated from CView?
   a. within the application window
   b. within a dialog window
   c. within a CDocument window
   d. within a frame window
6. Which subclass of CView creates a Text Editor program?
   a. CFormView
   b. CEditView
   c. CCtrlView
   d. CHTMLView
7. Which subclass of CView creates a window that can be edited in Dialog Editor?
   a. CFormView
   b. CEditView
   c. CCtrlView
   d. CHTMLView

8. Which version of the GetDocument() function is used with a program's release build?
   a. the inline version defined in the interface file of the CView-derived class
   b. the version defined in the implementation file of the CView-derived class
   c. the inline version defined in the interface file of the CDocument-derived class
   d. the version defined in the implementation file of the CDocument-derived class
9. An OnUpdate() function is called each time the document class changes or whenever the document class executes an ______________ function.
   a. Refresh()
   b. UpdateViews()
   c. UpdateAllViews()
   d. Update()
10. Which of the following tasks is not required in order for a class derived from CDocument to write data to, and read data from, files?
    a. instantiating a CDocument class object in the project application class
    b. creating data members to temporarily hold the data for the current document
    c. overriding the CDocument class's member functions to customize the creating, loading, and saving mechanisms of the document/view architecture
    d. overriding CDocument's Serialize() member function in order to read the document's data from and write the document's data to a file
11. The MFC Application Wizard automatically provides overridden implementations for the CDocument class's ______________ and Serialize() functions.
    a. OnOpenDocument()
    b. OnNewDocument()
    c. OnCloseDocument()
    d. DeleteContents()
12. Which of the following functions is used for reinitializing a CDocument class's data members when the user creates a new document?
    a. OnOpenDocument()
    b. OnNewDocument()
    c. OnCloseDocument()
    d. DeleteContents()

13. When a user creates a new document in an SDI application, MFC ________________.
    a. reuses the same document object
    b. creates a new document object
    c. builds an array of document objects
    d. copies the original document object's data members to a new document object
14. The ________________ function is used by the MFC framework to determine if a document has been modified since the last time it was saved.
    a. ChangedDocument()
    b. CleanDocument()
    c. LastModified()
    d. SetModifiedFlag()
15. ________________ refers to the ability for data to continue to exist after the program closes.
    a. Persistence
    b. Stability
    c. Dynamism
    d. Continuance
16. The process of storing data to and retrieving data from a persistent storage medium is referred to as ________________.
    a. encryption
    b. serialization
    c. compilation
    d. interpretation
17. Which of the following is required in a serialized class?
    a. an overridden OnFileSave() function
    b. an overridden DeleteContents() function
    c. an empty default constructor
    d. an empty default destructor
18. Which function of the CArchive class checks to see if a document is being stored?
    a. OnStoreFile()
    b. OnSaveFile()
    c. IsSaving()
    d. IsStoring()

19. Which operator is used with a CArchive object to write data to a disk file?
    a. <<
    b. >>
    c. ++
    d. <-
20. Which operator is used with a CArchive object to read data from a disk file?
    a. <<
    b. >>
    c. ++
    d. <-

PROGRAMMING EXERCISES

1. Assume that you have a document-based MFC program that saves contact information to files. The program gathers five pieces of information—first name, last name, address, city, state, ZIP, and telephone—and stores each piece of information in data members named m_sFirst, m_sLast, m_sAddress, m_sCity, m_sState, m_sZip, and m_sPhone. Add statements to the following member function named updateInfo() so that it reads data values from a document object named CContactsDoc and assigns the values to the view class's data members. For simplicity, assume that both the view class and the document class use the same variable names for the data members.


```
void CContactsView::updateInfo() {
}
```

2. Modify the following OnUpdate() function for the CContactsView class so that controls in the program's dialog window are reset to the original values when the user creates a new document.

```
void CContactsView::OnUpdate(CView* pSender,
     LPARAM lHint, CObject* pHint)
{
     // TODO: Add your specialized code here and/or
     //  call the base class
}
```

3. Modify the following OnNewDocument() function and DeleteContents() function so that the document class's data members are reinitialized to their original values when a user creates a new document.

```
BOOL CContactsDoc::OnNewDocument() {
     if (!CDocument::OnNewDocument())
          return FALSE;
     return TRUE;
```

```
}
void CContactsDoc::DeleteContents() {
     // TODO: Add your specialized code here and/or
     // call the base class
     CDocument::DeleteContents();
}
```

4. Modify the updateInfo() function from exercise 1 so that it marks the program as modified and updates any other document views.
5. Modify the following Serialize() function in the Contacts program's CContactsDoc class so that the data members listed in exercise 1 are written to and read from disk files.

```
void CContactsDoc::Serialize(CArchive& ar)
{
     if (ar.IsStoring())
     {
     }
     else
     {
     }
}
```

Programming Projects

1. Create a document-based version of the BugReport program you created in Chapter 10 that is used as a software development bug report. Save each bug report as a separate document.
2. Create a document-based version of the Interview application you created in Chapter 10 that is used for tracking, documenting, and managing the process of interviewing candidates for professional positions. Save each prospective employee's interview as a document.
3. A check box is a common type of Windows control that can be set to true (checked) or false (unchecked). Use the following steps to add a check box control to the Invoice program that can be used to determine whether an invoice has been paid.
   a. Add a check box control beneath the Group Box control. Use the Properties window to change the check box's resource ID to IDC_PAID and its caption to Paid.
   b. Add a DDX data member for the IDC_PAID control named m_bPaid with a data type of BOOL.
   c. Declare a data member for the IDC_PAID control named m_bPaid in the InvoiceDoc.h file.
   d. Add a BN_CLICKED message handler function for the IDC_PAID control named OnBnClickedPaid() that calls the updateDataMembers() function. Also,

add the statement `pDoc->m_bPaid = m_bPaid;` above the `pDoc->SetModifiedFlag(TRUE);` statement in the updateDataMembers() function to transfer the value of the IDC_PAID control to the associated data member in the CInvoiceDoc class.

e. Add the statement `m_bPaid = pDoc->m_bPaid;` above the `UpdateData(FALSE);` statement in the OnUpdate() function to update the display in the window if the value of the m_bPaid data member in CInvoiceDoc changes.

f. Add statements to the Serialize() function in the InvoiceDoc.cpp file that store the value of the m_bPaid data member to the invoice file and retrieve it from the invoice file. Also, add the statement `m_bPaid = FALSE;` above the CDocument::DeleteContents(); statement in the DeleteContents() function in InvoiceDoc.cpp to reinitialize the value of the m_bPaid data member each time a new document is created.

4. Another persistence technique that you may want to explore on your own involves a special Windows database known as the System Registry. The System Registry stores Windows system information along with initialization and configuration information for individual applications. Look for the System Registry topic in the MSDN Library and redesign the Invoice program so that the most recently used invoice number is stored in the System Registry. Each time you open the Invoice program, it should retrieve the invoice number from the System Registry, increment it by one, and then display the new number in the Invoice # edit box. The number stored in the System Registry should only be updated when the user saves a new invoice.

CHAPTER

12

DESIGNING THE VISUAL INTERFACE

In this chapter you will learn:

- About the Graphics Device Interface
- How to draw in a window
- How to work with graphic object classes
- How to work with menus and commands
- How to work with toolbars and buttons

If you want to view paradise, simply look around and view it.
Anything you want to, do it.
Want to change the world?
There's nothing to it.

—Willy Wonka, from the film *Willy Wonka and the Chocolate Factory* (1971)

PREVIEW: THE STOCK CHARTING PROGRAM

You will work with a simple Stock Charting program in this chapter in order to learn how to draw graphic objects and how to add menus and toolbar commands to an application. The Stock Charting program allows you to track a stock's value over a five-day period (Monday through Friday) using three separate charts: a line chart, a column chart, and a scatter chart. The charts in the Stock Charting program are simplified versions of the types of charts you may have seen in Microsoft Excel. Although the Stock Charting program would not be very useful in a real-world setting because of its limitations, it will give you a good idea of how to add and manipulate graphic objects in programs.

To preview the Stock Charting program:

1. Create a **Chapter.12** folder in your Visual C++ Projects folder.
2. Copy the **Chapter12_StockCharting** folder from the Chapter.12 folder on your Data Disk to the Chapter.12 folder in your Visual C++ Projects folder, and then open the StockCharting project in Visual C++.
3. In the Solution Explorer window, expand the Source Files folder. The project contains several classes with which you are familiar, including an application class, a frame class, a view class, and a document class. Open the CStockChartingView class's implementation file, **StockChartingView.cpp**, in the Code Editor window.
4. Locate the **OnDraw() function** in the StockChartingView.cpp file. You use the OnDraw() function to add graphic objects to an application's device context. A device context is a special data structure that stores information about the text and graphics displayed by an application. For the Stock Charting program, all of the code that adds graphic objects to the program's window is contained in the OnDraw() function. Figure 12-1 only shows portions of the Stock Charting program's OnDraw() function because the function is too long to list here. The first few statements following the function header are used for converting the stock values entered by a user to the pixels scale of the charts. Now, notice the CPen and CBrush statements. CPen objects determine the style and color of lines; CBrush objects control the color and pattern displayed in closed objects such as rectangles and circles. Also, notice the many statements that use the pDC pointer. The pDC pointer is a handle to the device context that you use to draw graphic objects on the screen. Finally, notice the `switch` statement toward the bottom of the function. The `switch` statement determines which chart to display according to the value in an enum variable named m_Chart. (You will learn about `enum` data types later in this chapter.) Code within each `case` label adds the appropriate graphic objects to the device context, depending on the selected chart.

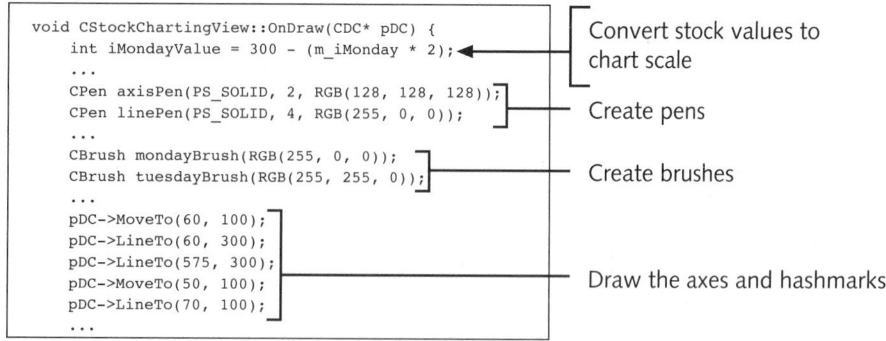

void CStockChartingView::OnDraw(CDC* pDC) {
int iMondayValue = 300 - (m_iMonday * 2);
...
CPen axisPen(PS_SOLID, 2, RGB(128, 128, 128));
CPen linePen(PS_SOLID, 4, RGB(255, 0, 0));
...
CBrush mondayBrush(RGB(255, 0, 0));
CBrush tuesdayBrush(RGB(255, 255, 0));
...
pDC->MoveTo(60, 100);
pDC->LineTo(60, 300);
pDC->LineTo(575, 300);
pDC->MoveTo(50, 100);
pDC->LineTo(70, 100);
...
Convert stock values to chart scale
Create pens
Create brushes
Draw the axes and hashmarks

Figure 12-1 Stock Charting program's OnDraw() function

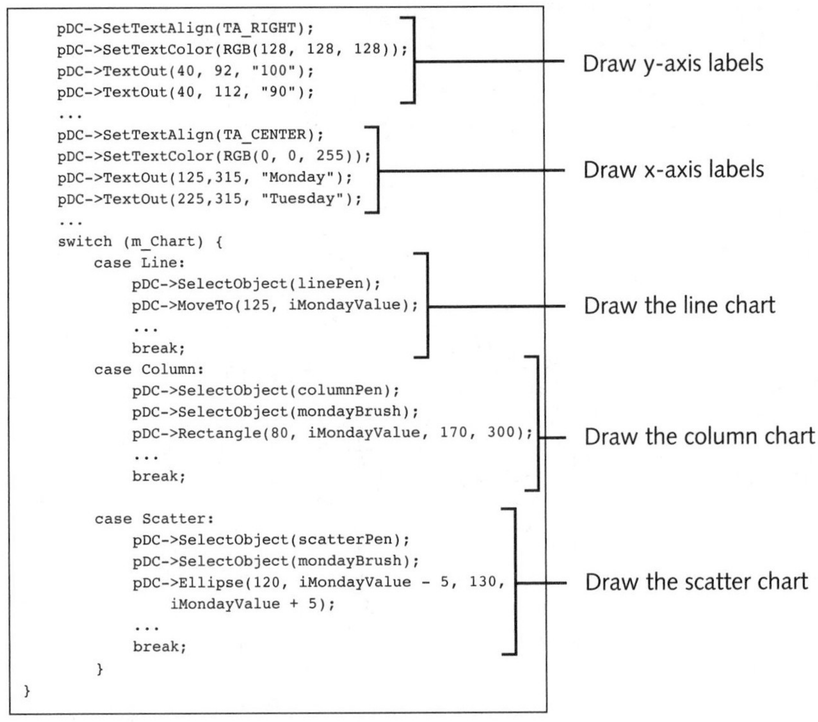
pDC->SetTextAlign(TA_RIGHT);
pDC->SetTextColor(RGB(128, 128, 128));
pDC->TextOut(40, 92, "100");
pDC->TextOut(40, 112, "90");
...
pDC->SetTextAlign(TA_CENTER);
pDC->SetTextColor(RGB(0, 0, 255));
pDC->TextOut(125,315, "Monday");
pDC->TextOut(225,315, "Tuesday");
...
switch (m_Chart) {
case Line:
pDC->SelectObject(linePen);
pDC->MoveTo(125, iMondayValue);
...
break;
case Column:
pDC->SelectObject(columnPen);
pDC->SelectObject(mondayBrush);
pDC->Rectangle(80, iMondayValue, 170, 300);
...
break;
case Scatter:
pDC->SelectObject(scatterPen);
pDC->SelectObject(mondayBrush);
pDC->Ellipse(120, iMondayValue - 5, 130,
iMondayValue + 5);
...
break;
}
}
Draw y-axis labels
Draw x-axis labels
Draw the line chart
Draw the column chart
Draw the scatter chart

Figure 12-1 Stock Charting program's OnDraw() function (continued)

12

5. Build and execute the program. The default chart type is the line chart, with each stock value set to a default value of 0. Try entering some new values in each of the edit boxes. When you change the value in each edit box, an EN_CHANGE event occurs, which executes event handlers that update the associated graphical value in the chart. Now, open the **View** menu. Notice the three commands at the bottom of the menu that you can use to change the type of displayed chart. Display the column chart and scatter chart by selecting their associated commands on the View menu. Now, examine the toolbar. At the right end of the toolbar are buttons that represent each chart type. Try clicking each button to display its associated chart. Both the menu commands and toolbar buttons execute the same WM_COMMAND messages used for command button events. Figure 12-2 shows an example of the Stock Charting program with the column chart displayed.

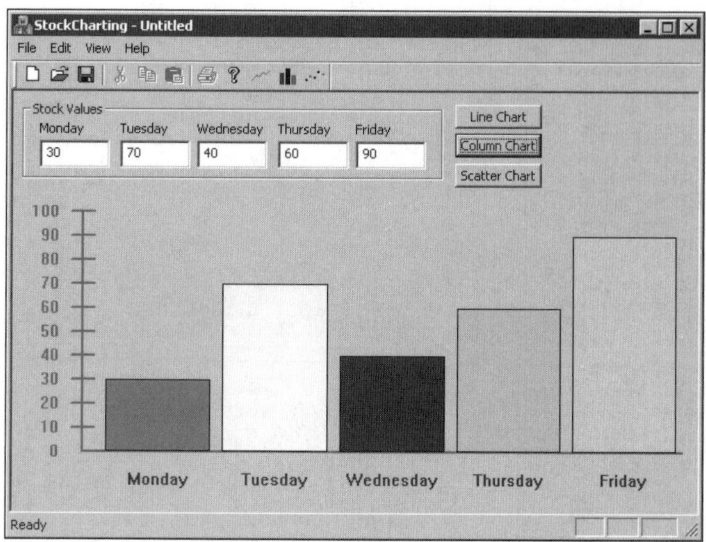

Figure 12-2 Stock Charting program with the column chart displayed

6. Press the **Close** button to close the Stock Charting program window.

INTRODUCTION

The first programs you created in this book were simple console applications that included little in the way of a visual interface, other than the text that was output to the screen. As your studies of Visual C++ have progressed, you have learned how to create Windows applications that include basic Windows operating system elements such as dialog controls and command buttons. This chapter brings you the next level of application development by introducing several techniques for designing the visual interface. The techniques you will learn include how to draw in an application window, how to modify the application window itself, and how to add menu commands and toolbar buttons to your application. Be aware, however, that you will learn only the basics of visual interface design. Nevertheless, you should learn enough in this chapter to be able to explore more advanced interface topics on your own.

THE GRAPHICS DEVICE INTERFACE

At one time or another in your work with Windows operating systems, you have probably come across the term device driver. A **device** is a generic term that refers to a particular piece of computer hardware, such as a monitor or printer. A **device driver** is a specialized type of program that allows the Windows operating system to communicate with a particular device. Many different types of devices, produced by numerous manufacturers, exist for personal computers. For Windows to communicate with a particular device, a driver must exist for it. Drivers for popular devices are available as part of the Windows operating system itself, whereas drivers for new or relatively obscure devices are usually available from the manufacturer of the device. Note that many types of drivers exist, including drivers that control a computer's drives, such as hard drives, CD drives, or floppy drives, and input devices, such as a mouse and keyboard. When you write a Windows application, however, you do not need to add any code to your program for directly communicating with the drivers for individual devices. If that were the case, then to write a Windows program, you would need to include code for the thousands of devices that are available today. Instead, the Windows operating system controls most types of devices by using drivers behind the scenes.

When designing a visual interface, you need to concern yourself with how the visual portion of your program appears on output devices such as monitors, printers, and plotters. The **graphics device interface**, or **GDI**, manages communication with different types of Windows graphical device drivers. In essence, the GDI acts as a translation layer between your application and the device to which it outputs. The GDI allows Windows applications to be device-independent by mapping the visual portion of an application to the appropriate output required by a given device driver. For example, monitors are available in different resolutions and color settings. A VGA monitor's resolution, for instance, is 640 columns by 480 rows of pixels; a Super VGA monitor's resolution is 1,024 columns by 768 rows of pixels. Additionally, some monitors can display only 256 colors, whereas other monitors can display millions of colors. The GDI manages the mapping of an application's visual interface to the appropriate resolution for any given monitor, and maps color values to a monitor's nearest available color. Similarly, the output to printers and plotters requires different mappings, depending on the type of printer or plotter you are using. Figure 12-3 illustrates how the GDI translates between Windows applications and devices.

12

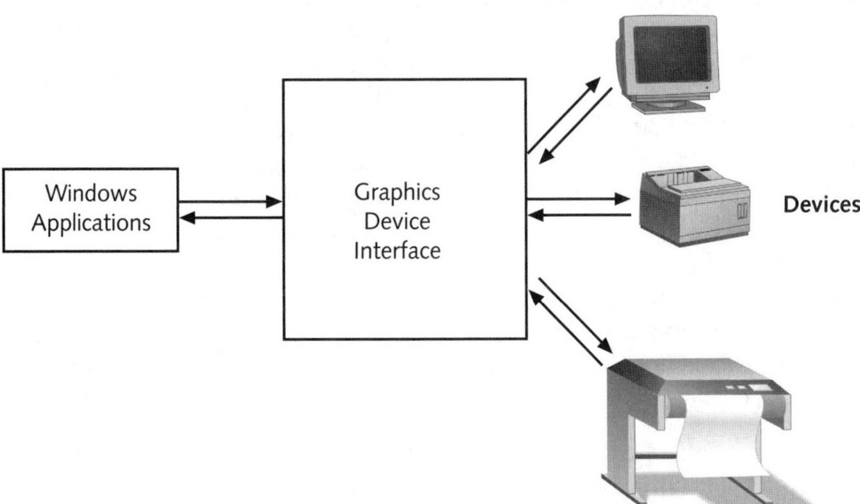

Figure 12-3 GDI translation between Windows applications and devices

One of the most important parts of the GDI as it relates to the design of a visual interface is the device context, which you will examine next.

Device Contexts

To draw in an application window, you must do so through a device context. A **device context** is a Windows GDI data structure that stores information about the text and graphics displayed by an application. When your application runs on a given device, the GDI translates the information stored in the device context to the format of the device driver. Essentially, you "draw" your text and graphics into the device context and then hand the device context off to the GDI, which translates the device context to the appropriate device driver when necessary. You can actually think of the device context as a canvas that you can use to paint the visual elements of your program. The data structure that represents a device context is created and manipulated by the classes listed in Figure 12-4.

Class	Description
CDC	Directly accesses and modifies an application's drawing information. This class is also the base class for device contexts.
CPaintDC	Represents an application's display information
CClientDC	Represents the client area of a window
CWindowDC	Represents the whole application window, including its frame
CMetaFileDC	Enables drawing into a Windows metafile

Figure 12-4 Device context classes

The most important of the device context classes listed in Figure 12-4 is the CDC class; this is the base class for the other device context classes. The MFC framework automatically instantiates a CDC object for you and supplies you with a pointer to the object in the inherited OnDraw() function. You use the CDC object pointer in the OnDraw() function to directly add and modify drawing information in the device context. You will learn about the CDC class and OnDraw() functions shortly. For now, understand that all drawing output is performed in the OnDraw() function through the CDC object pointer. You do not usually need to work directly with the other device context classes because the MFC framework manages them for you. However, you should understand the use of each device context class in case you need to design a more advanced user interface in the future.

Mapping Modes

Recall that you reference a window's pixels with x-axis and y-axis coordinates, beginning in the upper-left corner of a screen or window at an x-axis position of 0 and a y-axis position of 0. Pixel measurements are usually written in the format *x*, *y*, which means that the starting point, or point of origin, in the upper-left corner of the screen is written as position 0, 0. As you move right from the upper-left corner of the screen along the x-axis, or down along the y-axis, the pixel measurements increase. Therefore, a pixel position that is 100 pixels to the right along the x-axis and 200 pixels down on the y-axis is written as 100, 200. A device context uses this manner of measuring pixel positions as its default measurement system, or mapping mode. A **mapping mode** is a coordinate system that determines the units and scaling orientation in a device context. Figure 12-5 illustrates the default measurement system.

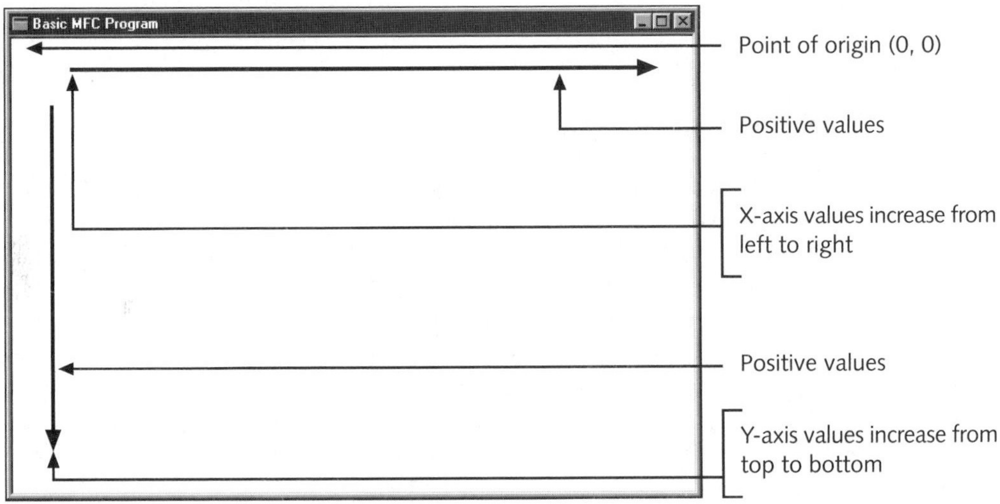

Figure 12-5 Default measurement system

12

Mapping modes begin with a prefix of *MM_*, followed by a description of the mapping mode. The default mapping mode illustrated in Figure 12-5 is named MM_TEXT. Figure 12-6 lists the eight mapping modes you can use in applications.

Mapping Mode	Description
MM_ANISOTROPIC	Units of measure are mapped to application-specific values. Axes are scaled independently. Orientation of x and y axes are user defined.
MM_HIENGLISH	Units of measure are mapped to 0.0001 inches. X-axis values increase from left to right. Y-axis values decrease from top to bottom.
MM_HIMETRIC	Units of measure are mapped to 0.01 millimeters. X-axis values increase from left to right. Y-axis values decrease from top to bottom.
MM_ISOTROPIC	Units of measure are mapped to application-specific values. Axes are scaled identically. Orientation of x- and y-axes are user defined.
MM_LOENGLISH	Units of measure are mapped to 0.01 inches. X-axis values increase from left to right. Y-axis values decrease from top to bottom.

Figure 12-6 Mapping Modes

Mapping Mode	Description
MM_LOMETRIC	Units of measure are mapped to 0.1 millimeters. X-axis values increase from left to right. Y-axis values decrease from top to bottom.
MM_TEXT	Units of measure are mapped to one pixel. X-axis values increase from left to right. Y-axis values increase from top to bottom.
MM_TWIPS	Units of measure are mapped to one twip, which is equal to 1/20th of a printer's point or 1/1440 inches. X-axis values increase from left to right. Y-axis values decrease from top to bottom.

Figure 12-6 Mapping Modes (continued)

All mapping modes begin with a point of origin of 0, 0 in the upper-left corner of the screen or window. However, for all of the mapping modes except MM_TEXT (the default), MM_ISOTROPIC, and MM_ANISOTROPIC, the values along the y-axis decrease instead of increase as you move away from the point of origin. Therefore, a pixel position that is 100 pixels to the right along the x-axis and 200 pixels down on the y-axis is written as 100, –200 using any of the mapping modes other than MM_TEXT, MM_ISOTROPIC, and MM_ANISOTROPIC. Figure 12-7 illustrates how y-axis values decrease as you move away from the point of origin.

You can change a mapping mode's point of origin from 0, 0 to another value using the SetViewportOrgEx() API function or the SetViewportOrg() member function of the CDC class.

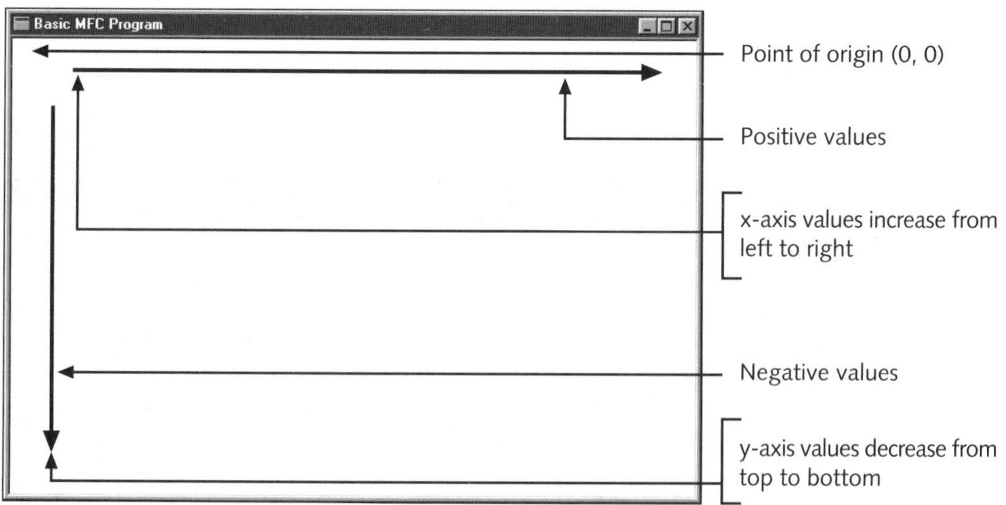

Figure 12-7 Axis values for all mapping modes except MM_TEXT, MM_ISOTROPIC, and MM_ANISOTROPIC

As mentioned previously, the default mapping mode is MM_TEXT. If you want to change the mapping mode in your application, then you need to execute the SetMapMode() function of the CDC class, which you will learn about shortly. Although there will be times when you will want to use a mapping mode other than MM_TEXT, the default mapping mode of MM_TEXT is sufficient for your studies in this chapter. For instance, you may need to use a more exact unit of measure than pixels. Additionally, if you are configuring a document to print, it is much easier to use the MM_LOENGLISH mapping mode. Because the MM_LOENGLISH mapping mode uses inches as its unit of measure, it is much easier to use when calculating where your document should print on an 8½ × 11 sheet of paper. If you were to use the MM_TEXT mapping mode, which uses pixels as its unit of measure, then you would need to convert the pixels to inches in order to accurately gauge your printing coordinates.

Working with Color

Although computer systems can display anywhere from 256 to millions of colors, the display of colors is the result of combining just three primary colors, red, blue, and green. Graphical computer systems, such as Windows, use the **red**, **green**, **blue**, or **RGB color system** for specifying colors. You create individual colors in the RGB color system using the **RGB() macro**. The color created with an RGB() macro is sometimes referred to as an **RGB triplet**. The syntax for using the RGB() macro is `RGB(`*`red, green, blue`*`)`. Each of the three parameters in the RGB() macro can accept an integer value ranging from 0 to 255, which indicates the intensity to use for each color. A value of 0 indicates that the color you are creating should include the minimum intensity of a primary color, and a value of 255 indicates that the color should include the maximum intensity of a primary color. By combining different intensities of the red, green, and blue primary colors, you can come up with millions of different hues. You create primary colors of red, green, or blue by using a full intensity value of 255 for one of the primary colors, but values of 0 for the other primary colors. For example, to display the color red, you use the RGB() macro as follows: `RGB(255, 0, 0)`. Black is represented by the minimum intensities for each primary color using the statement `RGB(0, 0, 0)`. White is represented by the maximum intensities for each primary color using the statement `RGB(255, 255, 255)`. Figure 12-8 lists RGB color values for some common colors.

Color	Red Intensity	Green Intensity	Blue Intensity
Red	255	0	0
Green	0	255	0
Blue	0	0	255
White	255	255	255
Black	0	0	0
Light Gray	192	192	192

Figure 12-8 Common RGB color values

Color	Red Intensity	Green Intensity	Blue Intensity
Dark Gray	128	128	128
Yellow	255	255	0
Cyan	0	255	255
Magenta	255	0	255

Figure 12-8 Common RGB color values (continued)

Even though you can come up with millions of colors with the RGB color system, the number of colors that can actually be displayed depends on the color capabilities of individual hardware devices such as monitors and printers.

Several of the device context functions that you will use in this chapter require RGB color parameters. For instance, the CreatePen() function, which is used for designating line thickness and color, requires an RGB color value as its third parameter. One way to pass the RGB color value to a function is to pass an RGB() macro, along with your desired color intensities, as the function argument. The following example shows how to pass a blue RGB color as the third parameter of the CreatePen() function using the RGB() macro. For now, do not worry about how the CreatePen() function works because you will examine it in detail later in this chapter.

```
CPen m_CurPen;
m_CurPen.CreatePen(PS_SOLID, 2, RGB(0, 0, 255));
```

You can also declare your own color variable using the Windows API **COLORREF data type**. You create a color variable by assigning the RGB triplet returned from the RGB() macro to a variable of the COLORREF data type. The following code shows another version of the CreatePen() function, but this time a COLORREF variable named blueColor is passed as the CreatePen() function's third parameter instead of an RGB() macro:

```
CPen m_CurPen;
COLORREF blueColor = RGB(0, 0, 255);
m_CurPen.CreatePen(PS_SOLID, 2, blueColor);
```

Once you create a COLORREF variable, you can extract the intensity value of each primary color using the GetRValue(), GetGValue(), and GetBValue() macros.

DRAWING IN A WINDOW

Although you have added dialog controls to some of the programs you have created, you have not actually drawn graphic objects in any of your windows. Graphic objects are lines, rectangles, and circles that you add to a device context. You can create lines, rectangles, and circles using different colors, line thickness, and fills. (Fills refer to colors and patterns that you apply to the interior of closed images such as rectangles and circles.) You can also draw text graphic objects into a device context that are similar to the Static Text controls you have added to dialog windows. Unlike Static Text controls, however, you can use different fonts and colors to format the text you draw into a device context. Figure 12-9 shows an example of some of the graphic objects that you can display in a window through the device context.

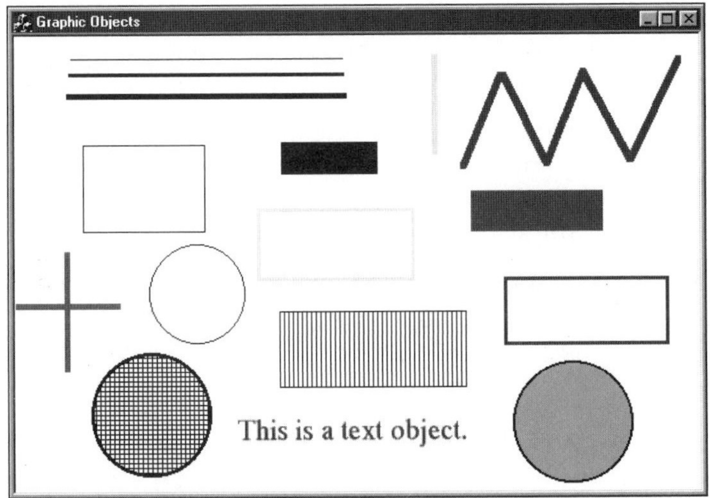

Figure 12-9 Graphic objects

Next, you will start creating the Stock Charting program. You will derive the program's CView class from the CFormView class in order to be able to use dialog controls in the application window. Later, you will add graphic objects to the same window containing the dialog controls.

To start creating the Stock Charting program:

1. Create a new project named **StockCharting** using the MFC Application Wizard. Save the project in the Chapter.12 folder in your Visual C++ Projects folder.
2. The MFC Application Wizard executes and starts to walk you through the steps involved in creating an MFC program. Click the **Application Type** tab, and then select **Single document** from the application choices. Be sure to leave the **Document/View architecture support** check box selected and the other options in the tab set to their default settings.
3. You can leave the Compound Document Support, Document Template Strings, Database Support, and User Interface Features tabs set to their default settings, so skip ahead and click the Advanced Features tab.

4. In the User Interface Features tab of the Advanced Options dialog box, select the **Maximized** check box. Leave the rest of the options set to their defaults and click the **Advanced Features** tab.
5. In the Advanced Features tab, clear all of the selected check boxes, and then click the **Generated Classes** tab to continue.
6. In the Generated Classes tab, select **CFormView** from the Base class combo box, and then click the **Finish** button.
7. Because you cleared the Printing and print preview check box in the Advanced Features tab, you will receive a dialog box confirming that no printing support will be available for the CFormView class. Click the **Yes** button to continue.

Next, you will add dialog controls to the CStockChartingView class's dialog window. You will add five Edit Box controls to the dialog window in which users can enter the stock value for each day of the week that they are charting a stock. You will also add command buttons that you will temporarily use to change the displayed chart type.

In some situations, you may want to limit the values that users can enter into controls. For example, in the Stock Charting program, the y-axis of each chart has a scale that begins with 0 and ends at 100. Therefore, users can only enter stock values between 0 and 100. A mechanism called dialog data validation, or DDV, which is related to DDX, assists in the validation of data when you exchange values between controls and variables, allowing you to limit the values users can enter. When you add DDX data members using the Member Variables tab in ClassWizard, certain data types, such as integer and floating point data types, support DDV by allowing you to set the minimum and maximum values that users can enter into a control, such as an Edit Box. For the stock value Edit Box controls in the Stock Charting program, you want to allow users to enter only values between 0 and 100. Once you call the UpdateData() function to exchange values between your dialog controls and their associated DDX data members, DDV checks to make sure that users entered values that are within the range you specified. For the stock value Edit Box controls, you will use the `int` data type, which supports DDV.

You may wonder why you are using `int` data types when stock values often include decimal portions. The device context functions you use to plot each value on the charts require that you pass integer values, not floating-point values. You could allow users to enter floating-point values, and then round off each value and cast it to the `int` data type. However, that would make the code unnecessarily complex. Remember, your purpose in this chapter is to study drawing functionality. Therefore, you will use the `int` data type.

To add dialog controls to the CStockChartingView class's dialog window:

1. After the MFC Application Wizard finishes creating the StockCharting program window, use Resource View to open the **IDD_STOCKCHARTING_FORM** dialog resource in the Dialog Editor.
2. Delete the Static Text control that reads **TODO: Place form controls on this dialog**.

3. As shown in Figure 12-10, use the form's sizing handles to resize it to approximately 400 pixels wide by 220 pixels high. You will need the extra space to display the charts. Note that the width and height of a selected dialog box (or any other selected control) displays in the IDE status bar.
4. Add the dialog controls that are also shown in Figure 12-10.

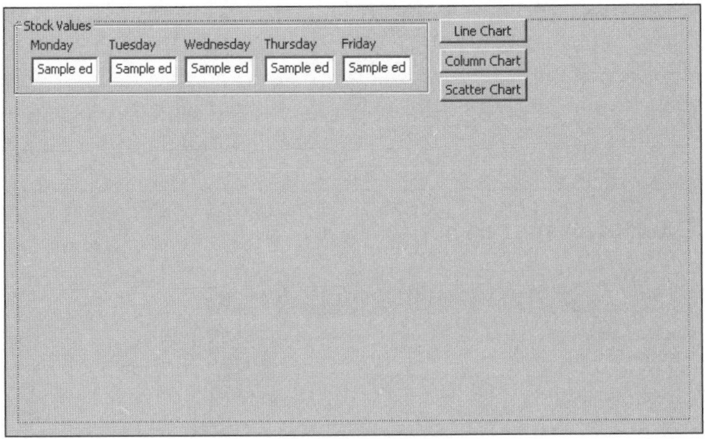

Figure 12-10 Stock Charting dialog controls

5. Use the table shown in Figure 12-11 to modify the resource IDs for each of the dialog controls.

Control	Resource ID
Monday	IDC_MONDAY
Tuesday	IDC_TUESDAY
Wednesday	IDC_WEDNESDAY
Thursday	IDC_THURSDAY
Friday	IDC_FRIDAY
Line Chart	IDC_DRAW_LINE_CHART
Column Chart	IDC_DRAW_COLUMN_CHART
Scatter Chart	IDC_DRAW_SCATTER_CHART

Figure 12-11 Dialog control resource IDs

6. When you are finished adding the controls to the dialog resource, use the Add Variable Wizard to add to the CStockChartingView class DDX data members for each of the stock value Edit Box controls using the variable names and data types shown in Figure 12-12. Also, set the minimum and maximum values for each DDX data member to 0 and 100, respectively.

DDV will use these values to validate the numbers entered by users. Figure 12-13 shows an example of the Add Variable Wizard after creating a DDX data member for the IDC_MONDAY resource ID, and setting its minimum and maximum DDV values.

Resource ID	Variable Name	Data Type
IDC_MONDAY	m_iMonday	int
IDC_TUESDAY	m_iTuesday	int
IDC_WEDNESDAY	m_iWednesday	int
IDC_THURSDAY	m_iThursday	int
IDC_FRIDAY	m_iFriday	int

Figure 12-12 DDX data member names and types

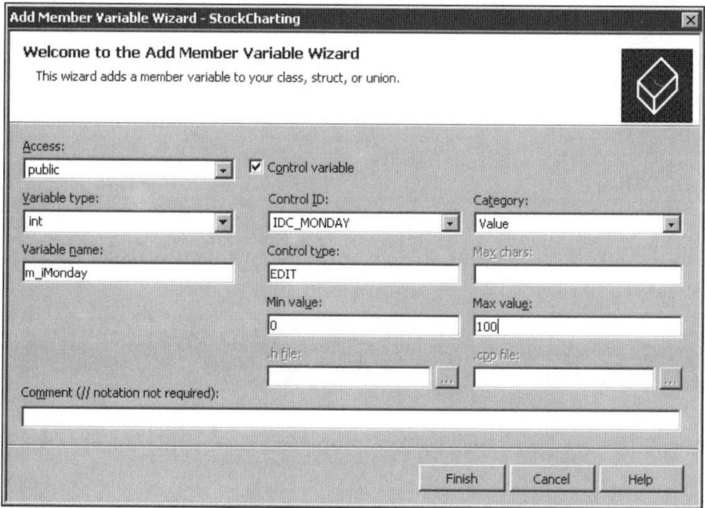

Figure 12-13 Add Member Variable Wizard after creating a DDX data member for the IDC_MONDAY resource ID and setting its minimum and maximum DDV values

The ability to draw into a device context is controlled by two functions: OnPaint() and OnDraw(). First, you will learn about the OnPaint() function.

Understanding the OnPaint() Function

All Windows applications must provide an event handler for the WM_PAINT message. The **WM_PAINT message** informs an application that its window must be redrawn, or *repainted*. Events that generate WM_PAINT messages include the user's resizing a window or a part of a window that is obscured by another window becoming visible again. A

WM_PAINT message is also generated by the UpdateWindow() function, which the MFC framework calls when an MFC program first executes. Calling the UpdateWindow() function allows an application to initially draw the contents of its windows. The message handler function for the WM_PAINT message is named **OnPaint()**, and is inherited from the CWnd class. The MFC framework automatically provides the OnPaint() function for handling any WM_PAINT messages it receives, as follows:

```
void CView::OnPaint() {
   // standard paint routine
   CPaintDC dc(this);
   OnPrepareDC(&dc);
   OnDraw(&dc);
}
```

The first statement in the OnPaint() function, `CPaintDC dc(this);`, declares an object named dc of the CPaintDC class. The dc object is the handle you will use to access an application's device context. Note that the CPaintDC device context class can only be used when responding to a WM_PAINT message. One of the requirements in an event handler that responds to a WM_PAINT message is that the handler must execute the BeginPaint() function at construction time and the EndPaint() function at destruction time. The constructor and destructor for the CPaintDC class automatically handle the calls to these functions. The second statement in the OnPaint() function `OnPrepareDC(&dc);`, is used for adjusting attributes of the device context. The default implementation of the OnPrepareDC() function does nothing. However, in order to handle special display and print capabilities such as pagination of multi-page documents, you override the OnPrepareDC() function in your derived CView class. The last statement in the OnPaint() function, `OnDraw(&dc);`, calls a function named OnDraw() and passes to it the address of the dc (device context) object.

You will never actually see the OnPaint() message handler in your programs because it is well hidden by the MFC framework. Also, you will not normally need to override the OnPaint() message handler in your programs. Because the OnPaint() message handler is hidden and you don't need to override it, you may be wondering where you add code that adds graphic objects to your window. You actually add your graphic object code to the OnDraw() function.

Overriding the OnDraw()Function

You use the **OnDraw() function**, which is inherited from the CView base class, to manage an application's device context. Essentially, the WM_PAINT message causes the OnPaint() event handler to execute, which, in turn, causes the OnDraw() function to execute. The most confusing part about drawing graphic objects through the device context is that the WM_PAINT message must go through the OnPaint() event handler to execute the OnDraw() function. You may think it would be easier to simply override the OnPaint() event handler and forget the OnDraw() function altogether. In fact, you can override the OnPaint() event handler and add all of your drawing code to the overridden function, if you so choose. However, graphic objects are not just displayed on the screen—they are also displayed in print preview and printed. The OnPaint() event handler prepares a "generic" device context that you can use for your graphic objects. Because it needs to be generic, the OnPaint() function cannot provide specific preview and printing functionality. This is one of the main reasons that the OnPaint() event handler is hidden by the MFC framework. The OnDraw() function, on the other hand, is used for adding specific functionality for the display and printing of graphic objects.

Next, you will override the OnDraw() function by adding a skeleton version of the function to the CStockChartingView class. The skeleton version of the overridden OnDraw() function that you add to the CStockChartingView class will not actually contain any functionality yet. You will add functionality to the OnDraw() function shortly.

To override the OnDraw() function in the CStockChartingView class.:

1. If necessary, open **StockChartingView.h** or **StockChartingView.cpp** in the Code Editor window.
2. Use the **Overrides** button in the Properties window to override the OnDraw() function in the CStockChartingView class. The new function is created, and your cursor is moved to the function definition.

The following code shows the OnDraw() function skeleton that you just added to the CStockChartingView implementation file:

```
void CStockChartingView::OnDraw(CDC* /*pDC*/)
{
  // TODO: Add your specialized code here and/or call the
base class
}
```

Notice that `CDC* pDC` is declared in the function header, creating an object pointer named pDC of the CDC class. You will use the **pDC pointer** as a handle for accessing the application's device context. By default, Visual C++ adds a comment block around the name of the pDC pointer; you will need to remove the comment block before you can use the pDC pointer in the body of the OnDraw() function. Recall that when the OnPaint() function called the OnDraw() function, it passed the dc object as an argument. However, the dc object, which represents the device context, was created using the CPaintDC device context class. Remember that the CPaintDC device context class is used only when responding to a WM_PAINT message. Therefore, the device context that was created with the CPaintDC class is passed to an object of the CDC class. Because the CDC class is the base class for the other device context classes, an object of the CDC class can be used to store an object of one of its derived classes. The passing of the pDC pointer to access an application's device context is illustrated in Figure 12-14.

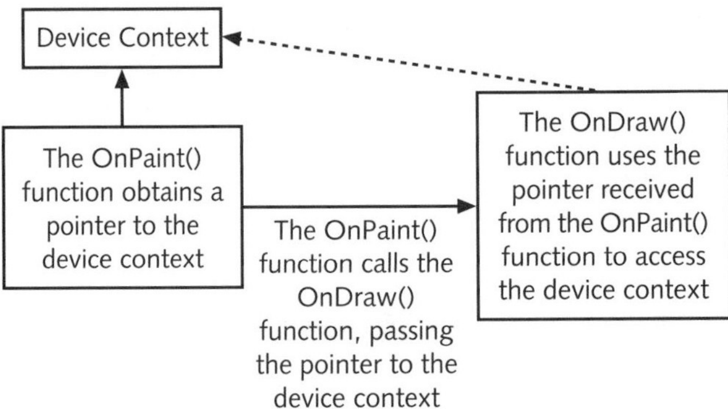

Figure 12-14 Passing of the pDC pointer to access an application's device context

Updating the Display

Before exploring individual drawing commands, you need to understand how to update the device context display—an important aspect of drawing. As you know, the OnDraw() function executes when the WM_PAINT message is generated, which occurs automatically when an application first loads or when the application window needs to be redrawn. However, what if you want to modify or replace your application's displayed graphic objects based on user input or program functionality?

To modify or replace the graphic objects that are already displayed in a device context, you must first call the Invalidate() function. The **Invalidate() function** notifies the update region that the window needs to be erased. The **update region** identifies portions of a window that need to be repainted. If an application's update region is not empty, then Windows generates a WM_PAINT message. The window is erased when the BegPaint() function executes in the OnPaint() handler. The OnPaint() handler then calls the OnDraw() function to update the display.

12

You can also notify the update region that only portions of a window need to be erased by using the InvalidateRect() and InvalidateRgn() functions. The InvalidateRect() function identifies a given rectangle as needing to be repainted. The InvalidateRgn() function identifies a specific region within a window as needing to be repainted. Passing a value of NULL to either of these functions adds the entire client area to the update region.

If you do not call the Invalidate() function to erase the device context before adding new graphic objects, then any new graphic objects you add will be placed directly on top of the old graphic objects. For example, the Stock Charting program loads the line chart by default. If you were to select the column chart and then the scatter chart without first erasing the device context with the Invalidate()function, the column chart would be placed on top of the original line chart, and then the scatter chart would be placed on top of the other two charts, as shown in Figure 12-15.

There are several methods for modifying and replacing graphic objects in the device context once you erase the window using the Invalidate() function. You will use an `enum` variable within a `switch` statement in the Stock Charting program to determine which chart to display. The `enum` variable you create for the Stock Charting program will be named m_Chart and will contain constants for each of the chart types: Line, Column, and Scatter. Next, you will create the m_Chart `enum` variable and `switch` statement in the Stock Charting program.

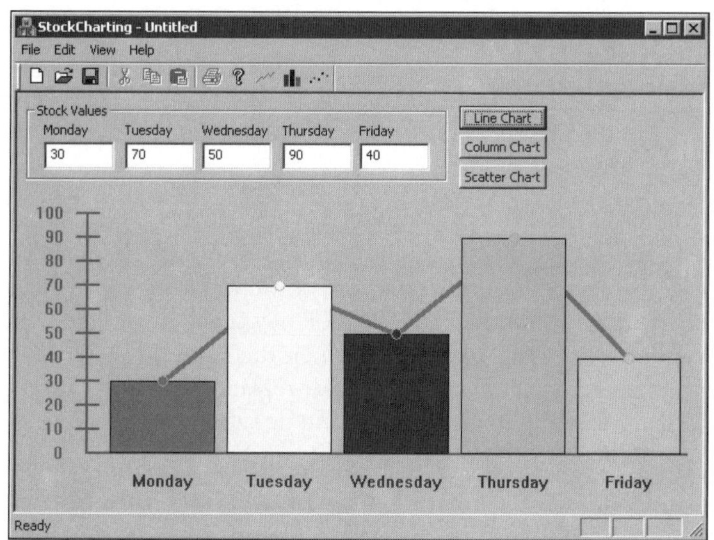

Figure 12-15 Stock Charting program without calls to the Invalidate() function

To create the m_Chart `enum` variable and `switch` statement in the Stock Charting program:

1. Open the **StockChartingView.h** file in the Code Editor window.
2. As shown in Figure 12-16, add the `enum` variable declaration to the first protected section, following the `DECLARE_DYNCREATE(CStockChartingView)` statement.
3. Next, open the **StockChartingView.cpp** file in the Code Editor window.
4. Replace the **`// TODO: add construction code here`** comment in the class constructor with the statement shown in Figure 12-17 to initialize the m_Chart variable to *Line*:

Start Page | StockCharting.rc...G_FORM - Dialog) | StockChartingView.h* | StockCh:

CStockChartingView | GetDocument

```
class CStockChartingView : public CFormView
{
protected: // create from serialization only
    CStockChartingView();
    DECLARE_DYNCREATE(CStockChartingView)
    enum {Line, Column, Scatter} m_Chart;

public:
    enum{ IDD = IDD_STOCKCHARTING_FORM };
```

Add this statement

Figure 12-16 enum variable declared in StockChartingView.h

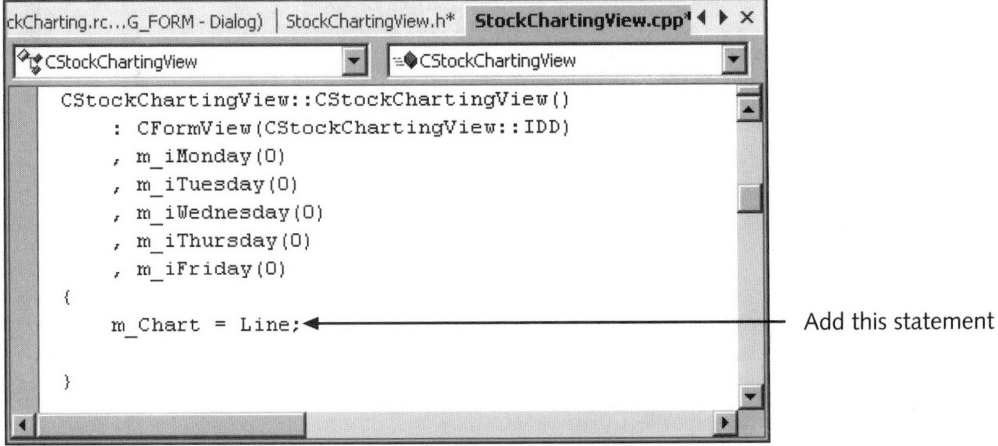

Figure 12-17 m_Chart variable initialized in CStockChartingView class constructor

5. Next, locate the OnDraw() function and add the **switch** statement shown in Figure 12-18. As you progress through the chapter, you will add code to each **case** label that draws the graphic objects for each chart type.

6. Also as shown in Figure 12-18, remove the comment block surrounding the pDC parameter.

Working with the CDC Class

Recall that the CDC class and its derived classes are used for accessing an application's device context. In addition to being the base class for other device context classes, the CDC class also contains all of the functions you need to draw in the device context. Later in this chapter, you will learn how to use some special graphics classes to change the display and formatting of drawn objects, but the CDC class is what you use to actually draw the objects. More specifically, to access the drawing functions in the CDC class, you use the pDC pointer that is passed to the OnDraw() function.

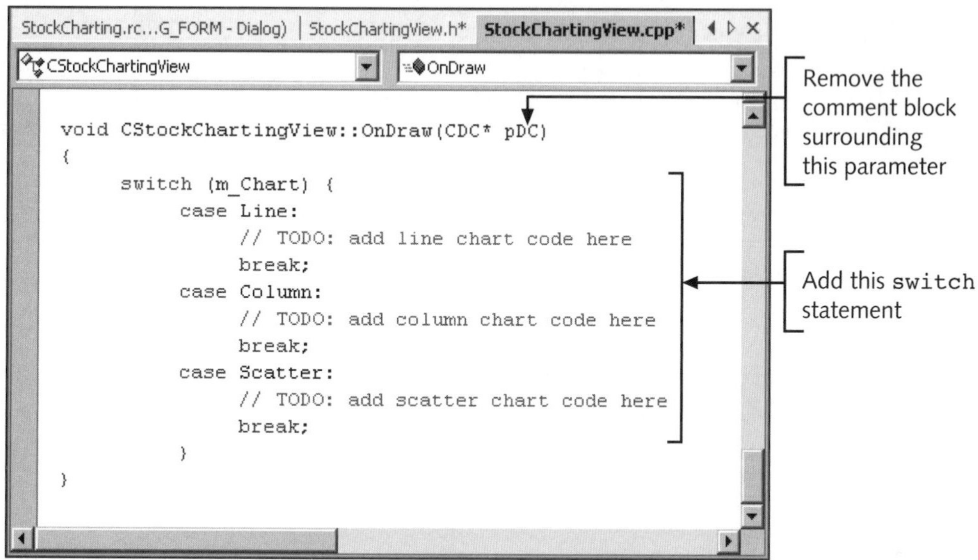

Figure 12-18 `switch` statement added to OnDraw()

The CDC class contains many functions for drawing and for working with the device context in general. The CDC Class topic in the MSDN Library provides a complete listing of CDC member functions. In this chapter, you will only work with the functions that you need to draw primitive graphic objects such as lines, rectangles, and circles, as well as functions for outputting text to the screen.

Drawing Lines

You use the **LineTo() function** to draw lines in the device context. The LineTo() function accepts two arguments: the x-coordinate and the y-coordinate of the line's ending position. You append the LineTo() function to the pDC pointer using the indirect member selection operator as follows: `pDC->LineTo(x, y)`. A line's starting position is drawn according to the current position. The **current position** is the starting point for any line or curve drawing function. The default current position is the mapping mode's point of origin, 0, 0. Therefore, to draw a line from the point of origin to position 100, 75 using the default MM_TEXT mapping mode, you modify the OnDraw() function as shown in the following code. Figure 12-19 shows the output.

```
void CGraphicsExampleView::OnDraw(CDC* pDC) {
   pDC->LineTo(100, 50);
}
```

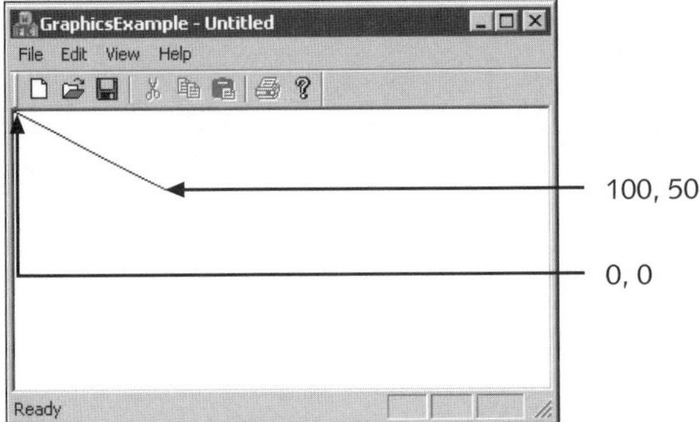

Figure 12-19 Output of a single LineTo() function

After you execute the LineTo() function, the x and y parameters you passed to it become the new current position. The following code shows how to create two connecting lines using the LineTo() function. Figure 12-20 shows the output.

```
void CGraphicsExampleView::OnDraw(CDC* pDC) {
   pDC->LineTo(100, 50);
   pDC->LineTo(150, 25);
}
```

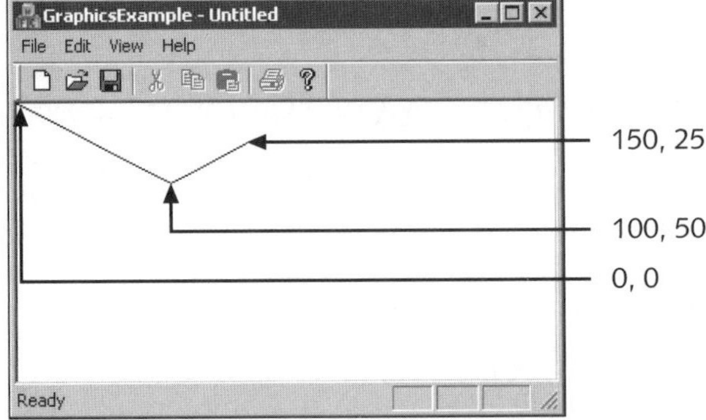

Figure 12-20 Output of two LineTo() functions

If you don't want your lines to start at the origin, 0, 0, you use the **MoveTo() function** to manually change the current position. You pass to the MoveTo() function an x parameter and a y parameter specifying the new current position. The following code shows a modified version of the OnDraw() function that uses LineTo() functions to draw a star. The first drawing statement calls the MoveTo() function to move the current position to 75, 255, which is the star's lower-left point. Then, each of the LineTo() functions draws a segment of the star. Figure 12-21 shows the output.

```
void CGraphicsExampleView::OnDraw(CDC* pDC) {
    pDC->MoveTo(75, 225);
    pDC->LineTo(150, 50);
    pDC->LineTo(225, 225);
    pDC->LineTo(50, 100);
    pDC->LineTo(250, 100);
    pDC->LineTo(75, 225);
}
```

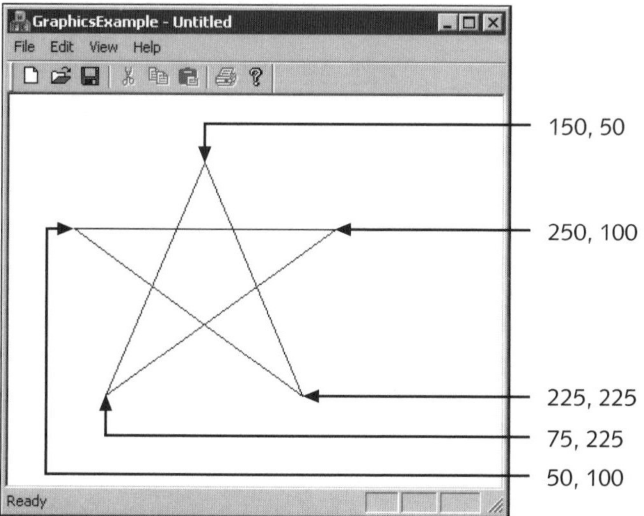

Figure 12-21 OnDraw() function that uses the MoveTo() function and LineTo() function to draw a star

Next, you will use LineTo() and MoveTo() functions to draw the axes for the Stock Chart program.

To use LineTo() and MoveTo() functions to draw the axes for the Stock Chart program:

1. Return to the **StockChartingView.cpp** file in the Code Editor window.
2. Add the statements shown in Figure 12-22 to the OnDraw() function. The first statement moves the current position to 60, 100, which is the point at which you will start drawing the y-axis. The second statement adds the y-axis by drawing a line to 60, 300, and the third statement adds the x-axis by drawing a line to 575, 300.

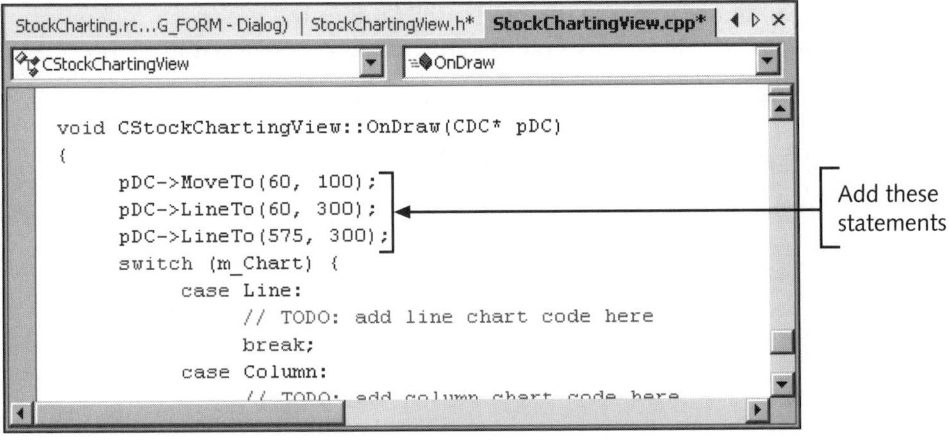

Figure 12-22 Line drawing statements added to the OnDraw() function

3. Next, above the **switch** statement, but after the statement **pDC->LineTo(575, 300);**, add the following statements to draw the hash marks along the y-axis. Hash marks appear along the y-axis every 20 pixels. Because the hash marks do not connect like the x-axis and y-axis, you must use a MoveTo() function to move the current position before drawing each hash mark.

```
void CStockChartingView::OnDraw(CDC* pDC) {
    ...
    pDC->MoveTo(50, 100);
    pDC->LineTo(70, 100);
    pDC->MoveTo(50, 120);
    pDC->LineTo(70, 120);
    pDC->MoveTo(50, 140);
    pDC->LineTo(70, 140);
    pDC->MoveTo(50, 160);
    pDC->LineTo(70, 160);
    pDC->MoveTo(50, 180);
    pDC->LineTo(70, 180);
    pDC->MoveTo(50, 200);
    pDC->LineTo(70, 200);
    pDC->MoveTo(50, 220);
    pDC->LineTo(70, 220);
    pDC->MoveTo(50, 240);
    pDC->LineTo(70, 240);
    pDC->MoveTo(50, 260);
    pDC->LineTo(70, 260);
    pDC->MoveTo(50, 280);
    pDC->LineTo(70, 280);
    switch (m_Chart) {
    ...
}
```

4. Build and execute the program. None of the program's functionality has been built yet, but you should see the axis lines as shown in Figure 12-23.
5. Close the Stock Charting program window.

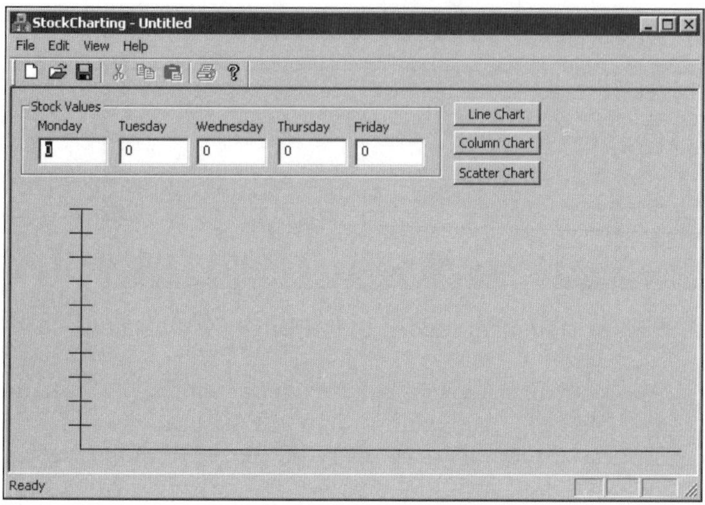

Figure 12-23 Stock Charting program axis lines

Next, you will use LineTo() and MoveTo() functions to create the Stock Chart program's line chart. Before creating the line chart, however, you need to understand the mathematics required to convert the numbers entered by users into values that correspond to the chart's grid system. Values in the MM_TEXT mapping mode increase as you move *down* the screen, which is the opposite of how your chart works. Values on your chart increase as you move *up* the chart. Additionally, the 0 points (or origin) of the x-axis and y-axis are not placed at the screen's 0 positions. As a consequence, the values a user enters do not directly correspond to values on the chart. You need some way to convert the users' values to the chart's values.

The x-values on the line chart are always placed at exact positions, 100 units apart. Monday's x-value is 125, Tuesday's x-value is 225, Wednesday's x-value is 325, Thursday's x-value is 425, and Friday's x-value is 525, as illustrated in Figure 12-24. These values are determined within the program and are not gathered from users, so you don't need to worry about converting them.

The value you are gathering from the user is the y-axis value, which represents the stock price. The 0 position on the y-axis is drawn at 300 pixels from the top of the window, and the 100 position on the y-axis is drawn at 100 pixels from the top of the window. Therefore, the y-axis displayed on screen is situated on a 200-pixel grid (300 – 100) that increases when you travel *down* the screen, instead of increasing as you go up the screen as your chart is supposed to do. You will need to do some math to get the value the user enters (from 0 to 100) to map correctly onto the y-axis.

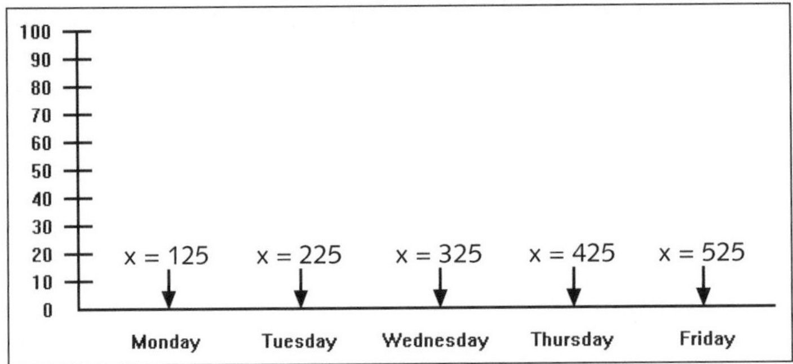

Figure 12-24 x-axis values

Each dollar that a user enters is equal to two pixels on the chart grid. Therefore, the first thing you need to do is multiply the value the user enters by two in order to get the value to correspond to the 200-pixel grid. After multiplying the stock value by two, you need to account for the fact that the mapping mode increases as you move down the screen, while your chart's value increases as you move up the screen. You account for this difference by subtracting the multiplied value from the 0 position, which is drawn at 300 pixels from the top of the screen. You will create local variables in the OnDraw() function and assign to them the values in the DDX data members, multiplied by two and subtracted from 300. The following code shows the local variable declaration and assignment you will add to the OnDraw() function for the Monday stock value:

```
int iMondayValue = 300 - (m_iMonday * 2);
```

12

Next, you will add code to the OnDraw() function that converts the stock values and displays the line chart.

To add code to the OnDraw() function that converts the stock values and displays the line chart:

1. Return to the **StockChartingView.cpp** file in the Code Editor window.
2. Immediately after the opening brace of the OnDraw() function, add the variable declarations and assignments shown in Figure 12-25 that convert the stock values.

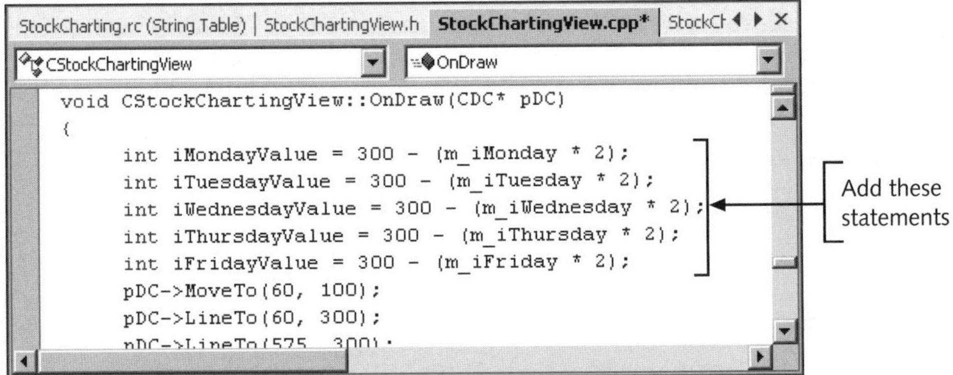

Figure 12-25 Variable declarations and assignments added to the OnDraw() function

3. Next, replace the **`// TODO: add line chart code here`** comment in the **`switch`** statement's Line **`case`** label with the statements shown in Figure 12-26. The first statement moves to the x-axis position of 125 and the y-axis position of the value assigned to the iMondayValue variable in the preceding step. Each subsequent statement then draws a line using the next stock value's associated local variable.

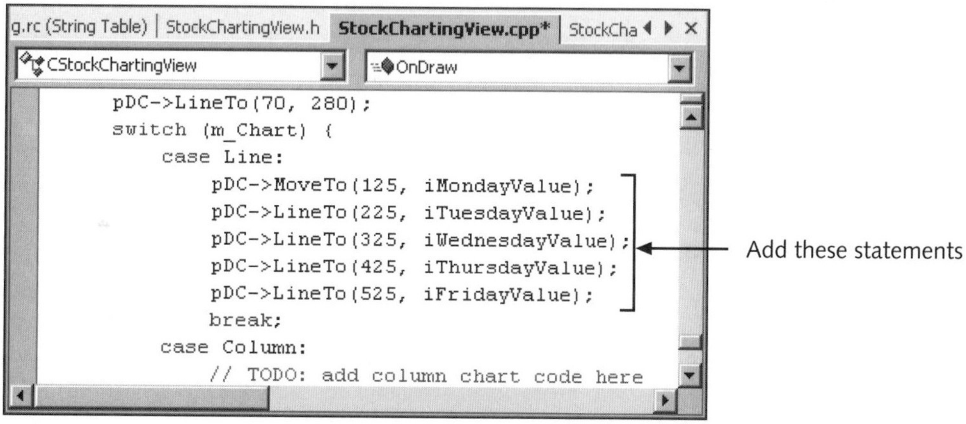

```
g.rc (String Table) | StockChartingView.h  StockChartingView.cpp* | StockCha
CStockChartingView                          OnDraw
    pDC->LineTo(70, 280);
    switch (m_Chart) {
        case Line:
            pDC->MoveTo(125, iMondayValue);
            pDC->LineTo(225, iTuesdayValue);
            pDC->LineTo(325, iWednesdayValue);
            pDC->LineTo(425, iThursdayValue);
            pDC->LineTo(525, iFridayValue);
            break;
        case Column:
            // TODO: add column chart code here
```

Add these statements

Figure 12-26 Line chart drawing statements added to the OnDraw() function

Before you can display the line chart, you need to add some message handlers to give the program its functionality. For each of the Edit Box controls, you will add EN_CHANGE message handlers that update the chart after the user enters a new value into one of the controls and moves to another control. You will also add to the IDC_DRAW_LINE_CHART resource ID a BN_CLICKED message handler that updates the display with the line chart when the user clicks the Line Chart command button.

To add message handlers to the Stock Charting program:

1. Add the following EN_CHANGE message handler functions to the CStockChartingView class for each of the Edit Box controls. The name of each message map function's resource ID is contained in a comment line above each function. The first statement in each function transfers the values in each control to its associated DDX data member. The Invalidate() function then erases the device context and raises a WM_PAINT message, which executes the OnDraw() function.

```
// IDC_MONDAY
void CStockChartingView::OnEnChangeMonday() {
```

```
      UpdateData(TRUE);
      Invalidate(TRUE);
}
   // IDC_TUESDAY
   void CStockChartingView::OnEnChangeTuesday() {
      UpdateData(TRUE);
      Invalidate(TRUE);
   }
   // IDC_WEDNESDAY
   void CStockChartingView::OnEnChangeWednesday() {
      UpdateData(TRUE);
      Invalidate(TRUE);
   }
   // IDC_THURSDAY
   void CStockChartingView::OnEnChangeThursday() {
      UpdateData(TRUE);
      Invalidate(TRUE);
   }
   // IDC_FRIDAY
   void CStockChartingView::OnEnChangeFriday() {
      UpdateData(TRUE);
      Invalidate(TRUE);
   }
```

2. Next, to the CStockChartingView class, add the following BN_CLICKED message handler function for the IDC_DRAW_LINE_CHART resource ID. The function contains the same statements as the Edit Box control function handlers, but it also contains a statement that assigns the m_Chart variable a value of *Line* to inform the **switch** statement in the OnDraw() function to display the line chart. The BN_CLICKED message handler for the IDC_DRAW_LINE_CHART resource ID will be necessary later when you want to redisplay the line chart after displaying the column or scatter charts.

```
void CStockChartingView::OnBnClickedDrawLineChart() {
   UpdateData(TRUE);
   m_Chart = Line;
   Invalidate(TRUE);
}
```

3. Rebuild and execute the program. You will not see a line chart at first because the chart starts at a default value of 0. Enter values in the edit boxes and see if the chart is updated correctly. Figure 12-27 shows the line chart after entering some values.

4. Close the Stock Charting program window.

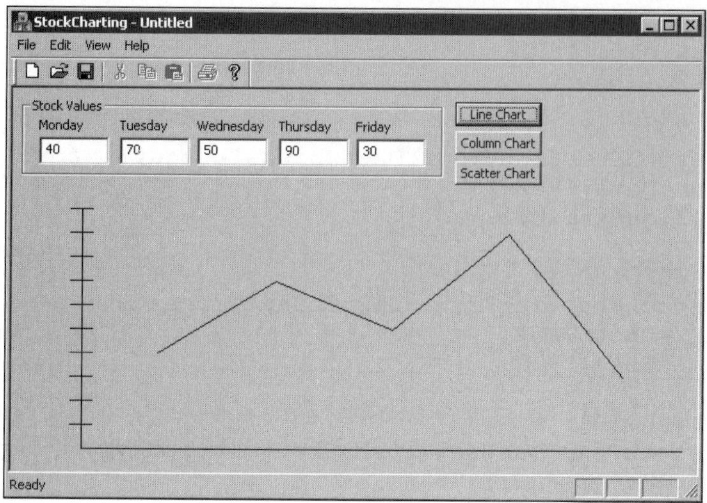

Figure 12-27 Line chart after entering values

Drawing Rectangles

You draw rectangles into the device context using the **Rectangle() function**. The Rectangle() function accepts four parameters: x1, y1, x2, and y2. The x1 and y1 parameters represent the rectangle's upper left corner, and the x2 and y2 parameters represent the rectangle's lower right corner. The following OnDraw() function with a Rectangle() statement draws the rectangle shown in Figure 12-28:

```
void CGraphicsExampleView::OnDraw(CDC* pDC) {
   pDC->Rectangle(50, 50, 200, 200);
}
```

There are many CDC functions for creating and manipulating rectangles. Later in this section, you will learn how to change a rectangle's line style and how to fill its interior with different colors or patterns.

Next, you will use rectangles to create the Stock Charting program's column chart. For determining the height of each rectangle (the height of each rectangle represents the value entered into each edit box), the column chart uses the same local variables that are declared and assigned values at the beginning of the OnDraw() function. However, you will use these local variables only to set each rectangle's y1 parameter, which represents the height of each rectangle. The x1, x2, and y2 parameters for each rectangle are set to permanent values. For example, the statement that creates the rectangle for the Monday stock value is written as follows:

```
pDC->Rectangle(80, iMondayValue, 170, 300);
```

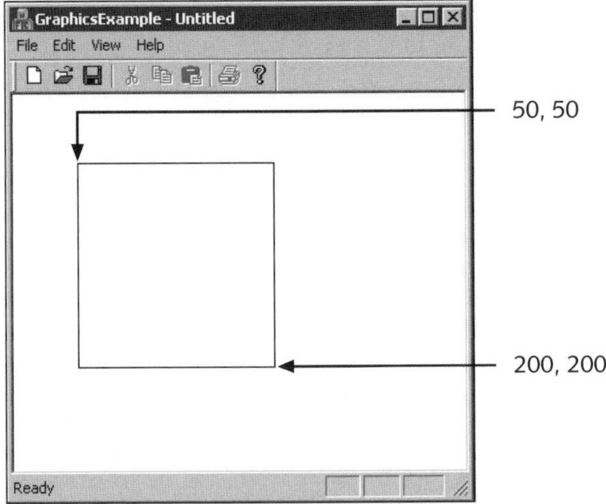

Figure 12-28 Output of a Rectangle() statement

To use rectangles to create the Stock Charting program's column chart:

1. Return to the **StockChartingView.cpp** file in the Code Editor window.
2. Replace the `// TODO: add column chart code here` comment in the `switch` statement's Column `case` label with the statements shown in Figure 12-29. Each statement uses the Rectangle() function to draw one of the chart's columns. The x1, x2, and y2 parameters are permanently set for each rectangle. However, each function determines the height of each column with an associated local variable as the y1 parameter.

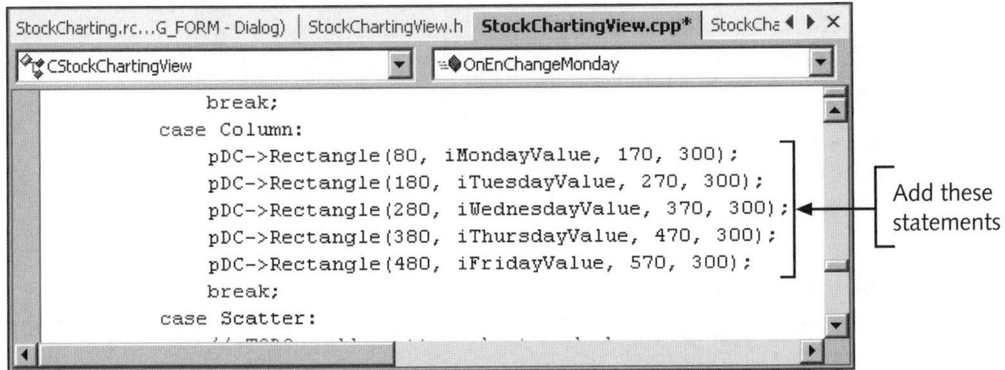

Figure 12-29 Rectangle drawing statements added to the OnDraw() function

3. Next, to the CStockChartingView class, add the following BN_CLICKED message handler function for the IDC_DRAW_COLUMN_CHART resource ID. The function contains the same statements as the message handler

function you added for the IDC_DRAW_LINE_CHART resource ID, except that the m_Chart variable is assigned a value of *Column*.

```
void CStockChartingView::OnBnClickedDrawColumnChart()
{
   UpdateData(TRUE);
   m_Chart = Column;
   Invalidate(TRUE);
}
```

4. Rebuild and execute the program. Click the **Column Chart** button and enter some values to see if the chart is updated correctly. Then, click the **Line Chart** button. The line chart should appear and display the same values that the column chart displayed. Figure 12-30 shows an example of the column chart after entering some values.
5. Close the Stock Charting program window.

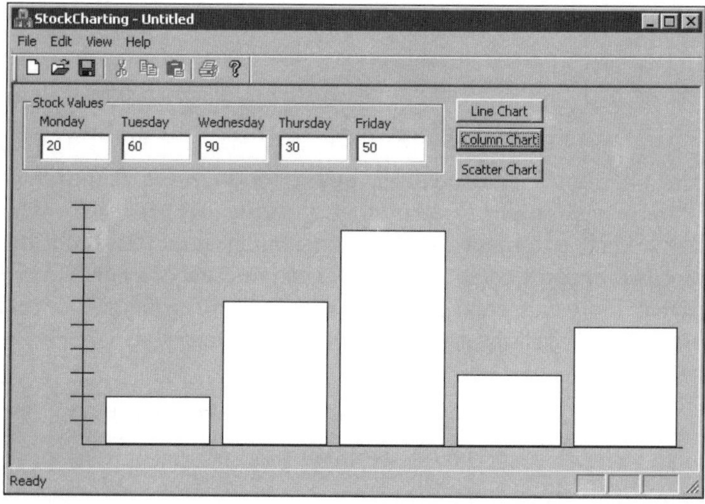

Figure 12-30 Column chart after entering values

Drawing Ellipses

In geometry, an ellipse is the mathematical term for an oval or circle. You use the **Ellipse() function** to draw ovals and circles in a device context. As with the Rectangle() function, the Ellipse() function accepts four parameters: x1, y1, x2, and y2. Instead of representing actual points on the ellipse, the x1, y1, x2, and y2 parameters represent the upper-left and lower-right positions of the ellipse's bounding rectangle. The **bounding rectangle** determines the height and width of an ellipse. An oval or circle contained by a bounding rectangle will be created to fill the height and width of the bounding rectangle. You do not actually see the bounding rectangle; it is more of a conceptual element for containing an oval or circle. Figure 12-31 illustrates an ellipse's bounding rectangle.

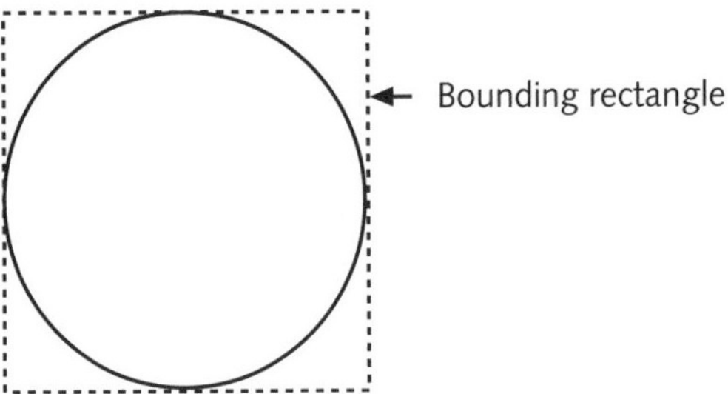

Figure 12-31 Ellipse's bounding rectangle

If you set the x1 and y1 parameters of the Ellipse() function to 0, then the ellipse's bounding rectangle will start in the upper-left corner of the client window. The following OnDraw() function contains a single Ellipse() function, whose x1 and y1 parameters are set to 0. Figure 12-32 shows the output.

```
void CGraphicsExampleView::OnDraw(CDC* pDC) {
   pDC->Ellipse(0, 0, 100, 100);
}
```

12

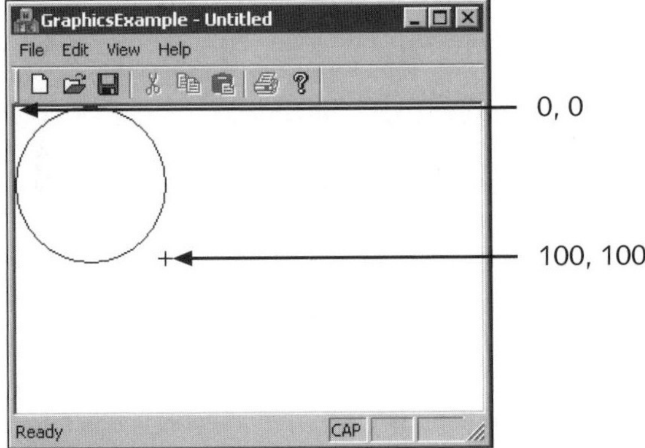

Figure 12-32 OnDraw() function with a single Ellipse() function

To create a perfect circle, the height and width of an ellipse's bounding rectangle must be equal. To create a bounding rectangle with an equal height and width, the value returned when you subtract the x1 parameter from the x2 parameter must be equal to the value that is returned when you subtract the y1 parameter from the y2 parameter. For example, the statement `Ellipse(50, 100, 150, 200);` creates a circle because both the height and the width are equal to 100. If the height and width of an ellipse's bounding rectangle are not equal, then the ellipse will be an oval. For example, the statement

`Ellipse(50, 100, 150, 300);` creates an oval because the width is equal to 100, but the height is equal to 200. The following OnDraw() function creates the two ellipses shown in Figure 12-33. The first ellipse is an oval, and the second ellipse is a circle.

```
void CGraphicsExampleView::OnDraw(CDC* pDC) {
   pDC->Ellipse(10, 10, 300, 50);
   pDC->Ellipse(50, 100, 150, 200);
}
```

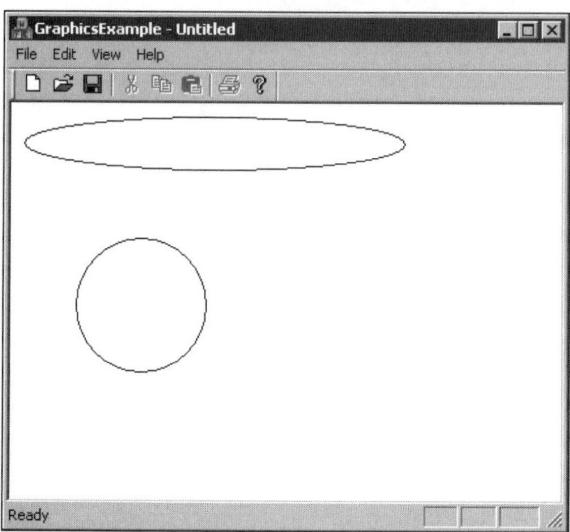

Figure 12-33 OnDraw() function with two Ellipse() functions

Next, you will create the Stock Charting program's scatter chart. You will use ellipses to represent each individual value plotted on the scatter chart. The scatter chart code uses the local variables to calculate the placement of each ellipse on the y-axis. However, the calculations are slightly different from those for the line and column charts. Each local variable represents the exact position of each stock value on the y-axis. In addition, you want each ellipse on the scatter chart to be a circle that is 10 pixels in diameter. To calculate the width of the bounding rectangle for each ellipse, you will hard-code the x1 and x2 parameters. To set the y-axis parameters so that the height of the ellipse is equal to 10, you will subtract 5 from the local variable to determine the y1 parameter, but add 5 to the local variable to determine the y2 parameter. For example, the statement that creates the ellipse for the Monday stock value is written as follows:

```
pDC->Ellipse(120, iMondayValue - 5, 130, iMondayValue + 5);
```

To create the Stock Charting program's scatter chart:

1. Return to the **StockChartingView.cpp** file in the Code Editor window.

2. Replace the `// TODO: add scatter chart code here` comment in the `switch` statement's Scatter `case` label with the statements shown in Figure 12-34. Each statement uses the Ellipse() function to draw one of the chart's circles. The x1 and x2 parameters are permanently set for each ellipse. To determine the height of each ellipse, each function subtracts a value of 5 from an associated local variable for the y1 parameter and adds a value of 5 to the same associated local variable.

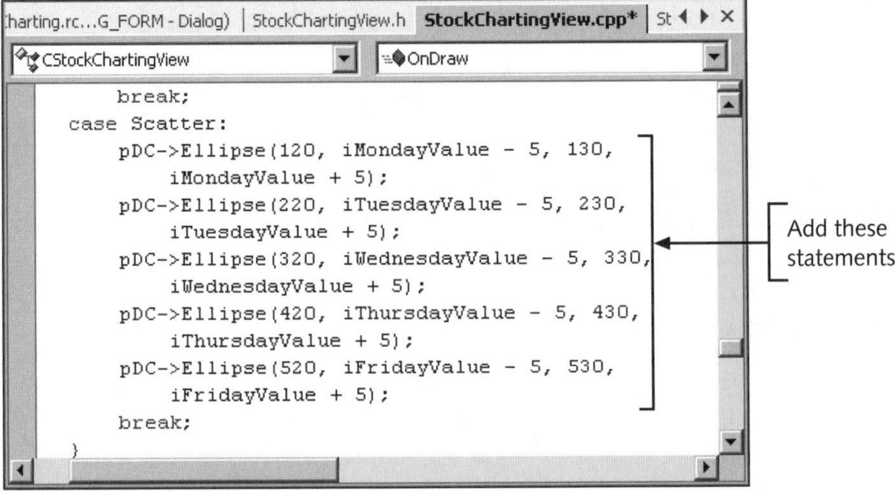

Figure 12-34 Ellipsis drawing statements added to the OnDraw() function

12

3. Next, to the CStockChartingView class add the following BN_CLICKED message handler function for the IDC_DRAW_SCATTER_CHART resource ID. The function contains the same statements as the message handler functions you added for the charts, except that the m_Chart variable is assigned a value of *Scatter*.

```
void CStockChartingView::OnBnClickedDrawScatterChart() {
   UpdateData(TRUE);
   m_Chart = Scatter;
   Invalidate(TRUE);
}
```

4. Rebuild and execute the program. Click the **Scatter Chart** button. Notice that when you first view the Scatter Chart, each of the ellipses is set to a value of 0, and they are therefore lined up with the x-axis. Next, enter some values to see if the chart is updated correctly. Then, try clicking the other two charts. Each chart should appear and display the same values that the scatter chart displayed. Figure 12-35 shows an example of the scatter chart after entering some values.

5. Close the Stock Charting program window.

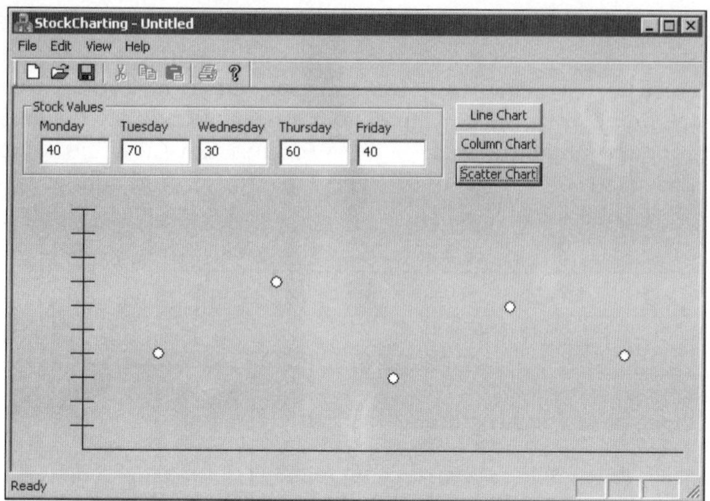

Figure 12-35 Scatter chart after entering values

Outputting Text

You add text to the device context using the **TextOut() function**. The TextOut() function accepts three parameters, using the syntax `pDC.TextOut(x, y, string)`. The *x* and *y* parameters represent the upper-left corner, where you want to place the text according to the mapping mode, and the *string* parameter is a CString variable or a literal string containing the text you want to be displayed. For example, in the following OnDraw() function, the text *Sample Text* is assigned to a CString variable named sText. The TextOut() function displays the contents of the sText variable at position 100, 100 in the device context. Figure 12-36 shows the output.

```
void CGraphicsExampleView::OnDraw(CDC* pDC) {
   CString sText = "Sample Text";
   pDC->TextOut(100, 100, sText);
}
```

Modifying the default font that Windows uses to display text graphic objects is a surprisingly difficult operation that is beyond the scope of this book. If you would like more information on how to modify the font for text objects, refer to the CFont class topic in the MSDN Library.

Notice that the text string displayed in Figure 12-36 is enclosed in a bounding rectangle. When you use the TextOut() function, a bounding rectangle is created for the text, similar to the bounding rectangle that is created for ellipses. The bounding rectangle for a text object is only as large as the text string itself.

The CDC class contains several functions for manipulating text objects. Two of the CDC text functions you will use in this chapter are the SetTextAlign() function and the

SetTextColor() functions. The **SetTextAlign() function** sets the horizontal and vertical text alignment for text objects according to the *x* and *y* parameters of the TextOut() function. You append the SetTextAlign() function to the pDC pointer with a member selection operator, just as you do for other CDC functions. To set the alignment you want, you pass to the SetTextAlign() function one of the alignment values listed in Figure 12-37. The TA_LEFT, TA_CENTER, and TA_RIGHT values align text according to the TextOut() function's x-value. The TA_BASELINE, TA_BOTTOM, and TA_TOP values align text according to the TextOut() function's y-value.

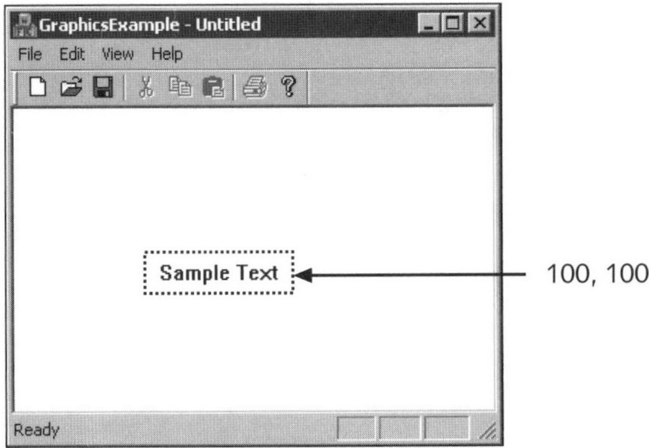

Figure 12-36 OnDraw() function with a single TextOut() statement

12

Value	Description
TA_BASELINE	The baseline of the text string aligns with the y-axis value.
TA_BOTTOM	The bottom of the bounding rectangle aligns with the y-axis value.
TA_CENTER	The bounding rectangle aligns in the middle of the x-axis value.
TA_LEFT	The bounding rectangle aligns to the left of the x-axis value.
TA_RIGHT	The bounding rectangle aligns to the right of the x-axis value.
TA_TOP	The top of the bounding rectangle aligns with the y-axis value.

Figure 12-37 SetTextAlign() function alignment values

TA_LEFT is the default horizontal alignment, and TA_TOP is the default vertical alignment.

In order to set text alignment, you must call the SetTextAlign() function before you call any TextOut() statements. Any TextOut() statements that follow a SetTextAlign() function will use that SetTextAlign() function's alignment setting until another SetTextAlign() function is called in the code. For example, the following code includes several SetTextAlign()

and TextOut() function calls. Each call to a SetTextAlign() function changes the alignment for any TextOut() objects that follow. Figure 12-38 shows the output.

```
void CGraphicsExampleView::OnDraw(CDC* pDC) {
   pDC->SetTextAlign(TA_BOTTOM);
   pDC->TextOut(50, 50, "Bottom Alignment");
   pDC->SetTextAlign(TA_BASELINE);
   pDC->TextOut(200, 50, "Baseline Alignment");
   pDC->SetTextAlign(TA_TOP);
   pDC->TextOut(350, 50, "Top Alignment");
   pDC->SetTextAlign(TA_LEFT);
   pDC->TextOut(200, 50, "Left Alignment");
   pDC->SetTextAlign(TA_CENTER);
   pDC->TextOut(200, 100, "Center Alignment");
   pDC->SetTextAlign(TA_RIGHT);
   pDC->TextOut(200, 150, "Right Alignment");
}
```

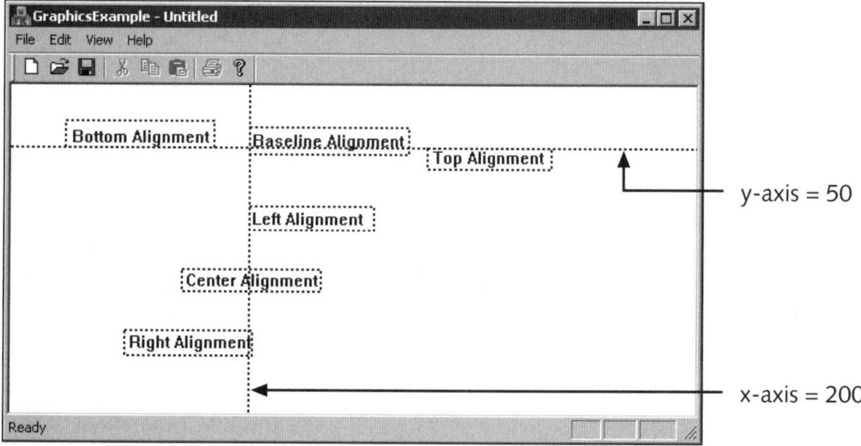

Figure 12-38 Output of SetTextAlign() and TextOut() function calls

The **SetTextColor()** function sets the color of any text objects displayed with the TextOut() function. You pass to the SetTextColor() function an RGB color value using either the RGB() macro or a COLORREF variable. Any TextOut() statements that follow a SetTextColor() function will use that SetTextColor() function's color setting until another SetTextColor() function is called in the code. For example, the following code displays three text objects. The first text object is set to a light gray color value, the second text object is set to a dark gray color value, and the third text object is set to black. Figure 12-39 shows the output.

```
pDC->SetTextColor(RGB(192, 192, 192));
pDC->TextOut(50, 50, "Light Gray Text");
pDC->SetTextColor(RGB(128, 128, 128));
```

```
pDC->TextOut(50, 100, "Dark Gray Text");
pDC->SetTextColor(RGB(0, 0, 0));
pDC->TextOut(50, 150, "Black Text");
```

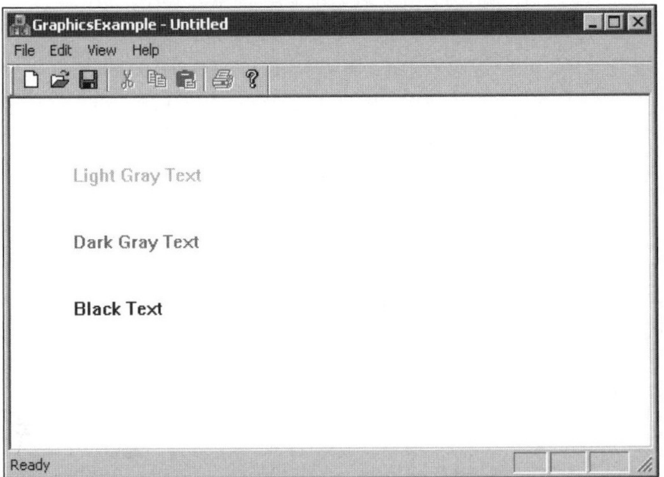

Figure 12-39 Output of SetTextColor() and TextOut() function calls

Next, you will add the axis labels to the Stock Charting program. The y-axis labels are right-aligned and set to dark gray. The x-axis labels are center-aligned and set to blue.

12

To add the axis labels to the Stock Charting program:

1. Return to the **StockChartingView.cpp** file in the Code Editor window.
2. Immediately above the `switch` statement in the OnDraw() function, add the following statements to draw the y-axis labels. The first statement sets the text alignment to right, the second statement sets the text color to dark gray, and the rest of the statements draw the text labels.

```
void CStockChartingView::OnDraw(CDC* pDC) {
...
    pDC->SetTextAlign(TA_RIGHT);
    pDC->SetTextColor(RGB(128, 128, 128));
    pDC->TextOut(40, 92, "100");
    pDC->TextOut(40, 112, "90");
    pDC->TextOut(40, 132, "80");
    pDC->TextOut(40, 152, "70");
    pDC->TextOut(40, 172, "60");
    pDC->TextOut(40, 192, "50");
    pDC->TextOut(40, 212, "40");
    pDC->TextOut(40, 232, "30");
    pDC->TextOut(40, 252, "20");
    pDC->TextOut(40, 272, "10");
    pDC->TextOut(40, 292, "0");
```

```
    switch (m_Chart) {
    ...
}
```

3. Next, above the **switch** statement in the OnDraw() function, immediately following the code you added in Step 2, add the following statements to draw the x-axis labels. The SetTextAlign() function changes the text alignment to center, and the SetTextColor() function changes the text color to blue.

```
void CStockChartingView::OnDraw(CDC* pDC) {
...
    pDC->SetTextAlign(TA_CENTER);
    pDC->SetTextColor(RGB(0, 0, 255));
    pDC->TextOut(125,315, "Monday");
    pDC->TextOut(225,315, "Tuesday");
    pDC->TextOut(325,315, "Wednesday");
    pDC->TextOut(425,315, "Thursday");
    pDC->TextOut(525,315, "Friday");
    switch (m_Chart) {
    ...
}
```

4. Rebuild and execute the program. Figure 12-40 shows how the new axis labels appear before entering any stock values.

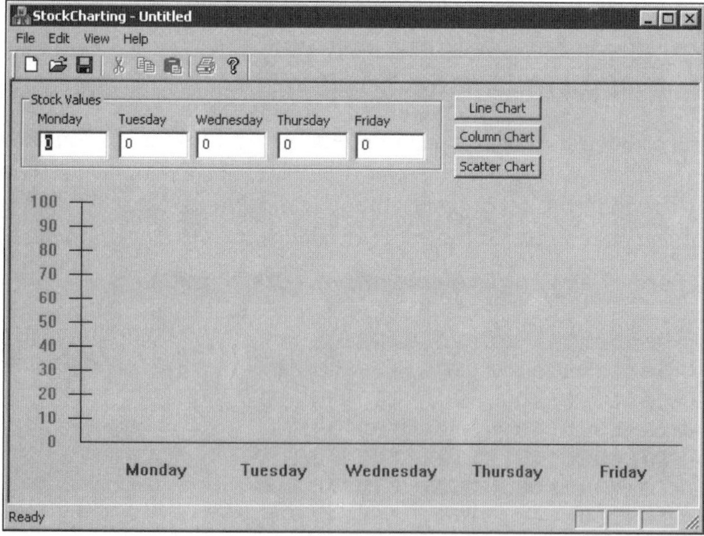

Figure 12-40 Stock Charting program after adding axis labels

5. Close the Stock Charting program window.

Graphic Object Classes

MFC includes several GDI classes for modifying the appearance of the graphic objects that you add to a device context. Some of the display elements you can select with the GDI classes include the size and colors of lines, the color and patterns used to fill the interiors of closed objects, and the fonts used to display text objects. The two graphic classes you will learn about in this chapter are the CPen and CBrush classes.

Working with Pens

When you draw any type of object that includes lines, you use a pen to draw those lines. A **pen** is an object created with the CPen class that determines a line's style, thickness, and color. You control the formatting of a pen with constructor functions. There are two constructors for creating a pen: a default constructor and a parameterized constructor. If you use the default constructor, then you must call the CreatePen() function to initialize the pen object. The **CreatePen() function** initializes a new pen with style, width, and color values. The syntax for using the CreatePen() function is as follows:

```
CPen variable;
variable.CreatePen(style, width, color);
```

The parameterized constructor uses a simpler syntax to declare and initialize a pen object in the same statement, as follows:

```
CPen variable(style, width, color);
```


Notice that you do not use the CreatePen() function with the parameterized constructor. Rather, the parameterized constructor for the CPen class calls the CreatePen() function for you.

The first parameter you pass when creating a new CPen object is the style parameter. The style parameter determines the line style (solid, dashed, and so on) with which you want to draw. Figure 12-41 lists some of the common style values you can pass to the style parameter.

Style	Description
PS_SOLID	Creates a solid line
PS_DASH	Creates a dashed line
PS_DOT	Creates a dotted line
PS_DASHDOT	Creates a line with alternating dashes and dots
PS_DASHDOTDOT	Creates a line with alternating dashes and double dots
PS_INSIDEFRAME	Creates a line that does not extend outside of an object's bounding rectangle
PS_NULL	Creates a pen that draws a blank line

Figure 12-41 Common pen styles

The CPen object width parameter determines the width of a line. If you pass a value of 0 to the width parameter, then the line thickness will always be one pixel wide, regardless of the mapping mode that is currently in use. However, if you pass a value of 1 or higher, then the line thickness will be set to the units of the mapping mode you are using, using the passed number. For example, if you pass a value of 3 and you are using a mapping mode of MM_TEXT, then the line thickness will be three pixels wide. If you are using a mapping mode of MM_LOENGLISH (which measures its units in increments of .01 inches), then the line thickness will be .03 inches wide.

The last CPen object parameter, color, determines the line color, using an RGB color value.

The dashed and dotted pen styles listed in Figure 12-41 work only if the CPen object width parameter is set to a value of 1. If you pass a value larger than 1 to the width parameter, then the PS_SOLID pen style will be used, regardless of which style parameter you pass to the CPen object.

Even though you declare and initialize a CPen object, the pen will not be applied to the device context until you pass the new object to the SelectObject() function. The **SelectObject() function** loads an object into the device context. In more simplified terms, you can think of the device context as being an artist. For your device context "artist" to use a different pen, you must use the SelectObject() function to actually hand it a new pen. The pen you last applied to the device context, using the SelectObject() function, will be used for all line drawing until you select a new pen into the device context. The following code shows how to use the CPen object to draw some lines that have different styles, thickness, and color. Figure 12-42 shows the output.

```
CPen solidPen(PS_SOLID, 1, RGB(0, 0, 0));
pDC->SelectObject(solidPen);
pDC->MoveTo(25, 50);
pDC->LineTo(300, 50);
CPen dashedPen(PS_DASH, 1, RGB(0, 0, 0));
pDC->SelectObject(dashedPen);
pDC->MoveTo(25, 75);
pDC->LineTo(300, 75);
CPen dottedPen(PS_DOT, 1, RGB(0, 0, 0));
pDC->SelectObject(dottedPen);
pDC->MoveTo(25, 100);
pDC->LineTo(300, 100);
CPen thickPen(PS_SOLID, 3, RGB(0, 0, 0));
pDC->SelectObject(thickPen);
pDC->MoveTo(25, 125);
pDC->LineTo(300, 125);
CPen thickerPen(PS_SOLID, 6, RGB(0, 0, 0));
pDC->SelectObject(thickerPen);
pDC->MoveTo(25, 150);
pDC->LineTo(300, 150);
CPen lightGrayThickPen(PS_SOLID, 6,
      RGB(192, 192, 192));
```

```
pDC->SelectObject(lightGrayThickPen);
pDC->MoveTo(25, 175);
pDC->LineTo(300, 175);
CPen darkGrayThinPen(PS_SOLID, 1,
       RGB(128, 128, 128));
pDC->SelectObject(darkGrayThinPen);
pDC->MoveTo(25, 200);
pDC->LineTo(300, 200);
```

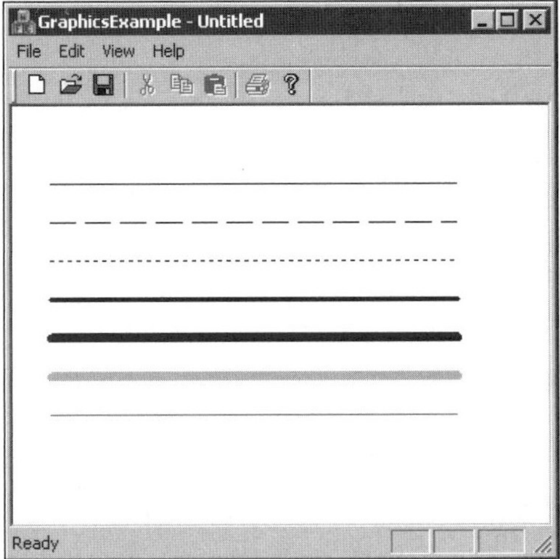

Figure 12-42 Pen examples

Although the preceding code and figure use LineTo() functions for simplicity's sake, you can also use pens with rectangles, ellipses, and other types of objects.

Next, you will add some pens to the Stock Charting program that you will use to add different line styles and line colors to the program's graphical elements.

To add some pens to the Stock Charting program:

1. Return to the **StockChartingView.cpp** file in the Code Editor window.
2. First, in the OnDraw() function, declare and initialize some pens, as shown in Figure 12-43. All of these pens use a solid border style. The axisPen is two pixels wide and dark gray, and will be used for the axis lines. The linePen is four pixels wide and red, and will be used for the line that is drawn by the line chart. The columnPen pen is one pixel wide and black, and will be used for the borders of the rectangles displayed by the column chart. The scatterPen is also one pixel wide and will be used for the borders of the ellipses in the scatter chart. The scatterPen is set to light gray so that the borders of the ellipses match the color of the dialog window—you want each ellipse to appear as a solid color on the scatter chart, with no visible border.

3. Also as shown in Figure 12-43, add the statement **`pDC->SelectObject (axisPen);`** to select the axisPen into the device context.

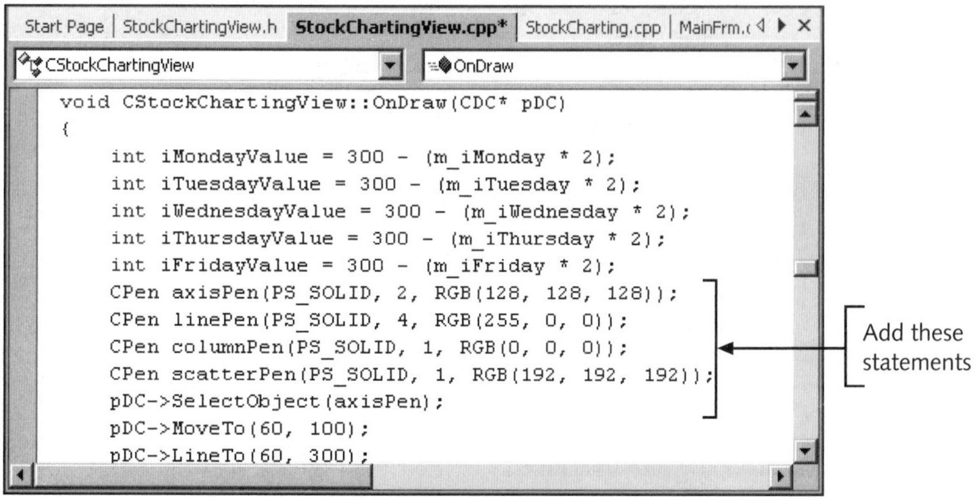
Start Page
StockChartingView.h
StockChartingView.cpp*
StockCharting.cpp
MainFrm.c
CStockChartingView
OnDraw
void CStockChartingView::OnDraw(CDC* pDC)
{
int iMondayValue = 300 - (m_iMonday * 2);
int iTuesdayValue = 300 - (m_iTuesday * 2);
int iWednesdayValue = 300 - (m_iWednesday * 2);
int iThursdayValue = 300 - (m_iThursday * 2);
int iFridayValue = 300 - (m_iFriday * 2);
CPen axisPen(PS_SOLID, 2, RGB(128, 128, 128));
CPen linePen(PS_SOLID, 4, RGB(255, 0, 0));
CPen columnPen(PS_SOLID, 1, RGB(0, 0, 0));
CPen scatterPen(PS_SOLID, 1, RGB(192, 192, 192));
pDC->SelectObject(axisPen);
pDC->MoveTo(60, 100);
pDC->LineTo(60, 300);
Add these statements

Figure 12-43 Pen statements added to the OnDraw() function

4. To select the linePen into the device context, add the following statement as the first statement in the `switch` statement's Line `case` label:

```
...
case Line:
   pDC->SelectObject(linePen);
   pDC->MoveTo(125, iMondayValue);
...
```

5. To select the columnPen into the device context, add the following statement as the first statement in the `switch` statement's Column `case` label:

```
...
case Column:
   pDC->SelectObject(columnPen);
   pDC->Rectangle(80, iMondayValue, 170, 300);
...
```

6. To select the scatterPen into the device context, add the following statement as the first statement in the `switch` statement's Scatter `case` label:

```
...
case Scatter:
   pDC->SelectObject(scatterPen);
   pDC->Ellipse(120, iMondayValue - 5, 130,
     iMondayValue + 5);
...
```

7. Rebuild and execute the program. Because the initial stock values are set to 0, you will see the red line that plots the values on the line chart visible along the x-axis. Figure 12-44 shows how the program with the new pens appears after entering some values for the line chart.

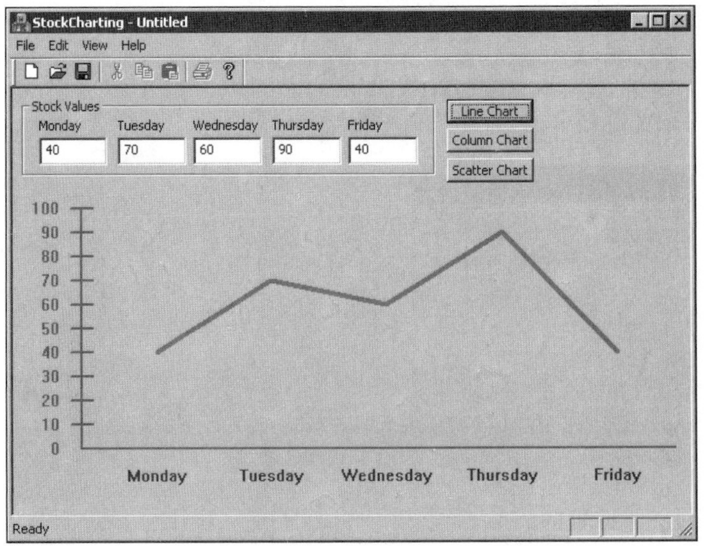

Figure 12-44 Line Chart after adding pens to the Stock Charting program

8. Close the Stock Charting program window.

Working with Brushes

When you draw any type of closed object, such as rectangles or ellipses, you can select the formatting of the brush that you use to fill those objects. A **brush** is an object created with the CBrush class that determines the color and pattern that is drawn in the interior of a closed object. As with the CPen class, there are multiple methods of constructing a brush. You will use the same method of constructing and initializing a brush with CBrush constructors that you used with the CPen class. The CBrush class, however, includes several overloaded constructors that allow you to construct brushes using different attributes; you will learn about two of those constructors. The first overloaded constructor creates a brush that fills an object with a solid color. The second overloaded constructor creates a brush that fills an object with a predefined pattern in a selected color.

The syntax for creating a brush that fills an object with a solid color is `CBrush` *`variable(color)`*`;`. You pass to the constructor an RGB color using the RGB macro or COLORREF macro. For example, to create a brush named darkGrayBrush(), you use the statement CBrush darkGrayBrush(RGB(128, 128, 128));. Once you create a brush, you must select it into the device context by using the SelectObject() function. The brush you last applied to the device context using the SelectObject() function will be used for all fills until you select a new brush into the device context. For example, the following code draws the two circles displayed in Figure 12-45:

```
CBrush darkGrayBrush(RGB(128, 128, 128));
pDC->SelectObject(darkGrayBrush);
pDC->Ellipse(25, 25, 100, 100);
CBrush lightGrayBrush(RGB(192, 192, 192));
pDC->SelectObject(lightGrayBrush);
pDC->Ellipse(125, 25, 200, 100);
```

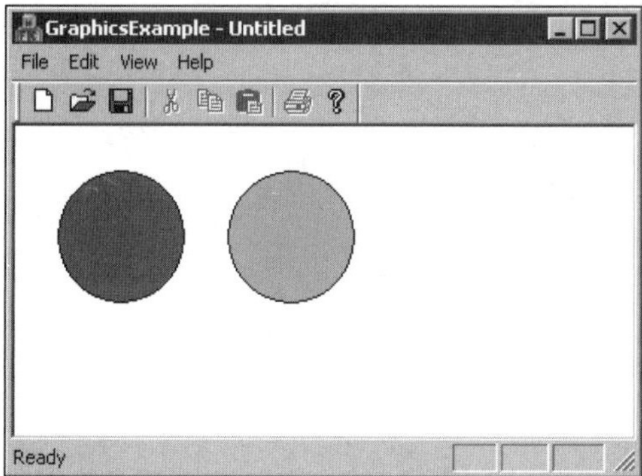

Figure 12-45 Circles filled by colored brushes

The syntax for creating a brush that fills an object with a predefined pattern in a selected color is `CBrush` ***`variable(pattern, color)`***`;`. The value for the *pattern* parameter can be any of the predefined values listed in Figure 12-46, and the *color* parameter is simply an RGB color with which you want to draw the pattern.

Value	Description
HS_BDIAGONAL	Downward 45-degree crosshatch
HS_CROSS	Horizontal and vertical crosshatch
HS_DIAGCROSS	45-degree crosshatch
HS_FDIAGONAL	Upward 45-degree crosshatch
HS_HORIZONTAL	Horizontal crosshatch
HS_VERTICAL	Vertical crosshatch

Figure 12-46 Brush pattern values

The following code draws the same circles from the previous example, but this time using the CBrush class that creates patterns. The brush pattern applied to the first circle is HS_HORIZONTAL, and the brush pattern applied to the second circle is HS_CROSS. Figure 12-47 shows the output.

```
CBrush darkGrayBrush(HS_HORIZONTAL, RGB(128, 128, 128));
pDC->SelectObject(darkGrayBrush);
pDC->Ellipse(25, 25, 100, 100);
CBrush lightGrayBrush(HS_CROSS, RGB(192, 192, 192));
pDC->SelectObject(lightGrayBrush);
pDC->Ellipse(125, 25, 200, 100);
```

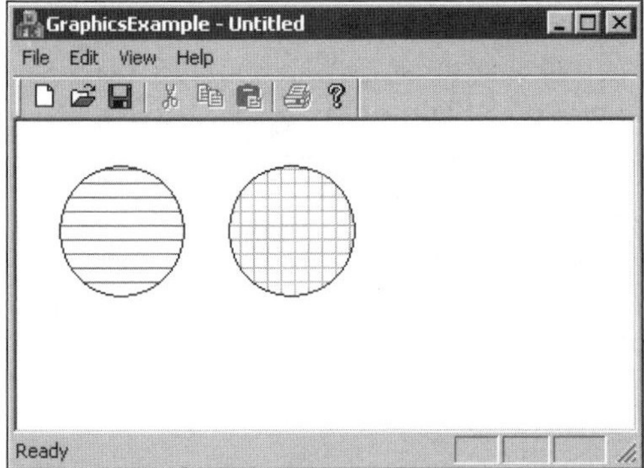

Figure 12-47 Circles filled by patterned and colored brushes

Next, you will add some colored brushes to the Stock Charting program that you will use to fill in the rectangles on the column chart and the ellipses on the scatter chart.

To add some colored brushes to the Stock Charting program:

1. Return to the **StockChartingView.cpp** file in the Code Editor window.
2. First, as shown in Figure 12-48, define the following brushes that you will apply to the rectangles in the column chart and the ellipses in the scatter chart. Each brush corresponds to a weekly stock. Add the brushes to the OnDraw() function after the code that defines the pens, which you added in the previous set of steps.

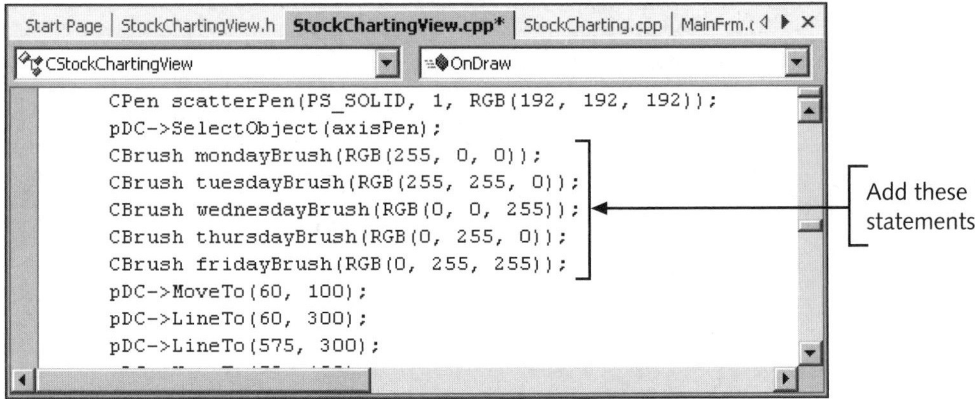

Figure 12-48 Brush statement added to the OnDraw() function

12

3. Next, add the following statements, which appear in boldface, to the Column and Scatter `case` labels in the `switch` statement. Each statement selects the appropriate brush into the device context, depending on which column or ellipse is to be drawn next.

```
...
case Column:
   pDC->SelectObject(columnPen);
   pDC->SelectObject(mondayBrush);
   pDC->Rectangle(80, iMondayValue, 170, 300);
   pDC->SelectObject(tuesdayBrush);
   pDC->Rectangle(180, iTuesdayValue, 270, 300);
   pDC->SelectObject(wednesdayBrush);
   pDC->Rectangle(280, iWednesdayValue, 370, 300);
   pDC->SelectObject(thursdayBrush);
   pDC->Rectangle(380, iThursdayValue, 470, 300);
   pDC->SelectObject(fridayBrush);
   pDC->Rectangle(480, iFridayValue, 570, 300);
   break;
case Scatter:
   pDC->SelectObject(scatterPen);
   pDC->SelectObject(mondayBrush);
   pDC->Ellipse(120, iMondayValue - 5, 130,
     iMondayValue + 5);
   pDC->SelectObject(tuesdayBrush);
   pDC->Ellipse(220, iTuesdayValue - 5, 230,
     iTuesdayValue + 5);
   pDC->SelectObject(wednesdayBrush);
   pDC->Ellipse(320, iWednesdayValue - 5, 330,
     iWednesdayValue + 5);
   pDC->SelectObject(thursdayBrush);
   pDC->Ellipse(420, iThursdayValue - 5, 430,
     iThursdayValue + 5);
   pDC->SelectObject(fridayBrush);
   pDC->Ellipse(520, iFridayValue - 5, 530,
     iFridayValue + 5);
   break;
```

4. Rebuild and execute the program. Enter some values and check the column and scatter charts to see if the rectangles and ellipses appear in color. Figure 12-49 shows an example of the Column chart after entering some values.

5. Close the Stock Charting program window.

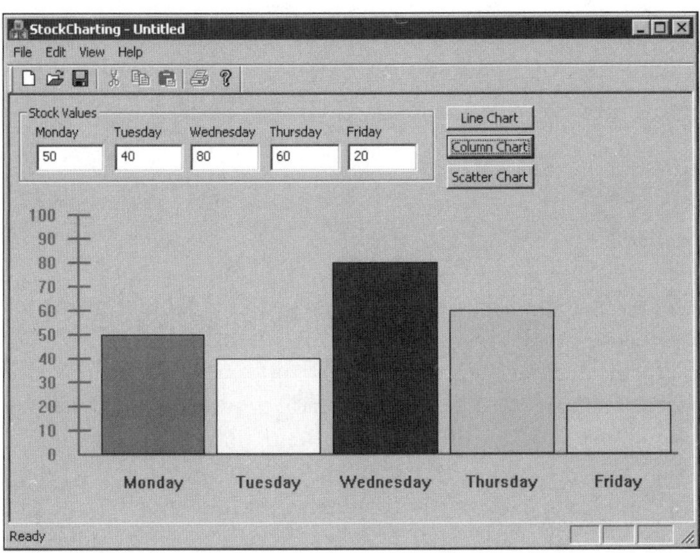

Figure 12-49 Column chart after applying brushes

MENUS AND COMMANDS

For the rest of this chapter, you will learn how to set up a program to execute commands using the menu and toolbar. Menus and toolbars are not exactly part of the device context, but they are important to the design of a Windows application's visual interface.

12

You have probably already noticed that MFC Application Wizard creates a menu for you whenever you build an MFC application. Menus are essential components of Windows applications. They allow you to execute commands that are contained within menus of choices. You can actually think of the commands on a menu as being very similar to the command buttons that you have used in dialog windows. Instead of being represented by a button, however, commands on a menu are represented by descriptive text.

In Visual C++, you use the Menu Editor to design and edit menus. If you open Resource View and expand the Menu folder, you will see the IDR_MAINFRAME resource that MFC Application Wizard automatically creates for you. By default, the menu resource includes File, Edit, View, and Help menus, with prewritten commands, such as the Copy and Paste commands, on the Edit menu. Figure 12-50 shows an example of the IDR_MAINFRAME menu resource in the Menu Editor, with the Edit menu displayed.

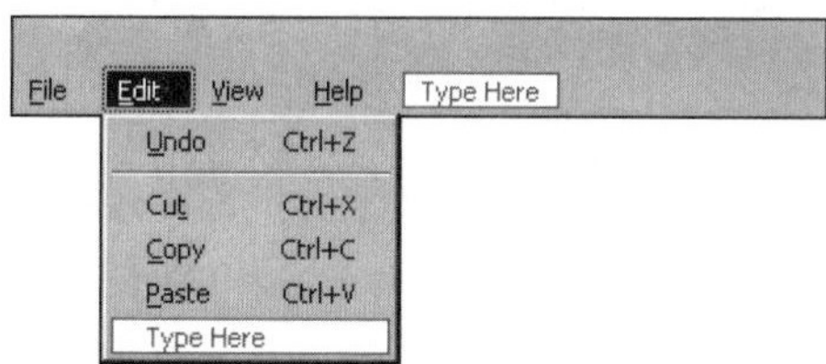

Figure 12-50 Menu Editor

Notice in Figure 12-50 that there is a box to the right of the Help menu that includes the text *Type Here*. You use this box to add a new menu to the menu resource. Clicking the menu box and typing a caption sets the Caption property in the Properties window. You can also set additional properties in the Properties window for the new menu item. Also, notice the box at the bottom of the Edit menu that also includes the text *Type Here*. You use this box to add new command items to a menu. After clicking the box to select it, you can type the text you want to appear as the menu command's caption, the same as you do for menus. The Properties window for each menu command also contains an ID drop-down list box in which you can enter or select a resource ID for a menu command. You can then use a COMMAND message and an associated message handler function to execute the functionality required by a command.

You can move menus and commands by positioning your mouse cursor on an element, pressing and holding the left mouse button, and then dragging the element to a new position. To delete an existing command, highlight the command you want to delete and then press the Delete key.

Menus and commands usually have an accelerator key associated with them. An **accelerator key** is an underlined character in a menu or command caption that defines a keystroke sequence that you can use to open a menu or select a command without using the mouse. For menus themselves, you open the menu by holding down the Alt key and pressing the underlined character on your keyboard. Once you open a menu, you can select a command by pressing its accelerator key. For example, most File menus include an Exit command. Notice in the preceding sentence that the *F* in File and the *x* in Exit are underlined. To open a File menu, you press Alt and the letter *F*. To select the Exit command once the File menu is opened, you simply press *x*.

To define an accelerator key in your menus and commands, you place an ampersand (&) in the caption before the letter you want to use as the accelerator key. For example, if you want to add a Delete command to the Edit menu, you click the empty box at the bottom of the Edit menu and then type an ampersand (&) and the letter you want to use as an underlined accelerator key. The caption &Delete creates a command with the D as the accelerator key as follows: Delete.

When you highlight a menu command, most programs display some text in the application's status bar that describes the command's purpose. For new menu commands, you use the Prompt property in the Properties window to set the text you want to appear in the status bar. Figure 12-51 shows an example of the Properties window for a new Delete command on the Edit menu. The menu command uses the letter *D* as an accelerator key and places the text *Deletes the current selection* in the application's status bar. Notice in the Edit menu that the *D* is underlined in the Delete command caption.

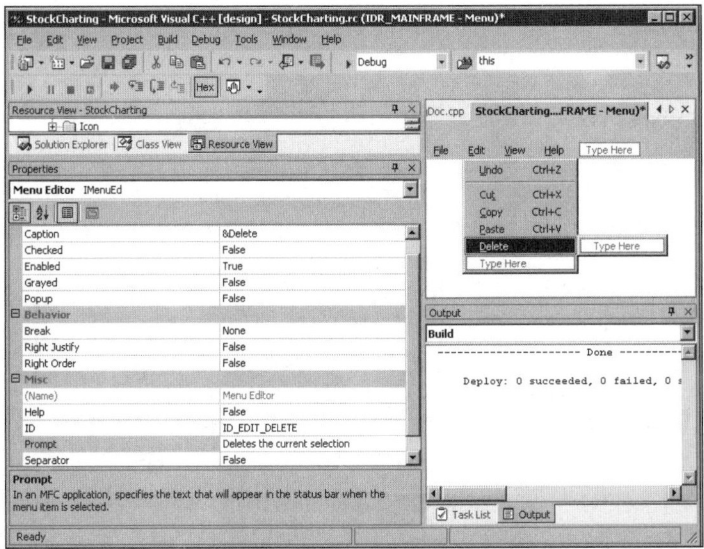

Figure 12-51 Adding a new menu command

Next, you will modify the Stock Charting program's View menu so that it includes commands to display each chart type.

To modify the Stock Charting program's View menu so that it includes commands to display each chart type:

1. Open **Resource View** and expand the **Menu** folder. Double-click the **IDR_MAINFRAME** resource ID to display the menu in the Menu Editor.
2. Expand the **View** menu in the Menu Editor and right-click the empty box at the bottom of the menu. Select the **Insert Separator** command from the Menu submenu on the View menu. The Insert Separator command adds a visual element to menus that groups related commands. After you select the Insert Separator command, a new empty box appears at the bottom of the View menu.
3. Click the new empty box at the bottom of the View menu and type a caption of **&Line Chart**. If necessary, display the Properties window. Change the ID property to **ID_VIEW_LINE_CHART**. After you enter the resource ID, select the new empty box at the bottom of the menu and then reselect the new Line Chart command. Modify the Prompt property box so it includes the following text: **Displays the line chart**.

4. Click the empty box at the bottom of the View menu, type a caption of **&Column Chart**. Change the ID property to **ID_VIEW_COLUMN_CHART**. After you enter the resource ID, select the new empty box at the bottom of the menu and then reselect the new Column Chart command. Modify the Prompt property box so it includes the following text: **Displays the column chart**.
5. Click the empty box at the bottom of the View menu, type a caption of **Sc&atter Chart**. Change the ID property to **ID_VIEW_SCATTER_CHART**. After you enter the resource ID, select the new empty box at the bottom of the menu and then reselect the new Scatter Chart command. Modify the Prompt property box so it includes the following text: **Displays the scatter chart**.
6. Use the Event Handler Wizard to map the COMMAND message handlers for the ID_VIEW_LINE_CHART, ID_VIEW_COLUMN_CHART, and ID_VIEW_SCATTER_CHART resource IDs. For instance, to add a COMMAND message handler for the ID_VIEW_LINE_CHART resource ID, first click the **&Line Chart** command on the View menu in the Menu Editor. Then, select **Add Event Handler** from the Menu submenu on the Edit menu to display the Event Handler Wizard. In the Event Handler Wizard dialog box, select **COMMAND** from the Message type list box, select **CStockChartingView** from the Class list box, and accept the suggested name of OnViewLineChart in the Function handler name box.

   Add the same statements to the new message handler functions that you added to the message handler functions for the IDC_DRAW_LINE_CHART, IDC_DRAW_COLUMN_CHART, and IDC_DRAW_SCATTER_CHART control buttons you created earlier. Recall that the message handlers for the control buttons execute the UpdateData() function, assign the correct chart type to the m_Chart data member, and then execute the Invalidate() function. After adding the message handler functions and appropriate statements for the ID_VIEW_LINE_CHART, ID_VIEW_COLUMN_CHART, and ID_VIEW_SCATTER_CHART resource IDs, the functions should appear as follows in the StockChartingView.cpp file:

```
void CStockChartingView::OnViewLineChart()
{
	UpdateData(TRUE);
	m_Chart = Line;
	Invalidate(TRUE);
}
void CStockChartingView::OnViewColumnChart()
{
	UpdateData(TRUE);
	m_Chart = Column;
	Invalidate(TRUE);
}
void CStockChartingView::OnViewScatterChart()
{
```

```
        UpdateData(TRUE);
        m_Chart = Scatter;
        Invalidate(TRUE);
}
```

7. Rebuild and execute the program. Test the new commands and see if they open each of the chart types correctly. Make sure that the status bar text and accelerator commands function correctly.
8. Close the Stock Charting program window.

TOOLBARS AND BUTTONS

Menus and toolbars are similar in that they both execute commands. Instead of having text commands as menus do, however, toolbars execute commands using graphical icons known as **buttons**. When you work with toolbars, you assign resource IDs to toolbar buttons, and then use COMMAND messages to map each button to a handler function. This procedure is almost identical to the way you map menu commands to handler functions. The main difference is that a menu is text based, whereas a toolbar is graphical.

You design and edit toolbars in Visual C++ using the Toolbar Editor. If you expand the Toolbar folder in Resource View, you will see the IDR_MAINFRAME resource. This is the same resource ID used by the menu resource. If you open the IDR_MAINFRAME resource in the Toolbar Editor, you will see several buttons already created for you, such as the Edit and Paste buttons. Buttons such as the Edit and Paste buttons execute the exact same commands as their counterparts on the Edit menu.

When you open the Toolbar Editor, a new Image Editor toolbar appears along with a Colors window that you use to edit or create button images. A new Image menu that contains tools for editing the button images also appears in the menu bar. At the far right of the toolbar is an empty button that you use to design a new button. The left portion of the Toolbar Editor, beneath the toolbar itself, displays a preview of the button you are editing. To the right of the preview window is the location where you design the button. Figure 12-52 shows an example of the IDE after opening the Toolbar Editor.

When you design a button, you color in the individual pixels that make up the button. You can see the individual pixels for the New toolbar button in the preview window in Figure 12-52. By default, the New button appears when you first open the Toolbar Editor. You can edit another existing button by clicking it to display it in the editing area. Like menu commands, you associate a toolbar button's resource ID with a COMMAND message and associated message handler function to execute the functionality required by the button. However, the Event Handler Wizard is not available to the Toolbar Editor, as it is for the Menu Editor. Instead, you must use the Events button in the Properties window to associate a toolbar button's resource ID with a particular function. Most commands executed by toolbar buttons usually have equivalent menu commands, so it is usually easier to simply use the same resource ID for a button that you do for a menu command. This allows the button and menu command to share the same COMMAND message map function.

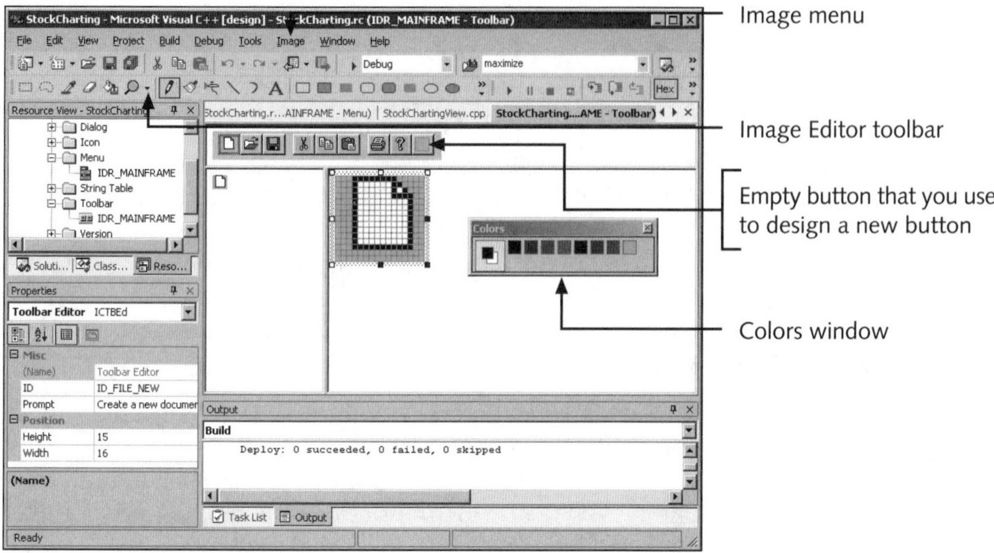

Figure 12-52 Toolbar Editor

You can move a button on the toolbar by clicking it with the left mouse button and dragging it to a new position while holding the left mouse button down. To delete an existing button, click and hold the left mouse button; holding the pointer over the button you want to delete, drag the button off the toolbar, and then release the mouse button.

When you move your mouse pointer over a toolbar button, many applications display a prompt in the status bar, the same as they do when you highlight a menu command. You use the Prompt text box in the Properties window to set the text you want to appear in the status bar for any toolbar buttons, the same as you do for menu commands. Although toolbars and buttons do not use accelerator keys, they usually have an associated ToolTip. As you should know, a ToolTip is a short description that appears when you hold your pointer over a button. You create a ToolTip by appending to the status bar text a \n and the text you want displayed in the ToolTip. Figure 12-53 shows an example of the IDE for a new Delete button. The text in the Prompt property box is *Deletes the current selection\nDelete*. This sets the status bar text to *Deletes the current selection* and the ToolTip to *Delete*.

Next, you will add to the Stock Charting program toolbar buttons that display the different types of charts.

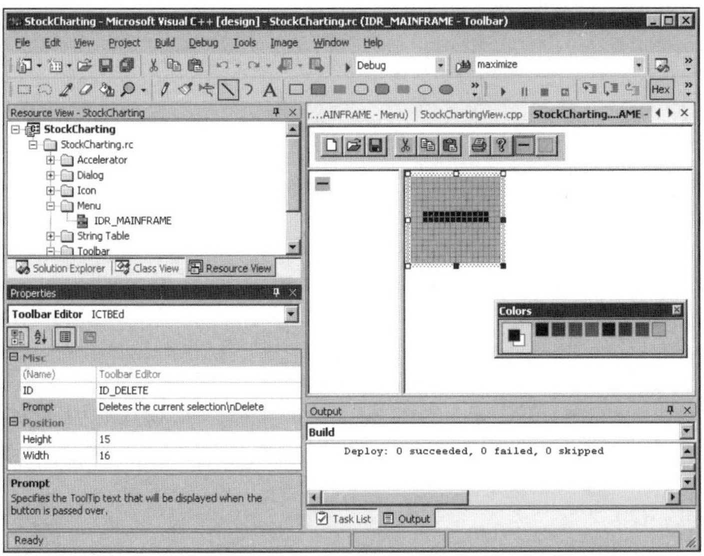

Figure 12-53 Adding a new Delete button

To add to the Stock Charting program toolbar buttons that display the different types of charts:

1. Expand the **Toolbar** folder in Resource View and double-click the **IDR_MAINFRAME** resource ID to display the toolbar in the Toolbar Editor.
2. The New button should be highlighted when you first open the Toolbar Editor. Click the empty button at the far right of the toolbar, then use Figure 12-54 as a model to design a button that displays the line chart.

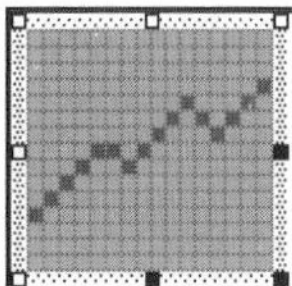

Figure 12-54 Line chart button

3. When you are finished designing the line chart button, change its ID property to the **ID_VIEW_LINE_CHART** resource ID that you created earlier for the Line Chart menu item. After you enter the resource ID, select the new empty button at the far right of the toolbar and then reselect the new line chart button. Modify the Prompt property box so it includes the following ToolTip text: **Displays the line chart\nLine Chart**.
4. Click the new empty button at the far right of the toolbar, then design a button for the column chart, using Figure 12-55 as a model.

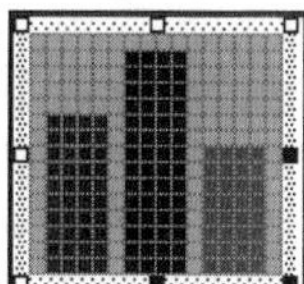

Figure 12-55 Column chart button

5. When you are finished designing the column chart button, change its ID property to the **ID_VIEW_COLUMN_CHART** resource ID that you created earlier for the Column Chart menu item. After you enter the resource ID, select the new empty button at the far right of the toolbar and then reselect the new column chart button. Modify the Prompt property box so it includes the following ToolTip text: **Displays the column chart\nColumn Chart**.
6. Click the new empty button at the far right of the toolbar and design a button for the scatter chart, using Figure 12-56 as a model.

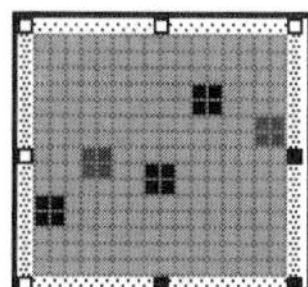

Figure 12-56 Scatter chart button

7. When you are finished designing the scatter chart button, change its ID property to the **ID_VIEW_SCATTER_CHART** resource ID that you created earlier for the Scatter Chart menu item. After you enter the resource ID, select the new empty button at the far right of the toolbar and then reselect the new scatter chart button. Modify the Prompt property box so it includes the following ToolTip text: **Displays the scatter chart\nScatter Chart**.
8. Rebuild and execute the program. Test the new toolbar buttons and see if they open each type of chart correctly. Make sure the status bar prompts and the ToolTips for each button function correctly.

Because toolbar buttons execute the same COMMAND message that menu commands do, you only need one message map function to handle the functionality of a menu command and toolbar button that share the same resource ID. Because you have already created COMMAND message maps for the resource IDs when you created the menu commands, you do not need to add any new message maps after creating the toolbar buttons.

9. Close the Stock Charting program window.

CHAPTER SUMMARY

- A device driver allows the Windows operating system to communicate with a particular device.
- The graphics device interface, or GDI, manages communication with different types of Windows graphical device drivers.
- The CDC class is the base class for device context classes.
- A mapping mode is a coordinate system that determines the units and scaling orientation in a device context. The default mapping mode is MM_TEXT.
- Graphical computer systems, such as Windows, use the red, green, blue, or RGB, color system for specifying colors.
- The WM_PAINT message informs an application that its window must be redrawn, or repainted.
- You use the OnDraw() function, which is inherited from the CView base class, to manage an application's device context.
- You use the pDC pointer as a handle for accessing the application's device context.
- The Invalidate() function notifies the update region that the window needs to be erased.
- You use the LineTo() function to draw lines in the device context.
- You use the MoveTo() function to manually change the current position.
- You draw rectangles in a device context with the Rectangle() function.
- You use the Ellipse() function to draw ovals and circles in a device context.
- You add text to the device context using the TextOut() function.
- A pen is an object created with the CPen class that determines a line's style, thickness, and color.
- The CreatePen() function initializes a new pen with style, width, and color values.
- The SelectObject() function loads an object into the device context.
- A brush is an object created with the CBrush class that determines the color and pattern that is drawn in the interior of a closed object.
- You design and edit menus in Visual C++ by using the Menu Editor.
- You design and edit toolbars in Visual C++ by using the Toolbar Editor.

Review Questions

1. The Windows operating system communicates with its computer hardware by using a ______________.
   a. hardware operator
   b. transmission facilitator
   c. communicator
   d. device driver
2. What does GDI stand for?
   a. Good Development Initiative
   b. Graphics Device Interface
   c. General Documentation Information
   d. Geared Delivery Integrator
3. What is the device context?
   a. an MFC dynamic link library
   b. a Visual C++ program
   c. a Windows GDI data structure
   d. a Windows API function call
4. What is the CDC object pointer in the OnDraw() function used for?
   a. to perform serialization for graphical objects
   b. to store information for a derived CDocument class
   c. to directly add and modify drawing information in the device context
   d. The OnDraw() function does not contain a CDC object pointer
5. What is the default mapping mode?
   a. MM_TWIPS
   b. MM_TEXT
   c. MM_LOENGLISH
   d. MM_HIENGLISH
6. Where is the point of origin for all mapping modes?
   a. the upper-left corner of the screen or window
   b. the upper-right corner of the screen or window
   c. the lower-left corner of the screen or window
   d. the lower-right corner of the screen or window

7. Which of the following RGB() macros returns the full intensity of the color blue?
   a. RGB(255, 0, 0)
   b. RGB(0, 255, 0)
   c. RGB(255, 0, 255)
   d. RGB(0, 0, 255)
8. What is the correct Windows API data type that you use to declare your own color variable?
   a. COLOR
   b. COLORRGB
   c. COLORPRIMARY
   d. COLORREF
9. Which of the following messages informs an application that its window needs to be redrawn?
   a. PAINT
   b. WM_PAINT
   c. DRAW
   d. REDRAW
10. The ______________ function notifies the update region that the window needs to be erased.
    a. Validate()
    b. Invalidate()
    c. Clear()
    d. OnPaint()
11. What is the correct syntax for drawing a line from the current position of 0, 0 to 100, 50?
    a. LineTo(100, 50)
    b. pDC.LineTo(100, 50)
    c. pDC->LineTo(100, 50)
    d. pDC->LineTo(0, 0, 100, 50)
12. Which of the following functions do you use to move the current position?
    a. MoveTo()
    b. CurrentPosition()
    c. GetPosition()
    d. SetPosition()

13. You use the ______________ function to draw ovals and circles in a device context.
    a. Circle()
    b. Oval()
    c. Round()
    d. Ellipse()
14. How do you set the size of an oval or circle?
    a. by setting the height and width of its bounding rectangle
    b. by passing a starting position, along with the oval or circle's circumference
    c. by passing the object's center point, along with its radius. For ovals, you must also pass an array containing *x*, *y* pairs representing the dimensions of the oval's curvature
    d. by passing eight *x*, *y* pairs representing equal positions on the oval or circle's circumference
15. The ______________ function sets the horizontal and vertical text alignment for text objects according to the x and y parameters of the TextOut() function.
    a. TextAlign()
    b. SetTextAlign()
    c. Justify()
    d. Align()
16. Which of the following functions sets the color of text objects?
    a. Color()
    b. TextColor()
    c. SetTextColor()
    d. Foreground()
17. Which is the correct syntax for declaring a pen object named curPen that is two pixels wide, dashed, and red?
    a. `CPen curPen(PS_DASH, 2, RGB(255, 0, 0));`
    b. `CPen variable(2, PS_DASH, RGB(255, 0, 0));`
    c. `CPen variable(RGB(255, 0, 0), 2, PS_DASH);`
    d. `CPen variable(2, RGB(255, 0, 0), PS_DASH);`
18. The ______________ function selects an object into the device context.
    a. DCObject()
    b. SetObject()
    c. GetObject()
    d. SelectObject()

19. What is the correct syntax to create a black brush named hatchBrush with an HS_CROSS pattern?
    a. `CBrush hatchBrush(HS_CROSS);`
    b. `CBrush hatchBrush(HS_CROSS, RGB(0, 0, 0));`
    c. `CBrush hatchBrush(RGB(0, 0, 0), HS_CROSS);`
    d. `CBrush hatchBrush(RGB(0, 0, 0), HS_CROSS, TRUE);`
20. Which special character do you use in the Prompt box for a menu or command resource to designate a character in a text string as the menu or command's accelerator key?
    a. @
    b. &
    c. %
    d. #
21. What special character(s) do you use to separate status bar text from ToolTip text in the Prompt box of a toolbar button's Properties window?
    a. &
    b. $
    c. \n
    d. /t
22. Which message is generated by both menu commands and toolbar buttons?
    a. BN_CLICKED
    b. WM_PAINT
    c. COMMAND
    d. EN_CHANGE

Programming Exercises

1. Write the statement that declares a COLORREF variable named brightYellow that stores a color of pure yellow.
2. Explain how the pDC pointer is passed between the OnPaint() and OnDraw() function in order to access an application's device context.
3. Use LineTo() and MoveTo() functions to create a drawing program that displays your initials in large block letters.
4. Write a statement that draws a rectangle that begins at position 5, 10 and ends at position 125, 200.
5. Write a statement that draws a perfect circle. The circle's bounding rectangle should start at position 10, 10 and be 200 pixels wide by 200 pixels high.

6. Write an OnDraw() function that uses TextOut() statements to print the 12 months of the year.
7. Modify the OnDraw() function you created in Exercise 8 so the text statements are aligned with the center of the bounding rectangle. Also, use RGB() macros to set the name of each month to a different color.
8. Write code that declares a new pen variable object and initializes the pen as a dotted line, five pixels in width, in the color blue. Also, write the statement that loads the new pen object into the device context.
9. Write code that declares a new brush variable object and initializes the brush with a 45-degree crosshatch pattern and with color red. Also, write the statement that loads the new brush object into the device context.

PROGRAMMING PROJECTS

1. Modify the line chart of the Stock Charting program so that each line segment is connected by a solid black circle.
2. Study the CFonts topic and the Text and Fonts topic in the MSDN Library to learn how to manipulate the typefaces displayed by text objects. Modify the axis labels in the Stock Charting program so that they use a serif typeface such as Times New Roman.
3. Add text labels for each stock value in the Stock Charting program that appear above the appropriate element in each chart. For example, if the Monday stock value is 80, then add a text object above the Monday column in the column chart that reads *$80*.
4. Add an overlay chart to the Stock Charting program. An overlay chart combines both a column chart and a line chart.
5. Modify the brush for the column chart of the Stock Chart program so that each column uses a different pattern.
6. Add a bar chart to the Stock Charting program. A bar chart differs from a column chart in that each rectangle increases in value from left to right instead of from bottom to top, as do column charts. Because the scale for a bar chart progresses from left to right, you will need to create a new coordinate system for the bar chart's grid.
7. Add controls to the Stock Charting program that you can use to compare two stock values. In other words, you will want to display the values for two stocks simultaneously in the Stock Charting program. Modify the line, column, and scatter charts so that they display both sets of values. Use a different color on the charts for each stock, such as a blue line for one stock and a red line for another stock. As another example, make all of the columns of the column chart for the first stock blue and make all of the columns for the second stock red.

8. Create a program that draws different types of objects based on a selection the user makes in an Objects menu or by clicking a toolbar button. Study the CDC class's member functions and include other object types in addition to the lines, rectangles, and ellipses you studied in this chapter. Create two additional menus: Lines and Fills. On the Lines menu, allow the user to select different line styles, sizes, and colors for the displayed object. On the Fills menu, allow the user to select different patterns and colors for the selected object.
9. You may have seen menu commands that include a check mark when that command's feature is currently active. You add a check mark next to a menu item by using the SetCheck() function of the CCmdUI class along with the ON_UPDATE_COMMAND_UI message handler. Search the MSDN Library for information on these topics and see if you can add a check mark next to the currently visible chart in the View menu of the Stock Charting program.

CHAPTER

13

CONNECTING TO DATABASES

In this chapter you will learn:

- About basic database structure
- About database management systems
- About structured query language
- How to connect to databases with MFC
- How to link dialog controls to database fields
- How to sort and filter records
- How to add and delete records

Knowledge is of two kinds: we know a subject ourselves, or we know where we can find information upon it.
Samuel Johnson (1709-1784)

PREVIEW: THE LIBRARY DATABASE PROGRAM

In this chapter, you will work with a Library Database application that demonstrates how to use MFC to access databases. The Library Database application stores information about fiction and nonfiction books, including the book title, author name, and publisher. Although the program is fairly simple, it demonstrates how you could write a much larger program that might actually be used by a library, for a corporate documentation database, or as an order entry database for a book vendor.

To preview the Library Database application:

1. Create a **Chapter.13** folder in your Visual C++ Projects folder.
2. Copy the **Chapter13_LibraryDatabase** folder from the Chapter.13 folder on your Data Disk to the Chapter.13 folder in your Visual C++ Projects folder, and then open the LibraryDatabase project in Visual C++.

3. Open **Solution Explorer** and expand the **Source Files** folder. The project contains several classes with which you are familiar, including an application class, a frame class, a view class, and a document class. The project also contains a class named CLibraryDatabaseSet, which is used for managing the information in a database.

4. Open the **LibraryDatabaseSet.cpp** file in the Code Editor window. If you scroll through the file, you will see some typical MFC functions. You will also see a DoFieldExchange() function, which is used for exchanging data between data members in the view class and records in the database. Figure 13-1 shows the LibraryDatabaseSet.cpp file's DoFieldExchange() function.

```
void CLibraryDatabaseSet::DoFieldExchange(CFieldExchange* pFX)
{
     pFX->SetFieldType(CFieldExchange::outputColumn);
     RFX_Text(pFX, _T("[BookID]"), m_BookID);
     RFX_Text(pFX, _T("[Title]"), m_Title);
     RFX_Text(pFX, _T("[Author]"), m_Author);
     RFX_Text(pFX, _T("[Publisher]"), m_Publisher);
     RFX_Int(pFX, _T("[Genre]"), m_Genre);
     RFX_Text(pFX, _T("[Description]"), m_Description);
}
```

Figure 13-1 DoFieldExchange() function

5. You cannot build and execute the program until you configure your system to recognize the database. However, Figure 13-2 shows an example of the Library Database application window.

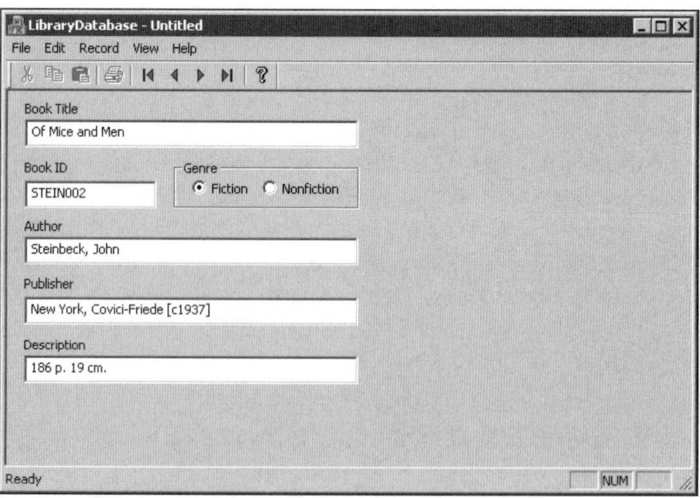

Figure 13-2 Library Database application window

6. Select **Close Solution** from the File menu to close the project.

The descriptions and publishing information for the records in the Library Database application were downloaded from the Library of Congress Online Catalog. If you would like to view the Library of Congress Online Catalog, visit *catalog.loc.gov/webvoy.htm*.

UNDERSTANDING DATABASES

The goal of this chapter is to learn how to use MFC to read, write, and modify database information. To accomplish this goal, it helps to first understand how databases work. Formally defined, a **database** is an ordered collection of information from which a computer program can quickly access information. You can probably think of many databases from your everyday life. For example, your address book is a database. So is the card file containing recipes in a kitchen. Other examples of databases include a company's employee directory and a file cabinet containing client information. Essentially, any information that can be organized into ordered sets of data, then quickly retrieved, can be considered a database. A collection of hundreds of baseball cards thrown into a shoebox is not a database, because an individual card cannot be quickly or easily retrieved (except by luck). However, if the baseball card collection were organized in binders by team, and then further organized according to each player's field position or batting average, then it could be considered a database because you could quickly locate a specific card.

The information stored in computer databases is actually stored in tables similar to spreadsheets. Each row in a database table is called a record. A **record** in a database contains a single complete set of related information. Each recipe in a recipe database, for instance, is a single database record. Each column in a database table is called a field. **Fields** are the individual pieces of information stored in a record. Examples of fields that might exist in a recipe database include ingredients, cooking time, cooking temperature, and so on. Database fields are created using data types, the same as C++ variables. In fact, the data types of many database programs are very similar to C++ data types. For instance, common data types that are found in many databases include string, integer, floating-point, and Boolean.

To summarize, you can think of databases as consisting of tables, which consist of records, which consist of fields. Figure 13-3 shows an example of an employee directory for programmers at an application development company. The database consists of five records, one for each employee. Each record consists of seven fields: Last_Name, First_Name, Address, City, State, Zip, and Extension.

Last_Name	First_Name	Address	City	State	Zip	Extension
Blair	Dennis	204 Spruce Lane	Brookfield	MA	01506	x305
Hernandez	Louis	68 Boston Post Road	Spencer	MA	01562	x412
Miller	Erica	271 Baker Hill Road	E. Brookfield	MA	01515	x291
Morinaga	Scott	17 Ashley Road	N. Brookfield	MA	01535	x177
Picard	Raymond	1113 Oakham Road	New Braintree	MA	01531	x213

Figure 13-3 Employee Directory database

The database in Figure 13-3 is an example of a flat-file database, one of the simplest types of databases. A **flat-file database** stores information in a single table. For simple collections of information, flat-file databases are usually adequate. With large and complex collections of information, flat-file databases can become unwieldy. A better solution for large and complex databases is a relational database. A **relational database** stores information across multiple related tables. Although you will not actually work with a relational database in this chapter, understanding how they work is helpful because relational databases are among the most common in use today.

Two other types of database systems you may encounter are hierarchical databases and network databases.

Relational databases consist of one or more related tables. In fact, large relational databases can consist of dozens or hundreds of related tables. Although relational databases may consist of many tables, you create relationships within the database by working with two tables at a time. One table in a relationship is always considered to be the primary table, whereas the other table is considered to be the related table. A **primary table** is the main table in a relationship that is referenced by another table. A **related**, or **child table** references a primary table in a relational database. Tables in a relationship are connected using primary and foreign keys. A **primary key** is a field that contains a unique identifier for each record in a primary table. A **foreign key** is a field in a related table that refers to the primary key in a primary table. Primary and foreign keys are what link records across multiple tables in a relational database.

There are three basic types of relationships within a relational database: one-to-one, one-to-many, and many-to-many. A **one-to-one relationship** exists between two tables when a related table contains exactly one record for each record in the primary table. You create one-to-one relationships when you want to break information into multiple, logical sets. It is important to understand that information in the tables in a one-to-one relationship can usually be placed within a single table. However, you may want to break the information into multiple tables to better organize the information into logical sets. Another reason for using one-to-one relationships is that they allow you to make the information in one of the tables confidential and accessible only by certain individuals. For example, you might want to create a personnel table that contains basic information about an employee, similar to the information in the table in Figure 13-3. Yet, you might also want to create a payroll table that contains confidential information about each employee's salary, benefits, and other types of compensation, that can be accessed only by the Human Resources and Accounting Departments. Figure 13-4 shows two tables, Employees and Payroll, with a one-to-one relationship. The primary table is the employee information table from Figure 13-3. The related table is a payroll table that contains confidential salary and compensation information. Notice that each table contains identical numbers of records; one record in the primary table corresponds to one record in the related table. The relationship is achieved by adding a primary key to the Employees table and a foreign key to the Payroll table.

Employees table

ID	Last_Name	First_Name	Address	City	State	Zip	Extension
101	Blair	Dennis	204 Spruce Lane	Brookfield	MA	01506	x305
102	Hernandez	Louis	68 Boston Post Road	Spencer	MA	01562	x412
103	Miller	Erica	271 Baker Hill Road	E. Brookfield	MA	01515	x291
104	Morinaga	Scott	17 Ashley Road	N. Brookfield	MA	01535	x177
105	Picard	Raymond	1113 Oakham Road	New Braintree	MA	01531	x213

Primary key

Payroll table

ID	Start_Date	Pay_Rate	Health_Coverage	Year_Vested	401K
101	1998	$21.25	No Coverage	NA	No
102	1993	$28.00	Family Plan	1998	Yes
103	1996	$24.50	Individual	NA	Yes
104	1991	$36.00	Family Plan	1996	Yes
105	1992	$31.00	Individual	1997	Yes

Foreign key

Figure 13-4 One-to-one relationship

A **one-to-many relationship** exists in a relational database when one record in a primary table has many related records in a related table. You create a one-to-many relationship in order to eliminate redundant information in a single table. Primary and foreign keys are the only pieces of information in a relational database table that should be duplicated. Breaking tables into multiple related tables in order to reduce redundant and duplicate information is called **normalization**. The elimination of redundant information (normalization) reduces the size of a database and makes the data easier to work with. For example, consider the table in Figure 13-5. The table lists each programmer's primary and other programming languages. Notice that each programmer's name is repeated for each programming language with which he or she is familiar. This repetition is an example of redundant information that can occur in a single table.

ID	Last_Name	First_Name	Programming_Language
101	Blair	Dennis	C
101	Blair	Dennis	C++
102	Hernandez	Louis	C
102	Hernandez	Louis	C++
102	Hernandez	Louis	Fortran
103	Miller	Erica	C
103	Miller	Erica	C++
103	Miller	Erica	Fortran
103	Miller	Erica	Java
104	Morinaga	Scott	C
104	Morinaga	Scott	Fortran
104	Morinaga	Scott	Java
105	Picard	Raymond	C
105	Picard	Raymond	Fortran

Figure 13-5 Table with redundant information

A one-to-many relationship provides a more efficient and less redundant method of storing this information in a database. Figure 13-6 shows the same information organized into a one-to-many relationship.

13

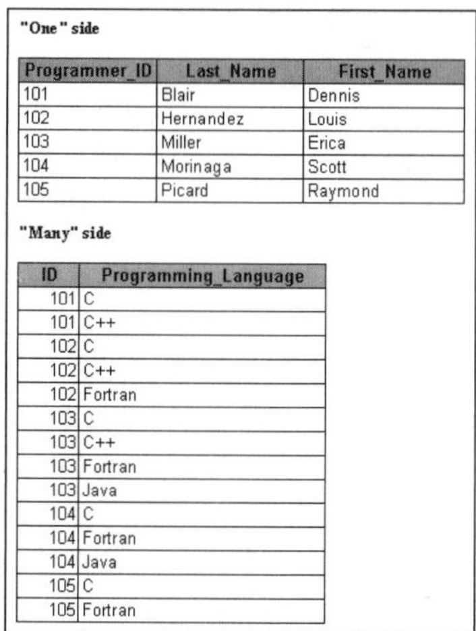

"One" side

Programmer_ID	Last_Name	First_Name
101	Blair	Dennis
102	Hernandez	Louis
103	Miller	Erica
104	Morinaga	Scott
105	Picard	Raymond

"Many" side

ID	Programming_Language
101	C
101	C++
102	C
102	C++
102	Fortran
103	C
103	C++
103	Fortran
103	Java
104	C
104	Fortran
104	Java
105	C
105	Fortran

Figure 13-6 One-to-many relationship

The "many" side of a one-to-many relationship is sometimes used as the primary table. In these cases, the relationship is often referred to as a many-to-one relationship.

Although Figure 13-6 is an example of a one-to-many relationship, the tables are not normalized because the Programming Language field contains duplicate values. Recall that primary and foreign keys are the only pieces of information in a relational database that should be duplicated. To further reduce repetition, you could organize the "many" table in Figure 13-6 into another one-to-many relationship. However, a better choice is to create a many-to-many relationship. A **many-to-many relationship** exists in a relational database when many records in one table are related to many records in another table. Consider the relationship between programmers and programming languages. Each programmer can work with many programming languages, and each programming language can be used by many programmers. To create a many-to-many relationship, you must use a junction table because most relational database systems cannot work directly with many-to-many relationships. A **junction table** creates a one-to-many relationship for each of the two tables in a many-to-many relationship. A junction table contains foreign keys from the two tables in a many-to-many relationship, along with any other fields that correspond to a many-to-many relationship. Figure 13-7 contains an example of a many-to-many relationship between a Programmers table and a Programming Languages table. The Programmers table contains a primary key named Programmer_ID, and the Programming Languages table contains a primary key named Language_ID. A junction table named Programming Experience contains two foreign keys, one corresponding to the Programmer_ID primary key in the Programmers table, and one corresponding to the Language_ID in the Programming Languages table. The Programming Experience junction table also contains a field named Years_Experience. You add records to the

Programming Experience junction table to build a list of the years that each programmer has been working with a particular programming language.

Programmers table

Programmer_ID	Last_Name	First_Name
101	Blair	Dennis
102	Hernandez	Louis
103	Miller	Erica
104	Morinaga	Scott
105	Picard	Raymond

Programming Languages table

Language_ID	Programming_Language
10	C
11	C++
12	Fortran
13	Java

Programming Experience junction table

Programmer_ID	Language_ID	Years_Experience
101	10	5
101	11	4
102	10	3
102	11	2
102	12	3
103	10	2
104	12	3
104	13	5
105	11	3

Figure 13-7 Many-to-many relationship

Database Management Systems

With a grasp of basic database design, you can now begin to consider how to create and manipulate databases. An application or collection of applications used to create, access, and manage a database is called a **database management system**, or **DBMS**. Database management systems run on many different platforms, ranging from personal computers, to client/server systems, to mainframes. Different database management systems exist for different types of database formats. A database management system that stores data in a flat-file format is called a **flat-file database management system**. A database management system that stores data in a relational format is called a **relational database management system**, or **RDBMS**. Other types of database management systems include hierarchical and network database management systems. Some of the more popular relational database management systems you may have heard of include Oracle, Sybase, Informix, and DB2 for mainframes, and Access, FoxPro, and Paradox for PCs.

Database management systems perform many of the same functions as other types of applications you might have worked with, such as word-processing and spreadsheet programs. For example, database management systems create new database files and contain interfaces that allow users to enter and manipulate data. One of the most important functions of a database management system is the structuring and preservation of the database file's structure. Additionally, a database management system must ensure that data is stored correctly in a database's tables, regardless of the database format (flat-file, relational, hierarchical, or network). In relational databases, the database management system ensures that the appropriate information is entered according to the relationship structure in the database tables. Many DBMS systems also have security features that can be used to restrict user access to specific types of data.

Two other important aspects of database management systems are their querying and reporting capabilities. A **query** is a structured set of instructions and criteria for retrieving, adding, modifying, and deleting database information. A **report** is the formatted, printed output of a database table or the results of a query. Most database management systems use a **data manipulation language**, or **DML**, for creating queries. Different database management systems support different data manipulation languages. However, **structured query language**, or **SQL** (pronounced like the word *sequel*), has become somewhat of a standard data manipulation language among many database management systems.

Many database management systems make it easier for users to create queries by hiding the data manipulation language behind a user interface. Figure 13-8 shows an example of Access's query design screen. Users can create queries by dragging fields from the table objects in the upper portion of the screen to the criteria grid in the bottom portion of the screen. Behind the scenes, Access creates the SQL code shown in Figure 13-9. SQL is Access's data manipulation language.

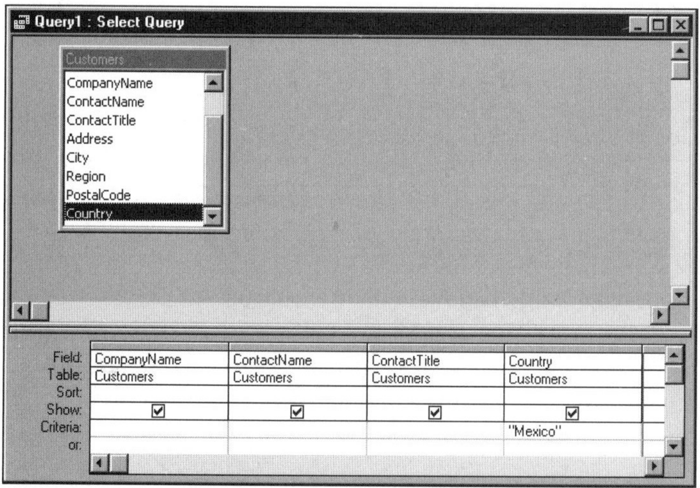

Figure 13-8 Access query design screen

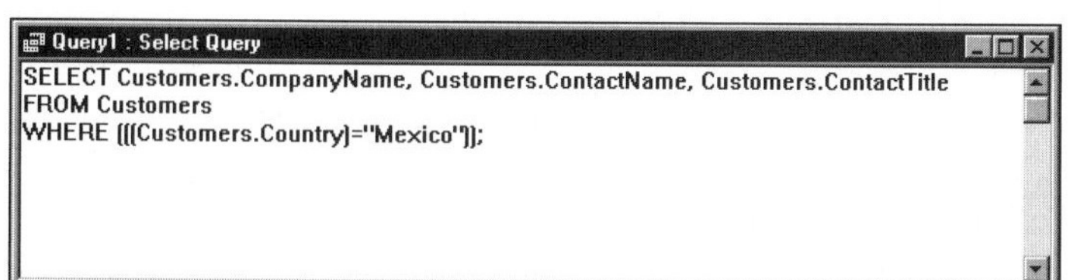

Figure 13-9 Access SQL code

Although working with an interface to design queries is fine for end users, to programmatically manipulate the data in a database, you must learn the database management system's data manipulation language. For example, when accessing databases with MFC, you must use a data manipulation language. Because SQL is the underlying data manipulation language for many database management systems, you will learn more about SQL later in this section so that you can better understand how MFC communicates with database management systems.

A great way to quickly write—and learn—SQL code is to use the Access query design screen to build and test your queries. You can then copy and paste the SQL string generated by the Access query design screen into your program code.

Many database management systems also use a data definition language, or DDL, for creating databases, tables, fields, and other components of a database.

It is important to understand that even though many database management systems support the same database format (flat-file, relational, hierarchical, or network), each database management system is an individual application that creates its own proprietary file types. For example, even though Access and Paradox are both relational database management systems, Access creates its database files in a proprietary format with an extension of .mdb, whereas Paradox creates its database files in a proprietary format with an extension of .db. Although both Paradox and Access contain filters that allow you to import each other's file formats, the database files are not completely interchangeable between the two programs. This situation holds true for most database management systems: They can *import* each other's file formats, but they cannot directly *read* each other's files.

In today's environment, it is often necessary for an application, such as an MFC program, to access multiple databases created in different database management systems. For example, a company may need an MFC application that simultaneously accesses a large legacy database written in dBase and a newer database written in Oracle. Converting the large dBase database to Oracle would be cost-prohibitive. On the other hand, the company cannot continue using the older dBase database because its needs have grown beyond the older database's capabilities. Still, the company must be able to access the data in both systems. To allow easy access to data in various database formats, Microsoft came up with the open database connectivity standard. **Open database connectivity**, or **ODBC**, allows applications that are written to comply with the ODBC standard to access any data source for which there is an ODBC driver. ODBC uses SQL commands (known as ODBC SQL) to allow an ODBC-compliant application to access a database. Essentially, an ODBC application connects to a database for which there is an ODBC driver and then executes ODBC SQL commands. Then, the ODBC driver translates the SQL commands into a format that the database can understand.

Structured Query Language

IBM invented SQL in the 1970s as a way of querying databases for specific criteria. Since then, SQL has been adopted by numerous database management systems running on mainframes, minicomputers, and PCs. In 1986 the American National Standards Institute (ANSI) approved an official standard for the SQL language. In 1991 The X/Open and SQL Access Group created a standardized version of SQL known as the Common Applications Environment (CAE) SQL draft specification. Even with two major standards available, however, most database management systems use their own version of the

SQL language. ODBC SQL corresponds to the X/Open and SQL Access Group's CAE SQL draft specification. Therefore, an ODBC driver for a specific database management system must support ODBC SQL.

If you ever work directly with an individual database management system, keep in mind that the ODBC SQL you learn in this chapter may not correspond directly to that database management system's version of SQL.

SQL uses fairly easy-to-understand statements to execute database commands. SQL statements are composed of keywords that perform actions on a database. Figure 13-10 lists several SQL keywords that are common to most versions of SQL.

Keyword	Description
FROM	Specifies the tables from which to retrieve or delete records
SELECT	Returns information from a table
WHERE	Specifies the conditions that must be met for records to be returned from a query
ORDER BY	Sorts the records returned from a table
INSERT	Inserts a new row into a table
INTO	Determines the table into which records should be inserted
DELETE	Deletes a row from a table
UPDATE	Saves changes to fields in a record

Figure 13-10 Common SQL keywords

The simple SQL statement `SELECT * FROM Programmers` selects all records (using the asterisk `*` wildcard) from the Programmers table. The following code shows a more complex SQL statement that selects the Last_Name and First_Name fields from the Programmers table if the record's City field is equal to Spencer. The results are then sorted by the Last_Name and First_Name fields using the `ORDER BY` keyword.

```
SELECT Last_Name, First_Name FROM Programmers
WHERE City = "Spencer" ORDER BY Last_Name, First_Name
```

SQL table or field names that include spaces are enclosed in brackets. For example, if the Last_Name and First_Name field names in the preceding code included spaces instead of underscore characters, you would write the statement as follows:

```
SELECT [Last Name], [First Name] FROM [Programmers]
WHERE [City] = "Spencer" ORDER BY [Last Name], [First Name]
```

Not all database management systems allow spaces in SQL table or field names. For this reason, many programmers prefer not to include spaces in SQL table or field names in order for their databases and SQL code to be compatible with database management systems that do not allow spaces.

By default, the MFC framework automatically places brackets around field names, even if they do not include spaces. For this reason, in any SQL statements you see in this chapter, brackets surround table and field names.

The MFC framework handles much of the work involved in assembling an SQL string. Therefore, for basic MFC database programs, you do not usually need to use any full SQL statements such as `SELECT * FROM [Programmers]`. However, you do need to understand how a SQL statement works because you will often need to define the parts of a SQL statement. Additionally, certain operations involving databases require that you write your own SQL statements. For example, later in this chapter you will learn how to narrow the record set returned from a database using the inherited m_strFilter data member. You must assign SQL statements to the m_strFilter data member using a statement similar to the following:

```
m_strFilter = "[Programming_Language] = 'C' OR 'C++'";
```

Refer to the MSDN Library for comprehensive information on ODBC SQL.

Connecting to Databases with MFC

You connect to databases with MFC using ODBC or OLE DB. You have already learned that ODBC allows applications that are written to comply with the ODBC standard to access any data source for which there is an ODBC driver. **OLE DB** is a data source connectivity standard promoted by Microsoft as a successor to ODBC. One of the primary differences between OLE DB and ODBC is that ODBC supports access only to relational databases, whereas OLE DB provides access to both relational databases and non-relational data sources, such as spreadsheet programs. OLE DB is somewhat advanced for your studies here because it requires a knowledge of COM (Microsoft's architecture for cross-platform development of client/server applications). In this chapter, you will use an ODBC database application to access an Access 2000 database. Although you are learning about databases, you should note that Access, and another popular DBMS, Paradox, are considered to be desktop database applications, not suited for large, enterprise-wide database systems that companies rely on for managing their businesses. Access and Paradox have their uses—both Access and Paradox databases are fairly easy to create and manage on a small scale. For mission-critical database applications, however, most companies use professional-strength, ODBC-compliant databases such as SQL Server, Oracle, Sybase, or Informix.

13

To create an ODBC database application, you must perform the following steps:

1. Create a Data Source Name to locate and identify the database.
2. Run the MFC Application Wizard to create the basic framework of an ODBC database application.
3. Add controls and code to display and manipulate the records in a database.

Next, you will learn how to create a Data Source Name to locate and identify the database and how to run MFC Application Wizard to create the basic framework of an ODBC database application. Later in this chapter, you will examine the steps involved in adding controls and code to display and manipulate the records in a database.

Creating the Data Source Name

To make it easier to access ODBC-compliant databases on 32-bit Windows operating systems, such as Windows NT, Windows 98, Windows 2000, and Windows XP, you create a Data Source Name to locate and identify the database. A **Data Source Name**, or **DSN**, contains configuration information that Windows operating systems use to access a particular ODBC-compliant database. The DSNs to which you can connect in a Windows environment are installed and managed using the ODBC Administrator utility in Control Panel. There are three types of DSNs: system, user, or file. The system DSN enables all users logged onto a server to access a database. A user DSN restricts database access to authorized users only. A file DSN creates a file-based data source, with an extension of .dsn, that can be shared among users. You will create a user DSN in this chapter.

To create the Library Database program, you will work with an existing Access 2000 database named Library.mdb. Because Access databases are ODBC-compliant, you can access them in an MFC program using either ODBC or OLE DB. The Library.mdb database consists of a single table named Books, with a primary key named BooksID. Next, you will create a user DSN for the Library.mdb database file.

The following steps were created on a computer running Windows 2000. The Control Panel options may appear different to you if you are running a different version of Windows.

To create a user DSN for the Library.mdb database file:

1. Copy the **Library.mdb** file from the Chapter.13 folder on your Data Disk to the **Chapter.13** folder in your Visual C++ Projects folder.
2. Click the Windows **Start** menu, and then select **Control Panel** from the Settings folder.
3. Depending on how your desktop is configured, click or double-click the **ODBC** icon in the Control Panel window. If you are using Windows 2000 or Windows XP, you will need to select the **Administrative Tools** folder in Control Panel to access the **ODBC** icon.

Depending on your version of Windows, the ODBC icon in the Control Panel window may have a different caption. For example, in Windows 98, the caption for the ODBC icon reads *ODBC Data Sources (32bit)*.

4. In the ODBC Data Source Administrator window, select the **User DSN** tab, if necessary. Figure 13-11 shows the User DSN tab.

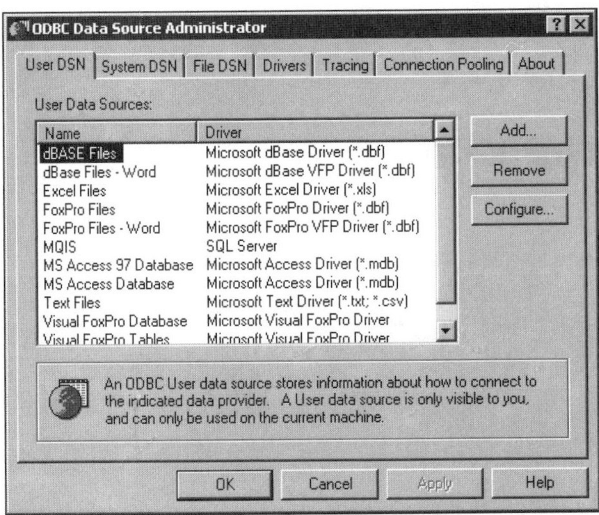

Figure 13-11 User DSN tab in the ODBC Data Source Administrator window

5. Click the **Add** button on the User DSN tab to display the Create New Data Source dialog box, as shown in Figure 13-12.

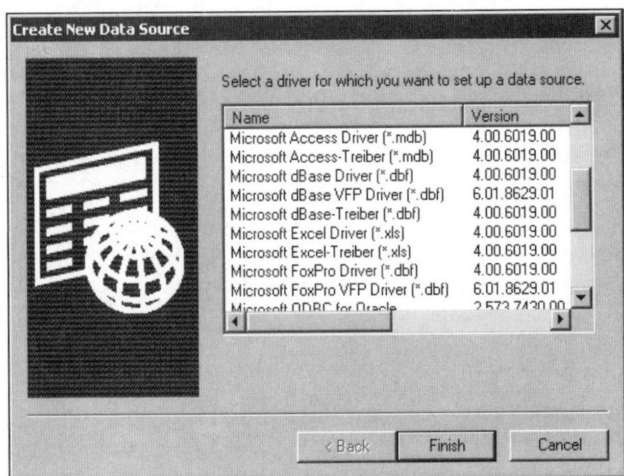

Figure 13-12 Create New Data Source dialog box

6. In the Create New Data Source dialog box window, select **Microsoft Access Driver (*.mdb)**, and then click the **Finish** button. The ODBC Microsoft Access Setup dialog box appears.

7. In the ODBC Microsoft Access Setup dialog box, type **Library** as the Data Source Name, and then click the **Select** button. In the Select Database dialog box that appears, select the **Library.mdb** file from the Chapter.13 folder in your Visual C++ Projects folder, and then click **OK**. The Select Database dialog box will close. Your ODBC Microsoft Access Setup dialog box should appear similar to Figure 13-13.

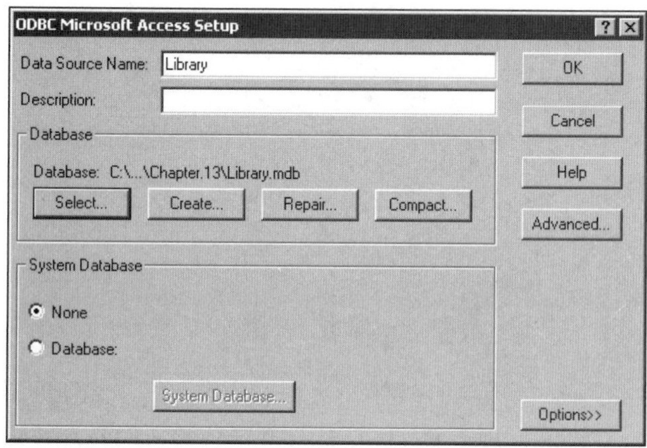

Figure 13-13 ODBC Microsoft Access Setup dialog box

8. Click **OK** to close the Microsoft Access Setup dialog box, and then click **OK** to close the ODBC Data Source Administrator window. Finally, close the **Administrative Tools** folder.

Creating an ODBC Database Application

The functionality that allows MFC to access ODBC-compliant databases is contained in the classes listed in Figure 13-14. MFC Application Wizard derives classes for you from the ODBC database classes, and the framework manages almost all of the function calls and data members required to connect to an ODBC database. However, you need to understand which classes are used in an MFC ODBC database application in order to be able to customize the application for your own needs.

All ODBC database applications begin with the CDatabase class. The CFieldExchange class manages the exchange of information between your application and the database. The MFC framework hides all of the details of the CDatabase and CFieldExchange classes from you, so you will not spend any time learning about them. The MFC framework automatically calls the CDBException class for any failures that occur when managing records in an ODBC database. The CDBException class is part of the Visual C++ exception-handling capabilities. You will not explore the CDBException class because exception-handling is an advanced topic, which this text does not cover.

Class	Description
CDatabase	Manages a connection to a database
CDBException	Returns exceptions for any failures that occur when managing records in an ODBC database
CFieldExchange	Manages the exchange of data between dialog controls and their associated fields in a database record, similarly to DDX, which handles the exchange of values between controls and variables
CRecordset	Represents the records returned from a database
CRecordView	Displays in dialog box controls the database records associated with a CRecordset object; derived from Cview

Figure 13-14 ODBC classes

Exception-handling is an advanced technique that allows programs to handle errors as they occur during the execution of a program.

The classes you need to explore include the CRecordSet and CRecordView classes. The CRecordset class represents records returned from a database, and the CRecordView class displays those records in a dialog box-style window that you can edit with the Dialog Editor. Before you can actually display the records represented by the CRecordset class, you must add controls to the CRecordView's dialog window for each field you want to display. Then, you must bind each control to its associated fields in the database record set. You will learn how to create data-bound controls in the next section.

The CRecordView class is very similar to the CFormView class you used in Chapter 11.

You can create two types of CRecordset objects: a snapshot or a dynaset. A **snapshot** is a static view of the records in a database. Any changes made to the database after you run your application, whether the changes are made by other users or by other CRecordset objects in your application, will not be reflected in your application's record set. In comparison, a **dynaset** is a dynamic record set that displays the most recent changes to a database each time you move from one record to another in a database application. Essentially, a snapshot queries the database only once when your application first executes. In contrast, a dynaset queries the database when an application first executes *and* each time a user moves to a different record. Snapshots are usually faster than dynasets because your application needs to query the database only once.

Dynasets are necessary in multiuser environments in which users need to work with a database's most current information. For example, a company may use a database to record inventory levels for items they sell. A sales associate could use the database to check if there is sufficient inventory to fill an order for a particular item, and then update the database with the current inventory level once he or she has filled the order. In order for one sales associate to see the most recent changes to inventory levels made by other sales associates, the inventory database needs to be created as a dynaset.

Later in this chapter, you will learn how to add and delete records from the Library Database application. For this reason, you will create the application's CRecordset object as a dynaset. Next, you will use MFC Application Wizard to create the Library Database project.

To use MFC Application Wizard to create the Library Database project:

1. Create a new project named **LibraryDatabase** using the MFC Application Wizard. Save the project in the **Chapter.13** folder in your Visual C++ Projects folder.
2. MFC Application Wizard starts. In the Application Type tab, select **Single document** from the application choices. Be sure to leave the **Document/View architecture support** check box selected. Then, click the **Database Support** tab.
3. As shown in Figure 13-15, the Database Support tab prompts you for the type of database support you want in your application. The first option, *None*, creates the application without database support. The second option, *Header files only*, adds basic database support to an application, but does not create any of the database classes. If you select the *Header files only* option, then you must manually derive your own classes from the database-specific classes. The third option, *Database view without file support*, creates an application that can read information from and write information to a database, but does not include support for additional files created with serialization. The fourth option, *Database view with file support*, creates an application that can read information from and write information to a database, and includes support for additional serialized files. Because the Library Database application does not need to work with any files other than the database itself, select **Database view without file support**. After you select *Database view without file support*, the Client type and Type options become available. Select **ODBC** as the Client type option and **Dynaset** as the Type option.
4. Click the Data Source to display the Select Data Source dialog box, which allows you to select the DSN that you want to make available to your database application. The File Data Source tab in the Select Database Source dialog box allows you to select file-based DSNs, whereas the Machine Data Source tab allows you to select system and user DSNs. Click the **Machine Data Source** tab, select the **Library** user DSN, and then click the **OK** button. Figure 13-16 shows an example of the Machine Data Source tab.

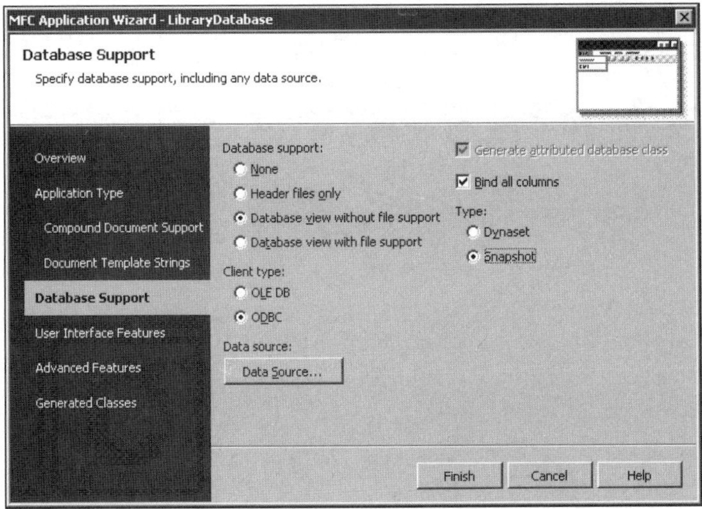

Figure 13-15 The Database Support tab in the MFC Application Wizard

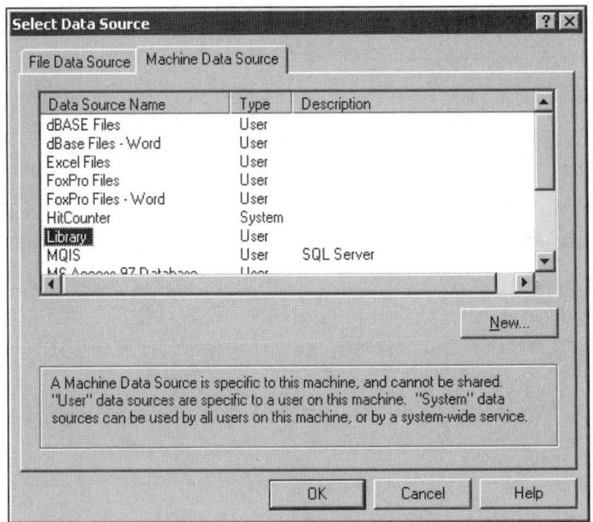

Figure 13-16 The Machine Data Source tab of the Select Data Source dialog box

5. After you click the **OK** button, you will receive a dialog box prompting you for a login name and password to access the database. Because the Library database does not require login information, leave both fields blank and click the **OK** button. You will see a Select Database Object dialog box that allows you to select the objects (tables, queries, and so on) from the database that you want to make available to your database application. Expand the **Tables** node. You will see that the Library.mdb database contains a single table named Books, as shown in Figure 13-17. Click once with your mouse to select the

table, and then click the **OK** button. After clicking the OK button, you will be returned to the Database Support tab of the MFC Application Wizard.

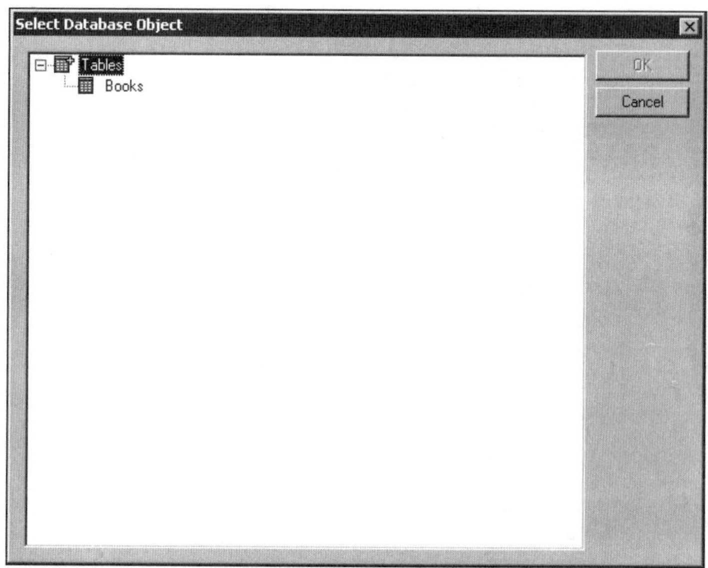

Figure 13-17 Select Database Object dialog box

6. Click the **Advanced Features** tab and clear all of the selected options.
7. The default options in the rest of the tabs in the MFC Application Wizard are fine, so click the **Finish** button to create the project.
8. Once the MFC Application Wizard finishes creating your project, use Solution Explorer to open the LibraryDatabaseSet.cpp file in the Code Editor window. The LibraryDatabaseSet.cpp file is the implementation file for the CLibraryDatabaseSet class, which derives from the CRecordset class. You will learn about the CRecordset class next. But first, locate and delete the #error preprocessor directive that reads as follows. Also delete the four comment lines that follow it.

   ```
   #error Security Issue: The connection string may contain
   a password
   ```

   After you click the Finish button, you will receive a security warning informing you that the connection string in the generated code may contain plain text passwords or other sensitive information. You can safely ignore this warning because the Library.mdb database does not require login information. However, the MFC Application Wizard will place a #error preprocessor directive that lists the same security warning in the CRecordset class. You need to remove the #error preprocessor directive in order to successfully compile the application. Click the **OK** button to continue.

   Next, you will examine the CRecordset class.

The CRecordset Class

The CRecordset class represents the records returned from a database. The CLibraryDatabaseSet class that the MFC Application Wizard built for you derives from the CRecordset class. Figure 13-18 shows the CLibraryDatabaseSet class implementation file.

```
class CLibraryDatabaseSet : public CRecordset
{
public:
     CLibraryDatabaseSet(CDatabase* pDatabase = NULL);
     DECLARE_DYNAMIC(CLibraryDatabaseSet)
// Field/Param Data
     CStringW     m_BookID;
     CStringW     m_Title;
     CStringW     m_Author;
     CStringW     m_Publisher;
     int    m_Genre;
     CStringW     m_Description;
// Overrides
     // Wizard generated virtual function overrides
     public:
     virtual CString GetDefaultConnect();         // Default connection string
     virtual CString GetDefaultSQL();    // default SQL for Recordset
     virtual void DoFieldExchange(CFieldExchange* pFX);     // RFX support
// Implementation
#ifdef _DEBUG
     virtual void AssertValid() const;
     virtual void Dump(CDumpContext& dc) const;
#endif
};
```

Data member declarations corresponding to each field in the database

Figure 13-18 LibraryDatabaseSet.h

One of the first things you should notice is the data member declarations that the MFC Application Wizard created in the public section of the CLibraryDatabaseSet interface file. A data member has been created that corresponds to each field in the database. Notice that for the name of each data member, the MFC Application Wizard uses the name of the field in the database, prefixed with m_ to identify the variable as an MFC variable. MFC Application Wizard also declares each data member using the corresponding data type for that field in the database. For example, the Author field is a text string field in the Library.mdb database. The corresponding data member in the CLibraryDatabaseSet class is named m_Author and is declared with a data type of CString using the statement: `CStringW m_Author;`.

Notice that the data types for the string fields, such as the Author field, are of the CStringW data type. The string data type in a database can be stored in either ANSI or Unicode format. MFC Application Wizard determines the data type of string fields in your target database and assigns a data type of either CStringA for ANSI or CStringW for Unicode. This more specific form of data type prevents the ODBC driver from performing unnecessary conversions, which could potentially slow your program. However, for the library program you are building, it is easier to change the string data types to CString and let the ODBC driver handle the conversions. Although not included in Figure 13-18 due to space limitations, the MFC Application Wizard includes comments

13

above the data member declarations in the LibraryDatabaseSet.h file that contain this same information. Next, you will modify the LibraryDatabaseSet.h file so that the data members corresponding to the fields in the database are of the CString data type.

To modify the LibraryDatabaseSet.h file so that the data members corresponding to the fields in the database are of the CString data type:

1. Open the **LibraryDatabaseSet.h** file in your Code Editor window.
2. Locate the following field data members in the public section:

```
CStringW    m_BookID;
CStringW    m_Title;
CStringW    m_Author;
CStringW    m_Publisher;
int   m_Genre;
```

Data member declarations corresponding to each field in that database

Modify the preceding declarations so their data types are of the CString data type instead of the CStringW data type. The modified data member declarations should appear as shown in Figure 13-19:

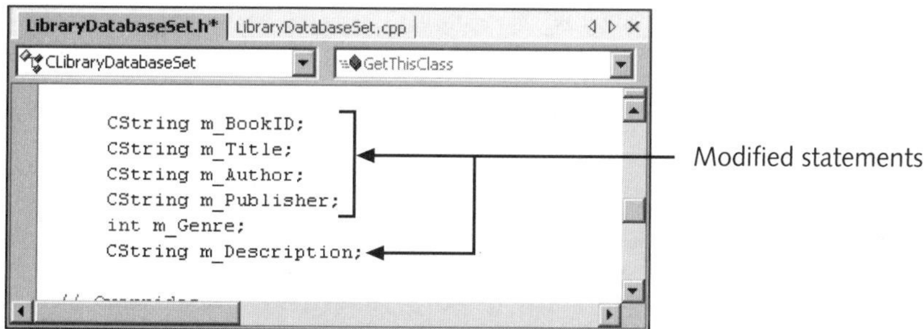

Figure 13-19 Modified data member declarations in the CLibraryDatabaseSet class

MFC handles the exchange of values between CRecordset data members and their corresponding fields in a database using a mechanism called **record field exchange**, or **RFX**. RFX is very similar to the MFC DDX mechanism, which handles the exchange of values between controls and variables. Whereas DDX uses the DoDataExchange() function to handle the exchange of values between controls and variables, RFX uses the DoFieldExchange() function to handle the exchange of values between CRecordset data members and their corresponding fields in a database. You will see the following declaration for the DoFieldExchange() function in the LibraryDatabaseSet.h file:

```
virtual void DoFieldExchange(CFieldExchange* pFX);
```

In the LibraryDatabaseSet.cpp file, you will see the following definition for the DoFieldExchange() function:

```
void CLibraryDatabaseSet::DoFieldExchange(
  CFieldExchange* pFX) {
  pFX->SetFieldType(CFieldExchange::outputColumn);
  RFX_Text(pFX, _T("[BookID]"), m_BookID);
```

```
        RFX_Text(pFX, _T("[Title]"), m_Title);
        RFX_Text(pFX, _T("[Author]"), m_Author);
        RFX_Text(pFX, _T("[Publisher]"), m_Publisher);
        RFX_Int(pFX, _T("[Genre]"), m_Genre);
        RFX_Text(pFX, _T("[Description]"), m_Description);
    }
```

You do not normally need to modify the DoFieldExchange() function. However, you should be aware that the statements within the DoFieldExchange() function are what enable the transfer of values between a derived CRecordset class's data members and the fields in a database.

The next thing to understand in the CLibraryDatabaseSet class is the constructor `CLibraryDatabaseSet(CDatabase* pDatabase = NULL);`. Notice the parameter for the constructor, `CDatabase* pDatabase = NULL`, which passes a pointer to a CDatabase object named pDatabase. Recall that the CDatabase class manages a connection to a database. Assigning a value of NULL to the pDatabase pointer in the CLibraryDatabaseSet class constructor informs the MFC framework to automatically construct a CDatabase object for you and to connect your program to the database.

For database applications with more than one CRecordset class, if a CDatabase object and connection already exist for a database, the MFC framework will pass a pointer to an existing database rather than create and connect to a new CDatabase object. Creating and connecting to a database object is resource-intensive, so it is much more efficient to work with a single database object instead of working with multiple database objects.

If you examine the LibraryDatabaseSet.cpp file, you will see the following definition for the class constructor:

13

```
CLibraryDatabaseSet::CLibraryDatabaseSet(CDatabase* pdb)
  : CRecordset(pdb)
{
  m_BookID = L"";
  m_Title = L"";
  m_Author = L"";
  m_Publisher = L"";
  m_Genre = 0;
  m_Description = L"";
  m_nFields = 6;
  m_nDefaultType = dynaset;
}
```

The L prefixes before the quotation marks in the preceding code are a special type of data mapping routine that converts a text value to its Unicode equivalent. See the Data Type Mappings topic in the MSDN Library for more information.

Notice that the CDatabase object pointer named pdb is passed to the constructor for the CRecordset base class. Also notice that the data members representing fields in the database table are initialized to default values. The initial values assigned to each data member will be quickly replaced with values in the database fields once the MFC framework calls the RFX DoFieldExchange() function. Finally, notice the definition for the m_nDefaultType data member, which determines whether you want the CRecordset object to be a dynaset or a snapshot. Because you selected dynaset when you ran the MFC Application Wizard, the m_nDefaultType data member is defined using the statement `m_nDefaultType = dynaset;`. However, if you had selected snapshot, the statement would read `m_nDefaultType = snapshot;`. You can modify the statement manually after running the MFC Application Wizard if you change your mind about what type of CRecordset object you want to use.

After the constructor for a CRecordset class executes, the MFC framework automatically calls the inherited Open() function of the CRecordset class. You will not see a declaration or definition for the Open() function in your classes that derived from CRecordset because the MFC framework uses the base class version of the function. However, you should be aware of the Open() function because it does much of the work in setting up the connection to a database.

When you pass a value of NULL to the pDatabase pointer in the derived CRecordset class constructor, the Open() function constructs a new CDatabase object and then calls the GetDefaultConnect() function to connect to the database. The MFC Application Wizard created an overridden version of the GetDefaultConnect() function for you that specifies the necessary information to connect to your database. If you examine the LibraryDatabaseSet.cpp file, you will find the following GetDefaultConnect() function definition:

```
CString CLibraryDatabaseSet::GetDefaultConnect() {
 return _T("DSN=Library;DBQ=C:\\Visual C++
Projects\\Chapter.13\\Library.mdb;DriverId=25;FIL=MS
Access;MaxBufferSize=2048;PageTimeout=5;UID=admin;");
}
```

The GetDefaultConnect() function contains a single statement that uses the special _T() data mapping function to return a text string that identifies the type of database (ODBC) and the DSN to connect to (in this case the Library DSN you created earlier), and other connection information. The database information string is returned to the Open() function, which uses it to connect to the database.

After the Open() function connects to the database by calling the GetDefaultConnect() function, it calls the GetDefaultSQL() function, which returns a string that the Open() function uses to build the default SQL statement that is executed against the database. If you examine the LibraryDatabaseSet.cpp file, you will find the following overridden GetDefaultSQL() function definition that is automatically supplied by the MFC Application Wizard:

```
CString CLibraryDatabaseSet::GetDefaultSQL() {
     return _T("[Books]");
}
```

The single statement in the GetDefaultSQL() function also uses the special _T() data mapping function to return a text string to the Open() function that contains the name of the table that you selected when you ran the MFC Application Wizard. Notice that the table name in the returned string is in SQL format. Once the Open() function receives the string, it constructs a SQL statement that simply returns all of the records in the tables you specified when you ran the MFC Application Wizard.

If you want the default SQL statement to be more explicit, you can modify the string returned by the GetDefaultSQL() function. For example, if you want the records returned from the database to be sorted by the Author field, then you can modify the `return` statement in the GetDefaultSQL() function as follows:

```
return _T("[Books] ORDER BY [Books].[Author]");
```

The preceding statement is only one method of sorting the records returned from an SQL query. Note that the GetDefaultSQL() function is used only to sort records when they are first returned from the database. You will see another method of sorting later in this chapter that you can use at any point in your program. For your version of the Library Database application, leave the GetDefaultSQL() function set to its default value of returning only the table name to the Open() function.

One final item about the CRecordset class that needs to be pointed out is where an object of the class is instantiated in a database application. An object of a derived CRecordset class is actually instantiated in the application's document class. This way, when you instantiate an object of the document class in the application class's InitInstance() function, an object of a derived CRecordset class is also instantiated. If you examine the LibraryDatabaseDoc.h file, you will see the following CLibraryDatabaseSet object declared in the public section:


```
CLibraryDatabaseSet m_LibraryDatabaseSet;
```

The CRecordView Class

The CRecordView class, which derives from CView, displays records from the CRecordset class in a dialog box-style window that you can edit with the Dialog Editor. Figure 13-20 shows the Library Database application's CLibraryDatabaseView class interface file that the MFC Application Wizard derived from CRecordView.

```
class CLibraryDatabaseView : public CRecordView
{
protected: // create from serialization only
     CLibraryDatabaseView();
     DECLARE_DYNCREATE(CLibraryDatabaseView)

public:
     enum{ IDD = IDD_LIBRARYDATABASE_FORM };
     CLibraryDatabaseSet* m_pSet;

// Attributes
public:
     CLibraryDatabaseDoc* GetDocument() const;

// Operations
public:

// Overrides
     public:
     virtual CRecordset* OnGetRecordset();
virtual BOOL PreCreateWindow(CREATESTRUCT& cs);
protected:
     virtual void DoDataExchange(CDataExchange* pDX);    // DDX/DDV support
     virtual void OnInitialUpdate(); // called first time after construct

// Implementation
public:
     virtual ~CLibraryDatabaseView();
#ifdef _DEBUG
     virtual void AssertValid() const;
     virtual void Dump(CDumpContext& dc) const;
#endif

protected:

// Generated message map functions
protected:
     DECLARE_MESSAGE_MAP()
};

#ifndef _DEBUG  // debug version in LibraryDatabaseView.cpp
inline CLibraryDatabaseDoc* CLibraryDatabaseView::GetDocument() const
   { return reinterpret_cast<CLibraryDatabaseDoc*>(m_pDocument); }
#endif
```

m_pSet pointer declaration

Figure 13-20 LibraryDatabaseView.h

Notice in the first public section in Figure 13-20 that the CLibraryDatabaseView declares a pointer named m_pSet of the CLibraryDatabaseSet class. It is through the m_pSet pointer that a CRecordView class communicates with its associated CRecordset class. However, as shown in the following code, the m_pSet pointer is initially assigned a value of `NULL` in the CLibraryDatabaseView class constructor:

```
CLibraryDatabaseView::CLibraryDatabaseView()
     : CRecordView(CLibraryDatabaseView::IDD) {
  m_pSet = NULL;
  // TODO: add construction code here
}
```

Now, notice the OnInitialUpdate() function that is declared in the LibraryDatabaseView.h file. The OnInitialUpdate() function is derived from CView and is called by the MFC framework after the view is first attached to the document, but before the view is displayed. It is in the OnInitialUpdate() function that you assign to the m_pSet variable a pointer to the derived CRecordset associated with a derived CRecordView class. The following code shows the OnInitialUpdate() function that the MFC Application Wizard defined for you in the CLibraryDatabaseView implementation file:

```
void CLibraryDatabaseView::OnInitialUpdate() {
     m_pSet = &GetDocument()->m_libraryDatabaseSet;
     CRecordView::OnInitialUpdate();
}
```

Recall that an object of a derived CRecordset class is instantiated in an application's document class. The CRecordset object that was declared in the document class for the Library Database application was named m_libraryDatabaseSet. Observe that in the first statement in the preceding code, the m_pSet variable is assigned as a pointer to the libraryDatabaseSet using the GetDocument() function of the CView class. Essentially, a CRecordView class communicates with its CRecordset class *through* the application's document class using the GetDocument() function. The second statement in the OnInitialUpdate() function calls the OnInitialUpdate() function for the CRecordView base class, while the last two statements adjust the size of the frame window to the CRecordView dialog window.

You learned in Chapter 11 that the GetDocument() function allows classes derived from CView to communicate with their associated document classes.

13

One final requirement for the m_pSet variable involves the virtual OnGetRecordset() function. In order to assign a pointer to a recordset object, a database application must override the OnGetRecordset() function and return the m_pSet pointer. The following code shows the OnGetRecordset() function that the MFC Application Wizard defined in the Library Database application's CLibraryDatabaseView implementation file:

```
CRecordset* CLibraryDatabaseView::OnGetRecordset() {
     return m_pSet;
}
```

Linking Dialog Controls to Database Fields

The reason you spent so much time learning about the m_pSet pointer in the last section is that the m_pSet pointer is necessary for the CRecordView class's dialog window to communicate with the CRecordset class's data members. In order for the CRecordView class's dialog window to communicate with the CRecordset class's data members, you need to add controls to a derived CRecordView class's dialog window. Then, you add to the

CRecordView class's DoDataExchange() function the appropriate DDX_Field functions listed in Figure 13-21 to handle the exchange of data between the dialog controls and the derived CRecordset class's data members.

Function	Description
DDX_FieldCBIndex	Synchronizes the index of the selected item in the list box control of a combo box control in a record view and an int field data member of a record set associated with the record view
DDX_FieldCBString	Manages the transfer of CString data between the edit control of a combo box control in a record view and a CString field data member of a record set associated with the record view
DDX_FieldCBStringExact	Manages the transfer of CString data between the edit control of a combo box control in a record view and a CString field data member of a record set associated with the record view
DDX_FieldCheck	Manages the transfer of `int` data between a check box control in a dialog box, form view, or control view object and an `int` data member of the dialog box, form view, or control view object
DDX_FieldLBIndex	Synchronizes the index of the selected item in a list box control in a record view and an `int` field data member of a record set associated with the record view
DDX_FieldLBString	Copies the current selection of a list box control in a record view to a CString field data member of a record set associated with the record view
DDX_FieldLBStringExact	Copies the current selection of a list box control in a record view to a CString field data member of a record set associated with the record view
DDX_FieldRadio	Associates a zero-based `int` member variable of a record view's record set with the currently selected radio button in a group of radio buttons in the record view
DDX_FieldScroll	Synchronizes the scroll position of a scroll bar control in a record view and an `int` field data member of a record set associated with the record view
DDX_FieldSlider	Synchronizes the thumb position of a slider control in a record view and an `int` field data member of a record set associated with the record view
DDX_FieldText	Manages the transfer of `int`, `short`, `long`, `DWORD`, `CString`, `float`, `double`, `BOOL`, or `BYTE` data between an edit box control and the field data members of a record set

Figure 13-21 DDX_Field functions

It is necessary to use the m_pSet pointer with the functions listed in Figure 13-21 in order to identify the CLibraryDatabaseSet class's record set and the fields in the record set. For example, you will use the DDX_FieldText() function to manage the exchange of data between the CLibraryDatabaseView class's dialog controls and the CLibraryDatabaseSet class's data members. The syntax for the DDX_FieldText() function when used to manage the exchange of data with the m_Author field is as follows:

```
DDX_FieldText(pDX, IDC_AUTHOR,
    m_pSet->m_Author, m_pSet);
```

The first argument, pDX, is a pointer to a CDataExchange object, which the MFC framework automatically supplies to establish the context of the data exchange. The second argument, IDC_AUTHOR, identifies the resource ID for the Author control in the CLibraryDatabaseView class's dialog box. The third argument uses the m_pSet pointer to point to the m_Author data member in the CLibraryDatabaseSet class, and the fourth argument uses the m_pSet pointer to identify the record set.

After adding DDX_Field functions to the derived CLibraryDatabaseView class's DoDataExchange() function, the derived CLibraryDatabaseSet class's RFX mechanism will then handle the data exchange between the class's data members and fields in the database. In short, the DDX mechanism handles data exchange between the dialog controls and a derived CRecordset class's data members, whereas the RFX mechanism handles data exchange between a derived CRecordset class's data members and a database's fields. Figure 13-22 illustrates how data is exchanged across a database application.

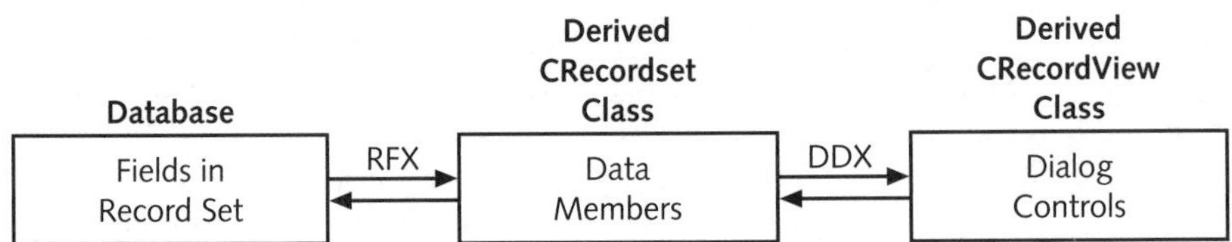

Figure 13-22 Data exchange across a database application

13

Next, you will add dialog controls to the CLibraryDatabaseView class's dialog window to display the fields in the Library Database program. You will use a new type of dialog control, Radio Button controls, to select a book's genre of fiction or nonfiction. A radio button appears as a small empty circle; when selected, it appears to be filled with a black dot. A radio button is usually contained within a group of other radio buttons, and you can select only one of the grouped radio buttons at a time. Figure 13-23 shows an example of a group of six radio buttons.

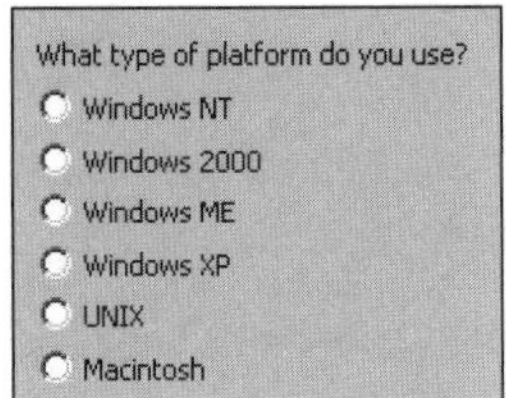

Figure 13-23 Radio buttons

The term *radio button* comes from car radios that have a group of push buttons, each of which is set to a radio station. In the same manner that you can select only one car radio button at a time, you can select only one Radio Button control contained within a group of other radio buttons.

Radio buttons are sometimes referred to as option buttons.

When used with a database, a single group of related radio buttons is used to represent a set number of choices that users can place in a single field. For example, you can enter only one of the six platform types in the database associated with the radio button group shown in Figure 13-23. In the code, you do not use a radio button's associated string, such as *Windows NT*, to refer to the radio button. Rather, you use an integer value that is associated with each radio button that is part of a group. The first radio button in a radio button group is represented by a 0, and each subsequent control in the group is represented by the next higher number. Therefore, the Macintosh control in Figure 13-23 is represented in a database field as the number 5.

Radio Button controls are recognized as being in the same group when the first control in the group has its Group property set to *True* in the Properties window. All radio buttons that follow are recognized as part of the same group until Visual C++ encounters another Radio Button control with its Group check box selected, which starts a new group. Additionally, the resource ID property of the first Radio Button control in a group is used to represent *all* of the Radio Button controls in the group; any resource IDs you assign to other controls in the group will be ignored. When used with a database, you associate the first Radio Button control's resource ID with a CRecordset data member. The MFC framework will automatically recognize which control in the group is selected and enter its integer value into the associated database field. Conversely, the MFC framework will also read each integer value in the database field that is associated with a radio button group and select the appropriate radio button when its record is displayed.

To add to the CLibraryDatabaseView class's dialog window dialog controls that will display the fields in the Library Database program:

1. Open the **IDD_LIBRARYDATABASE_FORM** resource in the Dialog Editor.
2. Delete the Static Text control that reads **`TODO: Place form controls on this dialog.`**.
3. Modify your dialog window so that it matches Figure 13-24.
4. Open the **Properties** window for the Book Title edit box and set its resource ID to **IDC_TITLE**.
5. Open the **Properties** window for the Book ID edit box and set its resource ID to **IDC_BOOKID**.

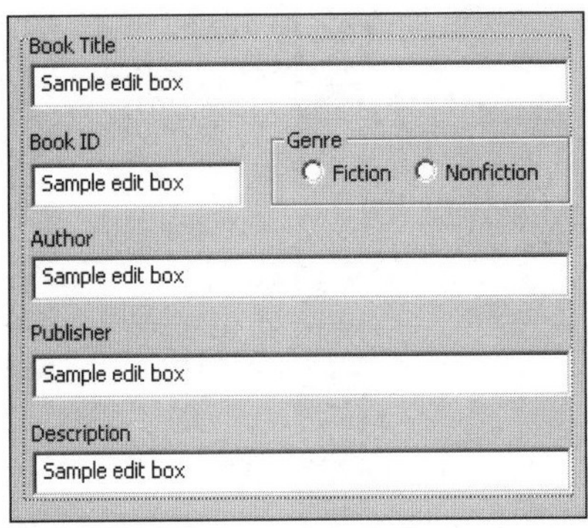

Figure 13-24 Library Database dialog controls

6. Open the **Properties** window for the Fiction radio button control and set its resource ID to **IDC_GENRE**. Also, change its **Group** property to **True** to designate the Fiction radio button as the first button in the IDC_GENRE group.
7. Open the **Properties** window for the Author edit box and set its resource ID to **IDC_AUTHOR**.
8. Open the **Properties** window for the Publisher edit box and set its resource ID to **IDC_PUBLISHER**.
9. Open the **Properties** window for the Description control and set its resource ID to **IDC_DESCRIPTION**.

Next, you will map the dialog control resource IDs to their associated field data members in the CLibraryDatabaseSet class. In previous chapters, you used the Add Member Variable Wizard to map dialog control resource IDs to their associated field data members, which automatically added DDX statements to the DoDataExchange() function. However, when working with a record set, it is easier to add the DDX_Field statements to the DoDataExchange() function manually.

13

To map the dialog control resource IDs to their associated field data members in the CLibraryDatabaseSet class:

1. Open the **LibraryDatabaseView.cpp** file in the Code Editor window and locate the DoDataExchange() function.
2. As shown in Figure 13-25, replace the comments in the DoDataExchange() function with DDX_Field statements.
3. When you are through adding the DDX_Field statements to the DoDataExchange() function, build and execute the project. The program should open to the first record, which is for the book *The 7 Habits of Highly Effective People*.

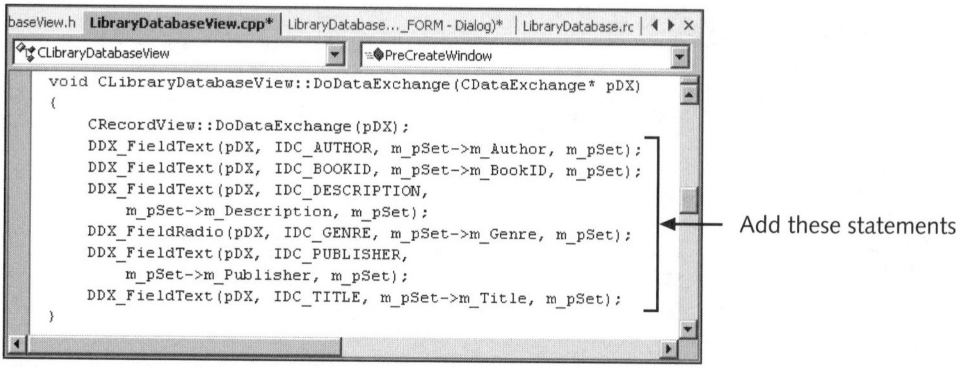

baseView.h | LibraryDatabaseView.cpp* | LibraryDatabase..._FORM - Dialog)* | LibraryDatabase.rc

CLibraryDatabaseView | PreCreateWindow

```
void CLibraryDatabaseView::DoDataExchange(CDataExchange* pDX)
{
    CRecordView::DoDataExchange(pDX);
    DDX_FieldText(pDX, IDC_AUTHOR, m_pSet->m_Author, m_pSet);
    DDX_FieldText(pDX, IDC_BOOKID, m_pSet->m_BookID, m_pSet);
    DDX_FieldText(pDX, IDC_DESCRIPTION,
        m_pSet->m_Description, m_pSet);
    DDX_FieldRadio(pDX, IDC_GENRE, m_pSet->m_Genre, m_pSet);
    DDX_FieldText(pDX, IDC_PUBLISHER,
        m_pSet->m_Publisher, m_pSet);
    DDX_FieldText(pDX, IDC_TITLE, m_pSet->m_Title, m_pSet);
}
```

Add these statements

Figure 13-25 DDX_Field statements added to LibraryDatabaseView.cpp

4. The MFC framework automatically added a Record menu and toolbar buttons that you can use to navigate to the first, previous, next, and last records in the database. The MFC framework also automatically added the code that manages the navigation functions associated with the menu commands and toolbar buttons for moving to and displaying each record in the record set. Practice navigating through the database using the menu and toolbar buttons. To see the navigation function performed by each button, hold your mouse over a button to display its ToolTip.
5. The MFC framework also manages any updates you need to make to records in the database. Whenever you make changes to a record, the MFC framework updates the record in the database when you move to another record in the record set—you do not need to manually save a record when you make changes. For practice, move to the record for the book *Tender Is the Night*. The book's author is incorrectly entered as *Hemingway, Ernest,* when it should be *Fitzgerald, F. Scott*. In addition, the book's genre should be *Fiction*, not *Nonfiction*. Make these changes to the record, and then move to the previous record using either the Record menu or the toolbar. Then, immediately move back to the *Tender Is the Night* record. The changes you made to the record should be visible.
6. Close the Library Database program window.

Manipulating Record Sets

You will often want to give users of your program the ability to manipulate record sets returned from a database. Two of the most common ways of manipulating record sets are sorting and filtering. Sorting presents database records in alphanumeric order based on a field in the record set. Filtering uses a given criterion to narrow records that the user can see. For example, suppose you have a sales database that lists revenue for each state in the United States. You can filter the sales database so that only the records for

California and New York are visible. Sorting and filtering do not change any data, nor do they change the number of records in the returned record set. Rather, sorting and filtering determine how the records are presented to the user and what records are visible to the user. First, you will learn about sorting.

Sorting

One way to sort records when they are first returned from a database, as you saw earlier in the chapter, involves modifying the **return** statement in the GetDefaultSQL() function. The following code uses the ORDER BY clause to sort the record set by the Author field in the Books table:

```
CString CLibraryDatabaseSet::GetDefaultSQL() {
  return _T(" [Books] ORDER BY [Books].[Author]");
}
```

The GetDefaultSQL() function is useful only for defining initial SQL criteria for the record set you want to be returned from a database.

When you derive a class from CRecordset, the derived class inherits a data member named m_strSort. You dynamically sort the records in a record set by assigning the field name by which you want to sort to the m_strSort data member. The MFC framework uses the field name in the m_strSort data member to construct an ORDER BY SQL statement to execute against the database. You assign values to the m_strSort data member from a CRecordView class using the m_pSet pointer to the associated CRecordset class. One way to use the m_strSort data member is in the OnInitialUpdate() function that runs when the application first executes. For example, the following modified version of the CLibraryDatabaseView class's OnInitialUpdate() function assigns the Author field to the m_strSort data member, which causes the database records to be sorted by author names when the program first executes:

13

```
void CLibraryDatabaseView::OnInitialUpdate() {
     m_pSet = &GetDocument()->m_libraryDatabaseSet;
     m_pSet->m_strSort = "[Author]";
     CRecordView::OnInitialUpdate();
}
```

Using the m_strSort data member in the OnInitialUpdate() function is essentially the same as adding an ORDER BY clause to the return statement in the GetDefaultSQL() function. For users to dynamically sort the records in the Library Database application, you need to add message handlers that assign the field to sort by to the m_strSort data member.

To use the m_strSort data member after the record set has been returned from the database, you must close the open record set using the Close() function inherited from the CRecordset class, assign a field name to the m_strSort data member, and then reopen the record set with the Open() method. Finally, you call the UpdateData() function to update the data displayed in the CRecordView class's dialog controls. For example to dynamically sort the Library Database application's record set by the Author field, you would add a message handler to the CLibraryDatabaseView class that executes the following statements:

```
m_pSet->Close();
m_pSet->m_strSort = "[Author]";
m_pSet->Open();
UpdateData(FALSE);
```

You may have noticed with the Library Database application that records are displayed in the numeric order of the BooksID field. This means that records are displayed in the order that they were added to the Books table, which isn't very useful to your users. Next, you will modify the Library Database application so that users can sort on author name and book title. You will add to the Record menu commands that execute each sort type.

To modify the Library Database application so that users can sort on author name and book title:

1. Open the Library Database application's menu in the Menu Editor.
2. Add a **separator**, a **Sort by Author** command, and a **Sort by Title** command to the Record menu, as shown in Figure 13-26. Modify the Sort by Author command's ID property to **ID_RECORD_SORT_BY_AUTHOR** and its Prompt property to **Sort the record set by author name**. Then, modify the Sort by Title command's ID property to **ID_RECORD_SORT_BY_TITLE** and its Prompt property to **Sort the record set by book title**.

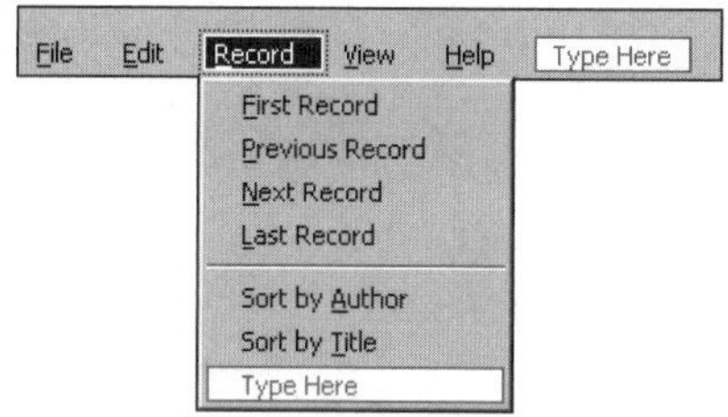

Figure 13-26 Adding new sort commands

3. Use the Event Handler Wizard to add to the CLibraryDatabaseView class the following COMMAND message map function for the ID_RECORD_SORT_BY_AUTHOR resource ID:

```
void CLibraryDatabaseView::OnRecordSortByAuthor()
{
      m_pSet->Close();
      m_pSet->m_strSort = "[Author]";
      m_pSet->Open();
      UpdateData(FALSE);
}
```

4. Use the Event Handler Wizard to add to the CLibraryDatabaseView class the following COMMAND message map function for the ID_RECORD_SORT_BY_TITLE resource ID:

```
void CLibraryDatabaseView::OnRecordSortByTitle()
{
   m_pSet->Close();
     m_pSet->m_strSort = "[Title]";
     m_pSet->Open();
     UpdateData(FALSE);
}
```

5. Rebuild and execute the program. Test the Sort by Author and Sort by Title commands on the Record menu to be sure the sort functions are working correctly. (You will need to navigate through the records in order to check if they were sorted correctly.)
6. Close the Library Database program window.

Filtering

Filtering works almost the same as sorting, except that it extracts a subset of the main record set instead of sorting it. Instead of using the m_strSort data member, you use the m_strFilter data member, which is also inherited from CRecordset. As with the m_strSort data member, you assign values to the m_strFilter data member from a CRecordView class using the m_pSet pointer to the associated CRecordset class. Instead of simply assigning a field name to the m_strFilter data member, you must also add an assignment statement that tells the MFC framework how you want to filter the record set. The MFC framework uses the assignment statement in the m_strFilter data member to construct a WHERE SQL statement to execute against the database. You must also close and reopen the record set using the Close() and Open() functions, the same as with the m_strSort data member. For example, you would use the following code to filter the records in the Library Database application so that only records in which the Author field is equal to *Hemingway, Ernest* are returned:

13

```
m_pSet->Close();
m_pSet->m_strFilter = "[Author] = 'Hemingway, Ernest'";
m_pSet->Open();
```

Be sure *not* to include the WHERE clause in the text string you assign to the m_strFilter data member. For example, the following assignment statement is incorrect:

```
m_pSet->m_strFilter
     = "WHERE [Author] = 'Hemingway, Ernest'";
```

When you filter records, the possibility exists that no records may match the filter expression that you assign to the m_strFilter data member. To be sure that there are records to display to the user, you use the GetRecordCount() function that is inherited from CRecordset to count the number of records in the record set. If the

GetRecordCount() function returns a value of 0, then no records matched the filter expression. The following code shows how to use the GetRecordCount() function within the example that filters for books by Hemingway. If the GetRecordCount() function returns a value of 0, then a message box informs the user that no matching records were found, the record set is closed, the m_strFilter data member is assigned an empty string, and then the record set is reopened. Assigning an empty string to the m_strFilter data member removes any previously assigned filter expression and instructs the MFC framework to return the entire record set.

```
m_pSet->Close();
m_pSet->m_strFilter
     = "[Author] = 'Hemingway, Ernest'";
m_pSet->Open();
int iNumRecords = m_pSet->GetRecordCount();
if (iNumRecords == 0) {
     AfxMessageBox("No matching records found.");
     m_pSet->Close();
     m_pSet->m_strFilter = "";
     m_pSet->Open();
}
UpdateData(FALSE);
```

Next, you will modify the Library Database application so users can filter records based on the type of book they are interested in. You will add commands to the Record menu that apply each filter. The filter will be applied to the Genre field in the Books table. Recall that Radio Button controls store integer values in database fields, starting with a value of 0 for the first control in a group. Because the Genre field is controlled by a radio button group, the first value in the group, Fiction, is stored as 0 in the database, whereas the second value, Nonfiction, is stored as the number 1. To filter the Library database to return only Fiction titles, you use the filter `m_pSet->m_strFilter = "[Genre] = 0";`. To filter the Library database to return only Nonfiction titles, you use the filter `m_pSet->m_strFilter = "[Genre] = 1";`. Finally, to reset the database to show all titles, you pass an empty string to the filter using the statement `m_pSet->m_strFilter = "";`.

To modify the Library Database application so users can filter records based on the type of book they are interested in:

1. Open the Library Database application's menu in the Menu Editor.
2. To the Record menu, add a **separator**, a **Show Fiction Titles** command, a **Show Nonfiction Titles** command, and a **Show All Titles** command, as shown in Figure 13-27. Modify the Show Fiction Titles command's ID property to **ID_RECORD_SHOW_FICTION_TITLES** and its Prompt property to **Show fiction titles only**. Then modify the Show Nonfiction Titles command's ID property to **ID_RECORD_SHOW_NONFICTION_TITLES** and its Prompt property to **Show nonfiction titles only**. Finally, modify the Show All Titles command's ID property to **ID_RECORD_SHOW_ALL_TITLES** and its Prompt property to **Show all titles**.

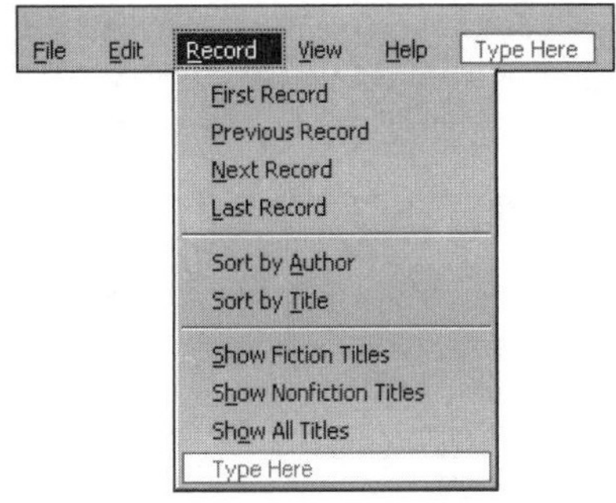

Figure 13-27 Adding new filter commands

3. To filter the database by fiction titles, use the Event Handler Wizard to add to the CLibraryDatabaseView class the following COMMAND message map function for the ID_RECORD_SHOW_FICTION_TITLES resource ID:

```
void CLibraryDatabaseView::OnRecordShowFictionTitles()
{
	m_pSet->Close();
	m_pSet->m_strFilter = "[Genre] = 0";
	m_pSet->Open();
	int iNumRecords = m_pSet->GetRecordCount();
	if (iNumRecords == 0) {
		AfxMessageBox("No matching records found.");
		m_pSet->Close();
		m_pSet->m_strFilter = "";
		m_pSet->Open();
	}
	UpdateData(FALSE);
}
```

13

4. To filter the database by nonfiction titles, use the Event Handler Wizard to add to the CLibraryDatabaseView class the following COMMAND message map function for the ID_RECORD_SHOW_NONFICTION_TITLES resource ID:

```
void CLibraryDatabaseView::OnRecordShowNonfictionTitles()
{
	m_pSet->Close();
	m_pSet->m_strFilter = "[Genre] = 1";
	m_pSet->Open();
	int iNumRecords = m_pSet->GetRecordCount();
	if (iNumRecords == 0) {
		AfxMessageBox("No matching records found.");

	   m_pSet->Close();
		m_pSet->m_strFilter = "";
		m_pSet->Open();
	}
	UpdateData(FALSE);
}
```

5. Finally, to remove any filters, use the Event Handler Wizard to add to the CLibraryDatabaseView class the following COMMAND message map function for the ID_RECORD_SHOW_ALL_TITLES resource ID:

```
void CLibraryDatabaseView::OnRecordShowAllTitles()
{
     m_pSet->Close();
     m_pSet->m_strFilter = "";
     m_pSet->Open();
     int iNumRecords = m_pSet->GetRecordCount();
     if (iNumRecords == 0) {
          AfxMessageBox("No matching records found.");
          m_pSet->Close();
          m_pSet->m_strFilter = "";
          m_pSet->Open();
     }
     UpdateData(FALSE);
}
```

6. Rebuild and execute the program. Test the Show Fiction, Show Nonfiction, and Show All Titles commands on the Record menu to be sure the filters are being applied correctly.
7. Close the Library Database program window.

Adding and Deleting Records

So far the Library Database application is quite functional. It allows users to modify existing records and sort and filter by different fields. However, it has two very big shortcomings in that you cannot add new records or delete existing records. For some types of databases, you may not want to allow users to add or delete records. For example, you would not allow users in a pubic library to add or delete records in the Library Database application. But suppose that the Library Database application is available only to library personnel who catalog and organize the library's collections of books and other media. Library personnel would certainly need to be able to add records to and delete records from the database.

Because there are many different methods of designing an interface for a database application (using menu commands, toolbars, controls, and so on), the MFC framework does not automatically create an option for adding records to a database. Additionally, the MFC framework does not create an option for deleting records because of the complexity of table relationships across relational databases. Therefore, it is up to you to write code for adding records to and deleting records from your database. In this section, you will write code that adds records to and deletes records from the Library Database application. Keep in mind that all databases are different and that the code listed in this section for adding records to and deleting records from an ODBC database may not necessarily work with other types of databases. Also, understand that the techniques in this section are quite rudimentary and would not be acceptable in a professional database application. For instance, the add record technique you will learn depends on the user navigating to another record in order for the new record to be properly saved. In a professional application, you could not count on this behavior from the user. For instance, the user may close the application before navigating to another record, assuming that the application itself will (and should) take care of the save details. However, the techniques you learn in this section are a good starting point for writing your own code that adds records to and deletes records from other types of databases.

Adding Records

The starting point for adding a new record is the AddNew() function that is derived from CRecordset. The **AddNew() function** prepares a new database record by setting the new record's field values to `NULL`. You then call the UpdateData() function with a value of `FALSE` to "clear" the dialog controls by assigning them values of `NULL`. You write your own message handler function to execute the AddNew() member function and the UpdateData() function, along with any other code required for your new records. The following code shows an example of a message handler function definition for the CLibraryDatabaseView class named OnRecordAdd() that executes the AddNew() function:

```
void cLibraryDatabaseView::OnRecordAdd() {
     m_pSet->AddNew();
     m_bAddRecord = TRUE;
     UpdateData(FALSE);
}
```

In the preceding code, notice the m_bAddRecord data member that is assigned a value of `TRUE`. Unlike updates to existing records, the MFC framework does not automatically update new records that are created with the AddNew() function. Instead, to save the new record to the database, you set your own user-defined (not inherited) Boolean variable to a value of `TRUE` as a flag that you will use in the OnMove() function (which you will learn about next). You can use any Boolean variable name you like, but names such as m_bAddRecord, m_bAddMode, and m_bAddNew are common.

13

The MFC framework automatically updates a record in the Library Database application (and in most types of database applications) when the user moves to a new record. The process of updating database records is managed by the CRecordView class's **OnMove() function**. However, in order to *save* a *new* record, you must override the CRecordView class's OnMove() function in your derived class. The following code shows a typical example of an overridden OnMove() function for the cLibraryDatabaseView class. The example includes two new functions that derive from CRecordset: the Update() function and the Requery() function. The **Update() function** saves new records to the database and is required in order to complete a new record operation that is started with the AddNew() function. The **Requery()** function updates a database application's record set.

```
void cLibraryDatabaseView::OnMove() {
     if (m_bAddRecord) {
          UpdateData(TRUE);
          m_pSet->Update();
          m_pSet->Requery();
          UpdateData(FALSE);
```

```
            m_bAddRecord = FALSE;
            return TRUE;
        }
        else
            return CRecordView::OnMove(nIDMoveCommand);
    }
```

The conditional expression in the preceding OnMove() function's `if` statement checks whether the user-defined m_bAddRecord data member is set to `TRUE`, indicating that the current record is a new record. The first statement in the `if` statement executes the UpdateData() function with a value of `TRUE` to copy the dialog control values to their associated data members in the CLibraryDatabaseSet class. Then, the `m_pSet->Update();` statement executes to save the new record to the database. Next, the Requery() function executes and updates the record set stored in the m_pSet pointer. The UpdateData() function executes again, but this time with a value of `FALSE`, to copy the updated values from the CLibraryDatabaseSet data members back into their associated dialog controls. Finally, the m_bAddRecord data member is assigned a value of `FALSE` and the OnMove() function returns a value of `TRUE`. Because the `else` statement executes for existing records, it calls the CRecordView base class version of the OnMove() function to allow the MFC framework to automatically handle any updates.

Next, you will modify the Library Database application so that it creates new records when the user clicks an Add Record command on the Record menu.

To modify the Library Database application so that it creates new records:

1. Open the **LibraryDatabaseView.h** file in the Code Editor window.

2. As shown in Figure 13-28, add a declaration for a BOOL data member named m_bAddRecord to the first protected section of the file.

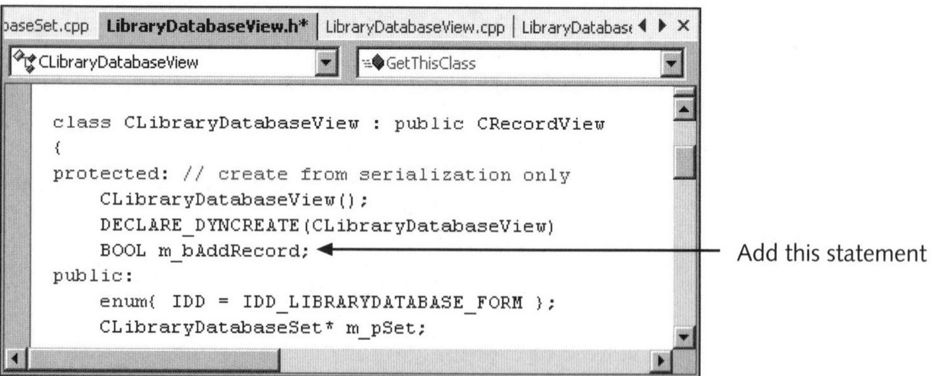

Figure 13-28 m_bAddRecord data member declaration added to LibraryDatabaseView.h

3. Next, open the **LibraryDatabaseView.cpp** file and replace the // TODO comment in the constructor with the statement shown in Figure 13-29 that initializes the m_bAddRecord data member to FALSE.

4. Open the Library Database application's menu in the Menu Editor.

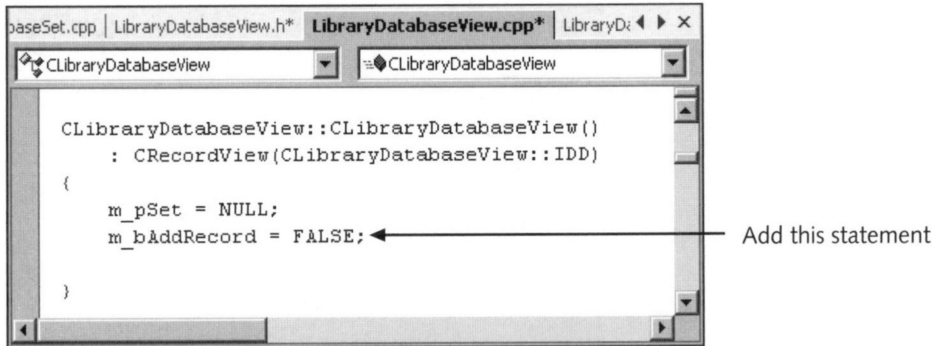

Figure 13-29 m_bAddRecord data member initiallized to FALSE

5. To the Record menu, add a **separator** and an **Add New Record** command, as shown in Figure 13-30. Modify the Add New Record command's ID to **ID_RECORD_ADD_NEW_RECORD** and its Prompt property to **Add a new record**.

Figure 13-30 Adding the Add New Record command

6. Use the Event Handler Wizard to add to the CLibraryDatabaseView class the following COMMAND message map function for the ID_RECORD_ADD_NEW_RECORD resource ID to add a new record to the database:

```
void CLibraryDatabaseView::OnRecordAddNewRecord()
{
     m_pSet->AddNew();
     m_bAddRecord = TRUE;
     UpdateData(FALSE);
}
```

7. Open Class View and select the CLibraryDatabaseView class. Then, use the Overrides button in the Properties window to override the OnMove() function.

After Visual C++ creates the new function, modify the function definition in the LibraryDatabaseView.cpp file as follows:

```
BOOL CLibraryDatabaseView::OnMove(UINT nIDMoveCommand)
{
     if (m_bAddRecord) {
          UpdateData(TRUE);
          m_pSet->Update();
          m_pSet->Requery();
          UpdateData(FALSE);
          m_bAddRecord = FALSE;
          return TRUE;
     }
     else
          return CRecordView::OnMove(nIDMoveCommand);
}
```

8. Rebuild and execute the program. Select the **Add New Record** command from the Record menu to create a new record and add the following information to the fields:

```
Book Title:      The Bridges of Madison County
Book ID:         WALLER001
Genre:           Fiction
Author:          Waller, Robert James
Publisher:       Thorndike, Me. : Thorndike Press, 1992
Description:     184 p. (large print) : ill. ; 23 cm.
```

9. After you finish entering the record, select any of the navigation commands to save the record to the database. Then, navigate through the database to review your new record.

10. Close the Library Database program window.

Deleting Records

Deleting records from a database is much simpler than adding them. Your two primary tasks are to call the Delete() and the MoveNext() functions that are inherited from the CRecordset class. The CRecordset class's **Delete() function** deletes the currently displayed record. Once you delete the current record, you use the **MoveNext() function** to navigate to the next record in the record set. Typically, you delete records using a message handler function named OnRecordDelete(), as follows:

```
void cLibraryDatabaseView::OnRecordDelete() {
     m_pSet->Delete();
     m_pSet->MoveNext();
}
```

The preceding function is sufficient for deleting a record. However, if the record you delete is the last record in the record set, then calling the MoveNext() function after deleting the record will move you past the end of the database, which means you will not have a valid record selected. In order to prevent this type of problem from occurring, you call the IsEOF() and MoveLast() functions after you call the MoveNext() function. The **IsEOF() function**, inherited from CRecordset, returns a value of `true` if your position in the record set is at the end of the file. If the IsEOF() function does return a value of `true`, then you should call the **MoveLast() function**, inherited from CRecordset, to navigate back to the last record in the record set, using code similar to the following:

```
if (m_pSet->IsEOF())
     m_pSet->MoveLast();
```

Other CRecordset functions that you can use to navigate through a recordset are the MoveFirst() function, which navigates to the first record in a record set, the MovePrev() function, which navigates to the previous record in the recordset, and the Move() function, which navigates to a specific record in the record set.

One more precaution you should take when deleting records is to check whether all of the records in the record set have been deleted, and then to clear the fields left over from the last visible record. After you execute the MoveLast() function, you should call the IsBOF() and SetFieldNull() functions. The **IsBOF() function**, inherited from CRecordset, returns a value of `true` if your position in the record set is at the beginning of the file. If the IsBOF() function returns a value of `true` after you execute the MoveLast() function, then your record set is empty. If your record set is empty, you should call the SetFieldNull() function, which is also inherited from CRecordset. The **SetFieldNull() function** receives a single parameter of `NULL`, which it uses to set all field data members in a derived CRecordset class to `NULL`. After executing the SetFieldNull() function, you should call the UpdateData() function with a value of `FALSE` to clear the values displayed in the dialog controls. The following code shows how to write the IsBOF() and SetFieldNull() functions:

13

```
if (m_pSet->IsBOF())
     m_pSet->SetFieldNull(NULL);
```

The following code shows a completed version of the OnRecordDelete() function:

```
void cLibraryDatabaseView::OnRecordDelete() {
     m_pSet->Delete();
     m_pSet->MoveNext();
     if (m_pSet->IsEOF())
          m_pSet->MoveLast();
     if (m_pSet->IsBOF())
          m_pSet->SetFieldNull(NULL);
     UpdateData(FALSE);
}
```

Next, you will modify the Library Database application so that it can delete existing records.

To modify the Library Database application so that it can delete existing records:

1. Open the Library Database application's menu in the Menu Editor.
2. Add a **Delete Current Record** command to the Record menu, as shown in Figure 13-31. Modify the Delete Current Record command's ID property to **ID_RECORD_DELETE_CURRENT_RECORD** and its Prompt property to **Delete the current record**.

Figure 13-31 Adding the Delete Current Record command

3. Use the Event Handler Wizard to add to the CLibraryDatabaseView class the following COMMAND message map function for the ID_RECORD_DELETE_CURRENT_RECORD resource ID to delete the current record from the database:

```
void CLibraryDatabaseView::OnRecordDeleteCurrentRecord()
{
      m_pSet->Delete();
      m_pSet->MoveNext();
      if (m_pSet->IsEOF())
            m_pSet->MoveLast();
      if (m_pSet->IsBOF())
            m_pSet->SetFieldNull(NULL);
      UpdateData(FALSE);
}
```

4. Rebuild and execute the program. Move to the last record in the database, which is the record for *The Bridges of Madison County,* the book you added in the last set of steps. Select the **Delete Current Record** command from the **Record** menu to delete the record for *The Bridges of Madison County*. After you delete the record for *The Bridges of Madison County*, the record for *The Art of War* appears.
5. Close the Library Database program window.

CHAPTER SUMMARY

- A database is an ordered collection of information from which a computer program can quickly access information.
- A flat-file database stores information in a single table.
- A relational database stores information across multiple related tables.
- An application or collection of applications used to create, access, and manage a database is called a database management system, or DBMS.
- Structured query language (SQL) has become a standard data manipulation language among many database management systems.
- Open database connectivity, or ODBC, allows applications that are written to comply with the ODBC standard to access any data source for which there is an ODBC driver.
- A Data Source Name, or DSN, contains configuration information that Windows operating systems use to access a particular ODBC-compliant database.
- The CRecordset class represents records returned from a database.
- A snapshot is a static view of the records in a database.
- A dynaset is a dynamic record set that displays the most recent changes to a database each time you move from one record to another in a database application.
- MFC handles the exchange of values between CRecordset data members and their corresponding fields in a database using a mechanism called record field exchange, or RFX.
- You use a DDX_Field function to handle the exchange of data between the dialog controls and the derived CRecordset class's data members.
- You sort a record set by assigning the field name you want to sort by to the m_strSort data member.
- You filter a record set by assigning a value to the m_strFilter data member.
- The AddNew() function prepares a new database record by setting the new record's field values to `NULL`.
- The Update() function saves new records to the database and is required in order to complete a new record operation that is started with the AddNew() function.
- The Requery() function updates a database application's record set.
- The Delete() function deletes the currently displayed record.

Review Questions

1. What is the name of one table's primary key when it is stored in another table?
   a. key symbol
   b. record link
   c. foreign key
   d. unique identifier
2. Breaking tables into multiple related tables in order to reduce redundant and duplicate information is called ______________.
   a. normalization
   b. redundancy design
   c. splitting
   d. simplification
3. A ______________ relationship exists between two tables when each record in a related table contains exactly one record for each record in the primary table.
   a. one-to-none
   b. one-to-one
   c. one-to-many
   d. many-to-many
4. A ______________ relationship exists in a relational database when one record in a primary table has many related records in a related table.
   a. one-to-none
   b. one-to-one
   c. one-to-many
   d. many-to-many
5. A ______________ contains a one-to-many relationship to each of two tables in a many-to-many relationship.
   a. union database
   b. flat-file link
   c. junction table
   d. bridge table
6. An application or collection of applications used to create, access, and manage a database is called ______________.
   a. a shell program
   b. a mainframe system
   c. a database management system
   d. three-tier client server design

7. Most database management systems use a form of ________________ for their data manipulation languages.
   a. C syntax
   b. C++ syntax
   c. Structured query language
   d. ActiveX data objects
8. A ________________ contains configuration information that Windows operating systems use to access a particular ODBC-compliant database.
   a. Dynamic link library
   b. SQL container
   c. ODBC interface unit
   d. Data Source Name
9. Which of the following is the type of CRecordset object that displays the most recent changes to a database each time you move from one record to another in a database application?
   a. snapshot
   b. dynaset
   c. recordset
   d. DBRecordset
10. Which of the following is the type of CRecordset object that displays a static view of the records in a database?
    a. snapshot
    b. dynaset
    c. recordset
    d. DBRecordset
11. What specific function in a derived CRecordset class handles the exchange of values between CRecordset data members and their corresponding fields in a database?
    a. UpdateData()
    b. DoDataExchange()
    c. DoFieldExchange()
    d. Update()

12. Which of the following is the correct header syntax for the constructor for a derived CRecordset class named CInventorySet?
    a. `CInventorySet::CInventorySet(CDatabase* pdb) : CRecordset(pdb)`
    b. `CInventorySet::CInventorySet(CDatabase* pdb)`
    c. `CInventorySet::CInventorySet(CDatabase* pdb) : CRecordset( )`
    d. `CInventorySet::CInventorySet( )`
13. Which of the following data members that are inherited from CRecordset determine the database access type of CRecordset object?
    a. m_nDefaultType
    b. m_pSet
    c. m_nType
    d. m_nDefault
14. Which inherited CRecordset function connects a database application to the database?
    a. GetDatabase()
    b. DefaultConnect()
    c. GetDefaultConnect()
    d. Connect()
15. In what class is an object of a derived CRecordset function instantiated?
    a. the derived CRecordset class itself
    b. the application class
    c. the frame class
    d. the document class
16. In what function do you assign to the m_pSet variable a pointer to the derived CRecordset associated with a derived CRecordView class?
    a. the derived CRecordView constructor function
    b. the OnInitialUpdate() function
    c. the DoFieldExchange() function
    d. the DoDataExchange() function
17. Which property in the Properties window identifies the first button in a group of radio buttons?
    a. Group
    b. Group Box
    c. Radio Group
    d. Radio

18. You sort the records in a record set by assigning the field name you want to sort by to the ________ data member.
    a. m_Order
    b. m_strAlpha
    c. m_Sort
    d. m_strSort
19. You filter the records in a record set by assigning the values you want to filter by to the ________ data member.
    a. m_Narrow
    b. m_strRefine
    c. m_Filter
    d. m_strFilter
20. Which of the following is the correct string for a filter that narrows a record set to include only records where the State field is equal to Massachusetts?
    a. `"WHERE [State] = 'Massachusetts'"`
    b. `"State = 'Massachusetts'"`
    c. `"WHERE [State] = Massachusetts"`
    d. `"[State] = 'Massachusetts'"`
21. What virtual function must you override in order to complete the process of adding a record to a database?
    a. OnLoad()
    b. UpdateAll()
    c. OnSave()
    d. OnMove()
22. The CRecordset class's ________ function deletes the currently displayed record.
    a. RemoveRecord()
    b. Remove()
    c. DeleteRecord()
    d. Delete()

23. Which code should you add to a function that deletes a record in order to be sure a valid record is displayed in the event that a user deletes the last record in a record set?

a.
```
if (m_pSet->IsEOF())
m_pSet->MoveNext();
```

b.
```
if (m_pSet->IsEOF())
m_pSet->MoveLast();
```

c.
```
if (m_pSet->IsEOF())
m_pSet->Last();
```

d.
```
if (m_pSet->IsEND())
m_pSet->MoveLast();
```

PROGRAMMING EXERCISES

1. Redesign the following table into a one-to-many relationship.

Employee_ID	Last_Name	First_Name	Hourly_Pay	Department
EMP001	Smith	Lucille	$32.50	Marketing
EMP002	Perez	Frank	$40.00	Legal
EMP003	Okayabashi	Mike	$22.00	Accounting
EMP004	Korso	Anthony	$28.00	Accounting
EMP005	Singh	Tasneem	$37.00	Legal

2. Redesign the following table into a many-to-many relationship.

Employee_ID	Last_Name	First_Name	Project_ID	Project_Name	Hours_On_Project
EMP001	Smith	Lucille	100-002	Ad campaign	14
EMP001	Smith	Lucille	100-003	Marketing brochure	9
EMP002	Perez	Frank	200-056	Vendor contracts	23
EMP005	Singh	Tasneem	200-056	Vendor contracts	17
EMP003	Okayabashi	Mike	300-010	Accounts receivable integration	8
EMP004	Korso	Anthony	300-010	Accounts receivable integration	12
EMP003	Okayabashi	Mike	300-012	Year-end tax returns	56

3. Assume that you have an ODBC database with a table named Courses that contains two fields, Course_Name and Student_Name. Write a SQL statement that selects just the Course_Name fields from the Courses table and sorts the records by the Course_Name field.
4. Modify the SQL statement in Exercise 3 so the statement selects all of the fields from the Courses table. Also, sort the returned records by both the Course_Name and the Student_Name fields. Be sure to use a single SQL statement to select and sort the fields.
5. Modify the following derived CRecordset class constructor so that it opens the database as a dynaset:

```
CEmployeesSet::CEmployeesSet(CDatabase* pdb)
     : CRecordset(pdb) {
     //{{AFX_FIELD_INIT(CTest4Set)
     m_Employee_ID = _T("");
     m_Last_Name = _T("");
     m_First_Name = _T("");
     m_Hourly_Pay = 0;
     m_Department = _T("");
     m_nFields = 5;
     //}}AFX_FIELD_INIT
     m_nDefaultType = snapshot;
}
```

6. Modify the following GetDefaultSQL() function so that it returns only records where the Shares field in the Stocks table is equal to 100.

```
CString CInvestmentsSet::GetDefaultSQL()
{
     return _T("[Stocks]");
}
```

7. Add a statement to the following OnInitialUpdate() function so that the database is sorted by the Net_Revenue field.

```
void CCorporationsView::OnInitialUpdate()
{
     m_pSet = &GetDocument()->m_CorporationsSet;
     CRecordView::OnInitialUpdate();
     GetParentFrame()->RecalcLayout();
     ResizeParentToFit();
}
```

8. Write a message handler function named OnPriceSort() for a Real Estate database application that sorts a record set by the Listing_Price field.
9. Write a message handler function named OnLocationFilter() for a Real Estate database application that filters a record set by the Property_Location field.
10. Add a dialog window to the Library Database application that allows users to filter the record set by a specific author's name.

11. Add the appropriate code to the following OnRecordAdd()and OnMove() functions to add new records to a database:

```
void cProductsView::OnRecordAdd() {
...
}
BOOL CProductsView::OnMove(UINT nIDMoveCommand) {
     // TODO: Add your specialized code here
          and/or call the base class
     return CRecordView::OnMove(nIDMoveCommand);
}
```

12. The following OnRecordDelete() function deletes the current record from a database. Add the appropriate code to display a valid record in the event that a user deletes the last record in the database. Also, add code that clears the fields left over from the last visible record in the event that a user deletes all of the records from the database.

```
void cCProductsView::OnRecordDelete() {
     m_pSet->Delete();
     m_pSet->MoveNext();
}
```

Programming Projects

For the following exercises, use an ODBC database management system that you have access to, such as Access, Paradox, or SQL Server, to create the database file where you will store the data. Create each project as an MFC application, and add the appropriate dialog controls to each class's dialog window to display and edit the fields in each database. Also, add code that allows users of each application to sort, filter, add, and delete records in the underlying database. Add menu commands and toolbar buttons that users can use to execute the sort, filter, add, and delete code.

1. Create a telephone directory database application. You should include standard telephone directory fields in the database, such as Name, Address, City, State, Zip, and Telephone Number.
2. Create a simple database application that stores airline surveys. Include edit box controls for the name of the airline, the flight number, and the date and time of the flight. Include edit box controls for the name of the airline, flight number, and date.
   - Friendliness of customer staff?
   - Space for luggage storage?
   - Comfort of seating?
   - Cleanliness of aircraft?
   - Noise level of aircraft?

Each radio button group should include the following buttons that allow users to select a rating for each question: No Opinion, Poor, Fair, Good, or Excellent.

3. Create a product review database application that customers can use to write reviews about software products. Use an edit box control where users can enter their detailed review. Include radio buttons that allow the user to rate the software by selecting a rating of No Opinion, Poor, Fair, Good, or Excellent. Include combo boxes that can be used to select the type of software (word processing, database, spreadsheet, and so on) and its required operating system (Windows XP, Windows 2000, and so on). Include any other controls and fields that you think should be included in a software review program.
4. Create an inventory database application that a car dealer can use to keep track of car inventories. Each car model should be saved as its own record in the underlying database. Include fields such as make, model, year, and base price, along with a field that stores the number of each car in inventory.
5. Database design techniques include the process of being able to identify and design five normalization levels: first normal form, second normal form, third normal form, fourth normal form, and fifth normal form. Search the Internet or visit your local library for information on these techniques and describe how to identify and design each normalization level.

Index

G

H

I

M

N

O

Q

R

X

Y